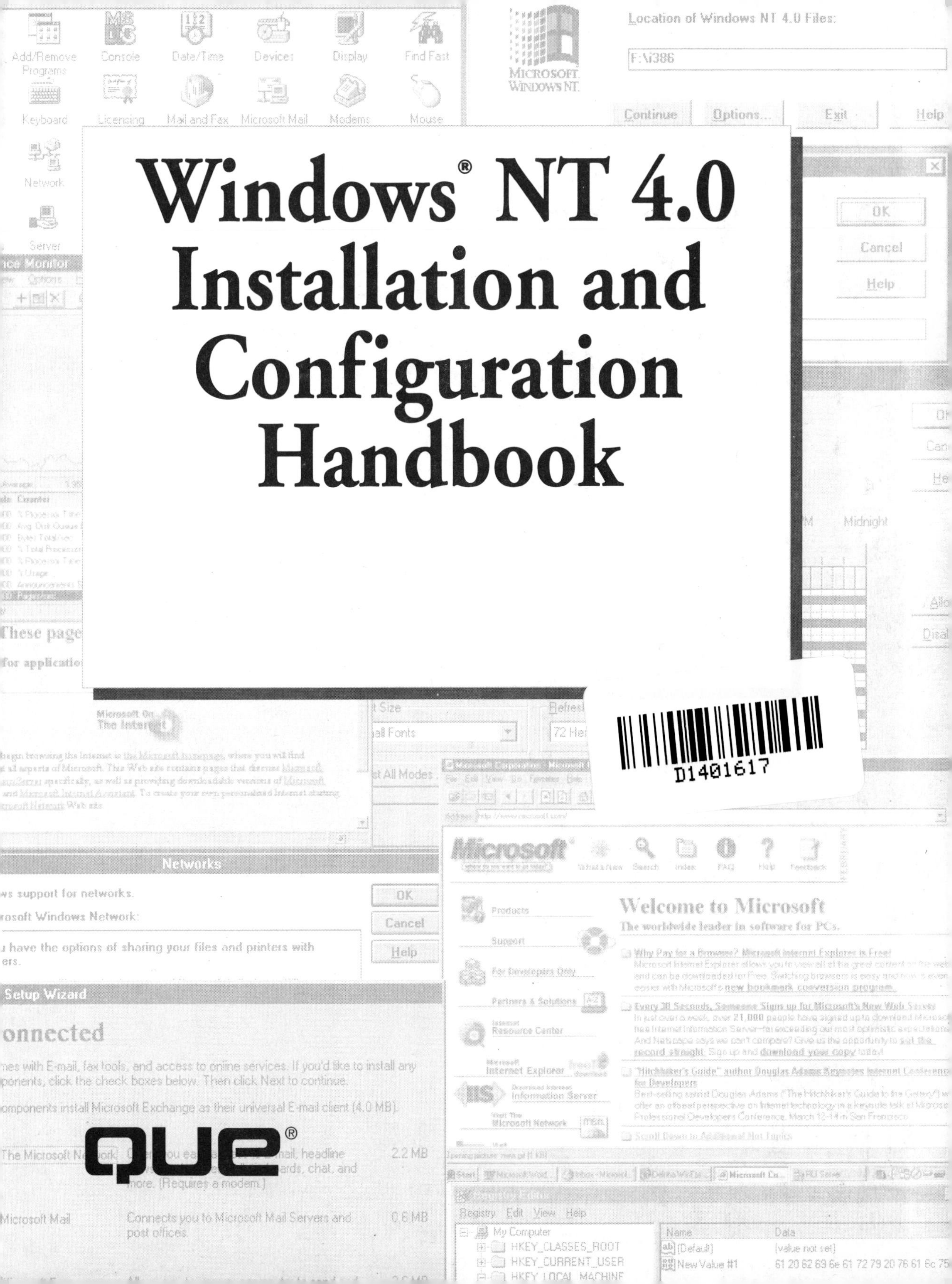

Windows® NT 4.0 Installation and Configuration Handbook
QUE®
D1401617

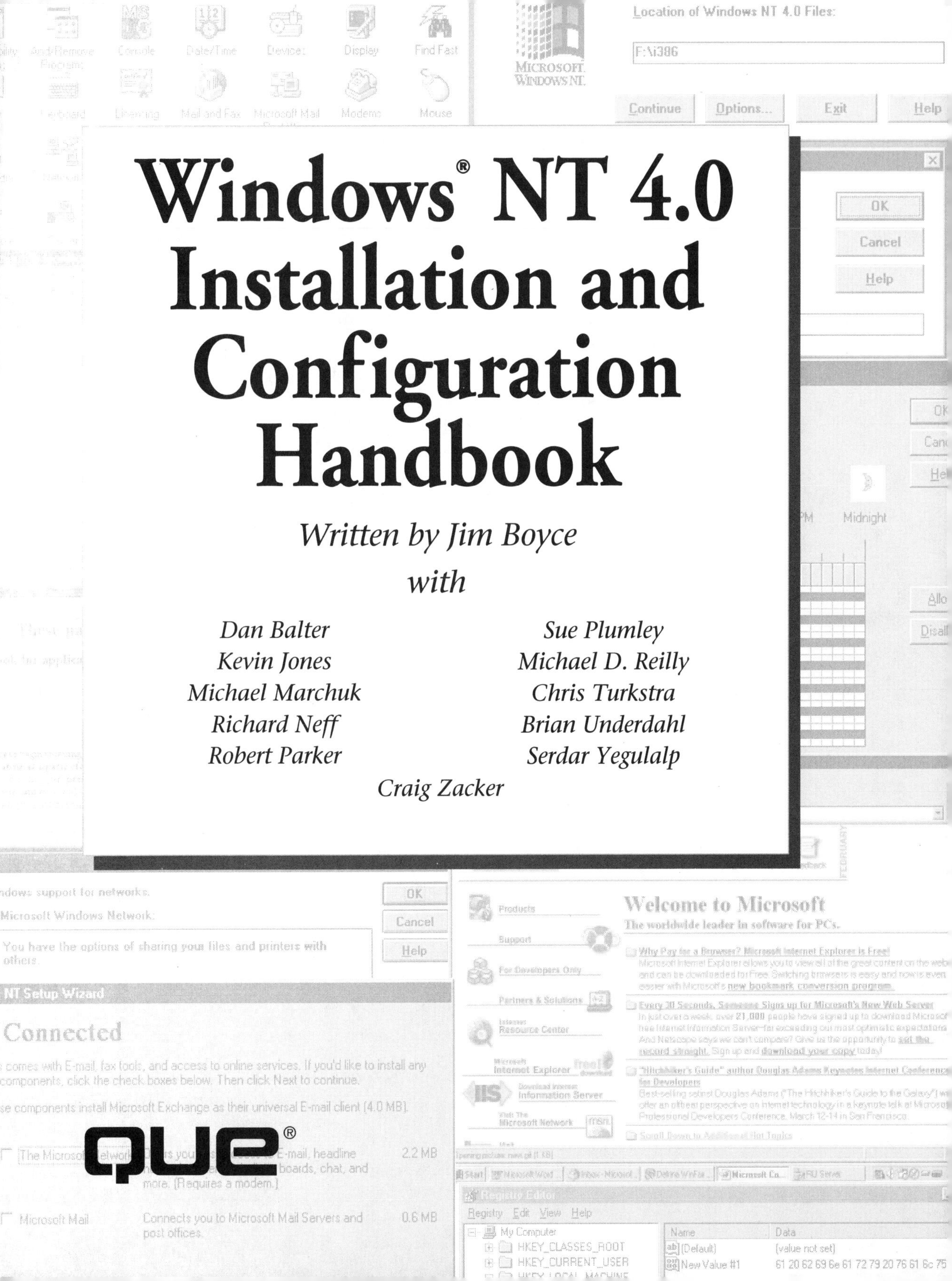
Windows® NT 4.0
Installation and
Configuration
Handbook
Written by Jim Boyce
with
Dan Balter
Kevin Jones
Michael Marchuk
Richard Neff
Robert Parker
Sue Plumley
Michael D. Reilly
Chris Turkstra
Brian Underdahl
Serdar Yegulalp
Craig Zacker
QUE®

Windows NT 4.0 Installation and Configuration Handbook

Library of Congress Catalog No.: 96-68990

ISBN: 0-7897-0818-3

98 97 96 6 5 4 3 2 1

Interpretation of the printing code: the rightmost double-digit number is the year of the book's printing; the rightmost single-digit number, the number of the book's printing. For example, a printing code of 96-1 shows that the first printing of the book occurred in 1996.

Screen reproductions in this book were created using Collage Plus from Inner Media, Inc., Hollis, NH.

Composed in *Stone Serif* and *MCPdigital* by Que Corporation

Credits

President
Roland Elgey

Publishing Director
Brad R. Koch

Editorial Services Director
Elizabeth Keaffaber

Managing Editor
Michael Cunningham

Director of Marketing
Lynn E. Zingraf

Acquisitions Editor
Elizabeth South

Product Director
Kevin Kloss

Production Editor
Julie A. McNamee

Editors
Elizabeth Barrett
Kate Givens
Thomas F. Hayes
Lori Lyons
Sarah Rudy
Nick Zafran

Strategic Marketing Manager
Barry Pruett

Technical Editor
John Nelsen
David Kipping

Technical Support Specialist
Nadeem Muhammed

Acquisitions Coordinator
Carmen Krikorian

Software Relations Coordinator
Patty Brooks

Editorial Assistant
Tracy M. Williams

Book Designer
Ruth Harvey

Cover Designer
Jay Corpus

Production Team
Marcia Brizendine
Jason Carr
Erin M. Danielson
Bryan Flores
Jessica Ford
Donna Wright

Indexer
Chris Wilcox

About the Authors

Jim Boyce, the lead author for *Windows NT Installation and Configuration Handbook*, is a contributing editor and columnist for *WINDOWS Magazine* and a regular contributor to other computer publications. He has been involved with computers since the late 70s, and has worked with computers as a user, programmer, and systems manager in a variety of capacities. He has a wide range of experience in the DOS, Windows, and UNIX environments. Jim has authored and co-authored over two dozen books on computers and software.

Dan Balter is a senior partner at Marina Consulting Group, a Microsoft Solution Provider located in Thousand Oaks, California. Dan works as an independent consultant and trainer who has been involved with several different network operating systems and PC application programs throughout his 12-year career. Dan takes pride in turning complex, technical topics into easy-to-understand concepts. He has specialized in integrating tax and accounting software into networked environments. Dan is certified as a Novell NetWare Engineer (CNE) and is very close to completing his certifications both as a Microsoft Certified Systems Engineer (CSE) in addition to attaining the Certified Network Professional (CNP) designation as awarded by the international Network Professionals Association (NPA). Dan graduated from U.S.C.'s school of business in 1983 and has been featured in over 25 personal computer training videos, including Windows NT and Windows 95, for KeyStone Learning Systems Corporation. Dan can be contacted by phone at 805-497-6100 or via the Internet at **73361.1611@compuserve.com**.

Kevin Jones has worked in the computer industry for 15 years. He has worked from large corporations, IBM and Unisys, down to very small startups. He has worked on such flagship products as dBase III and IV, PC Tools for Windows, and Norton Navigator. Currently, he is a principal software engineer with the Peter Norton Division of Symantec Corp. He has been actively working with Windows 95 since October of 1993.

Michael Marchuk has been involved with the computing industry for over 17 years. Michael currently manages the development research department for a midsized software development firm while consulting for small businesses and writing leading-edge books for Que. Along with his bachelors degree in Finance from the University of Illinois, he has received certification as a Netware CNE and a Compaq Advanced Systems Engineer.

Richard Neff is a Microsoft Certified Professional, certified as a systems engineer with elective exams in Microsoft Mail and Systems Management Server (SMS) and as a product specialist in Microsoft Excel 5.0 and Microsoft Word for Windows 2.0/6.0. He has a B.S. in computer science from VMI and has worked with personal computers for over 15 years. He currently writes a column called Unleashing Windows for the electronic magazine *ChipNet* found on America Online (keyword: **Chipnet**) or on the World Wide Web. He has formed his own computer consulting company, Network Technologies Group, which specializes in Novell Netware, Microsoft Windows NT, and Microsoft BackOffice solutions. Network Technologies Group is located in Blacksburg, Virginia, and also has a Web site at **http://www.bnt.com/~netech**. He can be reached by e-mail at **RickNeff** on America Online (**RickNeff@AOL.COM** over the Internet) or at **70761,3615** on CompuServe (**70761,3615@COMPUSERVE.COM**).

Robert Parker first caught the technical writing bug sitting in the Yale computer science department's machine room, tending systems with 256K of core memory. Since then, he has enjoyed a successful career documenting everything from bar code printers to wireless mice. He is currently a senior technical writer and associate Webmaster for Quarterdeck Corporation, which keeps him pleasantly occupied while he completes a doctorate in music.

Sue Plumley has owned and operated her own business for eight years; Humble Opinions provides training, consulting, and network installation, management, and maintenance to banking, education, medical, and industrial facilities. In addition, Sue has authored and co-authored over 50 books for Que Corporation and its sister imprints, including *10 Minute Guide to Lotus Notes, Special Edition Using Windows NT Workstation,* and *Easy Windows 95.*

Michael D. Reilly has 24 years of experience in computer data processing, including extensive experience on DEC's VAX series 780/785, SEL's 32/75, the CDC 3600, and Xerox 9300. He's been involved with personal computers since 1984. His background includes programming in Fortran, and developing applications in Microsoft Access, Oracle, and Progress. He has worked on the VMS, UNIX, DOS, Windows, and Windows NT operating systems. In 1990, he co-founded Mount Vernon Data Systems, Inc., a consulting company that specializes in client/server database applications. He is a Microsoft Certified Trainer for Windows NT, and has co-authored two books on Microsoft Access. Mike has an M.A. degree in physics from Queens' College, Cambridge University. You can reach him on CompuServe at **72421,1336**.

Chris Turkstra was the kid who was always disassembling his toys. He has been involved with PC technology since his first IBM PC in 1983. Chris is a technical architect who spends much of his time designing and implementing networked systems for clients. You can reach him at **75507.720@compuserve.com** or **turkstra@cris.com**.

Brian Underdahl is an author, independent consultant, and custom application developer based in Reno, Nevada. He's the author or co-author of over 25 computer books, as well as numerous magazine articles. He has also acted as a product developer and as a technical editor on many other Que books. His e-mail address is **71505,1114** on CompuServe.

Serdar Yegulalp is a technical editor with *WINDOWS Magazine*, and a regular beta tester for Windows 95, Windows NT, and NT products. Other research responsibilities include SCSI and document imaging hardware and software. You can reach Serdar at **syegul@cmp.com**.

Craig Zacker got his first experience with computers in high school on a minicomputer "with less memory than I now have in my wristwatch." His first networking responsibility was a NetWare 2.15 server and six 286 workstations, which eventually evolved into over 100 NetWare 4 Workstations, plus WAN connections to remote offices.

He's done PC and network support onsite, in the field, and over the phone for more than five years, and now works for a large manufacturer of networking software on the east coast as a technical editor and online services engineer.

Acknowledgments

Many people helped in the creation of this book in one way or another. Jim Boyce offers his thanks to:

Brad Koch for his support and developmental direction of this project.

Tom Barich for his invaluable help in putting together the project and authoring team.

Kevin Kloss, who did a great job molding and directing the project.

Julie McNamee and Theresa Mathias for an outstanding job of editing and fine-tuning the book.

Brian Underdahl, for putting together a terrific CD and related online materials.

John Nelsen for his outstanding job of technical editing. The book is much better because of his thoroughness and testing.

The staff of the production department of Macmillan Computer Publishing, for their usual fine job of turning text and illustrations into a real book.

We'd Like to Hear from You!

As part of our continuing effort to produce books of the highest possible quality, Que would like to hear your comments. To stay competitive, we *really* want you, as a computer book reader and user, to let us know what you like or dislike most about this book or other Que products.

You can mail comments, ideas, or suggestions for improving future editions to the address below, or send us a fax at (317) 581-4663. For the online inclined, Macmillan Computer Publishing has a forum on CompuServe (type **GO QUEBOOKS** at any prompt) through which our staff and authors are available for questions and comments. The address of our Internet site is **http://www.mcp.com** (World Wide Web).

In addition to exploring our forum, please feel free to contact me personally to discuss your opinions of this book: I'm **74201,1064** on CompuServe, and I'm **kkloss@que.mcp.com** on the Internet.

Thanks in advance—your comments will help us to continue publishing the best books available on computer topics in today's market.

Kevin Kloss
Product Development Specialist
Que Corporation
201 W. 103rd Street
Indianapolis, Indiana 46290
USA

Contents at a Glance

Contents

6 Customizing Setup 101

20 Integrating Windows NT in Novell Environments 439

21 Integrating Windows NT in UNIX Environments 465

22 Using Remote Access Services 483

VI Configuring Internet Services 515

23 Installing and Configuring Windows Messaging 517

Introduction

From its beginnings as OS/2 to its current release as Windows NT 4.0, Windows NT has grown into a powerful operating system that suits the needs of the network administrator as well as the average user. Windows NT Server is ideal for network, security, application, and Internet servers because of its security, speed, robustness, and integration. With the introduction of the popular Windows 95 interface to Windows NT 4.0, Windows NT Workstation is the ideal operating system for desktop business users because of those same features.

Whether you will be using the Server or Workstation version, installing and configuring a system with Windows NT is not as simple as installing and configuring Windows 3.x or Windows 95. A wide variety of new options are available, many of which you must consider before even beginning the installation. *Windows NT 4.0 Installation and Configuration Handbook* not only helps you understand these installation issues, but also steps you through the process of installing and configuring almost all aspects and features of the operating system.

What This Book Is About

Windows NT 4.0 Installation and Configuration Handbook covers a broad range of topics to help you install and configure Windows NT on Intel- and RISC-based systems. In most chapters, the material focuses on actual planning, installation, and setup issues, rather than user-related issues. For example, *Windows NT 4.0 Installation and Configuration Handbook* does not offer an explanation of how to use the accessory applications included with Windows NT or other features that are self-evident to the typical, experienced user. Instead, the book focuses on these key areas:

- Installing and configuring the operating system
- Installing and configuring optional features such as the Windows Messaging System
- Setting up and configuring network clients, protocols, and services
- Installing and configuring new hardware
- Fine-tuning critical systems such as memory and the file system for optimum performance, redundancy, and security
- Administering systems and users

- Setting up an Internet server and other Internet issues such as firewalls and security

Although the focus of this book is on installation and configuration, some chapters do cover a limited amount of information on using certain features in Windows NT. Generally, these features are covered because your understanding of the features will help you with installation and configuration tasks. For example, Chapter 1, "What's New In Windows NT 4.0," provides a brief primer on using the new Windows NT 4.0 interface, which will help you throughout the rest of the book.

The authors who have contributed to *Windows NT 4.0 Installation and Configuration Handbook* are experts in their areas, but have the unique ability of explaining their subjects in ways that a layman can easily understand. Most important, the authors write from practical experience.

Who This Book Is For

Windows NT 4.0 Installation and Configuration Handbook is intended for the intermediate to advanced user who needs a solid explanation of how to install and configure Windows NT Workstation and Windows NT Server. This includes advanced features such as Internet Information Server, which is bundled with Windows NT Server 4.0.

Because of the increasing popularity of Windows NT as a workstation operating system for business users, *Windows NT 4.0 Installation and Configuration Handbook* is geared toward not only the experienced network or system administrator, but also to the average experienced user. Whether you are setting up a single workstation or an entire system, this book provides you with a solid foundation of skills and techniques to set up and configure Windows NT to suit your needs.

We do assume, however, that you have some level of experience with Windows 3.x, Windows 95, or Windows NT 3.x, and are able to use the Windows interface. For example, you should know how to use the mouse, work with program menus and dialog boxes, and perform other common Windows tasks. Tasks that are not quite so obvious, however, we spell out for you. For example, you'll find step-by-step instructions on how to set up your modem in Windows NT—we'll tell you what programs to start and what buttons to click, so all you have to do is follow the instructions.

How This Book Is Structured

Windows NT 4.0 Installation and Configuration Handbook is divided into eight parts that take you from basic installation and configuration through more advanced topics such as configuring a Web or ftp server. The chapters are written to stand alone, so you don't have to keep referring from one chapter to another to set up or configure a particular feature in Windows NT. The following sections explain the parts of the book and what topics are covered in each.

Part I: Installing Windows NT

Part I explains how to set up and configure Windows NT 4.0 on all supported platforms, and also explains advanced setup topics such as network and distributed setup:

- Chapter 1, "What's New in Windows NT 4.0," explores the features that are new to version 4.0, including the new Windows 95 interface.
- Chapter 2, "Understanding Key Installation Issues," explores hardware, software, compatibility, and security issues you should understand before beginning the installation process.
- Chapter 3, "Planning the Installation," takes you step-by-step through the process of planning your workstation or server installation.
- Chapter 4, "Installing Windows NT," explains the step-by-step procedures for installing Windows NT on Intel- and RISC-based systems under a variety of situations.
- Chapter 5, "Network Installation and Configuration," helps you understand network protocols, clients, and services, and how to install them.
- Chapter 6, "Customizing Setup," explores the many ways you can customize the Windows NT Setup program to automate a variety of installation options and procedures.
- Chapter 7, "Distributed Setup," explains how to create and use a distribution share to enable installation across the network. Chapter 7 also explores the use of the Computer Profile Setup utility to further automate the setup process.

Part II: Administering Windows NT

Part II introduces you to concepts, techniques, and tools for administering and managing Windows NT workstations, servers, users, and environments:

- Chapter 8, "Understanding System Administration," provides an overview of key issues, concepts, and tools you'll use in subsequent chapters to manage Windows NT systems and users.

- Chapter 9, "Administering Servers and Sharing Resources," explains server-related management issues, including managing domains, the file system, and licensing, as well as monitoring and controlling server performance.
- Chapter 10, "Administering Users," teaches you to create and manage user accounts directly and through profiles and policies.
- Chapter 11, "Understanding and Modifying the Registry," explains a key topic for system administration: the Registry. You'll learn the significance of the Registry and how to use the Registry Editor to view and modify it.

Part III: Adding and Modifying Hardware

Adding and configuring hardware is an important aspect of optimizing Windows NT's performance. Part III explains how to install and configure a variety of common devices:

- Chapter 12, "Adding Multimedia Devices," explains installation and configuration tasks for CD-ROM drives, video adapters, and sound cards.
- Chapter 13, "Adding Modems," explains the process required to install various types of modems, including standard serial and parallel port modems, as well as ISDN devices. Chapter 13 also explains a key new feature in Windows NT communications: the Telephony API (TAPI).
- Chapter 14, "Adding Printers and Fonts," explains how to install printers and fonts and manage them through the Printers folder.

Part IV: Managing and Tuning Critical Sub-Systems

Part IV helps you begin to fine-tune the systems that have the most impact on Windows NT's performance. In addition to learning about key areas such as virtual and physical memory, disk and file-system structure, and data security, you'll also learn techniques and tips for optimizing those systems:

- Chapter 15, "Optimizing Physical and Virtual Memory," explains Windows NT's memory architecture and how you can optimize systems for best performance.
- Chapter 16, "Optimizing the File System," gives you a broad view of NTFS, disk compression, and other key disk-related issues.
- Chapter 17, "Ensuring Data Security," explores a range of data security topics including backup strategies and the use of fault-tolerant volumes.
- Chapter 18, "Optimizing Hardware: Processors, Video, and I/O Systems," explains ways you can improve system performance for video and other I/O devices.

Part V: Optimizing Networking and Communications

Part V examines a variety of topics that have become increasingly popular in the past few years: networking, the Internet, Remote Access Services (RAS), and communications. These chapters in Part V help you integrate NT systems in any network structure:

- Chapter 19, "Integrating Windows NT in Microsoft Environments," offers useful tips and techniques for integrating Windows NT in networks containing systems driven by other Microsoft operating systems and environments.
- Chapter 20, "Integrating Windows NT in Novell Environments," helps you not only integrate Windows NT systems in a Novell Netware network, but also replace existing Netware servers with Windows NT servers.
- Chapter 21, "Integrating Windows NT in UNIX Environments," explains how to tie together Windows NT systems and UNIX systems using X-Windows and other methods.
- Chapter 22, "Using Remote Access Services," provides an in-depth look at the features in Windows NT that enable you to connect to remote sites through dialup connections, and serve dial-in users to your own system and network.

Part VI: Configuring Internet Services

With the growing popularity of the Internet and new features in Windows NT for Internet support, businesses and individuals alike are turning to Windows NT as both a client and server platform for the Internet. The chapters in Part VI explore Internet issues in detail:

- Chapter 23, "Installing and Configuring Messaging System," explores the new e-mail feature, Windows NT Messaging System, that is included with Windows NT.
- Chapter 24, "Understanding and Configuring TCP/IP," provides an overview of TCP/IP and specific steps and tips for configuring and using TCP/IP as a protocol for Windows NT internetworking.
- Chapter 25, "Using Internet Programs," explains how to configure Internet clients such as Internet Explorer and Netscape to run under Windows NT. This chapter also explores other Internet utilities such as ftp and Telnet.

- Chapter 26, "Setting Up an Internet Server with IIS," explains how to use the Internet Information Service included with Windows NT Server 4.0 (and available separately from Microsoft) to create a full-featured Internet server with Windows NT.
- Chapter 27, "Implementing a Firewall," is a companion to Chapter 26, which explores the issues of server security. Chapter 27 explains how you can protect your Internet server with the use of a firewall.

Part VII: Customizing Windows NT

Part VII explores the many ways you can customize the Windows NT environment and interface. The chapters in Part VII teach you how to alter the appearance and function of Windows NT through the Control Panel and Registry:

- Chapter 28, "Customizing the Desktop," explains the many ways you can alter the visual and audio behavior of the Windows NT desktop. Chapter 28 also explains how to support multiple users with unique desktop settings on a single workstation.
- Chapter 29, "Customizing Hardware and System Settings," explores a variety of techniques you can use to control system-level features such as power management, date and time, and hardware profiles.

Part VIII: Appendixes

The appendixes to *Windows NT 4.0 Installation and Configuration Handbook* offer additional reference material you'll find useful when setting up and using Windows NT:

- Appendix A, "Working with the Registry Settings," lists critical and often undocumented Registry keys and settings.
- Appendix B, "What's on the CD," offers an overview and installation instructions for the *Windows NT 4.0 Installation and Configuration Handbook CD-ROM* that accompanies this book.

Conventions Used In This Book

In Windows NT, you can use either the mouse or keyboard to activate commands and choose options. You can press a command or menu hot key, use the function keys, or click items with the mouse to make your selections. In this book, command and menu hot keys are underlined as in the following example:

Choose File, Open to display the Open dialog box.

In this book, key combinations are joined by a plus (+) sign. For example, Ctrl+C means to hold down the Ctrl key, press C, then release both keys. The following example shows a typical command:

Choose Edit, Copy, or press Ctrl+C.

Occasionally, you might need to press a key, release it, then press another key. If you need to press Alt, then F, then O, for example, the command would be similar to the following:

Press Alt, F, O to display the Open dialog box.

Names of dialog boxes and dialog box options are written as they appear on your display. Messages that appear at the command prompt are displayed `in a special font`. New terms are introduced in *italic* type. Text that you type is shown in **boldface**. If you see an instruction to "Enter **some text**," it means to type the text **some text**, then press Enter. If the instruction tells you to "Type **some text**," it means to type the text but not press Enter.

Note

Notes provide additional information that might help you avoid problems or offer advice or general information related to the current topic.

Tip

Tips provide extra information that supplement the current topic. Often, tips offer shortcuts or alternative methods for accomplishing a task.

Caution

Cautions warn you if a procedure or description in the topic could lead to unexpected results or even data loss or damage to your system. If you see a caution, proceed carefully.

Troubleshooting

I'm having a specific problem with a Windows NT feature.

Look for troubleshooting elements to help you identify and resolve specific problems you might be having with Windows NT, your system, or network.

What About Sidebars?

Sidebars are sprinkled throughout the book to give you the author's insight into a particular topic. The information in a sidebar supplements the material in the chapter.

Margin cross-references like the one at the left direct you to related information in other parts of the book. Right-facing triangles indicate later chapters, and left-facing triangles point you back to information earlier in the book.

Internet references such as the following point you to sites on the Internet where you can find additional information about a topic being discussed.

On the Web

Microsoft's Internet Web Site

http://www.microsoft.com

Where To Go For More Information

Que offers other titles that will help you master the intricacies of Windows NT and related topics: *Special Edition Using Windows NT Workstation 4.0* and *Windows NT Workstation 4.0 Internet and Networking Handbook.*

For more information about these titles, Que, Macmillan Computer Publishing, and other Macmillan digital services, check out the Macmillan USA Information SuperLibrary on the Internet at **www.mcp.com**. You'll find a wealth of information, online shopping, and more. Or, check out the **MACMILLAN** forum on CompuServe.

For other online sources of information about Microsoft Windows NT, check the WINNT forum on CompuServe or connect to the Microsoft Web site at **www.microsoft.com**. ❖

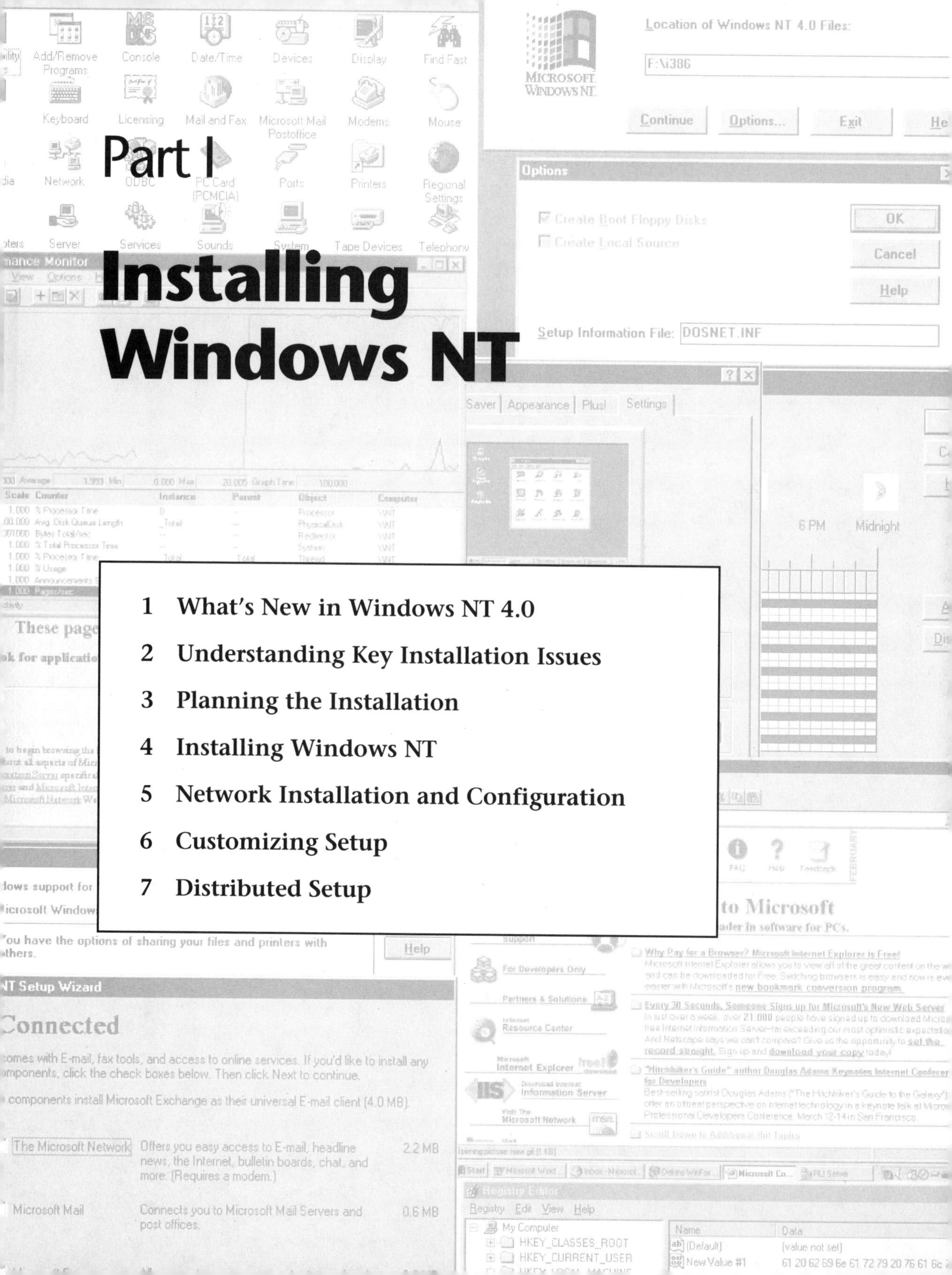

Part I

Installing Windows NT

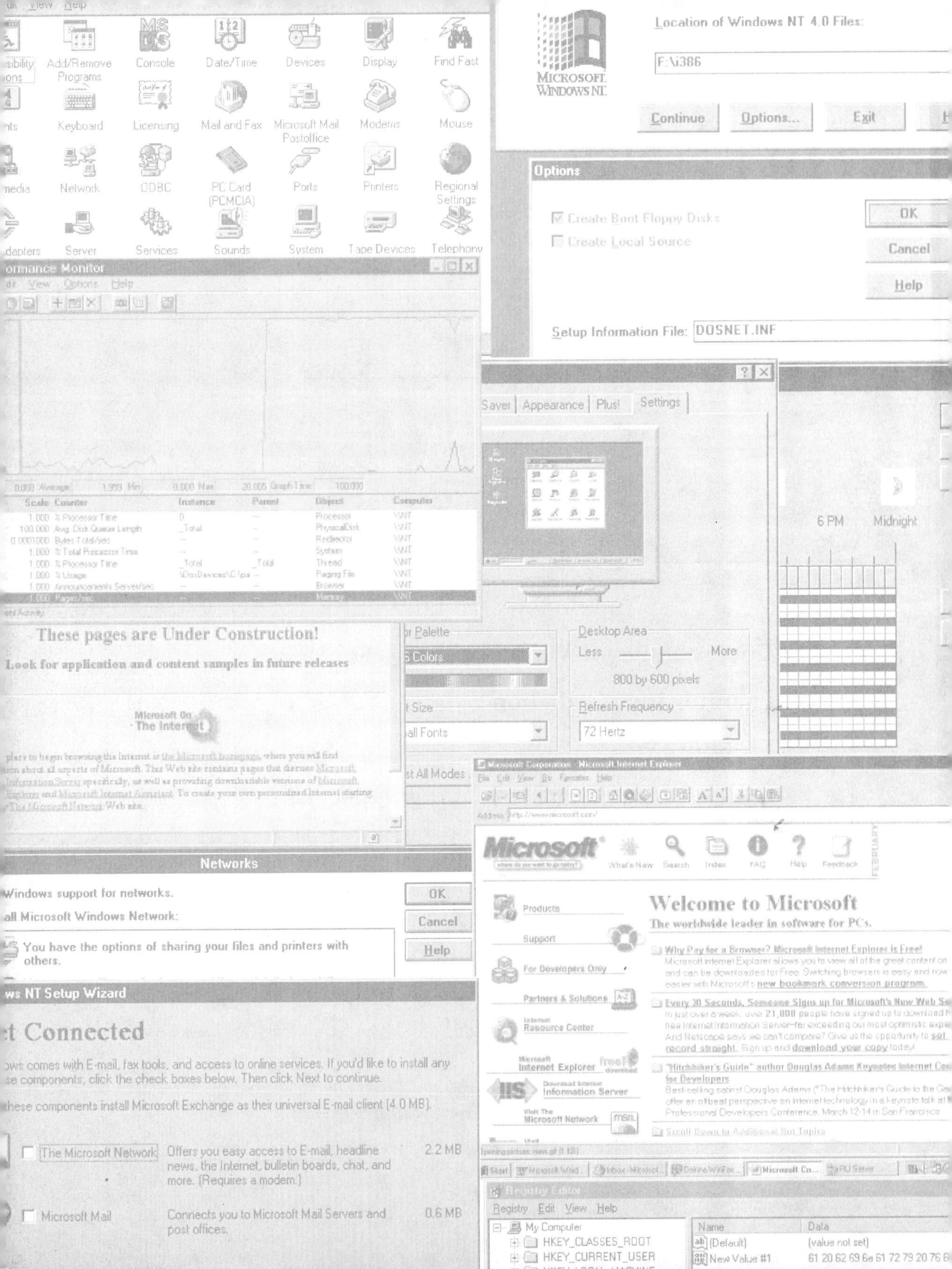

Location of Windows NT 4.0 Files:
F:\i386
MICROSOFT WINDOWS NT
Continue
Options...
Exit
Add/Remove Programs
Console
Date/Time
Devices
Display
Find Fast
Keyboard
Licensing
Mail and Fax
Microsoft Mail Postoffice
Modems
Mouse
Network
ODBC
PC Card (PCMCIA)
Ports
Printers
Regional Settings
Server
Services
Sounds
System
Tape Devices
Telephony
Options
Create Boot Floppy Disks
Create Local Source
OK
Cancel
Help
Setup Information File: DOSNET.INF
Saver
Appearance
Plus!
Settings
6 PM
Midnight
Desktop Area
Less
More
800 by 600 pixels
Refresh Frequency
72 Hertz
These pages are Under Construction!
Look for application and content samples in future releases
Microsoft On The Internet
Networks
Windows support for networks.
You have the options of sharing your files and printers with others.
OK
Cancel
Help
Welcome to Microsoft
The worldwide leader in software for PCs.
Products
Support
For Developers Only
Partners & Solutions
Resource Center
Internet Explorer
Information Server
Microsoft Network
Why Pay for a Browser? Microsoft Internet Explorer is Free!
Every 30 Seconds, Someone Signs up for Microsoft's New Web Se
"Hitchhiker's Guide" author Douglas Adams Keynotes Internet Co
for Developers
Scroll Down to Additional Hot Topics
Registry Editor
Registry Edit View Help
My Computer
HKEY_CLASSES_ROOT
HKEY_CURRENT_USER
Name
Data
(Default)
(value not set)
New Value #1
61 20 62 69 6e 61 72 79 20 76 6
et Connected
ows comes with E-mail, fax tools, and access to online services. If you'd like to install any se components, click the check boxes below. Then click Next to continue.
these components install Microsoft Exchange as their universal E-mail client (4.0 MB).
The Microsoft Network
Offers you easy access to E-mail, headline news, the Internet, bulletin boards, chat, and more. (Requires a modem.)
2.2 MB
Microsoft Mail
Connects you to Microsoft Mail Servers and post offices.
0.6 MB

CHAPTER 1

What's New In Windows NT 4.0

by Jim Boyce

Whether you are concerned more with appearances or function, you'll find many new features in Windows NT 4.0 to satisfy you. From system-level features such as support for hardware profiles to user-level features such as the new Windows 95-style interface, Windows NT 4.0 is full of new features.

This chapter offers an overview of those new features, including:

- Windows 95 user interface
- Windows Explorer
- Internet Explorer and other Internet tools
- Messaging System and its features
- Support for hardware profiles
- NDS-Aware Client/Gateway Services for NetWare
- Distributed Component Object Model (DCOM)
- DirectX
- Peer Web Services
- Point-to-Point Tunneling Protocol (PPTP) client
- Logon through Dial-Up Networking
- 486 emulator
- Autorun
- New Windows NT Server features such as the Internet Information Server

In addition to giving you a broad overview of Windows NT 4.0's new features, the following section about the new interface provides a brief primer to bring you up to speed with Windows NT's new look.

If you are already familiar with Windows 95 or the new Windows NT interface, you might prefer to skip to the section, "Internet Tools," to begin learning about other new features in Windows NT. Part VI, "Configuring Internet Services," also explores Internet features in Windows NT 4.0.

Windows 95 User Interface

One of the most notable features in Windows 95 is its new interface, which most users will agree is vastly improved over the Windows 3.x interface shared by previous versions of Windows NT. First introduced as the Shell Technology Preview, the Windows 95 interface is now firmly integrated into Windows NT 4.0.

As you become comfortable with the new interface, you'll realize that it resolves many of the previous interface's shortcomings while retaining those elements that worked well. Drag and drop has been expanded to many new areas. The Program Manager has been replaced by an integrated desktop. The File Manager has been replaced by Explorer, which gives you a view not only of your disks, but other resources such as the network, your e-mail inbox, the Control Panel, and more.

Note

This section of the chapter provides only a brief primer to the new Windows NT interface. For a more comprehensive explanation, refer to *Special Edition Using Windows NT Workstation 4.0* from Que.

Working with the Desktop

When you first boot Windows NT, you'll notice that the Program Manager, a venerable fixture in version 3.x, is gone. The new interface consists of an integrated *desktop* containing a selection of standard objects, as shown in figure 1.1.

The standard objects on the desktop include the following:

- *My Computer.* This folder contains folders for all the local disks connected to your system, all mapped network disks, the Control Panel, and Printers folder.
- *Network Neighborhood.* This folder contains icons for each computer in your workgroup or domain, as well as an icon labeled Entire Network that enables you to browse the entire network for resources.

- *Inbox.* This object opens the Windows NT Messaging inbox. Messaging provides an integrated inbox for your network and Internet mail, and custom message types.
- *Recycle Bin.* The Recycle Bin provides a storage area for deleted files, enabling you to recover files after they have been deleted. When you delete files from the Recycle Bin, the files are permanently deleted.
- *The Internet Explorer.* This icon appears only if you have installed Microsoft Internet Explorer, which is an Internet Web browser included with Windows NT.
- *My Briefcase.* A briefcase enables you to synchronize multiple copies of a file, such as on a notebook and desktop PC.

Many of these standard objects are explained in more detail in forthcoming sections. In addition to these standard objects, your desktop can contain other objects, including shortcuts and folders. Folders are explained next.

Fig. 1.1
The basic desktop is well-organized and uncluttered.

Caution

The standard desktop objects are created by settings in the Registry. Custom items that you add to the desktop reside in the folder \Windows\Desktop. To add an item to the desktop, you can simply copy, move, or create a shortcut to the object in the \Windows\Desktop folder. If you move an object to the desktop and then delete it, however, the object itself is deleted.

Understanding Folders

Two types of folders exist in the new Windows NT interface. *Disk folders* are really nothing more than directories represented by an icon. When you double-click this type of folder icon, a window appears that displays the contents of the folder (directory). These objects might include other folders (subdirectories or subfolders) as well as files (see fig. 1.2).

Fig. 1.2
Folders provide a graphical view of directories.

> **Note**
>
> The terms *folder* and *directory* are used interchangeably throughout this book.

You'll also see a second type of folder in the new interface. These folders don't represent directories, but instead are a special type of container for objects such as program icons, printers, and other non-disk objects. The Control Panel is a good example of this type of folder—it doesn't contain disk objects, but instead contains a variety of controls that enable you to configure your system's hardware and software (see fig. 1.3).

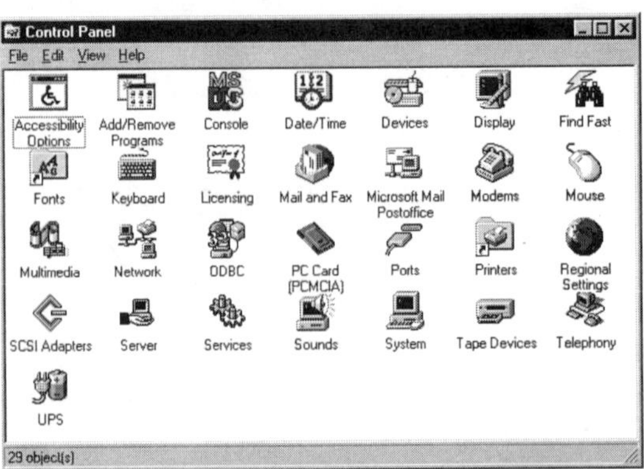

Fig. 1.3
The Control Panel is a special type of folder.

My Computer

My Computer is another of the special folders described in the previous section (see fig. 1.4). My Computer contains icons for each of the local disks connected to your system, mapped network disks, the Control Panel, and Printers folder. My Computer gives you quick access to all of your most often-used resources

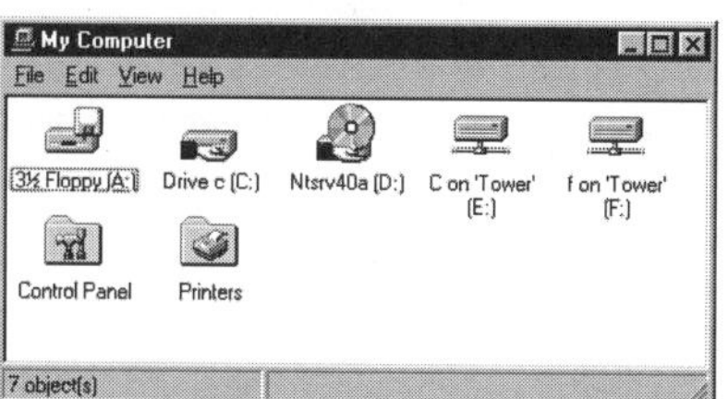

Fig. 1.4
My Computer contains your most commonly used resources.

> **Tip**
>
> If you prefer, you can change the name of the My Computer folder. Just right-click the folder and choose Rename. Or, click My Computer to select it, then click the icon's text. After the text is highlighted, enter a new name for the icon. Use this same method to rename any folder (the Recycle Bin cannot be renamed).

Network Neighborhood

The Network Neighborhood gives you quick access to network resources. When you open the Network Neighborhood, its window displays icons for each of the other computers in your workgroup or domain (see fig. 1.5). You'll also see the Entire Network icon, which enables you to browse the entire network for shared resources (such as computers that are not part of your workgroup). The Network Neighborhood can also contain special network objects such as network print servers.

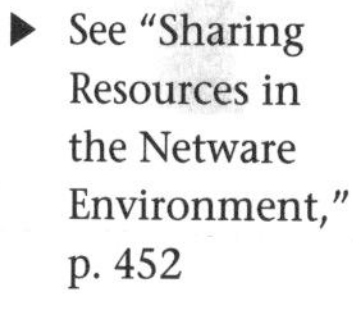

▶ See "Sharing Resources in the Netware Environment," p. 452

Fig. 1.5
The Network Neighborhood gives you quick access to network resources.

Double-click a computer's icon in the Network Neighborhood to display a folder containing icons for each of that computer's shared resources.

Tip

You can quickly map a local drive letter to a remote network disk. To do so, right-click either My Computer or the Network Neighborhood icon and choose Map Network Drive. Windows NT displays a simple Map Network Drive dialog box you can use to specify the drive letter and remote share name. To disconnect a network drive, right-click either My Computer or Network Neighborhood and choose Disconnect Network Drive. A dialog box appears that enables you to select the disk to disconnect.

The Taskbar

By default, the taskbar appears at the bottom of the desktop. You can, however, move the taskbar to any of the other three edges of the desktop simply by dragging it from one location to another. The taskbar contains the Start button, the *tray*, and an area in which running applications appear as buttons (see fig. 1.6).

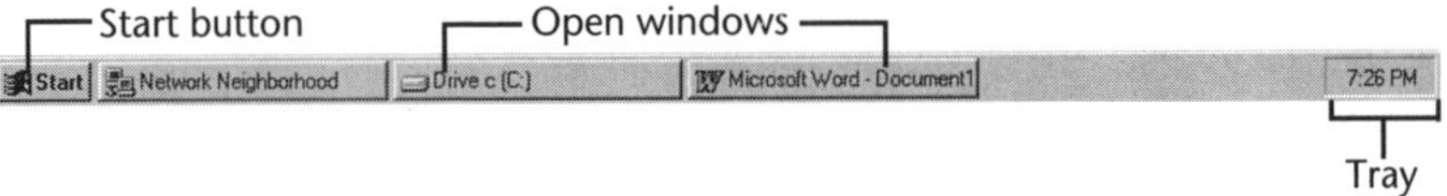

Fig. 1.6 The taskbar gives you quick access to running applications.

To select an application and bring it to the foreground, just click its button in the taskbar. To open the application's control menu, right-click the application's button.

Tip

To minimize all applications so that they are all on the taskbar, right-click an open space on the taskbar, and choose Minimize All Windows. To restore the desktop, right-click the taskbar and choose Undo Minimize All. If you're using a Microsoft Natural keyboard, you can press Win+M to minimize all windows, then press Win+Shift+M to restore the windows.

The tray serves a special purpose on the taskbar. In addition to displaying the clock, the tray also contains special indicator icons for tasks that are running as "hidden" programs. If your system contains a sound card, for example, a speaker icon appears on the tray. Clicking this icon opens a volume control you can use to set the card's volume.

Tip

To view the Date/Time Properties sheet, which enables you to set the time, date, and time zone, double-click the clock display in the tray.

The Start Menu

The Start menu essentially replaces the Program Manager as one of the primary means for starting programs and accessing resources in Windows NT. To open the Start menu, click the Start button, (which by default appears at the bottom of the display). By default, the Start menu contains the following items:

- *Programs*. The Programs menu essentially takes the place of program groups in the old Program Manager, giving you quick access to all of the programs installed on your system.
- *Documents*. As you work with documents, they are added to the Documents menu. You can open a recently used document by selecting it from the Documents menu instead of first opening the document's application. When you select a document from the Documents menu, the document's application opens automatically.
- *Settings*. This menu contains items for the Control Panel, Printers folder, and taskbar.
- *Find*. Use the Find menu to find files locally or on the network, other computers on the network, or topics on The Microsoft Network.
- *Help*. Use the Help menu item to open a Help folder that contains general Windows NT Help topics.
- *Run*. This item functions similarly to the Run command in Program Manager's File menu. Use it to start programs by entering their command lines (or browse for the program).

As you add applications and customize your system, additional items appear in the Start menu.

Tip

Right-click a blank area of the taskbar, choose Properties from the context menu, then click the Start Menu Programs tab to begin the process of customizing your Start menu. Or, simply add and remove shortcuts and other objects as desired from the \Windows\Start Menu folder.

Working with Folders and Other Objects

If you are familiar with Windows 3.x, Windows 95, or Windows NT 3.x, you should have no trouble working with folders and their contents. The following sections provide a brief overview.

Manipulating Objects

Typical objects that appear in folders include program icons, shortcut icons, other folders, and special objects such as network nodes. In most cases, you can move, copy, delete, and rename objects in a folder. To move an object from one location to another, simply drag it using the left mouse button. To copy the object, hold down the Ctrl key while dragging the object. To delete the object, select it and press the Del key.

▶ See "Working With Shortcuts," p. 20

You can also use the right mouse button to manipulate objects. To have the option of moving, copying, or creating a shortcut to an object, right-drag the object to its new location. Release the mouse button, and from the resulting context menu, choose Move Here, Copy Here, or Create Shortcut(s) Here, as appropriate.

Tip

The Windows NT 4.0 interface supports the Clipboard for copying and moving objects, including files. You can select one or more objects, then press Ctrl+C to copy them to the Clipboard, or press Ctrl+X to cut them to the Clipboard. Then, open the destination (such as a different folder) and press Ctrl+V to paste the objects to their new location. Note that when you copy or cut files to the Clipboard in this way, only a special filename list is placed on the Clipboard, not the files themselves. Windows NT then uses this filename list to accomplish the copy or move operation when you issue the Paste command (Ctrl+V).

Setting Object Properties

Many objects in the new Windows NT interface have *properties* associated with them. A file, for example, has a variety of properties including its name and file attributes (read-only, archive, hidden, and system). In most cases, you can change an object's properties. In the case of a file, for example, you can change the file's attributes.

To view an object's properties, right-click the object and choose Properties from the resulting context menu. A property sheet for the object appears. The appearance and contents of the property sheet vary according to the object. Figure 1.7 shows the property sheet for a Word document file.

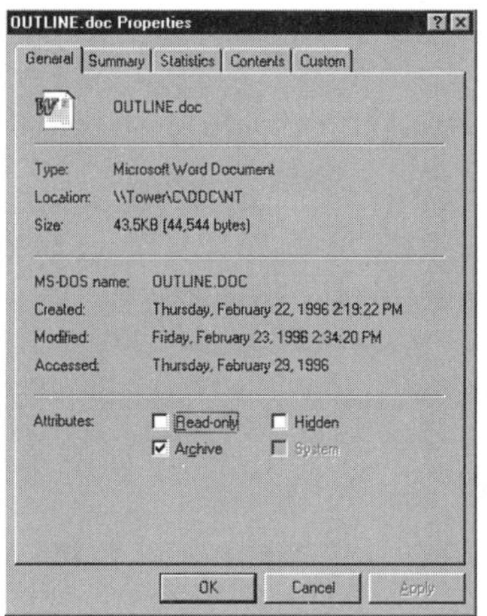

Fig. 1.7
This is the property sheet for a Word document file.

Changing Folder Options

When you browse through folders, Windows NT uses multiple folder windows by default to display the contents of the folders. For example, double-clicking a folder icon inside a folder window opens a new window to display the contents of the newly selected folder. If you prefer, you can configure the system to use a single folder window, simply changing the contents of the currently opened window to reflect the contents of the selected folder.

To set this behavior, choose View from the folder's menu, then choose Options to display the Options property sheet (see fig. 1.8). Select the view method you want to use from the two option buttons, then choose OK.

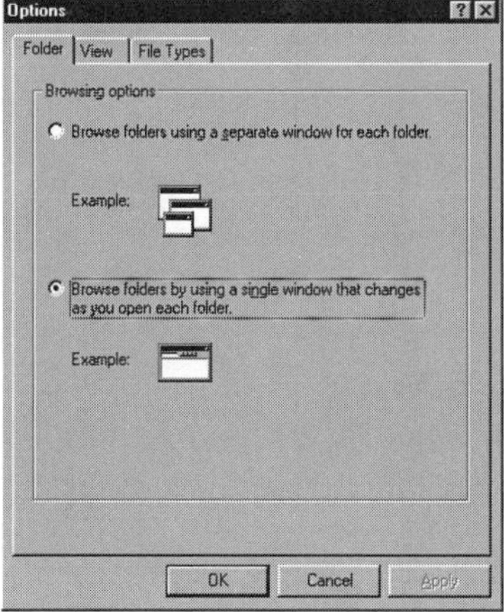

Fig. 1.8
Use the Options property sheet to control a folder's appearance and other options.

Tip

To close a window and all of its parent windows, hold down the Shift key and click the Close button (the X button in the upper-right corner of the window).

The View property page (see fig. 1.9) enables you to set other properties that define which type of files appear in the folder and whether their file extensions appear with their names. Note that these controls don't define whether the file actually resides in the folder, but simply determine whether they appear in the folder window or are hidden.

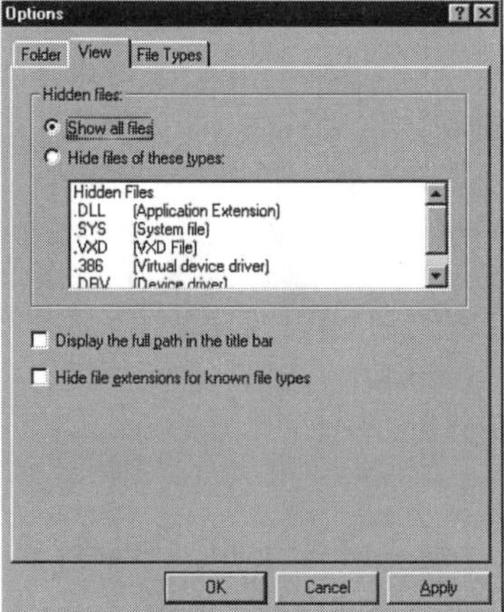

Fig. 1.9
Use the View page to define which types of files appear in the folder window.

Tip

To arrange icons in a folder and control other folder options, right-click inside the folder and choose a command from the resulting context menu. You also can create a new folder by right-clicking in the folder or on the desktop, and then choosing New, Folder.

Working with Shortcuts

A key feature of the new Windows NT interface is *shortcuts*. A shortcut is a *pointer* to an object such as a folder, program, or document. You might have a shortcut on the desktop to a folder, for example, but that folder might actually be located on a network server. Double-clicking a shortcut icon activates the object to which the shortcut points. You can identify a shortcut by a small curved arrow in the bottom-left corner of the shortcut's icon.

You can create shortcuts easily using drag and drop. To create a shortcut on the desktop, for example, locate the object for which you want to create a shortcut. Then, right-drag the object to the desktop. Release the mouse button and choose Create Shortcut(s) Here from the resulting context menu. Windows NT then creates a shortcut to the object. Once created, shortcuts can be moved, copied, and deleted like most other objects. For example, you might create a folder on the desktop for your most commonly used objects, then move or copy their shortcuts to this folder. To move the shortcuts, select them and drag them to their new location. To copy the shortcuts, hold down the Ctrl key while dragging the shortcuts to their new location.

Note

An important issue to understand is that manipulating a shortcut doesn't affect the object to which the shortcut points. Deleting a shortcut has no effect on the program or document to which it points, for example.

Working with the Startup Group

If you're familiar with Windows and Windows NT 3.x, you're probably familiar with the fact that you can set up programs to start automatically as soon as Windows starts. The same is true for Windows NT 4.0, although this feature is handled differently from previous releases.

In previous versions, you could cause programs to start automatically by adding them to the Startup program group in Program Manager. Windows NT 4.0, like Windows 95, uses a Startup folder for the same purpose. To view the contents of the Startup folder, choose Start, Programs, and Startup. The items listed in the Startup cascading menu are the items stored in the Startup folder. To cause a program to start automatically, simply place a shortcut to the program in the Startup folder (the Startup folder is located in \Windows\Start Menu\Programs\Startup).

Tip

You can control the way in which a program starts by modifying its shortcut properties. To do so, right-click the shortcut and choose Properties. When the object's property sheet appears, click the Shortcut tab to display the Shortcut property page. You can add command line switches or options in the Target text box, specify the program's startup folder with the Start In text box, specify a shortcut key for the shortcut, and specify the initial window state (minimized, normal, or maximized). To change the shortcut's icon, click the Change Icon button.

If you no longer want a program to start automatically, simply remove its shortcut from the Startup folder. If you've closed a program that normally starts from the Startup folder, and want to restart it, just choose Start, Programs, Startup, and choose the item you want to start.

Tip

To bypass the Startup group during startup (not start any of the programs it contains), hold down the Shift key while the system is starting. For example, type your password in the logon dialog box, hold down the Shift key, and choose OK. Continue to hold down the Shift key until the desktop appears and the hourglass pointer returns to an arrow pointer.

Using the Recycle Bin

The Recycle Bin provides a mechanism for retrieving deleted files and objects (such as shortcuts). When you delete an object, Windows NT moves the object to the Recycle Bin rather than deleting it. If you later decide you need the object, you can open the Recycle Bin and move it back to its original location (or any other location). When you empty the Recycle Bin, however, the items in it are deleted permanently.

The Recycle Bin appears and behaves much like any other folder. You can move objects in and out of the Recycle Bin using the same drag-and-drop techniques you use to move objects between folders. To empty the Recycle Bin, deleting all of the objects in it, right-click the Recycle Bin icon and choose Empty Recycle Bin from the context menu.

The Recycle Bin uses a certain amount of disk space on each disk to store deleted files. You can specify the percentage of disk space to allocate to the Recycle Bin according to your needs and the amount of free space available on each disk. To set the Recycle Bin's properties, right-click the Recycle Bin icon and choose Properties from the context menu. Use the Recycle Bin Properties sheet to control all disks globally or individually, disable the Recycle Bin, and control confirmation options (see fig. 1.10).

Caution

When the Recycle Bin becomes full, there is no indication of that condition and adding more files to the Recycle Bin results in some of the contents of the Recycle Bin being permanently deleted. Also, if you slide the size control for the Recycle Bin to zero while setting the Recycle Bin's properties, the Recycle Bin is emptied even if you press Cancel.

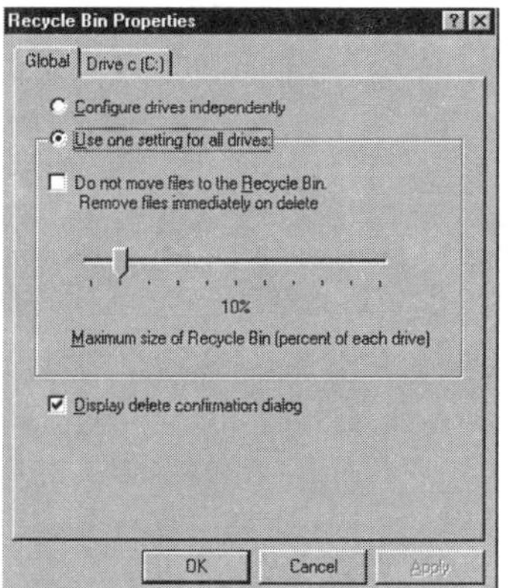

Fig. 1.10 Use the Recycle Bin Properties sheet to control Recycle Bin behavior and options.

Using Send To

Another useful feature in the new Windows NT interface is the Send To menu. Send To enables you to send an object to another object. For example, you can send a document to a printer without first opening the document's application. And, you can copy a file to a floppy disk by sending it to the disk. Or, you might want to mail the document through e-mail. Send To enables you to perform all of these tasks, as well as others.

To view the Send To menu, right-click the object you want to send, then choose Send To from its context menu. A cascading menu of destinations appears, and selecting an item sends the object to the selected destination. By default, the Send To menu contains a few predefined destinations, such as the system's floppy disks, mail recipient, and Briefcase.

You can add other items to the Send To menu simply by placing shortcuts to the object in the \Windows\SendTo folder. To add a printer to the Send To menu, for example, right-drag a printer from the Printers folder to the \Windows\SendTo folder and choose Create Shortcut(s) Here from the context menu.

Windows Explorer

Another key feature in the new Windows NT 4.0 interface is the Windows Explorer. Explorer is similar in function to the old Windows NT 3.x File Manager, except Explorer gives you access to other objects in addition to your disks, including the Control Panel, inbox, and Network Neighborhood. Figure 1.11 shows the Explorer window.

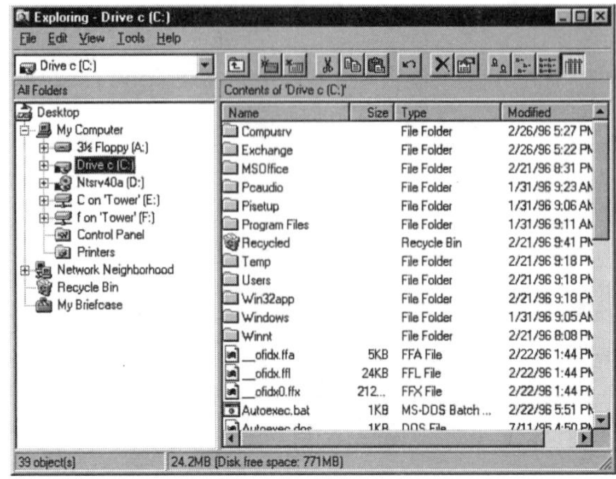

Fig. 1.11 Explorer gives you a view and access to most of the resources on your system and network.

The Explorer consists of a standard program window with two panes. The left pane, or *tree pane*, displays a hierarchical tree of the objects available from Explorer. The right pane, or *contents pane*, shows the contents of the currently selected object in the tree.

In general, the Explorer interface is self-explanatory for an experienced Windows user. The following are a few useful tips for features that are not obvious:

- *Using drag and drop.* In addition to using drag and drop to move and copy objects from the contents pane to another folder or the desktop, you can move and copy objects by dragging them from the contents pane to the tree pane, and vice versa. For example, you can move a file to a network disk simply by dragging it from the contents pane to the network disk's folder in the tree.

> **Note**
>
> Unlike with other types of files, dragging and dropping an EXE file copies the file, rather than moving it. To move an EXE file with drag and drop, hold down the Shift key while dragging the EXE file. Or, right-drag the file and choose Move Here from the context menu.

- *Selecting multiple items.* As in File Manager, you can select multiple items to copy, move, or delete in Explorer. To select multiple items in a series, click the first item in the series to select it, then hold down the Shift key and select the last item in the series. To select objects not in series, hold down the Ctrl key while clicking the object to select it. To select all items, press Ctrl+A.

- *Use right-click.* You can view the properties of almost any object in Explorer by right-clicking the object and selecting Properties from the context menu. The context menu also enables other tasks that vary from one object to another.
- *Activating a folder.* Explorer doesn't display the contents of a folder in the contents pane until you actually select the folder in either the tree or contents pane. This means you can select a folder to display its contents, then expand and collapse the tree to view other folder locations without opening them. This is useful, for example, when you want to move or copy objects to another folder. Just open the folder, select the objects, then manipulate the tree until you can see the destination folder. Then, drag the files from the contents pane to the other folder in the tree.
- *Sort the contents pane.* When you select the Details view for the contents pane (choose View, Details or click the Details toolbar button), the pane contains four columns: Name, Size, Type, and Modified. You can sort the view on any of these four columns just by clicking the column header. Clicking the column header again switches between ascending and descending order. The current sort order is used for subsequent folders, until you specify a different sort order.

When File Manager Is Better

Explorer is useful in a number of ways, most notably because unlike File Manager, it gives you a view of a much broader range of resources. For someone who is experienced with File Manager, however, Explorer can require an adjustment in the way you do things.

For example, Explorer unfortunately doesn't support MDI, so you're limited to only one window. You can, however, open multiple instances of Explorer to achieve the same effect as multiple document windows.

You might prefer to continue working with File Manager, at least for some tasks. To start File Manager, choose Start, Run, and enter **winfile** in the Run dialog box.

Internet Tools

You'll find plenty of Internet client and server tools in Windows NT 4.0. On the client side, one of the most important new features is the Internet Explorer.

Internet Explorer

Internet Explorer is Microsoft's World Wide Web client software (see fig. 1.12). With Internet Explorer you can browse the Web through a dial-up connection to an Internet service provider or through a hard-wired Internet connection.

Fig. 1.12
Browse the Web with Microsoft's Internet Explorer.

Internet Explorer is designed around the new Windows NT interface. In addition to using Internet Explorer to browse remote and local Web sites, you also can view local HTML and JPEG files with Internet Explorer.

ftp and Telnet

As with previous versions of Windows NT, version 4.0 includes ftp and Telnet utilities. The Telnet program is a Windows-based program that enables you to login to remote hosts through your system's Internet connection, whether dialup or hardwired (see fig. 1.13).

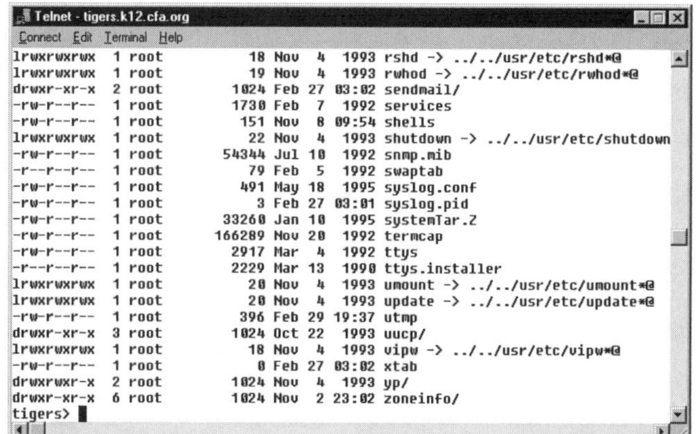

Fig. 1.13
Use Telnet to log in to a remote host.

The ftp utility included with Windows NT 4.0 is a command-line version of its ubiquitous UNIX counterpart. You can perform limited ftp retrievals with Internet Explorer. The ftp utility is useful for experienced ftp users and for higher-level ftp tasks such as retrieving or sending a selection of files.

▶ See "Using ftp and Telnet," p. 607

Messaging

Like Windows 95, Windows NT 4.0 includes the Microsoft Windows Messaging System, which enables you to send and receive e-mail through Microsoft's e-mail client, which also is included with Windows NT. Messaging supports various service providers that enable it to communicate with a variety of message servers (see fig. 1.14). Included with Windows NT 4.0 are service providers for Internet Mail and Microsoft Mail.

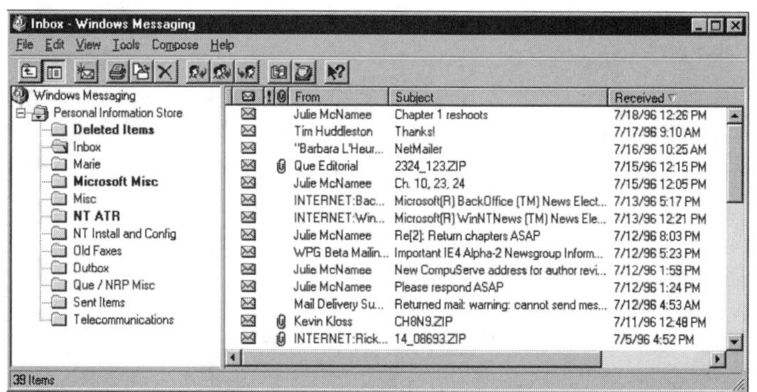

Fig. 1.14
The Messaging e-mail client provides an integrated messaging service.

▶ See "Configuring the Internet Mail Provider," p. 547

▶ See "Setting Up Microsoft Mail for Remote Mail," p. 557

The Internet Mail provider enables you to send and receive e-mail through an Internet mail server, either through a hardwired or a dial-up connection to the Internet mail server. The Internet Mail provider supports MIME mappings to filename extensions, automating transfer of MIME attachments.

The Microsoft Mail service provider for Messaging enables you to send and receive e-mail through a Microsoft Mail postoffice, including those created with other versions of Windows NT, Windows for Workgroups, and Windows 95. The Microsoft Mail provider supports remote mail, enabling you to connect to a Microsoft Mail postoffice through a Dial-Up Networking connection, enabling you to send and receive mail from a remote site.

Note

The remote capability for Microsoft Mail and Internet Mail in Messaging relies on Windows NT Dial-Up Networking and requires that the mail server be supported by a Dial-Up Networking dial-in server—either the mail server itself must also serve as a Dial-Up Networking server, or a Dial-Up Networking server must be connected to the same network as, and provide access to, the mail server. Note that the CompuServe Mail provider doesn't require Dial-Up Networking to support remote mail. CompuServe Mail uses its own dialer to connect to CompuServe.

Other New Features

In addition to the features already described, Windows NT 4.0 includes a selection of features that improve usability, networking, and hardware support. These features are described in the following sections.

Hardware Profiles

Like Windows 95, Windows NT 4.0 supports *hardware profiles*. A hardware profile is a configuration list of specific hardware. Windows NT enables you to create multiple hardware profiles and choose which profile to use in any particular Windows NT session. For example, you might create multiple configurations for a notebook computer, using one profile when the notebook is docked and another when it is undocked.

In general, Windows NT can detect which profile it should use based on the hardware it detects during startup. If Windows NT can't detect the correct profile (because the profiles are so similar, for example), it prompts you to specify which profile to use.

486 Emulator

Windows NT 4.0 for Reduced Instruction Set Computer (RISC) systems includes a new software emulator that enables these RISC systems to run Windows-based and MS-DOS-based applications that require 386-enhanced mode support or that look for an Intel 486 processor (or compatible). This feature broadens the available software base for RISC systems, although performance of applications running under the emulator will naturally be less than that of native applications.

NDS Support

The Client/Gateway Services for Netware, which is included in previous versions of Windows NT, has been updated to support Netware Directory Services (NDS). NDS support enables you to browse an NDS tree and connect to NDS volumes, and to connect to printers on the NDS tree. The Client/Gateway Services for Netware are essentially the same as in previous versions of NT, except that NDS is now supported.

Autorun

Like Windows 95, Windows NT 4.0 supports *autorun*, which enables Windows NT to automatically start audio and application CDs as soon as the CDs are inserted into the drive. To begin playing an audio CD, for example, you simply insert it into the drive. Windows NT detects the CD, recognizes it as an audio CD, and immediately begins playing the CD.

In the case of application CDs, Windows NT can start the application contained on the CD or open a window of options for the CD, depending on how the developer has structured the CD.

Note

An application CD must be designed to support autorun—older CDs do not support autorun. You must manually open these types of CDs as you have with previous versions of Windows NT.

Tip

To bypass autorun, hold down the Shift key when you insert the CD in the drive. To disable Autorun, set the following Registry key:

HKEY_LOCAL_MACHINE\System\CurrentControlSet\Services\CdRom\Autorun = 0

Distributed Component Object Model (DCOM)

In previous versions of Windows NT, Windows 95, and Windows 3.x, Object Linking and Embedding provided a mechanism for applications to work together cooperatively under a common interface. OLE also is the mechanism by which you build compound documents from data created by various applications.

The ability to use OLE across the network in these previous operating systems was very limited, at best. Microsoft has renamed OLE to Component Object Model (COM). In addition, Microsoft has expanded network support through Distributed Component Object Model (DCOM), which is a network-capable extension of COM. Through DCOM you can integrate applications and documents across a network, including the Internet.

DirectX

DirectX is a set of APIs (Application Programming Interfaces) geared toward enhancing multimedia performance. DirectX in Windows NT consists of DirectDraw 2.0, DirectSound 1.0, and DirectPlay 1.0. These APIs speed multimedia component performance by supporting hardware acceleration for graphics rendering and other new, common hardware features.

DirectDraw support has been expanded in Windows NT from previous versions of DirectDraw to include driver support for a selection of popular display adapters such as those from ATI and Matrox. You'll find more information about DirectX in Chapter 18, "Optimizing Hardware: Processors, Video and I/O Systems." You'll find a sample game called Roids in the \Ddraw folder on the Windows NT Workstation CD-ROM you can use to test DirectX performance.

Peer Web Services

Windows NT Workstation includes a set of utilities that enables you to easily set up your Windows NT Workstation computer as a personal Internet server. Peer Web Services lets your computer function as an ftp server, Web server, and news server. Peer Web Services is an ideal solution to publishing documents and files on intranets, and turns your computer into a solid platform for authoring Web documents that you publish elsewhere.

Note

If you need more robust or extensive Internet server support, consider the Internet Information Server (IIS), which is included with Windows NT Server 4.0. IIS also is available as an add-on to Windows NT Server 3.5x.

Dial-Up Networking Enhancements

Dial-Up Networking in Windows NT 4.0 includes enhancements to make it a more attractive method of creating and using wide-area networking. One new feature, the Point-to-Point Tunneling Protocol (PPTP) client, enables a Dial-Up Networking client to access resources on remote servers through a secure, encrypted protocol connection. PPTP enables you to create and access private virtual networks across a WAN connection through an Internet service provider or direct connection to the Internet. PPTP supports TCP/IP, IPX/SPX, and NetBEUI.

Another enhancement to Dial-Up Networking in Windows NT 4.0 is the ability to log on to a domain through a Dial-Up Networking connection. This enables you to authenticate your logon through a remote domain controller.

New Windows NT Server Features

In addition to the new features described in the previous sections, Windows NT Server includes more new features, many of which are targeted at making Windows NT a strong Internet server platform. The following sections describe these new features.

DNS Name Server

▶ See "Using DNS," p. 578

▶ See "Using WINS," p. 580

Windows NT Server 4.0 includes an RFC-compliant Domain Name System (DNS) name server. DNS provides for domain name resolution for IP routing, and is the primary mechanism by which Internet hosts resolve domain names to IP addresses.

You can configure the DNS server in Windows to use Windows Internet Name Server (WINS) for host name resolution, providing a more dynamic mechanism for address resolution.

Microsoft Internet Information Server (IIS)

In an effort to win a large share of the Internet server market, Microsoft has included its Internet Information Server (IIS) software with Windows NT

Server 4.0. IIS enables you to create a full-featured Internet server running Windows NT Server to include a Web server, ftp server, and gopher server. With the addition of the Exchange Server to your system, you can provide complete Internet services under NT.

Multi-Protocol Routing (MPR)

Windows NT 4.0 now supports multi-protocol routing, which enables a Windows NT Server to route IP and IPX protocols without the need for a hardware router. This enables you to connect LAN to LAN or LAN to WAN without additional routing hardware. However, the server must contain at least two network adapters. Windows NT also enables a server to relay BOOTP/DHCP messages across an IP-based LAN.

Remote Booting of Windows 95

The Remoteboot Service included in Windows NT Server 4.0 supports remote booting of Windows 95 clients, making it easy to support diskless Windows 95 computers on a LAN.

Remote Administration

Windows NT Server includes a new set of administration tools that run under Windows 95, enabling you to administer Windows NT servers from remote Windows 95 workstations. These tools were previously available separately.

DNS Support in UNC Names

You now can use DNS domain names in Uniform Naming Convention (UNC) pathnames. Previously, a UNC name had the format *server**resource*, in which *server* was the NetBIOS name for the server and *resource* was the name of the share resource. In addition to supporting this naming format, Windows NT also supports names in the form *host.domain**resource*, where *host.domain* specifies the domain name of the server, such as \\ftp.microsoft.com\pub. ❖

CHAPTER 2

Understanding Key Installation Issues

by Jim Boyce

Installing an operating system such as Windows 95 is a relatively simple task. Installing Windows NT, however, can be much more complicated. With complex security and compatibility issues to consider, getting all aspects of the installation right the first time can be a challenge. The whole process takes considerable thought and planning. This chapter gives you the background information you need to begin the installation process.

In this chapter, you learn

- An overview of Windows NT
- Compatibility issues
- File system issues
- Security issues
- An overview of Setup

If you are an experienced Windows NT administrator, most if not all the information in this chapter should be familiar to you. If you're relatively new to Windows NT, however, the following sections will be indispensable for helping you plan and carry out the installation.

An Overview of Windows NT

To fully understand your options for installing Windows NT and the consequences of installation, you need an understanding of Windows NT itself. The following sections cover the key concepts surrounding Windows NT.

A Brief History

Although Microsoft likely won't admit it, Windows NT rose from humble beginnings in OS/2, on which Microsoft and IBM collaborated in the late 1980s.

Eventually (and some would say *fortunately*), IBM and Microsoft suffered a falling out. IBM took over OS/2 for its own development, and Microsoft opted to redesign the operating system entirely to create Windows NT.

Late in 1988, Microsoft began the task of designing what would become Microsoft's vision of the operating system for the 1990s—Windows NT. Like its bantam-weight counterpart—Windows—Windows NT enjoyed mixed success throughout its first few years of existence. Starting around early 1995, however, Windows NT began to make major inroads into territory formerly held by UNIX, OS/2, and even DOS. Today, Windows NT is rapidly becoming the operating system of choice for many businesses, both large and small, for servers as well as for users. Many large companies are bypassing Windows 95 and moving to Windows NT.

The success of Windows NT is due partly to creative marketing, partly to Microsoft's sheer market leverage and clout, but mostly because Windows NT is simply a good operating system. Why? The next few sections give you a brief overview of Windows NT's features to answer that question.

Multitasking, Multithreading, and Multiprocessing

Early processors such as the 8088 did well to handle single tasks. As processors became more powerful, *multitasking* became more important and achievable. Multitasking refers to an operating system's ability to process multiple tasks, such as running more than one program at a time.

Two types of multitasking are used in today's operating systems—*cooperative* and *preemptive*. In cooperative multitasking, programs are designed (theoretically) to cooperate with one another for CPU time. That is, a program must give up control of the CPU to enable another program (task) to use the CPU. Windows 3.x uses this type of multitasking with mixed results. Properly designed programs function together quite well under Windows 3.x. A poorly designed program, however, can literally take control of the system, effectively halting all others.

Windows NT provides *preemptive multitasking*, in which the operating system, and not applications, determines how CPU time is allotted. In a preemptive multitasking environment, the operating system determines which program will have the CPU and for how long. A poorly designed program therefore has little effect on other programs—the operating system simply suspends the program and turns over control of the CPU to another program. Preemptive multitasking not only ensures that one program doesn't hog the CPU and other resources, but also results in smoother multitasking.

Note

Windows 3.x provides only cooperative multitasking, and Windows 95 provides both preemptive and cooperative multitasking. All versions of Windows NT have supported preemptive multitasking, but use cooperative multitasking for 16-bit Windows applications.

In addition to supporting multitasking, Windows NT supports *multithreading*, which is the ability to execute more than one sequence of instructions within the same task. Perhaps the simplest way to explain multithreading is to say that in a multithreaded operation, a task is divided into mini-tasks, called *threads*, which usually are generated by one event. Instead of handling the entire task sequentially, a multithreaded operating system can work on each thread of the task independently. The result is smoother operation and faster completion of the task, particularly with *multiprocessor* systems.

Multiprocessor systems, which are supported by Windows NT, contain multiple processors, or CPUs. In a uniprocessor system that contains only one CPU (like most of today's typical PCs), even multitasking operating systems such as Windows NT don't truly perform more than one task at a time. Instead, the CPU switches between tasks so quickly that it appears to be doing two (or more) things at once.

In a multiprocessor system, however, multiple tasks *can* be handled simultaneously. One CPU might be running operating system functions while a second CPU performs tasks for a program. It's like having multiple computers on your desktop.

Two types of multiprocessing systems exist: *asymmetric* and *symmetric* (see fig. 2.1). In asymmetric multiprocessor systems, each CPU handles a specific and unique set of tasks. One CPU might be running the operating system, for example, while a second CPU runs applications. The primary disadvantage to asymmetric designs is that the load on the processors isn't uniform. One CPU might be nearly idle while the other works at full tilt.

▶ See "Multiple Processors," p. 395

Windows NT, however, supports symmetric multiprocessor (SMP) systems. In an SMP system, the workload is distributed more evenly, with all tasks being distributed among the system's processors. Each processor might be handling a part of the operating system while also executing program threads. The result generally is faster, smoother performance.

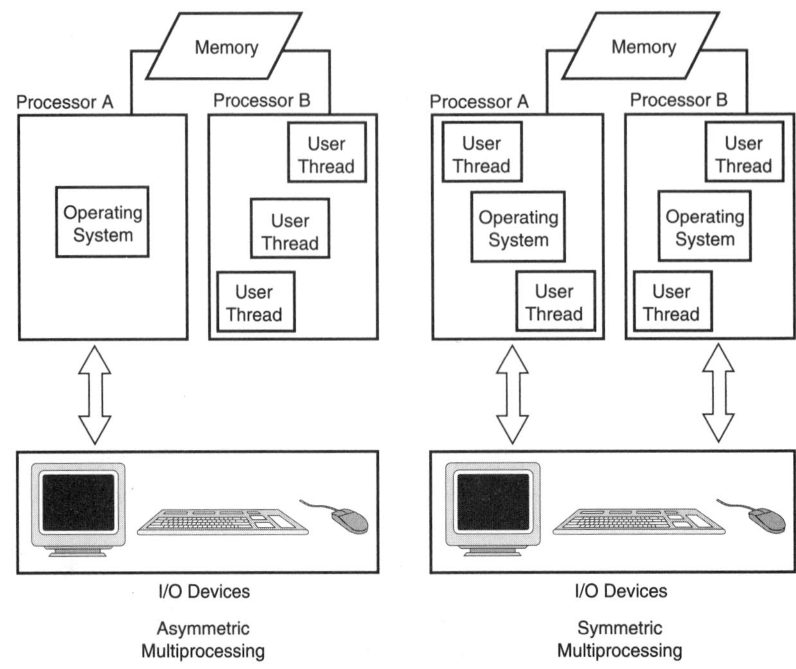

Fig. 2.1
Multiprocessor systems can be either asymmetric or symmetric.

Tip

If you're interested in switching to an SMP system but also must continue to run an operating system other than Windows NT (such as Windows 95), you can do so. Running an operating system such as Windows 95 on an SMP system simply results in all but one CPU being shut down for that session.

The File System

As a concession to backward compatibility, Windows NT fully supports the File Allocation Table (FAT) file system used by DOS on Intel-based systems. In addition, Windows NT provides its own file system called NTFS. There are numerous advantages to using NTFS in addition to, or in place of, the FAT file system:

- *Recoverability*. After a system failure or power failure, Windows NT can reconstruct the NTFS volume to a consistent state within a few seconds. NTFS also uses redundant storage for critical sectors, ensuring file system integrity even if a sector goes bad.
- *Security*. NTFS provides for a much higher degree of control over access to the file system. No file can be opened unless the user is given specific

permission to do so by a system administrator or the file's owner. Access is secured on a file-by-file basis, rather than by directory ownership and permissions.

▶ See "Controlling Resource Access," p. 226

- *Fault tolerance and redundancy.* While NTFS's recoverability ensures that the file system itself can be recovered after a system failure, it does not guarantee recovery of user files. Therefore, NTFS supports fault tolerance and redundancy features such as mirrored sets, stripes, and other levels of RAID (Redundant Array of Inexpensive Disks). This ensures continued access to files even when a disk fails, and also ensures recoverability of all files.

▶ See "Understanding Fault Tolerance," p. 377

- *Large volume sizes.* Unlike a FAT file system that uses 16-bit numbers to allocate disk space, NTFS uses 64-bit numbers, resulting in 2^{64} or more than 16 quintillion clusters, each of which can vary in size from 512 bytes on small disks to 4K on larger disks.
- *Multiple data streams.* Each unit of information such as name, contents, owner, and so on is implemented in NTFS as an object attribute, and each attribute consists of a single *data stream* of bytes. NTFS supports multiple data streams per file (include directories), making it easy to add new data streams and new information types to a file. This makes NTFS very adaptable and expandable.
- *Unicode support.* Unicode is a 16-bit character encoding method that enables different languages to be uniquely represented. Support for Unicode in NTFS eliminates the need for the code pages required by the FAT and HPFS file systems, and simplifies distributing data from one country to another.
- *Attribute indexing.* NTFS enables indexing of the file system based on attributes, which speeds up sorting and displaying of files. Although NTFS currently is structured only to index file name attributes, it could easily be modified to index by any other file attribute(s).
- *Bad-cluster remapping.* On fault-tolerant volumes, NTFS automatically retrieves a good copy of the data stored in a bad sector and dynamically maps the sector as bad, placing the data in a new, good sector.
- *Removable disks.* NTFS supports removable media such as Bernoulli disks, enabling these disks to be protected by the same levels of security as fixed disks.
- *POSIX support.* Windows NT includes POSIX support to enable you to run POSIX programs and shells. NTFS supports POSIX-related file mechanisms: case-sensitive file and directory names, file-change-time stamp, and hard links. NTFS currently doesn't support POSIX symbolic links.

If you intend to run only Windows NT on your system and not dual-boot to MS-DOS or Windows 95, converting your existing partition to NTFS will provide better performance and security. If you intend to continue using MS-DOS and/or Windows 95, however, converting to NTFS might not be a viable solution. For a more detailed explanation, refer to the section, "File System Compatibility," later in this chapter.

Scalability and Portability

As mentioned previously in this chapter ("Multitasking, Multithreading, and Multiprocessing"), Windows NT is a scalable operating system, meaning it can run on uniprocessor and multiprocessor systems. In addition, Windows NT is written primarily in the C and C++ languages, making it easily portable to new operating platforms.

Workstation versus Server

Windows NT comes in two versions: Workstation and Server. Windows NT Workstation is the best choice for user workstations, but also can act effectively as a server for relatively small workgroups (around 25 nodes). Windows NT Server is optimized to serve large workgroups and domains, and includes additional features not included with Windows NT Workstation, such as the Internet Information Server. For more information on Internet Information Server, refer to Chapter 26, "Setting Up an Internet Server with IIS."

◀ See "New Windows NT Server Features," p. 31

Although you can run the same types of programs under Windows NT Server as you can under Windows NT Workstation, the additional overhead in Server can lessen program performance. Using a server as a workstation also limits its performance as a server. Therefore, it's important for you to choose the Windows NT version that fits your needs.

Exploring Compatibility Issues

▶ See "Defining Your System Type," p. 65

Before you begin planning your Windows NT installation, you probably need to consider a number of compatibility issues that will determine how (and if) your existing programs will run, whether you'll be able to access your existing files, and so on. The following sections explore these compatibility issues.

Application Compatibility

Out of necessity to support a large installed application base and enhance the appeal of Windows NT, Microsoft built support into Windows NT for DOS and 16-bit Windows programs. Microsoft also added POSIX support to Windows NT. In version 4.0, however, support for OS/2 applications has been dropped.

In general, Windows NT can run DOS programs and 16-bit Windows programs written for Windows 3.x (referred to as Win16 programs). Many Win16 programs run equally well under Windows NT or Windows 3.x. Some Win16 programs, however, do not run under Windows NT. In particular, Win16 programs that require private virtual device drivers (VxDs) will not run under Windows NT.

Programs that conform to the Windows 95 compatibility logo requirements also run under Windows NT, so most Windows 95 programs will run fine under Windows NT. Microsoft allows for exceptions in compatibility, however, so the Windows 95 logo on a program is a good indicator but doesn't guarantee the program will run under Windows NT.

If you're upgrading your system from Windows 3.x or Windows 95 to Windows NT, or you intend to dual-boot between Windows 3.x/Windows 95 and Windows NT, verify your programs' compatibility. Check with the software publisher's technical support staff to determine if the version of the program you're using will run successfully under Windows NT. Or, connect to **http://198.105.232.4/BackOffice/infosrc.htm** to find instructions on downloading InfoSource, a directory of Windows NT-compatible hardware and software, training resources, and other Windows NT-related resources and data.

http://198.105.232.4/BackOffice/infosrc.htm Microsoft's BackOffice InfoSource links

On the Web

Tip

Many Windows NT programs are optimized for NT, taking advantage of such features as multithreading for improved performance. Consider upgrading to the NT version of an application even if your current version is compatible to take advantage of that optimization.

Integrating with Other Operating Systems

Because of its support for a wide variety of network protocols, Windows NT integrates easily with various other operating systems. Through its included TCP/IP protocol, Telnet, ftp, and third-party support for NFS, X-Windows, and other utilities, you can easily connect Windows NT systems to UNIX systems. Netware related services such as File and Print Services for Netware (FPNW) and Windows NT's Netware clients make it easy not only to connect Windows NT systems to Netware servers, but also to emulate Netware servers using Windows NT servers.

Note

For tips on using Windows NT in Novell networks, refer to Chapter 20, "Integrating Windows NT In Novell Environments." For help integrating Windows NT with UNIX systems, see Chapter 21, "Integrating Windows NT In UNIX Environments."

Naturally, Windows NT also integrates well with Microsoft's other operating systems and environments, including Windows for Workgroups and Windows 95. For help integrating Windows NT systems with systems based on Microsoft's other operating systems, see Chapter 19, "Integrating Windows NT in Microsoft Environments."

File system compatibility is another key installation issue to consider. The following section, "Understanding File System Issues," explores file system compatibility.

Understanding File System Issues

One key compatibility issue you need to consider is your file system(s). If you are upgrading from a previous operating system such as DOS or Windows 95, you must decide whether to upgrade your file system to NTFS. If you are using HPFS (High Performance File System), you need to convert your HPFS volume to either FAT or NTFS, because HPFS is no longer supported by Windows NT in version 4.0. These and other file compatibility issues are explored in the following sections.

The FAT File System

The File Allocation Table (FAT) file system has existed for many years, beginning its life on the PC in MS-DOS. Although FAT works well, it does have some disadvantages. First, FAT relies on 16-bit numbers to allocate disk space, limiting the number of clusters in a single volume to 2^{16} (65,536) clusters. This effectively limits the size of a volume.

FAT also can be very wasteful in file space allocation. FAT allocates space on the disk in *clusters*, which are groups of sectors (a sector being the smallest unit of storage space on a disk). The number of sectors in a cluster varies with drive and partition size, as shown in Table 2.1. Applying a little math to the numbers in Table 2.1 shows you that the size of one sector is 512 bytes, regardless of disk type. But, FAT allocates space by clusters, not by sectors, and this can lead to a considerable amount of wasted disk space.

Table 2.1 Clusters and Sectors Relationship

Type of Disk	Cluster Size in Bytes	Sectors Per Cluster
3 1/2-inch floppy	1,024	2
1.2M floppy	512	1
0-15M	4,096	8
16-127M	2,048	4
128-255M	4,096	8
256-511M	8,192	16
512M < 1G	16,384	32
1G or more	32,768	64

Note

These numbers apply to disks with a single partition and to logical drives in an extended partition.

Tip

Each sector also contains a 59-byte sector ID header that includes head, cylinder, and sector numbers; an address mark to indicate where the sector begins; and cyclical redundancy check (CRC) information to enable error detection in the sector ID header. The 59 bytes that comprise each sector are part of the reason a formatted disk contains less storage space than its theoretical unformatted capacity.

Consider this example: Assume you want to store a 60K file (61,440 bytes) on a 1G hard disk containing a single partition. The disk uses a cluster size of 32,768 bytes, 64 sectors per cluster (refer to Table 2.1). One cluster isn't large enough to accommodate the file, so two clusters are allocated to the file. These two clusters total 65,536 bytes, or 4,096 bytes more than required to store the file's contents, leaving eight empty sectors in the second cluster. Unfortunately, this means that almost 7 percent of the storage space is wasted. On a 1G disk, that amounts to 73M of disk space, assuming that all files waste 7 percent. Since sector slack actually could amount to 20 percent or more, you could be wasting as much as 200M on a large disk.

As you'll read in the upcoming section, "NTFS," the NTFS file system provides more efficient space allocation, and therefore is a better choice than FAT if maximum available space is critical.

It's important to note, however, that Windows NT fully supports the FAT file system. If you choose not to convert your existing FAT partition(s) to NTFS, Windows NT will be able to read and write to the file system without any problems.

NTFS

◀ See "The File System," p. 36

The NT File System, or NTFS, provides many advantages over the FAT file system (explained earlier in the section, "The File System"). These advantages include better performance, recoverability, fault tolerance, security, and more. In short, NTFS is an ideal option.

If you will only be using Windows NT on your system, you can convert your existing partition(s) to NTFS without any problems. Like DOS and other operating systems, Windows NT isolates the file system from your programs so they will have no trouble accessing files.

If you plan to use other operating systems on your computer, however, NTFS might not be a workable solution. This is because DOS, OS/2, and Windows 95 do not support NTFS and can't read NTFS. If you have one or more of these operating systems on your computer in addition to Windows NT, and you convert your file system to NTFS, these other operating systems will no longer be able to read the files in the NTFS volume. If these other operating systems are contained in that volume, they will no longer load.

One solution to this problem is to leave the existing file system intact and create a new partition for NTFS. You'll enjoy the benefits of NTFS for Windows NT without losing accessibility to your existing files for your other operating system(s). Unfortunately, creating a new partition for NTFS generally will mean resizing your existing partition, which requires deleting and recreating the partition. You'll first have to back up your entire existing file system and restore it after the repartitioning (assuming all the files will still fit in the reduced partition).

Note

Because Windows NT supports the FAT file system, Windows NT and programs you run under Windows NT will be able to access files in the FAT and NTFS partitions. Windows NT 4.0 no longer supports HPFS (High Performance File System used in OS/2), so neither Windows NT nor your Windows NT programs will be able to access an HPFS volume if one exists on your system.

These limitations only apply on the local computer, however. A Windows 95 computer, for example, can access a NTFS volume on a Windows NT computer across the network because file access then becomes a function of the network redirector, not the file system itself.

HPFS

Previous versions of Windows NT supported OS/2's High Performance File System (HPFS). Windows NT 4.0, however, drops HPFS support. A Windows NT 4.0 computer can't read or otherwise access an HPFS volume on a local drive. If your system contains an HPFS volume and you must be able to access its files in Windows NT, you must convert the HPFS file system to FAT or NTFS. The only way to achieve this is to copy the files from the HPFS volume to a FAT volume, which can be accessed by Windows NT or converted to an NTFS volume. Because Windows NT can't read HPFS, you'll have to copy the files from the HPFS volume using OS/2.

Disk Compression

Disk compression has been common in PCs for many years, and became popular with the introduction of DoubleSpace and DriveSpace in DOS and third party solutions such as Stacker. Windows NT, however, has been slow to support disk compression outside the NTFS file system.

Windows NT 4.0 supports compression, but not the type of on-the-fly compression provided by DriveSpace and other solutions for Windows 95 and DOS systems. Through File Manager or the Windows NT command line, you can compress and decompress individual files or directories. The compression process is not automatic—you must manually initiate the compression. Windows NT does, however, decompress the files automatically when you use them. You therefore enjoy the benefits of disk compression without the same level of performance drop occasioned by DriveSpace and similar compression utilities.

Because it doesn't support DriveSpace compressed volumes, you will have to reconfigure your system if you intend to use Windows NT on a system that also contains DOS or Windows 95 and compressed DriveSpace volumes. You'll be able to access the DriveSpace volumes while running DOS, Windows 3.x, and Windows 95, but not while running Windows NT. To access the files in the DriveSpace volume under Windows NT, you must copy the files to a noncompressed FAT volume or move the files to a network server.

▶ See "Using Disk Compression," p. 355

Understanding Security Issues

If you're moving from an operating system such as DOS or Windows 95 to Windows NT, you might not be familiar with many of the security issues surrounding Windows NT. The following sections bring you up to speed on Windows NT's security features to help you begin planning your Windows NT installation.

C-2 Security

Windows NT provides C2-level security, one of seven levels of security defined by the United States government. A C2-level system such as Windows NT must support the following security features:

- *Secure logon.* Users must identify themselves with a user name and password to gain access to the system. Unlike Windows for Workgroups and Windows 95, you must have a logon account and password created on the system by an administrator. You can't create your own logon on-the-fly.
- *Discretionary access control.* The owner of a resource determines which other users, if any, can gain access to the resource. If you create a file, you determine who else can access the file, and what level of access (read, modify, and so on) those others have to the file.
- *Auditing.* The system must track and record events relating to the security of the system and access to resources.
- *Memory protection.* Applications, files, and other resources must be protected from one another to prevent unauthorized access across the network.

> **Note**
>
> Although Microsoft's position has been that Windows NT will eventually support B-2 security (a higher level of security), no announcements have been made explaining when this will occur.

User Accounts and Privileges

As mentioned in the previous section, each user must have a preexisting account on the system in order to logon and gain access to the computer's and network's resources. On Windows for Workgroups and Windows 95 systems, a user can create an account and password on-the-fly by simply entering a new account name and password in the logon dialog box. With Windows NT, however, the account must have previously been created by an administrator. This provides a much higher degree of control over access to the computer and network.

Caution

Enabling users to dual-boot their systems between DOS or Windows 95 and Windows NT is a potential security risk. If the computer's local resources must be secure, you should not leave DOS or Windows 95 on the system or allow the user to boot to either of these operating systems. Because of the lower level of security with these two operating systems, it's possible for an unauthorized user to access restricted information on the system, and possibly the network. Windows NT plugs that security gap by requiring every user to have a valid account and password.

Windows NT supports a range of standard user groups, each with specific levels of access privileges. These standard groups are described in the following list:

- *Administrators.* Users who belong to the Administrators group have access to all resources on the system. Administrators can create user accounts and groups, assign permissions to resources, control sharing of resources, and shut down the system. Administrator access does not guarantee full access to all directories or files, however. A user can create a directory or file but not grant access to it to Administrators. Administrators can, however, take ownership of the directory or file.
- *Power Users.* Users in the Power Users group can manage user accounts and shared resources, and create resources for common access (such as folders and shortcuts). Power Users, however, don't have the same level of access as Administrators. A person in the Power User group, for example, can't take ownership of a file from the person who created the file.
- *Users.* This is the most common group, and the majority of the users on a system or network belong to this group. Users can create their own resources (such as files) and control access to those resources. Users, however, are restricted to the access rights assigned to them by Administrators.
- *Guests.* This group is designed for infrequent users of the system. Generally, access rights are severely restricted (often only to the files created by the guest users).
- *Replicators.* This group supports directory replication across a domain, and should contain only the domain user account used to log on to the replicator services of the primary domain controller and backup domain controllers in the domain.

- *Backup Operators.* This group enables the user to act as a backup operator, backing up and restoring files (such as to or from tape).

In addition to these groups, other groups are added for domains:

- *Domain Admins.* Users in this group administer the primary and backup domain controllers and workstations in the domain.
- *Domain Users.* This group enables users to work on computers within the domain.
- *Domain Guests.* This group enables guest users to connect to and use resources within the domain (subject to the limitations of the guest status).
- *Account Operators.* Members of this group can administer accounts within the domain through the User Manager for Domains utility. These members also can log on to domain servers, shut down domain servers, and use Server Manager to add computers to a domain.
- *Print Operators.* Users in this group can create, manage, and delete printer shares.
- *Server Operators.* Users in this group can manage primary and backup domain controllers in a domain.

In addition to these groups, Windows NT includes a set of special groups that you can use when assigning permissions:

- *Everyone.* This group includes anyone using the computer, including local and remote users.
- *Network.* This group includes all users connected to the computer over the network.
- *Interactive.* This group applies to anyone using the computer locally.
- *System.* This group applies to the operating system.
- *Creator Owner.* This group applies to users who create or own a resource.

Groups and permissions are explored in more detail in Chapter 10, "Administering Users." For now, understand that you must be prepared to create an Administrator account when you install Windows NT. After installation, you can run the User Manager to create additional accounts and apply appropriate group status and permissions to those accounts.

An Overview of Setup

The process for installing Windows NT is straightforward, and is explained in detail in Chapter 4, "Installing Windows NT." This section of this chapter gives you a brief overview of Setup so you'll know what to expect and can begin planning the installation. You can use this section as a "Quick Start" guide to installing Windows NT.

Installing Windows NT on New Systems

You can install Windows NT on a new system that contains no previous operating system and systems that contain only DOS. Windows NT Setup detects and installs support for the system's CD-ROM controller and drive, enabling Setup to install from the CD. Setup also partitions and formats the disk according to your specifications.

To start installation on these systems, follow these steps:

1. Turn off the computer and insert the Windows NT Setup Boot Disk in the boot floppy drive (usually, drive A), then turn on the computer.
2. When prompted to do so, insert Boot Disks 2 and 3, followed by the Windows NT CD.
3. Follow the instructions provided by Setup to complete the installation.

Upgrading a Previous Version of Windows NT

You can easily upgrade an existing Windows NT 3.x installation to version 4.0. To do so, you must have either local or network access to the Windows NT 4.0 file set (local CD or network distribution share). Initiation of Setup is performed from the Windows NT command prompt as follows:

1. At the Windows NT command prompt, connect to the drive on which the Windows NT 4.0 files are located. Then, change to the appropriate directory, such as I386 for Intel-based systems.
2. Enter the command **winnt32** to start Setup (or enter **winnt32 /b** to bypass creation of bootable floppy disks).
3. When prompted to do so, specify the local directory containing the copy of Windows NT you want to update.
4. Follow Setup's prompts to complete the upgrade process.

Upgrading Windows 3.x

The process for upgrading Windows 3.x (including Windows for Workgroups) to Windows NT 4.0 is similar to the process for upgrading a previous version of Windows NT. When you upgrade from Windows 3.x to Windows NT, Setup incorporates your currently installed programs and user settings, such as converting your Program Manager groups to Windows NT shortcuts and adding them to the Start menu.

Caution

If you upgrade your current Windows 3.x installation to Windows NT, you'll no longer be able to run Windows 3.x. If you need to continue to run Windows 3.x and Windows NT, create a multi-boot system as explained later in the section, "Creating Multi-Boot Systems."

To upgrade your existing Windows 3.x installation to Windows NT, follow these steps:

1. From the command prompt, connect to the drive containing the Windows NT 4.0 files (local CD or network distribution share). Then, change to the appropriate directory, such as I386 for Intel-based systems.
2. At the command prompt, enter the command **winnt** (or **winnt /b** to skip creation of bootable floppy disks).
3. When Setup prompts you to select the location of the Windows NT 4.0 files, select the directory appropriate to your type of system (such as I386 for Intel-based systems).
4. When prompted to do so, select the directory containing the Windows 3.x operating system you want to update.
5. Follow Setup's prompts to complete the upgrade process.

Note

Because of major differences between the Windows NT and Windows 95 Registries, Windows NT cannot upgrade a Windows 95 installation. You must install Windows NT to a new directory and reinstall any applications that require Registry settings. Prior to reinstalling an application, try running the application's executable file to see if it will run under Windows NT without reinstallation.

Creating Multi-Boot Systems

If you need or want to retain your existing operating system (DOS, Windows 3.x, or Windows 95), you can install Windows NT to a new directory. After installation, you'll be able to boot either Windows NT or your other operating system, as desired. At startup, the system presents a character-based menu enabling you to select which operating system you want to boot. If your previous operating system including multi-boot configuration files, you'll still have the ability to select that operating system's boot options, just as you did before installing Windows NT. If you've configured Windows 95 to display its boot menu, that boot menu appears after the system boot menu.

To create a multi-boot installation, follow these steps:

1. Connect to the directory containing the Windows NT 4.0 files (local CD or network distribution share). Then, change to the appropriate directory, such as I386 for Intel-based systems.
2. At the command prompt, enter the command **winnt** (or **winnt /b** to skip creation of bootable floppy disks).
3. Setup displays a list of the operating systems on your system. Press **N** and when prompted to do so, specify a new directory to contain Windows NT 4.0.
4. Follow Setup's prompts to complete the installation process.

You can also configure the system to boot an existing version of Windows NT 3.x, as well as Windows NT 4.0. To do so, follow the steps outlined previously, except in step 2, use the command **winnt32** (or **winnt32 /b**). When Setup displays the list of operating systems to upgrade, enter **N** and specify a new directory for Windows NT 4.0.

When you install Windows NT 4.0 to a new directory to create a multi-boot system with Windows 3.x, Windows 95, or Windows NT 3.x as the other operating system, Setup will not migrate your current user settings or applications to the new Windows NT 4.0 installation. You have to customize the settings after installation, and reinstall many of your applications in order to use them under Windows NT 4.0. This is primarily because the programs' DLLs and other support files must be copied to a location where Windows NT can locate them, and the programs' Registry settings must be incorporated into the new Windows NT 4.0 Registry.

Many programs, however, will work without reinstallation. Before you reinstall a program, try to run it. If the program doesn't use Registry settings or require its DLLs to be in a specific location, it's likely you'll be able to run the program without reinstalling it.

Tip

If you have to reinstall the program, you don't have to place it in a new folder. Backup any program support files you have customized (such as templates), then under Windows NT 4.0, reinstall the program in its current directory. After completing the installation, restore your customized files. The program should run under Windows NT 4.0 just as it does under your other operating system(s).

Installing on RISC Systems

Installing Windows NT 4.0 on a RISC-based system is slightly different from an Intel-based installation, and varies with the type of RISC system you're using. For installation instructions for specific RISC systems, see Chapter 4, "Installing Windows NT." ❖

CHAPTER 3

Planning the Installation

by Jim Boyce

Installing Windows NT is a multiphase process. The first phase is to understand the operating system and its overall impact on your systems, network, and the way you work. If you read Chapter 2, "Understanding Key Installation Issues," you should have a mental checkmark beside phase one. Phase two is to begin preparing your hardware for the installation.

In this chapter, you learn to

- Set up and prepare your hardware
- Back up critical files
- Evaluate and plan the file system
- Plan network options
- Define your system type

Although phase one includes physically setting up and connecting your computer's components, *Windows NT 4.0 Installation and Configuration Handbook* assumes you have the knowledge necessary to perform those steps. The coverage of hardware setup is therefore limited to steps specific to Windows NT, as you'll discover in the following section.

Setting Up and Preparing Your Hardware

Before you begin installing Windows NT, examine your system to verify that it's ready and configured for a trouble-free installation.

Checking Hardware Compatibility

Windows NT directly supports a variety of systems and peripherals through drivers included with Windows NT. Unfortunately, Windows NT's relatively low market share compared to Windows 3.x and Windows 95 means that most hardware vendors concentrate development efforts first on their Windows 3.x and Windows 95 support, then follow with Windows NT support. Smaller manufacturers often don't have the resources to develop for multiple operating systems. The result is that some hardware supported on these other operating systems is not supported or offers limited functionality under Windows NT.

Note

Support for your computer's CD-ROM drive and associated host adapter is particularly important because Windows NT installs from the CD. Windows NT supports a variety of SCSI and non-SCSI CD-ROM drives. Check the Hardware Compatiblility List (HCL) to make sure your adapter and drive are supported.

For example, one of the most popular mouse manufacturers, Logitech, provides full support for Windows 3.x and Windows 95—including expanded drivers to support middle-button function assignment. A Logitech mouse works fine under Windows NT's built-in driver, but it lacks the capability to use the middle button or to reprogram left- and right-button functions. Another example of limited compatibility is the Media Vision ProAudio Spectrum Pro, which enjoys full support under Windows 3.x and Windows 95, but lacks Sound Blaster compatibility under Windows NT.

Because hardware compatibility is a larger issue with Windows NT than with Windows 95, you should avoid potential problems by ensuring that your hardware is compatible to the degree you require under Windows NT before starting installation. This is particularly important if you're buying a new system for Windows NT.

To help you check your system's compatibility, Microsoft includes a hardware compatibility list (HCL) with Windows NT. The HCL lists the hardware that has been tested and certified as compatible with Windows NT, and includes footnotes for specific items detailing special driver requirements or limitations to compatibility. If you have not yet purchased Windows NT and want to access the HCL, you can do so through Microsoft's Internet sites, and CompuServe forums.

Microsoft's Web sites

http://www.microsoft.com/ntserver/hcl/hclintro.htm

http://www.microsoft.com/BackOffice/ntserver/hcl

Microsoft's ftp sites

ftp.microsoft.com\bussys\winnt\winnt-docs\hcl

CompuServe forums

WINNT, Library 1

MSWIN32, Library 17

If a hardware item isn't listed in the HCL, it still might be compatible. Some devices emulate more common devices. For example, many sound cards emulate Sound Blaster cards, which are supported by Windows NT. If your hardware isn't listed, check with the manufacturer to determine whether the hardware is supported directly by Windows NT or if the manufacturer offers a Windows NT driver for the device.

Verifying Firmware Version

If you're installing Windows NT on a DEC Alpha system, you need to verify that the correct firmware revision is installed on your system. (*Firmware* refers to the system configuration sofware installed in a computer's ROM.) If it isn't, you need to upgrade the system's firmware accordingly.

A README.TXT file is available that explains the firmware revisions needed for specific DEC Alpha systems. You can find the README.TXT file on CompuServe in Library 4 (Hardware Support) of the DEC4WNT forum. Or, you can retrieve the file via ftp from the /private/fwaxp directory at **gatekeeper.dec.com**. When you determine the correct firmware version for your system, you can retrieve the firmware and driver updates from the DEC Web site at **http://www.windowsnt.digital.com**.

DEC Web site

http://www.windowsnt.digital.com

DEC ftp site

gatekeeper.dec.com/private/fwaxp

CompuServe Forum

DEC4WNT, Library 4

Tip

For technical support or answers to questions regarding firmware updates, you can contact DEC technical support at (800) 354-9000 in the U.S. Outside the U.S., you can contact the local DEC representative.

Disconnecting the UPS

During installation, Windows NT Setup attempts to detect devices connected to the system's serial ports. This can cause problems with systems that are connected by serial cable to a UPS. If your system is connected to a UPS through a serial port, disconnect the system from the UPS before starting the installation process. The installation process is fairly quick, so the length of time the system will be unprotected by the UPS should be short.

Removing the Shell Technology Preview

The Shell Technology Preview is Microsoft's beta distribution of the Windows 95 interface for Windows NT. If you use the Shell Technology Preview (STP), you must uninstall it before upgrading your existing Windows NT installation to Windows NT 4.0.

To uninstall the STP, locate the SHUPDATE.CMD command that pertains to your installation type, such as \newshell\i386\SHUPDATE.CMD, from the directory in which you installed the STP. Then execute the command with the `/u` option to remove the shell preview:

```
\newshell\i386\shupdate.cmd /u
```

After you remove the shell and install Windows NT 4.0, you can restore your previous Start menu and desktop. To do so, open a command prompt and issue the following commands:

```
xcopy "%SystemRoot%\Start Menu" "%USERPROFILE%\Start Menu" /ec
xcopy "%SystemRoot%\Desktop" "%USERPROFILE%\Desktop" /ec
xcopy "%SystemRoot%" "%USERPROFILE%\Recent" /ec
```

Detecting and Disabling FPU Division Error

During Windows NT installation, Setup checks the CPU in your system for the floating-point division error that exists in early Pentium chips. If Setup detects the error, it prompts you to disable the FPU (Floating Point Unit). If you want to continue the installation process, however, you can do so. If you later decide to disable the FPU, you can use a utility called PENTNT that is included with Windows NT.

To use PENTNT, locate the file \i386\PENTNT.EX_ on your Windows NT CD. Open a command prompt, then issue the following command to expand the file to your hard disk:

```
expand d:\i386\pentnt.ex_ c:pentnt.exe
```

Substitute the appropriate source drive letter, and a different location on the hard disk for the expanded file if you want. Next, open a command prompt and enter the `PENTNT` command.

Tip

You might want to check your system's FPU prior to starting the Windows NT installation process to determine whether your Pentium CPU contains the FPU bug. If it does, you can install a newer chip without the bug. Use the directions described previously to expand and run the PENTNT utility. If your CPU doesn't contain the FPU bug, PENTNT will inform you of that fact.

Backing Up Critical Files

Another necessary step in installing Windows NT is to back up your system's critical files. Backing up the entire file system is the best option, because it ensures that all of your files are backed up. If you want to back up only some of your files, you'll find the following sections helpful for various types of systems. In addition, the sections discuss general backup strategies.

Choosing a Backup Method

The method you use to back up your system's files depends on the operating system you're currently using, whether your system is connected to a network, and the type of local backup hardware available to you (floppy, tape, CD-R). The following sections cover a variety of possibilities.

▶ See "Examining Backup Strategies and Media," p. 363

Note

CD-R refers to CD-Recordable, but CD-ROM refers to read-only CDs.

Local Backup Hardware

If you have relatively few document and data files on your system, simply copying them to floppy disk is a good option. If your system contains a tape drive, CD-R, Zip drive, or other backup hardware, you might prefer to back up your data files to this type of device. You should verify, however, that the device is supported under Windows NT 4.0. Also, verify that the backup software you will be using will run under Windows NT 4.0.

If the backup software runs only on your old operating system (such as DOS, Windows 3.x, or Windows 95), you'll have to retain the old operating system and create a dual-boot configuration. This will enable you to boot the old operating system, restore the files, then boot Windows NT to use them.

Network Backup

If your workstation is connected to a network, another option is to back up your files to a network server. If you're considering this option, consult your network administrator to determine whether space is available on a server and for help in backing up the files. The administrator probably will help you schedule the backup at a time when the increased network traffic from the backup won't have a major impact on other users.

◀ See "Creating Multi-Boot Systems," p. 48

As with a local backup, make sure the backup program you use to back up the files to the server will run under Windows NT 4.0. If not, you'll have to create a dual-boot system.

DOS Systems

On DOS systems, back up your existing CONFIG.SYS and AUTOEXEC.BAT files. If you're using a network, back up the network files, such as PROTOCOL.INI and any other network configuration files specific to your network type.

Windows 3.x Systems

On Windows 3.x systems, you should back up your CONFIG.SYS and AUTOEXEC.BAT files. In addition, back up the SYSTEM.INI and WIN.INI files from your Windows directory, as well as PROGRAM.INI, WINFILE.INI, CONTROL.INI, and PROTOCOL.INI. In fact, you should consider backing up all of the INI files in the Windows directory—this will give you backups of all your Windows system initialization files and your application INI files.

Windows 95 Systems

You should back up your Windows 95 Registry, initialization files, and system files. These include the following:

CONFIG.SYS

AUTOEXEC.BAT

WIN.INI

SYSTEM.INI

PROTOCOL.INI

USER.DAT

SYSTEM.DAT

IO.SYS

MSDOS.SYS

COMMAND.COM

Tip

If your system is a dual-boot system (DOS and Windows 95), you have four configuration files to back up. If you perform the backup from DOS, the files are CONFIG.SYS, AUTOEXEC.BAT, CONFIG.W40, and AUTOEXEC.W40. If you perform the backup from Windows 95, the four files are CONFIG.SYS, AUTOEXEC.BAT, CONFIG.DOS, and AUTOEXEC.DOS.

Although you could back up these files manually, Windows 95 includes a utility called Emergency Recovery Utility (ERU) that automates the process for you. ERU is contained on the Windows 95 CD in the folder \Other\Misc\Eru. To run ERU, locate the folder on the CD and double-click the ERU.EXE file. ERU first displays a dialog box that explains the function of ERU. Choose Next to continue and display the disk selection screen of the Emergency Recovery Utility dialog box (see fig. 3.1). Choose the Drive A button to store the files on floppy disk, or choose the Other Directory button to store the files on a local hard disk or network volume. Choose Next to continue. If you chose the Other Directory button, ERU prompts you to specify the disk and folder for the backup set.

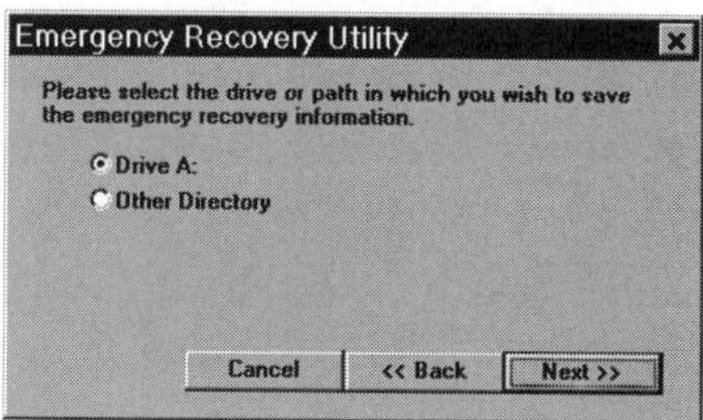

Fig. 3.1
Select the location for your backup files.

ERU lists the files it will back up (see fig. 3.2). If you want to back up all of the listed files, click Next. If you want to back up only some of the files, choose Custom to display an expanded dialog box you can use to select and deselect the backup of specific files (see fig. 3.3).

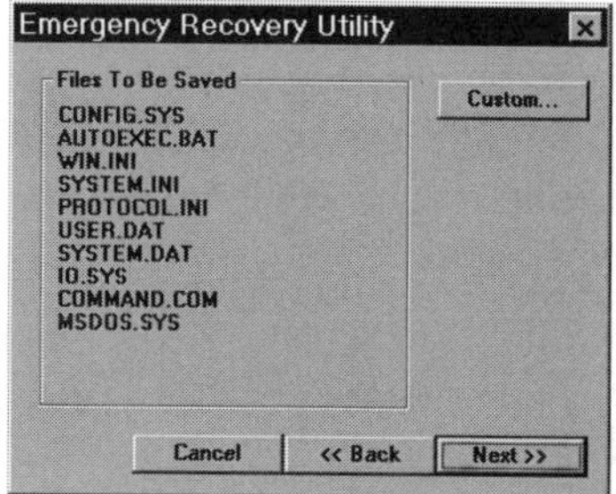

Fig. 3.2
ERU selects a default set of files it will back up.

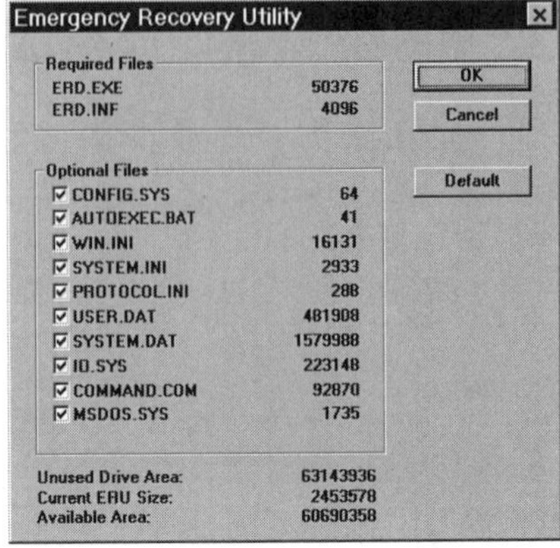

Fig. 3.3
You can selectively back up only some of the system's configuration files.

If you use the selective backup method, simply deselect the checkbox for each file you want to omit from the backup set. Then choose OK. ERU returns to the previous dialog box, removing the deselected files from the backup list. When you're ready to start the backup, click Next. ERU displays a status dialog box as the files are copied (see fig. 3.4).

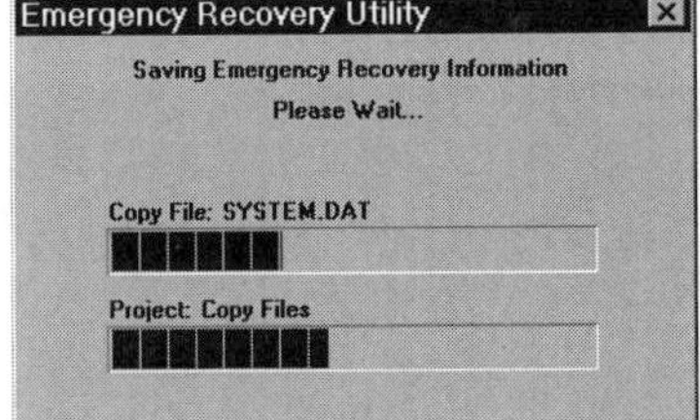

Fig. 3.4
ERU displays the status of the backup.

Tip

You can switch focus away from ERU's status dialog box to continue working in other applications. The status dialog box stays on top so you can monitor ERU's progress while you work.

If it becomes necessary to restore your Windows 95 files, boot your system to a Windows 95 command prompt. Execute the file ERD.EXE from the CD. The program will prompt you to select what files to restore.

Windows NT Systems

If you are upgrading your existing Windows NT system to Windows NT 4.0, you should first back up your Registry. To do so, you can use the REGBACK utility included with the Microsoft Windows NT Resource Kit. The REGREST utility, also included with the Windows NT Resource Kit, enables you to restore a Registry. If you don't have the Resource Kit or access to these two utilities, you can use a manual method to back up the Registry:

1. Shut down Windows NT.
2. Reboot the system to DOS using a dual-boot configuration or a DOS boot disk.
3. Copy the entire contents of the \WINNT\SYSTEM32\CONFIG directory to a disk. If you're using floppy disks, you'll require several disks to complete the copy.

If it becomes necessary to restore the Registry (after a failed upgrade, for example), again boot the system to DOS and replace all of the existing files in the \WINNT\SYSTEM32\CONFIG directory with the backup set.

In addition to backing up the Registry, consider backing up BOOT.INI, NTDETECT.COM, and NTLDR from the root directory of the hard disk to a floppy disk. These three files control the Windows NT boot process.

Creating and Updating a Repair Disk

In addition to backing up the files described in the previous section, you should have a Windows NT repair disk for your current Windows NT installation. If you don't have a current repair disk, create one before you upgrade to Windows NT 4.0. If you do have a repair disk, you should take the time to update it before upgrading to 4.0.

> **Note**
>
> During the installation of Windows NT 4.0, you have the option of creating a repair disk for 4.0. You should allow Setup to create the repair disk for you. However, you should have a repair disk for your current version prior to upgrading, because the two will not be compatible.

To create a repair disk, execute the program RDISK.EXE (Repair Disk Utility) in the \WINNT\SYSTEM32 directory. The Repair Disk Utility enables you to create a repair disk and update an existing repair disk (see fig. 3.5).

Click the Create Repair Disk button and follow the prompts to create the disk. To update your existing repair disk, insert the repair disk in drive A and choose the Update Repair Info button. Follow the prompts to complete the update.

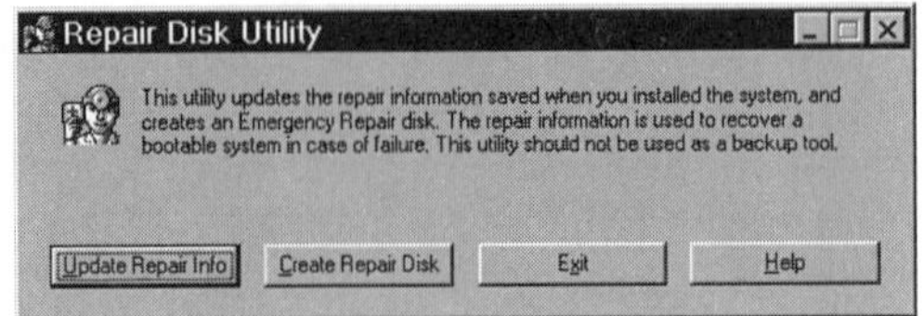

Fig. 3.5
RDISK.EXE enables you to create or update a repair disk.

Evaluating and Planning the File System

After you back up your important files, your next step is to analyze your existing file system and determine what changes you need to make to your file system to run Windows NT 4.0. The following sections provide an overview of the issues you need to consider.

> **Note**
>
> File system issues are discussed briefly in Chapter 2, "Understanding Key Installation Issues." For a more in-depth discussion of FAT, NTFS, and other file system issues, see Chapter 16, "Optimizing the File System." The following sections offer quick pre-installation tips on what to do for specific file systems.

FAT versus NTFS

◄ See "The File System," p. 36

Windows NT is fully compatible with the FAT file system used on DOS and Windows 95 systems. You can continue to use the FAT file system if you want. As explained in Chapter 2, "Understanding Key Installation Issues," however, the NTFS file system offers much better security and fault tolerance.

Unfortunately, DOS and Windows 95 don't support NTFS; therefore, they can't read NTFS volumes. If you currently use only Windows NT or plan to use only Windows NT after you upgrade, you can convert your existing FAT volume to NTFS. Setup will give you the option of doing so when you install or upgrade to Windows NT 4.0. There is nothing you need to do before the installation process to prepare for the conversion (unless you want to back up your file system first).

> **Note**
>
> See Chapter 4, "Installing Windows NT" for basic installation information.

If you will be using DOS or Windows 95 on the system in addition to Windows NT (dual-boot configuration) and you want to use NTFS, remember that DOS and Windows 95 cannot read any of the files in the NTFS volume. You have to repartition the hard disk to add an NTFS volume. To repartition the hard disk, follow these steps:

1. Back up the entire file system.
2. Delete the existing partition.
3. Using FDISK, create a new partition for the FAT volume, leaving space on the disk for the NTFS partition.
4. Format the FAT partition with FORMAT.
5. Reinstall the previous operating system.
6. Restore the files to the FAT volume from the backup set.
7. Run Windows NT Setup to create the NTFS partition.

Note

Adding an NTFS partition is a cumbersome process. Converting an existing FAT partition to NTFS is simple, however, and Setup can perform that task for you. You don't lose any of your existing files in the conversion. Because it is such a lengthy and involved process to add an NTFS partition to a fully partitioned disk, you should only retain the FAT file system if you must continue to also use DOS or Windows 95 on the system—otherwise, let Setup convert the FAT volume to NTFS.

Converting from HPFS

Unlike previous versions, Windows NT 4.0 doesn't support the HPFS file system. If your system contains an HPFS partition and you want to continue to access it under Windows NT 4.0, you have to convert the HPFS partition to an NTFS partition. To do so, you need the following utilities:

- *CONVERT.EXE*. This Windows NT utility converts a FAT or HPFS volume to NTFS. It is included with Windows NT.
- *BACKACC.EXE*. This OS/2 utility (which runs under OS/2) copies the HPFS access control lists to a file. After converting the volume to NTFS, you use the ACLCONV.EXE utility to incorporate the access control lists into the new NTFS volume.
- *ACLCONV.EXE*. This Windows NT utility incorporates the access control lists created by BACKACC.EXE into the converted NTFS volume.

◄ See "Understanding File System Issues," p. 40

Caution

The ACLCONV.EXE utility is included with earlier versions of Windows NT, but is not included with Windows NT 4.0. Therefore, you must convert the HPFS volume prior to upgrading to Windows NT 4.0.

To convert the HPFS volume to NTFS, follow these steps:

1. Boot the system to OS/2 and run the BACKACC.EXE utility to copy the access control lists to a file. Give the file a short name and place it in a directory (or on a floppy disk) that Windows NT can access.
2. Boot the system to your current version of Windows NT.
3. Run the CONVERT.EXE utility to convert the HPFS volume to NTFS, using the following example as a guide:

   ```
   CONVERT C: /FS:NTFS
   ```

   In this example, `C:` specifies the volume to be converted, and the `/FS:NTFS` switch specifies that the volume be converted to NTFS.
4. After converting the volume to NTFS, run the utility ACLCONV.EXE to restore the old HPFS security settings to the NTFS volume. The following is an example:

   ```
   ACLCONV backupfile /LOG:logfile
   ```

   In this example, you should replace `backupfile` with the name of the ACL backup you created under OS/2 in step 1. Replace `logfile` with the name of a log file in which you want ACLCONV to log error and status messages.

Integrating Compressed Volumes

As explained in Chapter 2, "Understanding Key Installation Issues," Windows NT doesn't support DriveSpace volumes, and Microsoft has no plans at this time to support DriveSpace in future Windows NT versions. If you have DriveSpace (or DoubleSpace) drives on your system that you need to access in Windows NT, you have to uncompress those volumes. If you still need to take advantage of compression, you can compress the files under Windows NT using the Explorer.

◄ See "Understanding File System Issues," p. 40

If you're running DOS, you must use the DRVSPACE utility included with DOS to uncompress the drive. If you're using Windows 95, choose Start, Programs, Accessories, System Tools, and DriveSpace to start the DriveSpace program.

> **Note**
>
> You need enough free space on the host drive to contain the uncompressed files; unfortunately, you might not have enough. If your system is connected to a network, check with the system administrator about backing up your compressed volumes to a network server. After the compressed volumes are safely backed up, you can delete them from your system. Then, install Windows NT 4.0, convert the file system to

NTFS, and begin copying the files to the NTFS volume from the network server. If necessary, you can compress the files using Explorer to gain enough space to contain the files.

▶ See "Using Disk Compression," p. 355

Planning Network Options

After you plan how to incorporate your existing file system under Windows NT 4.0, you need to consider your options for networking. The following sections provide a brief overview of networking issues you need to deal with during installation.

Domains and Workgroups

During installation, Setup prompts you to specify whether you want your system to become part of a workgroup or a domain. The following sections explain the difference between the two to help you determine which one applies to you.

Note

This chapter provides only an overview of workgroups and domains to enable you to decide which applies to your installation. For a detailed discussion of domains, domain management, and workgroups, see Chapter 9, "Administering Servers and Sharing Resources."

Understanding Workgroups

A *workgroup* is really nothing more than a logical grouping of computers on a network. Each computer has a unique name that identifies it in its workgroup. When you browse the network for shared resources, the resources shared by other computers in your workgroup are the ones you see first. The network can include multiple workgroups, and you can easily access the resources shared by computers in other workgroups. In essence, workgroups provide a means of organizing the display of shared resources in a logical manner. When you open the Network Neighborhood, for example, all of the computers in your workgroup appear in the window, which enables you to quickly locate resources in your workgroup (see fig. 3.6).

In a workgroup, security is handled on a server-by-server basis. This means that a user must have a valid account on each node that shares a resource. If your workgroup contains a centralized server and all shared resources are placed on that server, providing access to those resources is easy. Each user simply needs a valid account on that server.

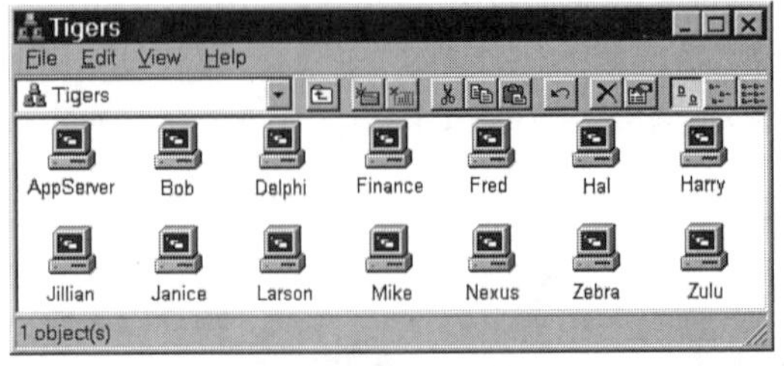

Fig. 3.6
Use workgroups to organize resources on the network.

▶ See "How Peer-to-Peer Sharing Works," p. 206

If you add multiple servers or want to access resources on a peer-to-peer basis, access becomes much more complex. If the workgroup contains 30 workstations, for example, and you want to access resources on all 30 workstations, you need 30 different accounts—one on each workstation. To simplify security and resource availability, therefore, you should consider using domains.

Understanding Domains

A *domain* is a group of computers that share a common user policy and security account database. In the domain, a *primary domain controller* (PDC) handles all security validation. *Backup domain controllers* (BDC) on the network can take over security validation if the PDC is unavailable. Only computers running Windows NT Server can act as domain controllers.

Securing access to resources across the network is greatly simplified in a domain. Instead of requiring a user to have an account on each node or server that shares a resource, the user only needs an account on the PDC. Other servers or workstations to which the user connects to access resources validate that user's access privileges through the PDC.

This provides simplified resource sharing, and it enables the user to log on to any workstation in the domain without needing an account on that workstation. The resources on that workstation are still secure because access to them is validated through the PDC. You might log on to a workstation, for example, but not be able to access any of the files on it.

Note

If your network contains multiple domains, managing security can become as complex as it is for workgroups. To simplify security management and resource distribution, you can create trust relationships between domains. In a *trust relationship*, one domain trusts another to provide security authorization. Users in a trusted domain can access resources in the trusting domain, even if they don't have an account in the trusting domain (subject to the resource's privilege assignments).

Defining Your System Type

During installation, Setup prompts you to specify whether your computer will be part of a workgroup, a PDC, or a BDC. A domain can contain only one PDC, but can contain multiple BDCs. Before running Setup, determine whether your computer will be a workgroup member, PDC, or BDC.

> **Note**
>
> You can promote a computer from a BDC to a PDC with Server Manager. When you do so, the current PDC is automatically demoted to a BDC. To convert a member of a workgroup to a domain controller, however, you have to reinstall Windows NT. This is why it is important to determine what your computer's function will be prior to running Setup.

Defining Other Network Options

In addition to determining what role your computer will play in the network, you need to decide before running Setup which network protocols, clients, and services you need to use. The protocols and clients you choose depend to a large extent on the other computers and servers on your network. If you're installing Windows NT Workstation 4.0 on a Netware network, for example, you should probably use the IPX/SPX protocol and Netware client, which will enable you to access resources on Netware servers.

The following sections offer an overview of options, protocols, clients, and services for various network environments.

Choosing a Protocol

Windows NT provides built-in support for the following network protocols:

- *NetBEUI.* NetBEUI is well-suited to small networks, but can't be routed. For this reason, NetBEUI is not a good choice for large networks, but the ease with which you can configure it makes it ideal for small networks that do not require routing.
- *NWLink (IPX/SPX).* Microsoft developed NWLink to be compatible with Novell Netware's IPX/SPX protocols. NWLink offers the advantages of Netware compatibility, routeability, and ease-of-configuration. NWLink is a good choice for all sizes of networks.
- *TCP/IP.* TCP/IP is one of the oldest protocols, but still provides excellent performance, reliability, and routeability. TCP/IP works well in any size network, and is a necessity for connecting to the Internet. The only disadvantage to TCP/IP is that it requires considerably more configura-

tion than NetBEUI and IPX/SPX. Through DHCP, however, you can greatly simplify TCP/IP configuration and management.

- *DLC.* The Data Link Control (DLC) protocol is included to enable you to connect Windows NT computers to IBM mainframes and access printers connected directly to the network, rather than to a server. It is not intended as a primary network protocol.
- *STREAMS.* This protocol originated on UNIX System V Release 4.0, and serves primarily to enable protocols developed for STREAMS to be ported to Windows NT.

When you install Windows NT, Setup installs NetBEUI and IPX/SPX by default. Unless you are connecting your computer in a mixed environment, you only need one network protocol. Any of the three primary protocols (NetBEUI, IPX/SPX, and TCP/IP) will work well, depending on the size of your network.

You can use multiple protocols, which makes sense in many situations. For example, if you connect to computers on your LAN through a wired connection but connect to the Internet through a dial-up connection, you might consider using TCP/IP in combination with IPX/SPX or NetBEUI. TCP/IP will serve as the protocol for your Internet connection, while your other protocol will handle LAN traffic.

Before installing Windows NT 4.0, decide what protocol is best for you based on your network environment. If you choose NetBEUI or IPX/SPX, you should not have to determine any settings prior to installation. If you choose TCP/IP, however, you must decide whether you will assign a specific IP address to your computer or use DHCP to retrieve an IP address from a DHCP server. If you decide to assign a specific IP address, you need to acquire a valid address. For detailed information on setting up TCP/IP, see Chapter 24, "Understanding and Configuring TCP/IP."

Note

You also should verify your network adapter's resource settings prior to starting the Windows NT installation. These settings include the adapter's base I/O address, IRQ, transceiver type, and possibly other settings depending on the card itself.

After you install Windows NT, you can add other network protocols and services if required. It's a good idea to limit the protocols and services you install during setup to a minimum, enabling you to test the network before you begin adding other protocols and services. ❖

CHAPTER 4

Installing Windows NT

by Michael Marchuk

If you've been reading through this book from the beginning, you're ready to finally begin installing Windows NT on your system. If you haven't read through the first few chapters, you should probably do so now. There are quite a few decisions you'll need to make during the installation process, and if you don't fully understand the decisions you're making, you could end up with a system that doesn't work the way you want or won't perform as well as it could.

In this chapter, you learn to

- Recognize the different parts of the installation process
- Install on new systems as well as those you want to upgrade
- Install your system from CD-ROM, disk, and over the network
- Keep the operating system you're using now and Windows NT on the same drive

Basic Installation

While the installation process is straightforward, there are many options to choose from when you finally start installing. This section covers what's happening during the installation process and how to implement the decisions you've made, like what type of file system to use, and whether to maintain your current operating system, for the type of installation you want.

Understanding Setup

The setup process for Windows NT attempts to hide much of the driver installation problems that have plagued DOS and OS/2 installations. Windows NT uses setup disks to self-boot the installation program. You probably received Windows NT on a CD-ROM with three installation disks. (Otherwise you received it on a boat-load of floppies.)

The setup floppies are used to load the bare minimum drivers to start the installation process. We'll cover more of the details later in this section, so for now just absorb the process.

During the installation with the setup floppies, Windows NT loads the drivers for the Hardware Abstraction Layer (HAL), mouse, keyboard, video, floppy drive, IDE/ESDI hard drives, and SCSI CD-ROMs. These drivers allow the Windows NT installation program to find the CD-ROM and begin installing the rest of the operating system.

Note

While it isn't necessary to have an SCSI CD-ROM drive, Microsoft strongly recommends that you have one. Most Intel-based computers don't come with an SCSI interface card. Rather, sound boards, proprietary cards, and IDE interfaces have become the way most manufacturers install a CD-ROM. SCSI interfaces are more expensive than these other connection options, although they do provide a much more flexible interface for peripherals.

Caution

Make sure you check with Microsoft's Hardware Compatibility List, which came with your Windows NT package. If you don't see your CD-ROM hardware listed as being compatible with Windows NT, you may not be able to install your new operating system. See the note later in this section which discusses hardware that is supported through retired Windows NT drivers.

After the installation program has been loaded, you are prompted to enter information related to the computer on which you are installing Windows NT. The information required of you during the setup process includes:

- The IRQ and memory settings for your network adapter boards
- Which file system you want to use for your hard drive (NTFS, FAT, or HPFS).
- Your domain or workgroup name for the network on which the computer will be connected.
- Administrator password.

- The directory to which you want to install the Windows NT system files.
- The network clients and protocols that you want to load.

Have this information at hand before you start your installation, and your setup of Windows NT will go much more smoothly.

Installing on New Systems

Whether you've decided to break in that new computer with Windows NT or you've had it with your old operating system and you want to start fresh, this installation provides you with the easiest installation routine. Not only will you not have to worry about maintaining any other operating systems, but you also won't have to deal with disk fragmentation, old programs and data files, or a hard drive organization scheme that just doesn't seem to work well anymore.

This installation assumes that you are going to reformat and possibly even repartition your hard drive to install Windows NT. When you begin this installation you'll only have two file system formats to choose from: NTFS and FAT.

During the setup process, the installation program asks about the partition on which you want to install Windows NT. You can either maintain the current partition and file system or repartition/reformat to create a new file system. Again, for a new system installation, we're assuming that any data you had on your system is safely stored away on floppies, the network, or somewhere else because you're planning to reformat.

◀ See "Evaluating and Planning the File System," p. 60

Choose the Format Drive option and select the file system that suits your needs. The installation program begins formatting your drive.

Note

The installation program really only formats the file system as FAT and flags the system for conversion to NTFS later on when the system reboots.

After the drive has been formatted, the installation program begins copying files for the second phase of the setup process from the CD-ROM, or disk to the hard drive. Once these files are copied, the system reboots and begins the second phase of the setup process which entails copying the rest of the files from the CD-ROM or disks and configuring the system to match your hardware and networking needs. Setup Wizards provide a step-by-step installation routine to make the setup process easier.

> **Note**
>
> Some newer systems include Multiple Central Processing Units (CPUs) to execute applications faster and provide a higher-end server environment for larger networks. Windows NT accommodates up to four CPUs in its default configuration and can work with more if the manufacturer has created a Hardware Abstraction Layer to handle their system.

Installing the Network During Setup

During Windows NT installation, the Setup Wizard prompts you through a number of steps to configure your workstation on a network. For example, Setup prompts you to specify if your computer will participate on a network, either through a hardwired connection (Network Interface Card (NIC) or ISDN adapter) or remote access through a modem. If you specify that the computer will participate on the network, Setup displays a network hardware search dialog box.

The easiest method for adding an adapter is to let Setup search for the adapter for you. To do so, click the Start Search button. Setup attempts to detect your NIC. If successful, Setup lists the adapter in the Network Adapters list when it finishes the search.

If Setup can't detect your NIC, or you don't want it to perform the search (if you haven't installed the adapter yet, for example), click the Select from List button instead of the Start Search button. Setup displays a Select Network Adapter dialog box you use to choose the brand and model of NIC installed in your computer. Or, if you have a driver disk supplied by the NIC's manufacturer, you can click the Have Disk button to select the NIC from the driver disk.

After you detect or select your NIC, click Next in the Setup Wizard. Setup displays a list of network protocols from which to choose. By default, Setup displays the TCP/IP, NWLink IPX/SPX, and NetBEUI protocols. Place a check beside each of the protocols you want to use (you can use multiple protocols if you wish). If you want to use DLC, STREAMS, or AppleTalk protocols, click the Select from List button to select these protocols. When you've added as many protocols as you need to the Network Protocols list, click Next.

Setup next prompts you to specify the network services you want installed. By default, Setup selects RPC Configuration, NetBIOS Interface, Workstation, and Server. The default set of services also includes Remote Access Service

(RAS), which you can use to connect to a RAS server through a modem. In addition, you can click the Select from List button to select additional services, as described in the following list:

- *Client Service for Netware.* This is the network client software for connecting to Netware servers.
- *FTP Server.* This service enables you to configure your computer as an ftp server for file transfer.
- *Microsoft TCP/IP Printing.* This service enables Windows NT to print to UNIX printers on the network using TCP/IP. The workstation (or server) on which this service is installed can act as a gateway to the UNIX printer, eliminating the need for other computers on the network to also run this service.
- *NetBIOS Interface.* This is Microsoft's implementation of the NetBIOS interface, and includes the NetBEUI protocol.
- *Network Monitor Agent.* This service enables remote network performance monitoring.
- *Remove Access Service.* The enables you to configure and use your computer for remote access, dialing into other computers (act as a client) or allowing other computer to connect to your own (act as a server).
- *RPC Configuration.* This service supports Remote Procedure Call (RPC) facility, which enables processes to be distributed across a network.
- *RPC support for Banyan.* This service provides RPC under Banyan networks.
- *SAP Agent.* The SAP Agent service enables Windows NT to handle SAP (Service Advertising Protocol) messages.
- *Server.* This service enables the computer to share its local resources.
- *Simple TCP/IP Services.* This service provides basic TCP/IP services, including networking and clients for ftp and Telnet.
- *SNMP Service.* This service enables the computer to be managed through the Simple Network Management Protocol (SNMP).
- *Workstation.* This service enables the computer to act as a client on the network.

When you've selected the service(s) you want, click the Next button, then click Next again to allow the services to install. If required, each service displays dialog boxes to prompt you for configuration information. For example, Setup prompts you to verify the IRQ, port address, and other settings for the NIC.

> **Note**
>
> Other services that require configuration during setup include Remote Access Service and TCP/IP. For information on configuring RAS, refer to Chapter 22, "Using Remote Access Services." For information on configuring TCP/IP, refer to Chapter 24, "Understanding and Configuring TCP/IP."

After all the services are installed, Setup informs you that it is ready to start the network. Click Next to allow Setup to start the network.

After the network is started, Setup prompts you for identification information for your computer. You can choose to join a workgroup or a domain. To join a workgroup, choose the Workgroup option button, then type the name of the workgroup in the associated text box. Or, choose the Domain option button if you want to join a domain, then type the domain name in the associated text box. If you also need to create an account in the domain, enable the Create Computer Account in the Domain checkbox. Then, choose Next. Setup prompts you for additional non-network information to complete the installation process.

You will also be asked whether you want an Emergency Disk created for you. You should always let Windows NT create an Emergency Disk to preserve your settings during the reinstallation of your system should something go wrong.

If you have chosen the NTFS file system, when your system reboots after installation, Windows NT converts the file system from FAT to NTFS before loading.

Upgrading Other Operating Systems

If you haven't read through the steps in the section "Installing on a New System" earlier in this chapter, you may want to go back and read through that section. It contains much of the same information that you'll need to know when upgrading your current file system to Windows NT.

Most people have computers that are working well for them now, but need additional security, flexibility, or power. If you have purchased Windows NT to upgrade your computer, this section is for you.

DOS/Windows 3.x

If you've waited to upgrade to Windows NT rather than Windows 95, you have a lot of company. Many corporations have taken the same strategy since Windows 95, while geared for network use, is still more focused as a home operating system. Many businesses want the security, protection, and ease of installation that Windows NT offers over other operating systems.

Assuming you've got the CD-ROM, hard drive space, and at least the minimum RAM and CPU specifications set forth by Microsoft, we can begin discussing the issues that surround upgrading your system from DOS or Windows 3.x to Windows NT. These issues can be separated into four major items:

- The FAT file system
- Disk compression software
- 16-bit applications
- Partition/hard drive sizes

Each of these items presents you with an opportunity and a headache. For example, the FAT file system that has served us well for all these years is hampered by the short file name restrictions and the limited partition sizes. In order to take advantage of your new operating system you should strongly consider moving to the NTFS file system. Once you've started using long file names, you'll wonder how you ever got along without them.

Additionally, you can choose to repartition your hard drive to one large partition to take advantage of your entire hard drive as one drive letter. However, this option requires a reformat of your hard drive so you'll need to back up your entire system and then proceed as a new system installation.

Another complication for installing onto a DOS or Windows 3.x system is the presence of disk compression software. Since you can't install Windows NT on a compressed drive, you'll have to decompress the drive and then install Windows NT. For most of us, the reason we installed the disk compression software is because our hard drives were inadequate for our needs. Decompressing the hard drive won't work if you've got 200M of data on a 100M hard drive. Perhaps a thorough pruning of your old applications and data will provide you with the ability to decompress your drive. If not, you may have to take the plunge and upgrade your hardware to accommodate your new operating system and all your data.

Finally, most of your 16-bit applications will work under Windows NT, but they can't handle long filenames and network browsing like 32-bit applications can. This may not affect you at first, but as you become accustomed to using long filenames with your 32-bit applications, you may become frustrated. While upgrading your application software will allow you to take advantage of your new operating system's features, we all know how much it hurts the pocketbook.

Windows 95

Upgrading Windows 95 to Windows NT is similar to upgrading from DOS and Windows 3.x to Windows NT. While you may have many 32-bit applications that allow you to manage long filenames and network browsing, you may have succumb to the urge to compress your hard drive with DriveSpace. If so, you will need to decompress your drive to install Windows NT.

When you upgrade from Windows 95 to Windows NT, your Registry settings will not be saved. All your applications that use the Registry for storing configuration options and all those auto-magical right-clicking associations will be gone. You will have to reinstall your software to reregister the items within the Windows NT Registry. As painful as it sounds, most people only have a handful of applications that require reinstallation. Some applications will work without reinstallation, but some of the neat features, such as WinZip's Add to Zip function within Explorer, won't be there.

Windows NT 3.x

One of the easiest operating systems to upgrade is a previous version of Windows NT. Microsoft has included that option within the installation program to streamline the setup process. Most of the setup options are read from your current Windows NT Registry and are used to upgrade the currently installed Windows NT components.

Also, since you are upgrading the same Registry, you shouldn't have to reinstall any of your current software or re-create any of your current users. Microsoft has made it very easy for Windows NT users to upgrade without much hassle. In fact, the installation process can be started from within Windows NT itself.

From within Windows NT, you can start the installation process by following these steps:

1. Run File Manager.
2. Change to the I386 directory on the CD-ROM.
3. Run WINNT32.EXE.

   This process asks you some questions about the installation.

> **Note**
>
> You need an additional 100M of hard drive space to accomplish the upgrade procedure because the setup files are copied to the hard drive before the second phase of the installation is started. Setup warns you if there isn't sufficient hard drive space.

If you are upgrading a previous version of Windows NT that is running on a partition formatted for HPFS, you may want to consider converting that partition to NTFS to provide you with all the security options of Windows NT in addition to the long filenames.

OS/2

Upgrading from OS/2 presents you with an option to convert your HPFS file system to NTFS. If you are not planning on a multi-boot system (one with multiple operating systems), then you should consider converting to NTFS. This provides you with all the security options of Windows NT in addition to the long filenames to which you have become accustomed.

Unfortunately, Windows NT does not support any OS/2 applications that use Presentation Manager or any 32-bit OS/2 applications. So unless you only use 16-bit character mode OS/2 applications, you'll have to purchase new programs to work with Windows NT.

Unless you are considering an environment in which you use both OS/2 and Windows NT on the same machine, you may be better off backing up your data to floppies, to the network, or to a hard drive formatted with FAT, and allowing Windows NT to reformat your hard drive for NTFS. This allows you to start fresh without the OS/2 system files and Presentation Manager applications hanging around on your hard drive. Again, this option is only for those who do not want to use OS/2 anymore.

Installing over a Network

Many companies can speed up the installation process by attaching to a network drive that contains a copy of the Windows NT setup files and installing from the network. This type of installation also works well for installing Windows NT on computers that have no CD-ROM drive. In order for this to work, though, there must be the ability to connect to a server on the network and at least 100M of free disk space on the workstation's hard drive to accommodate the Windows NT setup files.

> **Caution**
>
> Abide by the licensing policies that Microsoft has outlined when installing multiple machines with a single copy of Windows NT. Refer to your software license that accompanied your copy of Windows NT or contact Microsoft.

Attaching to the Network

The network installation of Windows NT can be accomplished on almost any type of network. As long as your workstation can get a drive letter pointing at the server on which the Windows NT setup files are located, you should be able to continue the installation.

Some networks on which this installation procedure is known to work include:

- Novell NetWare 2.x, 3.x, and 4.x
- Novell NetWare Lite 1.x
- Windows NT 3.x, and 4.x
- Windows 95
- Windows 3.11
- Banyan Vines
- LANTastic 5.x, and 6.x

Don't worry if your network operating system isn't listed here. The key is the ability to see a network drive letter from which the installation program can copy the files.

For example, if you were installing Windows NT from a NetWare 3.11 server, you would follow these steps:

1. Log in to the server that contains the Windows NT setup files. This assumes that you have rights to see the files on that server.
2. Create a DOS drive letter using the MAP command. For example: **MAP //MYSERVER/VOL1 G:**.
3. Run Windows.
4. Open File Manager and change to the drive letter you created with the MAP command in step 2.
5. Run the WINNT program to begin the copy procedure to the local hard drive and create boot floppies.

Running Setup over a Network

Once you've connected to the network, you will begin the fifth step as listed in the previous section. Running the WINNT program does two things:

- Creates boot floppies to install Windows NT on the local workstation.
- Copies the setup files to the local hard drive.

Because only local drives are available during the setup process, the setup files need to be located on the hard drive for the installation program. The boot floppies are required to begin the setup process.

> **Note**
>
> The setup floppies created during a network installation are not the same as those that come with the CD-ROM installation of Windows NT. If for some reason you need to re-create the original CD-ROM installation disks, you can run the WINNT application with the /OX option. This can be done from within the Program Manager by choosing File, Run and typing **Z:WINNT /OX** (where Z: is the network drive that contains the Windows NT setup files).

After the boot floppies are created, you need to restart the system with Setup Disk #1 inserted in the floppy drive. This initiates the setup process by loading the installation program and directing the installer to the local hard drive as the source of the complete Windows NT installation.

Installing Multiple Operating Systems

This section is for people who do not want to give up their older operating system in favor of running Windows NT exclusively. You may have some mission-critical business applications that require OS/2, or perhaps you have some reservations about giving up the DOS prompt that has served you well for many years. In any case, you may want to run multiple operating systems in a multi-boot configuration. Multi-boot means that when you start your machine, you have the option of which operating system to boot your computer with.

The boot configurations are managed by the BOOT.INI file that is read by the boot loader when your machine starts. Modifying this BOOT.INI file is covered in a section later in this chapter in the section titled "Modifying BOOT.INI."

Retaining Your Previous Version of Windows NT

If you currently have Windows NT running on your system, you will have the least difficult of the multiple operating system installations. Since you already have been through the process of installing Windows NT, you may have an NTFS file system in place. This limits your choices of multiple operating systems to only versions of Windows NT.

The installation program prompts you if it has found a previous version of Windows NT on your system. Since you want to maintain that version along with the new version of Windows NT, you'll need to install the newer version onto a different directory.

> **Caution**
>
> If you choose the same directory as the one in which your prior version of Windows NT was installed, you will upgrade your Windows NT installation and lose any chance of maintaining both versions.

The installation process continues as it has before, but now you are presented with the Boot Manager screen that will contain both the prior version of Windows NT and the version you just installed.

Retaining DOS/Windows 3.x

Keeping DOS and Windows 3.x around may be a choice that you make for one or more reasons such as:

- You are using a disk compression utility and have a compressed volume.
- You only want to experiment with a new operating system.
- Your current communications or utility programs won't work under Windows NT.

> **Note**
>
> While you cannot install Windows NT on a compressed volume, you can install NT on the uncompressed portion. When you are running Windows NT you won't be able to access the volumes that have been created with the disk compression software.

In any case, you may install Windows NT on your current FAT partition and use the Windows NT boot manager to choose which operating system you want to run when you boot your computer. You cannot repartition or reformat the drive that you have DOS and Windows 3.x on without losing data.

Retaining Windows 95

The installation of Windows NT on a Windows 95 computer is exactly the same as the installation onto a Windows 3.x setup. Make sure that you have enough hard drive space for both operating systems on an uncompressed drive volume. If you have used DriveSpace on your hard drive, you won't be able to access the compressed volume when you are running Windows NT.

Retaining OS/2

Should you want to keep OS/2 and Windows NT on the same computer, you have the option of maintaining the HPFS partition that OS/2 created. Windows NT installs onto the HPFS partition and replaces it.

If you want to keep the OS/2 boot manager instead of the Windows NT boot manager, you need to follow these steps to reactivate it:

1. Start Disk Administrator from within the Administrative Tools group in Windows NT.
2. Select the OS/2 Boot Manager Partition.
3. Choose Partition, Mark Active.
4. Reboot your system.

> **Note**
>
> You should not allow Windows NT to convert the HPFS partition since OS/2 won't be able to access the data on the NTFS partition.

Fine-Tuning System Startup Files

Some users like to get down and dirty with their operating systems. This section briefly covers the setup options that control how Windows NT boots up.

Modifying BOOT.INI

The BOOT.INI is a system file with two main parts. The first section specifies the default operating system and a time-out value specifying the wait period before automatically booting the system. The second section defines the operating systems that you have installed on your system that can be booted.

If you've set up your system as a multi-boot configuration between DOS and Windows NT, your BOOT.INI file may look something like this:

```
[boot loader]
timeout=30
default=multi(0)disk(0)rdisk(0)partition(1)\winnt35
[operating systems]
multi(0)disk(0)rdisk(0)partition(1)\winnt35="Windows NT Server"
c:\="MS-DOS"
```

You can edit the BOOT.INI file to change the operating system choices, but you have to first remove the read-only, hidden, and system attributes of the BOOT.INI file.

To change the attributes of the BOOT.INI file:

1. In File Manager, choose View, By File Type.
2. Click the Show Hidden/System Files checkbox and then click OK.
3. Select the BOOT.INI file and choose File, Properties or press Alt+Enter.
4. In the Properties sheet, remove the checks from the Hidden, Read Only, and System Attribute checkboxes. Click OK.

You can now edit the file using Notepad. Make sure you restore the hidden, read-only, and system file attributes after you've completed your edits.

Installing on a RISC System

Most RISC systems won't be shipped with Windows NT as the native operating system. RISC systems tend to run the manufacturer's version of the UNIX operating system. To install Windows NT on an ARC-compliant RISC system, your hardware must support the ability to boot from a CD-ROM. To install Windows NT on a RISC system:

1. Boot your system
2. From the ARC screen, choose the Run A Program option from the menu.
3. Type **cd:\system\setupldr** and press Enter. Note that some RISC systems require a different path than cd: when addressing the CD-ROM during bootup. Check your hardware vendor's documentation on the exact syntax required to access the CD-ROM.

The setup process now occurs in the same way that the Intel setup process does. Upgrading a previous version of RISC Windows NT is exactly the same as that of an Intel installation except the WINNT32 application is run from the directory that corresponds to the processor type you are using. See the section "Upgrading Windows NT 3.x" earlier in this chapter for more information on upgrading your RISC Windows NT setup. ❖

CHAPTER 5

Network Installation and Configuration

by Jim Boyce

Given Windows NT's target market, you're probably using Windows NT on a network. In the past, successfully connecting a computer to a network was a daunting task. Fortunately, Windows NT simplifies the task so it is almost fully automated.

In this chapter, you learn to

- Install network hardware
- Choose and configure protocols, clients, and services
- Use multi-protocol routing

The first step in connecting your computer to a network is installing the network hardware. If you are familiar with installing network hardware, you can skip to the section, "Choosing and Configuring Protocols." There's nothing unique to network hardware installation or configuration for Windows NT versus other network operating systems.

Installing the Network Hardware

Before you can install network protocols and services, you need to install and verify the operation of your network hardware. The complexity of this task depends on the type of network hardware and topology you choose. In all cases, however, the first step should be to configure and install the network adapter.

Configuring and Installing the NIC

The first step in installing your network hardware is to properly configure the network interface card (NIC). Generally, configuring a NIC requires specifying the card's IRQ and I/O base address. The NIC uses the IRQ line to signal the CPU that the NIC needs servicing by the CPU. The I/O base address is the memory address by which the CPU and NIC communicate.

Choosing an IRQ

Although some systems (EISA and MicroChannel) enable you to share IRQs among multiple devices, the majority of systems do not. Therefore, you generally must assign unique settings to the NIC—these settings cannot be used by any other device in the system.

Depending on the card's design, these settings are configured with jumpers or DIP switches on the NIC itself, or by running a configuration utility included with the NIC. With the latter, the configuration utility configures the card and stores its settings in ROM on the NIC.

If you have to configure the card manually because your card doesn't support auto-configuration, you first need to determine an available IRQ and I/O base address. If Windows NT is installed and functioning and you're simply adding a network adapter, an easy way to check available resources is to use WinMSD. To run WinMSD, choose Start, Run, enter **\Winnt\System32\Winmsd.exe** in the Open text box, and choose OK. You see the Windows NT Diagnostics property sheet.

To view the IRQs in use by devices in the system, click the Resources tab to display the Resources page (see fig. 5.1). If an IRQ is not listed in the Resources list, it is probably, though not necessarily, available for use by the NIC.

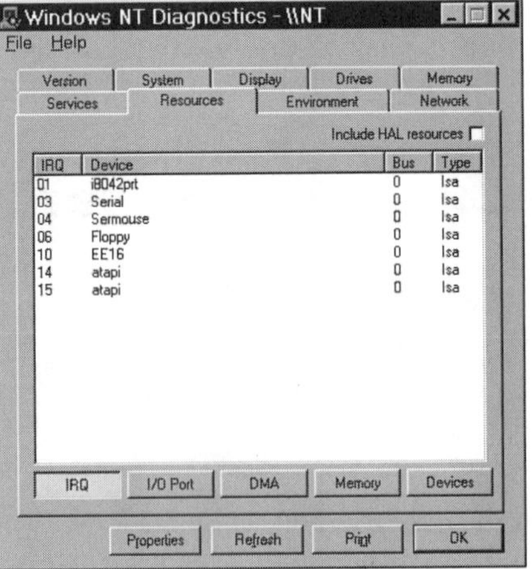

Fig. 5.1
You can view I/O address assignments with WinMSD.

Note

Although you can use WinMSD to view available resources, you can refer to Table 5.1 to see some common IRQ assignments. Some IRQs assigned to devices in your system might not appear in the WinMSD resource list. Your system's LPT1 port, for example, probably uses IRQ7, but doesn't appear in WinMSD's list.

Table 5.1 Common IRQ Assignments

IRQ	Use
2	Cascade to IRQ2
3	COM2 and COM4
4	COM1 and COM3
5	LPT2
6	Floppy disk controller
7	LPT1
8	Real-time clock
9	Cascade from IRQ2
10	Available
11	Available
12	PS/2 and Inport mice
13	Math coprocessor
14	Hard disk controller
15	Available

If you have not yet installed Windows NT but do have DOS or Windows 95 installed, you can use Microsoft Diagnostics (MSD) to view IRQ assignments. MSD is located in \Other\Msd directory folder on your Windows 95 distribution CD or disks, and is a DOS program. To run it, execute the MSD.EXE file. When the MSD main menu appears, click the IRQ Status button to view IRQ assignments. Be aware that, as with WinMSD, some IRQ assignments on your system might not appear in MSD's display.

Tip

When an interrupt is generated on IRQ8 through IRQ15, a corresponding interrupt is generated on IRQ9. Because IRQ9 is connected to IRQ2, an interrupt on IRQ8 through IRQ15 triggers a cascade interrupt on IRQ2. IRQ2 has a high system priority, so IRQ8 through IRQ15 therefore inherit that priority. For this reason, you should consider placing critical devices such as network adapters in the upper range of IRQs for performance reasons.

Choosing a Base Address

After you identify an IRQ for the NIC, you must assign a base address to the NIC. As explained previously, the I/O base address provides a memory location through which the CPU and peripheral device (such as an NIC) can communicate. A device typically uses a range of addresses, which is often called a *port.* Typically, 8-bit devices require an 8-bit address range, and 16-bit cards require a 16-bit address range. As with IRQs, most systems use common address settings. Table 5.2 describes these settings.

Table 5.2 Common Base Address Settings

Address	Device	Typical Address Range
200	Game Port	200-20F
260	LPT2	260-27F
2E8	COM4	2E8-2EF
2F8	COM2	2F8-2FF
300	NIC	300-31F
330	SCSI Adapters	330-33F
360	LPT1	360-37F
3C0	EGA	3C0-3CF
3D0	CGA	3D0-3DF
3E8	COM3	3E8-3EF
3F8	COM1	3F8-3FF

The documentation for your NIC probably recommends a specific base address—it's very likely that the recommended address is 300 or 330. There is no guarantee that these addresses (or whatever address is recommended) are unused. Check your system carefully to determine that the address you assign to the NIC is not already in use. If you're unable to determine the recommended address, install the card using its default setting (assuming that setting is not already in use).

If you're currently running Windows NT, you can use WinMSD to view base address assignments on your system. From the Windows NT Diagnostics property sheet, click the Resources tab to display the Resources page (refer to fig. 5.1). Choose the I/O Port button to display address assignments.

If you're using Windows 95 or DOS, you can use MSD to view some of your system's base address settings. These settings appear on the IRQ page (click the IRQ Status button on MSD's main menu).

After you configure your NIC, you're ready to install it in the computer and connect it to the network. The following sections explain how to add, remove, and modify network resources after Setup installs Windows NT. For information on how to install and configure network resources during Windows NT installation through Setup, refer to Chapter 4, "Installing Windows NT."

Managing Adapters

Although you probably will install your network adapters when you first install Windows NT, you can install and manage adapters at any time. The Network icon in the Control Panel enables you to manage NICs, as well as other network-related objects. The following sections explain how to manage NICs under Windows NT.

Adding and Removing NICs

To add or remove a NIC, open the Control Panel and double-click the Network icon. The Network property sheet appears (see fig. 5.2). You use this property sheet to manage NICs and other network properties.

The Adapters page lists the network adapters installed on your system. To add a network adapter, click the Add button. Windows NT displays the Select Network Adapter dialog box, which you use to select the adapter you're installing. After you select the NIC you want to add, choose OK. Windows NT reads the setup file for the NIC to determine what driver files to install, and might prompt you to specify the location of the driver files. Specify the drive letter containing the driver files (such as D for the CD-ROM drive). Windows NT automatically appends the required directory, so you generally only have to specify the drive letter. After locating the required files, Windows NT prompts you for setup information specific to the NIC, such as IRQ and other resource settings.

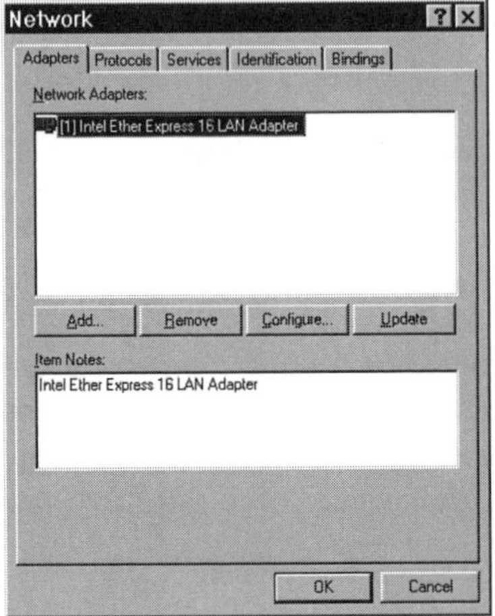

Fig. 5.2 You can accomplish most network configuration tasks through the Network object.

If the NIC you want to install is not included in Window NT's list of supported devices but you have a Windows NT driver disk supplied by the NIC manufacturer, click the Have Disk button on the Select Network Adapter dialog box. Windows NT prompts you for the disk and proceeds with the driver installation.

To remove a NIC from your system, select the NIC from the Network Adapters list on the Adapters page, then choose Remove. Windows NT prompts you to verify that you want to remove the selected adapter.

Setting NIC Properties

In addition to adding and removing network adapters, you can set the properties of installed adapters on the Adapters page. These properties typically include the NIC's resources (IRQ and base address), transceiver type, and other options.

To set an adapter's properties, select the adapter from the Network Adapters list and choose the Configure button. Windows NT runs a configuration routine that varies according to the NIC you select. Figure 5.3 shows a typical NIC configuration dialog box.

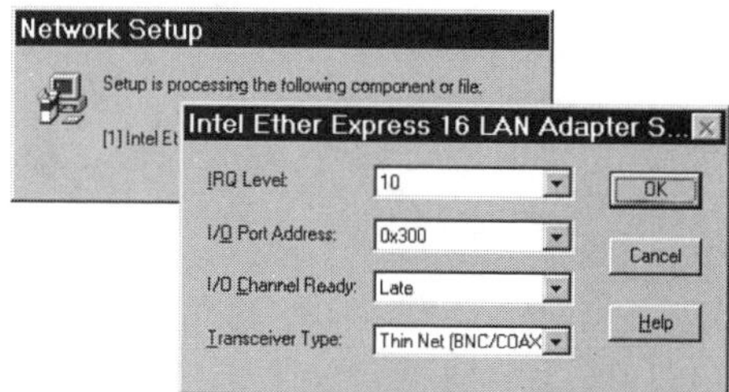

Fig. 5.3
NIC configuration dialog boxes vary from one NIC to another, but generally are similar.

Set the resources for the NIC, then choose OK to apply those changes. Choose Cancel to cancel the network adapter configuration.

Managing Protocols

To use network services, you must have at least one network protocol installed. You can use the Network property sheet to add, configure, and remove network protocols. To manage protocols, open the Control Panel and double-click the Network icon. When the Network property sheet appears, click the Protocols tab to display the Protocols page (see fig. 5.4).

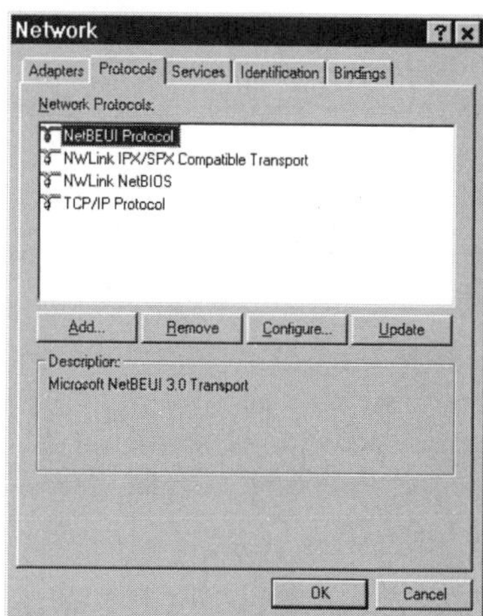

Fig. 5.4
Use the Protocols page to manage network protocols.

Adding Protocols

The Network Protocols list on the Protocols page lists the network protocols currently installed. To add other protocols, choose the Add button. Windows NT displays the Select Network Protocol dialog box (see fig. 5.5). Choose the protocol you want to install from the Network Protocol list.

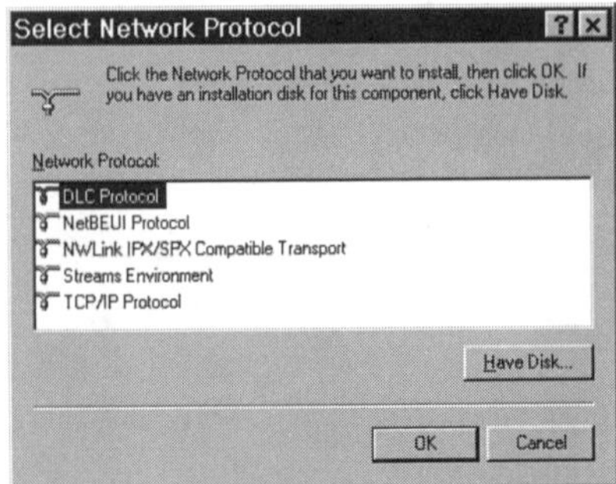

Fig. 5.5
Select the network protocol you want to install.

After you choose OK, Windows NT adds the protocol to your system but doesn't configure the protocol or bind it to the network adapter. To complete the process of adding the protocol, choose Close on the Network property sheet. Windows NT prompts you for any required settings, then binds the protocol.

> **Note**
>
> If you configured your system to use Dial-Up Networking, Windows NT detects that when you add a protocol and asks you if you want to enable the protocol for use under Dial-Up Networking.

Removing a Protocol

To remove a network protocol, double-click the Network icon in the Control Panel. When the Network property sheet appears, click the Protocols tab to display the Protocols page. If you want to remove a protocol completely, select the protocol from the Network Protocols list and click Remove (refer to fig. 5.4). Windows NT removes the protocol from your system and prompts you to restart the system for the change to take place. This removes the protocol for all adapters and services.

▶ See "Viewing and Changing Bindings," p. 97

> **Tip**
>
> Instead of removing a protocol from your system, you might want to disable the protocol from a specific adapter or service. To do so, use the Bindings page of the Network property sheet.

Configuring Specific Protocols

Some protocols, such as NetBEUI, do not offer any configurable options. Others, however, do enable you to configure various options that determine how the protocol functions on your system. You can configure protocols from the Protocols page of the Network property sheet. To display the Protocols page, open the Control Panel and double-click the Network icon. Then click the Protocols tab to display the Protocols page.

Of the five default protocols included with Windows NT, only the IPX/SPX and TCP/IP protocols are configurable. Because of its relative complexity, TCP/IP is covered as a separate topic in Chapter 24, "Understanding and Configuring TCP/IP." The following section explains how to configure the IPX/SPX protocol.

Configuring IPX/SPX

If you use the IPX/SPX protocol, you can configure a handful of options for it through the Control Panel. To do so, choose the Network icon in the Control Panel, then click the Protocols tab on the Network property sheet. From the Network Protocols list, choose NWLink IPX/SPX Compatible Protocol. Click the Configure button. Windows NT displays the NWLink IPX/SPX properties sheet shown in figure 5.6.

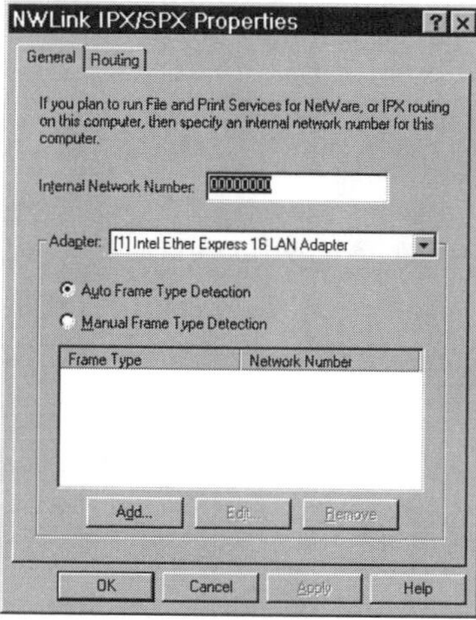

Fig. 5.6
Configure IPX/SPX through the NWLink IPX/SPX properties sheet.

> **Note**
>
> Unless you intend to run File and Print Services for Netware on your computer or use IPX routing, you should not have to configure the IPX/SPX protocol on your computer. The default settings should work properly.

On the General page, you can set general options for the IPX/SPX protocol. The following list explains these options:

- *Internal Network Number*. This option specifies the IPX node address of your computer. You can leave this value set at zero unless you are using IPX routing or intend to use File and Print Services for Netware.
- *Adapter*. Select from this drop-down list the adapter you want to configure. If your system contains only one network adapter, it's selected automatically.
- *Auto Frame Type Detection*. Select this option if you want NWLink to automatically determine the network frame type used by the selected adapter. If NWLink detects no frames at all, it defaults to 802.3.
- *Manual Frame Type Detection*. Select this option if you want to manually specify the frame type to be used by the adapter. Click the Add button to display the Manual Frame Detection dialog box. Enter the appropriate information in the dialog box, then click Add.

> **Note**
>
> To edit an existing frame type entry, select the entry from the list of frame types and click the Edit button. To remove an entry, select it and click the Remove button.

The Routing page enables you to control RIP (Routing Information Protocol) routing (see fig. 5.7). To enable IPX routing on a Windows NT Server, select the Enable RIP Routing checkbox.

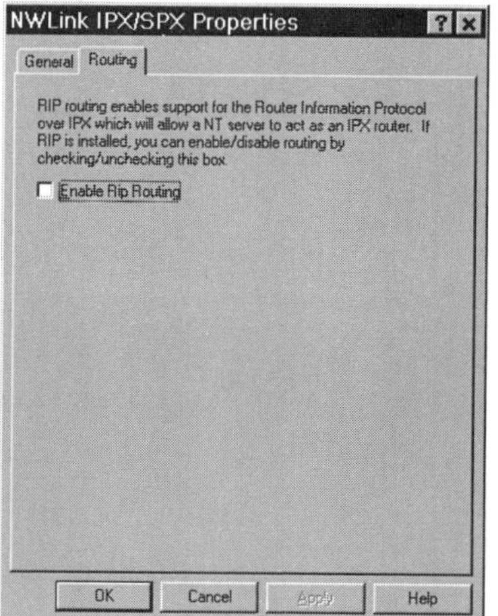

Fig. 5.7
Use the Routing page to enable or disable IPX routing.

Managing Services

In addition to at least one protocol, your Windows NT workstation or server requires various services to enable specific network functions. The Computer Browser service, for example, enables your computer to browse for resources on the network. The Workstation service enables your computer to access resources shared on the network. The number and type of services you use on your workstation or server depends on the protocols you use, whether you use RAS, and a host of other factors specific to each situation. Some services included with Windows NT are DHCP Server, FTP Server, and Remote Access Service. Other network features such as automated remote backup are often implemented as network services.

When you perform the network installation steps when you install Windows NT, Setup installs a basic set of services that enable your computer to access the network. You can add and configure other services at any time through the Control Panel. The next section explains how to add and remove network services. The following sections explain how to configure some of the most common Windows NT network services.

Installing and Removing Services

To view the network services currently installed, double-click the Network icon in the Control Panel. In the Network property sheet, click the Services tab to display the Services page (see fig. 5.8). Network Services lists the services currently installed on your computer.

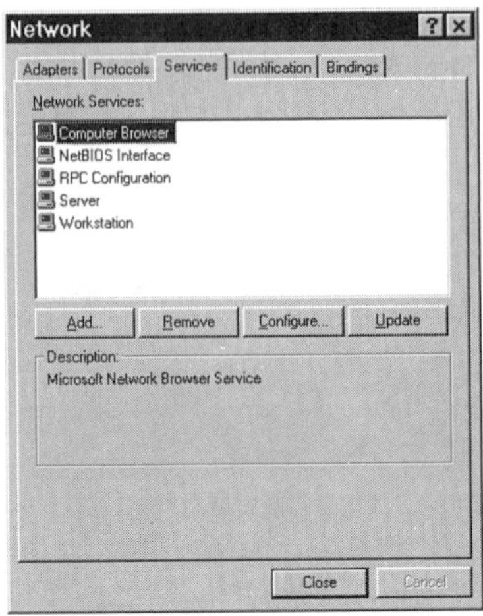

Fig. 5.8
The Services page displays the currently installed network services.

To add a network service, click the Add button to display the Select Network Service dialog box. Scroll through the Network Service list to locate and select the service to install, or click the Have Disk button if you want to install a third-party network service. When you choose OK, Windows NT installs the service and, depending on the selected service, might prompt you for additional configuration information. Figure 5.9 shows the configuration dialog box for the FTP Server service. Follow the prompts provided by Windows NT to provide the required configuration information and complete the service installation.

Fig. 5.9
If required, Windows NT prompts you for configuration information for the service.

To remove a network service, display the Services page of the Network property sheet. Select the service you want to remove, then click the Remove button.

Configuring Computer Browser

The Computer Browser service enables your computer to browse the network for shared resources. Under Windows NT Server, the Computer Browser service also supports browse requests from other computers on the network, supplying a list of available resources. The Computer Browser service is installed automatically when you install and configure network options during Setup, or when you add an adapter and protocol after Setup.

When you open the Network Neighborhood, it contains icons for each of the computers and other network objects (such as network printers) in your domain or workgroup. You also can browse other Windows NT domains (or workgroups) on your network by double-clicking the Entire Network icon in Network Neighborhood. In addition, you can browse LAN Manager domains on your network, but the names of the LAN Manager domains must be added under the Computer Browser service on the primary domain controller (PDC).

To add LAN Manager domains to the PDC and enable computers to browse those domains, follow these steps:

1. Log on to the PDC with Administrator privileges.
2. Open the Control Panel and double-click the Network icon.
3. Click the Services tab, select the Computer Browser service, and choose Configure.
4. In the Browser Configuration dialog box, type the name of the LAN Manager domain to add and click the Add button.

> **Note**
>
> Computer Browser on Windows NT Workstation is not configurable.

Configuring NetBIOS

Under Windows NT Server and Windows NT Workstation, you can configure the NetBIOS Interface service by changing lana (LAN address) numbers for NetBIOS network routes. To do so, select the NetBIOS Interface service from the Services page in the Network property sheet and choose Configure. Windows NT displays the NetBIOS Configuration dialog box shown in figure 5.10.

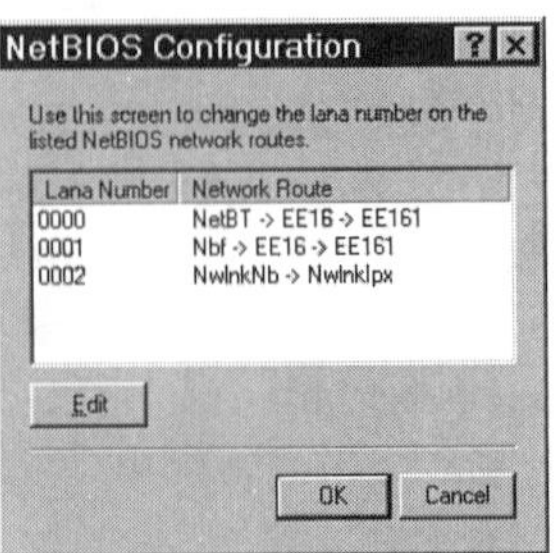

Fig. 5.10
You can edit lana numbers through the NetBIOS Interface service.

Select the lana number you want to change and click Edit to highlight the selected lana number. Type the new number and press Enter. When you're satisfied with the new lana number assignments, choose OK.

Configuring RPC

Remote Procedure Call (RPC) is a set of run time libraries and services that enable distributed applications to run on Windows NT. These distributed applications consist of multiple processes that cooperate to perform a task. Various processes in a task can run on different computers across the network.

Microsoft's implementation of RPC requires a *name service provider* to locate and register servers on the network. Microsoft RPC supports two name service providers: the Microsoft Locator and Distributed Computing Environment (DCE) Cell Directory Service. Because the Microsoft Locator is Microsoft's own name service provider, it is optimized for Windows NT. By default, RPC is configured to use Microsoft Locator. If you need to use DCE Cell Directory Service, you can configure your system to do so.

To configure RPC, display the Network property sheet and click the Services tab to display the Services page. Select the RPC Configuration from the list of installed services, and click Configure to display the RPC Configuration dialog box (see fig. 5.11).

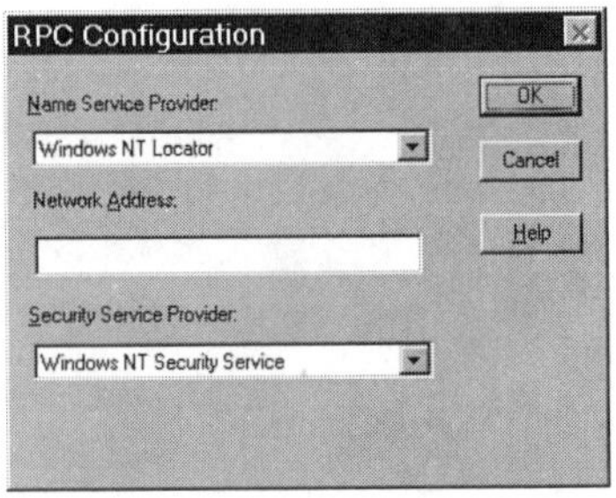

Fig. 5.11
Configure the name service provider in the RPC Configuration dialog box.

To select DCE, select DCE Cell Directory Service from the Name Service Provider drop-down list. Click in the Network Address text box and type the network address of the DCE name service provider. If the DCE Security Service is installed on your system, you can select it from the Security Service Provider drop-down list. If the DCE Security Service is not installed, security is handled through Windows NT. When you're satisfied with the RPC configuration, choose OK.

Configuring Server

Under Windows NT Workstation, the Server network service isn't configurable. Under Windows NT Server, however, you can set a few options for Server that enable you to optimize server performance for specific situations. To configure Server, select Server from the Network Services list on the Services page of the Network property sheet. Click the Configure button to display the Server dialog box shown in figure 5.12.

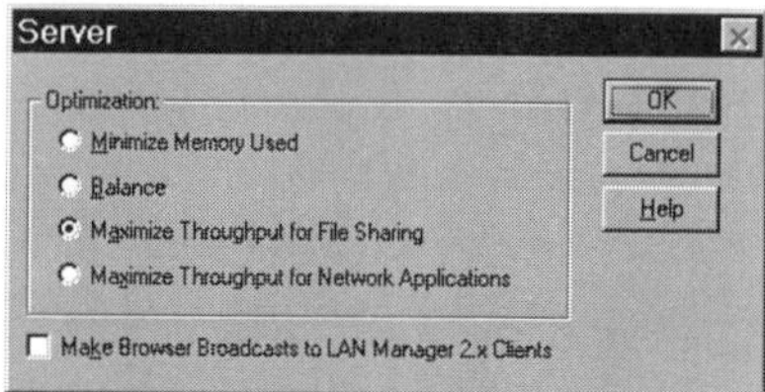

Fig. 5.12
Optimize server performance in the Server dialog box.

The following list describes the uses of the four option buttons on the Server dialog box:

- *Minimize Memory Used.* This option minimizes memory use by allocating enough memory for 10 client connections.
- *Balance.* This option allocates enough memory for approximately 64 connections and is the default setting for NetBEUI.
- *Maximize Throughput for File Sharing.* Choose this option to optimize file sharing performance on file servers installed on large networks.
- *Maximize Throughput for Network Applications.* Choose this option to optimize performance for servers providing distributed applications such as SQL Server.

In addition to these option buttons, the Server dialog box also contains a checkbox labeled Make Browser Broadcasts to LAN Manager 2.x Clients. Select this checkbox if your network includes a LAN Manager 2.x server and you want the server to browse resources on your server.

Updating Services

Occasionally, service software will be updated to include new features, to enhance performance, and to eliminate bugs. Rather than remove a service and reinstall it, you can simply update the service. To do so, display the Service page of the Network property sheet. Select the service you want to update and click the Update button. Windows NT prompts you for the location of the service update files. Enter the location for the files and choose Continue. Windows NT performs the service upgrade, prompting you for additional information if necessary.

Modifying Identification Settings

The fourth page of the Network property sheet is the Identification page. Click the Change button to view the Identification Changes dialog box. The controls on the Identification Changes page vary depending on whether your computer is acting as a domain controller. If your computer is a workstation or server (not a domain controller), you can change your computer's name and the workgroup or domain in which your computer belongs, and you can create an account for your computer in the domain (see fig. 5.13). If your computer is a domain controller, you can only change the computer's name and specify the name of the domain it controls (see fig. 5.14).

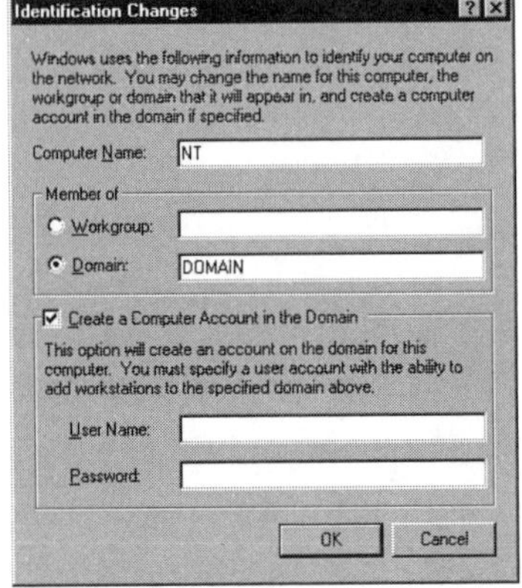

Fig. 5.13
On a workstation or server, you can change name, workgroup or domain, and create an account.

If you select the Create a Computer Account in the Domain checkbox shown in figure 5.13, Windows NT attempts to create an account on the domain controller of the specified domain. To create an account on the domain controller, you must enter a user name and the corresponding password for an existing account in the domain that has the necessary privileges.

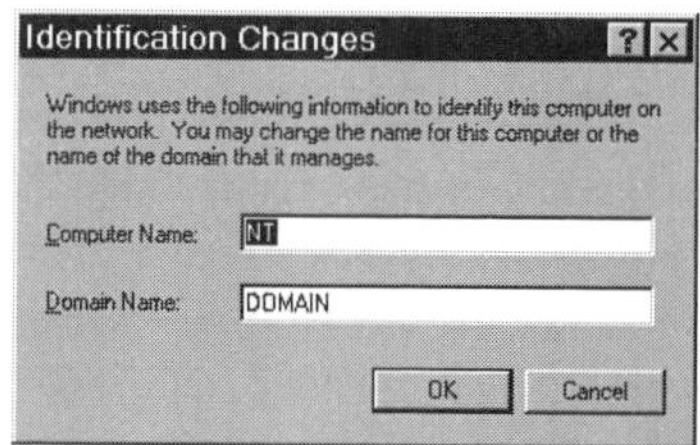

Fig. 5.14
On a domain controller, you can change only name and domain.

Viewing and Changing Bindings

The Bindings page of the Network property sheet enables you to view and modify network *bindings*, which define how the network services, protocols, and adapters interact. To view your computer's current bindings, double-click the Network icon in the Control Panel and click the Bindings tab to display the Bindings page (see fig. 5.15).

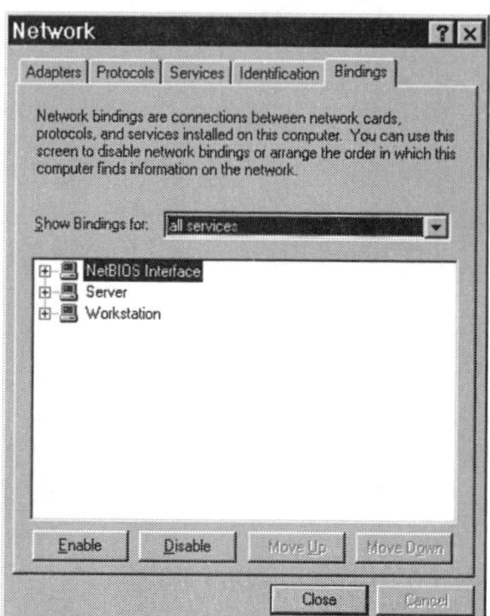

Fig. 5.15
View and modify bindings in the Bindings page.

By default, the Bindings page shows current bindings organized by service. You can view the bindings by service, protocol, or adapter by choosing the desired view from the Show Bindings For drop-down list.

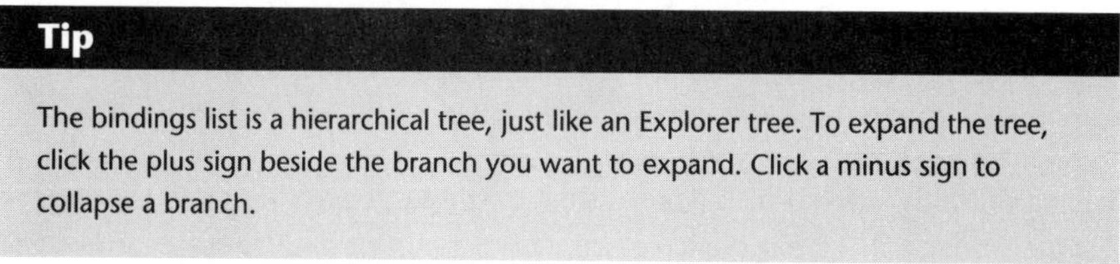

Tip

The bindings list is a hierarchical tree, just like an Explorer tree. To expand the tree, click the plus sign beside the branch you want to expand. Click a minus sign to collapse a branch.

Disabling Services, Protocols, and Adapters

The Bindings page enables you to easily disable specific services, protocols, and adapters. For example, you might have added TCP/IP, and only want to use it for RAS—not for your local LAN connection. Therefore, you would disable TCP/IP for the LAN adapter, but leave it enabled for the various RAS WAN wrappers (virtual NICs).

To disable a protocol for an adapter, choose All Adapters from the Show Binding For drop-down list. This organizes the display by adapter. Select the LAN adapter for which you want to disable the protocol. Expand the LAN adapter's branch. Click the protocol you want to disable and choose Disable. Windows NT places a red prevent symbol (a slash in a circle) beside the protocol to indicate that it is disabled (see fig. 5.16).

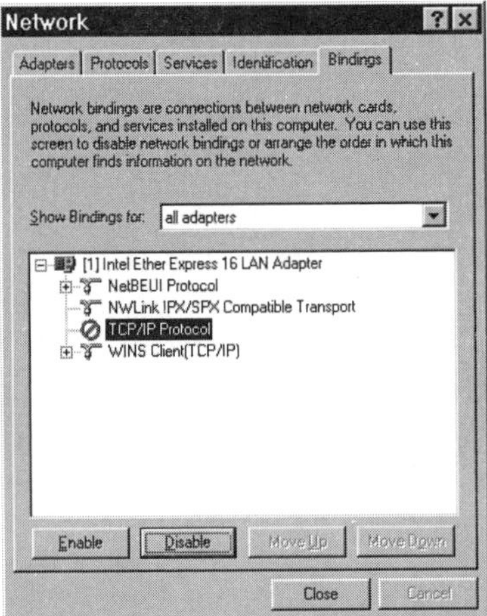

Fig. 5.16
Select a protocol and choose Disable to disable it.

To enable a protocol you have previously disabled, select the disabled protocol and choose the Enable button.

Tip

To disable a protocol completely (for all adapters and services), choose All Protocols from the Show Bindings For drop-down list to organize the list by protocol. Select the protocol you want to disable and choose Disable.

You can disable services and adapters using the same technique you use to disable a protocol. To disable a service, choose All Services from the Show Bindings For drop-down list to organize the list by service. Select the service and choose Disable. To disable an adapter, choose All Adapters from the Show Bindings For drop-down list. Select the adapter and choose Disable. After you enable and disable network services, adapters, and protocols according to your needs, choose OK. Windows NT makes the necessary changes and prompts you to restart the system so the changes can take place.

Note

Disabling a protocol, service, or adapter is not the same as removing it. Disabling it simply turns it off—removing it deletes the object from the system. If you think you might need the network object later, you should disable it. It's easier to re-enable an object than to reinstall it.

Using Multi-Protocol Routing

Windows NT Server can serve as a multi-protocol router, which connects multiple LAN segments. Basically, Windows NT Server acts as a router for IP and IPX traffic. When you install TCP/IP under Windows NT server, support for DHCP and BOOTP relay is installed automatically. Support for RIP (Routing Information Protocol), however, must be installed separately.

Note

The topics of routing and using Windows NT Server as a multi-protocol router are complex, and would take a number of chapters to cover in detail. This section of the chapter is intended for administrators who are familiar with routing and the issues involved with it. Therefore, only basic installation and configuration instructions are provided.

To support multi-protocol routing, the server must contain multiple NICs—one for each segment to be connected. The first step in setting up a Windows NT Server platform as a router is to install the adapter cards.

▶ See "Installing Windows NT Networking," p. 124

Next, you can install the RIP agent (either IP for TCP/IP or IPX for NWLink) that applies to the network protocol you want to route through the server. To do so, open the Control Panel and double-click the Network icon. Click the Services tab to display the Services page of the Network property sheet. Click the Add button, select the appropriate RIP agent from the list of available services, and choose OK.

When you install RIP for NWLink IPX/SPX compatible protocol, Windows NT informs you that NetBIOS Broadcast Propagation is disabled (see fig. 5.17). If you are using NetBIOS over IPX/SPX, choose Yes to enable the broadcast of type 20 packets.

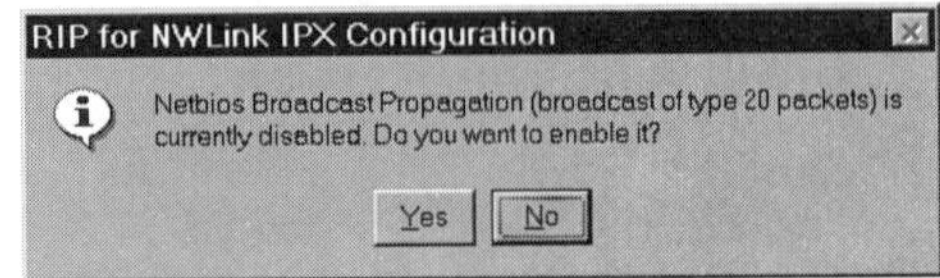

Fig. 5.17
Choose Yes to enable broadcast of type 20 packets if you're using NetBIOS over IPX/SPX.

> **Note**
>
> To configure BOOTP/DHCP relay services, select the TCP/IP protocol from the Protocols page of the Network property sheet. Choose Configure. Click the DHCP Relay tab to display the DHCP Relay property sheet so you can configure the agent.

CHAPTER 6

Customizing Setup

by Serdar Yegulalp

While Windows NT is relatively easy to install on most computers and is self-configuring for the most part, usually no two computers are going to follow exactly the same setup procedure. Windows NT has plenty of ways to handle the subtle but sometimes troublesome differences in hardware between machines.

In this chapter, you learn to

- Install from different media—network repositories and CD-ROMs
- Recognize all phases of Windows NT Setup, from the initial text-mode boot to the final GUI-mode configurations
- Troubleshoot problems with installation
- Interoperate with Windows 95, OS/2, and other operating systems
- Customize Windows NT Setup for specific environments and needs

Setup Procedures

Windows NT Setup consists of two major phases: a text-based phase, and a GUI phase, or graphical phase.

- The *text-based phase* loads in the machine-specific HAL or hardware abstraction layer, allows the user to make some preliminary driver and hardware choices, and loads in the majority of the Windows NT system files.
- The *GUI-based phase* loads in the remaining files, configures system settings, and loads network components. It also configures hardware that could not be set up initially, such as the graphics card.

There is no one way to set up Windows NT, just as there is no one way to use it. The two major ways to install Windows NT are from CD-ROMs, or a network directory. Floppy installation was supported up until Windows NT 3.51, but the number of floppy disks required to distribute Windows NT has become so large, floppy installations are impractical. (Floppies are still used to install drivers and system components, however.)

Installing from CD-ROMS on an IDE/ATAPI Controller

Windows NT's boot disks contain drivers for IDE/ATAPI drive controllers and should be able to recognize a CD-ROM based off an IDE/ATAPI controller without trouble.

> **Note**
>
> PCI-based IDE controllers will be recognized as an IDE/ATAPI controller device, even if no ATAPI devices are attached to it.

Installing from SCSI CD-ROMS

Windows NT's boot disks also contain drivers for the more popular varieties of SCSI host adapters and SCSI CD-ROMs. If either the host adapter or CD-ROM you are using is not detected by Windows NT during the installation cycle, you will need to supply the drivers yourself.

> **Tip**
>
> Some systems have the capacity to use a CD-ROM as a boot device. The CD-ROM for Windows NT 4.0 has been configured to operate with these computers. Check to see if your computer is capable of booting from CD-ROM. If so, you should be able to boot directly into the Setup program (WINNT).

Building Boot Disks for a CD-ROM

The three boot floppies that come with the CD-ROM for Windows NT aren't irreplaceable, and can be rebuilt using a command-line based utility called WINNT. If the disks are lost or damaged, or you're trying to build them for the first time, use the WINNT utility to create them.

Note

You need to have access to a CD-ROM from DOS, Windows 95, or Windows NT in order for the WINNT program to work. You cannot use Windows 3.1 or OS/2, either in DOS or Win-OS/2 mode, to build disks to install Windows NT.

If Windows NT Setup fails to identify your SCSI CD-ROM at boot time, make sure the CD-ROM is not set to use SCSI ID 0 or 1. Try another ID number and see what happens.

The WINNT program has the following command-line options:

```
WINNT [/S[:]sourcepath] [/T[:]tempdrive] [/I[:]inffile]
      [/O[X]] [/X ¦ [/F] [/C]] [/B]
```

- */S[:]sourcepath.* The /S options lets you specify, on the command line, where WINNT is to look for the Windows NT source files. You can supply a path to a drive, or to a computer on a network using the \\SERVER\SHARENAME[\PATH] convention. For instance, if you had Windows NT files on your server named NTSOURCE, in the directory named FILES, you would type \\NTSOURCE\FILES. This option defaults to the current directory.
- */T[:]tempdrive.* The /T option lets you tell WINNT where to store temporary files during setup. The default is the current drive. This option is useful when Windows NT tries to automatically choose a drive during setup that may not be immediately supported by it. With this, you can force Windows NT to install itself on a supported drive.
- */I[:]inffile.* /I lets you specify the name of the setup information file, which defaults to DOSNET.INF.
- */O.* This creates only the first three boot floppies for a full floppy disk set.
- */OX.* The /OX option creates boot floppies for a CD-ROM or floppy-based installation.
- */X.* /X forces WINNT to not create boot floppies, but simply to copy Windows NT files over to the hard drive and prepare the hard drive for booting directly into the graphical phase of Windows NT Setup.
- */F.* /F turns off file verifying when WINNT copies files to the target floppies. Turning off verification means the disk creation process will go faster, but there is the chance that a copied file will not be written correctly.
- */C.* When WINNT installs files to the boot floppies, it checks to see if

there is enough free space on each disk. Use the /C switch to disable the free-space check.

- */B*. The "floppyless operation" switch causes WINNT to copy all files over to the hard drive and continue the installation from there, without using boot floppies. This makes a good deal of the installation go faster, but it requires a good deal of hard drive space—at least 200M free—to make it work.

Running WINNT from DOS or Windows 95

Running WINNT under DOS or Windows 95 allows you to either create boot disks or to copy the Windows NT Setup files to your local drive. The former option is useful in that it can be invoked on just about any system that has a CD-ROM drive; the latter is useful in that it can speed things up enormously.

Building Boot Disks

To build the boot disks in DOS or 16-bit Windows, do the following:

1. Format three 3.5", 1.44M floppy disks. These will become your new boot disks.

> **Note**
>
> Windows NT doesn't format the floppies when copying files over to them, and doesn't check for physical disk integrity either. You have to do these things yourself. It does check for the integrity of the files copied over, but this option can be disabled.

2. Locate the directory on the CD-ROM that contains the processor version of NT that you need. In the previous cases, it will most likely be the I386 subdirectory, since the previous listed operating systems (Windows 3.x and Windows 95) only run on Intel-platform computers.
3. Log into the directory and type **winnt**, plus whatever command-line options are appropriate.
4. The program first prompts you for the pathname that contains the Windows NT source files (see fig. 6.1). If your CD-ROM is D, and you're installing the Intel version of Windows NT, the directory would be D:\I386. Supply whatever the appropriate drive and pathname is. Press Enter.

5. Insert each of the three disks as you are prompted to and press Enter. (see fig. 6.2)

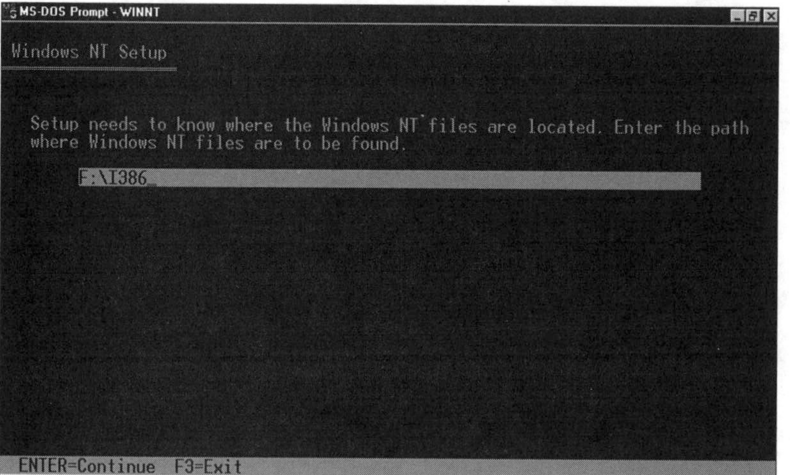

Fig. 6.1
If you haven't already told the WINNT program where to find its source files through the /S: option, it will ask you as soon as the program starts.

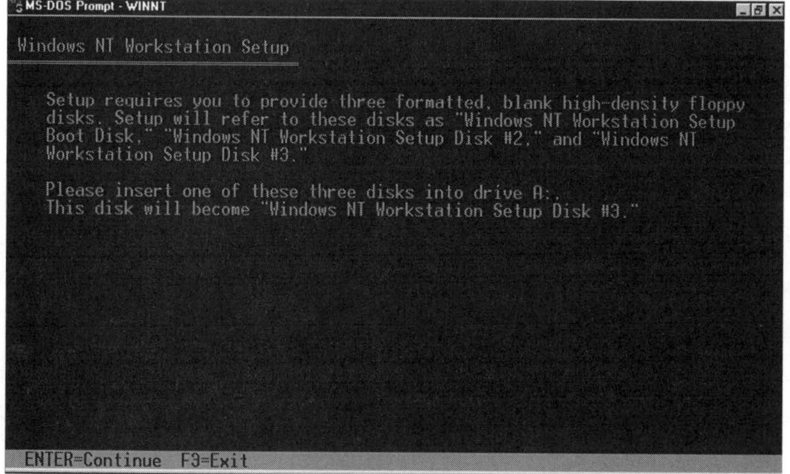

Fig. 6.2
The WINNT program prompts you to label and insert three disks.

Each disk has the appropriate files written to it (see fig. 6.3).

6. When the last disk has finished writing, the program will terminate. If you are planning to use these disks to install Windows NT immediately, leave that disk in the drive, since it is the first boot disk and will start automatically when you reboot the system.

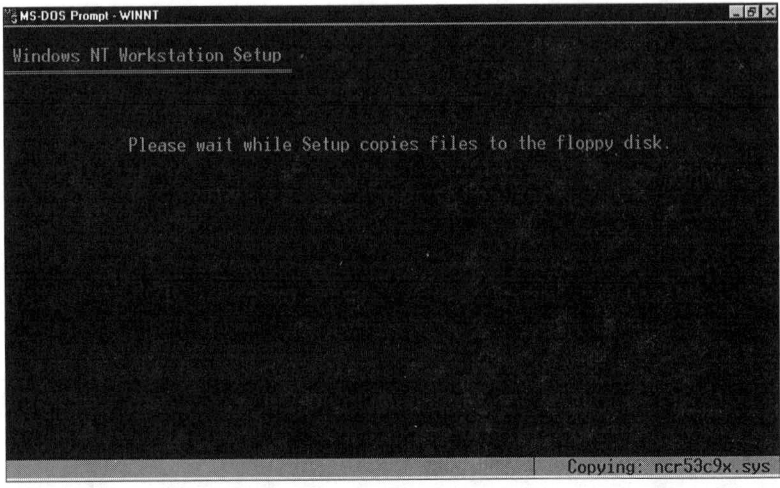

Fig. 6.3
WINNT tells you the name of each file as it copies it over to the target floppy.

Making a Local Copy of Windows NT Setup

To create a local copy of Windows NT Setup that will be activated when you next reboot your machine, do the following:

1. Locate the directory on the CD-ROM that contains the processor version of NT that you need. In the above cases, it will most likely be the I386 subdirectory, since the above listed OSes only run on Intel-platform computers.
2. Log into the directory and type **winnt /b**, plus whatever other command-line options are appropriate.
3. The program first prompts you for the pathname that contains the Windows NT source files (refer to fig. 6.2). If your CD-ROM is D: and you're installing the Intel version of Windows NT, the directory would be D:\I386. Supply whatever the appropriate drive and pathname is. Press Enter.
4. WINNT copies all the appropriate files into a temporary directory in the path specified by the /T: option. The default directory is WIN_NT.~RS on the boot drive. A progress bar shows how far along the copying procedure is.
5. When the last file has been written to the temporary directory, the program tells you to remove all disks from your drives and reboot. Pressing Enter terminates WINNT.

Running WINNT32 from Windows NT

WINNT cannot be run from Windows NT, but there is a separate version of WINNT, called WINNT32, that is designed to be run from within Windows

NT. It uses exactly the same set of command-line options and sports a graphical interface as well (see fig. 6.4).

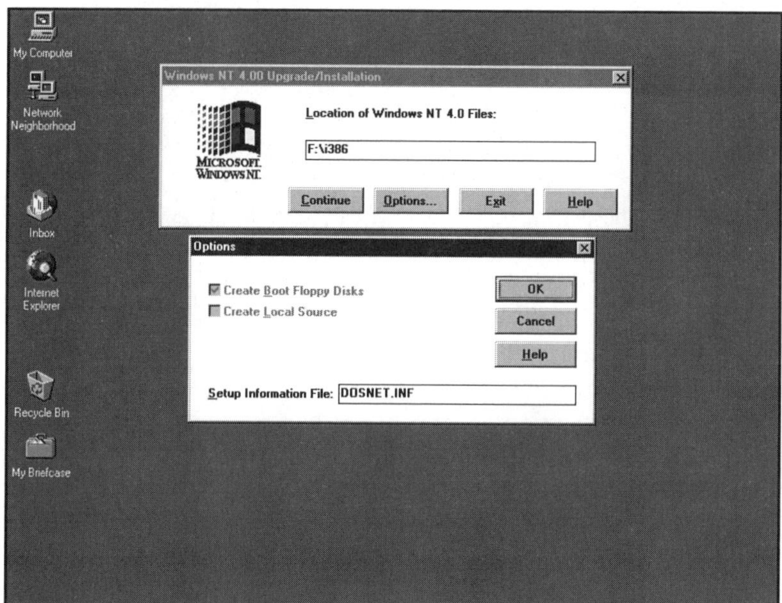

Fig. 6.4
WINNT32 runs from within Windows NT, versions 3.51 or 4.0, and uses the GUI to make the job of preparing for Windows NT installation that much easier.

Building Boot Disks from a Network Copy of Windows NT

If you have a copy of the Windows NT installation source files on a network, you can create boot disks using the WINNT or WINNT32 programs in almost exactly the same fashion as you did with the CD-ROM. Instead of logging to the directory on the CD-ROM that contains the proper Windows NT installation files, log on to the directory on the network that contains them and proceed from there.

Preparing the Computer for Windows NT

Windows NT deals with the underlying architecture of the computer differently than other operating systems. Before attempting to install, go into the configuration screens for your computer's BIOS and make the following changes.

- *Disable BIOS shadowing.* Windows NT does not use the BIOS to access hardware, so shadowing the BIOS is a waste of memory.

- *Disable video subsystem shadowing.* The same reasons apply here, since Windows NT doesn't use BIOS calls to access video hardware.
- *Disable hardware shadowing.* Most system BIOSes offer the ability to shadow certain segments of the memory that are reserved for adapter cards. Disable shadowing for these as well.
- *If your motherboard supports Plug-and-Play and you are given the option of disabling it, do so.* Plug-and-Play BIOSes can interfere with Windows NT's hardware detection.
- *Do NOT disable external CPU caching.* CPU caching is vitally important for faster performance. If you have this option, enable it.

Windows NT 4.0 also requires that the following be physically present at installation time:

- A 486DX processor or better. Windows NT 4.0 no longer supports 386 processors. Up to four processors can be present in the machine, and more than that can be supported with software drivers from various manufacturers.
- VGA display adapter or better. An SVGA adapter, with an 800 × 600 × 8-bit graphics mode available on it, is highly recommended as the minimum.
- 12,582,912 bytes (12M) of system RAM, although 16M or more is recommended.
- A CD-ROM drive is strongly recommended and just about mandatory at this point in Windows NT's evolution.
- A 3.5" floppy disk drive. Windows NT is no longer available on 5.25" disks.
- A mouse or other pointing device. Windows NT can be run exclusively from the keyboard, but it's a frustrating experience.
- At *least* 94,453,760 bytes free space on the drive that will hold the main Windows NT files. (At *least* another 16M is required on this drive or another drive for a paging file as well.) You'll need about twice this amount if you plan on doing a floppyless installation, since you need space to store the temporary files.

There are two possible ways a user can approach the task of partitioning media for use with NT:

- You can use whatever disk-partitioning programs are available in the current operating system (if you have one installed on the machine in question) to reserve space for Windows NT.

- You can use the disk-partitioning program built into Windows NT Setup to do the job.

There are significant advantages to using Windows NT Setup's own disk partitioning program:

- You can format the specified partitions, and use either the FAT or NTFS file systems.
- You can convert FAT or OS/2 HPFS partitions to NTFS.
- It's somewhat less cryptic than most disk-partitioning software, especially conventional FDISK. All the prompts are in plain English and include explanations of what's happening.

The single major disadvantage to using the Windows NT Setup partitioning program is that you have to run Windows NT Setup to use it.

Windows NT Installation: Step-By-Step

Now that you have prepared your system for Windows NT, it's time to actually install the operating system. In this section, we'll finally explore Windows NT installation in detail, with each step of the installation spelled out in detail and all options explained.

Before you start the installation, make sure you have satisfied all the following conditions:

- Your system is physically capable of receiving a Windows NT installation, as described above in "Preparing the Computer for Windows NT."
- You have a set of boot disks, or have prepared a boot disk set as described in the "Building Boot Disks from CD-ROM" section or the "Building Boot Disks from a Network Copy of Windows NT" section—or you have used the WINNT or WINNT32 program to copy the installation files to your local hard disk using the /B option.

Note

If you are going to start Windows NT installation from a three-floppy-disk set, make sure your system is not set up to skip the floppy drive in its boot sequences. Some systems are set by default to boot directly to the hard drive. This is usually governed through an option in the system BIOS. Check your computer's literature and BIOS settings to make sure.

Booting from Floppies

Here are the steps for starting Windows NT installation from a boot floppy set.

1. If your system is currently up and running, shut it down.
2. Insert the first disk of the boot floppy set into the disk drive and turn on the system.
3. As the first disk boots, you should see the following message: `Setup is inspecting your computer's hardware configuration.`
4. After a few moments, the screen turns blue with the legend "Windows NT Setup" at the top. At the bottom, you see "Setup is loading files" with the names of various installation files appearing next to it in parentheses.
5. Windows NT Setup asks you to change to disk #2 and press Enter. Insert the second disk in the boot disk series and press Enter. "Setup is loading files" reappears at the bottom of the screen.
6. After a few moments, the screen clears and the following message appears: Microsoft® Windows NT™ Version 4.0 (Build XXXX)1 System Processor [16 MB Memory] Multiprocessor Kernel. This description varies depending on the system you are installing on. (The build number is different with each minor revision of Windows NT, but at the time of this writing the build number was 1345.)
7. A few moments later, the first Windows NT Setup screen with user options appears. Skip to the section entitled "'Welcome to Windows NT Setup'"for further details.

Booting from a Local Hard Drive Copy

Here are the steps to follow when Windows NT Setup has been prepared to run on your local hard drive using the /B option in WINNT or WINNT32. You need only do the first step and the rest is automatic.

1. If your system is currently running, shut it down. Empty out all floppy drives and boot the system.
2. For a few seconds, you may see the Microsoft OS Boot Loader. This is a menu that lists all the available operating systems that can be booted. One of the options, Windows NT 4.00 Installation/Upgrade, is already highlighted. You need not do anything in order for it to continue loading Windows NT Setup.
3. After a few moments, the following legend should appear: Microsoft® Windows NT™ Version 4.0 (Build XXXX)1 System Processor [16 MB

Memory] Multiprocessor Kernel. (The build number is different with each minor revision of Windows NT, but at the time of this writing the build number was 1345.)

4. Soon after, the first Windows NT Setup screen with user options on it appears.

Welcome to Windows NT Setup

The first Windows NT Setup screen with user options has "Welcome to Setup" at the top in bold letters. From here, you have four choices.

- *Get More Information about Windows NT Setup By Pressing F1.* This option leads you into a series of screens that give some general information about Windows NT setup—what to expect at certain stages of the procedure, what certain keys do, and so on.
- *Repair a Damaged Windows NT version 4.00 Installation By Pressing R.* This can only be done if you have a Windows NT Repair Disk on hand (which is created during the final stages of Windows NT Setup).
- *Quit Setup By Pressing F3.* This aborts the setup and leads you to a screen where you can reboot in safety. If you are using boot floppies, nothing will have been written to the disk.
- *Set Up Windows NT By Pressing Enter.* As the menu would imply, start Setup by pressing Enter.

Mass Storage Device Detection

The first thing Windows NT Setup does is attempt to detect what mass storage devices are currently installed. Windows NT Setup runs through all the mass storage device drivers in its library. If you are using floppies to accomplish this portion of the install, you may be asked to change disks so all the needed device drivers can be loaded.

If you do not want Windows NT Setup to automatically detect mass storage devices, and instead want to specify them manually, press **S**. You will be taken to the screen that allows you to manually specify mass storage devices (see the later section entitled "Specifying Mass Storage Devices").

When Setup refers to mass storage devices, this includes any of the following:

- Proprietary CD-ROM controllers
- SCSI controllers or host adapters
- Drive arrays
- ATAPI/IDE controllers

After Windows NT Setup finishes checking your mass storage hardware against the drivers in its database, it displays the following line:

```
Setup has detected the following mass storage devices in your
computer:
```

Following this will be a list of all the detected devices. If no devices are detected, this does not necessarily mean that Windows NT Setup can't proceed. It just means that aside from conventional IDE or EIDE hard drives, no other forms of mass storage (SCSI, drive arrays, and so on) were found.

> **Note**
>
> Iomega Jaz and Zip drives are not detected at this stage of the install. Windows NT supports these devices, but they can't be used to hold a Windows NT installation.

You will be given two options at this point:

- *Specify Additional Controllers By Pressing S.* If you know you have a controller installed in your system that should be specified now, you can specify it by pressing **S** and choosing from a list of controllers. Also, if you have driver disks for a controller that isn't one of the ones normally supported by Windows NT, you can use this option to load it.
- *Continue By Pressing Enter.* Pressing Enter at this stage takes you to the next phase of installation.

Specifying Additional Controllers

When you press S from the Mass Storage Detection screen, you are presented with a list of controllers that have drivers already available for them in Windows NT Setup.

Follow these steps to install a driver already on the list:

1. If you are trying to install a driver on the list, use the up and down arrow keys to scroll through the list and select the needed driver.
2. Press Enter to select the highlighted driver. Windows NT Setup attempts to load the driver and match it to the piece of hardware it governs.
3. If Windows NT Setup can't find the device you requested, you get the following message: `The SCSI adapter, CD-ROM drive, or special disk controller you specified is not installed in your computer.`
4. If Windows NT Setup was successfully able to match the driver with a piece of hardware installed in your system, you are returned to the Mass Storage Device Detection menu with the newly installed hardware listed there.

Follow these steps to install a driver that you have a disk for:

1. Scroll to the bottom of the hardware list, to the selection that reads "Other (Requires disk provided by hardware manufacturer)" and press Enter.
2. Windows NT Setup then prompts you to insert the manufacturer supplied hardware driver disk. Insert the disk with the drivers you are trying to install and press Enter.
3. If Windows NT Setup cannot find any drivers on the disk, it prompts you again to insert the disk. Press Esc to cancel if you cannot find the right disk.
4. Once Windows NT Setup finds a disk with hardware drivers on it, it presents you with a list very similar to the one for the hardware drivers already available from within Windows NT setup. Scroll through the list with the arrow keys and press Enter to select the device you are trying to install drivers for.
5. Windows NT Setup attempts to load the driver and match it to the piece of hardware it governs. If Windows NT Setup cannot find the device you requested, you get the following message: `The SCSI adapter, CD-ROM drive, or special disk controller you specified is not installed in your computer.`
6. If Windows NT Setup successfully matched the driver with a piece of hardware installed in your system, you are returned to the Mass Storage Device Detection menu with the newly installed hardware listed there.

Once you have finished specifying and installing drivers for mass storage devices, and you have returned to the main Mass Storage Device Installation menu, press Enter to continue with Windows NT Setup.

Checking for Previous Versions of Windows NT

In the next phase of Windows NT Setup, the Setup program checks the computer for an existing installation of Windows NT. This can be an earlier Windows NT 4.0 beta, or an earlier version of Windows NT (from 3.1 through 3.51).

If Windows NT Setup finds another installation of Windows NT present on the same machine, it displays the drive path it found the other copy of Windows NT in and presents you with two options:

- *Installing Windows NT 4.0 Over the Older Version of Windows NT.* If you choose this option, the existing version of Windows NT will be upgraded to Windows NT 4.0. Existing user accounts and preferences, configurations, and security information will be migrated into the new installation. This is generally recommended, unless you are deliberately avoiding an upgrade (for instance, to have 3.51 and 4.0 on the same machine for the sake of side-by-side performance tests). When you choose this option, you aren't prompted for a pathname to install Windows NT into. Setup uses the path of the previous installation.
- *Installing a Fresh Copy of Windows NT into a New Directory.* If you choose this option, you will later be asked for a drive and path to install the new copy of Windows NT into.

> **Note**
>
> If you have more than one version of Windows NT installed on a machine, you will be given the option at boot-time to select which one of the versions you want to boot.

Major Hardware Components Menu

The next Windows NT Setup menu lists the major hardware components installed in your machine. Note that this is not a definitive list and is only meant to provide enough basic hardware compatibility to complete Setup. You will generally not need to change any of the settings listed here unless your hardware documentation demands it.

To change an option, use the arrow keys to move between the selections and then press Enter to view the possible choices.

The following options are present:

- *Computer.* The default option for this, at least for Intel x86-based computers, is "Standard PC" and covers the vast majority of computers manufactured. You will generally not need to change this option unless your computer's documentation specifies that you need to choose a different option here. For instance, many multiprocessor machines require a special driver here, as well as machines that use the C-Step i486 processor.
- *Display.* The default option for Display is "VGA or Compatible" and generally does not need to be changed. The only other option, aside from using a vendor-supplied driver, is "Standard VGA (640 × 480, 16

colors)" which is only included for the sake of compatibility with older or more obscure video cards that may not support other standard video modes.

- *Keyboard.* The default option here is "XT, AT or Enhanced Keyboard (83-104 keys)" which covers the vast majority of keyboards manufactured. Again, there will generally be no need to change this setting unless you are working with a nonstandard keyboard that comes with its own driver.
- *Keyboard layout.* The default keyboard layout will vary depending on the country version of Windows NT you are installing. Keyboard layouts are available for every country for which Windows NT has a version available.

Note

Western-language (non-Asian) versions of Windows NT do not come with language support or keyboard mappings for Asian languages. To obtain Asian-language support for Windows NT, you must have an Asian-language version of the operating system.

- *Pointing device.* The default pointing device varies depending on what Windows NT Setup has detected. Windows NT Setup has drivers to support all Microsoft and Microsoft-compatible as well as Logitech and Logitech-compatible mice. If no mouse is installed, the default device will be "No Mouse Or Other Pointing Device."

Caution

Running Windows NT without a mouse is difficult at best. If you don't already have a mouse installed, get one installed before continuing.

When you have finished making changes (if any), highlight the line that reads:

```
The above list matches my computer.
```

Press Enter to continue to the next stage of Windows NT Setup.

Partitioning Disks for Use with Windows NT

The next stage of Windows NT Setup displays all hard storage available on your computer, and lets you choose or create a partition into which to place your Windows NT installation.

Caution

Working with hard drive partitions is dangerous. Before making ANY changes to the partitioning scheme in your system, make sure that you are not destroying irreplaceable data.

As with the other menus, the up and down arrows are used to navigate between selections—in this case, the different available hard drive partitions. Pressing Enter selects a partition to deploy Windows NT onto. There are also two other options:

- *Create a Partition.* This option only works when you are highlighting an unpartitioned space on a hard drive. When you press C, you are prompted for how much room you want to allocate from the unpartitioned space. Type the amount of space (in megabytes) and press Enter. To bail out and head back to the Disk Partitioning menu, press Esc.
- *Delete a Partition.* This option lets you remove the highlighted partition and return it to unused space. When you press D, you are shown the partition you are about to delete and given one last chance to bail out. If you do, in fact, want to delete the partition, press **L**. If you want to go back to the Disk Partitioning menu without changing anything, hit Esc. Once the partition is deleted, you will be returned to the Disk Partitioning menu.

If you choose an unformatted partition, you will be allowed to format the partition as either a FAT volume or an NTFS volume. Each type of file system has its advantages and drawbacks.

- *FAT.* The old MS-DOS file system has lasted quite a while, albeit with a great many extensions and modifications. Windows 95 uses a slightly modified version of FAT (VFAT or FAT16), as does Windows NT, adding in such things as support for long filenames. Using FAT on Windows NT gives Windows NT more freedom to coexist with other operating systems, including MS-DOS, Windows 95, OS/2 and Linux. FAT's disadvantages are also many: age, security, a degree of structural instability when dealing with lots of files, and a limited volume size (2G maximum) which makes it unsuitable for use on large volumes that aren't partitioned into logical drives. It's best to use FAT only if you need to have coexistence with an operating system that requires it.

- *FAT32.* FAT32 is an enhanced version of conventional FAT, soon to be used exclusively for Windows 95. FAT32 allows you to use volumes greater than 2G, with 2K clusters. Because of this fundamental design difference, Windows NT 4.0 will not be equipped to support FAT32 volumes.
- *NTFS.* Windows NT's own file system, NTFS (which stands for, not too inappropriately, NT File System), has many features that put it several degrees above FAT. With an NTFS volume, Windows NT can support a whole host of security and safety features, including mirroring, event logging, striping, on-the-fly compression and decompression, and access control. It can also support far larger volumes and file sizes than FAT. Its single big disadvantage is that NTFS volumes cannot be accessed by anything other than Windows NT. If you are not intending to use other operating systems on the same machine, or need the security and safety features that NTFS provides, use NTFS.

Bear in mind that not every drive in a Windows NT machine has to be formatted the same. You can mix NTFS and FAT volumes freely on your computer. Performance is not significantly impacted if you mix file system types on the same machine.

When formatting a volume, you will be given a progress bar that tells you how far along the format procedure is.

Note

One advantage to using an existing FAT volume is that if you later decide to convert it completely to NTFS, you can do so without too much difficulty.

Choosing a Directory for Windows NT

After selecting and/or formatting a target volume for Windows NT to be installed into, you may be prompted to supply a directory name. Windows NT will be installed into this directory. The directory defaults to \WINNT.

If you elected earlier in Windows NT Setup to upgrade an existing Windows NT installation, you will not be given this prompt.

Unless you are specifically trying not to overwrite something in a directory already named \WINNT (such as an earlier version of Windows NT that you are preserving), you don't need to change the name.

Once you have settled on the name of the directory, press Enter to confirm your selection and continue with Setup.

Examining Hard Disk(s) for Corruption

Before copying Windows NT files into the target directory, Windows NT Setup prompts you as to whether you want to examine the disks in your system for corruption. Next to copying over the files, this is the second-most time-consuming part of Windows NT Setup, but it's well worth the investment. If Windows NT is installed onto a disk that is partially corrupt, your system may fail to boot or you may suffer data loss.

To begin the disk check, press Enter. If for some reason you want to skip the disk check, press Esc, and you will be moved to the next stage of Windows NT Setup.

During the disk check, the bottommost line on-screen lets you know what disk is currently being examined.

Copying Windows NT Files into the Target Directory

At this point, Windows NT Setup begins copying the Windows NT system files into the specified directory and partition. A progress bar on-screen, with a percentage counter, lets you know how far along the copying process is. Information about which file is currently being copied is shown in the lower-right-hand corner of the screen.

If you are installing Windows NT files from floppies, Windows NT Setup prompts you to change disks during the copying procedure. At each prompt, insert the specified disk and press Enter, and copying continues.

If there is an error during the copying procedure, Windows NT Setup informs you which file did not copy successfully, and offers you the option of retrying the file copy, skipping the file (and assuming whatever consequences could result from that file being missing), or quitting Setup entirely.

When copying has been completed, Windows NT Setup prompts you to press Enter to reboot the system. Remove all disks from the drives and press Enter. The computer reboots.

The First Reboot

After the first reboot, Windows NT should begin to load. The Windows NT kernel message should appear (the build number will vary):

```
Microsoft ® Windows NT ™ Version 4.0 (Build XXXX)
```

```
1 System Processor [16 MB Memory] Multiprocessor Kernel
```

Also note that after the kernel ID message, a number of periods appear. This is normal and indicates that Windows NT is continuing to load. If the machine is inactive for more than two minutes, and periods have stopped appearing, shut everything down and reboot again.

After a few moments, Windows NT starts up in GUI mode.

GUI Mode and Licensing Agreement

Generally, the first thing that appears once Windows NT switches to GUI mode is the licensing agreement. If you have a mouse attached, you will find that the cursor responds to the mouse movements as it does normally in Windows.

Assuming you have read and are familiar with Microsoft's licensing agreements, press Y or click Yes to continue. If you press N or click No, an error will be written to the Windows NT Setup log and the system will reboot. (You can resume setup simply by letting the system reboot.)

The Windows NT Setup Wizard

The next screen that appears is the Windows NT Setup Wizard. A Wizard is Microsoft's term for a graphical application that allows you to scroll back and forth freely between several screens full of options and make as many changes as you need before committing the choices you have made.

The first screen of the wizard is a simple welcome message; click Next to continue.

To go back to the previous screen at any time in the wizard, click Back.

Setup Options

At this point, Windows NT Setup lets you choose which of four varieties of Setup you want to use:

- *Typical.* Typical setup installs the default set of options that are recommended for the majority of computers. It is also the fastest of the Setup paths and asks the least number of questions from the user. Novice Windows NT users will probably do best with this version of Setup, since it goes the quickest.
- *Portable.* In the Portable version of Setup, Windows NT is installed with the options that best benefit users of portable computers.

- *Compact.* The Compact installation contains only what is absolutely essential to run Windows NT; none of the optional components are installed. You can elect to install optional components later, of course. This option is best for those who are running Windows NT with little space to spare.
- *Custom.* Custom Setup allows you to select the components you want to install and make other changes along the way as well. This option gives you the most flexibility in your installations, but is recommended for those who have had at least some experience with previous versions of Windows NT.

Choosing Custom is actually the best option here. With it we can explore the variety of configuration choices available in Windows NT Setup. If you choose any of the other options, some of the screens described here may not appear.

When you have selected a configuration option, click Next.

Name and Organization

In this screen, the user is prompted to type in his name and the name of his organization (optional). Windows NT uses this information to generate unique ID numbers for the computer and the installation of Windows NT you are configuring. You must type in a name in order for Windows NT Setup to proceed.

1. To select the Name field, press Alt+M or click the text box next to the word Name.
2. To select the Organization field, press Alt+O or click the text box next to the word Organization.
3. When you are finished, click Next to continue.

Computer Name

This screen prompts the user to provide a name for the computer, which will be used to uniquely identify it on any networks it is connected to.

Note

Your network administrator may have a specific name in mind for you to use, consult with him before filling out this field.

Computer names can be up to 15 alphanumeric characters, including spaces. If the choice of name is up to you, try to use a name that is descriptive. "MY COMPUTER" is not descriptive, while "DAVID'S NT BOX" is at least relatively descriptive.

Note

All letters entered in the Computer Name field are automatically converted to uppercase. This is normal, since network browsers for some operating systems can't handle upper- and lowercase computer names.

When you are finished, click Next to continue.

Administrator Account

The next screen prompts the user for a password that will be used with the Administrator account. Since the Administrator account allows a user an unprecedented level of access to the system, allowing him to change system settings and other user accounts as well, it should be guarded carefully.

Choose a password for the Administrator account and type it in. When you finish typing it, press the Tab key to advance to the Confirm Password text box and type the password in one more time. If you have not typed in a consistent password both times, you are warned of this with a dialog box, and you must type in both passwords again.

Caution

It is possible to leave the Administrator password blank by simply not typing anything into either field. This is not recommended, since it creates an enormous security loophole that anyone can exploit. Even if the system you are installing Windows NT on is not intended to be secure in the first place, it's bad practice to leave the Administrator password blank.

When you are finished, click Next to continue.

Emergency Repair Disk

In this screen, the user has the option of creating an Emergency Repair Disk. The Repair Disk contains backups of several crucial system files that can be useful in getting Windows NT back up and running in the event of a catastrophic failure.

Click Yes to tell Windows NT Setup that you want to create an Emergency Repair Disk. Click No to skip Emergency Repair disk creation.

If you don't want to create a repair disk at this point, you can always create one when you are actually running Windows NT by using the RDISK command (described later in the section, "Using the RDISK Command").

To create an Emergency Repair Disk, you need a blank, formatted disk. If you don't have one yet, prepare one and keep it handy, since the Emergency Repair Disk isn't written until later on in the installation process.

When you are finished, click Next to continue.

Select Components

The next stage of Windows NT Installation allows you to choose which components will be installed along with the Windows NT operating system.

> **Note**
>
> If you selected Typical or Compact Setup, you may not see this screen; instead, you are presented with a screen that allows you to choose whether you want to install optional components at all.

There are six major categories of optional components, some of which may have been preselected, depending on the type of installation you have chosen.

- *Accessibility Options*. This set of components allows Windows NT to be more easily used by the visually and physically handicapped.
- *Accessories*. The Accessories set of components contains many separate programs that make working with Windows NT a little easier: the Calculator, a full-function scientific calculator; Character Map, which lets you examine each installed typeface and select characters from them; Clipboard Manager, which lets you save, copy and export the contents of the Clipboard to a file or to another machine on the network; Clock (self-explanatory); several flavors of desktop wallpaper; Imaging, an applet that can display images in may different formats and accept input from TWAIN-compatible scanning devices; the Internet Jumpstart Kit, designed to allow users easy and quick connections to the Internet with either a modem or an existing network connection; Mouse Pointers, a collection of graphical and animated cursors; Object Packager, which allows you to create OLE-embedded objects; Paint, a simple graphics design program; Quick View, which lets you readily examine

the contents of most files; a set of Windows NT-specific screen savers; and the WordPad utility, which lets you read text files, Microsoft Word for Windows 6.0 and higher files, Microsoft Write files, and files that use RTF (Rich Text Format).

- *Communications*. There are three components in the Communications section: Chat, which allows two users on the same network to type messages to each other; HyperTerminal, a Windows NT version of Hilgraeve's communications software; and Phone Dialer, an application that stores and dials phone numbers through Windows NT's telephony extensions.
- *Games*. Four games are included with Windows NT: two card games (Freecell and the ever-popular Solitaire), Minesweeper, and Pinball. For best results, make sure you have a Windows NT-supported sound card before playing Pinball.
- *Windows Messaging Service*. All versions of Windows NT 4.0 come with the client version of Windows Messaging Service, Microsoft's new mail and information exchange paradigm. The Windows Messaging Service now also allows users to receive and send Internet mail, and is compatible with older versions of Microsoft Mail.
- *Multimedia*. The multimedia components include various sound schemes (collections of thematically related system event sounds), and applications for playing back and recording digital video and audio. You should deselect this option if you do not have sound hardware installed.

A checkbox next to the component name indicates whether the component has been selected. Click once on a component to highlight it, and click the checkbox to either select or deselect the components inside it. At the right of each component is a rough estimate of just how much disk space will be taken up by installing that component.

To select or deselect specific programs or files within a component, highlight the component and click the Details button. A screen that lists the files within that component appears, with checkboxes next to each file. When you are finished selecting or deselecting individual files, click OK to return to the main Components menu.

If the Details button is grayed out when you have a particular component highlighted, that component has no suboptions you can set.

When you are finished, click Next to continue.

Installing Windows NT Networking

The next major phase of installing Windows NT involves setting up Windows NT for networking. This includes configuring a network adapter (if you have one), setting network protocol options, and setting up Dialup Networking. Click Next to get past the "Installing Networking" opening screen.

The first set of networking options are for telling Windows NT Setup how the computer is connected to a network:

- *Do Not Connect this Computer to a Network at this Time.* Choose this option if the computer is not connected to a network at this time, or if you simply wish to install networking components later.
- *This Computer Will Participate on a Network.* This option is enabled by default and lists two suboptions that can be checked or unchecked independently: Wired to the Network means that you are directly connected to a network through an ISDN adapter or a network interface card. Remote Access to the Network indicates that you connect to the network through a dialup connection, or a modem. You can enable both of these options—for instance, if you use dialup networking to access the Internet, and use a network card to talk to a local-area network.

When you have finished selecting the appropriate options, press Next.

Network Adapter Search

The next phase of network installation involves locating and installing drivers for a network adapter card, if you have one. If you are only using Dial-Up Networking to access a network, you can skip this step by pressing Next.

Here are the steps to take when you reach this screen.

1. If you have a network card installed, click the Search button to have Windows NT Setup search for a network adapter. If the search is successful, the name of the adapter appears in the Network Adapters list. If Windows NT Setup can't find a network adapter, it tells you so.
2. If detecting automatically doesn't work, or if you have a network card that needs a driver provided by its manufacturer, click the Select from List button to display a list of all network cards that Windows NT has drivers for. Select the proper driver from the list and click OK to install it.
3. If you are installing drivers from a vendor-supplied disk, click Have Disk. A dialog box asking you for the drive and pathname to the drivers

appears, with "A:\" as the default path. Type the drive and directory where you have the drivers and click OK.

Once you have a network card driver installed, click Next to continue.

Note

If Windows NT Setup can't find your network card at all, make sure the hardware settings for the network card are correct. See the later section entitled "Troubleshooting Setup" for more information.

Network Protocols

In this screen, the user has the option to select and install networking protocols. Three options are presented at first:

- *TCP/IP Protocol.* The most common set of networking protocols in the world, the TCP/IP protocol stack is used by all computers that connect to the Internet, and many that don't. Because of its near indispensability, the TCP/IP protocol is checked by default.
- *NWLink IPX/SPX Compatible Transport and NetBEUI Protocol.* These are two protocols that are most commonly used by Novell Netware, but which are also used by Windows Networking. If you are connecting to other Windows machines or to a Netware server, enable both of these protocols.

By clicking Select from List, the user can bring up several other network protocol options. To install a protocol from this list, highlight it and press OK. You are returned to the main protocol menu, with the previously highlighted protocol added to the list of protocols to install and its checkbox enabled.

If you have vendor-supplied drivers for an additional protocol, you can install them by clicking the Have Disk button in the Select from List window. A window opens, prompting you for the path to the driver to install. Type the name of the path and click OK. If the driver is found, it will be added to the main protocol list.

Other protocols include:

- *AppleTalk Protocol.* The networking protocol used in Apple Computer's AppleTalk networking environment.
- *DLC Protocol.* Used for communications with some older IBM mainframes; included only for the sake of backward compatibility.

- *Point-to-Point Tunnelling Protocol.* This allows you to perform networking with the whole of the Internet as the backbone—in effect, browse the Internet as one giant server. This is indispensable if you plan on making your Windows NT machine an Internet server of any kind. For more on PPTP, see Chapter 2, "Understanding and Configuring TCP/IP."

When you're done selecting protocols, click Next to continue.

Network Services

The next screen contains a list of Windows NT services pertaining to networking that will be installed and activated. As with the protocols list, each service comes with a checkbox that allows you to specify if a service should be installed or not. If a service has a gray checkbox, it is required for networking and you cannot disable it.

The following options are installed by default with all forms of networking:

- *Remote Access Service.* This allows Windows NT to handle Remote Access functions, whether as a client or a server.
- *RPC Configuration.* This service governs remote procedure calls.
- *NetBIOS interface.* This service translates NetBIOS calls, incoming and outgoing, for use by Windows NT.
- *Workstation.* The Workstation service covers the client half of Windows NT's built-in networking (directory sharing, and so on).
- *Server.* This service is the server half of NT's built-in networking. The two must always be installed together.

Clicking the Select from List button brings up a list of alternative network services.

By clicking Select from List, the user can bring up several other network service options. To install a service from this list, click it to highlight it and press OK. You are returned to the main service menu, with the previously highlighted service added to the list of services to install, and its checkbox enabled.

- *Client Service for Netware.* This service allows you to browse and access Novell Netware servers and bindery trees. If you are going to be accessing any form of the Novell network, you should install this service. If you are using Windows NT Workstation, this item is named Gateway Services for Netware.
- *Microsoft Internet Information Server.* A simple but powerful World Wide Web, Gopher and ftp server that can be used to host considerably powerful intranet applications.

- *Microsoft TCP/IP Printing.* With this service, print jobs can be redirected via TCP/IP to another system's printer. Both systems must be running this service and TCP/IP as well.
- *Network Monitor Agent.* This is the new "bloodhound" service from SMS—a software sniffer for the network.
- *RPC Support for Banyan.* This services implements remote procedure calls for the Banyan VINES networking environment.
- *SAP Agent.* This service handles Netware-compatible Service Advertisement Packets, which allows a Windows NT server to be seen as a Netware server.
- *Simple TCP/IP Services.* These include finger, whois, ping and a few other minor but essential TCP/IP services.
- SNMP Service. The Simple Network Management Protocol service allows you to use universal methods for monitoring network actions—bridges, routers, and so on—on an in-band basis.

If you have vendor-supplied drivers for an additional service, you can install them by clicking the Have Disk button in the Select from List window. A window opens up, prompting you for the path to the driver to install. Type the name of the path and click OK. If the driver is found, it will be added to the main service list.

When you are finished with selecting services, click Next to continue.

Installing Selected Network Components

At this point, Windows NT Setup is ready to install networking components based on the choices you have made. If you need to go back and make changes, click the Back button, because this is the last chance you will have to make changes before Windows NT Networking is installed. Click Next to proceed with the installation.

You may be asked certain additional questions about your networking setup at this point. For instance, if you are installing RAS, you may be asked to install a modem, and the Add Modem Wizard is automatically invoked. Also, if you are installing a network adapter card, you may be asked for its interrupt channel and I/O address information. For more information on adding a modem, see Chapter 13, "Adding Modems."

Reviewing Network Bindings

When all network components have been installed and activated, you are shown a list of all network bindings. This is a description of what services and what protocols are "bound" or assigned to which adapters.

You will generally not need to change the assignments of bindings unless there are circumstances that demand it. If your network administrator has specific instructions about how protocols and services should be bound, consult with him before making changes.

The Network Bindings screen has the following options:

- *Show Bindings For.* By clicking here, you can review the bindings list in three different ways: by services, by protocols, or by adapters.
- *Enable.* Highlight an item and click Enable to enable it if it has been disabled.
- *Disable.* Highlight an item and click Disable to disable it.
- *Move Up/Move Down.* These two buttons let you shift the order in which items are prioritized. For instance, if you are reviewing the list of bindings by protocol, and one protocol is bound to two separate adapters, you can change the priority the protocol gives to those adapters by clicking one of them and then clicking either Move Up or Move Down.

When you are finished with making changes to bindings, click Next to continue.

Starting the Network

Now that all the software components are actually in place, Windows NT Setup attempts to start the network and determine if it is operational. If you need to go back and make changes to network settings, click Back. Otherwise, click Next to start the network.

Workgroup/Domain Selection

The next screen of Windows NT Setup allows you to choose if your computer will be participating in a Workgroup or a Domain.

> **Note**
>
> You cannot participate in a domain if you don't have permission to do so. Check with your network administrator to determine if your computer has permission to participate in the domain.

The workgroup/domain selection screen has the following options:

- *Computer Name.* This contains the name that the current computer has been registered under. It cannot be edited here.

- *Workgroup.* If you want the computer to join a Workgroup, click the radio button next to Workgroup and type the name of the Workgroup in the text box.
- *Domain.* If you want the computer to join a Domain, click the radio button next to Domain and type the name of the Domain in the text box.
- *Create a Computer Account in the Domain.* When you check this box and click Next, you are prompted to supply the name of an administrator for that domain, and a password. This administrator must have the ability to add workstations to the domain. Type the name and password and click OK.

When you have finished setting workgroup and domain options, click Next to continue.

Finishing Setup

At this point, you have finished specifying all the major options in Windows NT Setup. Before the last set of files can be copied over, however, a few more questions must be answered. Click Finish to start answering these questions.

Date/Time Properties

In this window, you are given the option to change the time and date of your computer, and to set the proper time zone that you are in.

Date & Time

Clicking the Date & Time tab brings up a screen in which you can set the following options:

- *Date.* To adjust the date, you can click the calendar to pick a specific day. Clicking the month and year boxes allows you to adjust which month and year the clock is set to.
- *Time.* By clicking the text box below the clock, you can type in the exact time. Also, by highlighting the hour, minute, or second in the text box, you can click the arrows to change their values up or down.

> **Note**
>
> Unless you know your computer's clock and calendar are wrong, you should not need to change the time and date.

Time Zone

Clicking the Time Zone tab brings up a world map and a list of all the available time zones. Click the drop-down list of time zones to select your correct time zone from among them.

Click the Automatically Adjust Clock for Daylight Saving Changes checkbox to allow Windows NT to automatically adjust your clock for Daylight Savings Time.

When you are finished setting your clock, calendar, and time zone, click Close to continue.

Select Video Adapter

▶ See "Installing Video Cards" p.263

At this point, Windows NT Setup attempts to automatically detect what video adapter you have installed in your computer, and opens the Display Properties sheet. A dialog box appears to inform you of the choice it has made. If it specifies the wrong adapter, you need to manually specify the correct adapter, or provide a vendor-written driver.

When you have finished configuring the video adapter, click OK.

Copying Files

The final phases of the install involve copying over what files there are left to copy, removing temporary installation files, and rebooting. If you elected to build an Emergency Recovery disk, you are prompted to insert it at some point, and the needed files are written to it.

Finally, you are presented with a screen that tells you to reboot your computer. You have finished Setup and are now ready to begin running Windows NT 4.0.

Troubleshooting Windows NT Setup

Many of the most complicated problems have the simplest solutions. Some of the more common problems that can crop up during Windows NT Setup, and some suggested solutions, are listed here.

- *The computer freezes at various points during Setup.* The most common reason for this problem is a faulty or improperly installed piece of hardware. Make sure all expansion boards and memory modules are properly installed and correctly seated. Also make sure the computer is not suffering from a ventilation problem. Many inexplicable system lockups are caused by inadequate cooling.

- *Setup aborts because it can't find a hard drive to install Windows NT onto.* This can happen if the wrong mass storage drivers are installed—for example, if ATAPI.SYS (the driver that governs most PCI IDE controllers) is loaded into a system that uses the CMD PCI IDE controller, which requires its own Windows NT drivers. Make sure the system you are using requires its own drivers for the hard-disk controller. This problem can also happen if the BIOS setup for the drive controller is not correctly configured, or if a Plug-and-Play BIOS has been enabled. Finally, it can happen if the drive itself is in some way malfunctioning or simply not hooked up correctly.
- *Setup cannot identify other hardware installed in the system—network cards, SCSI host adapters, and so on.* Again, the most common problem here is incorrect hardware configuration; make sure the hardware in question is not set to an unorthodox memory address. Windows NT is especially fussy about network interface cards being set to the correct address. Also, if you are specifying drivers manually rather than having Windows NT Setup install them automatically, make sure you are referring to the correct driver for the correct piece of hardware.
- *Windows NT Setup can't read certain files from the disk set, CD-ROM, or local copy.* If you are running from a floppy set, make sure the disk itself is not damaged (another reason not to use floppies, since they are far more prone to errors than just about any other medium). Check that CD-ROM drives are correctly terminated (if they are SCSI) and that the CD-ROM itself is free of visible defects and dirt. Finally, if you've installed from a network copy, make sure the network copy itself wasn't transferred from corrupted media.
- *A "blue-screen" STOP error occurs.* This type of error, both visually distinctive and universally dreaded, is so named for the display it produces: a white-text-on-blue-blackground screen full of memory dump information, with an error code at the top and a short list of the offending modules that may have caused the crash. When this appears, there has been some sort of unrecoverable error on the kernel level. Generally, it means that a driver or other system-critical component has failed, and the list of drivers at the top of the screen usually contains a clue as to which driver it might be. If you are upgrading from a 3.51 to a 4.0 installation, or are using 3.51 driver disks in a 4.0 installation, take care that you are not using drivers that need to be rewritten for 4.0. Video drivers are often the culprits for blue-screen crashes during Setup.

Customizing Setup

As we mentioned before, Windows NT Setup derives its list of files and some of its more important setup parameters from a file. By default, this file is named DOSNET.INF and is packaged with Windows NT.

DOSNET.INF is a text file and can be edited with any conventional text editor (such as Notepad or Write, or even the command-line program edit). Some of the options in DOSNET.INF can be edited to suit the whim of the administrator who is managing installations of Windows NT.

Changing Disk Space Requirements

If Windows NT is being installed along with other software, the administrator may want to ensure that enough space exists for both Windows NT and the programs in question. One way to automatically ensure this is to modify the amount of space that Windows NT checks for on the target drive, which is stored in DOSNET.INF.

> **Note**
>
> Modifying DOSNET.INF only works if you're installing from a boot disks set, either for a floppy set or a CD-ROM, or from a file set that has had its DOSNET.INF file modified. Installing directly from a CD-ROM does not make it possible to modify the DOSNET.INF file for distribution.

Another scenario where modifying the disk-space check is useful is if Windows NT is being installed with a relatively minimal amount of components, and can therefore fit on a system with relatively less free space.

Follow this procedure to change the minimum space requirements for Window NT.

1. Determine just how much more (or less) space you'll be needing for Windows NT. This is a tedious process, since it involves getting the exact amount of space required (or freed up) by adding (or removing) programs.
2. Use a plain-text editor (like Notepad or the edit command) to edit the DOSNET.INF file that is in the source files for Windows NT that you will be using. Find the following section, which should be near the top of the file:

   ```
   [SpaceRequirements]
   BootDrive = 1048576
   NtDrive  = 94453760
   ```

3. Change the NtDrive number to the exact amount of space, in bytes, that you will need.
4. Save the DOSNET.INF file. Install Windows NT normally.

> **Caution**
>
> Windows NT Setup can't double-check this number for you. If you change the values in the DOSNET.INF file, you are responsible for making sure they will work. Test them before deploying them.

Setting Up Master Files on a Server

One Windows NT deployment scenario that's showing more and more use is having Windows NT setup files accessible to users on a file server. This type of arrangement is especially useful for several reasons:

- Only one copy of Windows NT needs to be purchased (although the administrator will of course have to purchase the correct number of seat licenses from Microsoft).
- If there are additional files that the administrator wants to bundle with the Windows NT installation when a user runs WINNT to copy the files to his local drive, all he has to do is include them with the set and make changes to the DOSNET.INF file (described in the previous section).
- It makes version tracking easier and ensures tighter control over the distribution of copies. If the files are shared from an NTFS volume that has auditing and permissions enabled, it's possible to log every single user who accesses those files.
- For users with less experience, it makes the whole process of setting up, installing, and upgrading Windows NT almost completely automatic. The system administrator can provide the user with a simple batch file that runs the WINNT command with all the needed switches, and supplies the proper network path to the source files.

One simple way to provide master files through a server is to place the Windows NT CD-ROM into a CD-ROM drive and share out the \I386, \MIPS, and \ALPHA directories. The drawback to this scheme is that it forces the administrator to devote an entire CD-ROM drive to this single function. It also means much more wear and tear on the CD-ROM drive supporting it.

If you're planning to have Windows NT files served out to many people over a long period of time, it makes more sense to devote part of your server's own hard storage to it. Here is one suggested method of doing this:

1. Make sure you have enough space on your server to hold the Windows NT Setup files.
2. Create a directory on your server that will hold the shared files. Make sure that prospective users have read access to the directory in question.
3. From the command line or the Run menu option on the start button type: **xcopy /s <cdromdrive>:\<platformtype> <targetdirectory>.** For instance, if your CD-ROM was D:, you were running on the Intel chipset and the target directory was \NTINSTALL, the command would read: **xcopy /s d:\i386 \ntinstall**.
4. Share the directory across the network as needed.
5. Provide users with the name of the directory they need to connect to and installation instructions.

Customizing Protocol Setup

In some instances, an administrator who is controlling the distribution of the installation of Windows NT may want to change the way network protocols are handled. He may, for instance, want to disable the installation of certain protocols, both to speed things up and to prevent novice users from making potentially invalid choices. Or he may even want to decide whether to present them with a protocol setup menu in the first place.

In Windows NT Setup, these functions are controlled through the XPORTS.INF file, which is included with the Windows NT Setup files, albeit in compressed form. XPORTS.INF is a plain-text file that can be edited with any plain-text editor, and can easily be created by typing in the following examples.

Some default instructions are included with the XPORTS.INF file, and they go a long way toward explaining the workings of XPORTS.INF:

> This file allows a Network Administrator to customize over the network installations (installations using winnt.ext). This file can be modified on the network share containing the installation files. To install a transport by default, remove the ';' from the beginning of the line and set the value to the right of the '=' to 1. To not install a transport by default, set the value to 0. To suppress the dialog asking the user for confirmation or changes to the default transport, remove the ';' from the beginning of the !PromptForTransports line and set the value to 0.

A typical XPORTS.INF file contains lines like the following.

```
[DefaultProtocols]
Set !PromptForTransports = 1
Set !InstallNWLink = 1
```

```
Set !InstallTCPIP = 0
Set !InstallNetBEUI = 0
Set !PromptUserForProtocols = 1
```

Each of these lines describes a network component that can be set to be installed by default or ignored. Lines where the number after the equals sign is a zero (0) mean that the indicated protocol is *not* installed by default. Conversely, those with a one (1) after the equals sign mean that the indicated protocol *is* installed by default.

The "Set !PromptForTransports" line tells Windows NT Setup whether or not to even bother prompting the user with a dialog listing network protocol choices. Again, this is useful in situations where the administrator may want to minimize the amount of work the user has to do during an install, or simply to minimize the possibility of mistakes.

Note

Setting the !PromptForTransports value to zero doesn't mean that no protocols are installed; it simply means that no user prompting is provided. Protocols designated as defaults will install anyway.

Customizing Product ID

When a user installs from the Windows NT Server floppy disks or compact disc, Windows NT Setup asks the user to enter the Product ID. The network administrator should provide this information by default by changing a value in the INITIAL.INF file in the Windows NT Server master files.

To specify the Product ID in source files for network installation, edit the following line of INITIAL.INF to specify the Product ID for your site license:

```
ProductID=<###############>
```

For example, you might change this value to ProductID=942347978924567 if that is your Product ID number.

However, if you want the Product ID dialog box to appear during network setup so that each user can enter a value for the Product ID, then make sure that DisplayPidDlg="Yes" is in the INITIAL.INF file.

Installing over or with other Operating Systems

Windows NT has the advantage of being able to coexist with other installed operating systems. However, each operating system has its own peculiarities regarding booting and boot-sector management that Windows NT users need to keep in mind when configuring a multiboot system.

Because Windows NT has its own boot loader, other Microsoft operating systems such as Windows 3.1, MS-DOS, or Windows 95, can be booted from the Windows NT boot loader. Windows NT automatically recognizes the presence of other Microsoft operating systems and creates entries in the BOOT.INI file to enable them. (Details on how to modify the BOOT.INI file are listed in the following section.)

Installing with Windows 3.1 or Windows 95

Windows NT can be installed directly over Windows 3.1. If you install Windows NT into the directory that contained Windows 3.1, all the existing program settings and information are migrated to Windows NT. Note that once you do this, you have effectively changed your Windows 3.1 machine into a Windows NT machine, and you won't be able to boot Windows 3.1 or MS-DOS.

You can also choose to install Windows NT into a different directory than Windows 3.1. The existing Windows 3.1 installation won't be migrated, but you'll be given the option at boot-time of booting either Windows NT or Windows 3.1.

Attempting to install Windows NT over Windows 95 should be avoided. If you want Windows NT and Windows 95 to coexist in the same system, install them in discrete directories.

Caution

Installing MS-DOS or Windows 95 onto a Windows NT machine will destroy your Windows NT boot loader. If you plan to have either of these operating systems coexist on a Windows NT machine, install MS-DOS or Windows 95 first and *then* Windows NT.

Installing with OS/2

OS/2 has both some very good and bad points as far as multi-booting between operating systems goes.

On the good side is the IBM Boot Manager. The Boot Manager is a utility that installs in a primary partition on a hard drive and can be used to select, at boot time, which of one or more primary partitions to boot.

If you have a hard drive prepartitioned with several primary partitions on it and want to use Windows NT and OS/2 on separate partitions, leave an empty partition of about 1M at the front of the disk for the Boot Manager. Install Windows NT in the next partition, and then place Boot Manager in the first partition, marking that one as the active boot partition.

However, there are a few scenarios where Windows NT and OS/2 have trouble living together under the same roof.

OS/2, when installed on an MS-DOS drive, allows you to use a program called boot to swap the OS/2 and MS-DOS boot sectors. The nice thing about this scheme is that it allows you to do the same with the Windows NT or Windows 95 boot sectors as well. And since OS/2 does this automatically when it's installed on an MS-DOS drive, shouldn't it also do the same when installed on an NT drive, as long as said drive is using the FAT file system?

If only it did work like that. OS/2 won't allow you to install it on a partition with Windows NT on it without reformatting the partition first! (Windows NT also complains if it finds OS/2 files on a disk you've designated as a target for Windows NT during install, and suggests pretty much the same course of action. Windows NT support for HPFS and OS/2 applications have both been discontinued as of version 4.0.)

There is a way to get around this, but it's potentially dangerous and should only be done by advanced Windows NT users. It also only works if the partition Windows NT is already on is a FAT partition, since OS/2 can't read NTFS drives. (Note that this procedure only applies for systems with Windows NT already present, where someone wants to install OS/2.)

1. Boot MS-DOS or Windows 95.
2. In the root directory of the boot drive, type: **attrib -r -h -s *.***. This will make the hidden NT boot files—the things OS/2 sees and complains about—visible.
3. Type: **rename nt*.* xt*.***. This renames the NT boot files into something OS/2 will not have a complaint with.

Caution

Before you do this, make sure you don't have any critical files that match the wildcard xt*.*. Move them somewhere else before renaming your NT boot files.

5. Shut down and reboot. Install OS/2 normally.
6. After OS/2 finishes installing, restore the filenames by logging into the root directory and typing **rename xt*.* nt*.***.

Installing with Linux

Most breeds of Linux feature a boot-record manager called LILO (short for LInux LOader). LILO resides in the master boot record of a multi-partition hard drive, and allows you to specify which partition you want to boot.

Working with LILO to create a multi-boot system—Windows NT, Linux, and whatever else you want—strongly resembles working with OS/2 Boot Manager, in that the user should reserve partition space for all the operating systems involved before doing anything.

LILO can also be used to dual-boot a Linux system that uses the UMSDOS kernel to reside on a FAT-formatted partition, right alongside Windows NT. Since LILO resides in the master boot record of a hard drive, if the user ever decides to remove it, they will need to boot DOS or Windows 95 and use FDISK to do so.

One way to rewrite the master boot record of a hard drive is this:

1. In DOS or Windows 95, create a bootable floppy with the format a: /s command and copy FDISK.exe to it.
2. Boot the disk.
3. Log to the C: drive and type: **fdisk /mbr**. The master boot record of the drive will be rewritten with a FAT16/32-compatible version. ❖

CHAPTER 7

Distributed Setup

by Richard Neff

If you're a network administrator in a company with many Windows NT machines, upgrading to Windows NT 4.0 can be a daunting task. Going to every machine that needs to have Windows NT 4.0 installed or upgraded with the CD-ROM and boot disks certainly is the slowest method of setting up Windows NT in your organization. Fortunately, there are many options for distributing Windows NT 4.0 across your network.

In this chapter, you learn to

- Understand the difference between a distributed setup and a regular individual setup
- Understand the different methods used to set up a Windows NT computer across the network
- Create a Windows NT distribution share
- Use a Computer Profile Setup (CPS)
- Distribute Windows NT across the network using Microsoft Systems Management Server

Overview of Distributed Setup

Distributed setup methods are designed for a network administrator who has to install Windows NT on many computers in an organization. Performing the standard individual installation on multiple computers can take a long time. Distributed setup makes installation easier by creating a distribution share on a file server in the network and allows the administrator to install Windows NT from the share. The distribution share can also be customized to create exactly the configuration needed on individual workstations. The setup process can also be automated, further lessening the time needed to install multiple copies of Windows NT.

Understanding Distributed Setup

Distributed setup uses a network server, called a distribution server, to hold all the installation files used to install Windows NT on network computers. The installation files can be added, deleted, or modified on the distribution server to allow different configuration options to be automatically installed on client computers. The client machine then connects to the distribution server and installs Windows NT from the shared directory on the distribution server.

> **Note**
>
> The type of distributed setup method depends on your organization or network structure. It's highly recommended that you install Windows NT 4.0 using a pilot scenario before actually performing a large-scale installation. The pilot test allows you to experience problems on a small scale. You can then develop fixes to the problems before trying to do a "real" installation.

License Agreements

Of course, before attempting to distribute Windows NT over the network, be sure you follow the licensing agreements. Failure to follow the licensing agreements is a violation of the law and could cost your company significantly. Corporate users of software are more closely scrutinized for license compliance than individual users.

Creating and Using a Distribution Share

After Windows NT is installed on at least one computer, a distribution share needs to be created. Once the share is created, the Windows NT installation files can be copied to the share. From there, the installation files can be modified to customize the installation process for your organization. Separate shares need to be created for Windows NT Workstation and Windows NT Server.

To create a distribution share on a computer, follow these steps:

1. Create a new directory on the distribution computer. Remember, you need different shares if you want to have distribution shares for both Windows NT Workstation and Windows NT Server.
2. Copy the installation files from the Windows NT CD-ROM to the distribution share. You can use the directory structure of the CD-ROM which allows Windows NT to be installed on multiple platforms or you can

choose the directories you want to copy. For example, if you only use Intel platforms in your organization, you could just copy the \I368 directory from the CD-ROM.

3. Modify the installation files to customize the Windows NT Setup program for your organization. You may need to remove the Read-Only attribute from the files since they were copied from a CD-ROM.
4. Share the distribution directory. You should make it a read-only share to prevent users from accidentally modifying the installation files.

The distribution share can then be used to install Windows NT on a computer or be used to install additional files to a computer already running Windows NT 4.0. The distribution shares are designed to install Windows NT by using the winnt or winnt32 commands. To install Windows NT, connect to the distribution share and run either winnt, for MS-DOS and Windows 3.1 users, or winnt32, for users with earlier versions of Windows NT. This process can sometimes be automated through the use of batch files.

Creating a Single Share

Creating a single share is most commonly used with Windows NT Workstation. If your organization has only one Windows NT Server and you want to install Windows NT Workstation on the client machines, then only a single share is needed.

Creating Multiple Shares

Creating multiple shares is needed if you want to install Windows NT Workstation and Windows NT Server using distribution shares. Also, if you want to have distribution shares for older versions of Windows NT, you will need to have separate shares for all the versions of Windows NT. Multiple shares may also be used if you want to have different customized versions of Windows NT 4.0 setup files.

Installing Windows NT Unattended

You can install Windows NT unattended, that is without Windows NT prompting the user for information, by using an answer file. An *answer file* is used by the Windows NT Setup to retrieve the proper configuration settings without prompting the user. In order to use the unattended setup option, use the /u: switch followed by the answer filename after the winnt or winnt32 commands. For example:

```
winnt /u:c:unattend.txt
```

or

```
winnt32 /u:c:unattend.txt
```

You will also need to specify the distribution share for the Windows NT installation using the /s: parameter. So, if you had the source files located on the \\fileserver computer in the \winnt share and mapped to drive letter x:, the complete setup command would be:

```
winnt /u:c:unattend.txt /s:x:\
```

or

```
winnt32 /u:c:unattend.txt /s:x:\
```

Answer files are *not* needed when upgrading a Windows NT system with an unattended installation. However, they can be used to override settings currently used in the older Windows NT configuration.

Creating Answer Files Using the Setup Manager

The Windows NT Resource Kit provides a utility called the Setup Manager that allows answer files to be created or modified. The Setup Manager provides a graphical interface to select answer file options. The answer file is created or modified and can be used for an unattended installation. To run the Setup Manager, type the following:

```
setupmgr <answerfile>
```

where *<answerfile>* is the name of the answer file you want to create or edit. If no answer file is provided, the program will load with the default settings. Figure 7.1 shows the Setup Manager program.

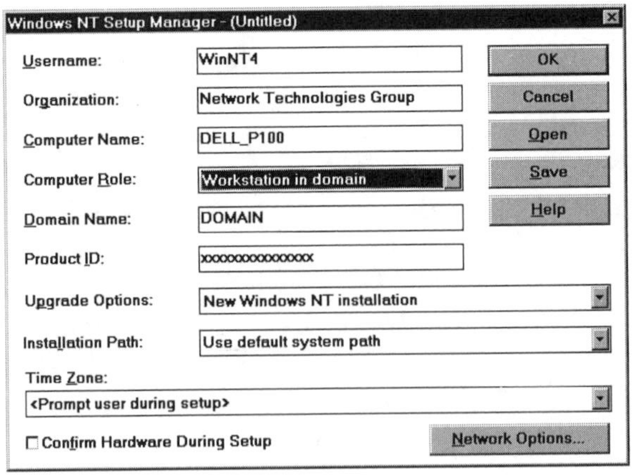

Fig. 7.1
The Setup Manager allows you to create answer files for unattended installations.

Using Computer Profile Setup (CPS)

The Computer Profile Setup (CPS) is useful if the computer equipment is similar or identical throughout the office. CPS uses the configuration of a computer, called the master system, and uses its settings to install and set up the other computers, known as the targets. The Windows NT CPS utility is found in the Windows NT Resource Kit disks and is designed to install Windows NT on Intel-based computers.

When using CPS to install Windows NT, the following steps are used:

1. A master system is created from an installed Windows NT 4.0 machine. This machine has Windows NT 4.0 properly installed and configured with the options to be used by the target machines.
2. The master system is then uploaded to a distribution server to allow access by other machines on the network.
3. The target computers are then used to copy the master system settings from the distribution server. The target machines are installed with the configuration used by the master system.
4. The duplicated systems should then be tested to ensure that the proper settings are used by the target machines.

Configuring the Master

The first step in using CPS is creating the master system. All the installed clients will use the configuration of the master system, so it must be properly installed and configured. Use a computer that contains the type of hardware adapters and devices that are used in your company.

After the master system has been installed and configured, you will need to upload the files to a distribution server.

To upload the master system to the distribution server, follow these steps:

1. On the master system computer, create a folder or directory to hold the CPS utility files.
2. Copy the CPS files from the Windows NT Resource Kit CD-ROM. These files are located in \i386\cps. You can use the XCOPY command or the Windows NT Explorer.
3. If needed, make any changes to the PROFILE.INI file using the Windows NT Notepad utility or another text editing program.
4. On the distribution server, create a directory to receive the master system files. This directory also needs to be shared on the network.

5. Finally, on the master system computer, type the following:

```
uplodprf -s:master directory -i:profile.ini [\dir1] [\dir2]
➥[\dirX]
```

The *master directory* is the UNC name of the directory to receive the files on the distribution server. The [\dir1], [\dir2], and [\dirX] options are additional directories on the master system that you want installed on the target computers.

Exporting to the Targets

After the master system is configured and copied to the distribution server, target computers can then have Windows NT installed. This installation does not necessarily have to be a purely network installation, although it is the most popular method. The following methods can be used to install the master system configuration to the target computers:

- Network adapter
- Serial or parallel port transfer
- Hard disk duplication
- Tape backup and restore methods
- Other large-media transfers, such as CD-R (Recordable CDs)

The difference between a CPS installation and merely copying the Windows NT files of the master system is that the CPS installation allows for the target computer to enter local machine information (user name, computer name, and so on). By merely copying the files, the target computer must have the local machine information manually configured.

However, target computers must have the same hardware devices and configuration as the master system. The exceptions to this are that target computers can have more memory or larger disk drives than the master system. However, if larger hard disk drives are used, they must be the same type (IDE, SCSI, and so on) as the master system. If your company has slightly different hardware devices attached to target computers, see the "Merging Profiles" section later in this chapter.

To distribute the master system configuration to the target computers over the network, follow these steps:

1. Create a bootable floppy disk using the DOS sys command or the /s format switch. After the system files are copied, add the network files, any SCSI drivers, or other network or boot device files. These files must allow the computer to be booted with the floppy disk and must allow access to the network and the disk drives. You will probably need to

copy the AUTOEXEC.BAT and CONFIG.SYS files for a machine to do this.

2. Copy the WINNTP.EXE file from the Resource Kit CD-ROM to the bootable floppy disk.
3. Boot the computer from the bootable floppy disk. Make a connection to the distribution share on the distribution server.
4. Type the following at the command prompt:

   ```
   winntp /r /s:\\servername\sharename /b
   ```

   where *servername* is the UNC name of the distribution server and *sharename* is the UNC name of the distribution share.

   The /r switch specified that a download of the distribution share is to occur rather than a normal CD-ROM installation.

   The /b switch is used to force the computer to reboot after the DOS-based setup has finished and continue with the graphical mode setup. When this option is used, the user must be sure that there is *not* a floppy disk in the a: drive.
5. The WINNTP tool copies the profile to the target computer from the distribution share and starts the Windows NT Setup program. The user name, machine name, and other local machine information is requested at this point, if the installation is not configured to be an unattended installation.
6. The Windows NT Setup program prompts the user to reboot the machine after the installation is completed. Remove the bootable floppy disk from the drive and reboot the machine. At this point, the computer should be completely installed with Windows NT and ready to use.

Merging Profiles

Many organizations do not have computers with hardware that is completely identical. Many companies standardize on a particular brand of computer, but those machines may contain different video cards, CD-ROM drives, and so on. If your organization has computers that are very similar, merging profiles allow you to use a CPS distribution system without requiring all the machines to have the same configuration as the master computer. CPS is used to create one profile from the master system and other profiles can be used for each of the different devices used in the company.

In order to have different profile configurations, you have to set up the original system profile and then create difference profiles. The difference profiles only contain Registry settings and device files that are needed for the item that is different from the original configuration.

To create difference profiles, follow these steps:

1. Create and upload a master system to the distribution server. For more information on creating and uploading the master system, see the section titled "Configuring the Master" earlier in this chapter.
2. On the master system computer, create a new directory or folder to hold the CPS utility files. If the master system is the same system used in the original configuration, this step may not be necessary.
3. Copy the CPS files from the Windows NT Resource Kit CD-ROM. These files are located in \i386\cps. You can use the XCOPY command or the Windows NT Explorer. Again, this may not be necessary if the machine was used to create the original master system configuration.
4. If needed, make any changes to the PROFILE.INI file using the Windows NT Notepad utility or another text editing program.
5. On the distribution server, create a directory that is different from the original master system directory. This directory will contain the difference profile. Be sure to also share this directory on the network.
6. On the master system computer, enter the following:

   ```
   uploadprf -h -s:differencedir -i:profile.ini [\dir1] [\dir2]
   ➥[\dirX]
   ```

   where *differencedir* is the UNC name to the directory created in step 5 on the distribution server. The [\dir1], [\dir2], and [\dirX] options are additional directories on the difference master system that you want installed on the target computers.

   The -h parameter specifies that only the hive is to be copied to the PROFILE.INI on the distribution server. This parameter is only used for difference profiles.

Once the difference profile has been uploaded to the distribution server, the user or administrator can download the profile to the target machine. In order for the profiles to be merged, the master profile will be specified, then the difference profile will be specified when using the WINNTP command.

To download the Windows NT profile using difference profiles, type the following:

```
winntp /r /s:\\servername\mastersharename,\\servername\diffsharename /b
```

where servername is the UNC name of the distribution server. The mastersharename is the UNC name of the distribution share for the original master system. The diffsharename is the UNC name of the difference profile share on the server. *No* spaces should be between the comma and the difference profile UNC name.

The /r switch specified that a download of the distribution share is to occur rather than a normal CD-ROM installation.

The /b switch is used to force the computer to reboot after the DOS-based setup has finished and continue with the graphical mode setup. When this option is used, the user must be sure that there is *not* a floppy disk in the a: drive.

Using Systems Management Server for Distributed Setup

Microsoft Systems Management Server (SMS), part of the BackOffice suite, is designed to handle software distribution over a client-server network. The advantage of using SMS over other types of distributed setup options is the amount of control and auditing the administrator has for an installation. SMS allows the network administrator to do the following:

- Query all the inventoried computers on the network to determine which machines have the necessary hardware requirements to run Windows NT 4.0.
- Remotely administer computers on the network to configure the machines for a Windows NT installation.
- Select and group the target machines to receive Windows NT.
- Allow the creation of packages that distribute a Windows NT installation with specific options on the target machines.
- Allow the creation of a job to execute the installation on the target machine(s). Jobs can also be monitored to verify the job status and results.

Systems Management Server is ideal for companies with over 100 networked computers or for networks that need centralized administration. Even for smaller companies, SMS can greatly reduce the amount of time needed to perform multiple Windows NT installations.

Introduction to Systems Management Server

Before using Systems Management Server to distribute and install Windows NT, a Windows NT Server machine must already be installed on the network. Also, Systems Management Server must be installed on a Windows NT Server. Systems Management Server has the following requirements:

- A Windows NT Server with 100M available on an NTFS partition. 1G is recommended for the distributed installation of Windows NT 4.0.
- A minimum of 24M of physical RAM on the Windows NT server.
- An SQL Server 4.2 or 6.x setup on the Windows NT server or network.

> **Caution**
>
> This is not meant to be a complete tutorial on Microsoft Systems Management Server. It's also assumed that you have a working SMS site on your network. If you have not completely installed a SMS server on your network and have not configured the clients to access SMS, see the SMS Administrator's Guide to install and set up SMS.

Once SMS is installed and configured on the network, the following steps, covered in more detail later in this chapter, allow the distribution and installation of Windows NT over the network:

1. Inventory computers on the network using Systems Management Server. A current inventory helps ensure the smooth distribution of a Windows NT installation.
2. Create SMS queries that specify the minimum requirements for a Windows NT installation on a computer.
3. Copy the Windows NT setup files to a shared directory on the distribution server.
4. Create Machine Groups for the Windows NT computers. This step is optional, but allows for better administration of the machines.
5. Create a package to install Windows NT on target computers using Windows NT setup scripts and SMS .PDF files.
6. Create a job to distribute and run the created package.
7. Monitor the job distribution status.

Tip

Before trying a large-scale distribution of Windows NT, try performing a distributed installation using SMS on a few machines. This may uncover any problems or errors during the installation and allow you to prevent those errors from occurring on a larger scale in a bigger deployment.

Performing Computer Inventories and Queries

The first step in using SMS to perform a large-scale installation of Windows NT is to determine which machines are even capable of running Windows NT. Furthermore, you may decide that the minimum requirements of running Windows NT are not suitable for the types of applications that are used in your company. SMS allows the administrator to inventory the computers on the network and query or search the network for computers with certain types of configurations.

You can customize SMS queries to find computers with different hardware properties. For example, you may not want computers with 16M of RAM memory to have Windows NT installed even though Windows NT can be installed on computers with 16M of RAM. SMS queries provide a flexible way of determining which computers on your network are able to use Windows NT at an acceptable speed.

To run an SMS query for computers capable of running Windows NT, follow these steps:

1. Start the SMS Administrator program. This is located in the Systems Management Server group (under Windows NT 3.x) or in the Systems Management Server folder (under Windows NT 4.0). In order to start the administrator program, you will be prompted for the SMS Administrator account name, password, and database. See the SMS documentation for more information on starting SMS.
2. The Microsoft SMS Administrator program is displayed (see fig. 7.2). The dialog boxes that are displayed may vary depending on which dialog boxes were open for the last SMS session.
3. Before a query can be run, you must define the query with the items to query for. These items include the processor type, memory, hard disk space, and so on. To create a new query, open the Queries dialog box by clicking the Queries icon (see fig. 7.2). The Queries dialog box shows any queries that have been defined.

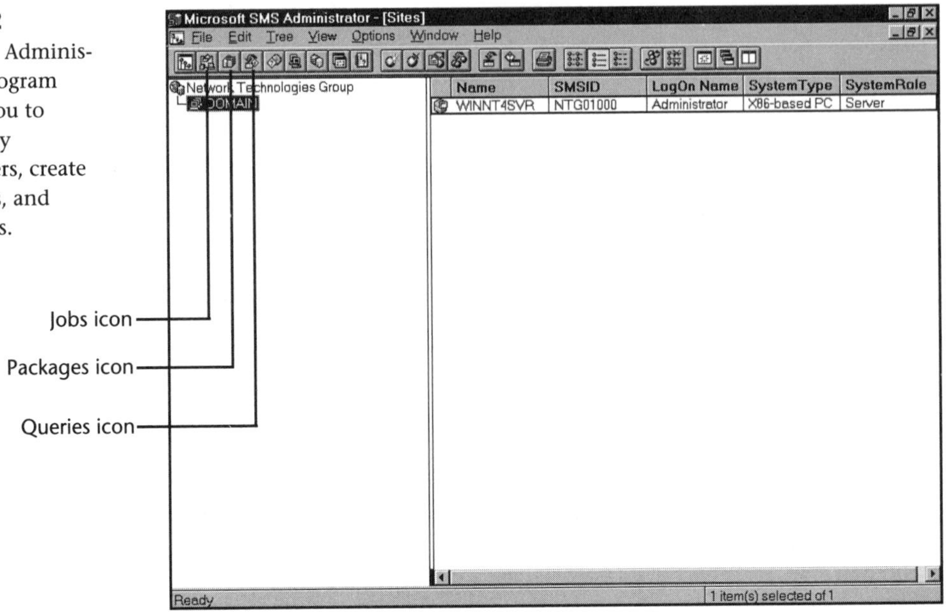

Fig. 7.2
The SMS Administrator program allows you to inventory computers, create packages, and send jobs.

Jobs icon

Packages icon

Queries icon

4. While the Queries dialog box is open, choose File, New. The Query Properties dialog box appears (see fig. 7.3) which will allow you to create a new query.

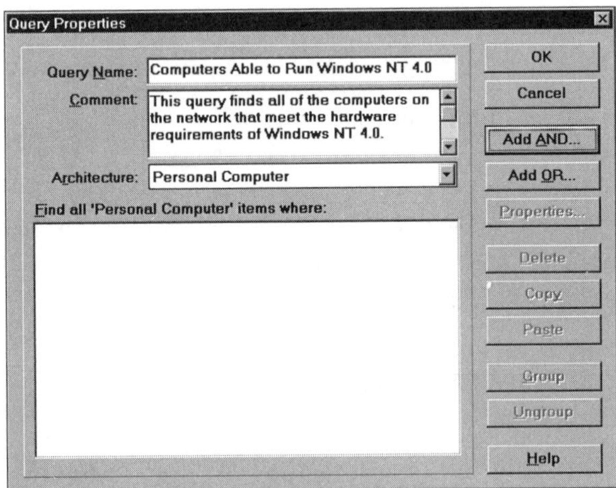

Fig. 7.3
The Query Properties dialog box allows you to create new queries.

5. In the Query Name box, type a name for the query. For example, Computers Able to Run Windows NT would be appropriate. You may also type a comment in the Comment box to further describe the function of the query.

6. The Add AND and Add OR buttons are used to select the criteria for the query. Click the Add AND button to enter the first item in the query. The Query Expression Properties dialog box appears (see fig. 7.4).

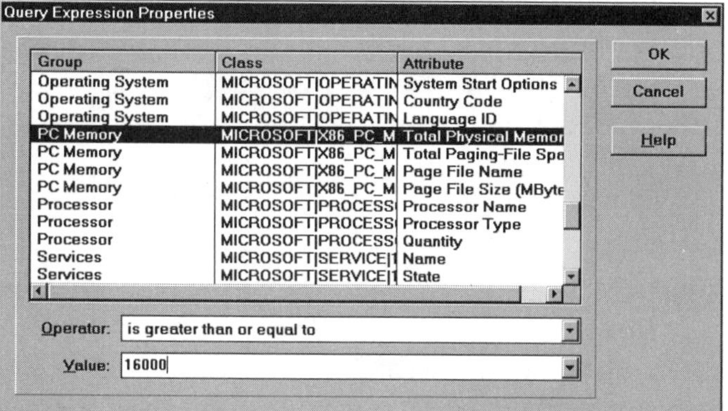

Fig. 7.4
The Query Expression Properties dialog box allows you to select the conditional items used in the query.

7. In the Query Expression Properties dialog box you can choose the different items to search for. For example, to find computers that have Pentium processors, select Processor in the group column. In the Operator text box, select the "is" item. In the Value box, select Intel Pentium from the drop-down list. In most instances you'll want to use the "greater than or equal to" item in the Operator box.

8. Continue to add items using the Add AND and Add OR buttons until you have all the items that you want to search for. After you have selected all the items, click OK.

9. To perform a query, choose File, Execute Query. The Execute Query dialog box appears (see fig. 7.5). You can select the query to run. You can also select the query from the Query dialog box and drag it to the site to run the query in the Sites dialog box.

10. After the query is started, the Query Results dialog box appears. As SMS finds computers that match the query criteria, the computers are added to the list. Keep in mind that on large networks, the Queries may take some time.

After a list of computers that meet the requirements for Windows NT in your organization are found, you can put the computers into a machine group for easier administration. This is an optional step provided to help make it easier to track the installation process of Windows NT 4.0 in your company.

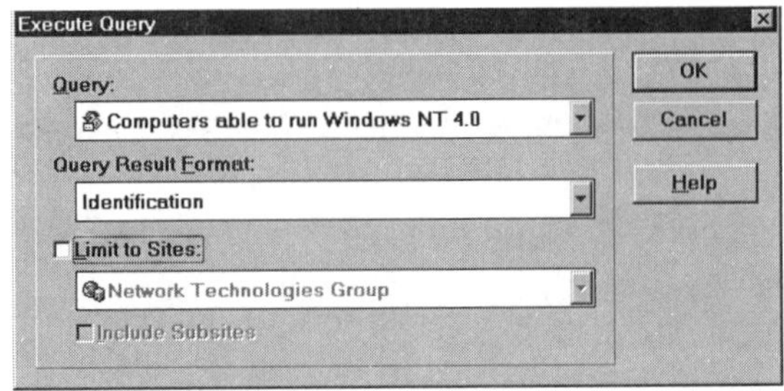

Fig. 7.5
The Execute Query dialog box allows you to select the query to run. The default query to run is the highlighted query in the Query dialog box.

To put the computers found in the query into a SMS machine group, follow these steps:

1. Start the SMS Administrator program. Provide the SMS Administrator account name, password, and database. See the SMS documentation for more information on starting SMS. The Microsoft SMS Administrator program is displayed.
2. Open the Machine Groups dialog box by clicking the Machine Groups icon on the toolbar. A Machine Groups dialog box appears. If there were any machine groups previously defined, they appear in this dialog box. (Do *not* close the Query Results dialog box.)
3. To add a machine group, choose File, New while the Machine Groups dialog box is active. The Machine Group Properties dialog box appears as shown in figure 7.6. Type the name of the new machine group you want to create in the Name text box. You can also type an optional comment about the machine group.

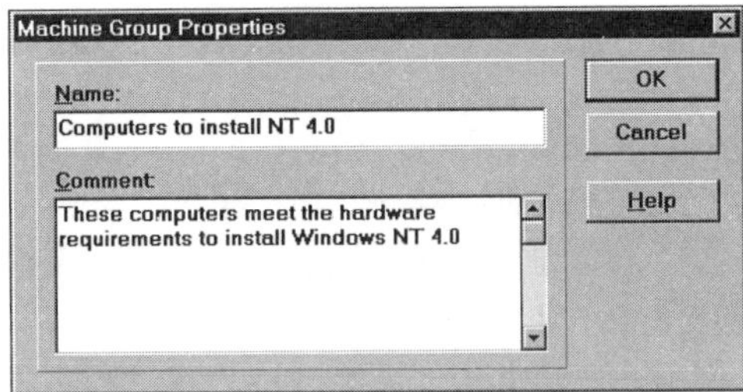

Fig. 7.6
The Machine Group Properties dialog box allows you to type a name for a new machine group.

4. Select the computers in the Query Results dialog box from the query you just ran. Use the mouse to drag the computers from the Query Results dialog box to the Machine Groups dialog box. The Add to Machine Group dialog box appears (see fig. 7.7).

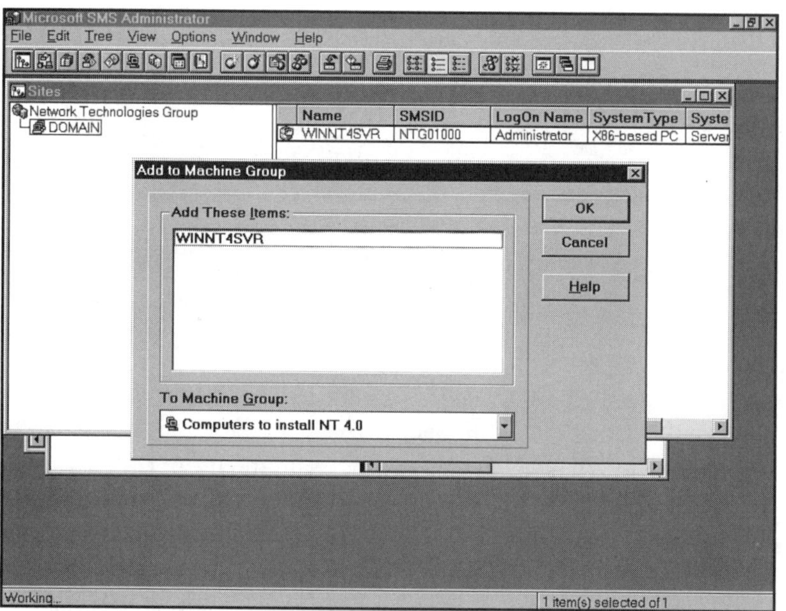

Fig. 7.7
The Add to Machine Group dialog box allows you to select the computers to add to the machine group. The machine group can also be changed.

5. The Add to Machine Group dialog box lists the computers to add to the machine group in the first list box. The To Machine Group drop-down list allows you to select the machine group where the computers will be added.
6. Be sure that the machine group that you just created is selected in the To Machine Group list and click OK.

Creating the Package

The next step is to create an SMS package for the Windows NT 4.0 setup. An SMS package contains the command and the parameters for the Windows NT Setup program. If you want to make the Windows NT Setup completely automated, you have to create an answer file (see the section titled "Creating Answer Files Using the Setup Manager" earlier in the chapter).

To create an SMS package to install Windows NT 4.0, follow these steps:

1. If it's not already started, start the SMS Administrator program. The Microsoft SMS Administrator program is displayed.
2. Open the Packages dialog box by clicking the Packages icon (refer to figure 7.2).
3. While the Packages dialog box is active, choose File, New to open the Package Properties dialog box (see fig. 7.8).

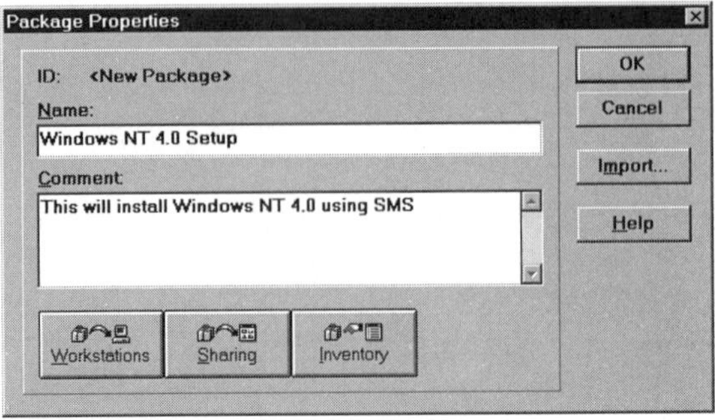

Fig. 7.8
The Package Properties dialog box allows you to configure the SMS package.

4. The Package Properties dialog box allows you to define the package to install Windows NT. In the Name box, type a descriptive name for the package. Optionally, you may also type comments for the package in the Comment box.
5. On the bottom of the Package Properties dialog box, there are three buttons: Workstations, Sharing, and Inventory. Since we want to have the Windows NT setup run on individual workstations, click the Workstations button. The Setup Package for Workstations dialog box appears.
6. In the Source Directory box, type the directory where the package files can be found. You may also click the Browse button to search the directory tree for the desired directory.
7. At the Bottom of the Setup Package for Workstations dialog box, you see a box titled Workstation Command Lines. Since we're creating a new package, there should be no command-line options in the box. Beside the box, click the New button to create a new command-line option. The Command-Line Properties dialog box appears (see fig. 7.9).

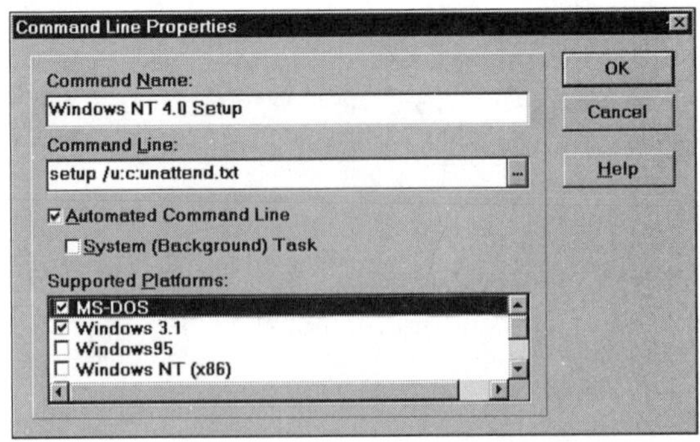

Fig. 7.9
The Command Line Properties dialog box allows you to enter the command to run with the appropriate parameters for the SMS package.

8. Under Command Name, give the command a descriptive name. This is *not* the command to be used. In the Command Line box, type the command with the parameters to be used with that command. For example, if you want to run the Windows NT Setup program with an answer file to be used, type: **winnt /u:**<*answer filename*> **or winnt32 /u:**<*answer filename*>. If you want the package not to prompt the user for input, check the Automated Command Line box. This is used for unattended installations. If you need the user to input information, be sure that the Automated Command Line checkbox is cleared. Also, be sure to check the computer types to run this package in the Supported Platforms list. When you are finished entering the appropriate information, click OK.

Sending the Job

After the package is created, a job is created to distribute the package to selected computers. After a job is sent, you can check the status of the job to see how the distribution process is going.

To create an SMS job to deliver the SMS package, follow these steps:

1. Start the SMS Administrator program.
2. Open the Jobs dialog box, by clicking the Jobs icon (refer to fig. 7.2).
3. While the Jobs dialog box is active, choose File, New. This will open the Job Properties dialog box (see fig. 7.10).

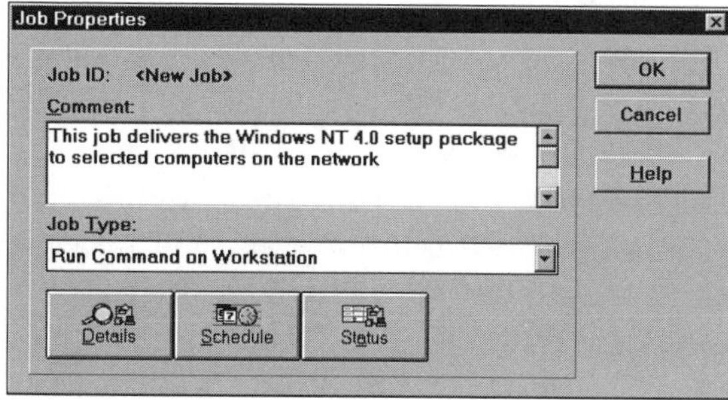

Fig. 7.10
The Job Properties dialog box allows you to enter the settings for an SMS job.

4. Entering a comment in the Comment box in the Job Properties dialog box is optional. If you want, you can type a descriptive comment for the job. To install Windows NT on workstations, be sure that the Run Command on Workstation option is selected in the Job Type drop-down list.

5. You should also see three buttons located at the bottom of the dialog box: Details, Schedule, and Status. To configure a new job for the Windows NT 4.0 distribution, click the Details button. The Details button will display the Job Details dialog box as shown in figure 7.11.

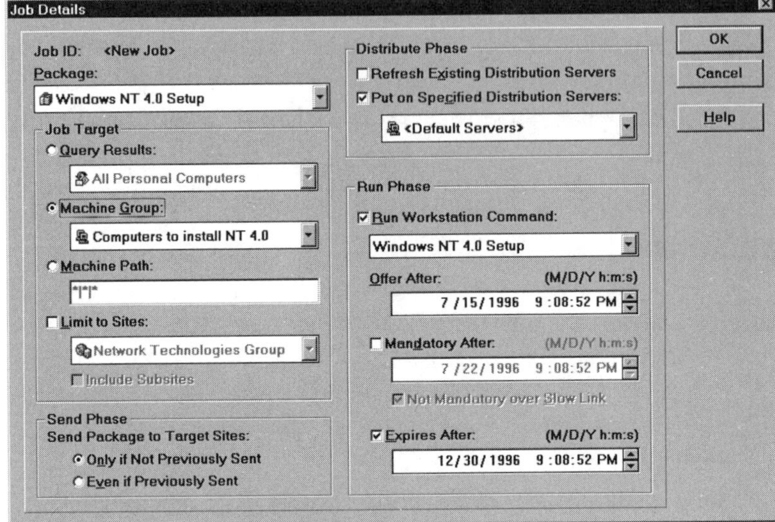

Fig. 7.11
The Job Details dialog box allows you to set many job options, such as the package to run, which computers to send the job to, and whether the job is mandatory.

6. Choose the package you created in the earlier procedure from the Package drop-down list.
7. In the Job Target box, you can choose which machines to send the job to. Usually, choosing a machine group is the easiest method of distributing the package to the correct computers.
8. In the Send Phase box, you can choose whether to send the package only if it has not been sent before or even if it has been sent before. In the Distribute Phase box, you can determine which SMS site servers to use to distribute the package. In the Run Phase box, you can set when the package is available to clients, whether it is a mandatory package, and when the job expires. Unless you are familiar with the different SMS options, it is recommended that you leave the default settings unchanged. After you are finished making selections in the Job Details dialog box, click OK until you return to the main SMS Administrator screen.

Once the job is configured, you should see it appear in the Jobs dialog box. If Pending is displayed in the Status column, the job can be modified. Once the Status column for the job changes to Active, the job can no longer be modified. The time it takes for a job to change from Pending to Active depends on the SMS network. Larger networks or networks with the SMS server also acting as a login server may take longer to send jobs than smaller networks or networks with a dedicated SMS server.

Monitoring the SMS Job

Once the job status changes to Active, the SMS job can be monitored. To monitor an active job, follow these steps:

1. Start the SMS Administrator program.
2. Open the Jobs dialog box, by clicking the Jobs icon (refer to fig. 7.2).
3. In the Jobs dialog box, select a job that displays Active in the Status column that you want to monitor. Choose File, Properties, or double-click the job. The Job Properties dialog box appears.
4. In the Job Properties dialog box, click the Status button at the bottom of the screen. The Job Status dialog box appears (see fig. 7.12).

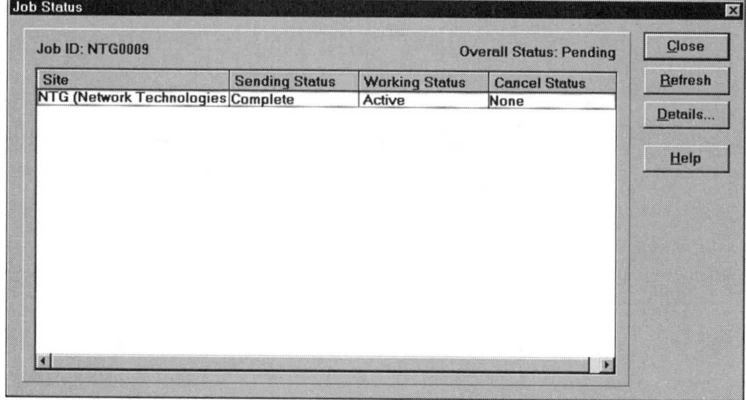

Fig. 7.12
The Job Status dialog box allows you to see the overall status of an active job.

5. If the job has had a chance to propagate across the network, you can click the Details button. Clicking the Details button opens the Job Status Details dialog box (see fig. 7.13).
6. You can click the Refresh button to recheck the status if the Job Status Details has been open for a while. When you are finished viewing the details, click the Close button.
7. When the Sending Status column displays Complete, the job has been sent. The Working Status column displays the working status of the job, and if the job has been canceled, the Cancel Status column will be used. Otherwise, the Cancel Status column will display None. When you are finished checking the status, click the Close button.

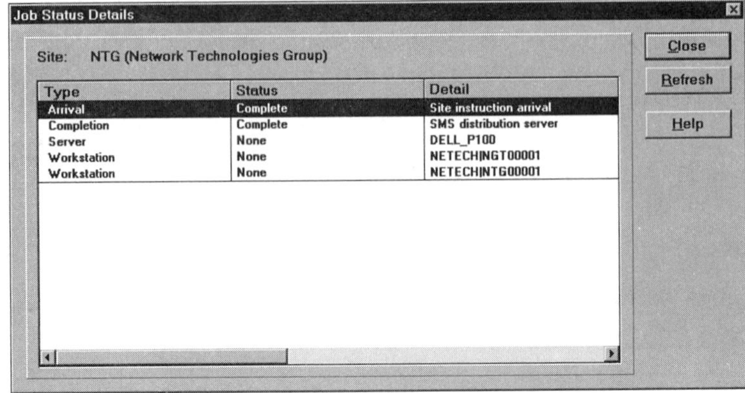

Fig. 7.13 The Job Status Details dialog box shows a listing of how the job is spreading across the network.

Using the Package on the Client Computer

Once the job has sent the package to the specified computers, the package will arrive in the user's SMS Package Manager. The SMS Package Manager is located in the SMS Client program group or folder. The SMS Client program group or folder is created when the SMS server inventories the client. If there is no SMS Client program group or folder on a client machine, read the SMS Administrator's Guide to set up the client.

All packages waiting to be executed are placed in the Pending Commands folder. If a package is not a mandatory package, the package must be run by the user. If a package is mandatory and the mandatory date is reached, a message appears informing the user that the package must be installed. The user may either immediately install the package or wait five minutes before the mandatory installation occurs. The five-minute wait allows the user to save any work if the package installation will cause the system to reboot (this is the case with a Windows NT installation). If user input is needed when running a package, a warning box appears informing the user that additional information is needed to complete the installation.

Figure 7.14 shows the Package Manager with a package to install Windows NT.

To select and install the Windows NT package using the Package Manager, follow these steps:

1. Double-click the Package Manager icon located in the SMS Client program group to start the Package Manager.
2. Open the Pending Commands folder by double-clicking the folder. You see a list of packages that have not been executed.

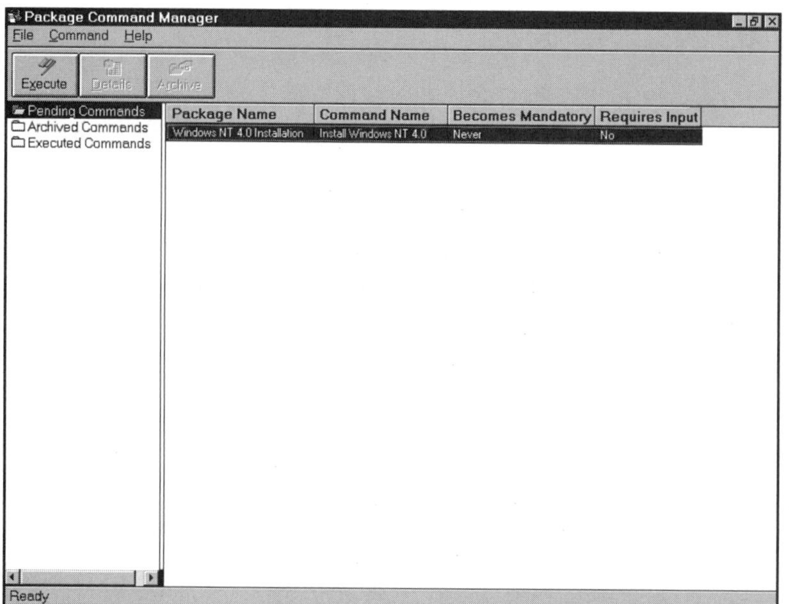

Fig. 7.14
The Package Command Manager on a client machine allows packages sent from the SMS server to be run on the client machine.

3. Select the package containing the Windows NT installation by clicking the package with the mouse button. If you want to select more than one package, hold down the Ctrl key when clicking packages.
4. Click the Execute icon on the toolbar or choose Command, Execute. The Execute icon is the first icon located on the toolbar. Once the package has been executed, it will be placed in the Executed Commands folder. ❖

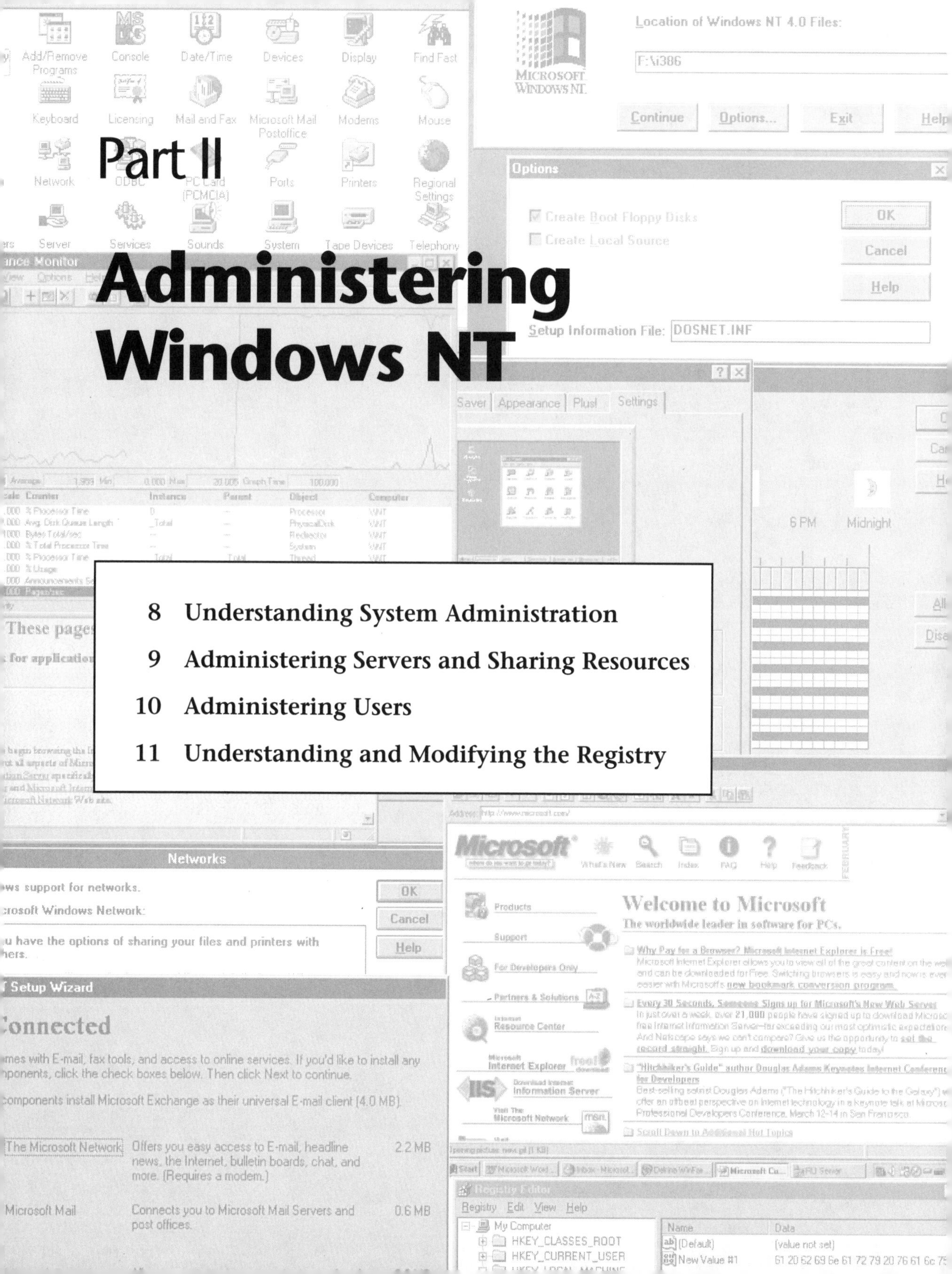

Part II

Administering Windows NT

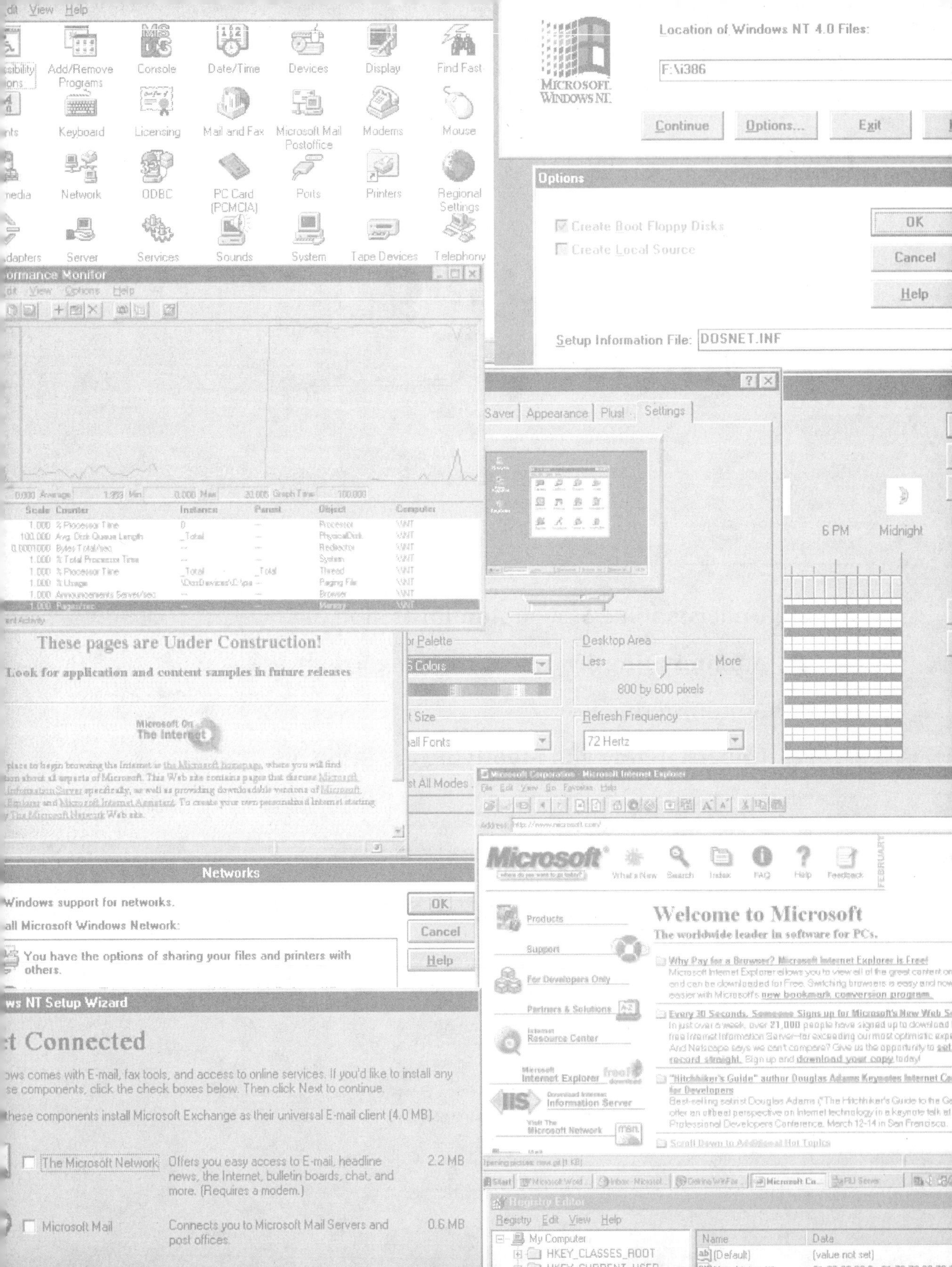

Edit View Help
Add/Remove Programs
Console
Date/Time
Devices
Display
Find Fast
Keyboard
Licensing
Mail and Fax
Microsoft Mail Postoffice
Modems
Mouse
Network
ODBC
PC Card (PCMCIA)
Ports
Printers
Regional Settings
Server
Services
Sounds
System
Tape Devices
Telephony
Location of Windows NT 4.0 Files:
F:\i386
MICROSOFT WINDOWS NT
Continue
Options...
Exit
Options
Create Boot Floppy Disks
Create Local Source
OK
Cancel
Help
Setup Information File: DOSNET.INF
Saver
Appearance
Plus!
Settings
6 PM
Midnight
Desktop Area
Less
More
800 by 600 pixels
Refresh Frequency
72 Hertz
These pages are Under Construction!
Look for application and content samples in future releases
Microsoft On The Internet
Networks
Windows support for networks.
all Microsoft Windows Network:
You have the options of sharing your files and printers with others.
OK
Cancel
Help
Microsoft Corporation - Microsoft Internet Explorer
Microsoft
Welcome to Microsoft
The worldwide leader in software for PCs.
Products
Support
For Developers Only
Partners & Solutions
Resource Center
Internet Explorer
Information Server
Microsoft Network
Why Pay for a Browser? Microsoft Internet Explorer is Free!
Every 30 Seconds, Someone Signs up for Microsoft's New Web Se
"Hitchhiker's Guide" author Douglas Adams Keynotes Internet Co
ws NT Setup Wizard
t Connected
ows comes with E-mail, fax tools, and access to online services. If you'd like to install any
se components, click the check boxes below. Then click Next to continue.
these components install Microsoft Exchange as their universal E-mail client (4.0 MB).
The Microsoft Network
Offers you easy access to E-mail, headline news, the Internet, bulletin boards, chat, and more. (Requires a modem.)
2.2 MB
Microsoft Mail
Connects you to Microsoft Mail Servers and post offices.
0.6 MB
Registry Editor
Registry Edit View Help
My Computer
HKEY_CLASSES_ROOT
HKEY_CURRENT_USER
Name
Data
(Default)
(value not set)
New Value #1

CHAPTER 8

Understanding System Administration

By Jim Boyce

Administration has the most impact on how the system and network perform. A finely tuned network doesn't happen by itself, nor does it continue to function well without some management. Even if you're running Windows NT Workstation, there still are management tasks you need to perform on the computer. This chapter introduces you to system and network administration under Windows NT.

In this chapter, you learn to

- Understand system administration tasks
- Manage the network
- Administer systems remotely

If you're an experienced system administrator for other operating systems, you probably have a good understanding of the tasks that need to be performed to keep the system running smoothly. Whether you're new to system administration or a pro, this chapter will give you the background you need to understand and apply system administration on Windows NT systems and networks.

Note

A complete treatment of system administration could fill a book of its own. This chapter provides primarily an overview of system administration on Windows NT systems. Chapter 9, "Administering Servers and Sharing Resources," and Chapter 10, "Administering Users," explain specific tools and techniques for managing systems and users. This chapter lays the groundwork for the following chapters and can be used by experienced administrators as a quick-start guide to system administration under Windows NT 4.0. The focus of these chapters is on the management tasks you'll need to perform in concert with, or shortly after, installing Windows NT.

Overview of System Administration

Although there is often some overlap between the two, you can divide system administration into two primary facets: server management and user management. A third facet, security management, is closely integrated with the other two.

Managing Servers

Managing a server involves a number of tasks. The number of tasks depends primarily on what services the server provides. On a database server, for example, managing the server also means managing the database and its associated software. On most servers, however, system administration comprises the following general tasks:

- Sharing file resources
- Sharing printer resources
- Managing the file system
- Managing domains and workgroups
- Managing software licenses
- Monitoring and tuning server performance

The following sections explore these general management issues to give you an idea of how these tasks are handled under Windows NT.

Sharing File Resources

Sharing file resources typically includes setting up shared directories and assigning user access privileges to those directories. The level of control you have over the shared resources depends on the type of file system on which the shared resource resides.

On a FAT file system, you can control access on a directory-by-directory basis, assigning access levels to each shared directory. You can assign access permissions to a directory by group and by user. The only privileges you can assign, however, are read, change, and full control—a fairly limited set of access privileges that offer little security flexibility.

You have many additional security options on an NTFS partition. In addition to controlling access on a per-directory basis, you can control access on a per-file basis. This capability gives you much greater flexibility than the FAT file system. For example, you can give access to a directory to a specific user, but restrict access by that user to specific files in that directory. Using NTFS also enables you to audit file access for added security.

Regardless of file system type, you manage shared disk resources through Explorer (see fig. 8.1). Explorer enables you to share and unshare directories and files, assign permissions, and perform other tasks, such as security auditing.

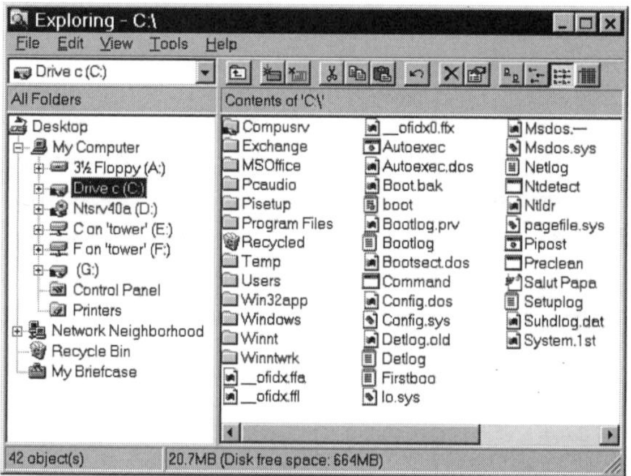

Fig. 8.1
You can use the Explorer to manage shared disk resources.

Tip

In previous versions of Windows NT, the primary tool you used to manage shared disk resources was File Manager. If you are more comfortable using File Manager, you can continue to do so under Windows NT 4.0. To run File Manager under Windows NT, open the Start menu and choose Run. Enter **winfile** in the Open text box on the Run dialog box. Or, create a shortcut to the file \WINNT\SYSTEM32\WINFILE.EXE.

Sharing Printer Resources

Another common system administration task is sharing and managing printers. Windows NT provides integrated access to local and remote printers through the Printers folder (see fig. 8.2). You can find the Printers folder in My Computer. Through the Printers folder, you can share local printers, install printers on remote workstations, and manage local and remote printers and their queues.

▶ See "Managing Printers," p. 204

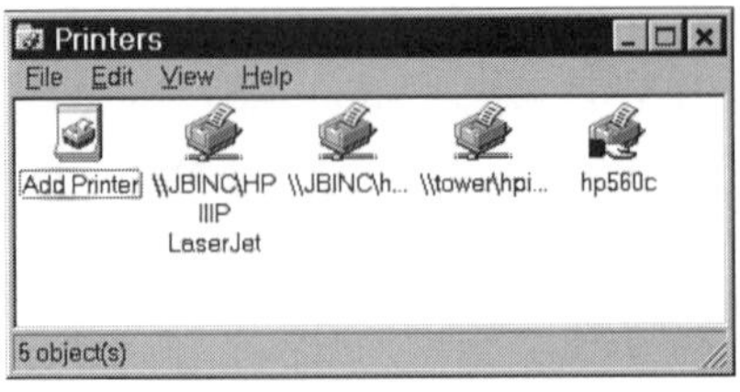

Fig. 8.2 Use the Printers folder to share and manage printers.

Windows NT's capability to install printer drivers across the network and to share remote printers enables you to manage all of your network's printers from a central location, including through a dialup connection to the network. Basically, you can control a remote printer in the same manner you control a local printer. Simply right-click the printer's icon in the Control Panel, choose Properties to display the printer's property sheet, and then set the properties according to your needs.

Managing the File System

Managing the file system is a major administrative function that includes managing disks (formatting, backup, compression, and so on), setting and managing access privileges for directories and files, and setting up and managing fault-tolerance options.

Most disk-related operations such as formatting, partitioning, and compression can be handled through the Disk Administrator (see fig. 8.3). You can also perform many of those same functions using Windows NT Explorer.

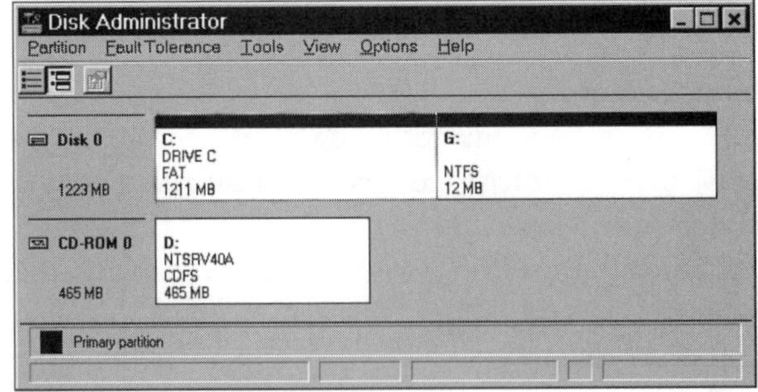

Fig. 8.3 Use the Disk Administrator to perform most disk-related tasks.

You can accomplish security-related tasks such as setting access privileges on directories and files in a variety of ways, but the most direct is to use Explorer. For example, to set access privileges on a directory, right-click the directory in Explorer. Choose Properties to display the directory's property sheet. Then, click the Security tab to display the Security page, which enables you to set permissions, control auditing, and view or take ownership of the directory (see fig. 8.4).

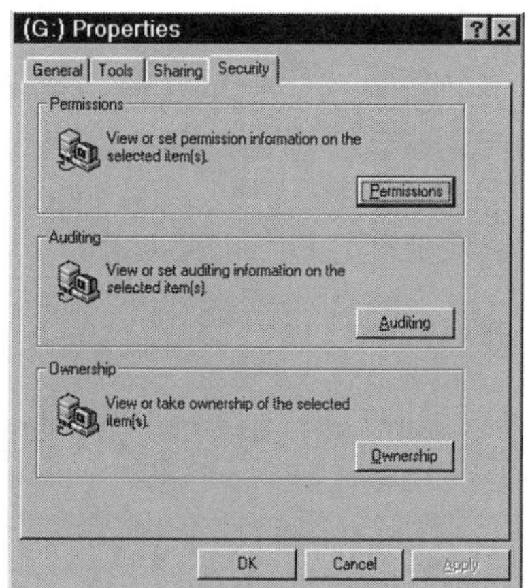

Fig. 8.4
Use the Security page to set a file or directory's security properties.

> **Note**
>
> Previous versions of Windows NT relied on File Manager for managing security and other directory and file options. All of these features have been incorporated into Explorer. If you prefer File Manager, you can continue to use it under Windows NT 4.0, as mentioned earlier.

Managing Domains and Workgroups

Another aspect of system administration involves managing domains and workgroups. A workgroup is a logical grouping of computers on the network that simplifies browsing for shared resources. Basically, workgroups give you a means of organizing computers and resources under a common workgroup name.

Domains add distributed security to the workgroup model. If a user has an account in the domain, he can log on to the network from any workstation in the domain. The user's access to shared resources on the network is determined by the privileges of his domain account. One Windows NT server in a domain serves as a primary domain controller (PDC). It manages security for the entire domain. Backup domain controllers (BDCs) serve as backups to the PDC.

◀ See "Understanding Security Issues," p. 43

◀ See "Domains and Workgroups," p. 63

▶ See "Creating and Managing Domains," p. 182

You can create a PDC only when you install Windows NT. Therefore, the only way to promote an existing server to a PDC is to reinstall Windows NT on that server. However, you can promote a BDC to a PDC through the Server Manager (see fig. 8.5). Promoting a BDC to a PDC automatically demotes the existing PDC on the domain to a BDC.

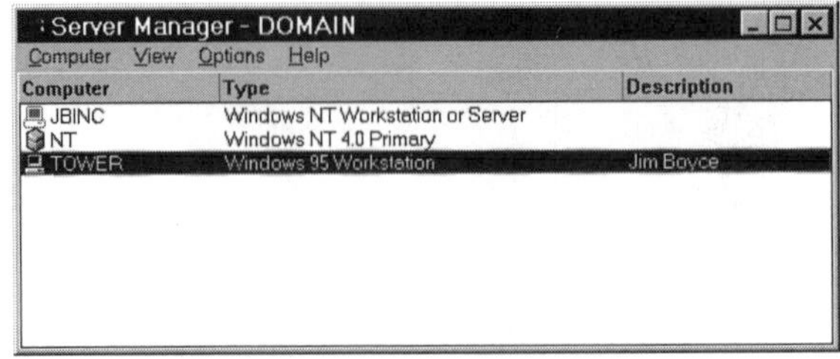

Fig. 8.5
You can use the Server Manager to manage a domain controller.

Creating workgroups is even easier than managing domains. On any computer, simply specify a new workgroup name in the Identification page of the computer's Network property sheet. Specifying the same workgroup on other computers adds those computers to the workgroup.

Managing Software Licenses

As the enforcement of anti-piracy laws becomes more commonplace, many companies are looking for solutions to ensure compliance with licensing restrictions for their operating systems and applications. Windows NT Server includes a Licensing icon in the Control Panel that enables you to specify the licensing mode your network uses and specify how licensing data is replicated across the domain network (see fig. 8.6). To access specific licensing options, double-click the Licensing icon in the Control Panel. In addition, Windows NT provides a License Manager utility that enables you to track product licenses (see fig. 8.7).

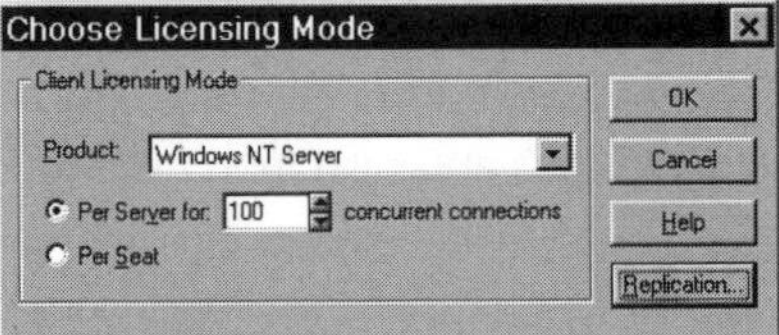

Fig. 8.6
Use the Licensing object in the Control Panel to specify client license options.

Monitoring and Tuning Server Performance

Ensuring fast and trouble-free server operation is a critical part of any administrator's job. Windows NT includes a number of tools that enable you to track and manage server performance. The Performance Monitor enables you to view the behavior and performance for processors, memory, cache, threads, and processes (see fig. 8.8). The Performance Monitor provides charting, alerting, and reporting features that display current activity and logging, as well as logging of past performance data.

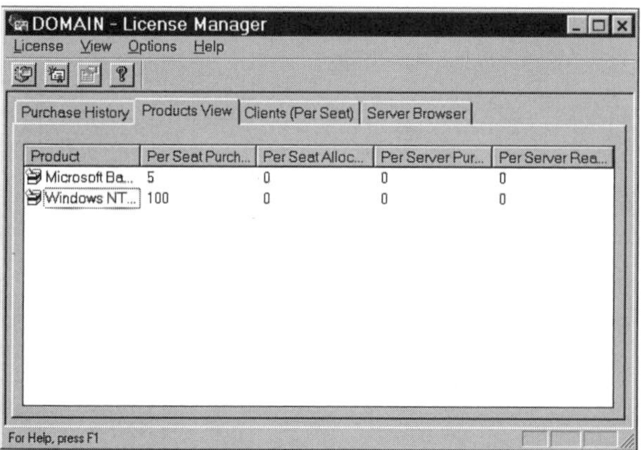

Fig. 8.7
Use the License Manager to track product licenses.

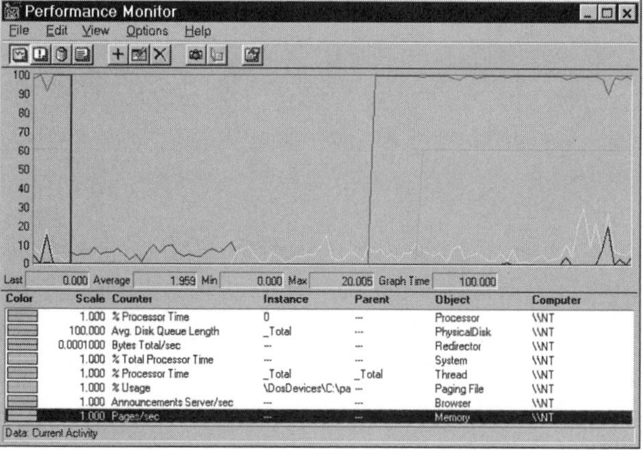

Fig. 8.8
Use the Performance Monitor to track system performance.

Unfortunately, performance problems are sometimes caused by hardware problems. To help you track down and troubleshoot problems, you can use the Windows NT Diagnostics (also called WinMSD) utility (see fig. 8.9). WinMSD provides information about system hardware, drivers, services, memory, and other information about the workstation or server to help you overcome problems and tune performance.

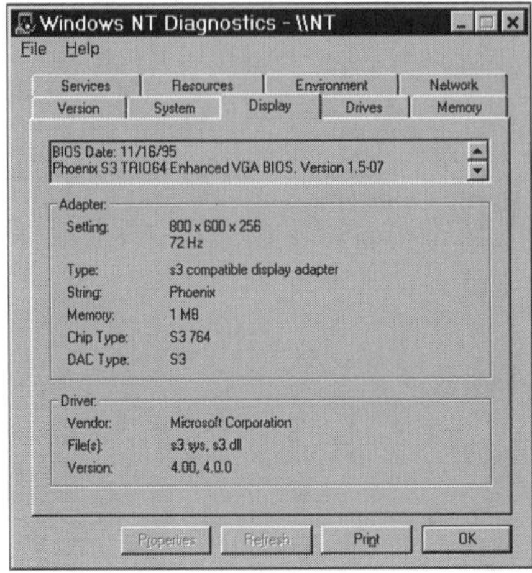

Fig. 8.9
You can use WinMSD to track and troubleshoot hardware and software problems.

Tip

The Windows NT Resource Kit contains additional tools for monitoring system and network performance.

Managing Users

Every administrator knows that managing user accounts and groups can take a considerable amount of time—particularly in dynamic organizations where the number or location of users changes frequently. Windows NT provides a good set of utilities that enable you to quickly create, delete, and modify user accounts and groups and assign access permissions.

▶ See "Creating and Modifying User Accounts," p. 211

For example, you can use the User Manager to manage all aspects of user accounts and groups. This includes creating and deleting accounts and groups, assigning group membership, applying security policies, and more (see fig. 8.10).

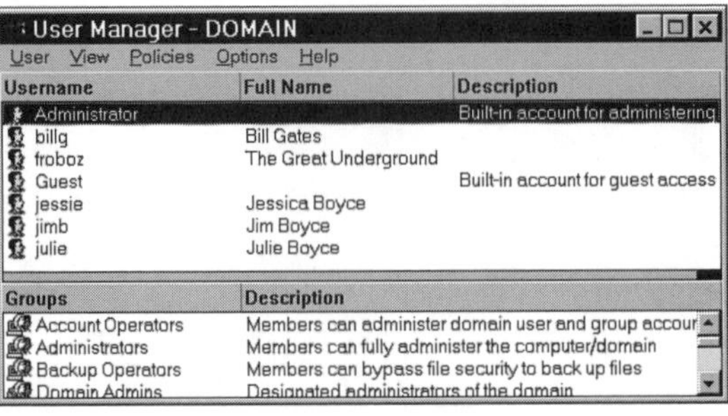

Fig. 8.10
The User Manager is a single tool for complete user account management.

As described in the section, "Managing Servers," earlier in this chapter, you assign access privileges using Explorer and the Printers folder (or File Manager and Print Manager).

To properly understand and apply the user management tools included with Windows NT, you need to understand the logon process. The following sections provide an overview.

▶ See "Managing Printers," p. 204

Understanding the Logon Process

When a user logs on from a Windows NT workstation, the logon dialog box prompts for a Username, domain or workgroup (From), and Password. The Username and Password text boxes need a user account name and its associated password. What the user selects for the From text box depends on whether the workstation is connected to a domain or is simply a member of a workgroup.

If the workstation is part of a domain, the user should specify in the From text box the name of the domain in which his user account is stored. The workstation then passes the logon request to the domain controller for the specified domain, which checks the security database for a matching account and password. If one is found, the domain controller directs the workstation to authorize the logon.

If the workstation is part of a workgroup, the user specifies in the From text box the name of the workstation from which he is logging on. The workstation then checks its internal security database for a matching account. If one is found, the logon succeeds.

Logon in Trusted Domains

You can create *trust relationships* between multiple domains on a network. In a trust relationship, one domain trusts another. The trusting domain recognizes all the users and global group accounts from the trusted domain, enabling users to log on at the workstation in the trusting domain. Basically, the trusting domain is saying to the trusted domain, "If a user can log on to workstations in your domain, I'll let him log on in my domain."

Trust relationships can be one-way or two-way. In a one-way trust relationship, domain A trusts domain B, but domain B doesn't have to trust domain A. In a two-way trust relationship, both domains trust each other. Also, trust relationships do not pass through to other domains. Domain A trusts domain B, and domain B trusts domain C, but that doesn't mean that domain A automatically trusts domain C. You must explicitly set up the trust relationship between domain A and domain C.

▶ See "Creating and Managing Domains," p. 182

When a user logs on from a trusting domain, he enters the name of the domain where his domain account resides in the logon dialog box. Windows NT then passes the logon request to the controller for that domain for authentication.

Remote Logon

WithWindows NT Remote Access Services (RAS), a user can log onto a RAS server through a dialup connection. Depending on how the RAS server is configured, the remote user can either gain access to the shared resources on the server, or to those resources and the resources on the network to which the RAS server is connected.

Remote logon is authenticated in much the same way as local logon. If the RAS server is not part of a domain, the remote user must have an account on the RAS server. If the RAS server belongs to a domain, the remote user can use a domain account to log on.

Using Remote Administration Tools

In addition to providing a good selection of system administration tools, Windows NT also gives you flexibility in how you apply those tools. The system administration utilities included with each Windows NT 4.0 platform for administration works across the LAN, and across a RAS connection. Therefore, you can manage remote domains and resources through a dialup connection to the remote network.

The tools for managing Windows NT from a Windows NT platform include:

- *Event Viewer.* This utility enables you to monitor security, system, and application events in your system.
- *Server Manager.* This utility enables you to view the status of users connected to the server, control shared resources, start and stop services, synchronize the domain, add computers to a domain, and perform other server-related management tasks.
- *User Manager for Domains.* With User Manager, you can view, create, and modify user accounts and groups; create trust relationships; and set auditing options.
- *DHCP Manager.* The DHCP Manager enables you to specify TCP/IP parameters and set other options for a DHCP server.
- *Remote Access Admin.* With the Remote Access Admin utility, you can start and stop RAS services on a RAS server, monitor port use, control

user access, view active users, and perform other RAS administration tasks.

- *Remoteboot Manager.* This utility enables you to manage remote booting of DOS- and Windows-based computers that boot across the network from a Windows NT server.
- *WINS Manager.* The WINS Manager enables you to perform configuration and management tasks on WINS servers.

In addition to the administration tools for the Windows NT platforms, Windows NT Server includes Windows 95-based versions of Event Viewer, Server Manager, and User Manager. These tools enable you to manage a remote Windows NT server or workstation across the LAN or a dialup connection from a Windows 95 workstation.

Installing the Tools

The Windows NT versions of the system administration tools are installed automatically when you install Windows NT. If you need to install them separately, the files are located on the Windows NT Server CD in the \CLIENTS\SRVTOOLS\WINNT folder. This folder contains folders for each of the supported Windows NT platforms: Alpha, Mips, Intel, and PowerPC. To install the Windows NT server tools, open the \CLIENTS\SRVTOOLS\WINNT folder and execute the SETUP.BAT file.

The Windows 95-based versions of the Windows NT system administration tools are located in the \CLIENTS\SRVTOOLS\WIN95 folder on the Windows NT Server CD. To install the tools under Windows 95, follow these steps:

1. On the Windows 95 workstation, open the Control Panel and double-click the Add/Remove Programs icon.
2. Click the Windows Setup tab to display the Windows Setup page.
3. Choose the Have Disk button to display the Have Disk dialog box.
4. Enter (or browse to) the \CLIENTS\SRVTOOLS\WIN95 path on the Windows NT Server CD, select the folder and choose OK, and then choose OK again.
5. In the Have Disk dialog box, select the Windows NT Server Tools checkbox, and then choose Install.

After you install the administration tools, you'll find shortcuts to the tools in the Start menu. To access these shortcuts, open the Start menu and choose Programs, Windows NT Server Tools.

Connecting Remotely

You can use the Windows NT administration tools across the LAN by simply opening the needed utility, then specifying which workstation, server, or domain you want to manage. If you want to manage a system through a dialup connection, however, you first must establish a connection to the remote LAN. The following sections briefly explain how to connect from Windows NT and Windows 95 computers.

Connecting from Windows NT

To connect to a remote server using Windows NT Workstation or Server, create a RAS connection to the server. For an explanation of RAS and how to create dialup connections, refer to the section, "Using RAS For Dial-Out," in Chapter 24.

Connecting from Windows 95

If you have not already done so, you need to create a Dial-Up Networking connection to the remote LAN containing the computer or domain you want to administer. To create a new connection to a RAS server on the remote LAN, follow these steps on the Windows 95 Workstation:

1. If you don't have a modem installed on the Windows 95 computer, first install the modem through the Modems icon in the Control Panel.
2. Open My Computer and double-click the Dial-Up Networking folder.
3. Double-click the Make New Connection icon. Windows 95 displays the Make New Connection Wizard (see fig. 8.11).

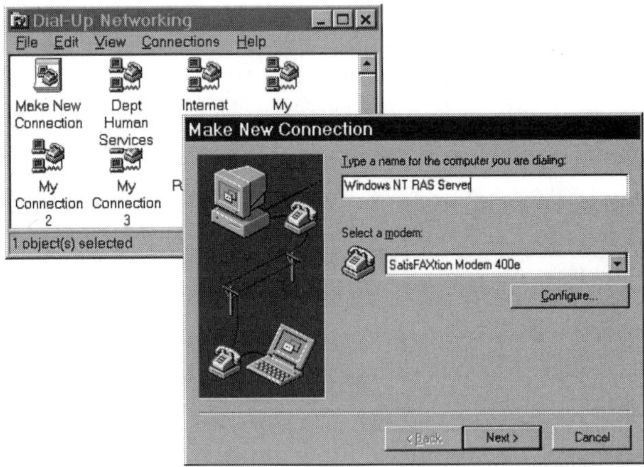

Fig. 8.11 Specify a name and modem for the remote connection.

4. Type a name for the connection in the Type a Name for the Computer You Are Dialing text box. Choose a modem from the Select a Modem drop-down list. If you need to configure the modem, click the Configure button and use the resulting Modem property sheet to configure the modem. Choose OK when you're done. Then choose Next.
5. Enter the area code and phone number for the remote dialup server in the Area Code and Telephone Number text boxes (see fig. 8.12). From the Country Code drop-down list, select the country in which the server is located. Then choose Next.

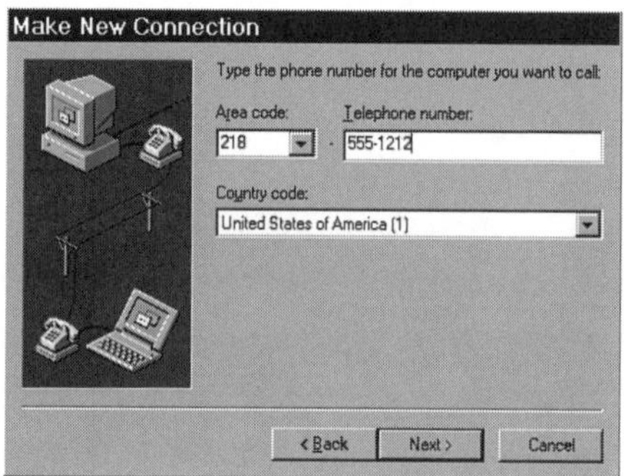

Fig. 8.12
Specify the area code and phone number for the connection.

6. Choose Finish to create the new connection and close the wizard.
7. In the Dial-Up Networking folder, right-click the connection you just created and choose Properties.
8. Click the Server Type button to open the Server Types dialog box (see fig. 8.13).

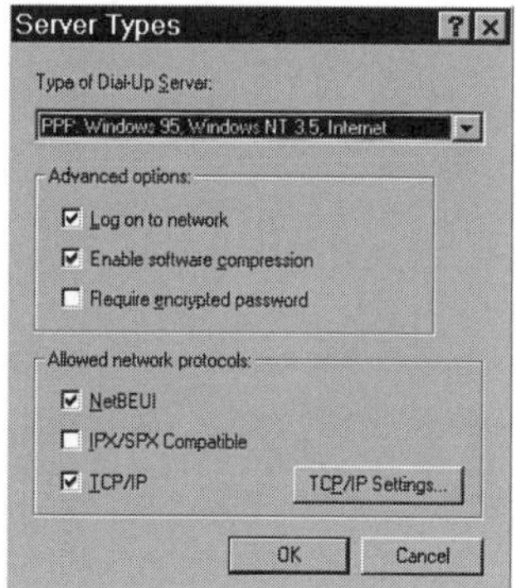

Fig. 8.13
Use the Server Types dialog box to set protocol and other connection options.

9. Select the PPP option from the Type of Dial-Up Server drop-down list.

> **Note**
>
> Although Windows NT 4.0 is not listed in the PPP option along with Windows 95, Windows NT 3.51, and Internet, Windows NT 4.0 uses the same PPP protocol for remote access as these other systems.

10. Verify that the Log on to Network checkbox is selected.
11. In the Allowed Network Protocols group, select the protocols you will need for the connection. If you are connecting only to administer the remote network, domain, and workstations, you only need to select the NetBEUI checkbox. Note, however, that the protocol you choose for the connection must be enabled by the RAS server to which you're connecting. If the remote server is configured to only support TCP/IP for dial-in, for example, you must use TCP/IP for your connection.

> **Tip**
>
> If you are using TCP/IP for your remote connection, you can use settings for the remote connection that are different from your local TCP/IP settings. To specify TCP/IP settings for the connection, click the TCP/IP Settings button to display the TCP/IP Settings dialog box (see fig. 8.14). Set the desired settings, and then choose OK.

Fig. 8.14 Enter TCP/IP settings for the connection in the TCP/IP Settings dialog box.

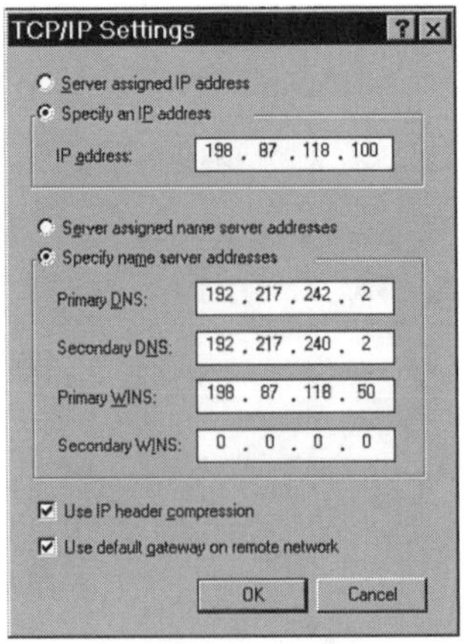

12. Choose OK, and then choose OK again to close the property sheet for the Dial-Up Networking connection.

When you need to connect to the remote network to administer its systems, open the Dial-Up Networking folder on your Windows 95 computer and double-click the connection's icon. After the connection is established, you can start the administration tools and connect to workstations, servers, and domains on the remote LAN. ❖

CHAPTER 9

Administering Servers and Sharing Resources

by Jim Boyce

As explained in Chapter 8, "Understanding System Administration," setting up and managing a networked system requires a lot of work. Fortunately, Windows NT provides a good set of utilities to help simplify system administration. This chapter focuses on servers, giving you an introduction of how to administer servers on a network.

In this chapter, you learn to

- Understand domains and trust relationships
- Create and manage domains
- Manage the file system
- Manage printers

Understanding Domains and Trust Relationships

As a network grows, keeping track of and supporting resources and users can become quite complex. Even on smaller networks, distributed resources can be difficult to manage. Under Windows NT, *domains* enable you to centralize user accounts while still enabling users to access the network and its resources from any point in the network. To administer servers effectively, you need to understand domains and their relationship to the network. Chapter 8, "Understanding System Administration," provides a brief introduction to domains. The following sections provide a more detailed explanation.

Understanding Workgroups and Domains

In Windows NT, as well as in Windows for Workgroups and Windows 95, a *workgroup* is a collection of computers on a network that are grouped together by a logical workgroup name. When you browse for resources on the network, you first see those computers on the LAN that are part of your workgroup. In Windows NT, for example, the Network Neighborhood displays an icon for each of the computers in your workgroup (see fig. 9.1).

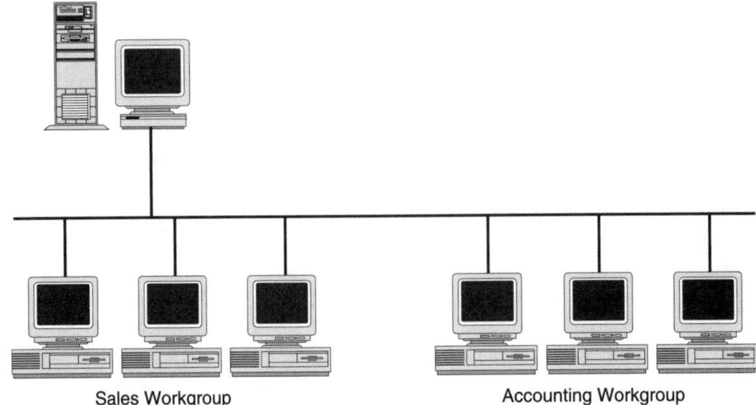

Fig. 9.1
Workgroups provide a means of organizing computers into logical groups.

A computer can belong to any workgroup on the network. In fact, it's very simple to change from one workgroup to another. Just open the Control Panel, double-click the Network icon, click Change on the Identification page of the Network property sheet, and specify a workgroup name. If the workgroup doesn't exist, you effectively create a new workgroup.

Workgroups simplify network browsing, but they do little—if anything—to simplify system administration. However, domains do simplify system administration. A *domain* is a group of computers that share a user account database. Domains enable centralization of account access and account management. Unlike a workgroup, in which a user must have an account on the computer he is logging on to, a domain user can log on from any workstation in the domain. More important for the administrator, however, is that you can administer accounts in one central location, which simplifies administration.

In addition to simplifying network administration, domains provide the same organization of resources to the network as workgroups. When a domain user browses the network for resources, he sees the resources organized by domain. The Network Neighborhood, for example, displays an icon for each computer in the user's domain. If the user needs to access a resource outside his domain, he double-clicks the Entire Network icon from the Network Neighborhood folder.

Primary and Backup Domain Controllers

Each domain includes one primary domain controller (PDC), and can (optionally) include one or more backup domain controllers (BDCs). The PDC stores the account and security database, and responds to access requests from workstations and servers in the domain. The PDC checks the validity of the account and password provided by the remote process, then approves or disapproves the access request. When you administer user accounts and privileges, you do so on the PDC. You do not, however, have to be logged on physically to the PDC. Instead, you can log on from any computer in the workgroup, including through a dial-up networking connection.

The BDC provides a backup to the PDC. The PDC replicates the user account database and related information to all BDCs on the network. If the PDC is unable to respond to an access request, the BDC handles the request. Although it isn't necessary to have a BDC on the network, you should create at least one.

Understanding Trust Relationships

A *trust relationship* is a special logical relationship between domains. In a trust relationship, one domain trusts another domain's users. The *trusting domain* allows users who have accounts in the *trusted domain* to access resources in its domain. For example, assume that domain A is the trusting domain, and domain B is the trusted domain. A user from domain B can access resources in domain A.

A trust relationship can be unidirectional or bidirectional. Just because domain A trusts domain B doesn't mean that domain B trusts domain A. You must explicitly set up the trust relationship between the two domains to be bidirectional if you want it to be so. Figure 9.2 illustrates the concept of trust relationships.

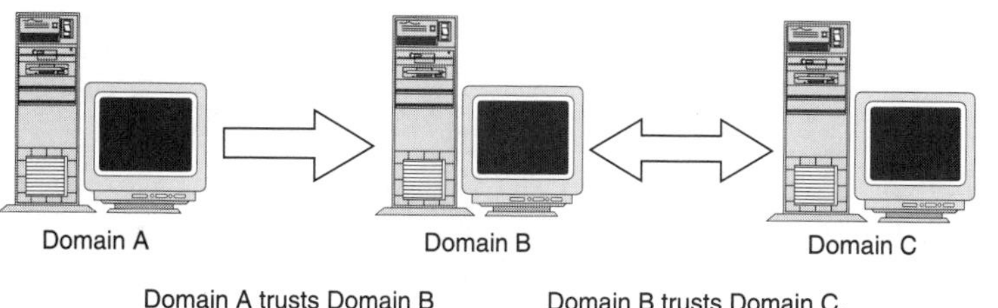
Domain A
Domain B
Domain C
Domain A trusts Domain B
Domain B trusts Domain C, and Domain C trusts Domain B

Fig. 9.2
You can create unidirectional and bidirectional trust relationships.

Domain trust relationships are not *transitive*. This means that trusts do not pass from one domain to another. For example, if domain A trusts domain B, and domain B trusts domain C, that doesn't mean that domain A trusts domain C. If you want domain A to trust domain C, you must explicitly set up the relationship between domain A and domain C. Figure 9.3 illustrates this concept.

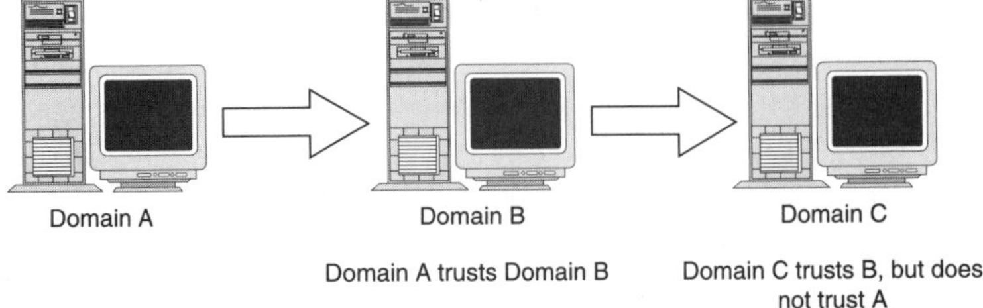
Domain A
Domain B
Domain C
Domain A trusts Domain B
Domain C trusts B, but does not trust A

Fig. 9.3 You must explicitly create trust relationships between domains.

> **Tip**
>
> Windows for Workgroups and Windows 95 clients on the network can enjoy the benefit of domains along with Windows NT clients. Setting the workgroup name of a Windows for Workgroups client to the name of a domain on the network adds that client to the domain. When the user browses for network resources, he sees the computers and other resources in the domain. If the user account and password supplied by the Windows for Workgroups user is a valid account in the domain, the user is automatically logged on to the domain when he logs on to Windows for Workgroups.
>
> You also can configure Windows 95 clients to log on to and become part of a domain. As with Windows for Workgroups clients, Windows 95 clients see the other computers in their domain when they browse for resources. To control Windows 95 domain logon, double-click the Network icon in the Control Panel. Click the Identification tab in the Network property sheet, and then enter the desired domain name in the Workgroup text box.

Creating and Managing Domains

Now that you have an understanding of how domains work, you're ready to begin creating and managing domains. This process includes creating a primary domain controller for each domain, and (optional) backup domain controllers.

You can create a domain in two ways:

- Create a new primary domain controller when you install Windows NT Server. This is explained in the section "Creating a Domain During Setup," later in this chapter.

- Use the Network property sheet (accessed from the Network icon in the Control Panel) to change the name of the domain on a primary domain controller to a new domain name. This is explained in the section "Moving a Domain (Renaming a Domain)," later in this chapter.

Before you begin creating and moving domains, however, you should understand how Security IDs (SIDs) work, because SIDs affect how and when you can create and move domains.

Understanding Security IDs

Windows NT Server assigns a Security ID (SID) to a PDC when you create the PDC. The SID then becomes a key component of the domain's security mechanism. As you add BDCs and computers to the domain, the PDC's SID is prefixed to those computers' names. When those other computers connect to the domain, they do so using the SID.

If you perform a new installation of Windows NT Server on an existing PDC, Setup will assign a new SID to the PDC—even if you specify the old domain name. Because the SID will be different, any BDCs or workstations that previously were members of the domain will not be able to find the new PDC. Therefore, you should never perform a new installation of Windows NT Server on an existing PDC. If the PDC is damaged in some way, you should allow the BDCs to handle security until you can get the PDC back up. If you are unable to do so, promote a BDC to be the PDC in the domain (see the section, "Promoting a PDC to a BDC," later in this chapter). Then, reinstall Windows NT Server on the old PDC, making it a BDC.

Note

Performing an upgrade on the PDC retains the SID and doesn't cause a loss of domain identity.

You also should never install a domain controller when the PDC is unavailable. Doing so will cause the server to become a PDC, which creates a second SID for the domain. Because the SID doesn't match the old PDC's SID, the new domain controller won't be able to function as a domain controller in the domain. To create a new domain controller in an existing domain, install the new domain controller while the existing PDC is available. This will cause the new controller to be installed as a BDC. Then, promote the BDC to a PDC while both domain controllers are active. This will automatically demote the existing PDC to a BDC.

Creating a Domain During Setup

When you install Windows NT Server, Setup prompts you to specify the security role of the computer. You can choose domain controller (primary or backup) or server. If you specify that the computer is to be a PDC, enter the name of the domain the server will control. Setup then searches the network to verify that the domain name you have specified does not already exist. Setup proceeds only if you have specified a new domain name.

Moving a Domain Controller to a New Domain

You can create a new domain by moving an existing domain controller to a new domain. To do so, follow these steps:

1. Open the Control Panel and double-click the Network icon.
2. Click the Identification tab of the Network property sheet to display the Identification page.
3. Click the Change button to open the Identification Changes dialog box (see fig. 9.4).

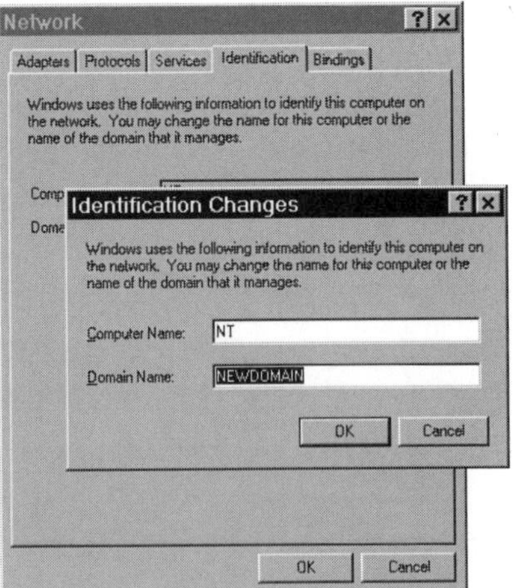

Fig. 9.4
Enter the new domain name in the Identification Changes dialog box.

> **Caution**
>
> If you intend to rename a domain, remember that you'll have to change the configuration of every existing workstation in the domain that you want to access the new domain. You also must reinstall the BDCs for the domain—you can't move them as you can a PDC. In addition, any trust relationships will have to be reconfigured. Finally, at the workstations you'll have to change all persistent connections to resources on the server to reflect the new name.

4. In the Domain Name text box, type the name for the new domain.
5. If you want to change the server's computer name, type a new name in the Computer Name text box.
6. Choose OK.

When you choose OK, Windows NT Server checks the network to determine if the domain name you specified is already in use. If the name is available, Windows NT Server displays a dialog box informing you of the consequences of changing domain names. Choose Yes if you want to continue with the name change, or choose No to cancel the process.

Managing Domain Controllers

In addition to creating and moving domains, you might have to perform additional domain administration tasks, such as the following:

- Creating a Backup Domain Controller (BDC)
- Promoting a BDC to a PDC
- Demoting a PDC to a BDC
- Synchronizing domains

Creating a Backup Domain Controller (BDC)

A BDC receives a copy of the user account database from the PDC, and handles requests for authentication when the PDC is unavailable. For example, if you must take down the PDC for maintenance, the BDC can handle logon authentication for the domain. Therefore, it is important that your network contain at least one BDC.

You can only create a BDC when you install Windows NT Server. Therefore, to promote a server to BDC status, you must reinstall Windows NT Server on it.

Promoting a BDC to a PDC

Occasionally, you will need to promote a BDC to PDC. For example, if you're going to shut down the PDC for maintenance, you should promote a BDC on the network to PDC. Doing so with the PDC online automatically causes the PDC to be demoted to a BDC.

◀ See "Basic Installation," p. 67

> **Note**
>
> If at all possible, you should promote the BDC when the existing PDC is online. Promoting the BDC while the PDC is online causes the PDC to automatically demote to a BDC. Also, very recent changes to the user database might not be incorporated in the BDC's database.

To promote a BDC to PDC, follow these steps:

1. Open the Start menu and choose Programs, Administrative Tools, Server Manager. The Server Manager opens.
2. Verify that no users are logged onto the system, or broadcast a message to all users that the system will be shut down temporarily.
3. When you're ready to proceed (when all users have logged off), choose View, Servers to view only servers on the network.
4. In the list of servers, select the BDC you want to promote to a PDC.
5. Choose Computer, Promote to Primary Domain Controller.
6. Server Manager warns you that promoting the BDC will close all client connections to the BDC and current PDC. If you're ready to proceed, choose Yes. Choose No if you want to cancel the task.

Demoting a PDC to a BDC

If you are unable to demote a PDC automatically by promoting a BDC to PDC, you can do so manually. For example, your PDC might suffer a hardware failure that takes it offline. You then can promote a BDC on the network to serve as PDC.

When you restart the original PDC, however, Windows NT Server displays a message that at least one service or driver failed during system startup. A little exploring in the Event Viewer will turn up a message that a PDC is already running in the domain. After you start the original PDC, follow these steps to demote it to a BDC:

1. Open the Start menu and choose Programs, Administrative Tools, Server Manager. The Server Manager appears.
2. Choose View, Servers to restrict the view to servers.
3. Select the server you want to demote.
4. Choose Computer, Demote to Backup Domain Controller.

Synchronizing Domains

In most cases, your network's BDCs will remain synchronized with the PDC. It is possible, however, for a BDC to become desynchronized from the PDC. To synchronize a BDC with a PDC, follow these steps:

1. Open the Server Manager.
2. Select the server you want to synchronize with the PDC.
3. Choose Computer, Synchronize with Primary Domain Controller (or choose Synchronize Entire Domain if you want to synchronize all domain controllers in the domain).

Creating and Removing Trust Relationships

If your network is large, it probably contains multiple domains. In many situations, creating trust relationships between domains can simplify administration and user access. Through trust relationships between domains, a user only needs an account in one domain to access other domains and their resources.

Creating a trust relationship requires two steps. First, the trusted domain must be configured to allow the other domain to trust it. Second, the trusting domain must be configured to trust the trusted domain. If each domain is managed by a different administrator, you'll have to coordinate setting up the relationship with the other administrator.

◀ See "Understanding Trust Relationships," p. 181

Use the following steps to create a trust relationship:

1. On the domain to be trusted, choose Start, Programs, Administrative Tools, User Manager for Domains.
2. In the User Manager, choose Policies, Trust Relationships to open the Trust Relationships dialog box (see fig. 9.5).

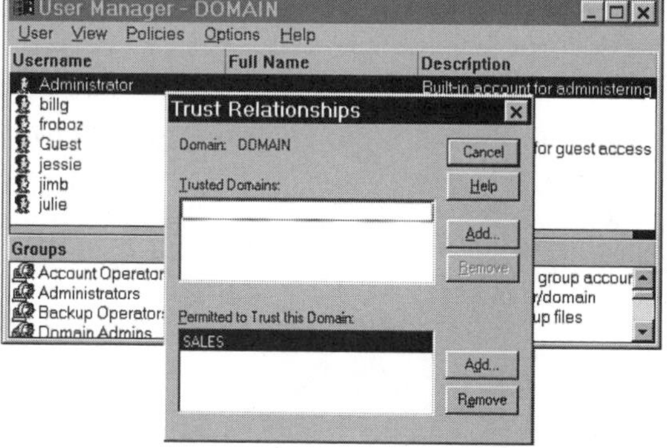

Fig. 9.5
Create trust relationships through the Trust Relationship dialog box in User Manager.

3. Choose the Add button next to the Permitted to Trust this Domain list. The Permit Domain to Trust dialog box opens (see fig. 9.6).

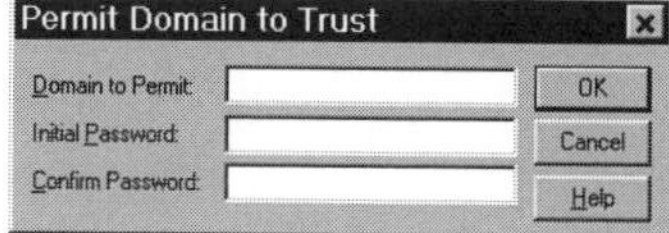

Fig. 9.6
Specify a domain name and optional password to enable other domains to trust the current domain.

4. In the Domain to Permit text box, type the name of the domain that will be permitted to trust the current domain.
5. (Optional) In the Initial Password and Confirm Password text boxes, enter a password that the administrator of the trusting domain must provide when she sets up the trust relationship from her domain.
6. Choose OK, then repeat steps 3 through 5 for additional domains you want to trust the current domain. When you're through adding domains, choose Close.
7. Acquire a password for the trust relationship from the trusted domain's administrator (refer to step 5).
8. Log on to the trusting domain as administrator and start the User Manager.
9. Choose Policies, Trust Relationships to open the Trust Relationships dialog box.
10. Choose the Add button next to the Trusted Domains list. The Add Trusted Domain dialog box opens (see fig. 9.7).
11. Type the name of the trusted domain in the Domain text box, and type the password for the domain acquired in step 7 in the Password text box. Choose OK.
12. The User Manager attempts to locate the domain on the network and validates the request to establish the relationship. If successful, the domain name will be added to the Trusted Domains list. If unsuccessful, User Manager displays an error message that the specified domain controller can't be found.

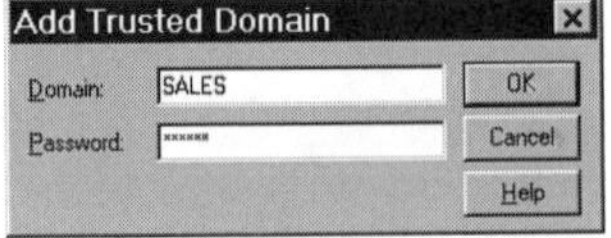

Fig. 9.7
Enter the domain and password for the trusted domain.

Adding and Removing Computers in a Domain

You can add workstations and servers to a domain through the Server Manager, which then enables the user of that workstation or server to join that domain. To add computers to a domain, follow these steps:

1. Log on to the server as Administrator, then open the Server Manager.
2. Choose Computer, Add to Domain. The Add Computer to Domain dialog box appears (see fig. 9.8).
3. Specify the function of the computer you're adding by selecting the appropriate option button.

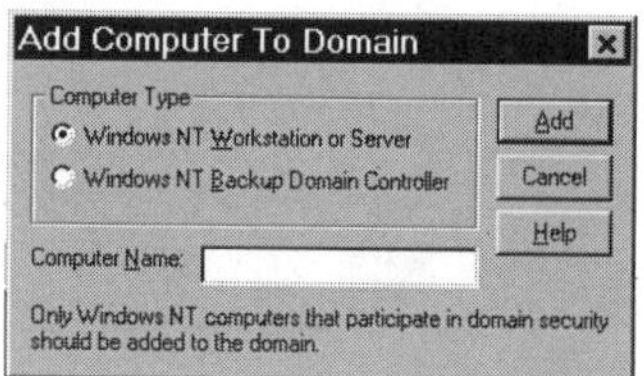

Fig. 9.8
Specify the computer name and computer's function to add a computer to the domain.

4. Type the name of the computer being added in the Computer Name text box.
5. Choose Add.
6. Repeat steps 3 through 5 for other computers you want to add.
7. When you're finished adding computers, choose Close.

It isn't absolutely necessary to add computers to the domain as just described. In the Identification Changes dialog box (double-click the Network icon in Control Panel, then choose Change from the Identification page), a user can cause Windows NT to create a computer account for him on the server (see fig. 9.9). To be able to do so, however, the user must supply the name and password of an account on the domain controller that has the authorization to add computers to the domain. You can assign this right to a group of users or to a single user account through the User Manager.

Members of the domain administrator's and server operator's groups always have the permission to add workstations to the domain, even if that right is not explicitly assigned to those groups. However, if you want to enable users to add their computers to domains by themselves, you can explicitly assign that right to a group or specific user account.

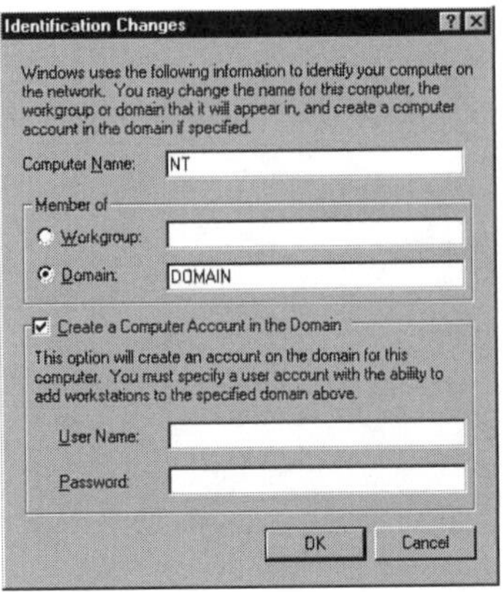

Fig. 9.9
With the correct account and password, a user can add his own computer to the domain.

To view or modify user or group rights, open the User Manager and choose Policies, User Rights. The User Rights Policy dialog box appears (see fig. 9.10). From the Right drop-down list, select Add Workstations To Domain. Click the Add button. From the Names list on the Add Users and Groups dialog box, select the group and/or user accounts to which you want to add this right. Choose Add. When you're finished adding names, choose OK.

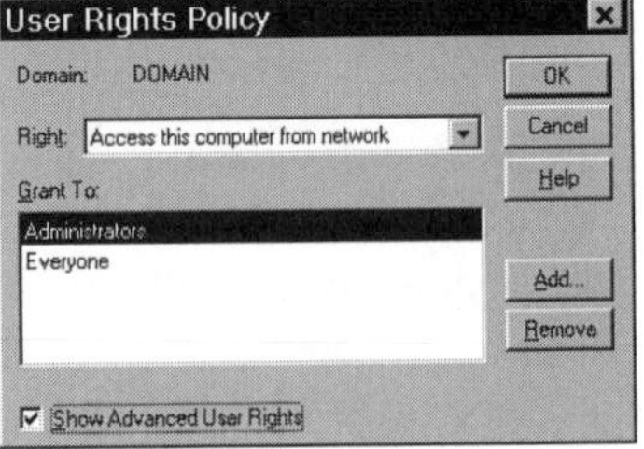

Fig. 9.10
Use the User Rights Policy dialog box to add rights to groups and users.

> **Tip**
>
> To view user names as well as group names in the Names list, click the Show Names button.

Using Server Manager

The Server Manager is the utility you will use most often to manage servers and their resources. To start the Server Manager, choose Start, Programs,

Administrative Tools, Server Manager. Or, execute the program \WINNT\SYSTEM32\SRVMGR. Figure 9.11 shows the Server Manager program window.

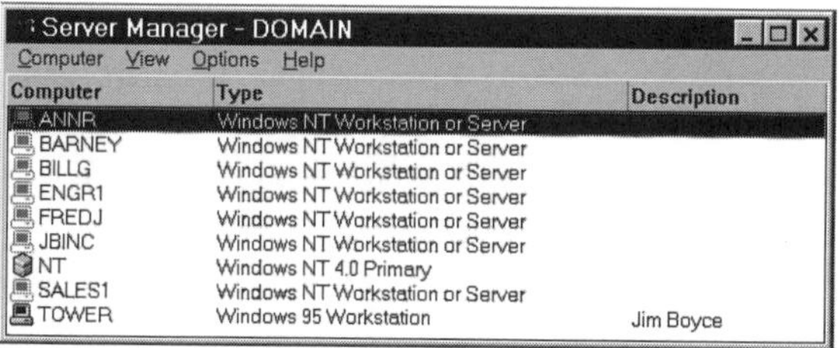

Fig. 9.11
Most server-related administration tasks can be performed with Server Manager.

The following sections explain the features in the Server Manager.

Selecting a Domain

Server Manager enables you to administer any domain in which you have the necessary privileges. When you start Server Manager, it displays the workstations and servers in your own domain. To choose a different domain, choose Computer, Select Domain. The Select Domain dialog box appears (see fig. 9.12).

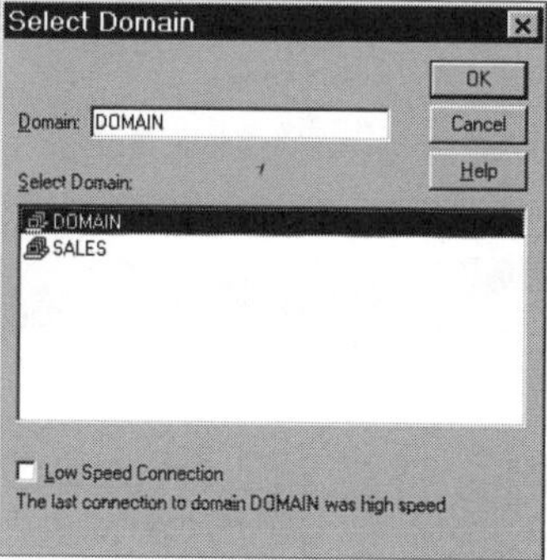

Fig. 9.12
Use the Select Domain dialog box to choose the domain to view.

The Select Domain dialog box lists all of the available domains (even if the domain's PDC or BDC is not available). To view a domain, select the domain from the Select Domain list or type the name of the domain in the Domain text box. Then, choose OK.

Troubleshooting

The name of a domain I want to administer appears in the Select Domain list, but when I select it and choose OK, Server Manager generates a message that the domain controller can't be found.

If a domain name appears in the Select Domain list, but you receive an error message that the domain controller for the domain can't be found, you might have a NetBIOS name problem. If you're connecting to a domain through a RAS connection, for example, the RAS connection might not be allowing NetBEUI (which would enable the remote domain PDC's NetBIOS name to be translated). Or, you might have disabled NetBEUI. To connect to the domain in these situations, enter the name of the domain's PDC in the Domain text box instead of the domain name.

If you're using TCP/IP, you can add the domain controller's name and IP address to the Lmhosts file to overcome this problem. Adding the name to Lmhosts causes its IP address to be resolved from its name.

Controlling Workstation and Server Views

With Server Manager, you can view the network in three ways: by server, by workstation, or by all. This enables you to focus on either servers or workstations, or view all computers on the network. To change the view, choose View, then choose Servers, Workstations, or All, depending on the type of view you want. If you want to further refine the view and see only those computers that are part of your domain, choose View, Show Domain Members Only.

Troubleshooting

When I choose Show Domain Members Only, Windows 95 workstations disappear from the list.

Windows 95 workstations whose workgroup names match the domain name appear in the computer list in Server Manager. They are not, however, true members of the domain, although their access to domain resources can be controlled through user accounts in the domain. When you choose Show Domain Members Only, therefore, these workstations disappear from the list.

Using a Low Speed Connection

If you are administering a domain, server, or computer across a LAN, most administration tasks will perform quickly. If you're administering across a slow link, such as through a Dial-Up Networking connection, many tasks can be very time consuming because a large amount of information must be transferred from the remote node and your local instance of Server Manager.

To help alleviate this problem, you can configure Server Manager for the low speed connection to the remote computer, which causes most automatic updating to be turned off. You then can use the View, Refresh command to update the display. Some actions, however, still cause automatic updates even if you've selected a low speed connection. These tasks include changing a computer's properties, managing services, and promoting a server to a PDC.

Tip

Press F5 to refresh the Server Manager display.

You can select a low speed connection in one of two ways:

- Choose Options, Low Speed Connection.
- Choose Computer, Select Domain. In the Select Domain dialog box that appears, select the domain you want to view and then select the Low Speed Connection checkbox.

Server Manager maintains the low speed connection status of the last 20 computers and domains you managed. If you last used a low speed connection to a domain, for example, the Select Domain dialog box automatically selects the Low Speed Connection checkbox accordingly and displays a message that the last connection to the computer was low speed. You can accept the default connection method or change it by selecting or deselecting the checkbox.

Tip

You can start Server Manager from a Windows NT command prompt and supply the name of a computer or domain to cause that computer or domain to be displayed as soon as the program appears. Or, you can create a shortcut to Server Manager and set its Target property to include the domain name and connection option. To set a low speed connection through the command prompt or Target property, add the /L switch to the command. The following example starts Server Manager to focus on the SALES domain with a low speed connection:

```
SRVRMGR SALES /L
```

Managing Server Properties

In addition to enabling you to control shared resources and services on a server, Server Manager enables you to control other aspects of server operation, which are referred to as the server's *properties*. To view a server's properties, select the server from the list in Server Manager, then choose Computer, Properties. Or, double-click the server name in the list. Either action opens the Properties dialog box shown in figure 9.13.

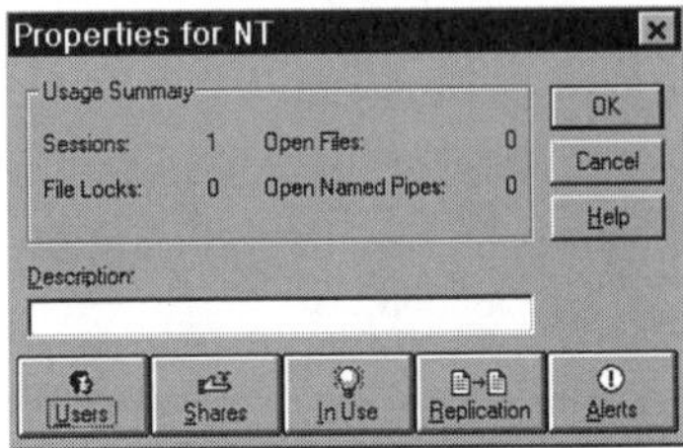

Fig. 9.13
Use the Properties dialog box to control a server.

The following sections explain these properties and how to control them.

Managing Connected Users

Through Server Manager, you can view the users who are connected to a server, view the resources they are using, and disconnect users from the server. For example, you might need to disconnect one or more users because you need to shut down the resource they are using.

To view user connections to the server, follow these steps:

1. Open Server Manager and double-click the server you want to manage. (You can also select the server and press Enter, or select the server and choose Computer, Properties.)
2. In the Properties dialog box, click the Users button to open the User Sessions dialog box (see fig. 9.14).

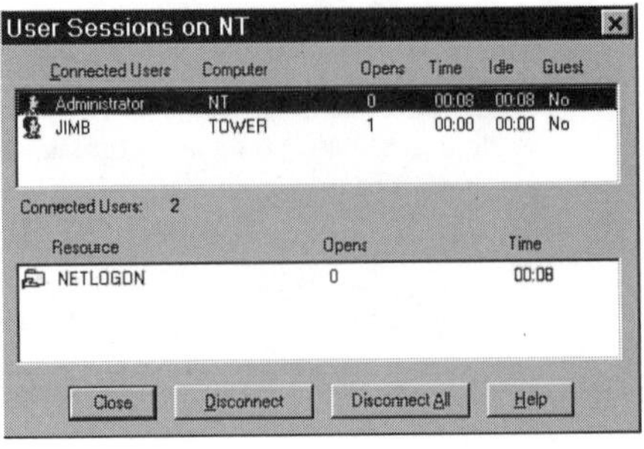

Fig. 9.14
The User Sessions dialog box lists all users connected to the server and the resources they are using.

3. From the Connected Users list, select the user whose connections you want to view. The resources opened by the user appear in the Resource list at the bottom of the dialog box.

To disconnect a user from all connected resources, select the user and click the Disconnect button. Server Manager warns you that disconnecting the user could cause a loss of data by the user. Choose Yes if you still want to disconnect the user, or choose No to cancel the operation.

To disconnect all users, click the Disconnect All button. Server Manager warns you that disconnecting the users might cause some to lose data. To continue, choose Yes. To cancel the disconnection, choose No.

> **Note**
>
> Although a user might have a resource open, disconnecting that user might not result in the user losing any data. For example, the user might simply have a folder open, but not have any files open. And, if the user is simply viewing the file and not modifying it, disconnecting the user won't cause a loss of data. You should, however, be careful about disconnecting users—someone who has worked for hours on a document would probably be very unhappy to find himself disconnected and his changes lost. You should broadcast a message before disconnecting users.

Managing Shares

In addition to letting you view which users are connected to specific resources, the Server Manager also enables you to view user connections by specific shares. You might, for example, want to remove a folder from sharing. Before doing so, you should verify that no users are connected to the share.

▶ See "Broadcasting Messages," p. 204

To view and manage share connections, open the Server Manager and double-click the server you want to manage. In the server's Properties dialog box, click the Shares button to open the Share Resources dialog box (see fig. 9.15).

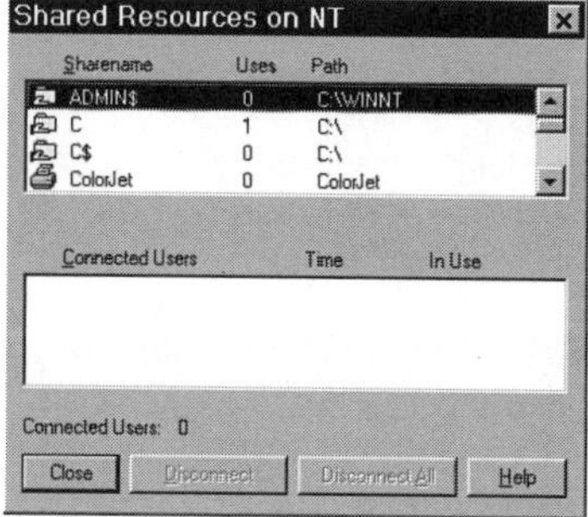

Fig. 9.15
View connections to specific shares through the Shared Resources dialog box.

The Sharename list displays all of the resources shared by the server, including disk and printer resources. To view connections to a share, select a share in the Sharename list. All users connected to that share are then displayed in the Connected Users list, along with connection time and whether the share is currently in use.

To disconnect a user from a share, choose Disconnect. To disconnect all users from a share, choose Disconnect All. As when disconnecting users from the server, you should make sure that disconnecting a user from a share will not cause the user to lose any data. If possible, you should warn the user through a broadcast message to disconnect from the share himself.

Managing Open Resources

The In Use button on a server's Properties dialog box lets you drill down even further to view opened resources. When you click the In Use button, Server Manager opens the Open Resources dialog box (see fig. 9.16). This dialog box lists specific files in use in a resource. You can use this dialog box to close the resource, or close all resources that are open. Again, be sure your users won't lose any data if you force close their shares.

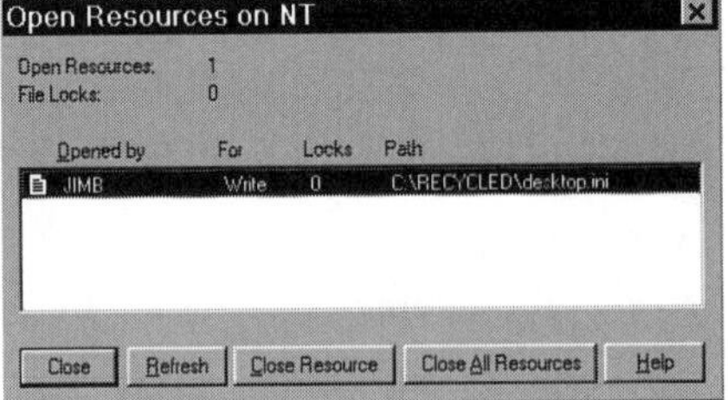

Fig. 9.16 You can close open resources through the Open Resources dialog box.

Configuring Handling of Alerts

Occasionally, *server alerts* will occur for a server. These alerts are generated by security and access problems, user connection problems, server shutdown, and printer problems. You can configure a server to broadcast alert messages to other computers and/or users.

To add a computer or user to the alert recipient list, follow these steps:

1. In Server Manager, select the server whose alerts you want to broadcast, then display its Properties dialog box by choosing Computer, Properties.
2. In the Properties dialog box, click the Alerts button to display the Alerts dialog box.

3. In the New Computer or Username text box, type the name of the computer or user to which you want the alerts to be broadcast, then choose Add.
4. To remove an existing computer or user from the list, select the computer or user from the Send Administrative Alerts To list, then choose Remove.
5. Choose OK to complete alert notification configuration.

Managing Directory Replication

Windows NT enables you to automate replication of directories across multiple computers and domains, enabling you to distribute and synchronize a set of files across the domains. Computers running Windows NT Server can act as both exporters and importers, replicating directories to other computers and importing directories provided by other computers. Workstations, however, can only import replicated directories.

A good example of files that should be replicated are logon scripts. You should replicate all user logon scripts to the BDCs, because the BDCs can authorize logon, and because a user's logon script should be located on the computer that authorizes logon to reduce network traffic. Therefore, you should group together your users' logon scripts into a logical directory structure, then export that directory structure to the BDCs.

Exporting Directories

To set up directory replication, first create a user account in the domain with the following properties:

- Password never expires
- Can log on 24 hours a day, seven days a week
- Is a member of the Backup Operators group

Give the account a logical name, such as RepDir. You can't name the account Replicator, because that name is already used by a local default group.

Next, create the set of directories you want to export. By default, the export directory is \WINNT\SYSTEM32\REPL\EXPORT (and the default import directory is \WINNT\SYSTEM32\REPL\IMPORT). In the \WINNT\SYSTEM32\REPL\EXPORT folder, you should create any additional folders you want to export. Then, open the Server Manager and double-click the server on which those directories reside. This opens the server's Properties dialog box. Click the Replication button to display the Directory Replication dialog box (see fig. 9.17).

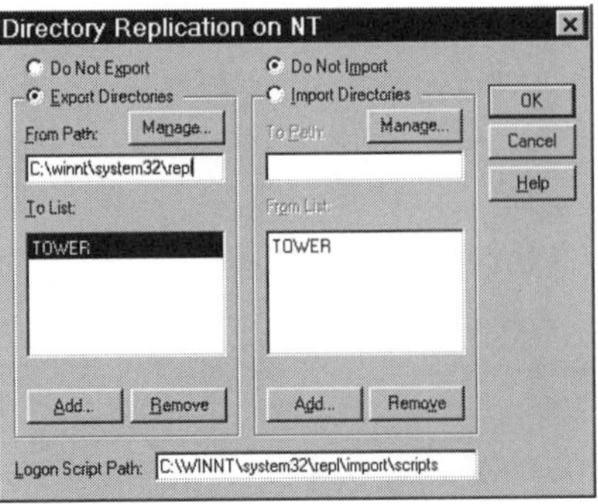

Fig. 9.17
Use the Directory Replication dialog box to replicate directories across domains.

To enable the export of a directory and its subdirectories, follow these steps:

1. Select the Export Directories option button to enable export.
2. In the From Path text box, type the path of the topmost directory of the directories you want to share.

> **Caution**
>
> In the From Path text box, make sure you specify the path to the directory to be exported—not the directory's parent directory. Specifying the parent directory causes all of its subdirectories to be exported, as well.

3. In the Directory Replication dialog box, choose the Add button under the To List box to display the Select Domain dialog box.
4. In the Select Domain dialog box, choose the domain containing the computers to which you want to replicate the directories.
5. When the list of computers in the domain appears, select the computer to which you want the directories replicated, then choose OK to add it to the To List.
6. Choose OK to close the Directory Replication dialog box. Depending on whether the Replicator service is running, Windows NT might stop, then restart the Replicator service (which happens automatically).

These steps export all of the directories in the target you specify. You can selectively prevent directories from being replicated by locking them. To lock directories and otherwise manage the replicated directories, follow these steps:

1. Choose the Manage button on the Directory Replication dialog box to display the Manage Exported Directories dialog box (see fig. 9.18).

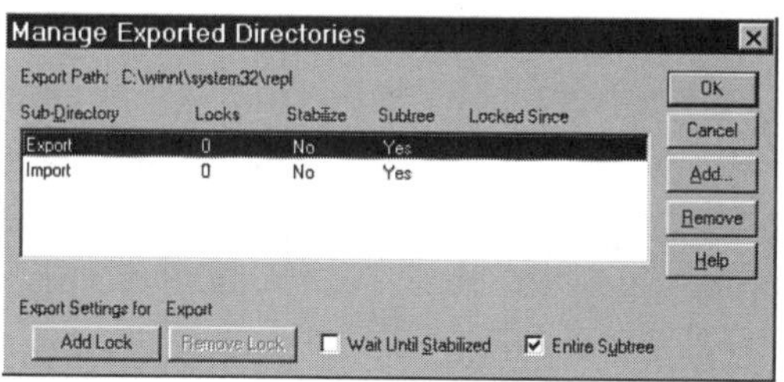

Fig. 9.18
Add subdirectories to be replicated using the Manage Exported Directories dialog box.

2. Set the options for the exported directory according to the following list of options and controls, then choose OK to return to the previous dialog box.

   - *Add Lock.* Use this button to add locks to the selected directory. Locking a directory prevents it from being replicated. A directory is replicated only when its Lock value is zero.
   - *Remove Lock.* Use this button to remove locks from the selected directory.
   - *Wait Until Stabilized.* When you select this checkbox, replication will not occur if any subdirectory or file in the selected directory has changed in the past two minutes. This option helps prevent partial replication, in which some files are not updated with others.
   - *Entire Subtree.* Select this checkbox to cause Windows NT to replicate all subdirectories and files under the selected directory. If this checkbox is not selected, only the first level subdirectory and its files are replicated.

Note

To remove a directory from replication, select the directory and choose the Remove button in the Directory Replication dialog box.

3. To add a subdirectory to the list, choose the Add button.
4. In the Sub-Directory Name text box of the Add Sub-Directory dialog box, type the name of the directory to be replicated, then choose OK.
5. Use the controls in the Manage Exported Directories dialog box to lock or set other options for the newly added directory.
6. When you're finished setting up the directories, choose OK. Choose OK again to close the Directory Replication dialog box.

Importing Directories

You use the Directory Replication dialog box to establish import of directories to a computer. The process is very similar to exporting directories:

1. Open Server Manager, select the computer you want to manage, and display its Properties dialog box by choosing Computer, Properties.
2. Choose the Replication button to display the Directory Replication dialog box.
3. Select the Import Directories option button to enable directory import.
4. In the To Path text box, specify the path to the local directory in which you want the imported directories stored (this is \WINNT\SYSTEM32\REPL\IMPORT by default).
5. Click the Add button under the From List to display the Select Domain dialog box.
6. Select the domain containing the computer from which you want to import, then select the computer itself.
7. Choose OK to close the Directory Replication dialog box, and then choose OK to close the Properties dialog box.

Troubleshooting

I added computers to the From List, and now the directories from the local domain no longer import. How do I reestablish the replication from the local domain?

By default, the From List is blank, and directories are imported from the local domain. When you add computers and other domains to the list, import no longer occurs from the local domain. To reestablish that replication, explicitly add the domain to the From List as you would any other domain or computer.

Managing Shared Directories

Although you can use the Explorer to manage shared directories, you also can use Server Manager to manage them. Using Server Manager has the advantage of bringing all shared directories into a single list, making it easier for you to view all shared directories at once.

To control the directory shares on a computer, open the Server Manager and select the server whose shares you want to manage. Choose Computer, Shared Directories to open the Shared Directories dialog box (see fig. 9.19).

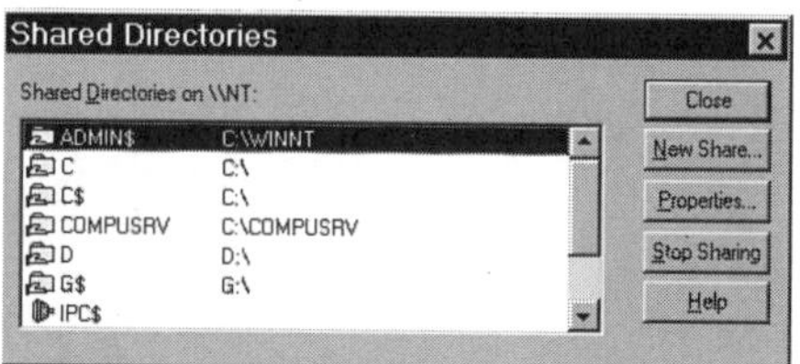

Fig. 9.19 Server Manager provides a centralized method for managing shared directories.

Changing a Share's Properties

You can easily change description, number of users allowed to connect, and permissions for a share. To do so, open the Shared Directories dialog box as explained in the previous section. Select the share you want to manage and choose Properties (or simply double-click the share's name). The Share Properties dialog box opens (see fig. 9.20).

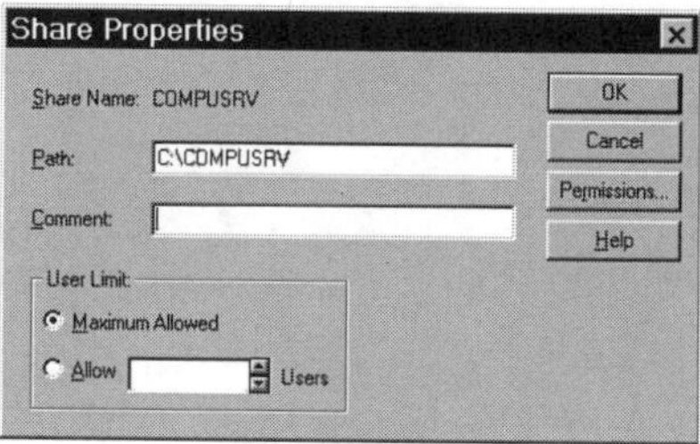

Fig. 9.20 Use the Share Properties dialog box to set a share's properties.

Use the Path and Comment text boxes to change the share's name and description. Use the controls in the User Limit group to specify how many users can connect to the share at one time. Click the Permissions button to display a dialog box that enables you to set explicit user and group permissions on the share.

> **Note**
>
> You can't change permissions on administrative shares such as C$.

▶ See "Understanding Permissions," p. 226

Creating a New Share

Although you can share directories using either the Explorer or File Manager, you also can share them using Server Manager. To share a directory, open Server Manager and select the server whose directory you want to share. Choose Computer, Shared Directories to open the Shared Directories dialog box. Choose the New Share button to open the New Share dialog box (see fig. 9.21).

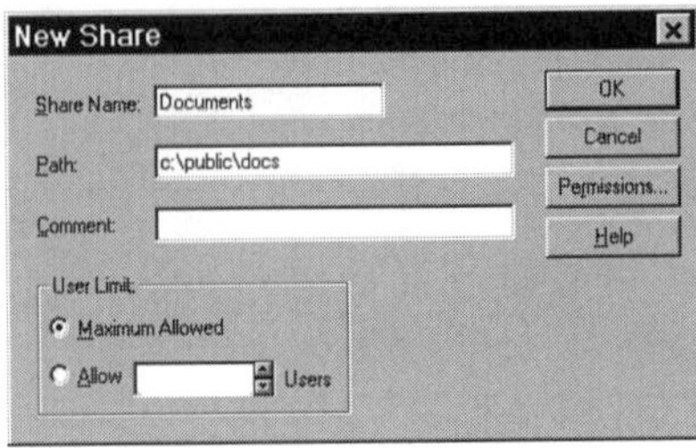

Fig. 9.21
You can create new shares with Server Manager.

The information you provide in the New Share dialog box is generally self-explanatory. For help in understanding permission, refer to Chapter 10, "Administering Users." For more information on sharing resources, refer to the section, "Configuring Peer-to-Peer Resource Sharing," later in this chapter.

▶ See "Controlling Resource Access," p. 226

Tip

To stop sharing a directory, select the directory in the Shared Directories dialog box and choose the Stop Sharing button.

Managing Services

A key feature of Server Manager is its capability to let you view the status of services running on a server, and to start and stop those services. You can perform these tasks even on remote servers, including those connected by Dial-Up Networking connections.

To view, start, or stop services on a server, open Server Manager and select the server with which you want to work. Choose Computer, Services to open the Services dialog box (see fig. 9.22). Most of the controls and buttons on the Services dialog box are self-explanatory.

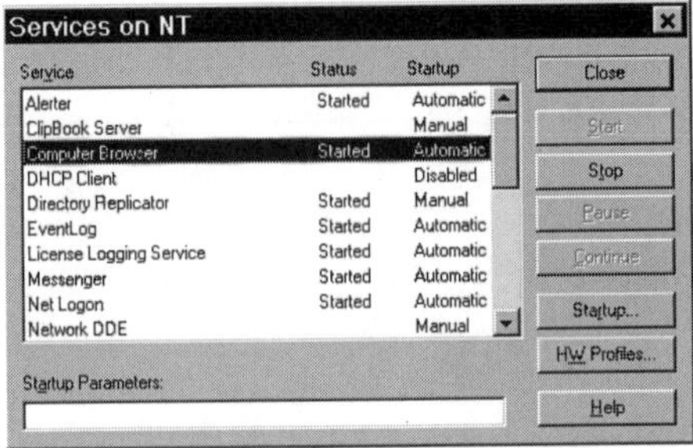

Fig. 9.22
View, start, and stop services through the Server Manager.

To control how a service starts, first select the service from the Service list, and then choose the Startup button to display the Service dialog box (see fig. 9.23).

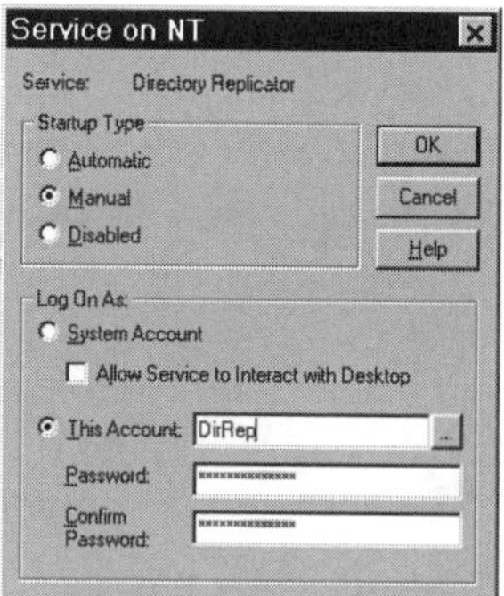

Fig. 9.23
Control service startup options with the Service dialog box.

The following list summarizes the options in the Service dialog box:

- *Automatic.* Select this option button to cause the service to start automatically when the server boots.
- *Manual.* Select this option button to require that the service be started by a user or other service.
- *Disabled.* Select this option to disable the service.
- *System Account.* Generally, services log on to the system account when they start. However, the Directory Replicator and Schedule services log on using other accounts. To specify which account a service uses to log on, click the ... button to the right of the This Account text box. Use the resulting dialog box to choose the existing account you want the service to use for logon.

> **Note**
>
> For the majority of services, the Log On As controls are dimmed because you can't change the logon account of most services.

- *Allow Service to Interact with Desktop.* Select this checkbox to provide an interface on the desktop that can be used by whomever is logged on when the service starts. This setting applies only to services logging on to the LocalSystem account.

- *This Account.* Use this control to specify an account to which you want the service to log on. By default, most services log on to LocalSystem. The Directory Replicator is an example of a service that logs on to a specific user account that you specify.

Broadcasting Messages

◀ See "Managing Directory Replication," p. 197

You will occasionally find it necessary to broadcast a message to all users who are logged on to a server. For example, you might need to take the server down for maintenance and need to inform users to log off by a certain time. Server Manager enables you to broadcast these types of messages.

To send a message, open Server Manager and select the server whose users you want to message. Choose Computer, Send Message. The Send Message dialog box appears (see fig. 9.24). Just type your message in the Message text box, then choose OK. The message is broadcast immediately to all users who are logged on to the selected server.

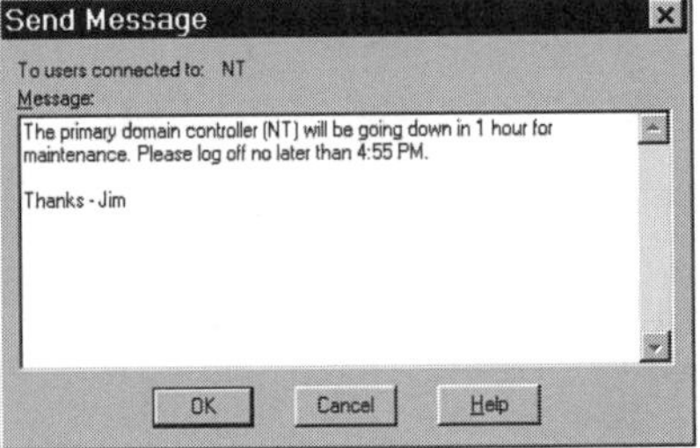

Fig. 9.24 Use Server Manager to broadcast messages to users connected to a server.

> **Note**
>
> The Messenger service must be running on your computer as well as any other Windows NT user to whom you want to send the message. Non-Windows NT clients such as Windows 95 and Windows for Workgroups do not receive the broadcast messages unless they are running WinPopup. For this reason, you should add WinPopup to the Startup folder/group on these clients.

Managing Printers

Another important aspect of setting up and administering a server is sharing and managing printers. Through new wizards and other mechanisms, Windows NT 4.0 simplifies printer installation and management over previous versions. While Chapter 16 details printer installation and configuration, there are a few aspects that are appropriate to discuss in this chapter because they relate directly to system management.

Managing Print Queues

As a system administrator, you're probably familiar with managing print queues. Rather than deal with the subject in depth, this section briefly explains how to access print queues using the new Windows NT 4.0 interface.

▶ See "Installing a Network Printer," p. 312

To access a printer's queue, locate the printer in the Printers folder, in the Network Neighborhood, or in the Explorer. Select the printer and press Enter, or just double-click the printer. The printer's queue window opens (see fig. 9.25).

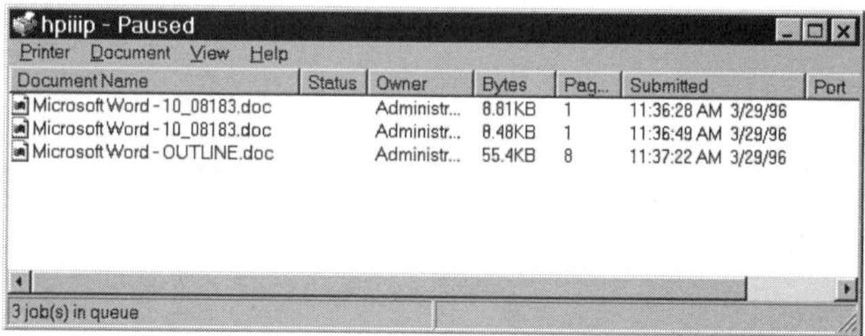

Fig. 9.25
Use a printer's queue window to control pending print jobs and other printer functions.

Any pending print jobs appear in the printer's queue window, including an indication of the job's status. In addition to pausing and resuming specific print jobs, you can pause and resume the printer itself, which places all pending jobs on hold.

If you have the necessary access privileges, you can set the properties of each document in the queue. Otherwise, you are restricted to setting properties only for jobs that you have created (depending on your group membership and corresponding access permissions).

To view and set a pending document's properties, double-click the document, right-click the document and choose Properties from the shortcut menu (or select the document and choose Document, Properties). A property sheet for the document appears, which lets you schedule the job, set its priority, set page and paper properties, and set specific printer properties for the print job (see fig. 9.26).

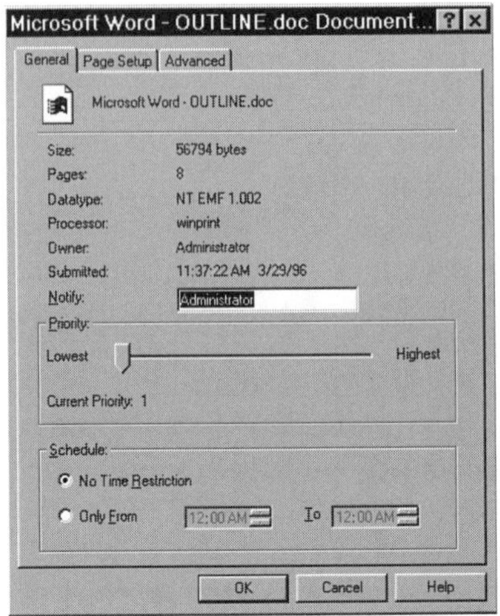

Fig. 9.26
Use a document's property sheet to control how and when it prints.

Configuring Peer-to-Peer Resource Sharing

In addition to supporting more traditional dedicated network resource sharing, Windows NT enables you to share resources on a peer-to-peer basis. In a peer-to-peer network, all Windows NT computers on the network, including those running Windows NT Workstation, can share disk and printer resources for other users to access. This ability enables any user to make his resources available to others. In some ways, however, peer-to-peer networking is a double-edged sword. It provides great flexibility in resource sharing, but complicates network security. To understand why that is true, you need to understand how peer-to-peer sharing works.

How Peer-to-Peer Sharing Works

With Windows NT, you can share resources from dedicated servers as well as from any Windows NT workstation. In addition, Windows for Workgroups computers on the network also can share their resources with Windows NT computers, and vice versa.

The process for sharing resources on a workstation is essentially the same as for a dedicated server. If the user's workstation has been configured to enable peer-to-peer sharing, he can set the sharing properties of a directory or disk using Explorer or File Manager, thereby giving other users access to it. He also can share his local printer through the Printers folder.

After the resource is shared, other users can access it just as they access resources shared by dedicated servers. When a user browses the network in Network Neighborhood, for example, he can see the resources shared by each workstation, as well as those shared by dedicated servers.

Note

The mechanics of sharing resources are explained in the following sections, "Sharing Disk Resources," and "Sharing Printer Resources."

As with resources shared by dedicated servers, you can connect to a peer-to-peer resource through UNC names and map them to local resources. You might, for example, map drive Z to a folder shared on a coworker's computer.

Essentially, resource sharing on a workstation is identical to sharing on a dedicated server. The only real difference is security.

Peer-to-Peer Security and Resource Availability

Any network environment is only as secure as its administrator and users make it. Users who leave scraps of paper lying around with their account and password information on them degrade system security, often without realizing it. In a peer-to-peer environment, security can become a problem, because users, rather than an administrator, have at least some control over how and when resources are shared.

Under Windows NT, however, even peer-to-peer resource sharing is secure. In order for a user to share a local resource, he must belong to a group that has that right, such as the Power Users group. If the user doesn't belong to a group that has the right to share resources, none of the sharing controls even appear in the user's interface. Controlling a user's ability to share resources is therefore easy—control the user's group membership accordingly. Or, explicitly add or remove the right to create shared objects.

The other point to understand about peer-to-peer resource sharing is that it is tied to the computer, not to an individual user. Shared resources will continue to be available even when the user who shared the resource is not logged on. For example, assume that Joe Blow is a member of the Power Users group, and shares a folder on his computer. Then, he logs off and Jane Doe, who is only a member of the Domain Users group, logs on to the same computer. Other users on the network still can access the folder shared by Joe, even though he isn't logged on to his computer. Also, Jane can't unshare the resource, or share additional resources, because she doesn't have the rights required to do so.

Because resources remain available even when the user who shared them is not logged on, you should have little trouble keeping resources available. As long as your users don't turn off their computers, any resources shared by their workstations will continue to remain available until removed by an administrator or other user with the appropriate rights.

Tip

If you want to retain control as an administrator over all shared resources, simply log on to a workstation as an administrator, share whatever resources need to be shared, then log off. Other users can use the workstation while it is sharing its resources, and will not have the ability to add new shares or modify the existing shares unless you give them the right to do so. You can control the shared resources from across the network, if needed (and even set up sharing from across the network).

Adding Sharing Ability

Members of the Administrators group have the right to share local resources. You can grant that right to other users in one of three ways: place the user in the Power Users group, create a special group for sharing and give that group the right to create shares, or give individual users the explicit right to share resources. Placing a user in the Power Users group has some potential security disadvantages. Power Users have many additional rights besides the ability to share resources. For example, Power Users can create and modify user accounts.

Note

The Power Users group exists only on Windows NT Workstation and on servers that are not domain controllers.

The best, most secure solution is to log on to the workstation as an administrator, share the necessary resources, then log off. If you want the user to be able to share resources, create a new group and add the right to that group. Then, place in that group any users who you want to be able to share resources. Or, add the right specifically to each user who needs it.

Tip

In a domain, you do not have to be physically present at a workstation to share its resources. Log on to the domain as Administrator, then browse the workstation in question for the resource you want to share. Set up the share as explained in Chapter 10, "Administering Servers," and in the sections, "Sharing Disk Resources" and "Sharing Printer Resources" later in this chapter.

Note

Your ability as an administrator to view resources across the network even when you have not set up those resources to be shared relies on Windows NT's creation of *hidden shares*. When you install Windows NT, secure shares are created for each disk and printer. These share names are post-fixed by a dollar sign ($), which prevents them from appearing in users' browse dialog boxes, effectively hiding them from users. When you browse the network as an administrator, you're actually browsing these hidden shares.

After you create the necessary group in User Manager, follow these steps to grant resource sharing rights to the group (or to an individual user):

1. In User Manager, choose Policies, User Rights to display the User Rights Policy dialog box.
2. Mark the Show Advanced User Rights checkbox.
3. From the Right drop-down list, choose Create permanent shared objects.
4. Click the Add button.
5. Click the Show Users button if you want to assign the right to individual users.
6. From the Names list, select the group(s) and user(s) to whom you want to give the right to share resources.
7. Choose OK, then choose OK again. ❖

CHAPTER 10

Administering Users

by Jim Boyce

Experienced administrators know that managing user accounts and network access is a major facet of system administration. In this chapter, you learn about the tools that Windows NT provides to simplify user and group account management. You also learn about access permissions and how to use those permissions to securely control access to resources.

In this chapter, you learn to

- Create and modify user accounts
- Control and restrict resource access
- Manage and distribute user profiles
- Use system and account policies

Creating and Modifying User Accounts

Unlike environments like Windows for Workgroups and Windows 95, Windows NT requires a user to have a preexisting user account either on the computer from which they are logging on, or on a domain. An administration task you'll perform fairly often is creating and managing user accounts. Windows NT simplifies the entire process by bringing all account control under one interface—the User Manager.

Overview of User Manager

The User Manager enables you to create user accounts and groups, assign users to groups, set access permissions for groups and individual users, create trust relationships, define account policies, and other administrative tasks. To start User Manager, choose Start, Programs, Administrative Tools, User Manager. Figure 10.1 shows the User Manager program window.

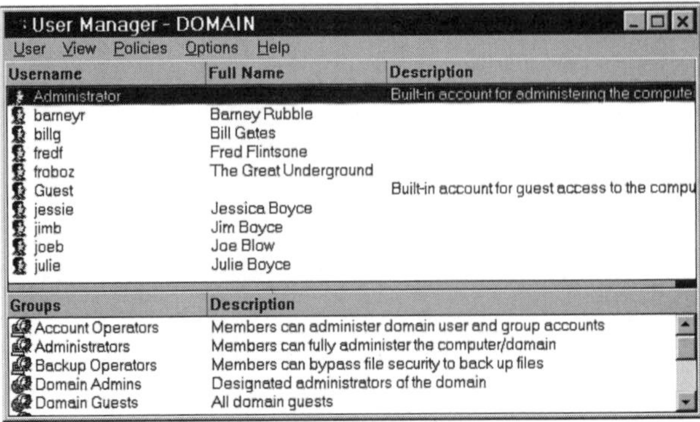

Fig. 10.1
You can manage accounts locally and remotely with User Manager.

> **Note**
>
> On a domain controller, User Manager for Domains performs the same function as User Manager, and is essentially identical except for the addition of a few features that enable you to select and work with domain-wide accounts. This chapter uses User Manager for Domains in all examples, but refers to both programs as simply User Manager.

User Manager enables you to perform the following administrative functions:

- Create and modify user accounts
- Create and modify groups
- Set account policies
- Grant user rights
- Set up auditing
- Create and modify trust relationships

To understand how to perform these tasks with User Manager, you first need to understand the concept of groups and individual user accounts.

Understanding Accounts and Groups

You must have a valid, preexisting user account to log on to a computer running Windows NT. If the workstation is participating in a workgroup and not a domain, you must have an account on that workstation itself. If you are logging on from a computer in a domain, you must have an account in the domain (or in a trusted domain).

A user account identifies each user with a name and other optional information, and defines how and when a user can log on, what resources the user can access, and what level of access the user has to those resources. Basically, the user account defines all aspects of the user's access to the computer and network. Each user account includes a password for security.

In addition to existing as an individual account, users can belong to specific *groups*. A group is a collection of users who have similar job or resource access needs. Groups simplify resource administration by enabling you to assign and control permissions on a broad basis. Instead of assigning permissions for a specific resource to every user, you can assign a specific set of rights to a group, then give those rights to users simply by making them members of the group. In this way, groups provide a means of logically organizing users and their access rights.

Windows NT supports two types of groups:

- *Global groups.* Global groups can contain user accounts only from within the domain in which the group is created. A global group can be granted permissions in other domains through a trust relationship between the domains.
- *Local groups.* A local group can contain users and global groups, which enable you to collect users from multiple domains into one group and manage them collectively. Local groups can only be assigned permissions in the domain in which the group is created.

> **Note**
>
> Unless yours is a very large, multidomained network, it is likely that most of the groups you create will be global groups.

Windows NT includes a selection of built-in user accounts and groups. The Administrator account, which you create when you install Windows NT, is essentially a built-in account. You can't delete or disable the Administrator account, but you can rename it. The Guest account is another built-in account. You can't delete the Guest account, but you can rename and disable it.

Table 10.1 describes the built-in groups supported by Windows NT—they are also listed in the following sections.

Table 10.1 Built-In Groups

Group	Type	Automatic Contents
Administrators	Local	Domain Admins
Domain Admins	Global	Administrator

(continues)

Table 10.1 Continued

Group	Type	Automatic Contents
Backup Operators	Local	None
Server Operators	Local	None
Account Operators	Local	None
Print Operators	Local	None
Power Users	Local	Setup User
Users	Local	Domain Users
Domain Users	Global	Administrators
Guests	Local	Domain Guests, Guest
Domain Guests	Global	Guest
Replicator	Local	None

Administrators

Members of the Administrators group enjoy almost complete access to and authority over the domain, server, or workstation containing the group. A member of the Administrator group can access any file or directory on a FAT file system. However, Administrators don't have complete, automatic access to directories and files on NTFS systems. Unless the owner of a file or directory grants access, even Administrators can't access the resource. An Administrator can, however, take ownership of the resource to gain access to it.

Domain Admins

◀ See "Understanding File System Issues," p. 40

◀ See "Evaluating and Planning the File System," p. 60

Every domain includes a global group named Domain Admins that is automatically added to the local Administrators group. Therefore, all members of Domain Admins are domain administrators. You can assign a user as a domain administrator two ways: add the user to the Domain Admins group, or add the user to the local Administrators group in the domain. By adding the Domain Admins group to the Administrators group in other domains, you enable the designated users to administer multiple domains with a single account in their home domain.

Backup Operators

This local group is designed to enable users to perform backup functions. Users in the Backup Operators group can back up and restore files, log on to the system locally, and shut down the system. Backup Operators cannot change security settings or perform other administrative tasks.

▶ See "Examining Backup Strategies and Media," p. 363

Server Operators

The Server Operators group is designed to enable its members to manage servers. Users in this group can log in to the system locally, share and unshare resources, format disks on the server, back up and restore files, and shut down servers.

Account Operators

Users in this group can create and manage user accounts in the domain. They can create and modify user accounts and groups, but can't assign user rights. Instead, they can create accounts and assign those accounts to groups that have been set up by an administrator.

◀ See "Using Server Manager," p. 190

Print Operators

The Print Operators group can log on to servers locally, shut down a server, and share, unshare, and manage print printers.

Users

The most common group is Users. Members of this group can't log on locally to a primary or backup domain controller; instead, they must log on from a client on the network (domain, workstation, or server).

▶ See "Managing Printers," p. 204

Power Users

Power Users are like users with some administrative rights. Power Users can create and modify user accounts (only modifying those they create). They can add accounts to the Users, Guests, and Power Users groups. Power Users can also share and unshare files and printers on local workstations or servers.

Domain Users

All user accounts in a domain automatically become members of the Domain Users group. The Domain Users group is part of the local Users group, which makes all of its members users of the domain.

Guests

Members of the Guests group on a domain have rights similar to Users. They can log on through a network client and access domain resources. Like Users, they cannot log on locally to a server—they must do so across the network.

Domain Guests

The Guest user account typically is included in the Domain Guests group, which is a member of the local Guests group. Members of the Domain Guests and Guests groups enjoy guest privileges in the domain to which they are logged on. To grant guest privileges across multiple domains, include the Domain Guests group in the local Guests groups of the other domains that trust the logon domain.

Replicator

See "Managing Directory Replication," p. 197

The Replicator group is a special group that facilitates file and directory replication.

Applying Accounts and Groups

The most important point to understand is that groups enable you to simplify administration and resource access. Instead of having to grant specific rights to each user, you simply create groups with specific rights, then assign users to those groups as needed. It's also important to understand that a user can be a member of many groups, and that one group can contain another group. In addition, you can add specific rights to a user if that one user is the only one who needs those rights—you don't have to create a group with those specific rights. You might consider doing so anyway, however, because you might have another user in the future who also needs the same rights.

In the following sections, you learn how to use User Manager to create and manage accounts and groups.

Controlling Views and Selecting Users

You can sort the view in User Manager to display names according to their account names or long names. By default, User Manager sorts by account name. To switch between these view methods, choose View, Sort by Full Name or choose View, Sort by Username.

After you select the view you prefer, you can select one or more user accounts from the list. To select an account, just click it. To select more than one account (so you can apply changes to all the selected accounts with one operation), hold down the Ctrl key and select accounts. If you want to select all accounts that belong to a specific group, choose User, Select Users. User Manager displays the Select Users dialog box (see fig. 10.2). Click the group whose member accounts you want to select, then click the Select button. Repeat the process until all of the desired accounts are selected. Then, choose Close to return to User Manager.

To work with the user database for a domain other than your home domain, choose User, Select Domain. From the Select Domain dialog box that appears, choose the domain you want to administer and choose OK.

Creating User Accounts

User Manager is the tool you use to create and modify user accounts. When you create an account, you specify general information such as the user's name and password. You also apply permissions and set other logon restrictions. The following sections explain the steps for creating a user account.

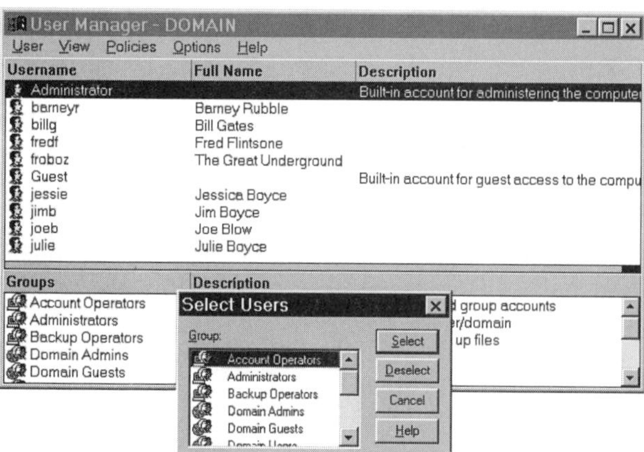

Fig. 10.2 Select all members in a group using the Select Users dialog box.

> **Note**
>
> The following sections explain how to create an account. To modify an account, just double-click the account in User Manager, then use the techniques and controls explained in the following sections to set account properties.

Specifying General Account Information

To begin creating a user account, choose User, New User to open the New User dialog box shown in figure 10.3. In the Username text box, type the name for the new account. This is the name by which the user will log on to the computer or domain.

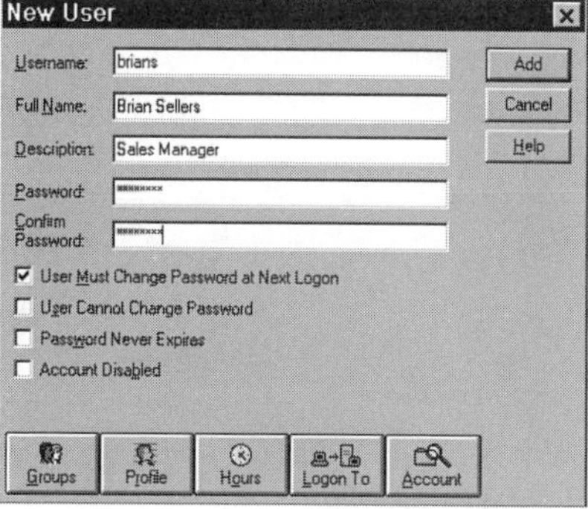

Fig. 10.3 Start the account by specifying basic information such as username and password.

Next, type the user's full name in the Full Name text box. Type a description if you want, such as the user's office location or job title, in the Description text box. In the Password text box, type the password you want to assign to the account. Then, in the Confirm Password text box, type the password again. This is the password the user will provide with his account name when he logs on.

The four checkboxes on the New User dialog box control general account properties:

- *User Must Change Password at Next Logon.* Select this checkbox to force the user to change his password the next time he logs on. Windows NT will prompt the user to change the password.
- *User Cannot Change Password.* Select this checkbox to prevent the user from being able to change his password.
- *Password Never Expires.* Select this checkbox if you want the user's password to continue to be valid indefinitely. You or the user can change the password at any time.
- *Account Disabled.* Select this checkbox to disable the account. You might create a template account to use for creating other accounts, and disable the template account to prevent users from possibly logging on with it. Or, you might disable an account if it won't be used for a while.

Tip

If a user forgets his or her password, just assign a new password to the account, then give the user the new password.

Setting Group Membership

In addition to specifying general information, you need to specify to which groups a user belongs. To do so, click the Groups button on the New User dialog box to open the Group Memberships dialog box (see fig. 10.4).

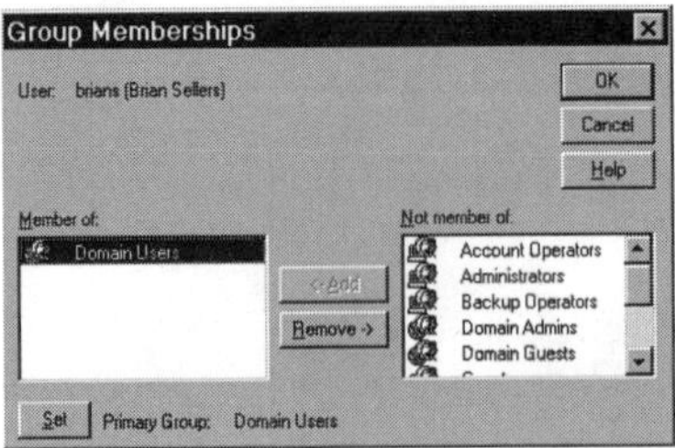

Fig. 10.4 Use the Group Memberships dialog box to specify group membership for an account.

Depending on the type of environment in which you're creating the account (domain or not), User Manager will automatically add the account to the Users or Domain Users group. Other groups you can add appear in the Not

Member Of list. To add other memberships, select the desired group and choose the Add button. To remove a group membership for a group, select the group from the Member Of list and choose Remove.

You can specify the group to be assigned as the primary group. The primary group association only affects users who log on using Windows NT Services for Macintosh or who run POSIX programs. To specify the primary group, select a group in the Member Of list and click the Set button.

When you're satisfied with the group membership assignments for the account, choose OK.

Choosing a Profile

The next step in creating an account is to specify a user profile, home directory, and logon script. To do so, click the Profile button on the New User dialog box to open the User Environment Profile dialog box (see fig. 10.5).

> **Note**
>
> Some services add to the options you can set in the User Environment Profile dialog box. This section covers the default properties.

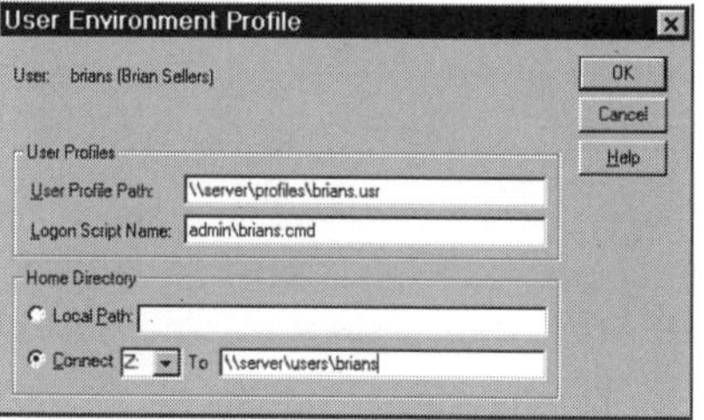

Fig. 10.5
Set a user profile, home directory, and logon script.

A profile is a special file Windows NT uses to store user settings such as desktop configuration, colors, sound assignments, and other user-definable properties. Each computer maintains a default user profile. If a user logs on and no profile is specified, the default profile is used. This profile then becomes the user's profile.

> **Tip**
>
> To support roaming users who log on from various nodes, store the profile on a network server that will be available to the user each time he logs on. This will provide the user with the same consistent, custom interface settings each time he logs on, regardless of the computer he uses.

To specify a user profile for the account, type the path to the profile file in the User Profile Path text box. For example, you might type **\\SERVER\PROFILES\BILLG.USR**, which defines the path to the file in UNC format. If you're working with multiple accounts, you can use an environment variable in place of the user's name. For example, assume you're working with six accounts, so you can't specify a single file for the profile. Instead, you enter something similar to **\\SERVER\PROFILES\%USERNAME%.USR**. User Manager replaces the variable %USERNAME% with each user's name to create or read the appropriate profile.

▶ See "Managing User Profiles," p. 230

In the Logon Script Name text box, enter the path to the logon script file for the account. You can specify the name of a batch file (BAT), command file (CMD), or executable file (EXE). Typically, logon scripts are stored in the *SYSTEMROOT*\SYSTEM32\REPL\IMPORT\SCRIPTS directory.

The Home Directory area of the User Environment Profile dialog box lets you specify the location of the user's home directory. This is the directory Windows NT will make active when the user logs on. In most cases, the user's home directory is the directory in which he stores his personal files.

◀ See "Managing Directory Replication," p. 197

You can specify a home directory on the user's local computer or on a server. To specify a local directory, select the Local Path option button, then type the local disk and directory, such as **C:\Users\Fredf**, in the Local Path text box.

Note

If a user logs on from the same computer all the time, you should use a local home directory on the user's computer to save network traffic and server disk space. Users who roam and log on from various nodes should have a home directory on a server so their home directory "follows" them and is always available.

To specify a shared network directory as the user's home directory, select the Connect option button. Then choose a drive letter from the Connect drop-down list. In the To text box, type the UNC path to the shared directory, such as \\SERVER\USERS\FREDF.

Tip

If you're working with multiple user accounts, you can use the %USERNAME% environment variable in the home directory path. User Manager replaces the user's name with the environment variable.

Setting Logon Hours

To specify when a user can log on to the system, click the Hours button in the New User dialog box to open the Logon Hours dialog box (see fig. 10.6). You might, for example, allow logon only during the week—not on weekends.

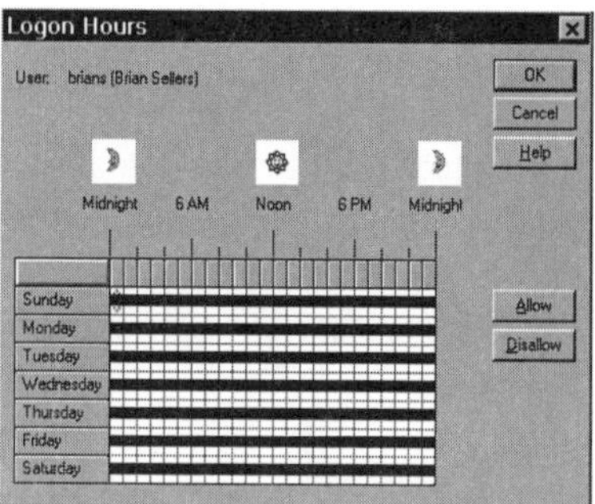

Fig. 10.6 You can control when a user has access to the system.

> **Note**
>
> The Logon Hours, Logon To, and Account buttons appear on the New User dialog box only if you are running User Manager for Domains.

By default, the user can log on at any time. To disallow logon during a specific period, select the period of time to disallow in the desired days, then choose Disallow. To disallow the same hour in every day, click the gray bar at the top of the hour column to select the hour for the entire week. Then choose Disallow.

> **Note**
>
> Disallowing logon applies only to server logon—it does not affect the user's capability to log on to a workstation locally. You might, for example, disallow logon to a server during a specific period every week to run backups on the server.

Setting Logon Restrictions

In addition to controlling when a user can log on, you can specify from which computers the user can log on to a domain. This enables you to restrict the computers a user can use to access the domain. To control logon, choose the Logon To button on the New User dialog box to open the Logon Workstations dialog box (see fig. 10.7).

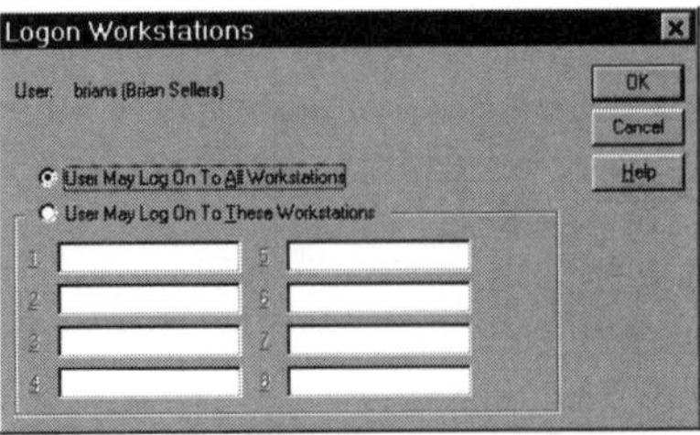

Fig. 10.7
You can specify from which computers a user can log on.

If you want to enable the user to log on to the domain from any computer, select the User May Log On To All Workstations option button. To restrict access to specific workstations, select the User May Log On To These Workstations option button. If you select the second option, you can enter up to eight workstation names in the text boxes.

Setting Account Type and Expiration

Most accounts in a domain are global, but you can create a local account. To specify the account type and expiration, choose the Account button on the New User dialog box to open the Account Information dialog box (see fig. 10.8).

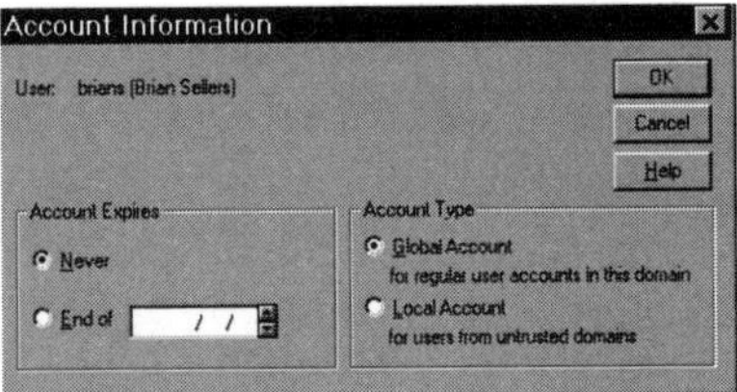

Fig. 10.8
Specify when the account expires, and the account type.

You might want to cause an account to expire for a variety of reasons. For example, the user might be a temporary employee, or the user only needs the account during a specific project. To specify that the account should expire, select the End Of option button and then use the End Of up- and down-arrows to set the date on which the account will expire. The account will expire on midnight of that date. If you don't want the account to expire, select the Never option button, which is the default.

You can also use the Account Information dialog box to specify the type of account. Select the Global Account or Local Account option button, depending on your requirements. In a domain, most accounts will be global.

Creating Groups

In addition to creating and modifying user accounts with User Manager, you can create and manage groups. After you create a group, you can add existing user accounts to that group. The following sections explain how to create local and global groups.

Creating a Local Group

To create a local group, choose User, New Local Group. The New Local Group dialog box appears (see fig. 10.9). In the Group Name text box, type the name you want to give the new group. You can use any combination of upper- and lowercase letters, except for the following:

“ / \ [ ] : ; | = , + * ? < >

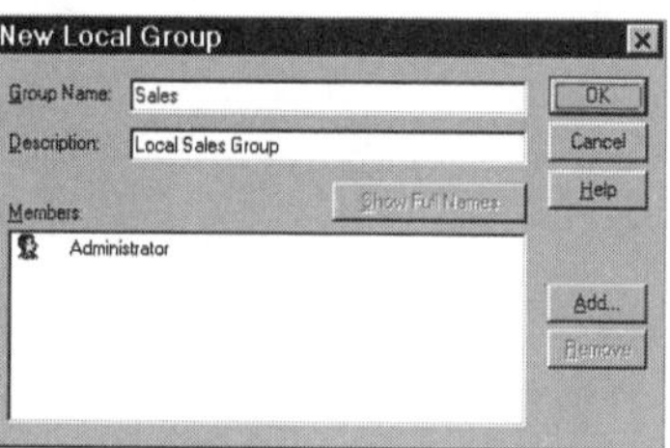

Fig. 10.9
Create local groups using the New Local Group dialog box.

In the Description text box, you can type a description for the group.

Next, you can begin assigning users to the group. Or, you can leave that task for later. To put it off, just choose the OK button. To add users now, click the Add button to display the Add Users and Groups dialog box (see fig. 10.10).

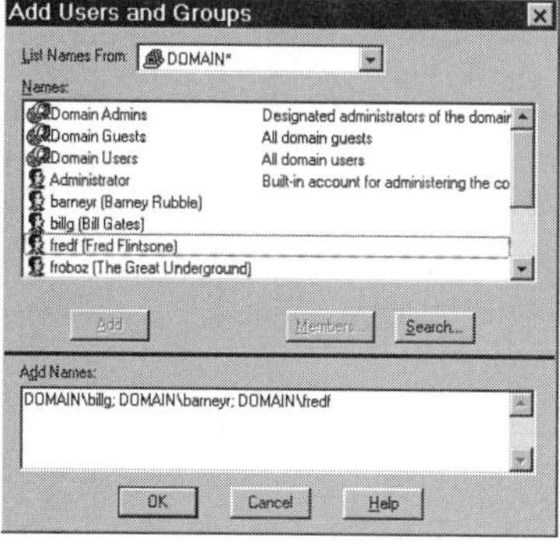

Fig. 10.10
You can add users to a group using the Add Users and Groups dialog box.

From the Names list, select all the groups and users you want to add to the new group. Then, choose Add. If you want to view the members of a listed group, select the group and choose the Members button. To delete a user or group from the list, click in the Add Names text box, highlight the name to be deleted, then press Delete. To search for a name or group locally or in a specific domain, choose the Search button.

Creating a Global Group

You create a global group in much the same way you create a local group. In User Manager, choose User, New Global Group to open the New Global Group dialog box (see fig. 10.11). As when creating a local group, type the group name in the Group Name text box and type a description in the Description text box.

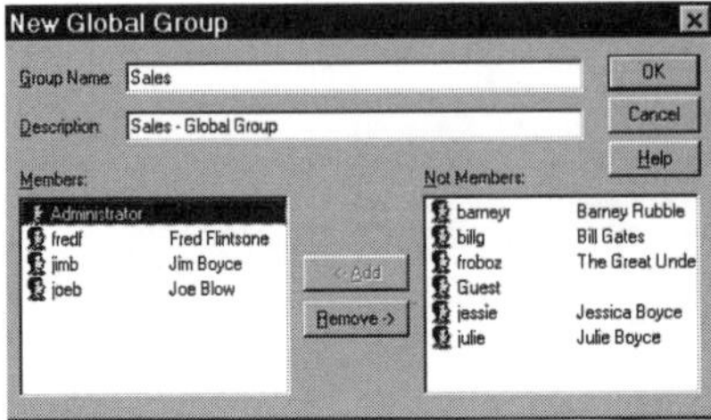

Fig. 10.11 Use the New Global Group dialog box to create global groups.

To add users to the group, select their names from the Not Members list and choose Add. To remove users from the group, choose their names from the Members list and choose Remove.

Understanding and Assigning Access Rights

A *right* grants a user (or group) the authority to perform a specific action. When a user logs on to an account to which a right has been granted (either directly or through group membership), that user can perform the task associated with the right. The following list describes the specific user rights:

- *Access this computer from the network.* This right enables a user to connect to the computer from across the network.
- *Add workstations to a domain.* With this right, a user can add workstations to a domain, which enables those workstations to recognize the domain's user accounts and global groups (enabling logon from those workstations).
- *Back up files and directories.* This right enables the user to back up files and directories on the computer, and supersedes file and directory permissions. Note that this right does not enable the user to view file or directory contents unless he has explicit permission to do so.
- *Change the system time.* With this right, the user can set the computer's system clock.
- *Force shutdown from a remote system.* This right enables the user to force a system to shut down from a remote node (such as a dialup connection).

- *Load and unload device drivers.* This right allows the user to dynamically load and unload device drivers. When you're managing a domain, this right applies to the PDC and BDCs. Outside of a domain, the right applies only to the computer on which the right is assigned.
- *Log on locally.* With this right, a user can log on to the system locally. In most cases, you don't want users to have the right to log on locally to a server, PDC, or BDC for security and performance reasons.
- *Manage auditing and security log.* This right, enables a user to manage auditing of files, directories, and other objects.
- *Restore files and directories.* With this right, a user can restore files that have previously been backed up. Note that having backup permission does not give a user restore permission, and vice versa.
- *Shut down the system.* This right enables the user to shut down the computer.
- *Take ownership of files or other objects.* With this right, a user can take ownership of files, directories, and printers. When you're managing a domain, this right applies to the PDC and BDCs. Outside of a domain, the right applies only to the computer on which the right is assigned.
- *Bypass traverse checking.* This right enables a user to traverse directory trees, even if she lacks the permission to traverse a directory. This right doesn't supersede ownership or permissions—if you don't have the necessary permission to see the contents of a directory, you still won't see its contents, although you can traverse the directory.
- *Log on as a service.* This right is designed to allow processes to register with the system as a service.

Note

Don't confuse rights with permissions—they are different. *Rights* apply to system-wide objects and tasks, and *permissions* apply to specific objects such as files and printers.

Generally, you control user rights by placing the user in a group whose rights you've already assigned. You also can assign rights on an account-by-account basis. To assign rights, open User Manager and choose Policies, User Rights. The User Rights Policy dialog box appears (see fig. 10.12).

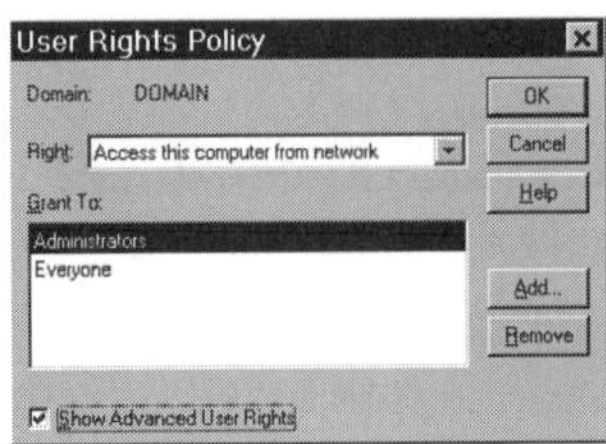

Fig. 10.12 Assign user rights to groups with the User Rights Policy dialog box.

From the Right drop-down list, choose the right you want to assign. Then, if the desired group is not already listed in the Grant To list, choose the Add button to display the Add Users and Groups dialog box (see fig. 10.13).

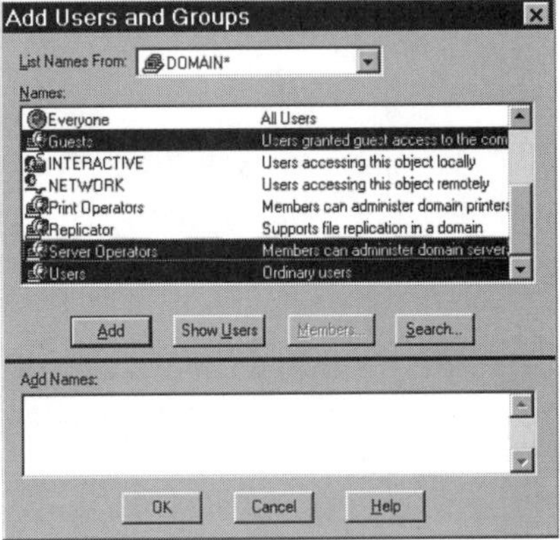

Fig. 10.13 You can assign the selected right to any combination of users and groups.

If you only want to assign the selected right to various groups, select the groups from the Names list and choose Add. To add the right to specific users, click the Show Users button to cause User Manager to display individual accounts as well as groups in the Names list. Choose the names from the list, then choose Add. When you're satisfied with the list, choose OK to return to the User Rights Policy dialog box. Repeat the process for any other rights you want to assign.

Controlling Resource Access

Now that you understand user accounts and groups, it's time to start using them to control access to shared resources. First, you need to understand permissions.

Understanding Permissions

In Windows NT, *permissions* determine the authority a user has to access certain types of resources, such as files, directories, printers, and other objects and services. The permissions that apply to specific objects depend on the object's type. The permissions for a printer, for example, are different from the permissions for a file. In addition, file permissions vary according to the type of file system being used. You have much finer control over access on NTFS file systems than FAT file systems.

Note

On an NTFS volume, you can set file and directory permissions independently. On FAT volumes, you can only set directory permissions. On both file systems, you can set permissions for shared directories. Permissions on NTFS volumes apply to local users, but this is not the case for the FAT file system. However, you can restrict access to FAT volumes simply by preventing local logon.

You can apply the following permissions to directories on NTFS volumes:

- *No Access.* This permission prevents the user from accessing the directory in any way, even if the user belongs to a group that has been granted access to the directory.
- *List.* With this permission, the user can only list the files and subdirectories in this directory and change to a subdirectory of this directory. The user can't access new files created in the directory.
- *Read.* This permission enables the user to read and execute files.
- *Add.* With this right, a user can add new files to the directory, but can't read or change existing files.
- *Add & Read.* This right combines the Read and Add permissions.
- *Change.* A user can read and add files to a directory, and change the contents of existing files.
- *Full Control.* A user can read and change files, add new files, change permissions for the directory and its files, and take ownership of the directory and its files.

You can assign the following rights to files on NTFS volumes:

- *No Access.* This prevents the user from accessing the file, even if she belongs to a group that has been granted access to the file.
- *Read.* This right enables the user to read and execute files.
- *Change.* The user can read, modify, and delete the file.
- *Full Control.* This right enables the user to read, modify, delete, set permissions for, and take ownership of the file.

A set of additional permissions enable you to control access to printers. These printer-related permissions are:

- *No Access.* This permission prevents any access to the printer and its queue.
- *Print.* Users with this permission can print to the printer, but can't change the queue or any other printer properties.
- *Manage Documents.* This permission enables a user to control settings for individual documents in the queue, and to pause, resume, restart, and delete documents in a queue. It does not provide print permission, which must be granted separately.
- *Full Control.* This permission gives a user complete control over a printer, including printing and managing documents. The user also can delete a printer and change its properties.

Applying Permissions

You typically set permissions when you share an object, and you can modify those permissions at any time. You can set permissions using more than one method, which vary according to the type of resource. The following sections explain how to set permissions on disk and printer resources.

◀ See "Managing Shared Directories," p. 200

Setting Disk Resource Permissions

You can share directories and files through Explorer or File Manager. This section focuses on Explorer to explain how to apply permissions.

Before you can set permissions on a directory, you must share the directory. To do so, follow these steps:

1. Open Explorer (or a folder window), then locate and select the directory.
2. Right-click the directory and choose Sharing to open the Sharing page of the directory's property sheet.
3. Select the Shared As option button.
4. Windows NT uses the directory name as the default share name. If you want to use a different name, highlight the name in the Share Name text box and type a different name.
5. (Optional) Type a comment for the share in the Comment text box.
6. In the User Limit group, specify the maximum numbers of users who can connect to the share, or select the Maximum Allowed to allow an unlimited number of users to access the share.
7. Click the Permissions button to open the Access Through Share Permissions dialog box (see fig. 10.14).

8. To change a permission, select the group you want to change from the Name list, then select the desired permission from the Type of Access drop-down list.
9. To add a group or user, click the Add button to display the Add Users and Groups dialog box.

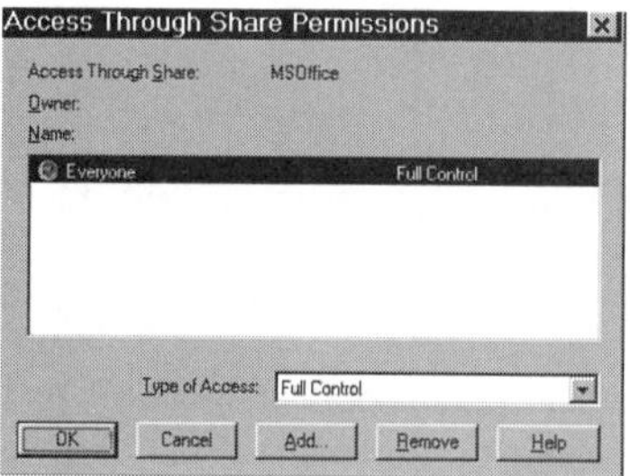

Fig. 10.14
By default, Windows NT grants full control to everyone.

10. Select the users and groups you want to add, then choose Add, followed by OK.
11. Repeat step 8 to change the permissions for specific groups and users, and then choose OK.

> **Note**
>
> To set permissions on a directory that is already shared, open Explorer and select the directory. Or, open a folder window and select the directory. Then, right-click the directory and choose Sharing. Click the Permissions button to begin changing or adding permissions.

You can set permissions on individual files only on NTFS volumes. To set permissions on files, select the files in Explorer, then right-click a file in the selection and choose Properties. Click the Security tab, and then click the Permissions button to open the File Permissions dialog box (see fig. 10.15). Adding and modifying group and user permissions is then similar to the process described previously for directories.

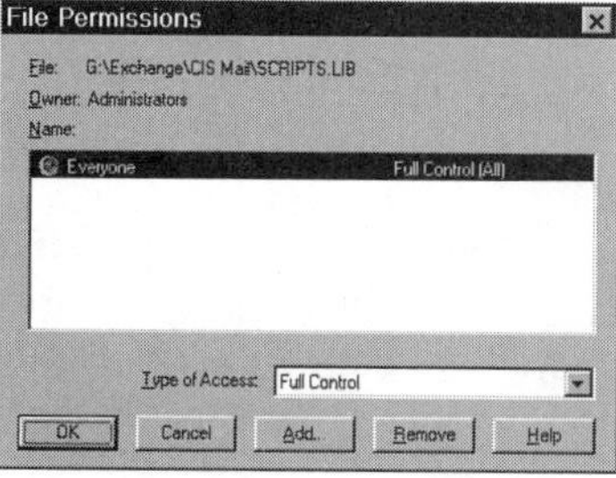

Fig. 10.15
You can set permissions on individual files on NTFS volumes.

Setting Printer Permissions

You set printer permissions in much the same way you set disk permissions:

1. After you have shared the printer, open the Printers folder and right-click the printer. Then, choose Properties.
2. Click the Security tab to display the Security property page.
3. Click the Permissions button to open the Printer Permissions dialog box (see fig. 10.16).

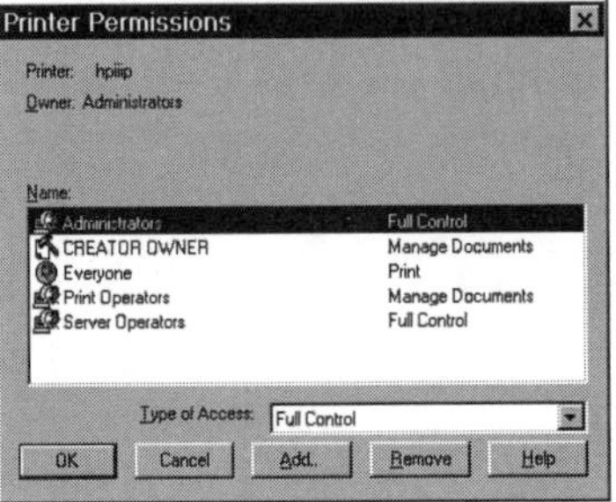

Fig. 10.16
Use the Printer Permissions dialog box to set printer permissions.

4. To change an existing group's permission, select the group from the Name list and select the desired permission from the Type of Access drop-down list.
5. To add a user or group, click the Add button to display the Add Users and Groups dialog box.
6. Select the users and groups you want to add, then choose Add, followed by OK.
7. Choose OK to close the Printer Permissions dialog box.

Managing User Profiles

User profiles enable a user's desktop settings and other interface and operating parameters to be retained from session to session. If a user's profile is stored on a server on the domain, the user can have the same interface and settings regardless of which computer he uses to log on to the domain. In addition, profiles enable you to control the types of changes a user can make to his working environment.

Understanding Profiles

A *profile* is a group of settings stored in a special type of Registry file that works in conjunction with a set of folders and shortcuts to create the user's working environment. When a user logs on, Windows NT reads the user's profile and structures the Windows NT desktop according to the settings in the profile. These settings include such things as desktop colors, sounds, and other Control Panel settings; specific accessory application settings (Notepad, WordPad, and so on); network printer connections; and other user environment settings.

The first type of profile you can assign to a user is called a *personal profile*. The personal profile can be changed by the user from one logon session to another, subject to certain restrictions in the profile itself. This type of profile enables a user to make changes to her profile and retain those changes for future logon sessions.

The second type of profile is called a *mandatory profile*. A mandatory profile is almost identical to a personal profile, except that changes do not carry from one session to another. You can give a user the capability to change certain settings even with a mandatory profile, but those changes are not stored permanently in the user's profile. The profile reverts to its original state for the next logon session.

Tip

The only difference between a personal profile and a mandatory profile is the name of the Registry file. A personal profile has the file extension DAT, and a mandatory profile uses the file extension MAN.

If a user has no profile, Windows NT uses a *default profile* from the user's logon workstation. That profile is then saved as the user's profile for future logon sessions.

Profiles serve two purposes:

- Profiles provide a unique user interface configuration for each user, and allow that configuration to move with the user from workstation to workstation.
- Profiles enable the administrator to control the types of changes a user can make to his working environment.

Profiles are created automatically when you log on to a system and make changes to the user environment. In previous versions of Windows NT, the User Profile Editor enabled you to create and modify user profiles. The User Profile Editor has been replaced by the System Policy Editor, which installs automatically when you install Windows NT Server (it is not included with Workstation). The System Policy Editor provides finer control over each workstation's and user's profile, so you should consider using the system policy rather than profiles to control user restrictions.

Supporting Transient Users

If you have users who log on to the domain from different workstations, you probably want those users to have a consistent interface, regardless of the workstation they log on from. The way to achieve this is to place the users' profiles on the domain controller, and replicate the profiles (and logon scripts, if applicable) across the network. When you create the users' accounts, specify the network location for the profile. When the user logs on, Windows NT will read the profile across the network and configure the workstation accordingly.

> **Note**
>
> When you are configuring profiles for transient users, remember that hardware settings could easily vary from one workstation to another. Make sure the profiles you create can be supported by the workstations from which the users will be logging on.

Setting Account Policies

The *account policy* determines how passwords are handled for all user accounts and it controls global logon parameters. To specify account policy settings, first open User Manager and select the domain whose account policy you want to set. Then, choose Policies, Account to open the Account Policy dialog box (see fig. 10.17).

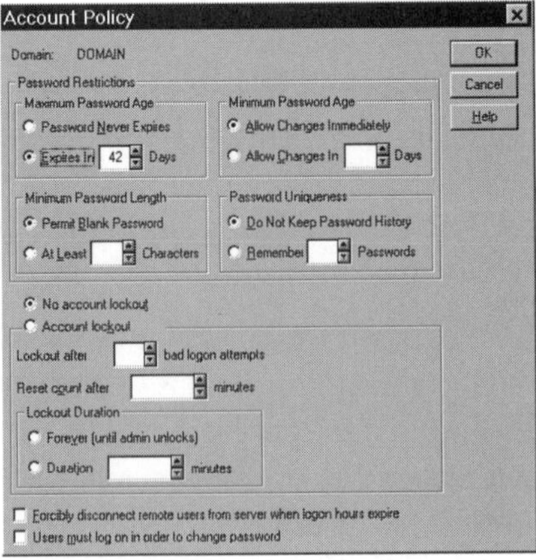

Fig. 10.17 Specify global logon parameters using the Account Policy dialog box.

The following list summarizes the settings you can specify in the Account Policy dialog box:

- *Domain (or Computer).* This read-only entry specifies the name of the domain or computer whose account policy you're modifying.
- *Maximum Password Age.* Use this group to specify when, if ever, user passwords expire. You can specify a value between 1 and 999 days, or select Password Never Expires to allow users to keep the same password indefinitely.
- *Minimum Password Age.* Use this group to specify how long a password must be used before the user can change it.
- *Minimum Password Length.* Use this group to specify the minimum number of characters each password must be. You can specify a value from 1 to 14 characters as the minimum. For best security, you should not use the Permit Blank Password option.
- *Password Uniqueness.* This group enables you to control whether a user can reuse an old password. If you don't care how often or how soon a user can reuse a password, select the Do Not Keep Password History option button. Otherwise, specify a value from 1 to 8.
- *No Account Lockout.* If you select this option, users are never locked out of the system—regardless of the number of failed login attempts they make (such as specifying an incorrect password).
- *Account Lockout.* Use this option and group to specify how many failed logon attempts a user can make before being locked out of the system, and how soon the user can reattempt logon.
- *Forcibly Disconnect Remote Users From Server When Logon Hours Expire.* Select this checkbox if you want the user to be automatically logged off when the logon time defined for their account expires.
- *Users Must Log On In Order To Change Password.* If you select this checkbox, a user whose password has expired must have an administrator set a new password for his account. If this checkbox is not selected, the user can change his password without notifying the administrator.

When you're satisfied with the account policies, choose OK to close the dialog box. ❖

CHAPTER 11

Understanding and Modifying the Registry

by Serdar Yegulalp

When Windows 3.0 and 3.1 were the kings of the Windows roost, all system settings were stored in a set of plain-text initialization files. These files were known more commonly as INI files because of their common three-letter file extension of INI. Because Windows itself tended to be less complex, a plain-text file did the trick nicely, as it had worked before with CONFIG.SYS for DOS.

When Windows 3.0 was expanded into Windows for Workgroups and Windows NT, Microsoft realized that the INI file structure had severe inherent problems. The files were hard to maintain; they often bulked up over time with settings from programs long deleted. The files also became harder to organize, because of the multitude and diversity of Windows applications being written.

With the introduction of Windows NT, a whole new approach was needed—one that would also be in line with Windows NT's goals of security and stability. What Microsoft came up with was the *Registry*: a unified database that contains all system and program settings in a regimented, organized fashion.

The Registry is designed to replace not only INI files, but CONFIG.SYS and AUTOEXEC.BAT as well. The only time Windows NT allows INI files to exist is when 16-bit programs generate and work with them.

When Microsoft designed Windows 95, it incorporated the Registry structure into its design. It seems probable that the Registry will continue to be used in future versions of Windows.

In this chapter, you'll learn about

- The structure of the Registry—keys and values
- The types of data stored in the Registry: binary, text, and DWORD values
- Using the REGEDIT program, which lets you make changes to the Registry
- Importing and exporting Registry entries
- Connecting to a network Registry

An Overview of the Registry

The Windows NT Registry is organized into two main files:

- *USER.DAT*. As the name implies, this section of the Registry stores all settings specific to individual users, from their Desktop settings to their Startup menu contents.
- *SYSTEM.DAT*. This branch of the Registry stores Windows NT's general hardware and software settings.

Several layers of protection guard the data in these files. All Registry files are stored in an encrypted binary format that can't be read without the proper tools and user authorization. It's not possible to hack the Registry with a plain-text editor. Also, the Registry files are marked as read-only, hidden system files to prevent them from being deleted or discovered accidentally, even by someone with administrator privileges.

You use a program called the Registry Editor to view and edit the Registry. The Registry Editor will only be used to show segments of the Registry for the examples in this chapter; however, later in the chapter you will learn how to use the Registry to actually make changes.

Keys

All the data in the Registry is stored as *values*. These values are organized and grouped into headings and subheadings called *keys*.

The left pane of the Registry Editor lists all the keys in the Registry (see fig. 11.1). The keys are grouped into headings and subheadings, much like the levels of an outline. For example, the HKEY_CURRENT_USER key contains a number of other keys that relate to the current user's settings, such as AppEvents (which governs things like sound effects assigned to system actions) and Keyboard Layout. Each of these keys may have keys under them, and so on. There is no realistic limit to the number of key levels.

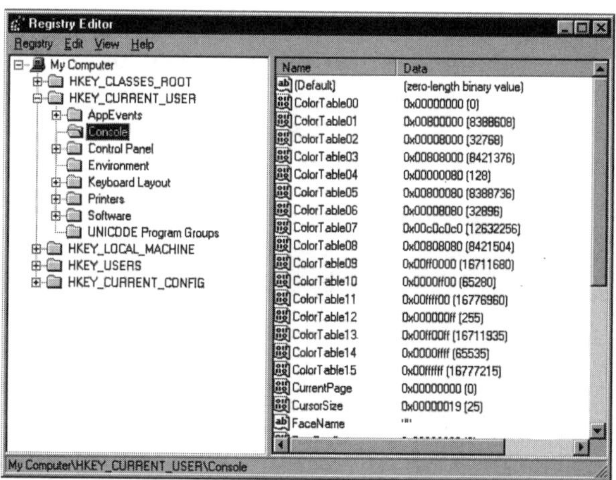

Fig. 11.1
This segment of the Registry displays the current user's console settings.

Keys are referred to by listing all of their parent keys (from the top down in the hierarchy) separated by slashes. For example, the highlighted key in figure 11.1 would be referred to as My Computer\HKEY_CURRENT_USER\Console. (The topmost key is the name of another computer if you're looking at a network Registry.) Because most of the Registry references in this chapter are on the local machine, I'll leave off "My Computer" in future examples.

Values

When you select a particular key, the right pane of the Registry Editor lists all the values assigned to that particular key. In figure 11.1, the Console key has many values attached to it. For example, the HistoryBufferSize value, which contains the size of the history buffer (the number of previous commands remembered by the Run command in the Start button), is currently set to 50 (or 32 in hexadecimal).

There is no realistic limit to the number of values that can be assigned to a key.

There are three types of values:

- *String values.* String values are alphanumeric strings of any length. In the Registry Editor, strings are indicated by being enclosed in quotation marks. For example, the FaceName key in figure 11.1 is a zero-length string value.
- *Binary values.* Binary values are strings of binary data entered in hexadecimal format, and can be of any length. Binary values are listed in the Registry as strings of hexadecimal pairs, such as "EF DB OC 26 45 A0."

- *DWORD values.* DWORD values are 32-bit hexadecimal numbers and can be entered in either decimal or hexadecimal format. DWORD values are listed in the Registry Editor in both hexadecimal and decimal format. For example, the CursorSize entry has a DWORD value of 0x00000019 in hexadecimal, or 25 in decimal. The decimal number is in parentheses.

> **Caution**
>
> Binary values or binary key names should generally be left alone, unless you're working from very specific instructions on how to change them (and have a good reason for doing so). The slightest change in some of these entries can prove fatal to your system.

Key Organization in the Registry

In the previous figure 11.1, five main keys are listed in the left pane of the Registry Editor. All Windows NT Registries have these five main keys. Each key is devoted to a different aspect of the system and user configurations, as shown in figure 11.2.

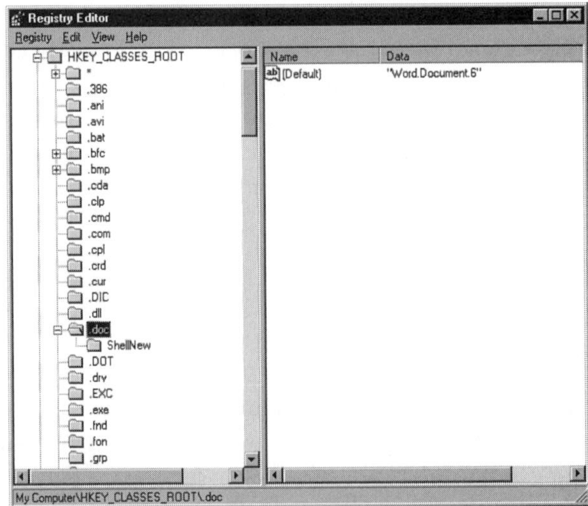

Fig. 11.2 The HKEY_ CLASSES_ROOT KEY contains both file extensions and file object names.

HKEY_CLASSES_ROOT

The HKEY_CLASSES_ROOT key stores file associations and extensions, as well as information about the programs they are associated with. Two kinds of data are stored as keys in HKEY_CLASSES_ROOT:

- *File extensions.* The three-letter extensions that both NTFS and FAT use to designate different types of files are listed as keys. The type of object they represent is stored as a string value. For example, figure 11.2 shows that the file extension `.doc` represents a file of type `"Word.Document.6"` (which refers to Microsoft Word version 6). File extensions have a dot as the first character of their key name.
- *Object descriptions.* File extensions can be associated with object descriptions, which are sets of keys that tell Windows NT more about a specific kind of file other than what its extension should be. In figure 11.3, the `Word.Document.6` object has a number of sub-keys that tell Windows NT what kind of icon to associate with it (the DefaultIcon key) and what commands to use when a user asks to execute or print the file. The right pane contains the string value associated with opening the file. In this case, Windows NT will run Word for Windows with the filename passed to it as an argument.

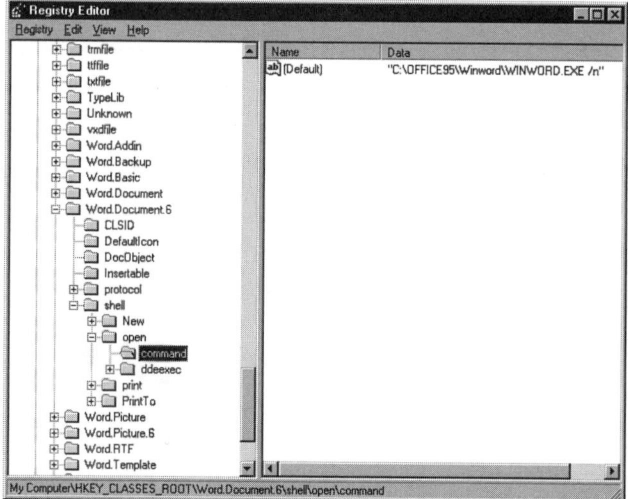

Fig. 11.3
Object descriptions in the Registry match with file extensions, telling the operating system how to represent them and what to do with them.

> **Note**
>
> Keeping object descriptions and file extensions discrete allows for more flexibility in the way programs work, among other things. For example, if future versions of Microsoft Word used WRD as their file extension, the WRD extension could be associated with the `Word.Document.6` object without breaking any existing settings.

The whole process of associating file extensions with object types and program actions doesn't have to be done by hacking the Registry directly; it's normally done through choosing View, Options and then working on the File Types tab when you're in Explorer.

HKEY_CURRENT_USER

HKEY_CURRENT_USER contains the settings for the user logged in at the root console (see fig. 11.4). All of the user settings are originally stored as keys in HKEY_USERS; they are copied to HKEY_CURRENT_USER when a user logs on.

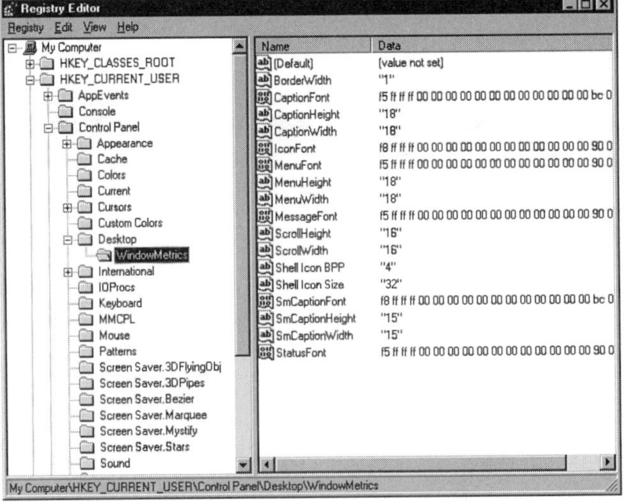

Fig. 11.4
The HKEY_CURRENT_USER key contains settings that vary for each user logged in.

HKEY_CURRENT_USER usually contains these sub-keys:

- *AppEvents.* The AppEvents key is subdivided into EventLabels and Schemes. Schemes contains the names of specific system events and the multimedia events (typically WAV sounds) associated with them. EventLabels contains plain-English names for each application event.

- *Console.* Contains settings that govern the appearance of the user console (the command line, not the desktop). Examples of console settings include whether or not Insert mode is turned on by default.
- *Control Panel.* The keys under Control Panel contain all the desktop settings that are changed through Control Panel, including custom colors, window metrics, mouse sensitivity settings, and so on.
- *Environment.* Miscellaneous environment settings that are holdovers from MS-DOS and older Windows versions, including SET= strings.
- *Keyboard Layout.* Data on which keyboard layout is operable.
- *Printers.* Binary-stored settings for each installed printer. The best way to modify this is by choosing the Printers icon and making changes from there because the individual settings aren't called out.
- *Software.* Settings for specific programs, grouped by manufacturer. When you expand this key, you usually see an entry for Microsoft and entries for specific Microsoft programs under it (including Windows NT). If you have Netscape's Netcruiser installed, Netscape will have its own key, and so on.
- *UNICODE Program Groups.* Used by Windows NT to refer to programs that use Unicode internally.

Note

Some HKEY_CURRENT_USER keys may contain more entries than the ones listed here. This is not abnormal; some programs (and future versions of Windows NT) will do this deliberately. The only time you should worry is if a key seems to consist of garbage characters or can't be deleted. (Always be very careful when deleting keys, however.)

HKEY_LOCAL_MACHINE

The HKEY_LOCAL_MACHINE key contains the keys that describe the hardware, security, and software settings of the machine. It describes anything that isn't linked to a specific user, but rather to the machine as a whole.

HKEY_LOCAL_MACHINE usually contains the sub-keys described in the following sections, although there may be others depending on your system's configuration.

HARDWARE

HARDWARE lists both the hardware installed in your system and the resources allocated to the hardware. The following sub-keys are used under

HARDWARE to further describe what's installed and how:

- *DESCRIPTION.* Describes what devices are actually installed by using ID numbers, and contains binary strings to describe the devices' configuration states. Generally not user-editable.
- *DEVICEMAP.* Lists how the devices are organized and labeled according to the device hierarchy that Windows NT uses. DEVICEMAP also lists where the precise device descriptions are to be found elsewhere in the Registry. For example, the KeyboardClass key tells Windows NT where to find and what to call all devices in the Keyboard class of device. Right now there's only one such device: \Device\KeyboardClass0. Its driver resources are in HKEY_LOCAL_MACHINE\SYSTEM\ControlSet001\Services\Kbdclass.
- *RESOURCEMAP.* Lists the physical resources occupied by hardware devices, such as the IRQ for a COM: port.

SECURITY

As the name implies, SECURITY contains Windows NT's storehouse of security information, such as user privileges and passwords. Don't be surprised if you open this key in the Registry and don't see anything. No user—not even the Administrator—is allowed to edit or even see the entries in SECURITY.

SOFTWARE

The SOFTWARE key contains the following keys.

- *Classes.* This is the source from which the HKEY_CLASSES_ROOT key is copied.
- *Description.* Contains other detailed information about installed software. Nothing user-modifiable shows up in here.
- *Microsoft.* Contains settings specific to Microsoft-related applications. Other manufacturers, such as Netscape, may install their own keys in SOFTWARE to hold settings for their programs as well.
- *Program Groups.* Holds information about program groups that have been added to the Start button's Programs option since Windows NT was first installed. This key is useful for tracking what to remove when an application is uninstalled.

- *Windows 3.1 Migration Status.* Contains information about Program Manager groups and overall system settings if you've installed Windows NT over a Windows 3.1 or Windows for Workgroups installation.

SYSTEM

The SYSTEM key is home to backup copies of the system hardware profiles and device lists. It also holds options that were selected during Windows NT Setup.

For example, the SYSTEM\Setup key contains a value named WinntPath, which is a string value that contains the MS-DOS pathname from where Windows NT files are to be installed (such as new drivers). If you originally installed from a subdirectory on a hard drive and want to force Windows NT to get new files from a CD-ROM drive instead, change the WinntPath setting to the path for your CD-ROM drive. For example, if your CD-ROM drive is D: and you installed from the I386 subdirectory, set WinntPath to `D:\i386\`.

HKEY_USERS

HKEY_USERS is the original repository for user-specific keys that get copied to HKEY_CURRENT_USER when a user logs on. There are always at least two child keys in HKEY_USERS: .DEFAULT and the Administrator user profile. .DEFAULT lists the default HKEY_CURRENT_USER options for newly created user profiles. More keys get created as more users are added to the system database.

If you open HKEY_CURRENT_USER, you'll see that the Administrator profile is not referred to with a key named "Administrator," but with a unique serial number. This serial number is used system-wide for allocating security; it prevents fraudulently created user accounts, or user accounts created after the fact, from being able to access restricted resources.

Assume you have a user named WillD who has a certain directory shared specifically with him. If you delete his user account and create a new one with exactly the same username, password, and so on, he still won't be able to re-access the shared directory with that account. He'll have to get that directory re-shared to his new account. As with many other things in Windows NT, the access control is not based on something as simple as the username, but rather the underlying user serial number (see fig. 11.5).

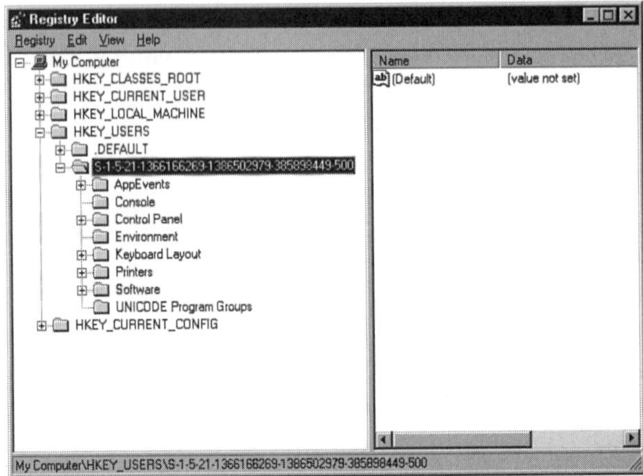

Fig. 11.5
The HKEY_USERS key, with its unique user ID numbers.

Caution

Never attempt to change user serial numbers. You'll corrupt Windows NT's security, and possibly render your system unusable in the future. Changing settings associated with an HKEY_USERS repository is one thing; hacking the actual user number is another.

This is especially true for the Administrator account. If you ruin the Administrator account, you will have to reinstall everything to get back into Windows NT. At the very least, you'll have to use a Windows NT Emergency Repair Disk.

HKEY_CURRENT_CONFIG

The HKEY_CURRENT_CONFIG key contains a few critical hardware configuration settings that are used by Windows NT to determine the hardware configuration to use when the system is booted. Typically, this is just the video hardware settings, but other settings that would be critical for starting Windows NT correctly would also be kept here.

Differences Between the Windows NT and Windows 95 Registries

As mentioned at the beginning of the chapter, both Windows 95 and Windows NT use the Registry to store settings for the operating system and for applications. However, there are enough differences between the way Windows NT and Windows 95 use the Registry to make many of the techniques used for modifying the Registry on one platform unusable on the other. This difference was far more distinct in Windows 3.51 and Windows 95 than it is now with Windows NT 4.0. This is because Windows NT 4.0 incorporated many of the changes made to Windows 95, such as the revised shell. However, there are still enough differences between the way Windows NT uses the Registry and the way Windows 95 uses the Registry to make them worth noting:

- *Hardware configurations*. Windows NT handles hardware entirely differently than Windows 95, not only by disallowing direct reads or writes to hardware devices, but by storing device descriptions and settings in the Registry in a totally different fashion. Some of the details about how devices are referenced in the Registry were covered earlier in the chapter.
- *Security*. Windows 95 is not designed to be inherently secure. Granted, the password system in Windows 95 prevents a casual intruder from getting past your screen saver, but Windows NT is designed to be inherently far more secure. Certain parts of the Registry, such as the HKEY_LOCAL_MACHINE\SECURITY key, are not viewable or editable by users or even Administrators.

There is a significant reason for mentioning this: A Windows 95 user who becomes a Windows NT user may try implementing one of the many Registry changes that alter Windows 95's functioning in one way or another. An example is the key HKEY_CURRENT_USER\Control Panel\desktop\WindowMetrics. In Windows 95, adding the value `MinAnimate="0"` turns off the "flying windows" animation that takes place when you minimize a window. In Windows NT, the same change has no effect. This is an innocuous example, but if a Windows 95 hacker tries to change something not so innocuous without knowing exactly what he's doing, serious damage could result. If you're planning to make *any* changes to the Windows NT Registry, make sure those changes work for Windows NT and not simply Windows 95.

Using the Registry Editor

You use the Registry Editor program to view or make changes to the Registry. Because making changes to the Registry can be risky, the Registry Editor is not on any of the submenus on the Start menu—not even for the Administrator accounts.

To run the Registry Editor, follow these steps:

1. Open the Start menu and choose Run.
2. Type **regedit** in the Open list box and press Enter. The Registry Editor opens as shown in figure 11.6.

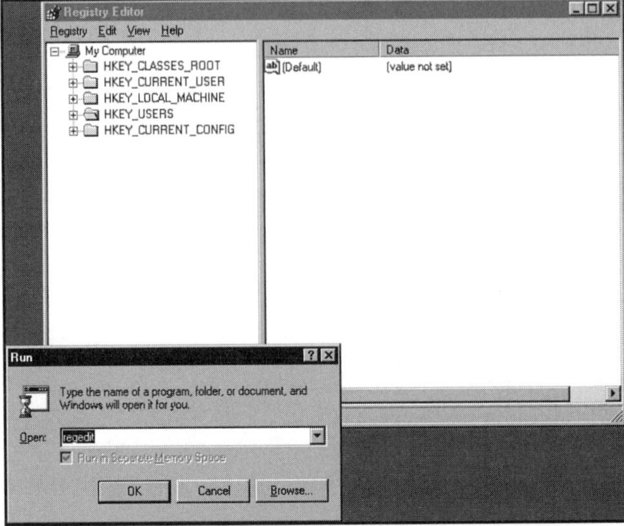

Fig. 11.6
The Registry Editor, immediately after being opened.

The only reason to look at or make changes to the Registry is if there's no other way to get to the data you need. If you can make the changes you want in another, safer way—such as through the Control Panel—try that first before hacking around with your system's settings.

Caution

If you have to make changes to the Registry, be very cautious. The Registry Editor has the power to *completely* mess up your system. (Go back and read that sentence again!) It's safe to use the Registry Editor to browse settings, but be sure you know *exactly* what you're doing before you change anything. What may seem like a trivial change may not turn out to be trivial at all.

Adding Keys

Generally, only applications will add or delete keys to or from the Registry. Adding keys to the Registry is less destructive than deleting keys, because a key that doesn't refer to anything is usually ignored by the operating system. Nevertheless, adding keys is still something that should not be taken lightly.

To add keys to the Registry, use the following procedure.

1. Open the Registry Editor if you haven't already done so.
2. In the left pane of the Registry Editor, select the key that will be the parent for the new key (see fig. 11.7). In other words, choose the key that you want the new key to go under.

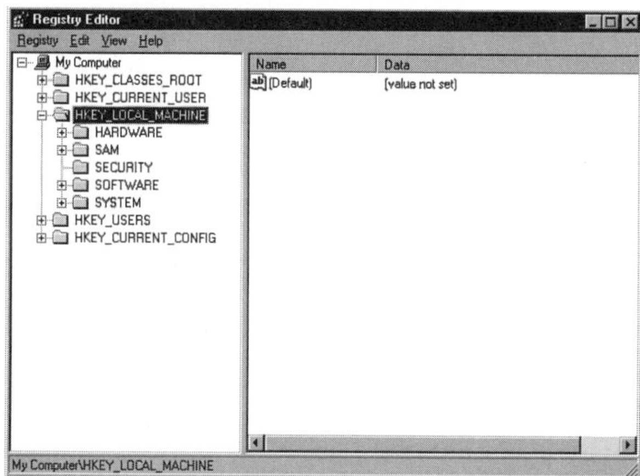

Fig. 11.7
The selected key will be the parent for the newly created key.

3. From the Registry Editor menu, choose Edit, New, Key. You can also right-click the parent key and choose New, Key (see fig. 11.8).

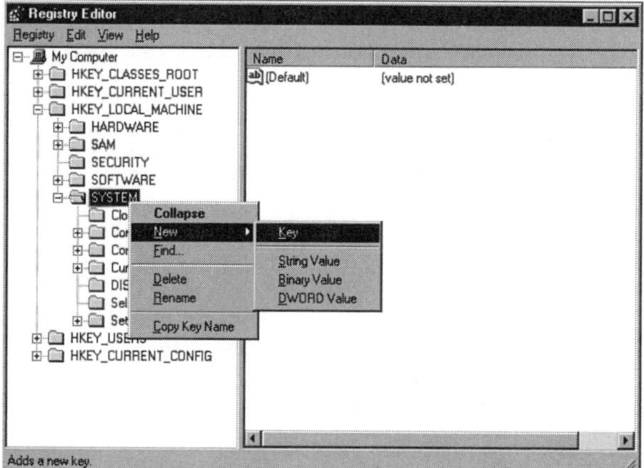

Fig. 11.8
Right-clicking the parent key gives you a shortcut menu from which you can choose to create a new key.

4. A new key labeled `New Key #1` appears (see fig. 11.9). This is the default name for a newly created key. At this time, you can type a name for the new key, because the key's name will be activated for editing. If you don't want to change the name yet, press Enter.

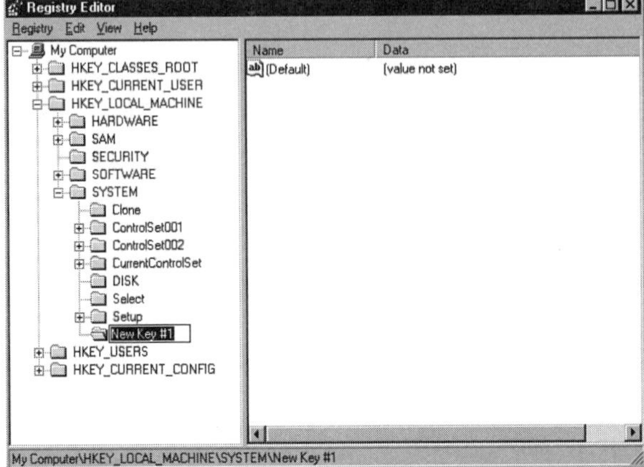

Fig. 11.9 The newly created key, with its name field in edit mode.

Deleting Keys

Deleting a key is far riskier than adding one. Again, always know what you're deleting and why before you run the risk of destroying potentially irreplaceable system settings.

> **Caution**
>
> Deleting a key also deletes all values and keys under that key. Make sure the key you're removing doesn't have child values that could be important.

To delete a key, follow these steps:

1. If you haven't started the Registry Editor, do so.
2. In the left pane of the Registry Editor, select the key you want to delete (see fig. 11.10).

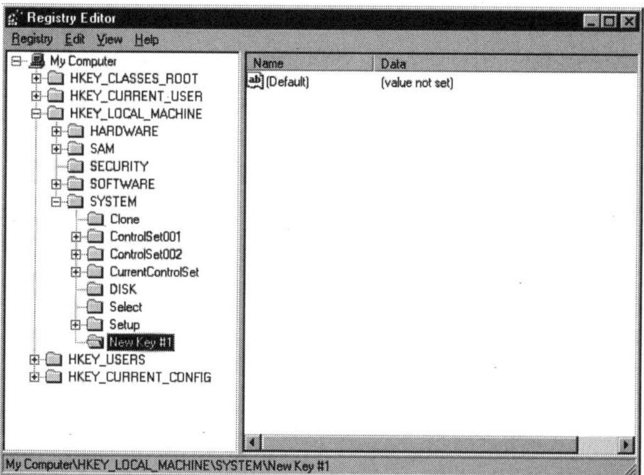

Fig. 11.10
The newly created key to be deleted is highlighted here.

3. Press the Delete key. Alternately, you can right-click the key and select the Delete option, or you can choose Edit, Delete from the Registry Editor menu.

> **Note**
>
> Certain keys cannot be deleted by default. For example, HKEY_CLASSES_ROOT cannot be removed. If a key cannot be deleted, the Delete options on the Registry Editor Edit menu and on the shortcut menu will be grayed out.

Adding Values

As with adding keys, adding values that aren't recognized by the system or applications software isn't recommended. Similarly, adding values has less of a chance of adversely affecting the system than deleting values.

To add a value to a key, follow these steps:

1. In the Registry Editor, select the key to which you want to add the value from the left panel (see fig. 11.11).

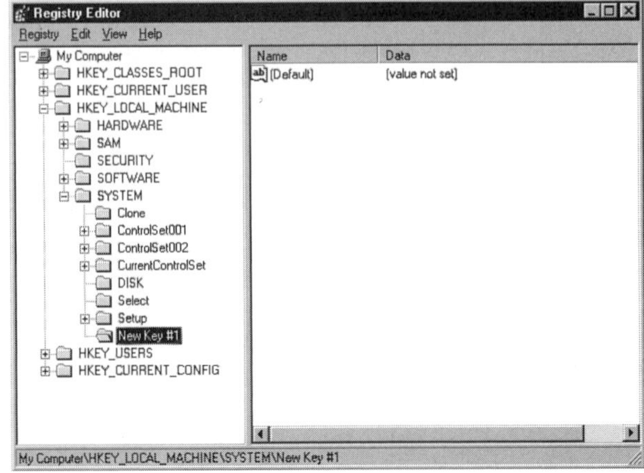

Fig. 11.11
You will add a value to the selected key (which is the key created in the previous section).

2. From the Registry Editor menu, choose Edit, New. Then, choose String Value, Binary Value, or DWORD Value, depending on the kind of value you want to add. Alternately, you can right-click the selected key in the left pane and then choose New and the desired value type from the shortcut menu (see fig. 11.12). You can also right-click in the right pane to open the New menu.

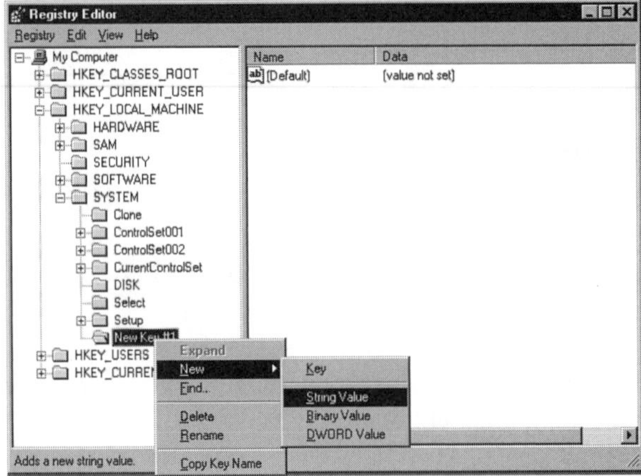

Fig. 11.12
Select the type of value to create: binary, string, or DWORD.

3. The newly created value has a default name of `New Value #1`, and the name of the value is open in Edit mode (see fig. 11.13). Type a new name for the value, or press Enter to leave the name as is.

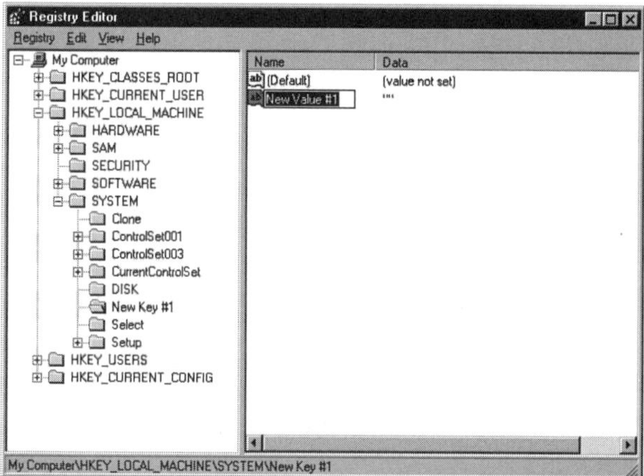

Fig. 11.13
The new value is ready to be renamed.

Deleting Values

Deleting values, as with deleting keys, is potentially dangerous. Also, individual values can't be protected from deletion the way individual keys can. *Any* value visible in the Registry Editor can be deleted.

To delete a value from a key, follow these steps:

1. Select the key that contains the appropriate value in the left pane of the Registry Editor (see fig. 11.14).

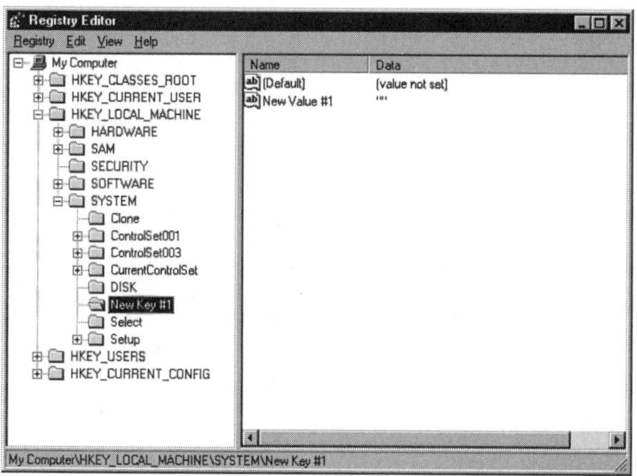

Fig. 11.14
The highlighted key has values that will be deleted.

2. Select the value you want to delete in the right pane (see fig. 11.15).

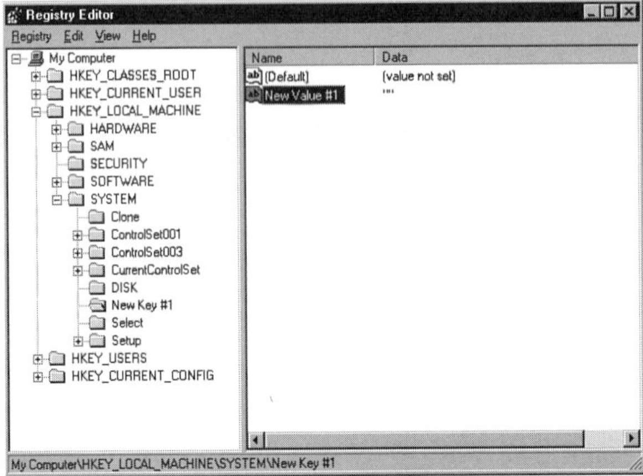

Fig. 11.15
The value to be deleted is highlighted.

3. Press the Delete key. You can also right-click the value and choose Delete from the shortcut menu (see fig. 11.16). Or, you can choose Edit, Delete from the Registry Editor menu.

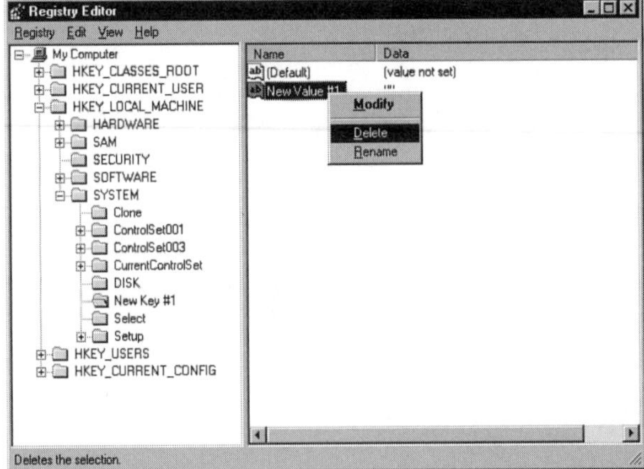

Fig. 11.16
Right-click to open the shortcut menu and choose Delete.

4. The program asks you whether you want to delete the listed value (see fig. 11.17). This is your last chance to prevent deleting the listed value. If you really want to do this, choose Yes.

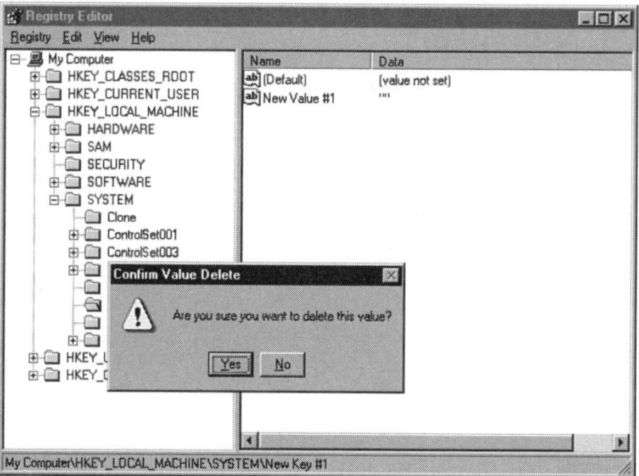

Fig. 11.17
Your last chance to back out before the value is permanently removed.

5. The value should disappear from the right pane of the Registry Editor.

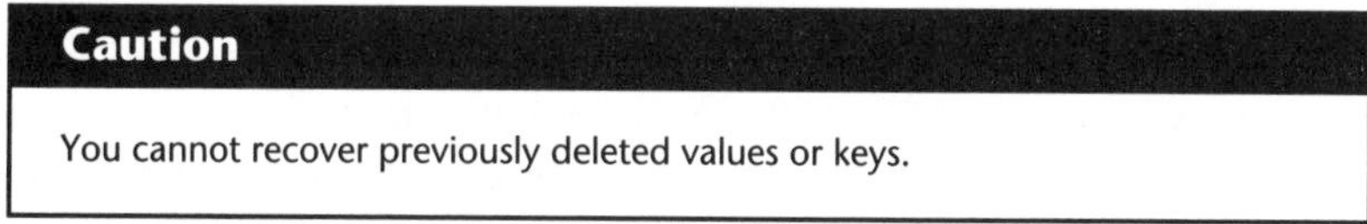

Caution

You cannot recover previously deleted values or keys.

Modifying Existing Values

Editing an existing Registry value is simple, but it carries the same risks that go with all other Registry modifications. Never change a value unless you are certain of what you're doing.

To change an existing value, follow these steps:

1. Select the key that contains the value you want to change in the left pane of the Registry Editor (see fig. 11.18).

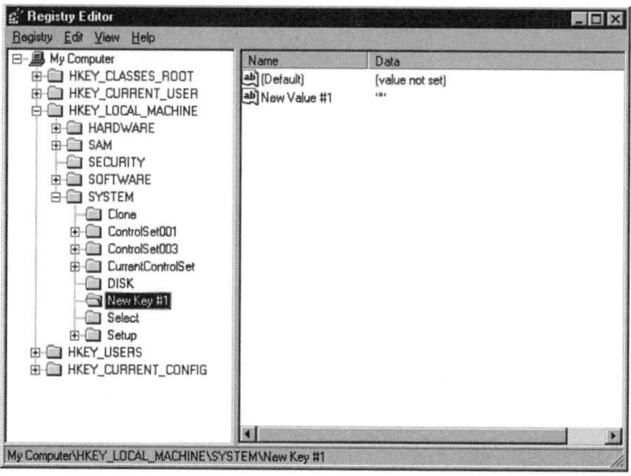

Fig. 11.18
The key with the value to be changed is highlighted.

2. In the right pane, select the value itself (see fig. 11.19).

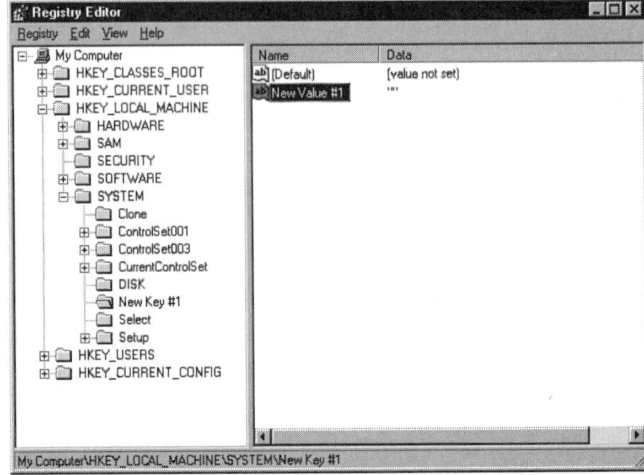

Fig. 11.19
The value to be edited is highlighted.

3. To change the name of the value (not the data stored in the value), press F2 (see fig. 11.20). You can also right-click the value and choose Rename from the shortcut menu. Or, you can choose Edit, Rename in the Registry Editor.

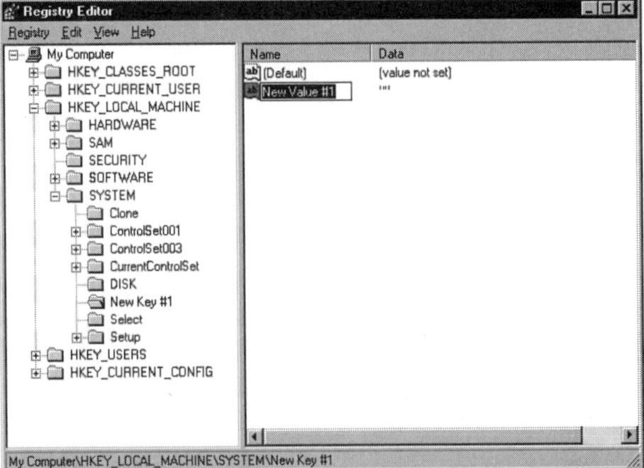

Fig. 11.20
The name of the value is ready to be changed.

4. To change the data stored in the value, choose Edit, Modify in the Registry Editor. Alternately, you can right-click the value and choose Modify from the shortcut menu (see fig. 11.21).

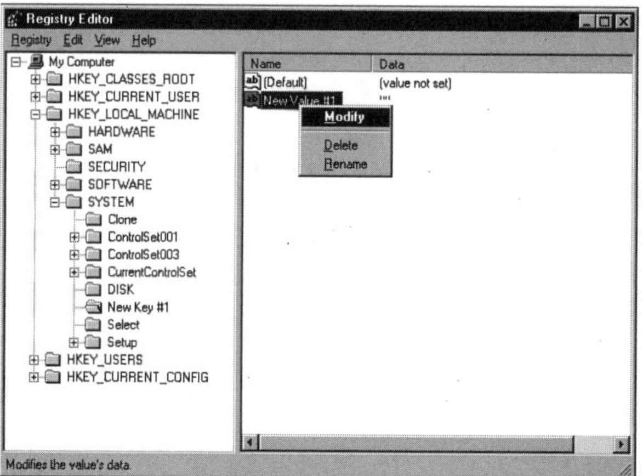

Fig. 11.21
The shortcut menu's Modify option.

5. When changing binary values, you will be prompted to type in the data in hexadecimal pairs (see fig. 11.22). The right side of the edit window shows you what you're entering as ASCII. You can also click the ASCII side of the window and type the data as ASCII. You'll see hexadecimal representations appearing in the left column.

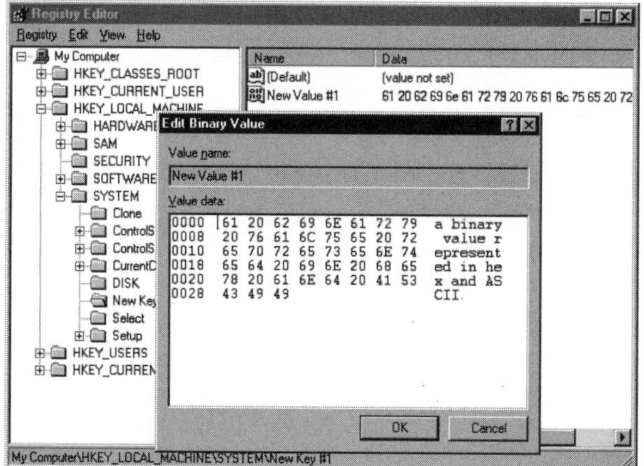

Fig. 11.22
Editing a binary value.

6. When changing string values, you're prompted to type the string as ASCII (see fig. 11.23).

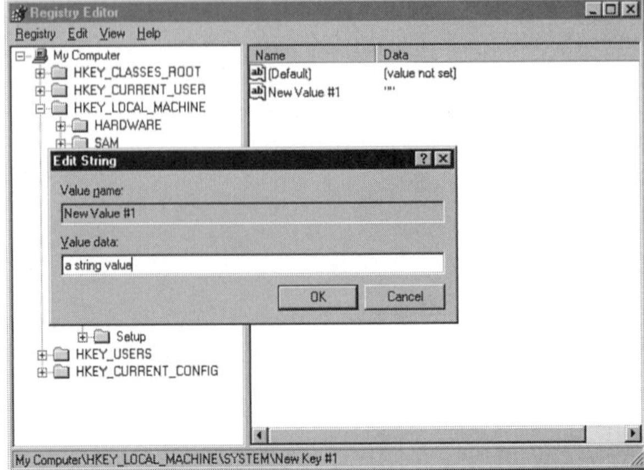

Fig. 11.23
Editing a string value.

7. When changing DWORD values, you're prompted to type the DWORD value as a number (see fig. 11.24). You can choose between typing in the value as hexadecimal or as decimal by selecting the appropriate radio button in the edit window.

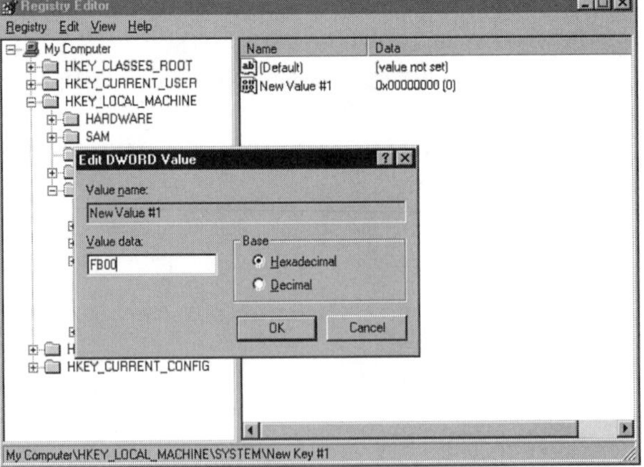

Fig. 11.24
Editing a DWORD value.

Importing Registration Files to the Registry

Registration files are lists of Registry entries, usually bundled with an application or a driver, that contain information that must be merged with the Registry before the application or driver can be used.

Registration files have the extension REG and are formatted as plain-text ASCII files. Each line in the REG file has three components: the location and name of the value to be inserted, an equal sign, and the value itself.

The following is a segment of the REG file that deals with the WordArt component of Microsoft Office:

```
HKEY_CLASSES_ROOT\MSWordArt.2 = Microsoft WordArt 2.0
HKEY_CLASSES_ROOT\MSWordArt.2\protocol\StdFileEditing\verb\0 =
&Edit
HKEY_CLASSES_ROOT\MSWordArt.2\protocol\StdFileEditing\server =
C:\WINDOWS\MSAPPS\WORDART\WRDART32.EXE
HKEY_CLASSES_ROOT\MSWordArt.2\Insertable
HKEY_CLASSES_ROOT\MSWordArt.2\CLSID = {000212F0-0000-0000-C000-
000000000046}
```

Merging a registration file into the Registry is usually done automatically by an installation program, but if you need to perform the procedure manually, here's how:

1. Open the Registry Editor.
2. Choose Registry, Import Registry File.
3. In the Import Registry File dialog box, supply the name of the registration file to merge in and choose Open (see fig. 11.25).

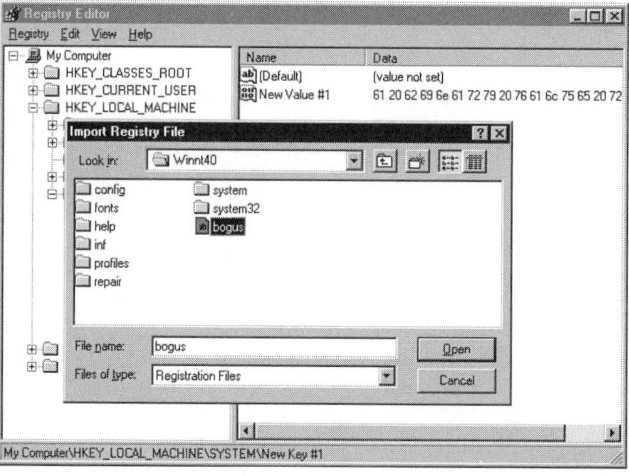

Fig. 11.25
Providing the name of a REG file to be imported.

Caution

If you merge a registration file that refers to existing keys or values, the older key values will be overwritten.

Exporting the Registry to a File

You can also export the Registry to a single REG file that follows the same format as the registration files merged into it. This is useful for many reasons:

- Backing up the Registry.
- Analyzing the Registry outside of the Registry Editor, which has some limitations as far as editing and searching.
- Manually removing binary errors or illegal entries in the Registry.

To export the Registry to a REG file, follow these steps:

1. Open the Registry Editor.
2. Choose Registry, Export Registry File.
3. In the Export Registry File dialog box, type a name under which to save the Registry file and press Save (see fig. 11.26).

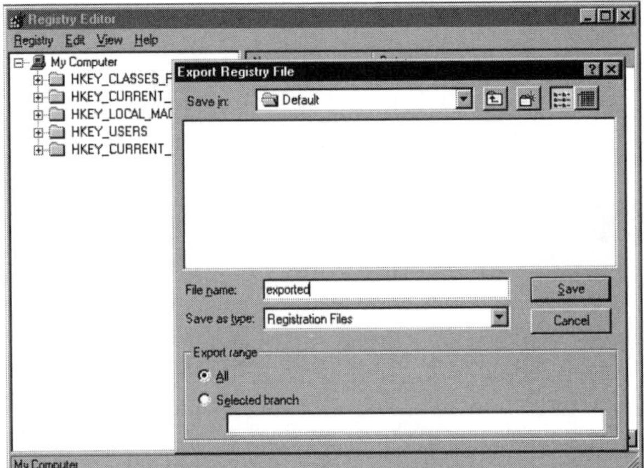

Fig. 11.26 Choose a file name to export the Registry under.

Portions of the Registry as well as the whole of the Registry can be exported to REG files. Here's how to export a portion of the Registry:

1. Open the Registry Editor.
2. In the left pane of the Registry Editor, select the key branch you want to export.
3. Choose Registry, Export Registry File.
4. In the Export Registry File dialog box, type a name to save the Registry file under.

5. In the Export Range area, select Selected Branch. The name of the highlighted key branch should appear in the associated text box.
6. Choose Save to save the file.

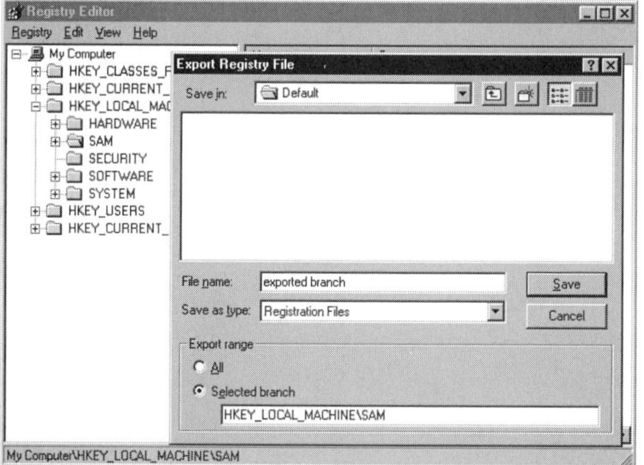

Fig. 11.27
Choosing a file name under which to export a Registry branch.

Connecting to Network Registries

You can use the Registry Editor to connect to a registry on a remote machine. The same functions possible with the Registry Editor normally, such as adding, removing, changing keys and values, and importing and exporting, are available.

Note

You can only connect to a remote registry when you have the remote registry service running on the target machine (which is not enabled by default) and when that machine also has remote administration enabled (which is also off by default).

To connect to a remote registry, follow these steps:

1. In the Registry Editor, choose Registry, Connect Network Registry.
2. Type the name of the computer whose registry you want to connect to. For a list of available machines, choose Browse.
3. When you finish editing the remote registry, choose Registry, Disconnect Network Registry. ❖

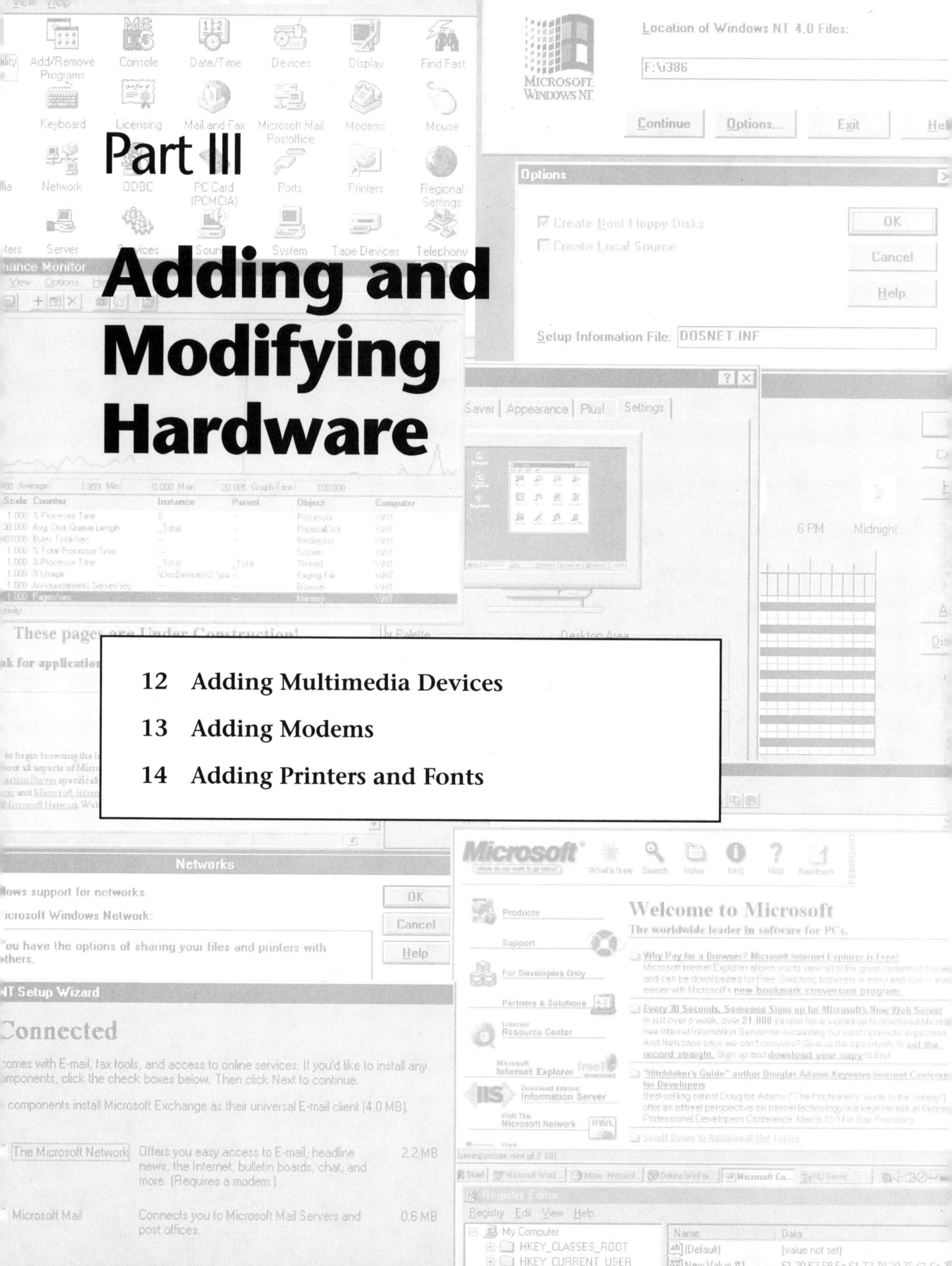

Part III
Adding and Modifying Hardware

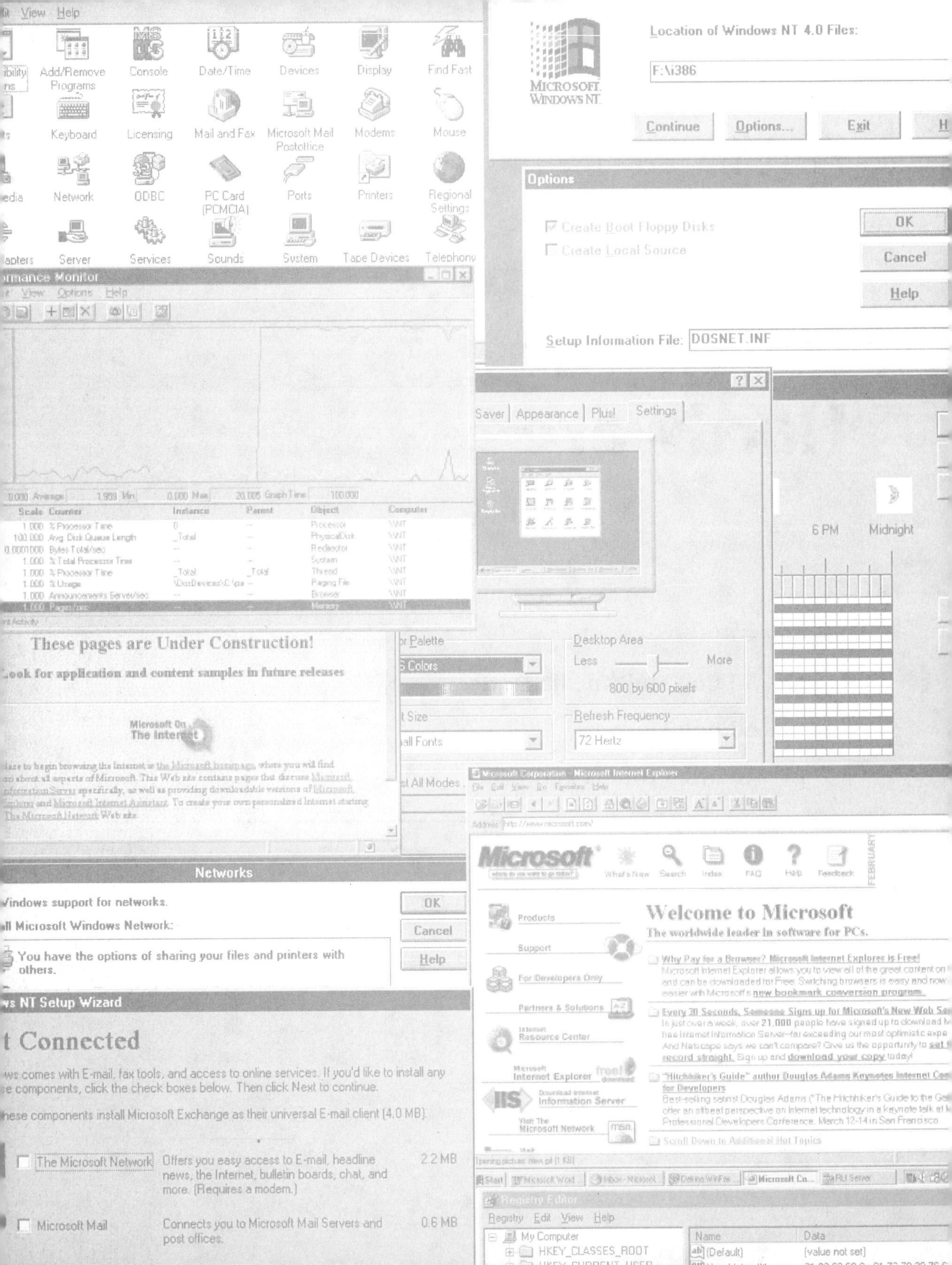

View Help
Add/Remove Programs
Console
Date/Time
Devices
Display
Find Fast
Keyboard
Licensing
Mail and Fax
Microsoft Mail Postoffice
Modems
Mouse
Network
ODBC
PC Card (PCMCIA)
Ports
Printers
Regional Settings
Server
Services
Sounds
System
Tape Devices
Telephony
Location of Windows NT 4.0 Files:
F:\i386
MICROSOFT WINDOWS NT
Continue
Options...
Exit
Options
Create Boot Floppy Disks
Create Local Source
OK
Cancel
Help
Setup Information File:
DOSNET.INF
Saver
Appearance
Plus!
Settings
6 PM
Midnight
Desktop Area
Less
More
800 by 600 pixels
Refresh Frequency
72 Hertz
These pages are Under Construction!
Look for application and content samples in future releases
Networks
Windows support for networks.
Microsoft Windows Network:
You have the options of sharing your files and printers with others.
OK
Cancel
Help
Microsoft Corporation - Microsoft Internet Explorer
Welcome to Microsoft
The worldwide leader in software for PCs.
Products
Support
For Developers Only
Partners & Solutions
Why Pay for a Browser? Microsoft Internet Explorer is Free!
s NT Setup Wizard
t Connected
ws comes with E-mail, fax tools, and access to online services. If you'd like to install any
e components, click the check boxes below. Then click Next to continue.
hese components install Microsoft Exchange as their universal E-mail client (4.0 MB).
The Microsoft Network
Offers you easy access to E-mail, headline news, the Internet, bulletin boards, chat, and more. (Requires a modem.)
2.2 MB
Microsoft Mail
Connects you to Microsoft Mail Servers and post offices.
0.6 MB
Registry Editor
Registry Edit View Help
My Computer
HKEY_CLASSES_ROOT
Name
Data
(Default)
(value not set)

CHAPTER 12

Adding Multimedia Devices

by Serdar Yegulalp

Unlike many other mission-critical operating systems, Windows NT supports a variety of multimedia devices. This includes CD-ROM drives (SCSI or ATAPI), sound cards, and video boards—especially the kind of high-performance video and audio hardware that a high-performance operating system like Windows NT can get the most out of.

This chapter covers installing and configuring three of the most common varieties of multimedia hardware:

- Video cards
- CD-ROM drives, both ATAPI and SCSI
- Sound cards

Installing Video Cards

A video card classifies as a kind of multimedia device—definitely more so now than ever before. Practically every manufacturer of video card offers something extra in their hardware: video playback or MPEG decoding, video capture or NTSC output, and even audio.

Windows NT includes support for most major brands of video cards created. There's strong manufacturer-level support for video hardware as well. Most new video cards include a Windows NT driver in the box.

Note

WinNT 3.5x drivers are incompatible with Windows NT 4.0.

Video Card Issues

Because of the way Windows NT handles video drivers, installing a video card under Windows NT is fundamentally different than installing, for example, a sound card. Windows NT depends far more on its installed graphics card working correctly than most other operating systems. For that reason, Windows NT requires that the user shut down and reboot every time the user reconfigures video card drivers.

Windows NT has also been designed to take into account what can happen if a video card isn't properly installed, whether because of faulty drivers or bad hardware. A malfunctioning video driver can render Windows NT unbootable, and therefore unusable.

To this end, one of the standard boot options for Windows NT is Windows NT 4.00 (VGA mode), which boots the system using a backup set of "plain vanilla" VGA drivers. These drivers only provide 16 colors and 640 × 480 resolution, but they do make it possible to boot the system. If you find that an installed video driver is not working properly, boot using the Windows NT 4.00 (VGA mode) and pick up where you left off to correct the problem.

Installation

To install a video card under Windows NT, follow these steps:

Caution

Don't attempt to physically install a video card in a computer running Windows NT without first setting up the needed drivers.

1. From the Control Panel, double-click the Display icon. The Display Properties sheet appears (see fig. 12.1)
2. Click the Settings tab to view the Settings page (see fig. 12.2).
3. Choose the Change Display Type button to open the Display Type dialog box (see fig. 12.3).

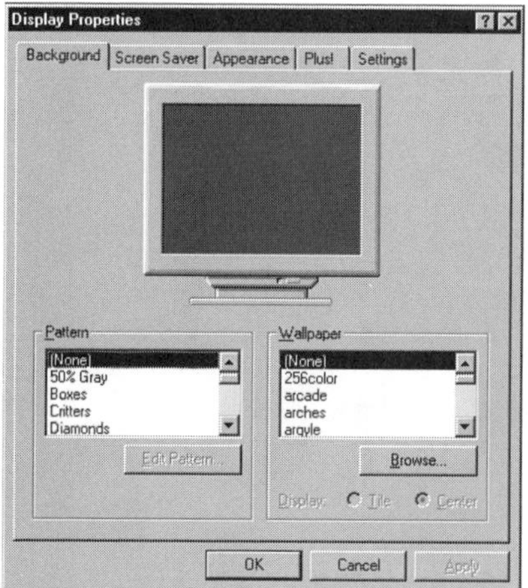

Fig. 12.1
The Display Properties sheet, from the Control Panel.

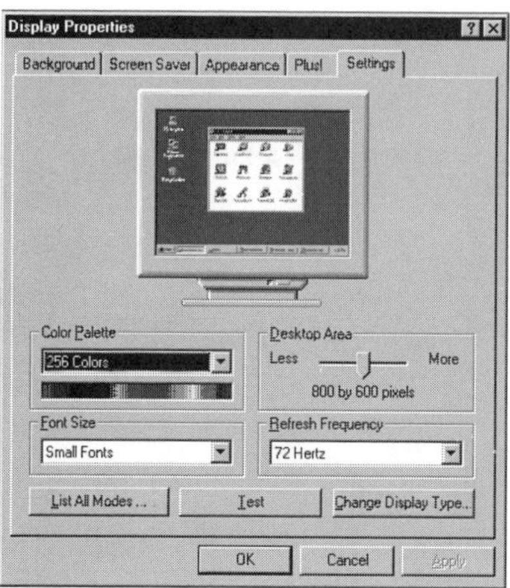

Fig. 12.2
The Settings page of the Display Properties sheet.

4. In the Adapter Type area, choose the Change button. The Select Device dialog box appears (see fig. 12.4).

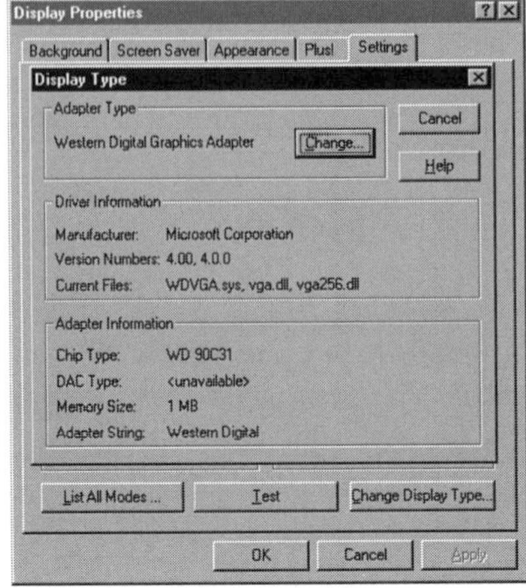

Fig. 12.3
The Display Type dialog box, from the Settings tab.

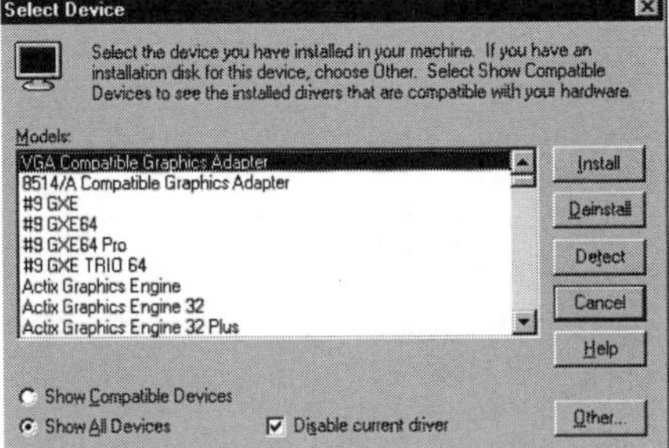

Fig. 12.4
Changing the display adapter type.

5. If the adapter you're installing came with its own disk of drivers, choose the Other button and insert the driver disk. In the Install From Disk dialog box that appears, supply the proper path to the drivers and press Enter (see fig. 12.5).

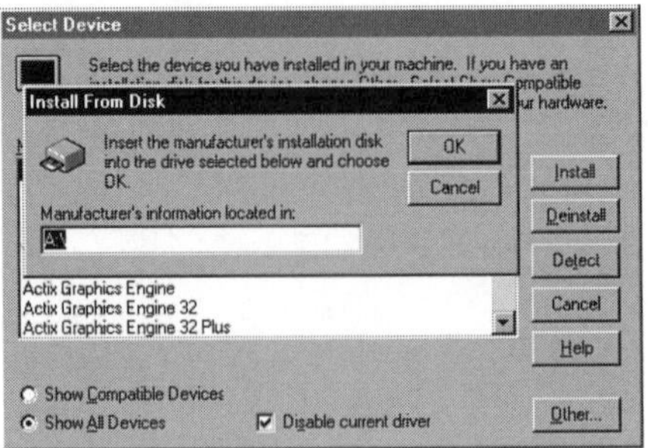

Fig. 12.5
Supply the path to your drivers here.

6. If the adapter you're installing is listed in the Models list, select the closest possible match to your video card from that list and choose Install. You will be warned that this change will modify your system configuration (see fig. 12.6). Choose Yes.

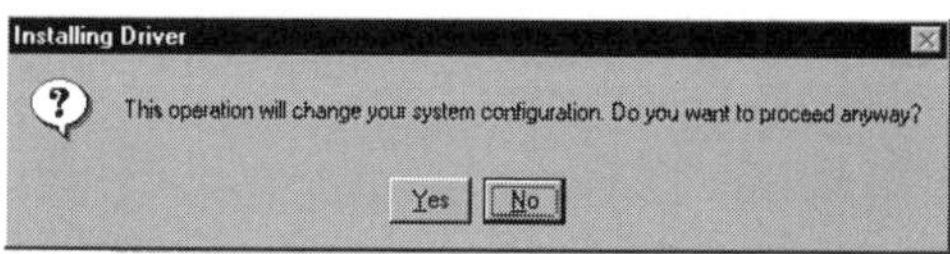

Fig. 12.6
Confirm the change.

7. You may be warned that the driver you are installing already exists on your system (see fig. 12.7). If you are trying to overwrite a corrupted driver with a fresh copy, choose New. If you don't mind using the existing driver, choose Current.

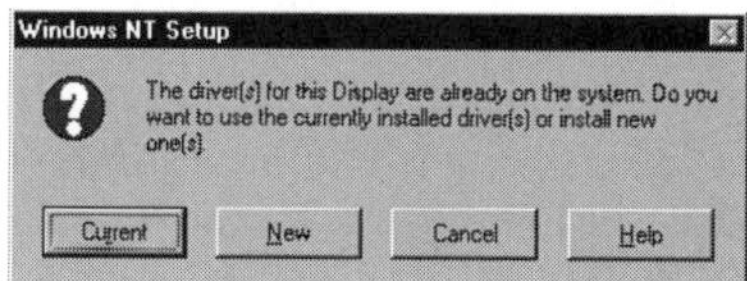

Fig. 12.7
Choose how to work with an existing driver.

8. Windows NT now informs you that the driver was successfully installed (see fig. 12.8).

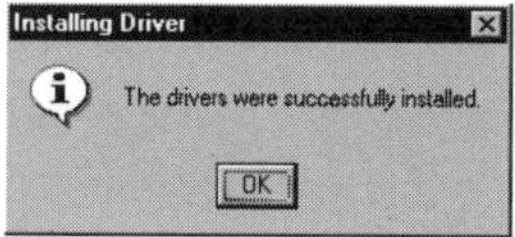

Fig. 12.8
The driver has been installed.

9. Windows NT also informs you that the driver could not be dynamically started (see fig. 12.9). This is normal. It simply means that the video driver is too crucial to the system's operation to be stopped and started again. Choose OK and then shut down and restart the system.

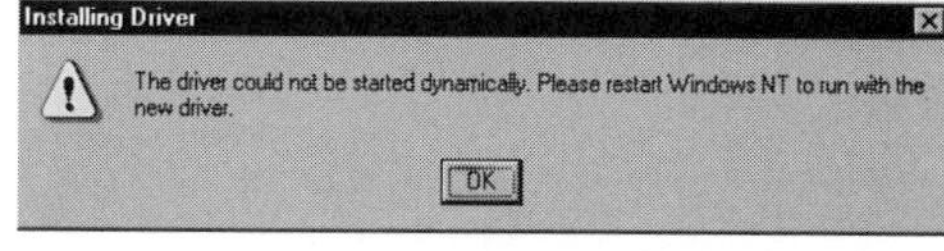

Fig. 12.9
Choose OK from here then shut down. Your new video card should start when you reboot.

10. Install your new video card. Boot Windows NT. The new card should work when you restart your system.

Troubleshooting Video Cards

With video cards under Windows NT, the worst thing that can go wrong is that Windows NT may refuse to boot. Or, the system may boot but the display will be unreadable or of the wrong dimensions. If this happens, simply reboot the system and use the Windows NT 4.00 (VGA mode) boot option to remove or reset the offending driver.

Here's a list of options to work with when debugging video cards under Windows NT:

- *Make sure you have the exact video card driver.* Some chipsets, like the S3, have many types of drivers that may seem interchangeable. They are not. The differences between the Diamond Stealth Pro and the Diamond Stealth 64 VRAM, for example, are significant enough that Diamond authored different drivers for each card. Check the *exact* name of the card with the manufacturer if you have to.
- *Check your card's hardware settings.* Older video cards—and even some newer ones—have jumpers or DIP switches that govern critical settings, such as timer interrupts or IRQs.
- *Check the way IRQ9 is being used.* Many newer video cards (mostly PCI-based) are automatically assigned the use of IRQ9 by the computer. This works in most cases, especially if nothing else uses IRQ9. A few systems that have other hardware reserved for IRQ9 experience problems because of this. If your video hardware allows it, you may want to try disabling the use of IRQ9 for video. Alternately, you can find out what other hardware is trying to use IRQ9 and redirect or disable that.

Installing a CD-ROM Drive

CD-ROM drives have gone from being luxuries—buggy and badly supported ones at that—to being very necessary computer components. Windows NT has a strong stake in CD-ROM technology, especially because Windows NT, and increasing amounts of Windows NT software, are all being deployed on CD-ROMs. Having a CD-ROM drive on a Windows NT machine should be a cardinal rule. It simplifies many of the tasks of system administration, such as loading software and getting updates.

CD-ROM drives come in three basic types, depending on the kind of controller they're based on:

- ATAPI, or IDE
- SCSI
- Proprietary

Installing an ATAPI/IDE CD-ROM Drive

A great advantage of ATAPI CD-ROM drives is that they connect directly to a conventional IDE controller. This reduces the amount of additional hardware you have to cram into what may be an already-overburdened computer.

ATAPI CD-ROM drives are often recognized by older BIOSes as being just another kind of hard drive. Newer BIOSes will recognize them for what they are—a CD-ROM drive—and list them as such. Either way, Windows NT will be able to detect them and make use of them automatically.

To install an ATAPI CD-ROM drive under Windows NT, follow these steps:

1. Shut down your Windows NT machine.
2. Find an IDE controller for the new CD-ROM drive. Newer model computers are outfitted with two IDE controllers, which are usually on the motherboard although they can also be on their own controller card. Each IDE controller can hold a maximum of two devices: one attached at the end of the controller data cable and the other attached at the middle.

> **Tip**
>
> Install CD-ROM drives on their own IDE chain if possible. This prevents the hard drive and the CD-ROM drive from reducing the performance of the other.

3. Check the CD-ROM drive manual for the proper jumper settings. If there is more than one IDE unit on a chain, one of the units has to be designated a *master*, and the other a *slave*. Set the jumpers to their correct positions.

> **Note**
>
> Boot devices must be master devices. If you have your CD-ROM drive on the same IDE chain as your boot drive, the boot drive must be set as a master device and the CD-ROM drive must be set as a slave.

4. Attach the CD-ROM drive to the IDE chain you selected. Follow the procedures appropriate for installing the drive in your system's chassis. Make sure the CD-ROM drive is receiving power as well.

5. Boot the system and check its ROM BIOS settings. Make sure the controller and drive you have the CD-ROM drive attached to have been enabled in BIOS. If possible, set the controller to auto-detect the CD-ROM drive. Setting the drive type to None usually doesn't allow the drive to be seen by software.

> **Note**
>
> If your BIOS is relatively recent (updated since January 1995), it should have the capability to recognize ATAPI CD-ROM drives for what they are. Check to see if the CD-ROM drive is showing up in your system BIOS. If it isn't, refer to the section "Troubleshooting CD-ROM Drives," later in this chapter.

6. Restart the system and open My Computer. If everything went well, you should see a CD-ROM drive icon in My Computer (see fig. 12.10).

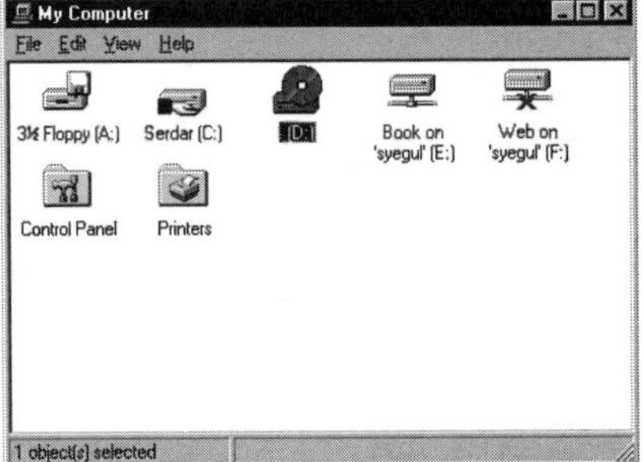

Fig. 12.10 The CD-ROM drive icon under My Computer.

Installing an SCSI CD-ROM Drive

In some ways, installing an SCSI CD-ROM drive is not that different from installing an ATAPI/IDE CD-ROM drive. You still have to be sure you're installing the CD-ROM drive with the correct configuration so it doesn't conflict with other devices. On the bright side, Windows NT automatically detects attached SCSI CD-ROM drives without any prompting from the user.

> **Caution**
>
> To make use of an SCSI CD-ROM drive, you have to have an SCSI host adapter in your system. Some systems have this as part of their motherboard, while others feature it as an adapter card. Either way, this section assumes you already have some kind of SCSI host adapter installed and enabled under Windows NT.

To install an SCSI CD-ROM drive for use in Windows NT, follow these steps:

1. Shut down your Windows NT machine.
2. Examine the SCSI host adapter and device chain you plan to install the SCSI CD-ROM drive on. Make sure you have a device ID number free for the CD-ROM drive, and that you have the proper cabling.

> **Tip**
>
> Depending on your host adapter, Windows NT may not be able to detect a CD-ROM drive installed as device 0 or 1. Try setting it at 2 or higher to get the best results.

3. Set the CD-ROM drive's device ID number and termination. If you are installing the CD-ROM drive at either end of the SCSI chain, it must be terminated. Make sure the CD-ROM drive is receiving power as well.
4. If the CD-ROM drive is an internal model, follow the procedures appropriate for installing the drive in your system's chassis.
5. If your host adapter allows you to check the adapter and attached devices, which are usually activated through a key combination at boot time, boot the system and activate your host adapter's configuration. Make sure the CD-ROM drive is visible there.
6. Boot Windows NT and open My Computer. If all has gone well, you should see a CD-ROM drive icon there.

Installing a Proprietary CD-ROM Controller

Some CD-ROMs, such as those bundled with audio hardware by Creative Labs or Sony, use a proprietary interface and controller for their CD-ROM. Proprietary CD-ROM controllers are getting scarcer because more CD-ROM manufacturers are using either ATAPI or SCSI to get up-to-date. However, there are still plenty of existing proprietary controllers.

Proprietary controllers usually require you to set jumpers or switches that control which IRQ, DMA, or memory addresses they use. They also take up an expansion slot inside the computer, usually an ISA slot.

Some proprietary controllers are also part of a sound card, and are installed as one. The following instructions deal with what to do in just such a case.

> **Note**
>
> If the proprietary card comes with specific instructions and drivers for installing the card under Windows NT, follow those instructions instead.

To install a proprietary controller and CD-ROM under Windows NT, follow these steps:

1. Ensure that your system has bay space for the CD-ROM and a free slot for the controller.
2. Run Windows NT Diagnostics, which you can find by opening the Start menu and choosing Administrative Tools. Check free IRQs, DMAs, and memory spaces against what the controller card may need.
3. Change jumper settings on the controller card to fit the available free memory settings.
4. Shut down the computer.
5. Install the adapter card in the appropriate expansion slot and follow the procedures appropriate for installing the CD-ROM drive in your system's chassis. Make sure the CD-ROM is receiving power as well.
6. Start Windows NT and open My Computer. If Windows NT automatically recognizes the proprietary card type, you should see the CD-ROM drive icon in My Computer.

Some proprietary cards are also sound cards, which have a CD-ROM controller built in. To install them, follow these steps:

1. Open the Control Panel and double-click the Multimedia icon (see fig. 12.11).

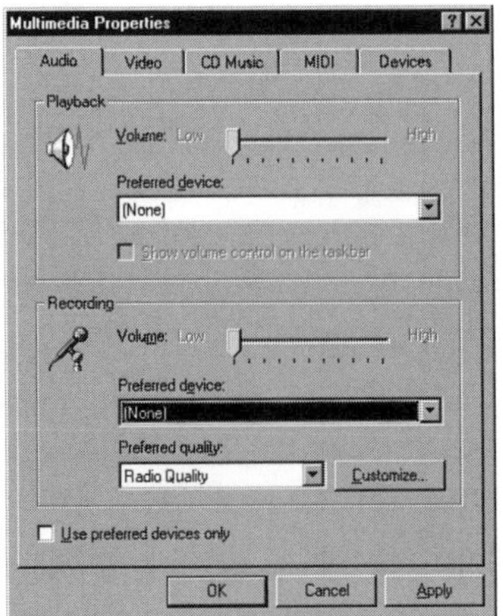

Fig. 12.11
The Multimedia properties sheet, activated from the Control Panel.

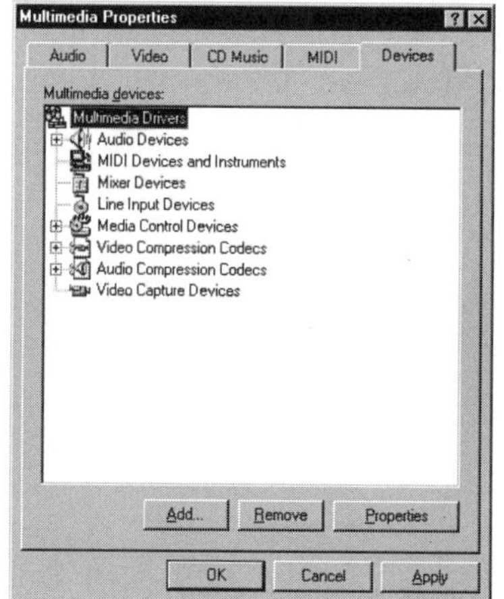

Fig. 12.12
The Devices tab in the Multimedia window.

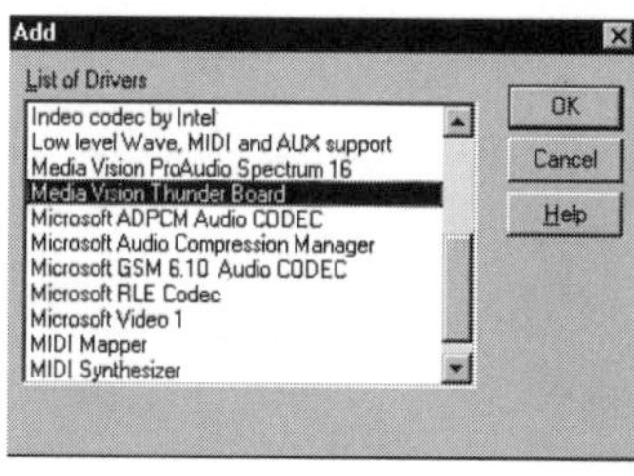

Fig. 12.13
The Add dialog box appears when you click the Add button.

2. Select the Devices tab as shown in figure 12.12.
3. Click the Add button to open the Add dialog box as shown in figure 12.13.
4. Choose the card that most closely matches the description of the one you have installed. Click OK and the Install Driver dialog box appears as shown in figure 12.14.
5. You may be prompted to insert disks or your Windows NT CD-ROM, and to provide a pathname. Remember that on the CD-ROM, the pathname depends on the processor version you're using. Intel users would look in \i386 for their files.
6. Depending on the card you are installing, Windows NT may prompt you for the card's settings. Fill in the needed text boxes and click OK.
7. Windows NT may have to shut down and restart at this point. After restarting, open My Computer and look for a CD-ROM drive icon.

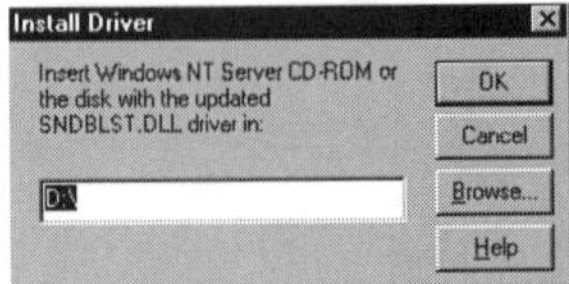

Fig. 12.14 Adding the card with the proprietary controller on it.

> **Tip**
>
> If you want to change the drive letter of a CD-ROM, run Disk Administrator and do it in the same fashion as you would for a conventional hard drive.

Troubleshooting CD-ROM Drives

Many of the common problems with CD-ROM drives under Windows NT are usually due to something simple, which is easily detected and even more easily avoided with a little foresight. If you've followed all the instructions and something still doesn't seem to be right with your CD-ROM drive, take a look at this list of symptoms and solutions:

- *The CD-ROM drive doesn't show up at all.* First, make sure the CD-ROM drive is receiving power. If it's an internal model, try switching plugs. If it's an external model, try changing power cords. Make sure the data cables are functional and connected properly. Both SCSI and ATAPI/IDE data cables are polarized: they only go in one way—the right way. However, it's still possible to attach a cable with bent or broken pins at one end, or with a short in the middle. Check the host adapter or IDE BIOS settings—both in hardware and in Windows NT—to make sure everything matches. If your SCSI host adapter has a self test, try running that to see if the adapter is bad. Check that drive references in the IDE setup have the controller with the CD-ROM enabled and active.
- *The CD-ROM drive shows up more than once.* This is a common problem with SCSI CD-ROM drives and is usually due to the CD-ROM drive being set to the same device number as another device on the chain, including the host adapter (which is usually set to device #7). Change the device number on the CD-ROM drive to something not in use.
- *The CD-ROM drive works far too slowly for its speed or generates a lot of errors.* If this is a SCSI CD-ROM drive, make sure that SCSI chain is properly terminated at both ends and that the data cables along the chain are hooked up and in good condition.

- *No music from the CD-ROM drive.* Every CD-ROM drive has a slightly different wiring scheme to allow music from an audio CD to be piped from the CD-ROM drive into the sound card or to an auxiliary connector. Make sure you followed the wiring scheme correctly for your card, and that the speakers or headphones are getting power. Also, some CD-ROM drives use a special cable to carry audio to the sound card. Make sure your sound card supports this. Under Multimedia in the Control Panel, click CD Music and make sure the headphone slider isn't set too low for you to hear anything. Also, check the CD-ROM volume slider in the Volume Control applet; make sure it isn't set to zero or muted out completely.

Installing a Sound Card

Sound cards are at the same time some of the most hotly desired and flat-out hated pieces of hardware available. The majority of software is augmented with sound in some way, and there's no denying the dramatic difference between a game like *Doom*™ with and without bone-jarring sound effects.

The hatred that surrounds a lot of sound hardware is the trouble it takes to get them installed and keep them running. Most sound cards require that the user set jumpers or switches that determine what IRQ, DMA, and memory address settings the card will use.

Windows NT goes a long way toward solving this problem by providing a few tools that make installing sound cards a little easier. One of them is the Windows NT Diagnostics utility, which gives you precise information about free IRQ, DMA, and memory settings. You can use it to check against the settings available to the card you're trying to install.

Note

Sound cards that are supported under Windows 95 may not be supported under Windows NT. For example, at the time of this writing, the sound cards manufactured by Advanced Gravis do not have NT support drivers. If you are purchasing a sound card for Windows NT, consult the card manufacturer before purchasing to ensure that Windows NT drivers are available for it.

Installing a Sound Card

To install a sound card under Windows NT, follow these steps:

1. Under Windows NT, run the Windows NT Diagnostics program, available in the Administrative Tools folder under the Start button. Check free IRQs, DMAs, and memory spaces against what the controller card may need.
2. Set the jumpers and/or switches on the card to a setting that doesn't conflict with existing hardware and that is supported by the card.
3. Shut down the computer. Install the card and the auxiliary hardware supported by the card (such as speakers, microphone, and so on).
4. Boot Windows NT. Open the Control Panel and double-click the Multimedia icon.
5. Select the Devices tab (see fig. 12.15).

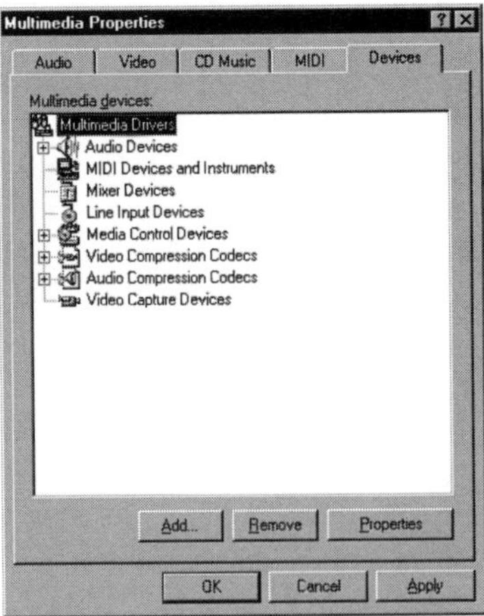

Fig. 12.15
The Devices page lists the multimedia devices available.

6. Click the Add button to open the Add dialog box as shown in figure 12.16.
7. Choose the card that most closely matches the description of the one you have installed. Click OK.

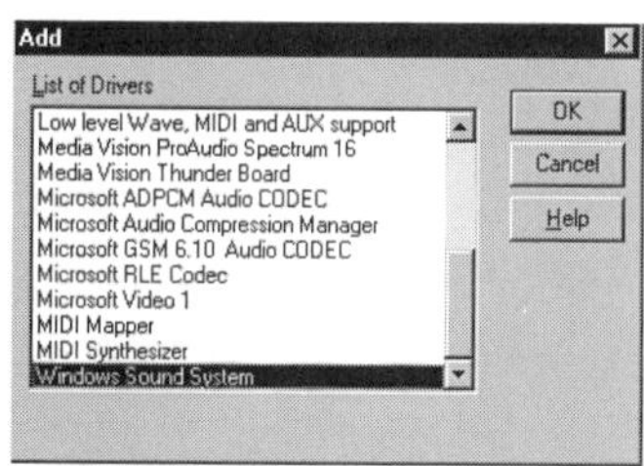

Fig. 12.16
Adding a device.

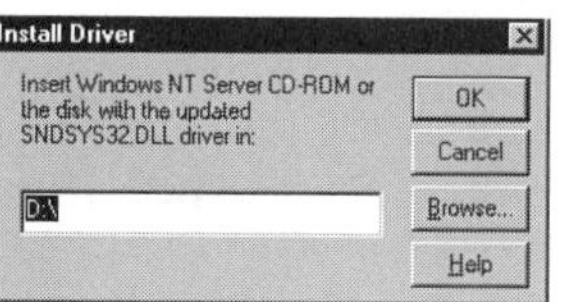

Fig. 12.17
Provide the pathname to the drivers.

8. You may be prompted to insert disks or your Windows NT CD-ROM and to provide a pathname. Remember that on the CD-ROM, the pathname depends on the processor version you're using. Intel users would look in \i386 for their files. If your sound card came with Windows NT-specific drivers, supply those instead.
9. Depending on the card you're installing, Windows NT may prompt you for its settings. Fill in the needed information and click OK.
10. You may have to shut down and restart Windows NT at this point. After restarting, open the Control Panel, double-click Multimedia, and select the Devices tab. Look under the Audio Devices subsection in the Multimedia Devices list (see fig. 12.18).

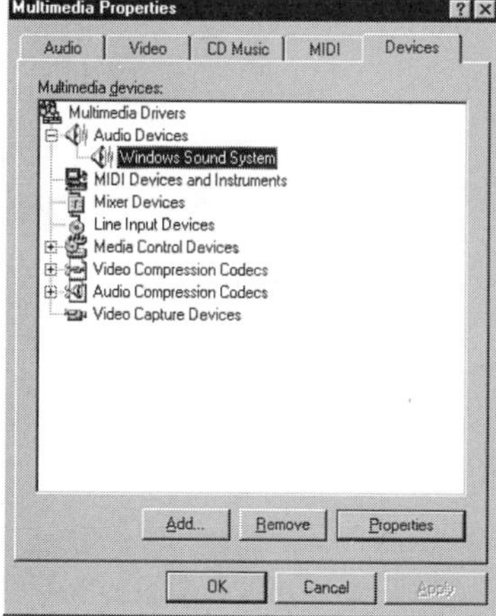

Fig. 12.18
The installed audio device, as listed under Audio Devices.

Troubleshooting Sound Cards

As with CD-ROM drives, the majority of what can go wrong with a sound card can be traced to simple and easily fixable problems. The problems rarely require replacing apparently defective hardware. Some common problems are:

- *Sound playback is distorted or sounds play in an endless loop.* Aside from the sound card not producing any sound at all, this is the most common sound card problem. The culprit here is a conflict between the sound card and another hardware device. Make sure the sound card isn't occupying a setting that another hardware device (including system devices, such as mice and conventional hardware controllers) is using.
- *No sound at all.* This common problem is sometimes the easiest to fix, because it can be traced to a host of simple little problems. Has the connection to the speakers come unplugged? Are the speakers receiving power? Are they turned up? Are the volume controls in Windows 95 (available as an icon on the taskbar or in the Multimedia icon of the Control Panel) at zero? If you go through all of these and find nothing wrong, see if you have the next symptom.
- *No listing for the card in the Multimedia Devices list.* This indicates that the sound card driver was not installed correctly. Go back through the installation procedure and make sure there are no errors, such as missing drivers, disks that don't read correctly, and so on.
- *WAV playback is OK, but there is no sound from the CD-ROM drive.* Make sure the CD-ROM drive is wired correctly to deliver sound to the sound card, and that the mixer controls for the CD-ROM drive are enabled and not set at zero. ❖

CHAPTER 13

Adding Modems

by Serdar Yegulalp

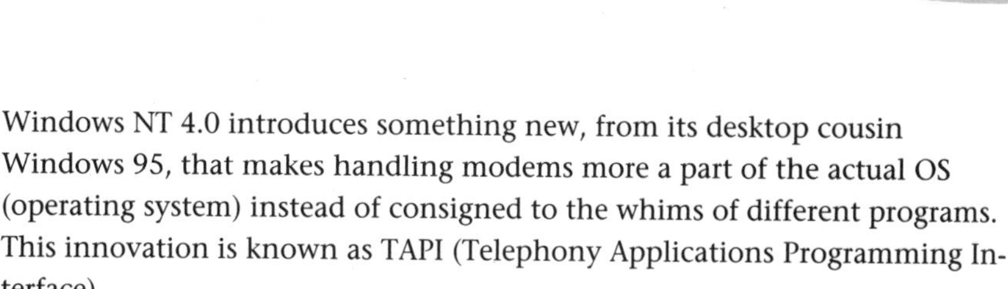

Windows NT 4.0 introduces something new, from its desktop cousin Windows 95, that makes handling modems more a part of the actual OS (operating system) instead of consigned to the whims of different programs. This innovation is known as TAPI (Telephony Applications Programming Interface).

Previous versions of Windows NT handled modems in much the same fashion as conventional Windows and Windows for Workgroups: they didn't, at least not directly.

TAPI changes all that because it's a standardized way for programs to talk to modems with the operating system as an intermediary. Normally, if a program wants to have the modem go online and dial a number, it has to say, "Send this command string to the modem and tell me the result." However, the command string could be anything depending on the type of modem you have. Not only that, but the program has to take into account what could happen if the dialing fails, if the modem simply isn't there, and so on.

With TAPI, the operating system does all the direct handling of the modem. A library of vendor-written drivers contains all the needed configuration strings and modem commands.

In this chapter, you learn to:

- Install and configure a modem
- Configure Telephony options

Installing a Modem

The following steps cover installing a modem, whether it's an internal or external model. If you already have a modem installed in your system, you can skip ahead to step 5.

1. Unpack your modem and familiarize yourself with the installation instructions.
2. If your modem is an internal model, read the modem documentation to determine how to set which port the modem will be using, and make sure that it is set to use a previously unoccupied port in your machine. You may need to disable an existing COM port in your computer to make room. Read your computer's own documentation to learn how to disable ports in the computer's BIOS configuration.
3. If your modem is an external model, make sure you have the proper type of external COM port available, the proper cabling for it, and the port itself correctly enabled in hardware.
4. Shut down the computer and install or connect the modem according to the instructions. Power up the computer again.
5. Open the Start menu and choose Settings, Control Panel. You can also open Control Panel from My Computer.
6. Double-click the Modems icon to open the Install New Modem Wizard (see fig. 13.1).

   The Install New Modem Wizard only appears if you have not installed any modems. After you successfully install a modem, double-clicking the Modem's icon gives you a list of currently installed modems. You can still access the Install New Modem Wizard from the modem list by clicking the Add button.

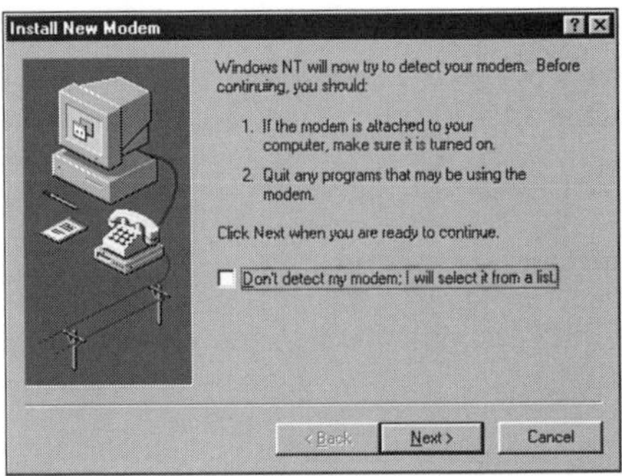

Fig. 13.1
The Install New Modem Wizard can detect your modems automatically or let you choose from a list of manufacturers.

7. The user has two choices at this point: to manually specify a modem, or to allow Windows NT to search for one itself. It may be best to start by seeing if you can manually specify the modem, since searching automatically can take time depending on the machine being used, and can sometimes return inaccurate results. Click the Don't Detect... checkbox and then click Next. You will be presented with the Install New Modem window (see fig. 13.2).

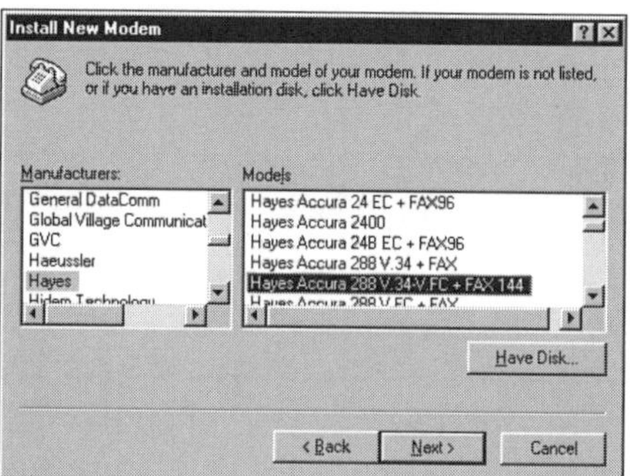

Fig. 13.2
The database of modem drivers available in Windows NT is organized first by manufacturer and then by model.

8. The left pane of the Install New Modem window, labeled Manufacturers, lists all the manufacturers of modems in the modem database. Select the maker of your modem by using the mouse to scroll through the list and clicking the proper manufacturer. You can also select quickly by selecting the Manufacturers window by clicking anywhere in it and typing the first few letters of the manufacturer's name.
9. Once you have selected the manufacturer, the right pane of the Install New Modem window, labeled Models, lists all the models of modems from that manufacturer. Select the model of your modem by using the mouse to scroll through the list and click the proper model name. You can also select quickly by selecting the Models window by clicking anywhere in it and typing the first few letters of the model name.
10. If your modem isn't listed here and you have been provided with a disk that contains Windows NT-specific drivers for it, insert the disk, click the Have Disk button and provide a path to the disk. Windows NT will then search the disk for Windows NT-compatible modem drivers and display a list of its findings. Install the driver you need by highlighting it and clicking OK.

Tip

If you don't know the manufacturer or model of your modem, use auto-detection to determine what modem is installed. However, many modems (especially from lower-end manufacturers) don't return accurate description information to the computer they're attached to.

To auto-detect a modem from the Install New Modem Wizard, leave the Don't Detect My Modem... checkbox on the wizard's first screen unchecked, and then click Next.

Note

Also note that ISDN modems are listed, detected, and handled in the same manner as a conventional modem. They are not listed as network cards.

11. Once you have a make and model of modem selected, click Next. The next window in the Install New Modem Wizard allows you to choose which port the modem is attached to (see fig. 13.3).

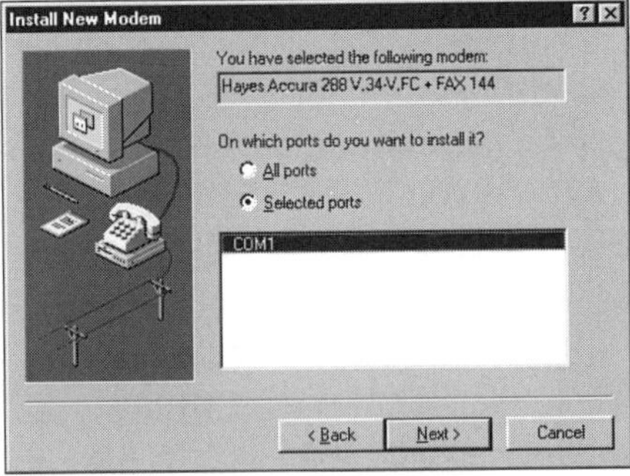

Fig. 13.3 Choose which port the modem is attached to from a list of ports installed in your system.

12. Choose the port your modem is attached to by clicking its name from the list. Click Next to continue.
13. The final screen of the wizard should appear. Click Finish to conclude the modem installation (see fig. 13.4). You may be asked to insert driver disks for your modem—either a third-party driver disk or the Windows NT CD-ROM. The wizard will also ask you for a path to the drivers. Insert the disk and type a pathname to the drivers, then click OK.

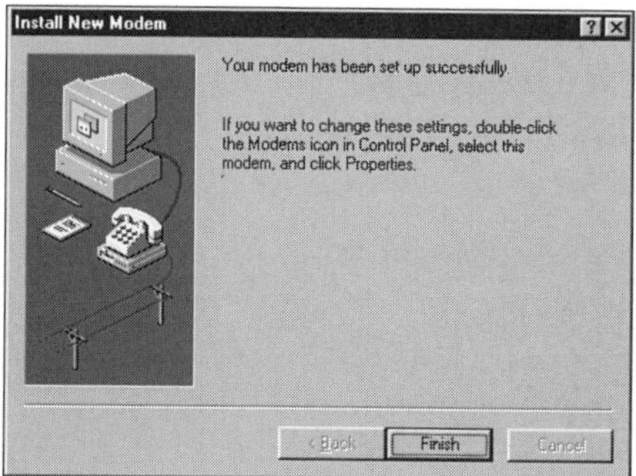

Fig. 13.4
Clicking Finish at the end of the Wizard installs the modem driver.

Configuring a Modem

There are many configuration options that allow you to get exactly what you need out of your modem. Not every modem will connect perfectly with every modem out-of-the-box, so you need to adjust baud rates or flow control options or whatever else is needed for a successful connection.

To edit the configuration options for a modem, open the Modems Properties sheet by double-clicking the Modems icon in the Control Panel (see fig. 13.5).

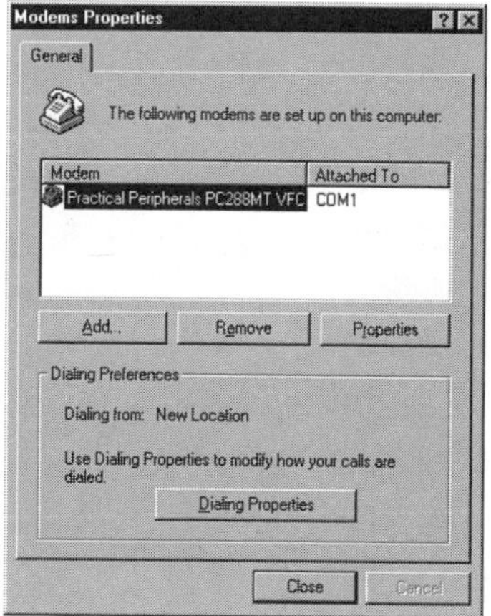

Fig. 13.5
The Modems Properties sheet lists currently installed modems and their connections.

The following options are available in the Modems Properties sheet:

- *Add.* Click this button to add another modem to the Modem list. When you click this button, the Install New Modem Wizard opens.

- *Remove.* Click this button to remove the highlighted modem. You are asked whether you really want to do so before the modem is removed.
- *Properties.* Click this button to change the properties of the highlighted modem.
- *Dialing Properties.* Click this button to open the Dialing Properties sheet. This is the same as double-clicking the Telephony icon in Control Panel. For more information, see the section "Configuring Telephony Options" later in this chapter.

The Properties Sheet for a Modem

Double-clicking a modem listed in the Modems Property sheet will bring up that modem's property sheet (Practical Peripherals in this case), which is divided into two tabs: General and Connection (see fig. 13.6).

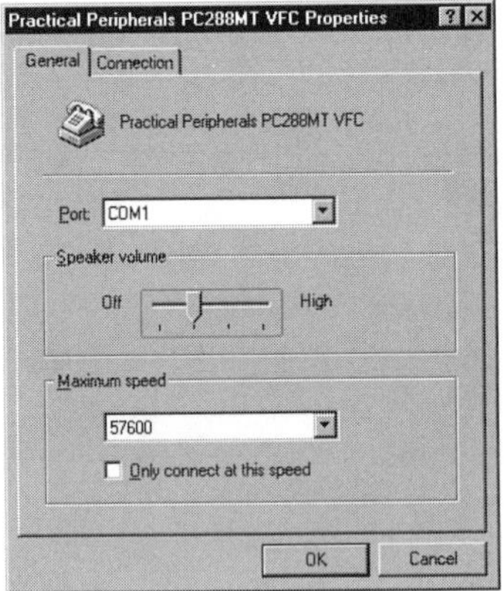

Fig. 13.6
The Modem Properties sheet lets you change port assignments, the speaker volume, and the maximum connection speed.

The General Page

On the General Page, the more commonly used modem parameters are stored and can be changed, such as the modem's speaker volume and baud rate (refer to fig. 13.6).

- *Port.* If you want to change the port assignment for a specific modem, click the Port drop-down list to select the proper port for this modem from a list of valid ports.
- *Speaker Volume.* Drag this slider to select the desired volume for your modem's internal speaker.

> **Note**
>
> Some modem drivers, especially the generic-class drivers, only have two speaker settings: on and off. Don't be surprised if you try to drag the slider and find you can't position it in the middle.

- *Maximum Speed.* Open this drop-down list to select the maximum speed at which your modem can connect. If you want to ensure that the modem connects only at that speed, select the Only Connect at this Speed checkbox.

> **Note**
>
> The default setting for Maximum Speed for most modems is 57,600 baud—even for modems that operate at 28,800 baud. Leave this setting at 57,600 baud for the best results, unless you're trying to force a lower-speed connection. Some modems are able to connect at 115,200, and it's worth experimenting with the higher speeds to see if you can achieve increased performance.

The Connection Page

The Connection page holds modem parameters that relate specifically to the kind of connection the modem will make when it dials (see fig. 13.7).

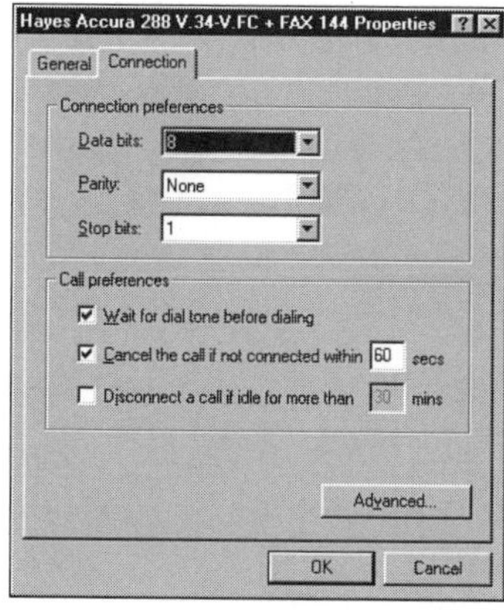

Fig. 13.7
The Connection page holds options that relate to how connections are handled.

Connection Preferences

The items in the Connection Preferences section deal specifically with the kind of data in an established connection.

- *Data Bits.* Open this drop-down list to change the number of data bits used when trying to connect. You can select anywhere from 4 to 8 data bits. The default is 8.
- *Parity.* Use this drop-down list to change the kind of parity used in the connection. Windows NT supports the following kinds of parity: even, odd, mark, space, and no parity. The default is no parity.
- *Stop Bits.* Choose the number of stop bits used when making a connection from this drop-down list. Windows NT supports one, one-and-a-half, and two stop bits—the default is one stop bit.

Call Preferences

The Call Preferences section deals with options pertaining to making a call with the modem, as opposed to the data connection. These parameters are optional, and should only be changed if necessary.

- *Wait for Dialtone Before Dialing.* Select this checkbox if you want the modem to dial only when it hears a dial tone. This option is selected by default, so deselect it if you want to do "blind" dialing.
- *Cancel the Call if not Connected Within __ Seconds.* Select this option to provide a value in seconds that is the maximum time-out for the modem to detect a carrier. Deselect this option if you want the modem to take as long as it needs to connect.
- *Disconnect a Call if Idle for More than __ Minutes.* If you select this checkbox and provide a value in minutes, Windows NT disconnects a call when no data has gone over the wire for the specified amount of time.

Advanced Connection Settings

The Advanced Connection Settings dialog box governs flow control, error correction, modulation, logging, and extra initialization strings the user wants to pass to the modem (see fig. 13.8).

To open the Advanced Connection Settings dialog box click the Advanced button on the Connection page.

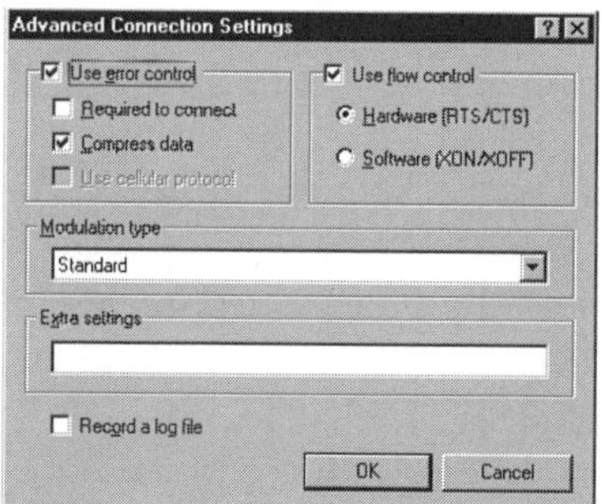

Fig. 13.8
Some of the more sophisticated modem configuration options are in the Advanced Connection Settings dialog box.

> **Caution**
>
> Modem drivers come with their own properly configured initialization strings for each brand of modem. Don't specify an additional configuration string unless you know it's needed. If you do, you might experience degraded modem performance or you might not be able to connect reliably—if at all.

Use Error Control Section

When you select the Use Error Control checkbox, you enable the use of error control in the modem and you enable all the options in the Use Error Control section that pertain to it. Making changes to these controls is optional.

- *Required to Connect.* Select this checkbox if you want to ensure that error correction is used every time you establish a connection. It is deselected by default.

> **Note**
>
> If the modem can't ensure error correction in a connection with another modem, it disconnects. If you select this checkbox and are consistently experiencing hang-ups when you dial a given number, try deselecting this checkbox to see if this improves your connection.

- *Compress Data.* Select this checkbox to ensure that data sent over the modem is compressed before it is transmitted. Doing this provides a greater level of throughput on most modems. This option is selected by default.
- *Use Cellular Protocol.* Select this checkbox to ensure that connections over a cellular modem are reliable.

> **Note**
>
> Use Cellular Protocol is only used for modems defined as cellular modems in the modem driver database. Most modems have this checkbox deselected; therefore, it is deselected by default. You cannot force this option.

Use Flow Control Section

When you select the Use Flow Control checkbox, you enable the use of flow control in the modem and the options that control it. These changes are optional and may not need to be changed from their default settings unless you are trying to connect to another modem that demands you have flow control enabled.

- *Hardware (RTS/CTS).* Select this option to ensure that all flow control is handled by your hardware, such as your modem. This is the default option, because most modems support flow control in their hardware.
- *Software (XON/XOFF).* Select this option if your modem does not directly support flow control and you want to use software signals to govern it instead.

Modulation Type

The Modulation Type drop-down list contains the major types of data modulation available in your modem. Only change this option if you're attempting to dial to a modem that requires nonstandard modulation.

There are two modulation types:

- *Standard.* This is the default setting and is the usual type of modulation supported by most modems.
- *Nonstandard (Bell, HST).* This setting is typically used by modems not used in North America.

Extra Settings

You can type a command string to be passed to the modem upon initialization in the Extra Settings text box. Because most modems already have the initialization strings they need for the best performance in their drivers, there is usually no need to change this setting.

For example, if you needed to pass the string "ATZ2" to the modem before dialing, you would type ATZ2 in the Extra Settings text box.

Record a Log File

Select the Record a Log File checkbox to create an ongoing list of calls, errors, and modem initialization details in a file named MODEMLOG.TXT. This file is kept in the main Windows NT directory.

If you have trouble connecting, staying connected, or getting maximum throughput, select this checkbox and read the file that results.

Configuring Telephony Options

Telephony is the term for hardware and software that deals with telephone equipment. Here it refers to the locale settings for phone dialing used by Windows NT and the actual drivers that comprise the Windows NT telephony subsystem.

To open the Telephony window:

1. Open the Start menu and launch Control Panel.
2. Double-click the Telephony icon in Control Panel.

You can also get there by clicking the Dialing Properties button in the Modem Properties sheet (see fig. 13.9).

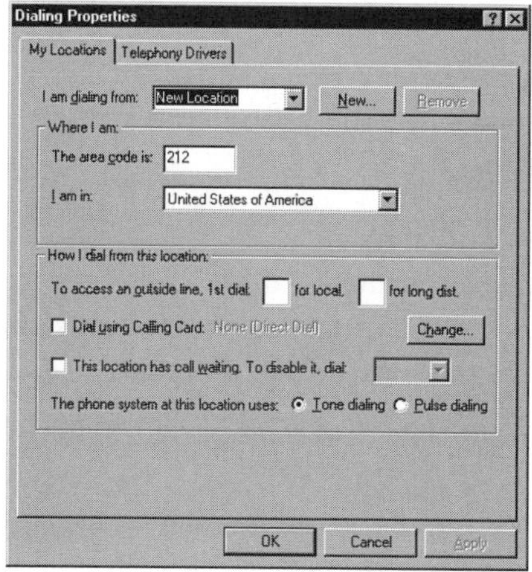

Fig. 13.9
The My Locations page of the Dialing Properties sheet contains information about where you're dialing from.

Windows NT understands that a computer can be in different places at different times—and not just because it's a portable computer. To this end, the Telephony subsystem registers where a computer is dialing from and the proper options to use in each case. Each set of settings is called a location.

My Locations Page

The My Location page of the Dialing Properties sheet lets you choose from a list of installed locations (or create your own) and change the settings that go with that location. Default settings are created for these when you first install a modem, and do not need to be changed by the user unless he or she wants to do so.

- *I Am Dialing From.* You can change the name for the default setting in this drop-down list by typing a new one. If you're dialing from home, for example, just type **Home**.
- *New.* Click the New button to create a new location (with the default title of New Location, of course).
- *Remove.* Click this button to remove the currently selected location. This option is not available when you only have one location left.

Where I Am

The Where I Am section allows you to describe where you're dialing from. If you set up a location to dial from, then you must also provide the following information:

- *The Area Code Is.* Type the area code you are dialing from in this text box. Area code conventions can vary depending on what country you're in.
- *I Am In.* Choose the name of the country from which you're calling from this drop-down list. The default for the U.S. version of Windows NT is United States of America.

How I Dial from This Location

The How I Dial from This Location section governs how calls are placed from the location you're in. You will need to provide these settings if you are using a call location as described in the previous sections.

- *To Access an Outside Line, 1st dial.* Enter the prefixes needed to dial local and long distance calls. Most business telephone systems require dialing a 9 before placing an outside call. In such a case, type **9** in both text boxes. These text boxes are empty by default.
- *Dial Using Calling Card.* Select this checkbox if you want to dial using a calling card. This option is deselected by default, and there is no card selected when it is enabled. Click Change to provide a calling card number.
- *This Location Has Call Waiting. To Disable It, Dial.* Select this checkbox if you have call waiting. This also enables the drop-down list that

contains three of the most common call waiting disable codes: 1170, *70, and 70#. If your telephone system uses a different code, type it in.

- *The Phone System at this Location Uses: Tone Dialing, Pulse Dialing.* Choose Tone or Pulse to select the kind of dialing done through your phone system.

Telephony Drivers Page

The Telephony Drivers page lists all the drivers that govern telephony currently installed in Windows NT (see fig. 13.10). Windows NT comes preinstalled with all the drivers needed to operate telephony properly, so you should not have to modify anything out-of-the-box. However, Microsoft or third-party manufacturers might supply additional drivers later on.

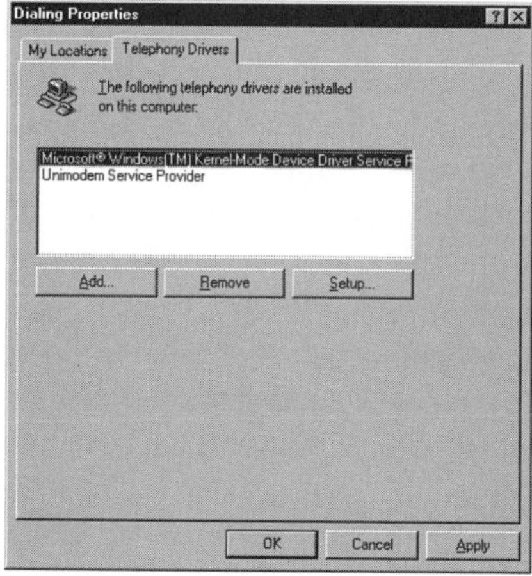

Fig. 13.10 All drivers that govern telephony are listed in the Telephony Drivers page.

Modem Troubleshooting

Most modems work well with the default settings provided for them by Windows NT's TAPI drivers. But things can go wrong. You can have dropped connections, garbled data, or a modem that doesn't seem to be working at all.

Fortunately, the most common problems are usually the simplest, and you can solve the majority of modem problems with a little patience and thought.

Problems: No Dial Tone, No Answer from the Modem

- *Are you able to get a dial tone from the phone line through a conventional phone?* If you can, there might be something wrong with the cable connecting the modem to the phone jack. If not, there might be something wrong with the phone jack.

- *Is the modem plugged in and turned on? Are the phone and data cables connected correctly?*
- *If you have an external modem, is your select port enabled and functioning, and is the data cable correctly set up?* Some external modems use 25-pin cables, and some users have mistakenly plugged the other end into their LPT port. (Some external modems do use LPT ports for high throughput, but most don't.)

Problems: Garbled Data, Constant Hang Ups

- *Is your driver set for exactly the same model number and manufacturer as your modem?* Make sure the port you're using is not also assigned to a different device somewhere else.
- *Are the data bits, stop bits, parity, and other settings correct?* Some older computers (such as the dialups for the computer service, CompuServe) require different modem settings than the default.
- If you get better results with a different modem or with lower baud rates, you might be dealing with a modem on the other end that works in a nonstandard fashion and responds better to different settings. Experiment by turning off error correction, compression, lower baud rates, and so on until you can connect reliably.
- Are you using a leased line that has a different voltage or connection requirement than a conventional phone line? Some modems are not designed to work with leased lines and can be damaged if you plug them into one. ❖

CHAPTER 14

Adding Printers and Fonts

by Serdar Yegulalp

Windows NT lets you install and configure printers with ease—whether they are connected locally by an LPT: or COM: port, or accessed via a network. Windows NT also makes it possible to allow other people on your network to print to your printer. You control who has the authority to do so.

Because most printers don't have more than a few fonts built into their hardware (and printing with the same fonts over and over again gets boring really fast), Windows NT also lets you install and use TrueType fonts on installed printers. For printers that come with their own soft fonts, Windows NT has controls to allow you to upload and manage soft fonts.

In this chapter, you learn to

- Install a local or network printer with the Add Printer Wizard
- Configure existing printers through the Printer Properties sheet
- Troubleshoot problems specific to local and network printers
- Install and manage TrueType fonts

Installing a Local Printer

Most standalone computers—even Windows NT machines—have some kind of local connection to a printer. Even if they don't, it's a good idea to have at least one printer driver installed. Some programs refuse to work, or behave badly, unless a printer driver has been installed.

Before you try to install a printer, make sure you know the following:

- What make and model your printer is
- Which port the printer is attached to

Caution

If you aren't sure of any of this information, get the needed information from the person responsible for setting up the printer, such as your system administrator. Don't try to guess your way through this.

Using the Add Printer Wizard

Windows NT uses the Add Printer Wizard to guide users through each stage of installing and configuring a printer, both local and remote. This section shows you how to install a locally connected printer.

Note

When you install Windows NT, it doesn't auto-detect printers. The responsibility of installing printers falls to the user or system administrator running Windows NT.

The Add Printer Wizard can install any of the printer drivers provided with Windows NT, which covers nearly every commonly used printer. But if you're using a recently introduced printer with its own Windows NT drivers, the Add Printer Wizard lets you install those as well—as long as you have the disk provided with the printer that contains the Windows NT 4.0 drivers.

Tip

Many NT users are concerned about getting proper driver support for their hardware, because the amount of hardware directly supported by NT isn't as large as the amount of hardware supported by Windows 95. If you don't see your printer's manufacturer or model listed when you use the Add Printer Wizard, check your printer's manual to see if it's compatible with another popular brand of printer. For example, most laser printers claim some form of compatibility with the LaserJet line of printers from Hewlett Packard. If this is the case, then you would find out which LaserJet model your printer can emulate and use that driver for it.

Follow these steps to install a locally connected printer in Windows NT:

1. Open the Start menu and choose Settings, Printers. The Printers window appears (see fig. 14.1). You can also open the Control Panel and double-click the Printers icon.

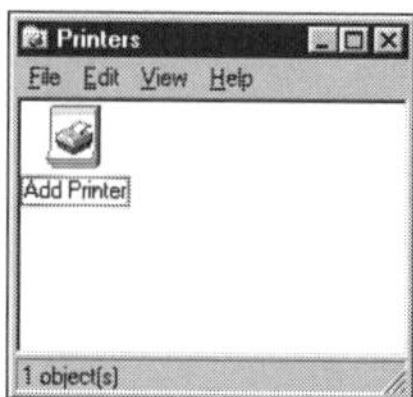

Fig. 14.1
The Printers window lists all currently installed printers, along with the Add Printer Wizard.

2. Double-click the Add Printer icon. The Add Printer Wizard appears (see fig. 14.2).

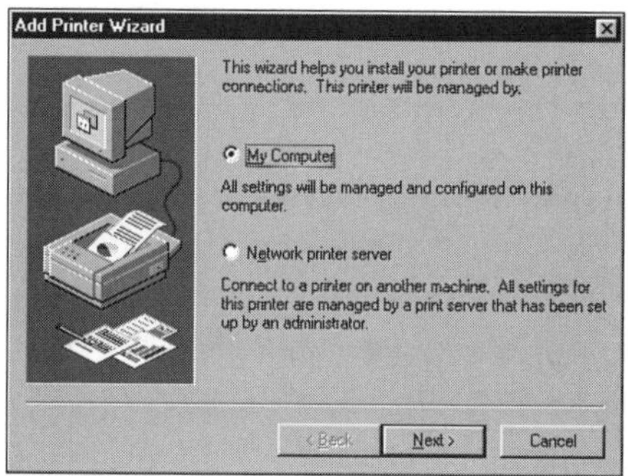

Fig. 14.2
The Add Printer Wizard works for both local and remote printers.

3. Select My Computer for a locally connected printer. Choose Next.

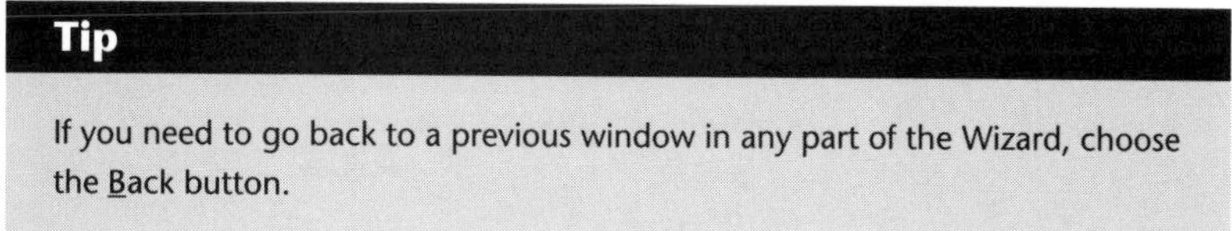

Tip

If you need to go back to a previous window in any part of the Wizard, choose the Back button.

4. The next Add Printer Wizard screen allows you to tell Windows NT which port your printer is attached to (see fig. 14.3). Check the port your printer is connected to.

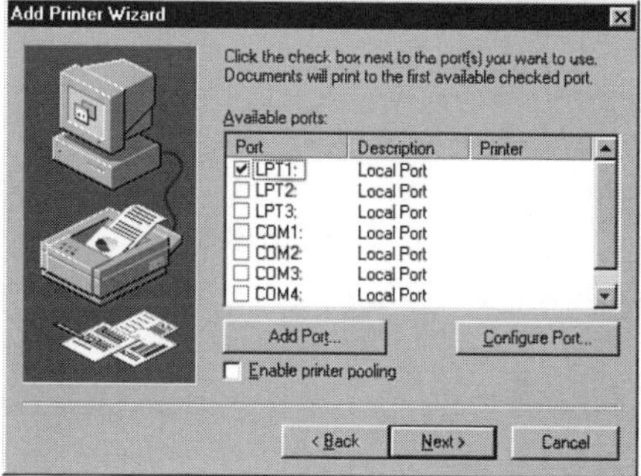

Fig. 14.3
You can select more than one port for a given printer, or print directly to a file.

Note

The "FILE:" entry in the port list means that the printer will direct its output to a dump file on a drive. The user specifies the name of the file at print time. This can be useful if you want to provide a copy of the print job to someone else, for instance.

Most programs will let you print to a file regardless of what you've selected here, but if you're certain you're always going to be printing to a file, choose this. Also, if you don't have a printer installed but you're probably going to use software that requires the presence of a printer driver, such as some desktop publishing programs, choose a popular printer brand (the Hewlett Packard LaserJet 4 PostScript is a good choice) and connect it to the "FILE:" port.

5. By selecting more than one port, you can tell Windows NT to attempt to print to several ports in the order that they appear on the list. This is useful if you have several printers of the same model attached to your computer and want to avoid queuing more than one job per printer at a time. Check off the ports that apply.
6. Clicking the Configure Port button will let you edit specific details concerning how Windows NT handles that port while printing. For an LPT port, Windows NT will let you set the number of seconds Windows NT will wait for a response from a printer before returning an error condition (see fig. 14.4).

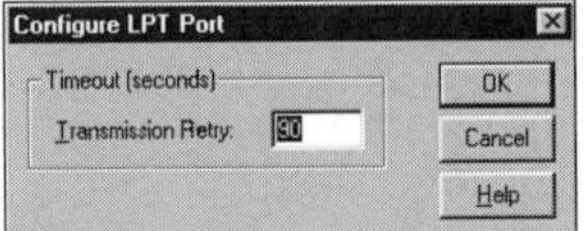

Fig. 14.4
The dialog box for configuring an LPT: port lets you choose the time interval between retries. 90 seconds is a good number to stick with.

7. Clicking the Configure Port button on a COM: port will let you control specific settings for that port, or add or delete other COM: ports (see fig. 14.5). If you have a printer set to use a COM: port and you haven't configured your COM: settings yet, this would be a good time to do so. Otherwise, click Next.

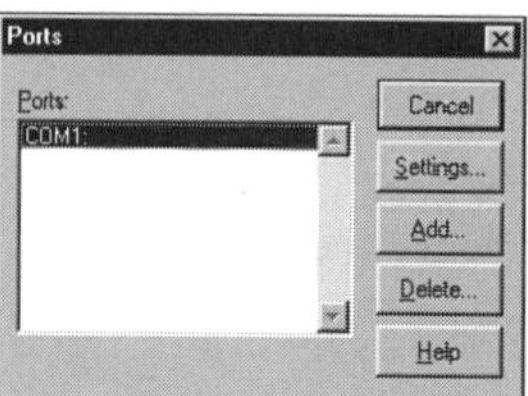

Fig. 14.5
The COM: dialog box that appears when you click Configure is the same one you get when you double-click the Ports icon in Control Panel.

8. The Manufacturers pane contains a list of all printer makers who have provided drivers for Windows NT (see fig. 14.6). Select the maker of your printer.

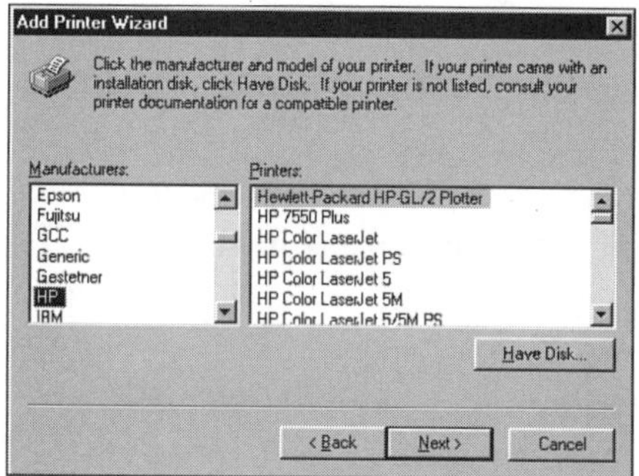

Fig. 14.6
Choose the make and model of your printer.

Tip

By typing the first few letters of the manufacturer while in the Manufacturers list, you can move quickly to the name you want without having to scroll to it. This also applies to the Printers list.

9. The Printers pane contains a list of all the drivers for printers provided from the selected manufacturer. Select the exact model of your printer and choose Next.

Note

If you already have the drivers needed for the printer you've chosen (for example, if you previously installed the printer under Windows NT 4.0 and removed it for some reason), the Add Printer Wizard asks if you want to keep the existing driver or replace it with a new copy (see fig. 14.7). Windows NT

continues

continued

recommends you keep the existing driver; this is safe in most cases. If you're certain the old driver has become corrupted, replace it with a fresh copy.

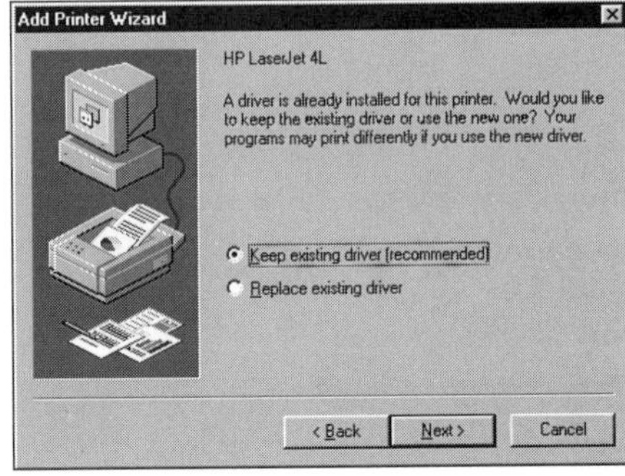

Fig. 14.7
If a driver for the printer you've selected is already present, this message appears.

10. In the Printer Name text box, type a name for this printer—preferably something short and descriptive. You can assign a longer description to a printer later. If you want this to become your default printer, select Yes (see fig. 14.8). Choose Next.

Note

This is *not* the same as a share name for your printer. The share name is the name shown for your printer when displayed in the Network Neighborhood. You will have an opportunity to assign a share name later.

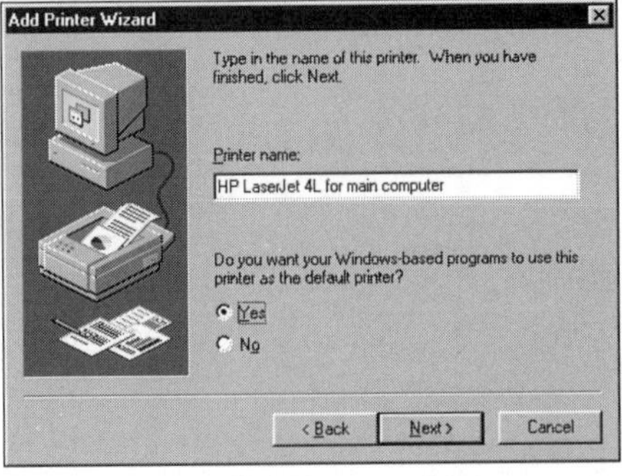

Fig. 14.8
A short name for your printer will do here. You also get to choose if you want to make this your default printer.

11. The next screen of the Add Printer Wizard allows you to control the sharing of your printer (see fig. 14.9).

If you want to have your locally connected printer recognized as a printer on the network, select Shared and then type a name in the Share Name text box. This can be any sequence of characters, including spaces and numbers.

If you want to allow systems that connect to your printer to have the proper driver for the printer downloaded to them when they connect, select the appropriate type of driver from the list box. Drivers are available for Windows 95 and Windows NT 3.1, 3.51, and 4.0 machines that use the x86, Mips, or Alpha chipsets. (Windows NT 4.0 machines also support the PowerPC.)

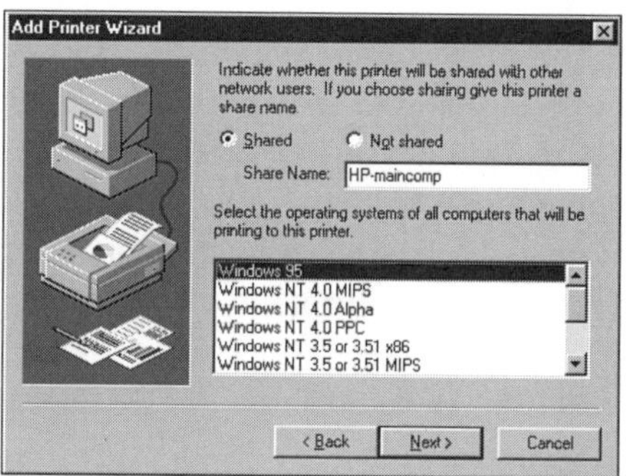

Fig. 14.9 Enable Sharing when you want your printer to be accessible over a network.

12. With all the basic configuration options set, Windows NT can print a test page for you after installing the needed drivers. Select Yes to print a one-page document with some sample graphics and text on it (see fig. 14.10). Choose Finish.

> **Note**
>
> If the text page doesn't print or if it looks distorted, save it and refer to it when reading the section, "Troubleshooting Locally Connected Printers," later in this chapter.

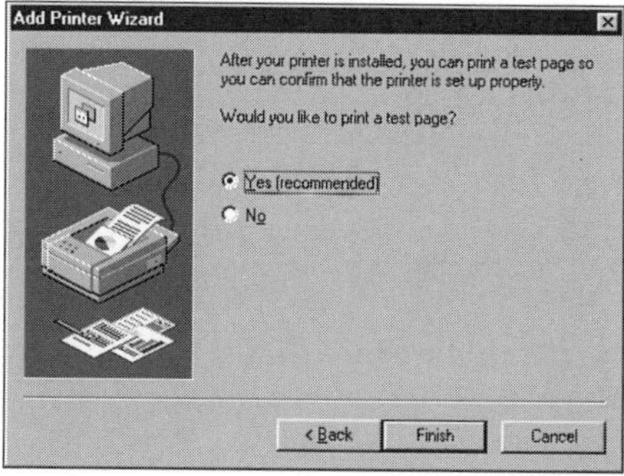

Fig. 14.10 Windows NT lets you print a test page before concluding the printer installation.

13. After choosing Finish, Windows NT probably prompts you for the appropriate Windows NT disks or CD-ROM. If you're installing from a network, provide the correct network directory or share path.

If everything copies successfully from the disks, the Printer Properties sheet appears with your new printer installed and an icon representing it. You've now completed the basic installation of your local printer and are ready to configure it. If you chose to print a test page, it should come rolling out of your printer right about now as well.

Configuring a Local Printer through the Properties Sheet

When you right-click a printer icon in the Printers window, you can choose the Properties menu option from the shortcut menu. As with many other Windows NT system objects (like My Computer or the Recycle Bin), the Properties sheet lets you configure that item's individual settings. With printers, you can change drivers or port settings, reassign names to printers, redirect output and virtual port trapping, control job scheduling, and do many other things.

The General Page

The first tab on the Printer Properties sheet is the General tab. All of the most basic data about the printer is on this page (see fig. 14.11).

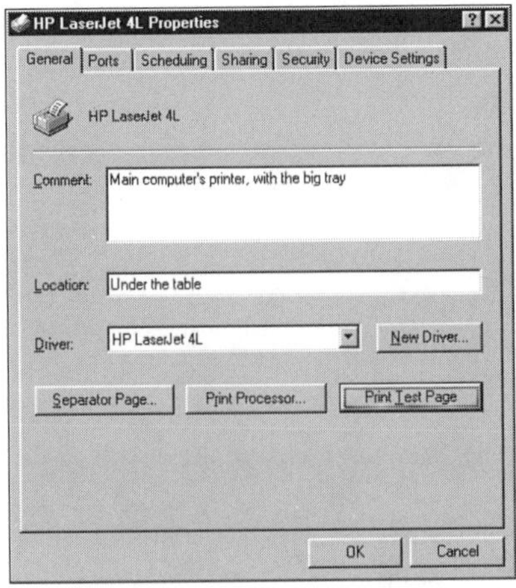

Fig. 14.11
The General page of the Properties sheet gives basic information about the printer, including administrator comments and physical location.

- *Comment.* This text box can contain any comments you want to supply for the printer. Users with access to the printer can view these comments when they open the printer's properties sheet.

- *Location.* This text box describes the printer's location. This text box is also available to any other user with access to the printer.
- *Driver.* This list box indicates what driver is currently installed for this printer. If you make a mistake when installing the driver or if you change the printer to another model later on, you can change the driver without having to reinstall the printer. Choose the New Driver button to choose the driver from the Manufacturers and Printers lists.
- *Separator Page.* Choosing this button lets you enable, disable, or change the look of this printer's separator page. A *separator page* lists the name of the user in large letters, the name of the print job, and the time and date of the printout. It works much like one of those plastic bars at the grocery store—you place it between your groceries and another customer's groceries to keep them separate. A separator page is really only useful for network or shared printers, where you have jobs from more than one user at a time.
- *Print Processor.* The Print Processor feature lets you control which Windows NT system component handles the rasterizing of print jobs. Different printer processors may allow you to send different data types to the printer. The default print processor is named **winprint** and can handle all the major varieties of printer data: RAW, NT EMF, and TEXT. You will generally not need to change this option.
- *Print Test Page.* Choose this button to produce a test page. This is the same test page you had the option of printing when you first installed the printer. A text page is useful if you change drivers or configurations and want to be sure the printer is still responding correctly.

The Ports Page

Click the Ports tab to view the Ports page of the Printer Properties dialog box (see fig. 14.12). Visually and functionally, the Ports page is the same as the Available Ports list in figure 14.5. The only difference here is the Enable Bidirectional Support checkbox, which should be selected for most LPT: ports. If the checkbox is grayed out, the port probably doesn't have bi-directional support or is already being used to the best of its capabilities.

By choosing Add Port, Delete Port, or Configure Port, you can change the allocation of ports to match your physical hardware setup if the two are different or have been changed since you last configured ports in Windows NT.

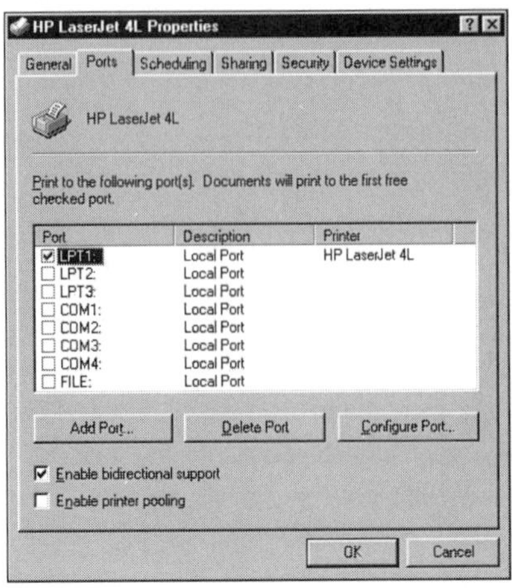

Fig. 14.12
The Ports page is the same as the one that appears when you double-click the Ports icon in the Control Panel, except for the bidirectional support option.

The Job Scheduling Page

The options on the Job Scheduling page let you control priorities for print jobs as well as their spooling behavior (see fig. 14.13). You also have precise control over the printer's availability.

- *Available.* The Available area of the Job Scheduling page has two main choices:

  Always. The printer is always available.

  From, To. By filling in these fields with time codes in the correct format (which varies depending on the locale-specific configuration of your Windows NT installation), you can specify a time interval for when the printer is available.

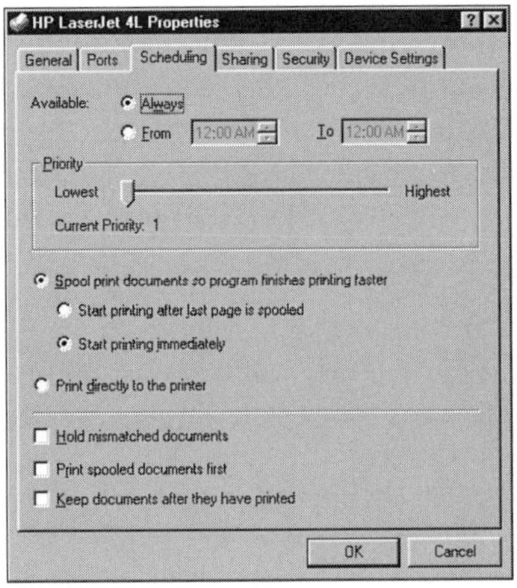

Fig. 14.13
On the Job Scheduling page, you can control just when the printer is available and how jobs are to be spooled through it.

Note

The restrictions you place on a printer's availability may not necessarily be true in reality, but if you have a printer in a room which is to be secured during certain hours—or that is annoying to hear rattling away at three in the morning—it's nice to have control over when the printer is alive and when it's not.

Tip

You can't specify multiple time segments for the From and To options (such as, 9-10 AM and 5-6 PM).

You can do this a different way, however. Install two separate printer devices under Printers that use the same driver and point to the same port. However, use different From and To specifications. Label each printer so there's no confusion, and add comments in the Comment text box of the General tab for each printer about when they are available.

- *Priority*. Aside from the order in which print jobs are received, Windows NT ranks spooled print jobs in order of priority. Obviously, higher-ranked jobs get to go to the head of the queue when introduced into the spooler. Set the Priority control to the proper level for the computer you're currently using.
- *Spool Print Jobs So Program Finishes Printing Faster*. Spooling basically means buffering. By selecting this option, Windows NT acts as an intermediary between the program doing the printing and the printer itself. It takes the entire program's printout at once and feeds it to the printer in manageable chunks. By having the operating system handle this, the burden is no longer on the program, which could get tied up for quite a while when printing.

Note

The opposite of this option, by the way, is Print Directly to the Printer. By printing directly to the printer, you may get a faster response from the printer but it will almost certainly tie up your computer longer. Note that some programs, like Word 7.0 for Windows NT and Windows 95, have the capability to spool print jobs on their own.

- *Start Printing After Last/First Page Is Spooled.* Selecting one of these options enables you to decide when Windows NT starts feeding the print job to the printer: either when the program is finishing its print job or when it's beginning. If you have programs that print excruciatingly slowly or that perform a lot of multi-page print jobs, and you hate waiting for hard copy, the first page option is probably best.
- *Print Directly to the Printer.* Selecting this option disables Windows NT-level spooling entirely. All print jobs go right from the program to the printer, with all the delays that might imply. As mentioned previously, if you have programs that spool printing internally and you don't want to bother with the memory or processor overhead of an OS-level spooling subsystem (and you're not working with a shared printer), you might want to elect this option.
- *Hold Mismatched Jobs.* If a spooled job doesn't finish printing, Windows NT can hold the job until the problem is fixed (whatever it may be). The user can then resend the job.
- *Print Spooled Jobs First.* When you select this checkbox, any jobs that have been sent directly to the printer will be deferred in favor of job that have been spooled.
- *Keep Jobs After They Have Been Printed.* After a spooled job has been sent to the printer, its print job does not vanish from the queue list. It stays there until you remove it manually. Using the queue of expired print jobs is a useful way to track what jobs have gone through the printer.

The Sharing Page

The options in the Sharing page governs permissions over the printer, if it's shared out over a network. Because the printer is not currently shared, the Not Shared option is selected (see fig. 14.14).

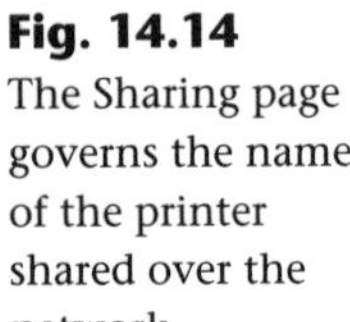

Fig. 14.14
The Sharing page governs the name of the printer shared over the network.

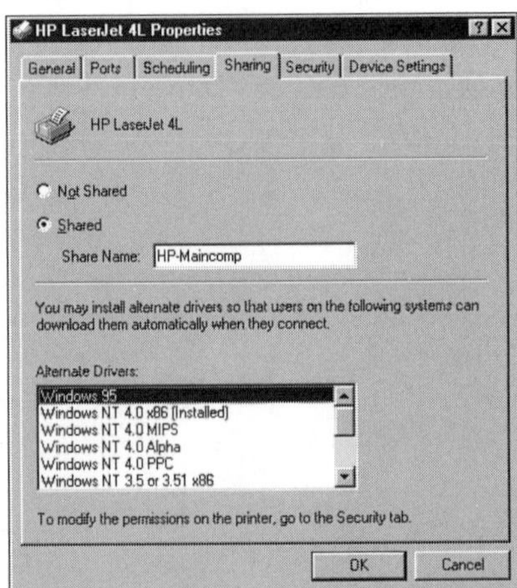

To share the printer, choose Shared and type a name (uppercase letters, numbers, and spaces are acceptable) for the printer in the Share Name text box. A *share name* is what a network user will see of the printer when they browse the Network Neighborhood.

The Security Page

The Security page allows you to control three aspects of security for a shared printer: permissions, auditing, and ownership (see fig. 14.15). Not every user has access to these options; for this example, however, assume you are logged in as an Administrator and consequently have access to everything.

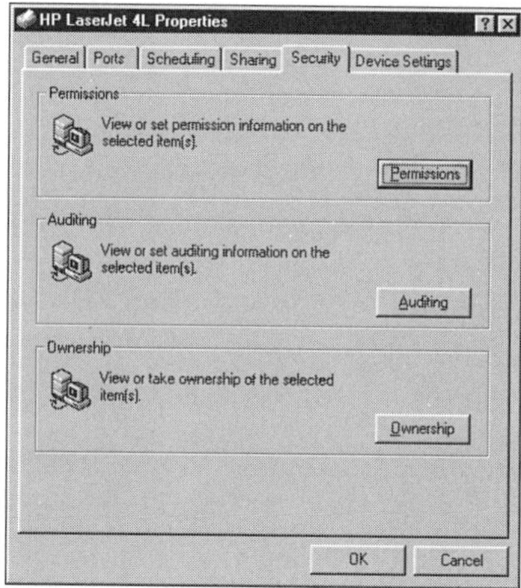

Fig. 14.15
The Security page options allows you to control permissions, auditing, and ownership.

Permissions. Choose the Permissions button to open the Printer Permissions dialog box (see fig. 14.16). Here you can edit what users and user groups can perform actions to the printer and what those actions can be.

Each user or user group listed in the Name box has a level of access assigned to them, which is listed on the right. You can change the access level for a given user or user group by selecting that group from the list, and then selecting the new access level from the Type of Access drop-down list.

There are several types of access:

- *Full Control.* The designated user or user group has total control over the printer. They can change settings, print, stop jobs in progress, and so on.
- *Manage Documents.* Users or user groups with this level of access are capable of printing to the printer as well as deleting jobs in progress. They cannot make changes to settings.

- *Print.* Those with this level of access can only print to the printer; they can't delete jobs in progress or change settings.
- *No Access.* The designated user or user group has no rights to this printer. They can't use it, print to it, or edit its attributes. They can see the printer—they just can't do anything with it.

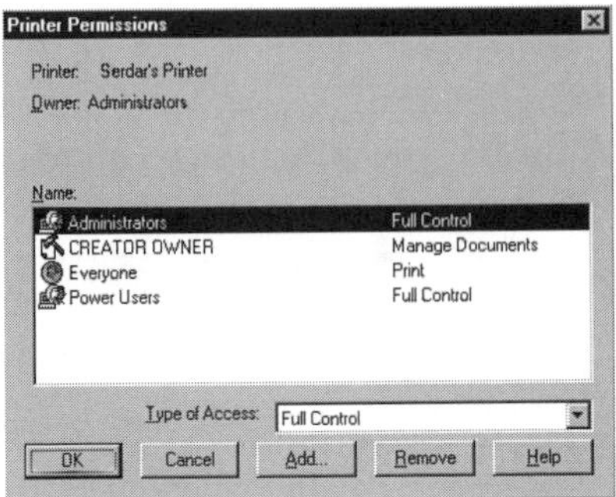

Fig. 14.16
The Printer Permissions dialog box lets you control just how much individual users or whole user groups can do on a particular printer.

Choosing the Add and Remove buttons lets you add names from a master browse list of user names or delete the highlighted name from the Name box.

Auditing. Choose the Auditing button to open the Printer Auditing dialog box (see fig. 14.17). Here, you can change how specific printer events are logged to the Windows NT security log.

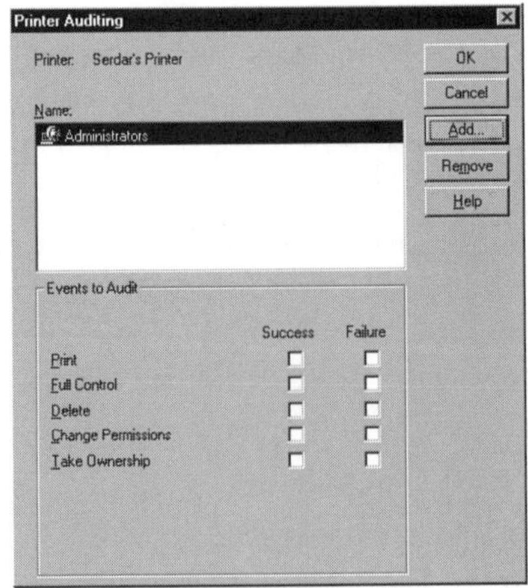

Fig. 14.17
The Printer Auditing dialog box governs what printer events are logged for what users and user groups.

> **Note**
>
> For auditing to work here, it must first be enabled for specific users or user groups. You do this through the User Manager utility, also known as the User Manager for Domains utility in Windows NT Server.

To change auditing for a specific user or event, follow these steps:

1. Make sure the user name or group you want to set auditing for is in the Name list. If it isn't, choose Add and use the Add Users and Groups dialog box to include the names you want (see fig. 14.18).
2. Select the user or group whose auditing behavior you want to change.
3. Select the checkboxes that indicate what events to audit. If you want to audit events that are not successful (either because of lack of permission or a failure of equipment or software), select the Failure boxes of the events you want logged.
4. Press OK to finish.

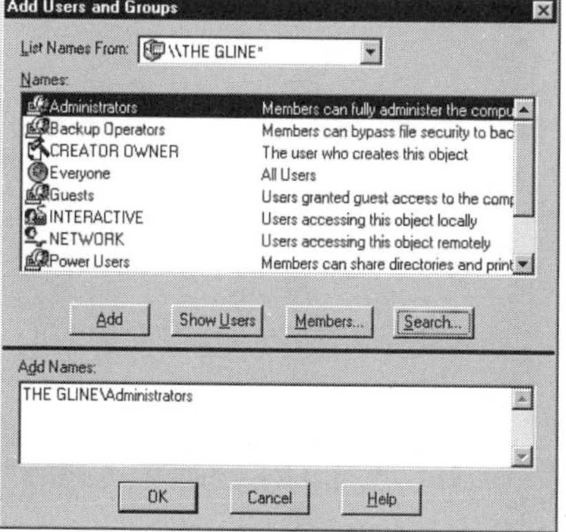

Fig. 14.18 Use the Add Users and Groups dialog box to include names that aren't in the Name list.

Ownership. Choose the Ownership button to open the Owner dialog box (see fig. 14.19). To take ownership of a printer, choose the Take Ownership button. Ownership of a printer is more symbolic than anything in Windows NT 4.0; it's meant to show which user is intended to do the actual management of the printer.

Fig. 14.19 The Owner dialog box describes the current owner of the printer.

> **Note**
>
> Only Administrators can take ownership of printers. Ownership cannot be given to users; it can only be taken by administrators.

The Device Options Page

The Device Options page lists any miscellaneous options that are specific to individual models of printers. Every printer's Device Options page will look different than the one shown here for this reason.

Figure 14.20 shows the Device Options for the Hewlett Packard LaserJet 4L. For example, the Page Protect option (toggled off in this example) is displayed here because it is specific to this model of printer.

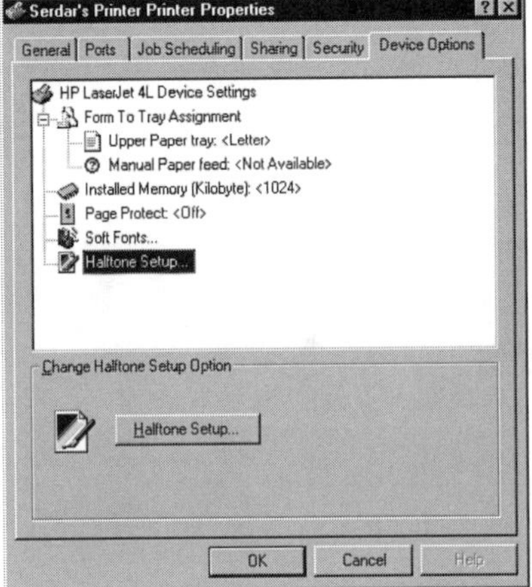

Fig. 14.20 The Device Options page for the Hewlett Packard LaserJet 4L. Every printer shows different options.

Troubleshooting Locally Connected Printers

Most of the problems that occur while installing and configuring a locally connected printer aren't hard to resolve, and probably can be found in this section, which lists simple, commonplace oversights.

No Printout, No Connection, Time Out

Here are some common problems that result in the printer timing out or producing no printout at all:

- *Is the printer receiving power, and are all the cables and connections to the printer OK?* Check to see that the pins on both ends of the signal cable (and in the computer and the printer) are all intact. Make sure nothing is bent, broken, or missing. Cable problems can also cause distorted or garbled printouts.

- *Is the printer offline?* Most printers go online by default when they're turned on, but make sure the printer is actually online. If it seems to be but still isn't responding, try resetting the printer or taking the printer offline and then back on again.
- *Is there paper and toner in the printer? Has the printer developed a paper jam or is the toner cartridge not properly inserted?* These are often overlooked, but common problems that can be easily solved.
- *Are the printer ports configured correctly in the hardware and the software?* Some computers allow the user to change the memory address and interrupt settings of COM: and LPT: ports. If they've been changed from the standard settings, Windows NT may not be able to talk to them properly. Reset them to their original factory settings. Or, if they were changed to prevent conflicts with other hardware, change Windows NT's ports settings to match their hardware settings.
- *Is the port hardware itself functioning?* A port that's not based off the motherboard but is on a standalone plug-in card might not be working.

Garbled Printout, Wrong Fonts

Here's a list of common problems that can cause a printout to come out looking garbled.

- *Do you have the correct printer driver for your printer installed?* If you're using a PostScript driver, make sure your printer supports PostScript. Also, make sure this support is enabled in your printer's hardware. Not all PostScript printers have PostScript support enabled by default.
- *Are your printer's font substitution tables configured correctly?* If you're seeing completely incorrect fonts being printed, your printer may be substituting the wrong fonts.

  To look at the font substitution table for your printer (if it has one), open Printers, right-click the icon for your printer, choose Properties, and then choose the Device Options tab. Look for the Font Substitution Table option in the list at the top and expand it. A list of system fonts and what gets substituted for them in the printer appears (see fig. 14.21). Click a font to see a list of possible substitutes if you'd rather use one of them instead (Download as Soft Font should be the topmost entry in the list).

If you still can't get the correct fonts to print (even after resetting font substitutions), set all the listed fonts to Download as Soft Font and see what happens.

> **Note**
>
> Some printers (mostly non-PostScript models) don't have a Font Substitution Table option. For this example, I used the HP LaserJet 4ML, which is a PostScript printer.

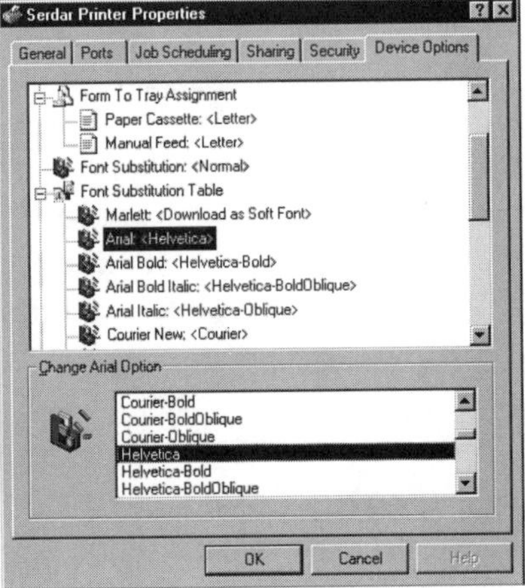

Fig. 14.21
The Font Substitution table for the HP LaserJet 4ML PostScript printer.

> **Note**
>
> Make sure the fonts you specify really are the fonts you want downloaded. Print examples of the font to see if it matches what you need. Sometimes the "wrong font" turns out to be the one actually being specified, with nothing being wrong except the user's expectations!

- *Does the amount of RAM specified in the Device Options page match the amount of RAM actually installed in your printer?* If you've specified too large of a number, the printer will almost always print incorrectly.

Installing a Network Printer

Windows NT lets you install printers shared over any Windows NT-compatible network. Installing a network printer isn't that different from installing a locally connected printer, but there are a few steps in the Add Printer Wizard that have to be followed differently.

1. Launch the Add Printer Wizard. There are two ways to do this: Open the Start menu and choose Settings, Printers; or double-click the Printers icon in the Control Panel. Choose Next.

> **Note**
>
> You can't install a network printer unless it's attached to the network and has been correctly installed on the computer it's physically attached to.

2. When the wizard prompts you to choose a locally connected or network printer, choose Network (see fig. 14.22).
3. Windows NT browses the network looking for printers. Open the branches for the part of the network where the printer you want to connect to is and click OK.

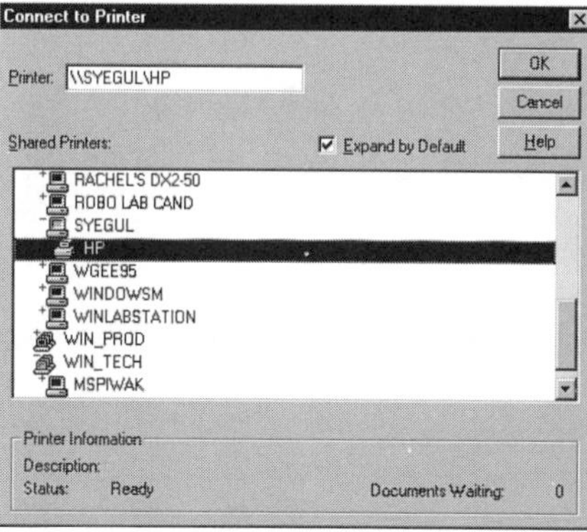

Fig. 14.22
The Connect to Printer dialog box allows you to search for all printers in the Network Neighborhood.

If you don't already have the driver for the printer you're trying to connect to installed locally, Windows NT may prompt you to insert the appropriate disks. When Windows NT is finished installing the required drivers, the final page of the wizard and the printer's properties sheet appear. Choose Finish on the wizard.

The biggest difference between the properties of a locally connected printer and the properties of a network printer is in the port assignment. If you click the Ports tab of the Printer Properties sheet for a network printer, there will be an additional port selected (see fig. 14.23). This new port is named for the network connection the printer is on, and is usually identified as a LAN Manager Printer Port.

> **Tip**
>
> If you know the network connection name of your printer (for example, \\SYEGUL\HP is shown here), you can create a new port in the Ports page with that name and connect to a network printer manually.

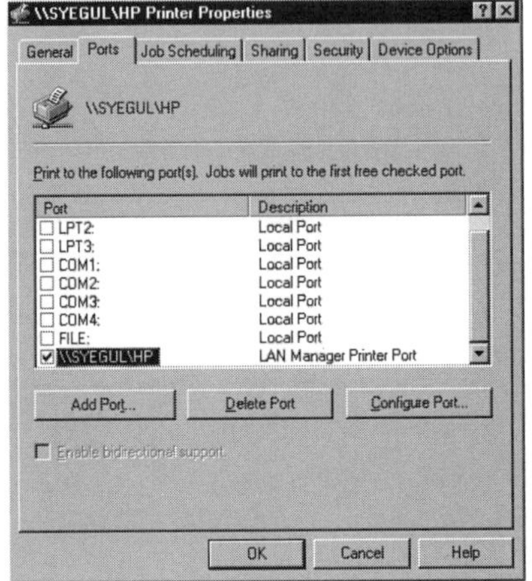

Fig. 14.23
The Ports page for a network printer shows the name of the printer's network connection as a port.

Troubleshooting Network Printers

When attempting to print to a network printer, all the problems that can plague a locally connected printer can arise. But there are additional problems that can go wrong with a network printer. The following is a brief list of issues to check if a network-connected printer is not functioning properly:

- If you're printing to a print server, such as a NetWare print queue, make sure the print server computer is online and functioning properly. You may need to consult with the systems administrator in charge of the print server.

> **Note**
>
> You might also want to check out the earlier section, "Troubleshooting Locally Connected Printers."

- *Is the printer correctly connected to the print server computer?* Make sure the print server can print to the printer locally before attempting to attach to it through the network.

■ *Is the print queue stalled or paused?* If someone has taken one of the printers offline for changes or maintenance and not notified users about it, the print queue will stack up one print job after another. This is something you should bring up with the systems administrator.

Installing TrueType Fonts in Windows NT

Windows NT uses TrueType fonts to enhance its displays and printed documents. A number of basic fonts come preinstalled with Windows NT: Arial, Times New Roman, Courier, and so on. However, most Windows NT users will eventually want to expand the list of available fonts.

To install fonts in Windows NT for use on displays and in printers, follow these steps. Be sure you have ready the disk with the fonts to install.

1. Open the Start menu and choose Settings, Control Panel. The Control Panel opens (see fig. 14.24).

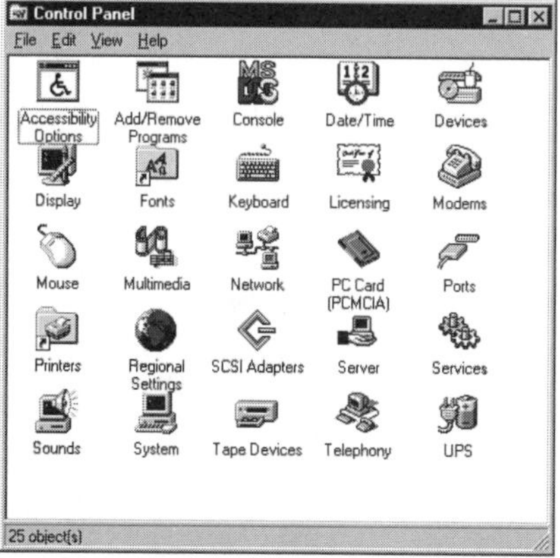

Fig. 14.24
The Control Panel contains the shortcut to the Fonts folder.

> **Tip**
>
> Another way you can get to the Fonts folder is through Explorer. Fonts is a subfolder of the main Windows directory.

2. Double-click the Fonts icon in Control Panel. The Fonts window opens (see fig. 14.25).
3. In the Fonts window, choose File, Install New Font. The Add Fonts dialog box appears (see fig. 14.26).

4. Use the Add Fonts dialog box to browse to the directory or to the disk where you have the fonts to install. The names of the fonts stored in that directory or disk appear in the List of Fonts list.

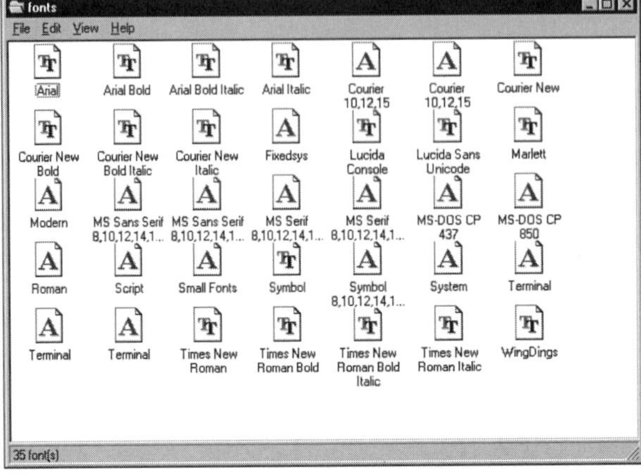

Fig. 14.25
The Fonts window lists the names of all currently installed fonts in Windows NT.

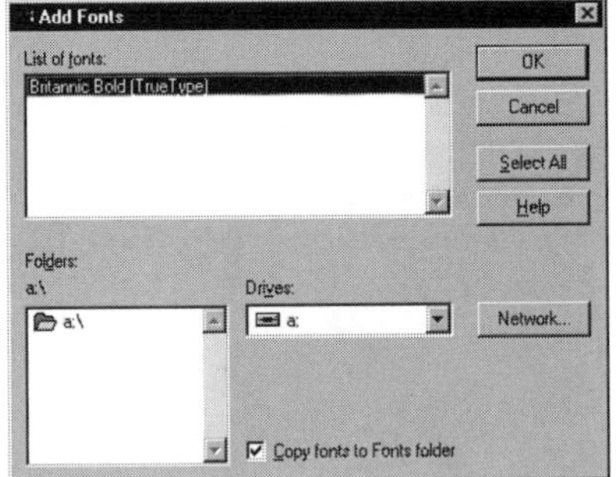

Fig. 14.26
Browse the directory containing the fonts you want to install.

5. Select the fonts you want to install from the List of Fonts list. To install them all, choose Select All. Choose OK.

> **Note**
>
> If you have specific kinds of fonts stored in separate hard disk directories (such as having all decorative fonts in a directory called \Decorative) and you want to refer to them from those directories, deselect the Copy Fonts To Fonts Folder checkbox. Windows NT will leave the fonts where they are and refer to them where they are. The Copy Fonts To Fonts Folder checkbox is selected by default, because fonts are usually installed from disk or other removable media.

6. The newly installed fonts should appear as icons in the Fonts folder (see fig. 14.27).

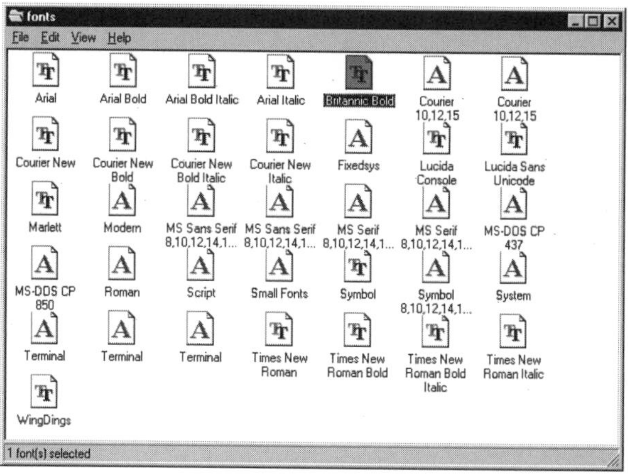

Fig. 14.27
The newly installed Britannic Bold font is now visible in the Fonts folder.

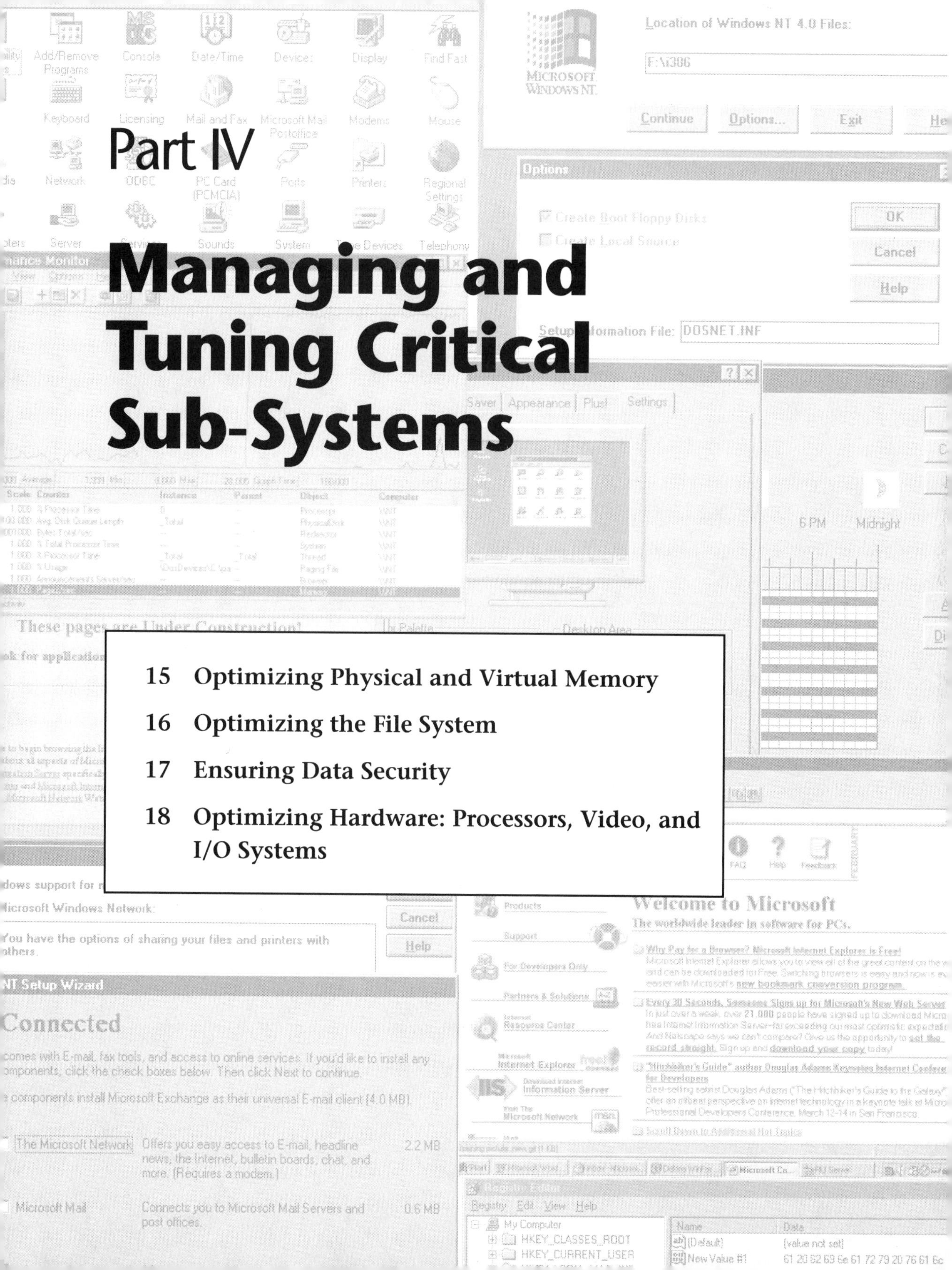

Part IV

Managing and Tuning Critical Sub-Systems

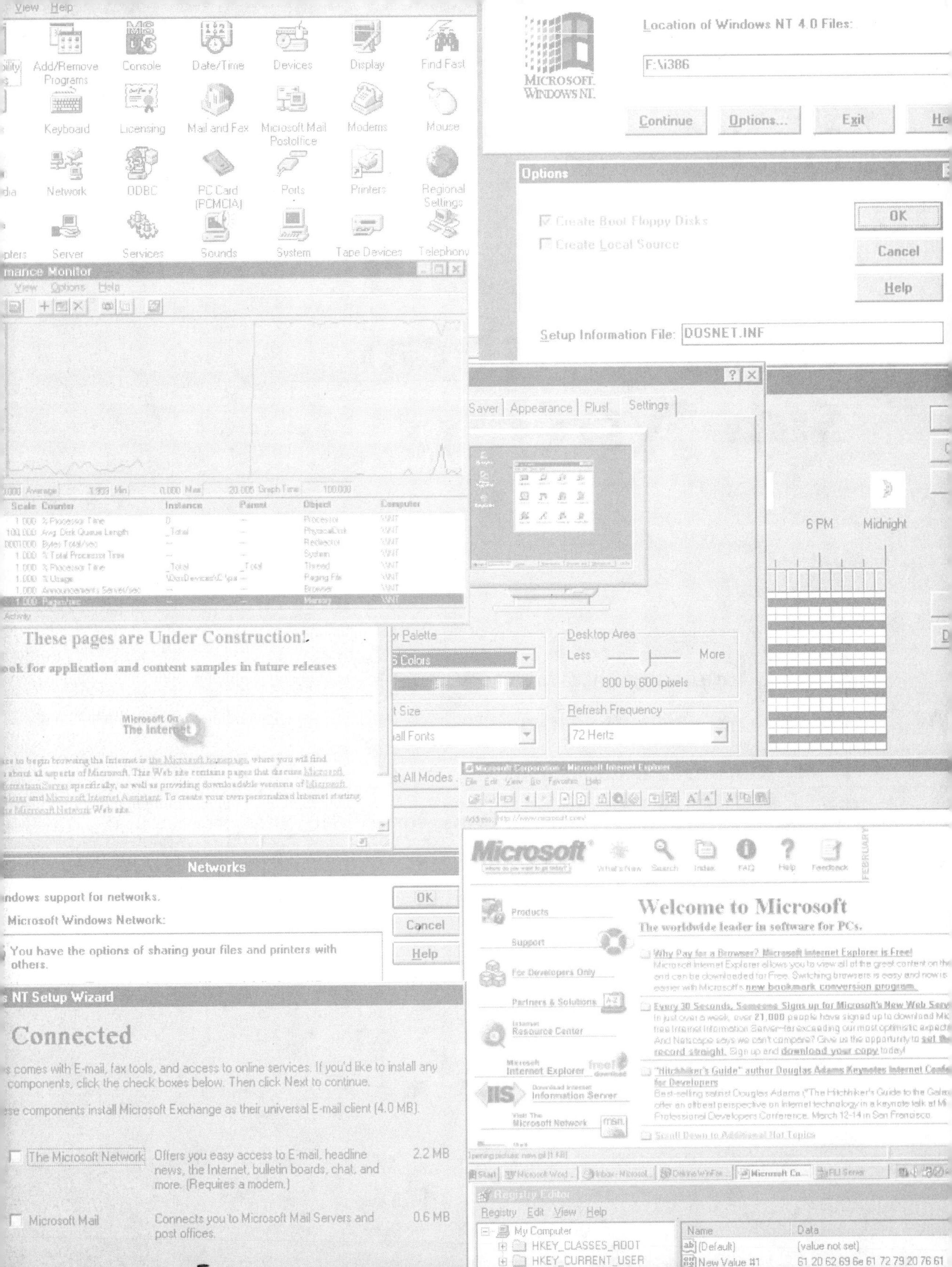

View Help
Add/Remove Programs
Console
Date/Time
Devices
Display
Find Fast
Keyboard
Licensing
Mail and Fax
Microsoft Mail Postoffice
Modems
Mouse
Network
ODBC
PC Card (PCMCIA)
Ports
Printers
Regional Settings
Server
Services
Sounds
System
Tape Devices
Telephony
MICROSOFT. WINDOWS NT.
Location of Windows NT 4.0 Files:
F:\i386
Continue
Options...
Exit
Options
Create Boot Floppy Disks
Create Local Source
OK
Cancel
Help
Setup Information File: DOSNET.INF
Saver
Appearance
Plus!
Settings
Desktop Area
Less
More
800 by 600 pixels
Refresh Frequency
72 Hertz
6 PM
Midnight
These pages are Under Construction!
Microsoft Corporation - Microsoft Internet Explorer
Microsoft
Welcome to Microsoft
The worldwide leader in software for PCs.
Products
Support
For Developers Only
Partners & Solutions
Resource Center
Internet Explorer
Information Server
Microsoft Network
Networks
OK
Cancel
Help
Microsoft Windows Network:
You have the options of sharing your files and printers with others.
NT Setup Wizard
Connected
The Microsoft Network
Offers you easy access to E-mail, headline news, the Internet, bulletin boards, chat, and more. (Requires a modem.)
2.2 MB
Microsoft Mail
Connects you to Microsoft Mail Servers and post offices.
0.6 MB
Registry Editor
Registry Edit View Help
My Computer
HKEY_CLASSES_ROOT
HKEY_CURRENT_USER
Name
Data
(Default)
(value not set)
New Value #1

CHAPTER 15

Optimizing Physical and Virtual Memory

by Serdar Yegulalp

Perhaps the single most critical issue of Windows NT performance is memory. Memory, even more than processing power in most circumstances, determines just how much Windows NT can flex its muscles. This is especially true in client/server environments where the emphasis may not be on processing power, but simply on having enough memory on the server machine running Windows NT to address each client's application needs.

Also, Windows NT is designed to be a fault-tolerant operating system. Fault tolerance and application protection all come with a price, however, and that price is the memory needed to support such a scheme.

Windows NT 4.0, as opposed to previous versions of Windows NT, puts physical memory at more of a premium. The new, more elaborate shell design, ported from Windows 95, is one reason for this. Also, a new host of system components have been introduced: TAPI, PCMCIA support, and so on. Obviously, not all of these items will be occupying memory at once, but using them as part of day-to-day Windows NT operations does mean that more memory will be used.

Another, more indirect, reason for Windows NT 4.0 being more demanding on memory than its predecessors is the increase in memory demands made by larger applications. Not every application requires 16M or 24M of RAM to execute, but the most powerful and well-written applications always put memory at a premium—especially industrial-strength graphics or engineering applications, which gobble tons of memory for sophisticated math.

In this chapter, you learn to

- Recognize the difference between physical and virtual memory
- Use guidelines to decide how much physical memory to install in a specific Windows NT system
- Optimize memory performance

Physical versus Virtual Memory

Windows NT makes use of two kinds of memory: physical memory and virtual memory.

- *Physical memory.* Memory that exists as RAM chips mounted in the computer.
- *Virtual memory.* Disk space used to mimic the behavior of RAM chips.

Physical memory, or RAM, has the advantage of speed, but the disadvantage of high cost. One megabyte of RAM for a PC sells for many times more than 1M of hard storage in any medium.

More Is Better...

Why is all of this significant? Well, as mentioned previously, Windows NT's memory demands can be partially alleviated through the creative use of disk space. By taking chunks of live memory that aren't actually being used and temporarily storing what's in them on the hard drive—a technique known as *swapping* or *paging*—it's possible to get far more use out of the memory you do have.

This scheme, while it does give any Windows NT machine a performance boost, has its limitations.

- *The size of the hard drive.* Windows NT takes up about 100M. If you're running Windows NT on a small hard drive, you won't have as much room for swap space, to say nothing of data or third-party programs.
- *The speed of the hard drive.* A slow hard drive—or a slow drive controller, for that matter—will bring Windows NT to a grinding crawl, especially when it starts swapping heavily.
- *The speed of the computer.* Swapping eats CPU cycles. The less time spent swapping, the more time spent actually running applications.

The best-equipped machine, with the biggest, fastest drives available and the highest-grade controller and CPU, will swap a lot faster than a machine with third-rate hardware in any of those categories, of course. But ultimately, the best performance will come from the machine that swaps the least. And for that to happen, there has to be enough physical RAM in the machine to keep the amount of swapping down. (No Windows NT machine will ever not swap, but the best of them swap very, very little.)

...But How Much Is Enough?

The single biggest question everyone will probably be asking at this point is: So how much physical memory *do* you need for good performance?

The starting magic number is 16M. Windows NT will perform reasonably well in 16M of RAM, provided that not too many big applications are running concurrently. Windows NT really requires 24M or more to achieve top-flight performance if you're running a mix of applications—something like three or four applications from Microsoft's 32-bit Office suite, for example.

Physical Memory Guidelines

Here is a list of pointers to give you an idea of just how much physical memory should be installed in a Windows NT machine, depending on the tasks involved.

- As mentioned at the beginning of this section, the absolute minimum amount of physical memory for any computer running Windows NT should be 16M.
- Add at least another 4M for each kind of networking service. If you're installing Dial-Up Networking, Windows Networks, and Netware Networks as services in Windows NT, then you should estimate another 2M per service. If you're using your machine as a network server, take the final number and add 50 percent.
- Add 16M if you are working regularly with graphics. This includes programs like AutoCAD, Adobe Photoshop, QuarkXpress, or any photo-realistic image rendering software.
- Add 8M for fault tolerance and system protection. This includes such things as disk mirroring and striping, software that allows you to use Windows NT to create main and backup domain controllers, backup software, virus protection software, and disk defragmentation software. While these programs may not each be that big (although a few of them can be), they do add up if you run them concurrently.
- Add 16M if you are doing application development. Development environments like Visual C++ and Visual Basic need memory for themselves and for the applications being generated with them.

For most applications, 32M will be quite satisfactory. For heavy duty graphics and server applications, 48M will do the job. Only very demanding configurations require 64M.

For example, if you have a computer running Windows Networking that is being used to do desktop publishing, the math would run as follows: 16M (base memory) + 2M (Netware) + 16M (DTP software) = 34M, rounded off to 36M. Note that this is a rough minimum. You probably could make this an even 32M, depending on performance considerations, because not all of the 16M of base memory would be in use at any one time.

Determining how many things will be running at once will allow you to get a better idea of your estimates. If you don't plan to use more than two of the categories or features previously listed at any one time, you can slim down your estimates slightly.

Improving Memory Performance

In order to minimize memory utilization, you should reduce the amount of memory that is in constant use. Here are some suggestions:

- *Reduce the number of display colors.*
- *Reduce the display resolution.*
- *Use no desktop wallpaper, or use smaller wallpaper with a lower bit depth.* These suggestions applied in earlier versions of Windows, and they're still applicable in Windows NT. Displays with 16- or 24-bit color depth, 800 × 600 resolution or greater, and desktop wallpapers all take up live RAM or waste processor time being swapped in and out.
- *Turn off unneeded services and drivers.* This can be a high-risk adventure because services and drivers aren't always documented in plain English. For example, if you don't plan on using the parallel port with Windows NT, you can disable the parallel port services. The parallel port driver isn't an especially memory-consuming one, but it serves as a good example of how this sort of thing is done, and it illustrates how some services are interdependent. To learn how to disable unneeded services and drivers, see the next section, "Disabling Unneeded Services."

> **Note**
>
> If the device or driver you selected is an integral part of the system and can't be deactivated, you will be told so. It's actually not that easy to damage Windows NT by shutting off devices or drivers, but it's better not to tempt fate.

- *Use a separate hard drive for swap memory.* Paging eats up CPU time and forces a drive to labor quite a bit. With this in mind, if you're configuring a fairly high-end Windows NT machine, investing in a second (or third) hard drive and devoting at least part of it to swap space makes good sense. The main disk can be reserved for applications and the operating system itself, and the amount of time wasted for the disk to split time between two or more things—paging and regular system operations—comes way down. A computer running Windows NT should be outfitted with at least 1G of hard disk storage—not just for the operating system and its support files, but for swap space. Read the section "Changing Virtual Memory Settings," for more information on this.

> **Note**
>
> You have to have some swap memory on your boot drive for crash logging (unless you don't use that service), but try to put the majority of your swap file space on a different physical drive. At the very least, put the swap space in a different partition of that drive.

- *Do not install networking if it's not needed.* If you don't plan on using networking, don't add it in at install time. This includes Dial-Up Networking which can gobble up to 2M of RAM, even when it's not in use.
- *With physical memory, use consistent sets of chips.* One of the most important rules about purchasing and installing RAM in a computer is that it's a very bad idea to mix RAM chips of different speeds or even from different manufacturers. The results can be unpredictable, ranging from the computer simply not performing well to the computer not working at all. Use as many identical chips as you can, right down to the lot number and manufacturer.
- *Use 32-bit programs instead of 16-bit counterparts.* Every time a 16-bit program is launched, Windows NT has to spawn a virtual machine to handle it. This eats memory. Use as many 32-bit programs as possible unless there's only a 16-bit version available.

  If you have the memory to support it, enable 16-bit applications to run in their own memory space. By doing this, each 16-bit application that Windows NT runs is executed in its own virtual machine, with about 2M of program space per virtual machine. If a 16-bit program crashes, it's protected from other 16-bit programs and doesn't bring them down as well. See "Setting Memory Space for 16-bit Programs" later in this chapter.

Disabling Unneeded Services

To disable a driver or service, follow these steps:

1. Determine the proper name for the driver or service that is to be deactivated. Because there are dozens of drivers and services that ship with Windows NT, and many more are offered by manufacturers to support specific pieces of hardware, you may have to ask your local Windows NT guru which drivers correspond to what.
2. From the Control Panel, double-click the Devices icon. The Devices dialog box appears (see fig. 15.1).

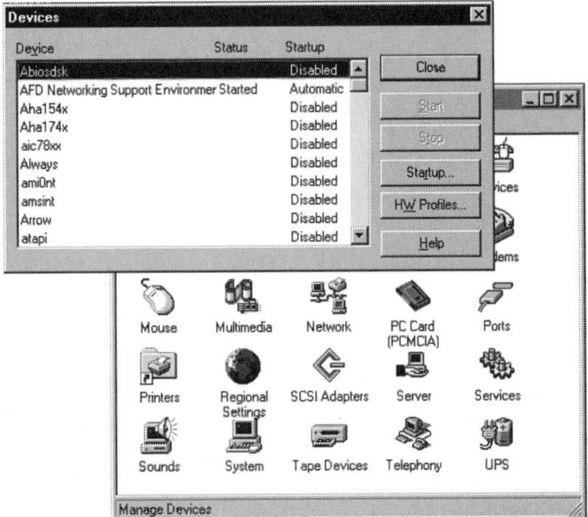

Fig. 15.1
The Devices dialog box lists all available devices.

3. In the Device list, select the name of the device or driver you want to disable. Click the Startup button. The Device dialog box appears (see fig. 15.2).
4. Select the Disabled radio button.

   Or

   If you still want the device to be able to manually be enabled during a Windows NT session, select Manual instead.
5. Click OK and then click Close.

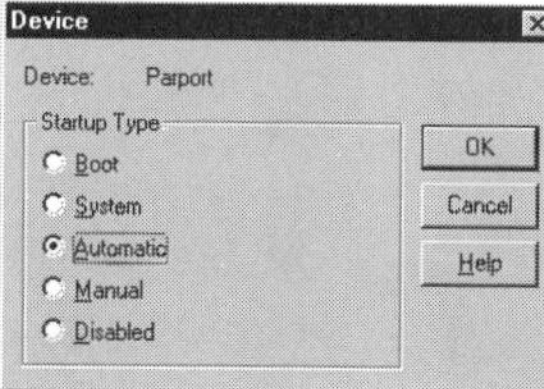

Fig. 15.2
You can change the startup parameter of a device.

Setting Memory Space for 16-bit Programs

To set the memory space for a 16-bit program, follow these steps:

1. Create a shortcut for the program if you haven't done so already.
2. Right-click the shortcut and choose Properties. You can also press Alt+Enter. The Properties sheet appears as shown in figure 15.3.

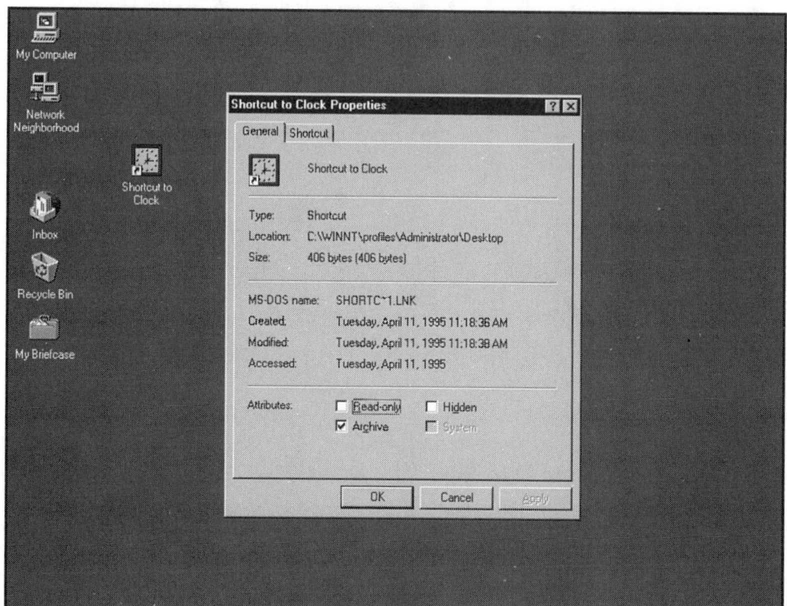

Fig. 15.3
Properties for the shortcut are shown on the General page.

3. In the Shortcut to Clock Properties sheet, click the Shortcut tab.
4. Select the Run in Separate Memory Space checkbox (see fig. 15.4). If this is a 32-bit program, the checkbox will be grayed out by default.
5. Click OK.

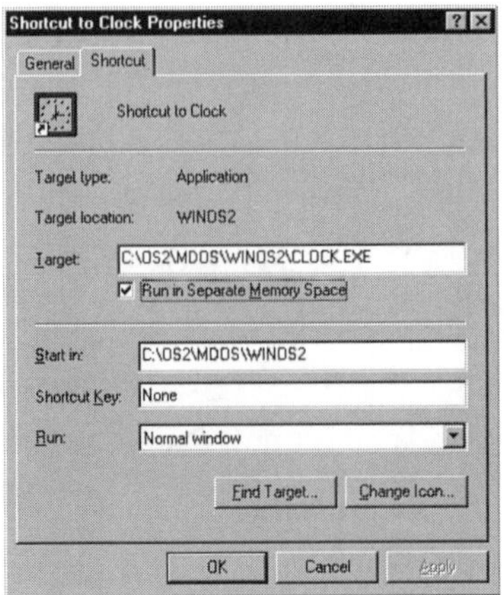

Fig. 15.4
The Run in Separate Memory Space checkbox is selected.

Changing Virtual Memory Settings

When you install Windows NT, it configures itself as having one swap file on the boot drive. The swap file is usually 16M in size, but has the potential to grow. Obviously this won't be the best possible choice for all machines.

To access the virtual memory settings on a Windows NT machine, follow these steps:

1. Open the Control Panel and click the System icon.
2. From there, click the Performance tab.
3. Then click the Change button in the Virtual Memory dialog box (see fig. 15.5).

The Drive list at the top of the Virtual Memory dialog box lists all the paging files (or swap files) in your Windows NT system. The two numbers listed under Paging File Size are the initial and maximum size of the paging file, respectively. The following lists the virtual memory options and gives an explanation of each:

- The *Initial Size* number is the size in megabytes of the selected paging file when first created. By default, this is set to the amount of physical memory you have in the system.

- The *Maximum Size* number dictates the maximum size in megabytes of the selected paging file.

  The ideal maximum size for a page file is anywhere from two and a half times to four times the amount of physical memory installed in the system. Tend toward the lower end of that spectrum if you use your system in a less demanding way, and toward the higher end if you do more demanding work.

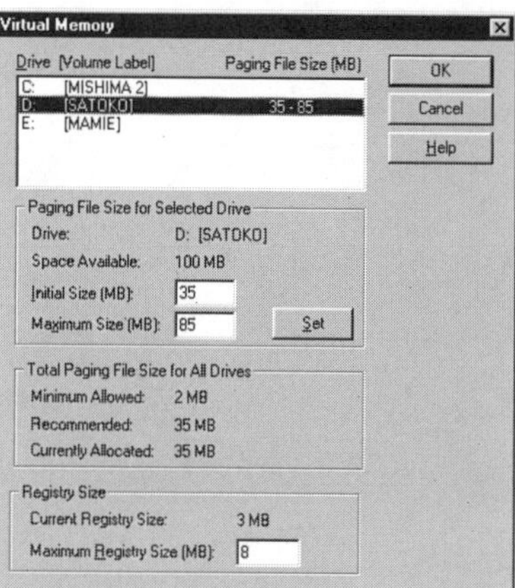

Fig. 15.5
The Virtual Memory dialog box allows you to change virtual memory settings.

> **Note**
>
> The Maximum Size is a way of keeping Windows NT from wasting too much space on a swap file. It's been determined that after a certain point, swap space is wasted. The hard drive acreage that the swap file takes up would be better used as storage.

Setting the Paging File Sizes

To set the paging file sizes, follow these steps:

1. In the Drive list, click the drive of the paging file size you want to set.

> **Note**
>
> If you are setting aside a section of a physical drive that's not your boot drive for swap space, this is the place to specify it. Reduce the swap file on your main drive to 16M and put the majority of the swap space on the other drive.

2. In the Initial Size text box, type the number in megabytes that you want to use as the initial size of the swap file (see fig. 15.6). The amount of physical memory present in the system is good as a baseline figure. If you notice the system behaving sluggishly, especially early in the session, set this number higher and see if that helps.

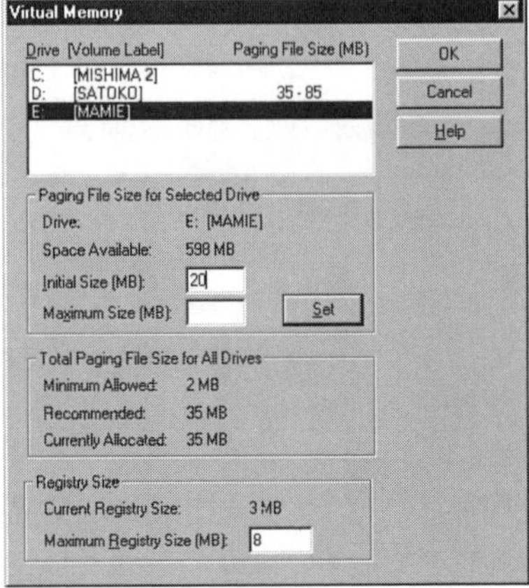

Fig. 15.6
Change the Initial Size parameter by typing a number in the Initial Size text box.

3. In the Maximum Size text box, type the number for the maximum size of the paging file (see fig. 15.7). Two and a half times the installed memory in the system is a good number to start with.

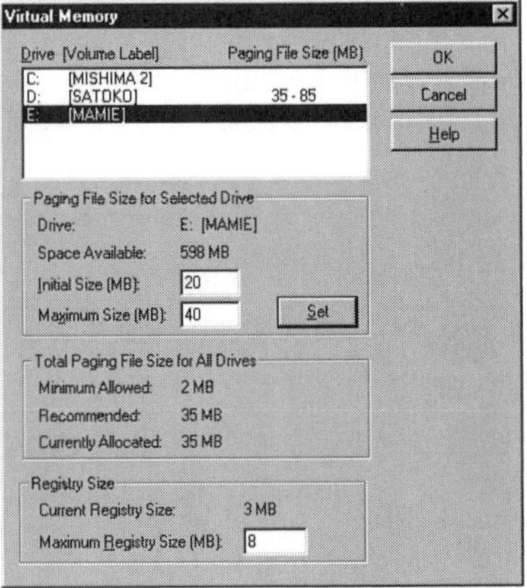

Fig. 15.7
Change the Maximum Size parameter by typing a number in the Maximum Size text box.

4. Click Set to establish the changes and then click OK in both the Virtual Memory dialog box and the System Properties sheet.

Changing Network Server Memory Demands

Windows NT's Server service lets you adjust the way memory is demanded and allocated to file sharing and network functions. This is one of the less commonly exploited memory-management options. It is very useful if you're not running Windows NT as a server, because you can save a fair amount of memory by allocating it only where it is needed.

Note

You cannot use this technique on systems that do not have the Server service loaded and active, such as systems that don't use networks.

To change the way Server allocates memory, do the following:

1. Open the Control Panel and double-click the Network icon. The Network dialog box appears.
2. Click the Services tab to view the Services page.
3. Select Server from the Network Services list and click Properties. The Server dialog box appears.
4. Select the Minimize Memory Used option if you're only running networking to access a few connections at a time. Most people who use Windows NT as a desktop environment will want to do this.
5. Select Balance if you are using a fair number of different kinds of networking options, such as NetBEUI and TCP/IP.
6. Select Maximize Throughput for File Sharing if you're using the system primarily as a file server, or if you have many shared folders.
7. Select Maximize Throughput for Network Applications if you are using the system for other network functions besides file sharing. ❖

CHAPTER 16

Optimizing the File System

By Michael Reilly

Windows NT supports several file systems, allowing backward compatibility while preparing for the future. Between the well-known FAT (File Allocation Table) file system and the new NTFS (New Technology File System), Windows NT offers a range of features and capabilities. Of course, no one file system does it all, so knowing the benefits and drawbacks of each will allow you to make an informed decision about which file system to use, and under what conditions. In this chapter, we discuss each of the file systems, point out their strengths and weaknesses, and describe how they fit in your Windows NT network.

In this chapter, you learn

- Which file systems are supported by Windows NT
- The features and limitations of each file system
- Why you should use NTFS for large disk drives
- How to create volume sets
- How to compress data on NTFS drives

Overview of the File System

Windows NT version 4.0 supports three file systems. The old standby, the FAT file system offers backward compatibility and efficiency on smaller disks. The new generation file system, NTFS, provides recoverability, security, and the ability to comfortably handle large disks. Windows NT also supports CDFS. This is, as the name implies, a file system that is specific to CD-ROMs. Because the CDFS file system is not an option for use with hard disks, and has no user-modifiable parameters, we will leave it out of this discussion, and concentrate on FAT and NTFS.

The FAT File System

This file system has been around since before the original PCs and is beginning to show its limitations. It does work well for smaller disks, below 200M, but its upper limit is 4G per partition. Therefore 4G is also the maximum file size.

The FAT file system allocation table is 16 bits wide. The minimum segment of the disk which can be tracked using the allocation table is called a cluster, and with 16 bits, there can only be 2^{16} clusters in any volume. That is 65,536 clusters, less what the FAT takes for itself. On disks up to 127M, the cluster size is actually set to 2048 bytes. But beyond that, the cluster size increases as the size of the disk goes up, in order to keep the total number of clusters below the 65,536 limit. The following table shows what happens to cluster size as the size of the disk increases:

Disk Size (M)	Cluster Size (Bytes)
0-127	2048
128-255	4096
256-511	8192
512-1023	16384

What does this mean for the user? Well, one cluster is the smallest entry in the file allocation table. So every file must occupy at least one cluster. If you have a batch file, for example, which is only 80 bytes long, it still occupies one cluster. So on a 600M hard disk, 16304 bytes would be wasted for just this one file. The percentage of the disk lost in this way increases with disk size. Of course, if most of your files are large graphics images, then you need not worry, but most of us have a lot of INI files, bitmaps for wallpapers, and so on. So a significant portion of the disk space is lost.

One answer is to partition the disks so that each volume is smaller than say 255M. But with 1G disks considered entry level, and 1.6, 2, and 2.5G disks becoming available even on desktop systems, you can end up with a large number of logical drives. Perhaps it is time to replace the FAT file system on your big hard drives. It does make you wonder about those appliance stores that sell computers with big hard drives—all formatted as the C: drive.

The above discussion does not apply if a DOS-based disk compression is used, such as DriveSpace, DoubleSpace, or Stacker. These compression techniques essentially treat the entire drive as one large file that contains compressed versions of the real files, and so the wasted space is recovered. Actually, some of the supposed compression benefit arises not from the compression algorithm, but from this more efficient use of disk space.

The search mechanism used by the FAT file system is a linked list. This means that the file's directory entry contains the beginning FAT entry number for this file. This FAT entry contains the FAT entry number of the next cluster, or a marker that shows that this is the last cluster of the file. So a file that occupies 12 clusters will have 12 FAT entries and 11 FAT links. It is an efficient system for smaller files at first, but as files become fragmented, read and write times become longer and the system appears to run more slowly. Obviously, it becomes less efficient as the file sizes grow.

The root directory of a FAT partition is limited to 512 entries. Most users do not keep many files at the root level, but for those who do, this limit can be puzzling, especially as it only applies to the root directory. And in any directory, the filename and directory length is limited to 255 characters. Under DOS, the old limit of eight characters for the filename plus three for the extension meant that filenames were cryptic and not very informative. Newer operating systems such as Windows NT and Windows 95 can work around this limitation but with some caveats, as we will see later in this chapter.

Tip

The FAT file system has less overhead and can show faster total throughput compared to an NTFS with drive sizes under 1G. Therefore, if security is not an issue, and your drive is not very large (or partitioned), you may want to seriously consider using FAT instead of NTFS on the Windows NT Workstation.

Understanding NTFS

NTFS was introduced in 1993 with the first release of Windows NT. During the design phase of NTFS, the driving force was the need for a recoverable file structure which would support enterprise data without the risk of files being lost, or data corrupted, as can happen on FAT partitions. Additional requirements included security, and the ability to store huge data files on disks much larger than those that the FAT file system can handle.

Large Disk Capacities

NTFS was designed from the outset to handle very large disks. The maximum file and partition size is 16 Exabytes, or 2^{64} bytes. In case you are wondering how big an Exabyte is:

1024 Megabytes = 1 Gigabyte (G)

1024 G= 1 Terabyte (T)

1024 T = 1 Petabyte (P)

1024 P = 1 Exabyte (E)

So 16E should be a safe upper limit for a few years. NTFS is not at its best with smaller disks, partly because of how it handles the directories, but also because there is about a 5M overhead with any NTFS disk. This is one reason (security being another) why NTFS does not work with floppy disks, although this could change with some of the newer, 100M+ floppy disk drives being developed by Compaq and others.

Recoverability

When Windows NT was in early development, there were no plans for an additional file system. It became apparent that for the operating system to succeed at an enterprise level, it would have to have a more robust file system than anything currently available on personal computers. The key was the recoverability of the files to ensure that data was not corrupted or lost. If the system crashed, or a disk failed, then files would not be corrupted. Recoverability was added to Windows NT using a database-like model in which disk accesses are treated like transactions. If the transaction does not complete properly and entirely, then it is rolled back, and removed completely.

Fault Tolerance

Disk fault tolerance is implemented in software on Windows NT server only, not on Workstation. For a full discussion of fault tolerance, see Chapter 17, "Ensuring Data Security." Windows NT Workstation does allow stripe sets to be built for performance reasons. In a stripe set, the data is distributed across several physical hard disks. But there is no fault tolerance, and if one disk in the stripe set is lost, all of the data in the set is lost.

Security

Windows NT allows multiple users to log in to a computer, with different settings for each user. But what if some files should be available to certain users, and not to others? Windows NT was designed as a network operating system, with built-in capabilities for file and print sharing. A user can share resources on the network and can access resources which have been shared on the network. But how can a file be shared and accessible to some users, and off-limits to others? The answer in Windows NT is to assign permissions to files and directories, controlling the level of access to these files. Each file has an Access Control List, which is compared against a user's Security Access Token. If the user has the required permissions, then access to the file is granted. The FAT file system has no mechanism for assigning permissions, whereas NTFS was designed with security in mind.

NTFS permissions apply to local users logging on to the computer; when you share the resource across the network, share permissions also apply, and are effective on any share, including FAT disks. The most restrictive permissions apply, so that if a user has Full Control permission on a share, and Read-Only on the NTFS directory, they will still only be able to read the file. We will talk in more detail in the section "Assigning Security on NTFS" later in this chapter about how permissions are set on NTFS volumes.

NTFS and the Windows NT I/O Manager

As far as the Windows NT I/O system is concerned, NTFS is nothing more than another driver loaded into the operating system, which is used for processing I/O requests. NTFS can be layered on top of or below other drivers in the I/O Manager's layered file model, as shown in figure 16.1. Because NTFS is a loadable driver, it can be replaced with an upgraded version, or with a whole new file system, with minimal disruption. Applications running within the Win32 or other application subsystems call the I/O Manager, which then call NT system services, which then find the correct loaded drivers and call them.

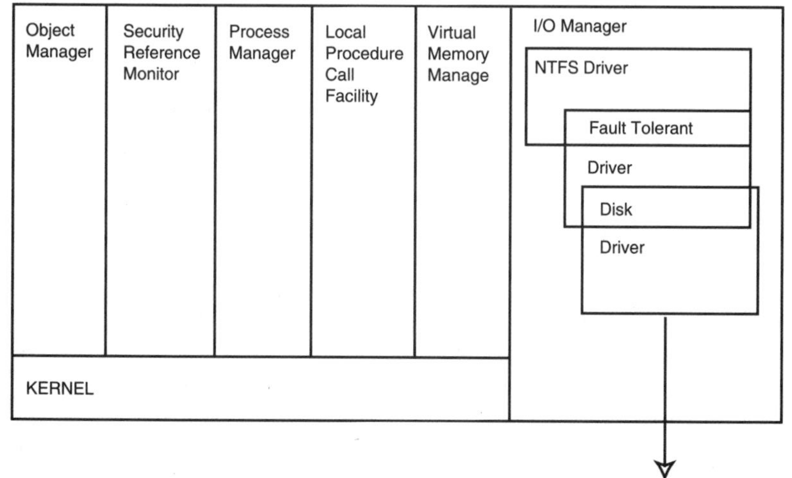

Fig. 16.1
NTFS is another driver in the Windows NT I/O system.

The layered drivers exchange I/O requests via the NT Executive I/O Manager. Using the I/O Manager as the vehicle for communicating allows each driver to maintain its independence. A driver can be loaded or unloaded without affecting the other drivers. Also the NTFS driver exchanges information with the Log File Service, the Cache Manager, and the Virtual Memory Manager, as shown in figure 16.2, in order to optimize memory usage and provide for recoverability. The Log File Service (LFS) keeps a log of disk writes, which is used in the recovery process for the NTFS volume if the system crashes.

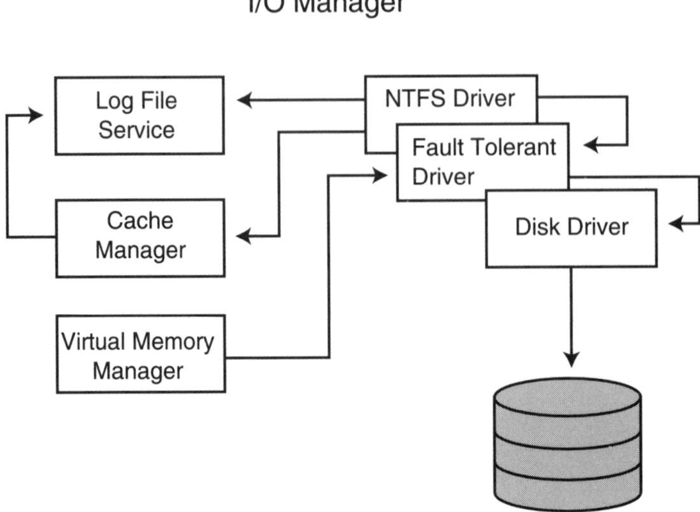

Fig. 16.2
NTFS interacts with other drivers in the Windows NT Executive.

NTFS Volumes

NTFS uses the term volume to denote a logical disk drive. The volume may be a primary partition, a logical disk in an extended partition, or it may be a section of space on a disk that would be considered a non-DOS partition. Essentially, a volume is an area of disk space that Windows NT has designated as a logical disk drive. It does not even have to be contiguous space on one disk, as you will see later in this chapter, in the section "Creating NTFS Volume Sets."

B-Tree File Management

NTFS uses B-tree file management to keep track of file locations on the disk. This technique offers several benefits over the linked-list technique used in the FAT file system. The filenames are stored in sorted order, so lookups happen faster. On larger volumes, B-trees grow wide rather than deep, so NTFS does not show a significant performance drop as the directories become larger.

The B-tree data structure minimizes the number of disk access needed to find an entry (see fig. 16.3). In the master file table (discussed later in this chapter), the directory's index root attribute contains filenames that act as indexes into the second level of the B-tree. Each filename in this index root attribute contains a pointer that points to an index buffer. This index buffer contains filenames that precede the name of the file in the index root attribute. By precede, we mean that they would sort before the file in the index buffer. For example, if *filen* is a first-level entry in the B-tree, the index buffer might contain entries for *filea, fileb, filec,* and so on. NTFS is able to perform a binary search using these index buffers, resulting in rapid file retrieval.

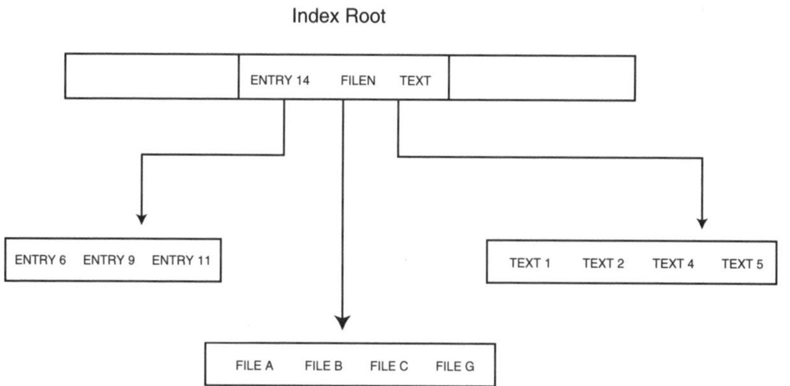

Fig. 16.3
B-tree sorting provides an efficient file search for NTFS.

The NTFS Structure on Disk

Like FAT, NTFS also uses the cluster as its smallest allocation unit. The size of the cluster, or cluster factor, is determined by the NTFS format utility. The Disk Administrator Format command does not allow any options, but formatting from the My Computer folder or from the command prompt, you can control the cluster size, as shown in figure 16.4. NTFS supports cluster sizes of 512, 1024, 2048 and 4096 bytes. The default cluster sizes in NTFS are shown in the following table:

Disk Size (Megabytes)	Cluster Size (Bytes)
0-511	512
512-1023	1024
1024-2047	2048
2048 and up	4096

These default values are a compromise between the wasted space inherent in a large cluster size and the fragmentation that can occur with a small cluster size. Internally, NTFS only references clusters, and is therefore independent of physical sector sizes.

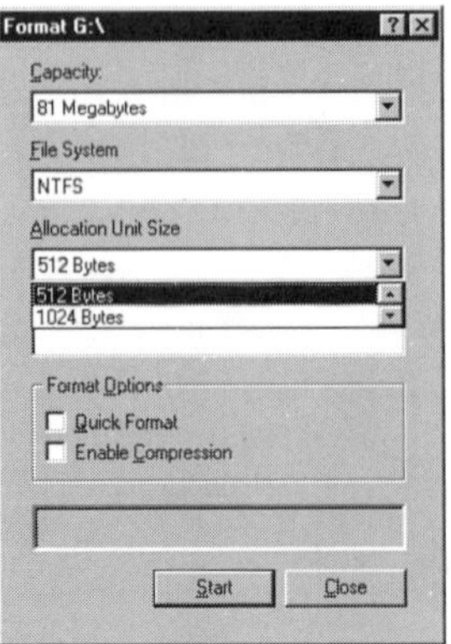

Fig. 16.4
The cluster size can be specified when formatting from the My Computer folder.

NTFS has a file known as the master file table (MFT) which contains one row for each file on the volume—it even includes an entry for the MFT itself. There are instances where a file is very fragmented, and then it may require more than one record on the MFT. If so, the first record in the MFT which refers to the file is called the base file record, and it contains the locations of the other records in the MFT that refer to this file. Each volume also contains a boot file and a set of files that contain information about all of the files stored on this volume (called metadata files). These files are used as the basis for the file system structure.

A file on an NTFS volume has an associated 64-bit identifier, called a file reference. This number is generated as a combination of a file number and a sequence number. The file number provides the position of the file within the MFT, and the sequence number is used for internal consistency checking. It is incremented by one every time the MFT file record position is reused.

Using NTFS

The real test is whether NTFS delivers on its promises. Regardless of its internal structure, it must perform well and offer benefits to the users before they will adopt it as a standard, and indeed, it does meet expectations.

Benefits of NTFS

NTFS offers very solid security: good enough for Windows NT to attain the U.S. Government approval as secure at the C-2-level. Of course, C-2-level security involves other issues as well, but a robust, secure file system is an essential component. Security can be thought of as the balance of two conflicting requirements; allowing users access to what they need while keeping them out of everything else. By treating every file and directory as an object, and setting permissions on those objects, access can be controlled to the individual file and user level if needed. On the other hand, it is also easy to make the system open, so that anyone with a valid logon can get to the resources.

NTFS offers an auditing capability that is designed like all Windows NT auditing, as a security feature, not an accounting feature. It can track who has accessed a file successfully, and who has tried to break into a file or directory and failed. This auditing does involve some overhead, but can be useful in identifying problems.

The other major benefit of NTFS is that it is a recoverable file system. Although the idea of a recoverable file system that could survive a system crash was not new in the mainframe world, it was an innovation in the personal computer world, where the reliability of hardware and software was less than perfect.

Converting to NTFS

The conversion from a FAT file system to an NTFS file system is not difficult, and it can be done with data in place on the disk—the existing files will be converted as part of the file system upgrade. But the conversion should be approached with just a little caution. The reason for the caution is that it is not possible to convert back to FAT from NTFS. The only way to restore the FAT partition is to back up the data, remove and rebuild the partition, format it as FAT, and restore the data. It is always a good idea to back up the data before any conversion, just in case something goes wrong.

The conversion can be requested during Windows NT installation, or it can be done later.

On Windows NT Installation

When you install Windows NT, you can do so onto a completely blank disk, with no previous file system, or you can install onto a disk with the FAT file system in place. (Of course, if you are upgrading to Windows NT 4.0 from a previous version, the disk may already be an NTFS volume). If you are installing on a FAT partition, during the installation process you will be given the opportunity to convert the file system to NTFS, for the disk partition on which Windows NT is to be installed. If you choose this option, the conversion is performed as part of the installation process.

On Demand

If you wish to retain the data on the disk, the conversion from a FAT partition to NTFS has to be done using the CONVERT utility from the command prompt. The syntax is:

```
convert  drive:   /fs:ntfs
```

where drive is the drive letter, and the /fs indicates which file system to use. The /fs:ntfs is really redundant, as the conversion only works one way, but perhaps it is there to make sure that you really mean to convert to NTFS. The conversion will happen immediately if the drive is not in use. If it is in use, then you will be offered the option of marking it for conversion the next time the system is started. Obviously, the system partition can only be converted during the startup process because it is always in use. If an application has a file open on the disk, or even if File Manager or Explorer are pointing at that drive, the drive is considered to be in use. When the system starts, at the blue screen where the disk integrity is normally checked, you will see a series of messages telling you that the volume is being converted to an NTFS volume.

Caution

There is an option on the Disk Administrator menu under Tools called Change Format. This will convert a partition from FAT to NTFS, or from NTFS to FAT, but it does so by formatting the drive, and so the data is lost. You might expect that a Change Format command would retain the data, but in fact, it just acts like a Format command. Fortunately, it does warn you that all of the data will be lost if you proceed, but it is still not clear why Windows NT has no way of calling the conversion routines from within Disk Manager.

Assigning Security on NTFS

One of the design criteria for NTFS was that it be a secure file system. It is not possible to access a file on an NTFS drive unless you have the necessary permissions. Let's look at how those permissions are assigned.

Permissions

Windows NT allows you to set permissions on directories and files on NTFS volumes, down to the individual file level. Let us look first at directory permissions. Select a directory in Explorer or within a folder. Then right-click to pop up the dialog box, and choose Properties. Select the Security tab, as shown in figure 16.5.

From here, the next step is to set up the permissions, so select the Permissions button to open the Directory Permissions dialog box, as shown in figure 16.6.

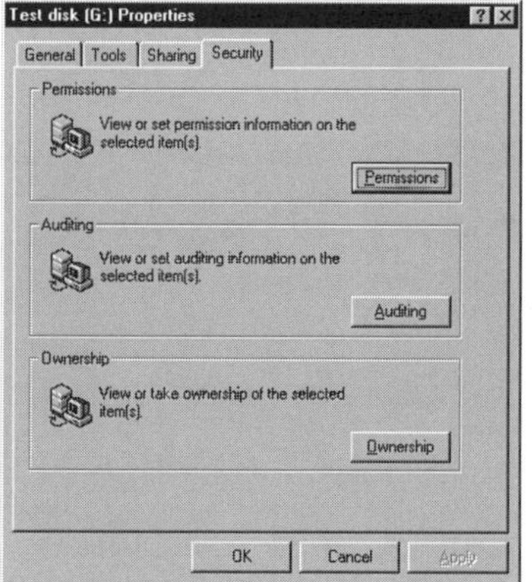

Fig. 16.5
Click the Permissions button on the Security page.

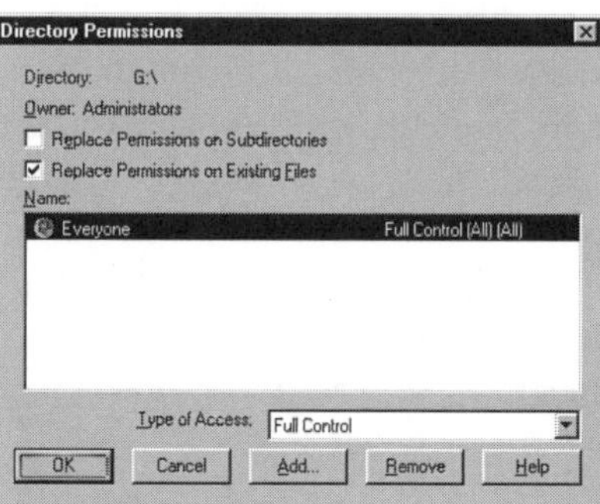

Fig. 16.6
This is what you'll see if you select a directory and open its properties sheet, then move to the Permissions button on the Security sheet.

To add permissions, click the Add button, and select the users or groups from the list which appears, as shown in figure 16.7.

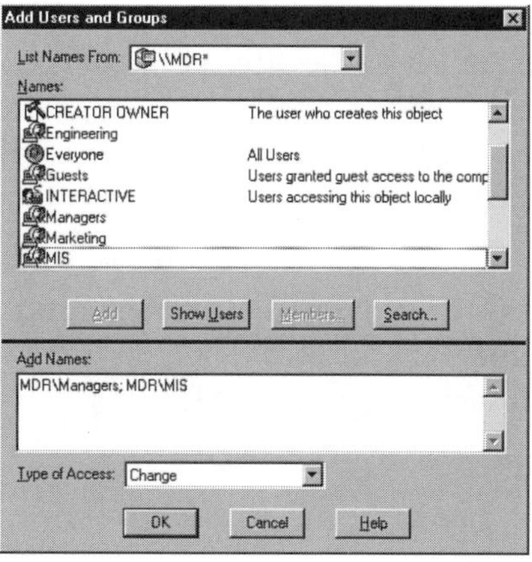

Fig. 16.7
Add the users and groups with the appropriate permission level chosen.

Now the required permissions have been added, they can be modified, as shown in figure 16.8.

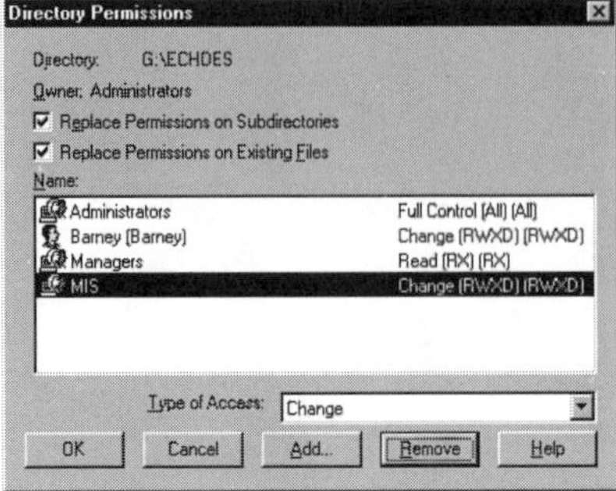

Fig. 16.8
The group Everyone has been removed and other access levels set.

Notice that the option to Replace Permissions on Subdirectories has been set, so that these permissions will apply to all the subdirectories below the one selected. We also want to check the Replace Permissions on Existing Files. When you click OK, you will be prompted to confirm that you wish to change the permissions on the files and subdirectories, as shown in figure 16.9.

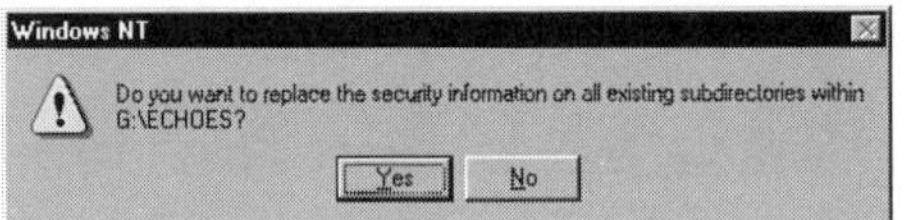

Fig. 16.9
This action is optional, but it does make administration simpler if you work from the top down like this.

If you wish to set permissions on files, the technique is exactly the same, but this time, you set permissions for the selected file only, as shown in figure 16.10. Notice that Marketing has been designated as having No Access, so nobody who is a member of the marketing group will be allowed to access this file.

The permissions can also be set from the Security, Permissions menu option in File Manager. For those who are used to Windows NT 3.51 and earlier, this will be familiar, and is shown in figure 16.11.

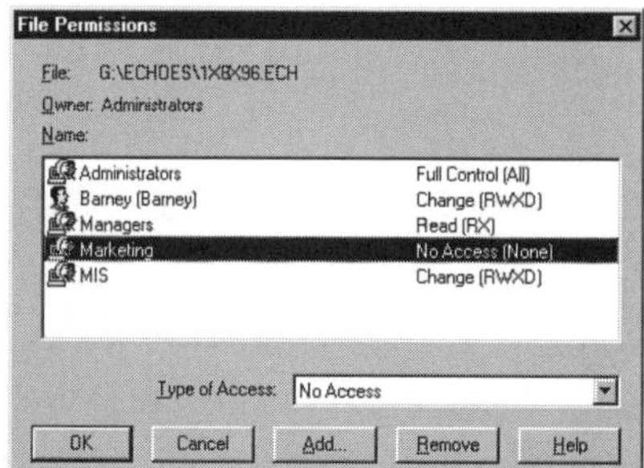

Fig. 16.10
We decided that members of the Marketing group should be denied access to this file.

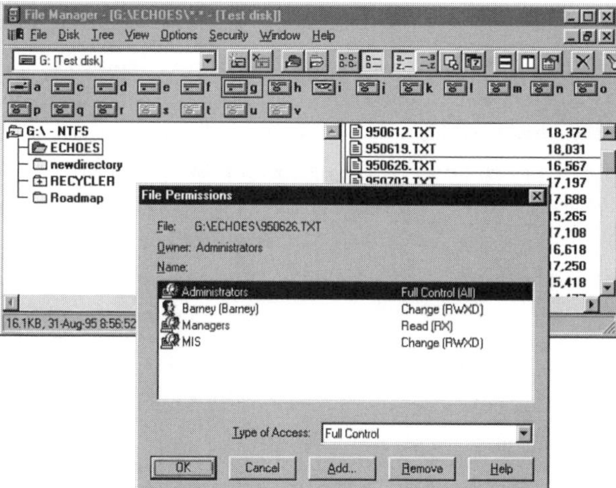

Fig. 16.11
For those readers who are familiar with earlier versions of Windows NT, this is familiar territory.

The five predefined access permissions are No Access, Read, Change, Full Control, and Special Access. Each permission level carries with it the ability to perform a certain combination of tasks. The tasks are Read(R), Execute(X), Write(W), Delete(D), Set Permissions(P) and Take Ownership(O). The table below shows how the tasks are associated with the various permissions.

Permission	R	X	W	D	P	O
No Access						
Read	y	y				
Change	y	y	y	y		
Full Control	y	y	y	y	y	y
Special Access	?	?	?	?	?	?

Special Access can be any combination of the six tasks, and is set by selecting the desired combination of permissions, as shown in figure 16.12.

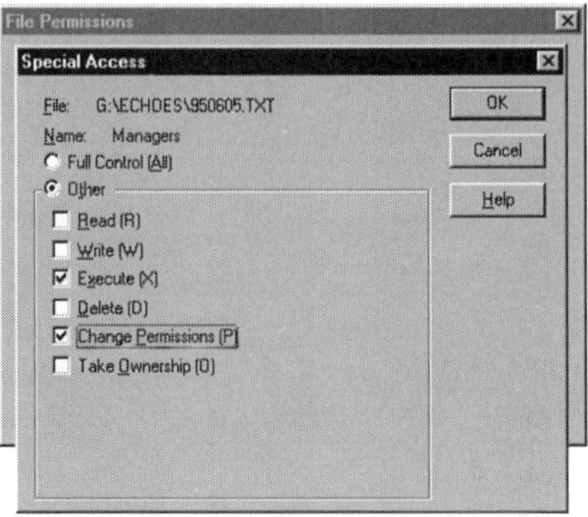

Fig. 16.12
You can set any combination of permissions for Special Access.

Whenever a disk is formatted as an NTFS volume, by default, everyone has full control. This effectively means that there is no security on the disk. In an environment that needs to be secure, the first step is to remove the group Everyone from full control, and then assign permissions to the users who need to access this volume. Note that removing the group Everyone means that nobody will be able to access the disk, so assign Full Control to the administrators local group at the root directory.

The permissions on NTFS directories are set in the same way as the permissions on files. The difference is that Special Directory Access sets Special Access rights for new and existing directories, and Special File Access sets Special Access rights for new and existing files.

Whenever you set permissions for a directory, the permissions are changed for that directory and for any existing files in the directory. By default, the permissions on existing subdirectories and the files they contain are not changed. If you want your new permission setting to apply down the directory tree, select the Replace Permissions on Subdirectories checkbox when you set the permissions.

Once permissions are set, new files or subdirectories created in the directory inherit their permissions from the current directory permission settings.

Auditing

You have to log on as a member of the Administrators group in order to audit files and directories. If you wish to audit file access, auditing has to be turned on in User Manager first. Specifically, auditing of File and Object Access must be selected, with success, failure, or both chosen for auditing, as shown in figure 16.13. To do this, follow these steps:

1. Select the Start menu and choose Programs, Administrative Tools, and then User Manager.
2. In the User Manager window, choose Policies, Audit to open the Audit Policy dialog box.

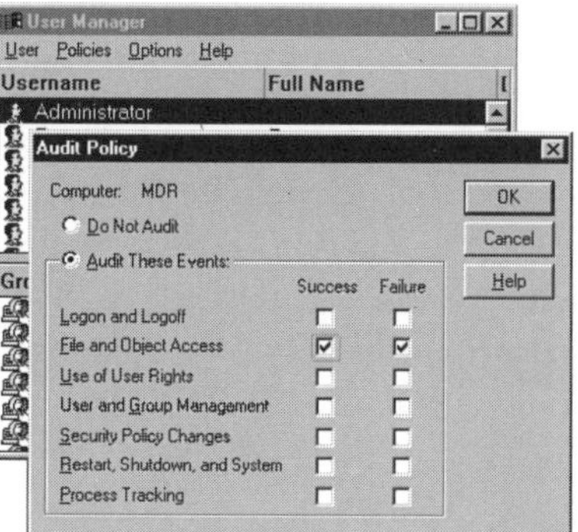

Fig. 16.13 Auditing has to be turned on here for it to work at a file or directory level.

Then you can set up auditing to track file usage on directories and files from the Properties sheet, using the Security tab just as you did for Permissions, as shown in figure 16.14. You can also choose Security, Auditing in File Manager.

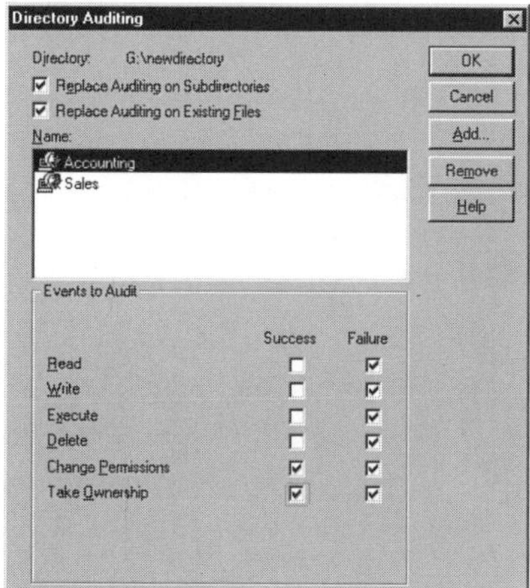

Fig. 16.14 Set up auditing to track file usage.

If you attempt to set up auditing here without turning it on first in User Manger, you will see an error message, and then the auditing dialog box will close so that you can switch to the User Manager and turn it on.

Auditing can be turned on only for selected users. In fact, you have to specify which users to audit: until you do, you can't turn on auditing. Different users can have different levels of auditing assigned, so that a user who is experiencing technical difficulties might have file access failures monitored, whereas a suspected hacker might have both success and failure monitored. Discretion is advised when auditing file access, as turning it on for everyone on all files will mean a performance hit because of the additional overhead.

Once auditing is in place, it has to be monitored through the Event Viewer, found in the Administrative Tools group. The Event Viewer logs include System, Application, and Security, and it is the Security log that contains the audit information. Logs can be sorted by most recent first or oldest first, and can be filtered by several parameters. Filtering by user will isolate the activities of a specific user, and you can examine the log on another computer, using the Log, Select Computer option to connect to another user's computer. The ability to examine logs remotely can be a big help in troubleshooting problems.

Ownership

The Properties Sheet for any file or directory includes an Ownership button on the Security page that shows who currently owns the files on the NTFS volume (see fig. 16.15).

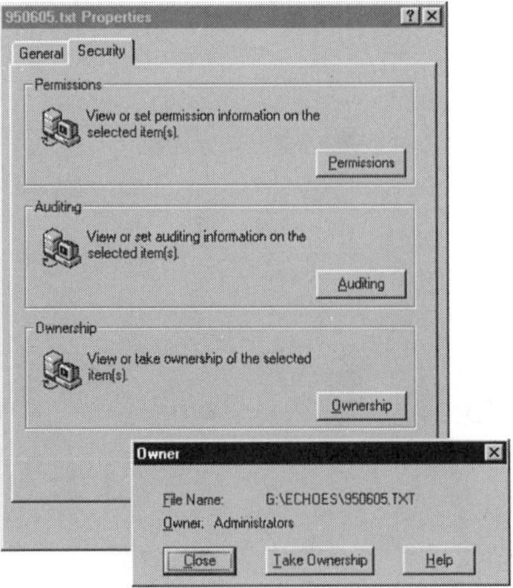

Fig. 16.15
The administrator owns this file.

Normally, the creator of a file will be the owner. The system administrator can always take ownership of a file, which is done from this menu. Actually, anyone who has Full Control permissions or Take Ownership permission can take ownership of a file. This means that if someone has locked everyone else out of their files, and then quit, the system administrator can always take ownership of the files, and therefore gain access to what those files contain. Alternatively, using the Special Access Permissions, the administrator can give someone else the authority to take ownership of the files.

While it is possible to take ownership of a file, it is not possible to assign ownership to an individual, for security reasons. The administrator can only *permit* a user to take ownership, but then the user has to actually *take* ownership of the file.

An exception to the normal rules of file ownership is that whenever a file is created by any member of the Administrators group, the file is owned by the Administrators group, not by the person who created the file. This is yet another reason why the system administrator should build a second account for his or her own use, and only log on with administrator privileges when necessary to perform administrative tasks.

Permissions and Ownership Issues When Moving and Copying Files

When a new file is created in any directory, it inherits the permission settings of that directory. But what happens when a file is copied into a directory, or moved? When a file is copied, the copy process creates a new file. So the new file will inherit the permission settings associated with the target directory. The same applies when a file is moved from a different disk. The move process creates a file on the new disk, with the new permissions from the target directory. Then the file is deleted from the original disk. But there is one situation that calls for extra care when the file is moved from another directory on the same disk. The file will show up in the new directory, but with the permissions that it had in its original directory. Why is this? Well, if we look at what really happens when a file is 'moved' from one directory to another on the same disk, the explanation becomes clear. The file does not really move; only the directory address of the file changes, but it is the same file in the same disk space. A new file has not been created with new directory permissions, as happens when the file is moved from another disk. So the original file retains its original permissions, even when these differ from the permissions on the directory and the other files in the directory.

Similar logic applies to ownership of the file. When the owner copies it, the owner is creating the copy, and therefore owns the copy, even if the copy is placed in a directory owned by someone else. However, if the owner or administrator has given someone else the authority, then another user can make a copy of the file, and becomes the owner of the copy. Part of the reason for this is a security issue. An employee with top secret clearance cannot copy files into a directory owned by a low-level employee and 'frame' that employee by making it appear that he was stealing files. The top-secret employee would still be the owner of the files, regardless of their location.

Using the Disk Administrator

The Disk Administrator, located in the Administrative Tools group, is a graphical tool used to create, delete, and configure partitions; format disks; assign drive letters; and (on Windows NT Server only) set up fault-tolerant disk arrays. Figure 16.16 shows the Disk Administrator interface.

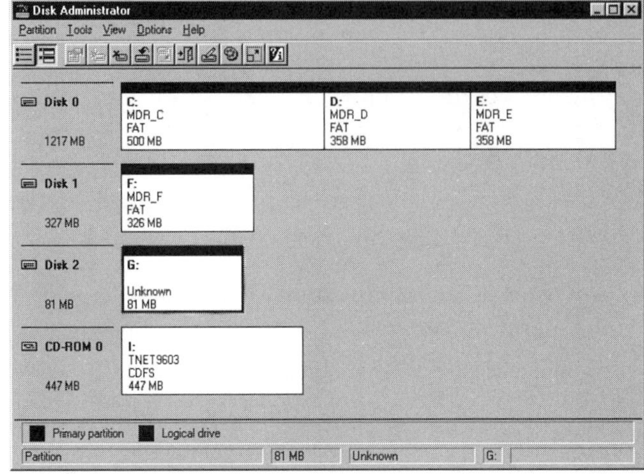

Fig. 16.16
The Disk Administrator shown here has been customized with the Options, Customize Toolbar menu item so that additional buttons are shown on the toolbar.

Different colors are used to indicate primary and extended partitions, volume sets, and stripe and mirror sets, which are discussed in Chapter 17 in the section, "Creating and Managing Fault-Tolerant Volumes." These colors can be customized, as can the toolbar in this version of Disk Manager.

The first time you use the Disk Administrator utility, or when you add a new disk to the system, it will tell you that it is going to write a signature to the disk. The signature identifies the disk so that even if it moved to another computer, the disk can still be recognized.

Creating and Using a Partition

To create a partition using the free space on a disk, right-click the area of free space and choose the Create option to create a primary partition, or the Create Extended option to create an extended partition, as shown in figure 16.17.

A dialog box opens that permits you to specify how much of the free space to allocate to the new partition, as in figure 16.18. In this case, we just made the partition equal to the size of the disk.

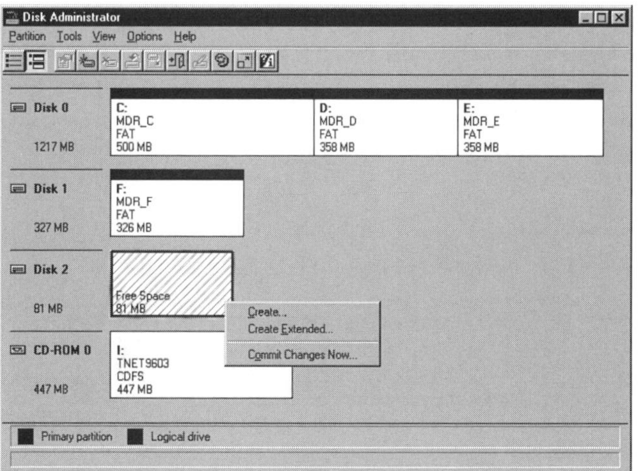

Fig. 16.17
Each area on the disk has an associated shortcut menu, which changes depending on how that area is configured.

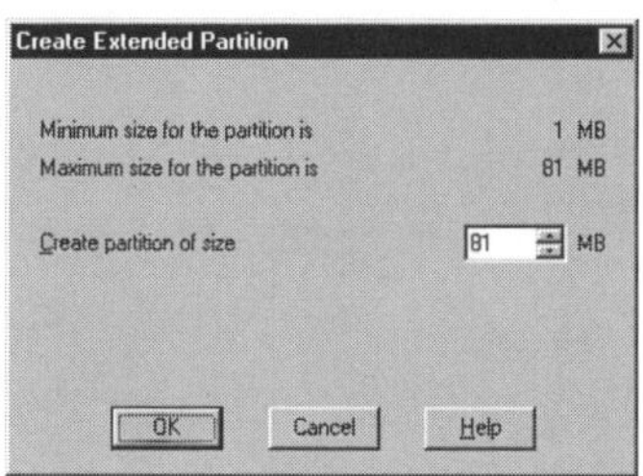

Fig. 16.18
Specify the amount of the free space to allocate to this partition.

At this point, we just have a partition with free space, and so we need to create a logical drive within the partition. Figure 16.19 shows the creation of a 40M drive within the 81M partition.

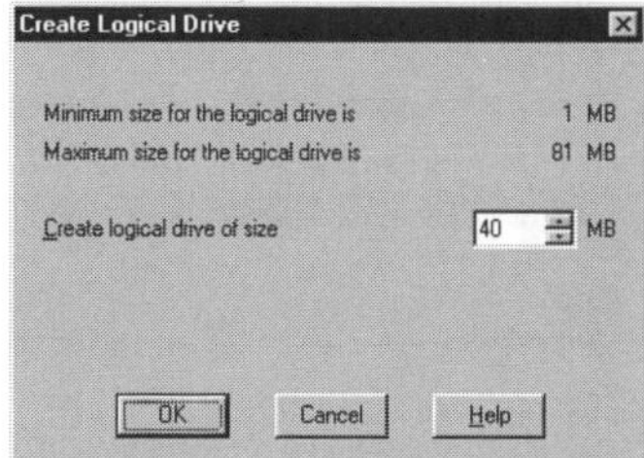

Fig. 16.19
A logical drive of 40M will be created on this 81M partition.

Now that the drive has been created, we commit the changes (more on this later) and then format the drive as NTFS by choosing Tools, Format.

Creating NTFS Volume Sets

An NTFS volume set is a collection of disk partitions that are treated as a single partition. A volume set can be created from within the Disk Manager by selecting one or more areas of free space (hold the Ctrl key down as you click each area to ensure that all the areas are selected) and then choosing Partition, Create Volume Set. In the example shown in figure 16.20, a 30M partition was created on Disk 2. Then this partition and the remaining free space were selected, and right-clicked to pop up the menu.

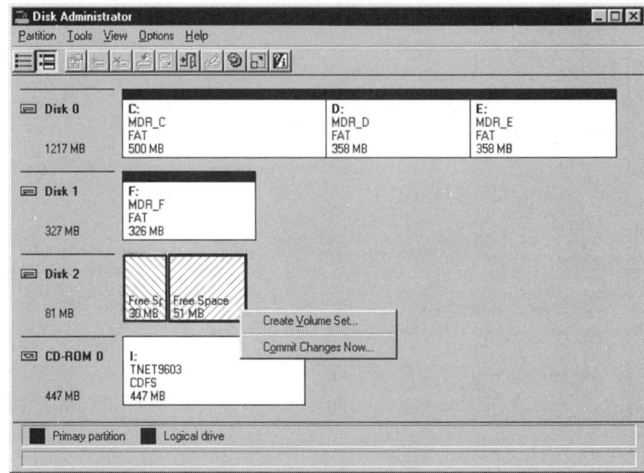

Fig. 16.20 We selected the existing partition and the remaining free space.

From this menu, we selected Create Volume Set, and added the remaining disk space to the set, as shown in figure 16.21.

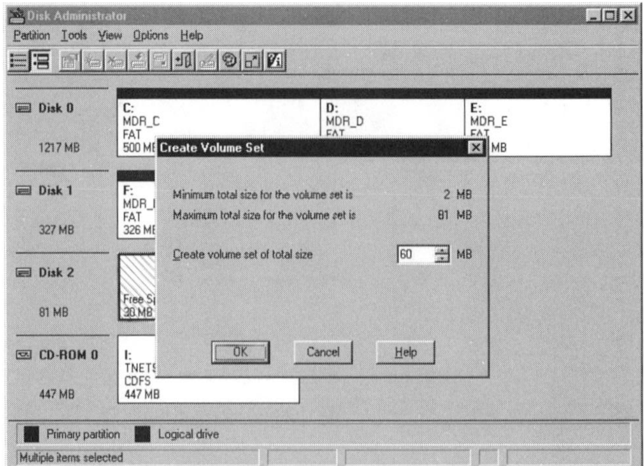

Fig. 16.21 The additional free space is added to the partition to create a volume set.

Notice that the color of the bar at the top of the volume has changed—the default is yellow for a volume set. The areas selected do not have to be on the same physical disk. In theory, you can create a volume set by combining space on an IDE disk, and space on an SCSI disk. Once the partition has been created, commit the changes, as described later in this chapter, and then you can format the partition as an NTFS or FAT volume.

The partition that contains the boot sector or the operating system can't be part of a volume set. DOS does not recognize volume sets, so be careful how you use this feature on any dual boot machine. There is no fault tolerance in a volume set, as there is no redundant data stored on the volume set. There is no way to reclaim any part of the volume set without deleting the entire volume set, which would mean losing the data it contains, or at least, having to back up the data and restore it.

Extending NTFS Volumes

NTFS volumes can be extended in order to increase the available space. In other words, you can add space to the NTFS volume without having to reformat it, and without losing any data. Just like when you create a volume set, it is the *logical* volume that is extended, and the additional space does not have to be the next section of the physical disk. In fact, the new space does not even have to be on the same physical disk. The ability to extend a volume is very useful, for example, to a database administrator. Suppose that the database was placed on a 500M disk, and has reached the limits of that disk. You can install another 500M disk, and add the space on the new disk to the original volume, so that the drive now looks like a 1G disk. You can extend the volume more than once, adding sections of multiple disks to the volume. Windows NT handles the translation from physical to logical disks, giving the user a wide range of options.

Extending the volume on one disk with unused space on that disk is relatively safe. On the other hand, extending the volume over more than one disk increases the risk of a disk failure affecting your data. If one disk fails, the data will probably be irrecoverable. And you can't remove disks from the set, as we mentioned earlier. So if you have extended the volume to give your database more breathing room, you may wish to move it to a larger single drive at the first opportunity.

To extend a volume set, you must select the volume to be extended, and the free space (more than one area of free space if you wish) by holding down the Ctrl key as you select each one. If you do not select an existing volume and at least one area of free space, the Extend Volume Set option will remain dimmed. Disk Administrator will offer to automatically restart the system after you quit and save your changes. (You can delay the restart if necessary.) On the restart, it formats the additional space as NTFS without affecting any existing files on the original volume or volume set. There is no way to extend a volume set without this system restart, so if you are a database administrator, back up and take down your database before starting this procedure.

In figure 16.22, we built and formatted a logical drive in a 30M partition, and then selected it and the remaining free space on the disk. Now we can extend the volume set, even though we have data on this drive.

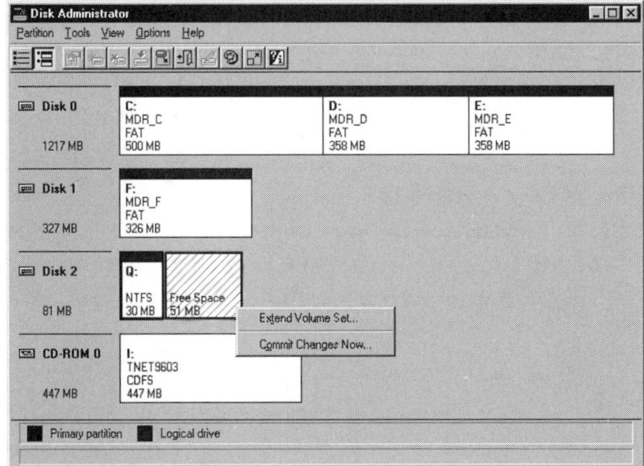

Fig. 16.22
The additional free space is added to the drive to extend a volume set.

Only NTFS volumes can be extended, and you cannot extend a stripe or mirror set. There is no way to extend a FAT volume set without first converting it to NTFS, or removing it and rebuilding the set. After a volume set is extended, it's a good idea to rebuild the emergency repair disk for your installation of Windows NT so that it will have the correct disk configuration information. If you don't, and have to use an old version of the emergency repair disk, you risk losing all the information in the volume set.

Committing Changes

When you make changes in Disk Manager, such as converting free space into a new partition, the changes are normally not made until you close Disk Manager. This is a safety feature which allows you to change your mind if you selected the wrong disk, for example. Even when you add or delete a partition, when you exit from Disk Manager, you will be asked if you wish to make the changes final, and you will have the opportunity to discard the changes.

But suppose that you want to format a new partition. The Tools, Format command is dimmed because the partition has not actually been built yet. Rather than exiting from Disk Manager and then starting it again, you can choose Partition, Commit Changes Now to force the changes to be committed. The partition is created, and now you can format it. This option is useful if you wish to commit some changes, and then proceed with further changes, such as creating a partition and then making it part of a stripe or mirror set.

Formatting NTFS Volumes

A partition can be formatted as NTFS from within Disk Manager with the Tools, Format option. If it's already formatted, as either FAT or NTFS, the menu option shows as Change Format. You can format a drive from within the My Computer folder, or from Explorer, in each case by right-clicking the drive letter, and then selecting the Format option from the pop-up menu. And of course, there is always the command prompt option. Use the command

```
FORMAT /FS:NTFS
```

in order to format a drive with the NTFS file system.

Default Permissions on NTFS Drives

As mentioned earlier, when a drive is formatted with the NTFS file system, the default permission is that Everyone has Full Control. This is probably not what you want on an NTFS volume, so you should use the Security menu to set the permissions you really want, and then remove the group Everyone from the list, or at least from Full Control. You will need to assign some permissions, rather than leave the permissions box empty, or nobody will have permission to access the disk.

Caution

Do not attempt to make a secure volume by assigning the No Access permission to Everyone, of course, or nobody will be able to access the disk.

Removing Partitions

NTFS partitions are most easily removed from within Disk Manager. FAT partitions, of course, can be removed by Disk Manager or FDISK, but some older versions of FDISK have problems with NTFS volumes created in non-DOS partitions. So the best approach is to remove NTFS partitions from Windows NT. The Partition, Delete menu option will do the trick, and again, the deletion is not final until you exit from Disk Manager or commit the changes. Alternatively, you can right-click the drive, and select Delete from the pop-up menu.

Deleting the system partition is trickier, because you can't delete a partition that is in use.

Assigning Drive Letters

Within Windows NT, you can assign any available drive letter to any of the logical drives. There is no requirement, as there is in DOS, to have contiguous drive letters starting at C:. Nor is it necessary to label the primary partitions first, then the drives within the extended partitions. Windows NT gives you complete flexibility in assigning drive letters. By choosing Tools, Drive Letter from Disk Administrator, you can specify a drive letter, as shown in figure 16.23.

The changes take place immediately without rebooting, as shown in figure 16.24.

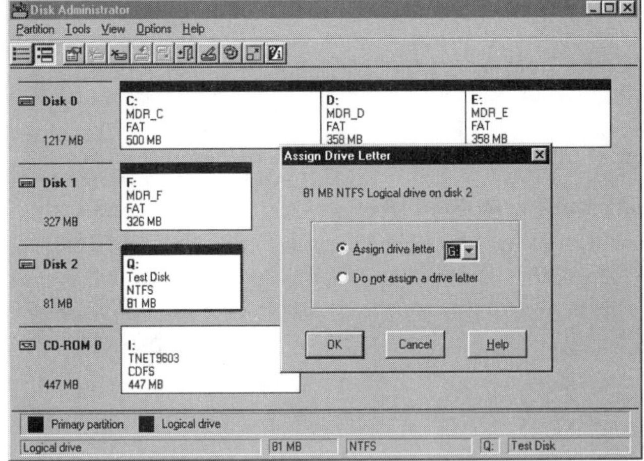

Fig. 16.23
Windows NT Disk Administrator allows very flexible assignment of drive letters.

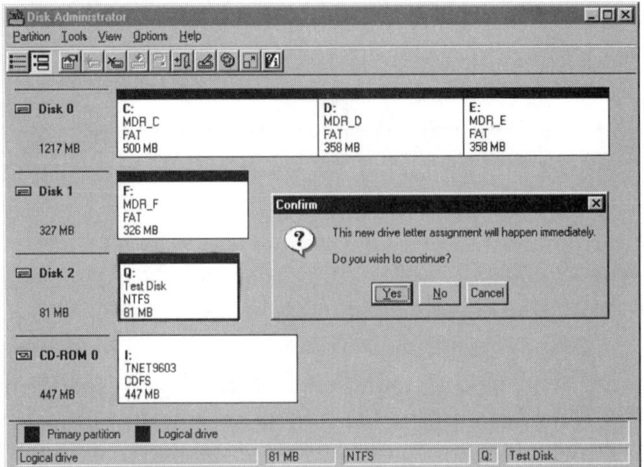

Fig. 16.24
Disk Administrator updates the drive letters immediately.

You can even specify that a drive does not have a drive letter. Of course, you will not be able to access the drive until you give it a letter—but then nobody else can either, so there may be times when you need to hide a drive and can use this option. It might be useful, for example, to install a 'hot swap' drive, assign it a drive letter for testing, then deactivate it until needed. Or if you have more than 24 drives, you can leave some of them without a drive letter until you need them.

By the way, for those of you who have multiple connections to other systems, and are running out of drive letters, you can map a network drive as B:, as long as you only have one floppy drive in the computer.

Reassigning drive letters is often useful when you wish to add another hard disk, and keep the CD-ROM drive letter the same (handy if you installed software from a CD-ROM drive, and more so if you run software from the CD-ROM directly). Or you may wish to change the CD-ROM drive letter to one further down the alphabet, to allow room for adding hard disks without having to change the drive letter of the CD-ROM. Then you can install and run software from the CD-ROM without having to edit the program locations in the Registry or the Startup Program list. (Windows NT, like all Windows software, still lacks the ability to specify that a program has moved from drive D: to drive E:. The only option seems to be to remove and reinstall the program, or manually edit all references to it.)

Using Disk Compression

Disk compression was introduced to Windows NT in version 3.51. Windows NT only supports compression on NTFS volumes, not on FAT volumes. It works very differently from the disk compression in DOS and Windows 95. The mathematical basis for the compression algorithms is similar to that of DoubleSpace or DriveSpace, but Windows NT does not convert the entire volume to a compressed disk, and so there are no 'phantom' drives to contend with. Instead, Windows NT offers disk compression that can be turned on and off at an individual directory or file level.

How Disk Compression Works on NTFS

NTFS divides a file into compression unit 16 clusters long (which translates to 8K for 512 byte clusters). Then it determines whether compressing the unit will save at least one cluster of storage. If compression will not show a gain of at least one cluster, then NTFS writes the unit to the disk as a 16-cluster run with no compression. But in the case where the data in the 16-cluster unit will compress to 15 or fewer clusters, NTFS allocates only the number of clusters required, and writes the data to the disk. NTFS reads and writes at least one compression unit at a time when accessing compressed data. It tries to store compression units in contiguous locations, so that it can read them with a single I/O operation. Using a 16-cluster compression unit size reduces internal fragmentation, because the larger the compression unit, the less the overall disk space needed to store the data.

The NTFS compression algorithm uses a three-byte minimum search rather that the two-byte minimum employed by DoubleSpace. This enables a much faster compression and decompression (roughly twice as fast) with a penalty of about two percent compression for the average text file.

Should Data Be Compressed?

The designers of Windows NT were not in favor of disk compression, and probably still are not. But when disk compression became widely used in DOS and again in Windows 95, the demand for compression in Windows NT increased. In the end, the Windows NT team came up with a solution that avoids the complexity of switching drive letters, maintains security, and allows more options about what is compressed and what is left uncompressed. The compression techniques chosen were biased in favor of performance over the theoretical maximum possible compression ratio. Given that hard disk prices are falling rapidly, and memory costs are coming down more slowly, this seems like a smart decision. Thanks to the way NTFS looks up files on the disk, only one lookup operation is needed to find a compressed file on a disk, compared to three disk-accessed needed to locate a file in a DoubleSpace compressed disk. This means that NTFS pays no penalty when looking for a compressed file, and offers better performance with compressed files than DoubleSpace on FAT does.

The opposition to disk compression was based on the premise that compression is not appropriate on a server, and that is still true. NTFS compression is definitely biased toward Workstation users. The purpose of the server is to provide the requested data to the client as efficiently as possible. If all the data has to go through the CPU and be uncompressed, the load on the CPU will increase dramatically and the system will provide poor response. As a general rule, data accessed by clients from a server system should not be compressed. On the other hand, files that are rarely used, and then only on the local computer, can be compressed. Microsoft's position is that in benchmark tests, some heavily accessed servers have shown significant and unacceptable performance degradation after compression was implemented, and they advise against using compression on servers.

How to Compress Data

Compressing data in Windows NT is actually simpler than using DOS compression, as it is an option in My Computer, Explorer, and File Manager. In My Computer and Explorer, select the files or directories you want to compress, and right-click to open the shortcut menu. The Compress and Uncompress options are on this menu. The Compression attribute can be set on or off from the Properties sheet of this menu. The Properties sheet also shows the original and the compressed file sizes (see fig. 16.25).

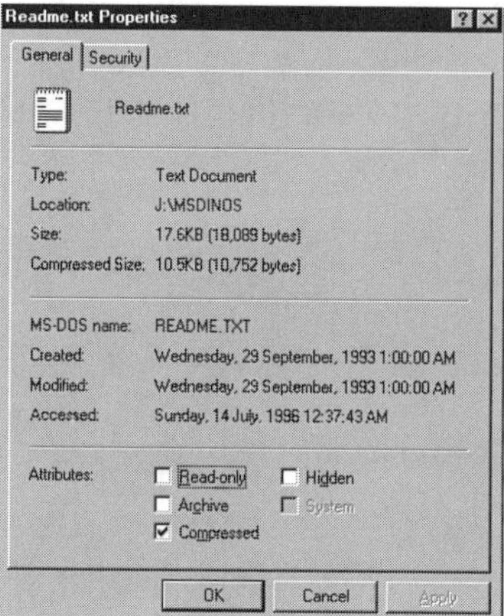

Fig. 16.25
Check a file's compression size on the General page.

Note that it is possible to compress a directory, but leave the files in it uncompressed. You will be prompted about whether the compression should be applied to the folders (or files and subdirectories) contained in the folder (or directory) that is being compressed. If you compress a folder or directory, but not its contents, the compression will apply only to any new folders or files placed in that folder or directory.

As with DOS compression, the file size is shown just as it was before it was compressed. However, the disk size also does not change, unlike DOS compression where the disk appears to be larger. When files are compressed on an NTFS disk, the free space will increase, but the total disk space is not changed. Using the pop-up menu to open the properties sheet for any file will show both the original file size and the compressed file size.

In File Manager, the Files, Compress and Files, Uncompress menu options can be applied to selected directories and files. File Manager uses a different color to indicate compressed files and directories, but My Computer and Explorer do not have any such visual indication that a file is compressed. They do not even show file attributes (Hidden, System, and so on) which is too bad, as compression is a new attribute that could also be shown.

By the way, for those who still insist on using the command line, there is a new command, COMPACT, which will compress files on NTFS volumes. For a full listing of the switches associated with this command, type **COMPACT /?** at the command prompt.

Moving and Copying Compressed Files

The same logic applies with compressed files as when we discussed the ownership and security permissions on files in Windows NT. If the file is copied or moved from another disk, then it takes on the compression properties of its new directory. But if it is moved to a new directory on the same disk, the compression attribute is unchanged. So you may find a compressed file in a directory that otherwise contains uncompressed files, as shown in figure 16.26.

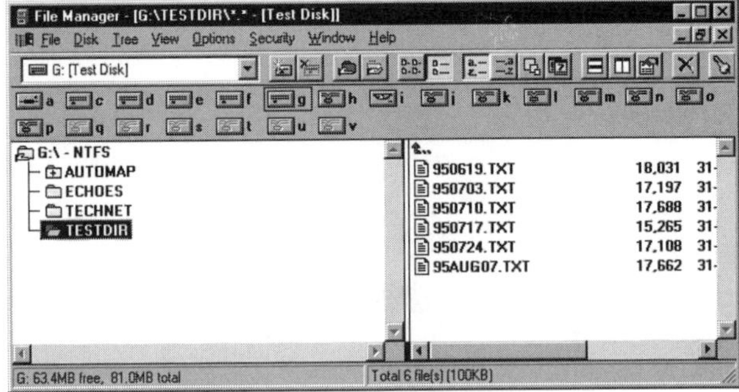

Fig. 16.26
These files were moved here from another directory on this disk and so retain the compression attribute.

Compatibility Issues

As we mentioned, the methods used for compression within Windows NT, DOS, and Windows 3.1 are totally different. Obviously DOS and Windows 3.1 cannot read Windows NT compressed partitions, as compressed files are only stored on NTFS volumes. In other words, to take advantage of the data compression in Windows NT, you must use NTFS and give up DOS compatibility. Or if you want DOS compatibility, then you have to leave the disks as FAT, and give up compression and other benefits of NTFS.

The reverse is also true: Windows NT cannot read DOS DoubleSpace or DriveSpace disks. So if you want to dual-boot the system, and access the FAT disks, you can't compress them.

Understanding and Using Long Filenames

The ability to handle long filenames was another item on the list of requirements when NTFS was designed. The old DOS 8+3 filename standard was viewed as a serious limitation, and was already outdated technology. For POSIX compliance, case-sensitive filenames were mandatory. Not only does Windows NT allow long filenames on NTFS partitions, it also allows them on FAT partitions, as does Windows 95.

Long Filenames on NTFS

Under Windows NT, filenames on either FAT or NTFS volumes can be up to 255 characters. They can contain spaces and multiple periods. Anything after the last period is assumed to be a file extension. NTFS filenames can include Unicode characters.

Integrating with Other File Systems

Many users have systems that dual-boot Windows NT and another operating system, such as DOS with Windows for Workgroups. Some partitions are FAT, others are NTFS. And even on a sever running nothing but NTFS, files can be requested over the network by a client running a DOS-based operating system. So part of the design for NTFS included the ability to make the files visible to other operating systems.

Compatibility

Not only must the files be visible to other operating systems, they must also be readable. When a file is copied or moved from an NTFS disk to a FAT disk, the file must be written with a name that can be read by the target file system. To do so, an algorithm was developed to convert the long filenames to shorter names that follow the naming standards of the DOS operating system. These shortened names are what shows in the File Manager when you choose View, All File Details, as seen in figure 16.27. They are also what you will see when you use the DIR/X command at the command prompt. To make them visible from Explorer or a folder within Windows NT 4.0, you will have to use the file Properties sheet, which is not as convenient.

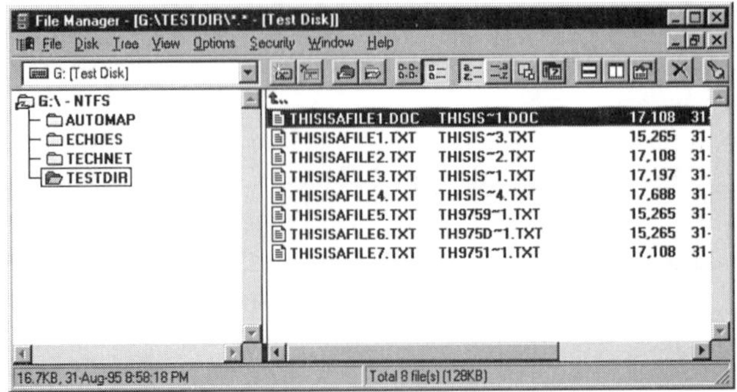

Fig. 16.27
File Manager is the easiest way to examine the long and short filenames.

Translating Long Filenames to Other File Systems

The method used to convert long file names to FAT-compatible filenames is as follows:

1. Remove illegal characters, spaces, Unicode characters, and leading and trailing periods.
2. Remove all embedded periods except for the last one.
3. Truncate the string before the period (if there is one) to six characters.
4. Append the string "~1" to the six character string before the period.
5. Truncate the string after the period to three characters.
6. Make the entire name uppercase, to avoid names which differ only in case.
7. If the generated name duplicates an existing filename, increment the ~1 string.
8. If the increment process results in a ~5, use a hashing algorithm to generate a different name, retaining only the first two characters.

This sequence is intended to produce compatible filenames, and is just one of many ways in which the file names can be generated. So while it may be of interest to know how it works, developers can't count on this exact scheme being used in future releases of Windows NT. The important point is that each file has a short filename which DOS programs can use, and a long filename that 32-bit software can use.

Newer software, including anything written for Windows 95, can recognize the long file and directory names, but older 16-bit applications cannot. So a problem arises with applications such as Word and WordPerfect. Double-clicking a DOC file will start Word, but if the directory name is too long, Word won't be able to find the file. This is not really a problem, as the File, Open menu option will still work and allow you to find the file. When Word saves the file, it may be set up to create a backup copy of the old version. The long filename will remain with the document file, but the backup copy will not have a long filename, because Word can't create the long filenames. For the same reason, if you use the File, Save As option to save the file with a new name, you will be limited to the 8+3 file names that Word understands. ❖

CHAPTER 17

Ensuring Data Security

by Richard Neff

Because many users and businesses rely on data stored on computers, protecting that data is a very important part of an operating system. Hardware, especially hard disks, may fail; minimizing the effects of computer failures is critical. Backup protection and fault tolerance are two major features that Windows NT provides to minimize the risk of lost data.

Backups of data are the first link to ensuring data security. The Backup program provided with Windows NT allows data to be copied to a storage medium and later restored. With Windows NT, disk fault tolerance allows data to remain safe even in the event of a hard drive failure.

In this chapter, you learn to

- Determine appropriate backup strategies and media
- Backup and restore data using the Backup utility
- Create and implement mirrored and duplexed drives
- Create and implement disk striping with parity checking
- Restore data when fault-tolerant devices fail
- Learn about UPS systems and protecting server data

Examining Backup Strategies and Media

Because many vital types of information are stored on computers, loss of that data can be catastrophic. Data should always be backed up to ensure that it can be recovered should the computer's disks fail. Therefore, it's important to have a good backup strategy implemented to minimized the risk of losing data. You must also choose the correct media to store your backup information.

There are many types of media that can be used to store extra copies of computer data. The type of media used depends on the particular needs and requirements of the user. Floppy disks, tape drives, and other storage devices are types of media often used to store extra copies of data.

Floppy Disks

Floppy disk drives usually are standard equipment with most personal computers and can store small amounts of data from 360K to 1.44M. Since they are so commonplace, they are often used to back up data on personal computers. However, due to the small amount of data stored on a disk, floppy disks are not the preferred media to store the entire contents of a hard drive. To do so often takes hundreds of disks and backup time is tediously long. Floppy disks are better used to copy a few important files for safekeeping.

Tape Drives

Tape drives are the most common media to back up large amounts of information, such as an entire hard drive, in a reasonably fast and inexpensive fashion. Tapes last between 5 to 10 years depending on the quality of the tape. Tape drives can store anywhere from 120M to 8G or more on a single tape. Tape drives can be single tape drives where tapes are manually changed when they are full and tape autoloaders that automatically change a full tape with a blank one. Tape autoloaders are used to effectively increase the storage capacity on computers with large storage requirements such as database servers on a network.

Quarter-Inch Cartridge (QIC)

The Quarter-Inch Cartridge (QIC) standard uses a quarter-inch wide tape with nine parallel tracks. The QIC standard is divided into different types based on the tape's storage capacity. The QIC standard also uses data compression to allow more data to be stored on the tape. The storage capacity can vary from 60M to 1.4G or more, depending on the QIC type used. QIC tapes and drives are usually the least expensive type of tape backup.

4mm Digital Audio Tape (DAT)

Although more expensive than QIC types of drives, 4mm Digital Audio Tape (DAT) drives offer more storage capacity and speed. These types of tape drives are more commonly found on high-end workstations and servers. 4mm DAT also uses data compression to increase the storage capacity of a tape. 4mm DAT tapes can store from 2G to 4G of data.

8mm Digital Audio Tape (DAT)

Although similar to 4mm DAT, 8mm Digital Audio Tape (DAT) is twice the width of 4mm DAT and is able to hold more information on a single tape. 8mm DAT is usually found on larger network installations to back up multiple servers in a network. As with 4mm DAT, it uses data compression to help increase the capacity of tapes. An 8mm DAT tape can store from 4G to 8G of data.

Other Backup Media

Other storage media exists to which data can be copied, such as Zip drives, Compact Disk-Recordable (CD-R) disks, or Magno-Optical disks. These devices hold anywhere from 1M to 660M of data depending on the device. Many of these devices require special drivers and may not be supported in the Windows NT Backup utility.

Tape Backup Methods

There are many backup strategies available to back up data while keeping costs and the number of tapes to a minimum. While backing up an entire drive with all files, even if they have been backed up previously, provides the best backup protection, it's the most costly, uses the most tapes, and may not be practical for all situations.

Other methods often use a combination of full backups and incremental backups where only the files that are new or not copied on the last backup are copied to the backup media. The most common implementation is the Grandfather-Father-Son backup method.

The Grandfather-Father-Son Method

The Grandfather-Father-Son backup method is a fairly simple and commonly used method of tape rotation. There are four daily tapes (for example, Monday-Thursday), four weekly tapes (for example, Fridays), and 12 monthly tapes (January through December). The daily tapes, known as the sons, are used at the end of the listed day. The weekly tapes, known as the father tapes, are used at the end of the day on Friday, with Weekly1 being the first Friday of the month, and so on. The 12 monthly tapes, known as the grandfather tapes, are used on the last day of the corresponding month.

Usually the daily tapes are not full backups, but incremental backups. The Weekly and Monthly tapes are usually full backups. The Grandfather-Father-Son backup method allows for recovery throughout the entire year using the monthly tapes. The rotation of tapes also helps to minimize the risk of lost data if a tape is damaged. This method is also one of the simplest to manage.

Table 17.1 describes the tape rotation of the Grandfather-Father-Son method.

Table 17.1 Grandfather-Father-Son Tape Backup Method

Tape	Description
Daily	Four tapes are labeled Monday through Thursday and a backup, usually incremental, is performed at the end of the corresponding day.
Weekly	Four tapes are labeled Weekly1, Weekly2, Weekly3, and Weekly4. A backup, usually a full backup, is performed at the end of the day on Friday.
Monthly	Twelve tapes are labeled January through December and a full backup is performed on the last day of the corresponding month.

Other Backup Methods

Another tape backup method is the Ten-Tape method. The Ten-Tape method rotates all the tapes evenly and provides a backup history for about 12 weeks. This method uses a series of four-week cycles. In the first four-week cycle, the four tapes are labeled Monday through Thursday. This is similar to the Grandfather-Father-Son method described previously. On the first Friday, a tape is made and only used once in the series. The next Friday, a different tape is used to back up the data. So, you will end up with four tapes with the different Friday backups. Again, at this point, it is similar to the Father and Son tapes of the Grandfather-Father-Son method.

After the four-week cycle, the tapes are moved up in the schedule. For example, the Tuesday tape becomes the Monday tape. The Monday tape is rotated "out" and one of the two unused tapes becomes the last Friday tape. This process continues every four weeks, with tapes moving up in the tape order. Although harder to manage than the Grandfather-Father-Son method, it helps to evenly distribute the use of the tapes. It also requires fewer tapes than the Grandfather-Father-Son method.

A third tape backup method is the Tower of Hanoi method. The Tower of Hanoi method is named after the mathematical game where disks are moved around three pegs. Seven tapes are typically used instead of the 10 to 20 that are used with the other methods. Tape sets are labeled A, B, C, and so on. The tapes are mathematically determined into the appropriate order. This method is used by some automated programs and is difficult to maintain manually.

Other backup methods can be used to safeguard data on Windows NT systems. While the three methods listed are the most common, other methods may provide a better solution for a user's or organization's needs. Determining the best backup solution depends on such factors as the overall cost of tapes, the ease of tape management, the length of the backup history, and so on.

Tip

If you are a casual user, you may not need to make daily backups. You may want to just make weekly or monthly backup tapes.

Off-Site Backup Storage

For the best data security, some backups should be kept away from the computer site so that if physical damage occurs at the site, data can be restored on a repaired or replacement computer. In many instances, a network administrator will take the backups to a home location or a predefined corporate location for safekeeping. Usually, weekly system backups are taken off-site; however, this is dependent on the needs of a particular organization. Current logs should be kept on the status of off-site tapes. Home users using Windows NT 4.0 may incorporate off-site storage, such as taking the tapes to a personal bank box or safe, if the situation warrants.

Applying Backup Strategies

Windows NT 4.0 has a Backup utility in the Administrative Tools folder. To start the Windows NT 4.0 Backup program, click the Start button, then choose Programs. When the Program list is displayed, choose Administrative Tools, then Backup.

When the Backup program starts, you see two windows: one lists the machine's drives and the other lists the tape devices connected to the computer (see fig. 17.1). You'll also see a menu and a toolbar for backup functions.

If you don't have a recognized tape drive on your computer, you'll see an error message displayed when you first start the Backup program. If you don't have a recognized tape drive on your system, you won't be able to use the Windows NT Backup utility to back up files (see fig. 17.2). Although you may be able to select files in the Drives window, you will not be able to back them up if no tape device is available.

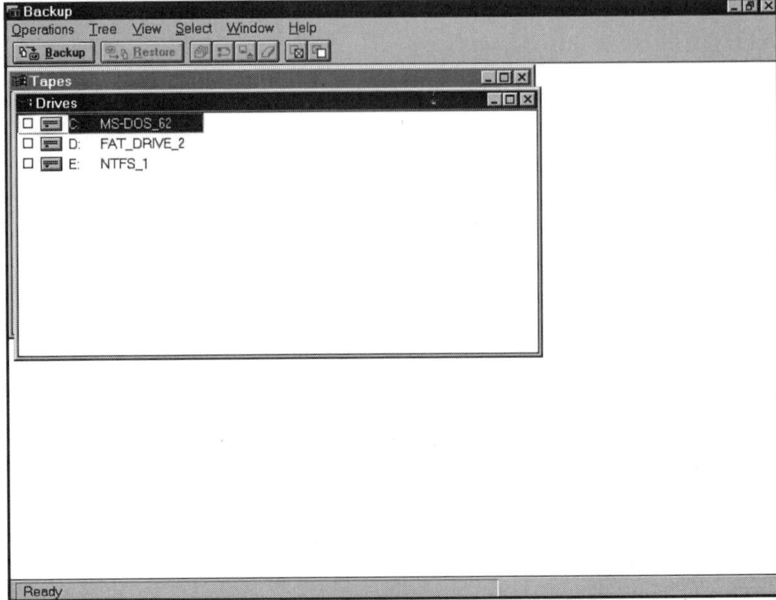

Fig. 17.1
The Backup utility main screen shows the Drives window.

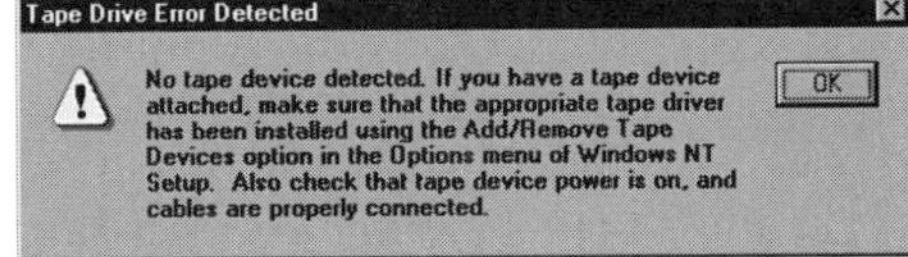

Fig. 17.2
You must have a tape drive for the Backup utility to back up data files or this error message will be displayed.

Permissions Required to Perform Backups

You need to have the Backup Files and Directories user right to back up all the files on a Windows NT system. The Administrator and Backup Operators groups have this right by default. If you do not have this user right, you will only be able to back up files you have created or otherwise been given access.

Backing Up Data with the Backup Utility

Backing up data with the Windows NT Backup utility is very straightforward. The Backup utility windows are similar to the Windows NT Explorer in both look and functionality. In the windows for the drive and file listing, you can either click the checkbox to back up all the files on an entire drive, or you can double-click the drive to see the first-level directory tree of that drive. You can then select files and directories by clicking the checkbox beside them, or you can continue to double-click directories to expand them (see fig. 17.3). To unselect an item that has been checked, simply click the checkbox to clear it.

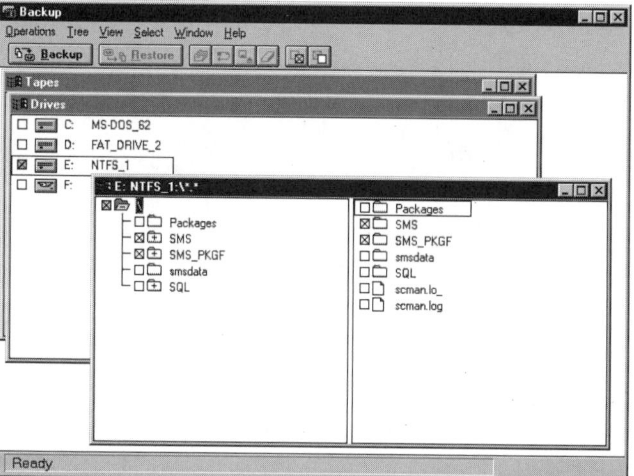

Fig. 17.3
You need to select items in the Drives window before starting the backup.

> **Note**
>
> While the Windows NT Backup program can be used to handle complete system backups, restoring the entire system can be a complex process. In almost all instances when an entire drive fails, Windows NT will have to be reinstalled, then the Backup utility will be able to restore the rest of the system. For protection of an entire system drive, see the section "Understanding Fault Tolerance" later in the chapter.

The group of files and directories selected is known as the backup set. Once you have created a backup set, you can simply click the Backup button in the toolbar at the top of the screen, or you can choose Operations, Backup to start the backup. The Backup Information dialog box appears allowing you to select different backup options. Figure 17.4 shows the Backup Information dialog box.

The Backup Information dialog box contains many options concerning the tape information, backup set information, and log information. Listed below are the different options found on the Backup Information window.

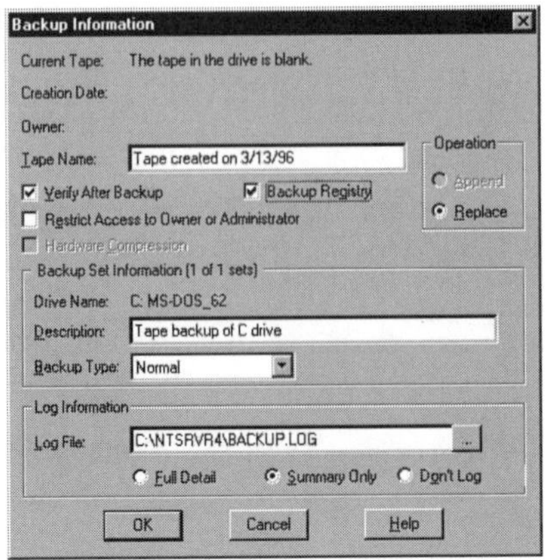

Fig. 17.4
Before the backup is started, the Backup Information dialog box will be displayed.

- *Current Tape.* If the tape currently has a name, it displays the tape name.
- *Creation Date.* Displays the date of the last backup on the tape.
- *Owner.* The account of the user who first created a backup set on the tape.
- *Tape Name.* You can input a new name for the tape here. The name can be no more than 32 characters long. This option is not available with an Append operation.
- *Operation.* Choosing Append adds the backup set to the end of the current backup set on the tape. Replace overwrites the current backup set on the tape.
- *Verify After Backup.* If checked, this verifies the information written to the tape after the backup is performed.
- *Restrict Access to Owner or Administrator.* Allows only the owner of the tape, the Backup Operators group, or an Administrator to read, write, or erase the tape. This option is not available with an Append operation.
- *Hardware Compression.* Enables hardware compression to be used if the device supports hardware compression. This option will be grayed out if hardware compression is not supported (see fig. 17.4).
- *Backup Registry.* Makes a copy of the local Windows NT Registry and places it on the tape if the drive containing the Registry is selected.
- *Backup Set Information.* Contains the drive name, the description, and the type of backup (Normal, Copy, Incremental, Differential, or Daily) for each backup set. Table 17.2 lists the different types of backups that can be performed and gives an explanation of each.
- *Log Information.* Describes the type of log information to record as well as the filename of the log file. The Log Information box allows for three

types of logging: Full Detail, Summary Only, and Don't Log. Full Detail logs events and errors with the verbose messages. The Summary Only option logs with just a quick summary of the event or error. The Don't Log option provides no logging of the backup process.

Table 17.2 Backup Types

Backup Type	Description
Normal	Backs up all data selected and marks each file as backed up.
Copy	Backs up all selected files, but doesn't mark as backed up. Keeps the archive file attribute for the files the same.
Incremental	Backs up and marks only the files that have changed since the last backup in the file selection.
Differential	Backs up the files that have changed since the last backup in the file selection, but doesn't mark as backed up.
Daily	Backs up, but doesn't mark as backed up, only the selected files that have been modified on the day of the backup.

Monitoring the Backup Status

Once you choose the OK button in the Backup Information dialog box, the backup process starts with the settings you specified. Once the backup process starts, the Backup Status dialog box appears (see fig. 17.5).

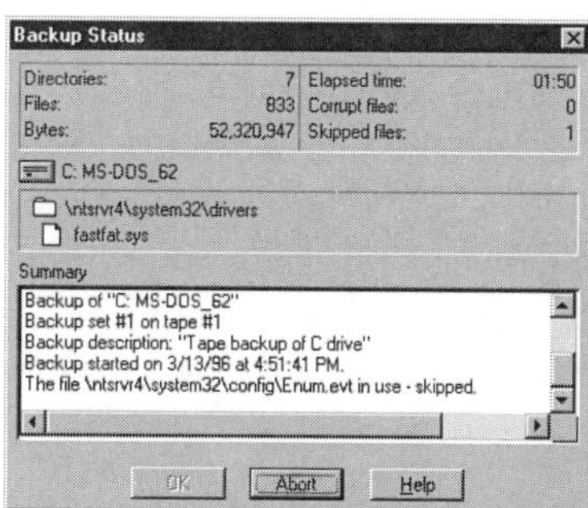

Fig. 17.5 Once the backup is started, you can monitor the process by viewing the Backup Status window.

The Backup Status dialog box displays the following information:

- Directories processed
- Files processed
- Bytes processed

- Time elapsed in hours, minutes, and seconds since the backup was started
- Number of corrupt files encountered
- Number of skipped files due to read errors or open/locked files
- Selected disk, directory, and file currently being copied to tape
- Summary information showing an event log of the current backup process

If you need to stop the backup process before it is completed, click the Abort button. You'll see a message asking if you want to abort the operation or continue the backup process.

Restoring Data with the Backup Utility

The second major function of the Windows NT Backup utility is the restoration of files from a backup tape. The Windows NT Backup utility allows you to do a full restoration or selected-files restoration on a tape set.

Tip

Be sure to test your backup and restore procedure beforehand to ensure that when you need to copy data off of a tape, you can be sure the procedure will work properly. After important files have been deleted or corrupted is a very bad time to discover that the backup/restore procedure did not work.

To restore files from a tape or tape set to the hard disk, insert the tape that contains the files you want into the tape drive. Then open the Tapes window by clicking the Restore or Maximize buttons in the title bar, if the window is not already displayed. The tape name appears to the right of each tape icon in the left panel of the Tapes window. The right panel in the Tapes window displays information such as: the drive that was backed up, the backup set number, the tape number, the backup type, the date and time of the backup, and a description of the backup.

In order to restore files from a tape or tape set, you need to load the tape's catalog. The *catalog* displays a list of any other backup sets on the tape. By default, the information in the Tapes window displays information about the first backup set on the tape.

To load a catalog of a tape's backup sets, follow these steps:

1. Select the tape of the catalog you want to load from the Tapes window.

2. Choose Operations, Catalog. You can also double-click the icon of the tape or select the Catalog button (icon with index cards on it) on the toolbar.
3. The Backup program searches the tape for a complete list of the backup sets on the tape. A status box appears that allows you to stop the catalog process if needed.
4. After all the individual backup sets have been displayed, you can select a backup set to load by double-clicking the backup set's icon.

> **Note**
>
> When restoring files, the backup type used is very important. If incremental or differential backups were used, you will first need to restore a complete backup, then the incremental or differential backup to restore an entire directory with the most recent files. For individual files, you may only need to restore the files from the incremental or differential backup tape.

Once the catalogs of a tape are loaded, you can copy all the files on a tape, restore individual backup sets on a tape, or copy individual files in a backup set. To select all the files on a tape to be restored, check the tape in the left side of the Tapes window. To restore a backup set, click the checkbox of the tape set or tape sets that you want to restore. To select individual files, check the checkbox of the files you want to copy from the tape set.

After you have selected which items you want to bring back from the tape, click the Restore button on the toolbar or choose Operations, Restore. The Restore Information dialog box appears (see fig. 17.6).

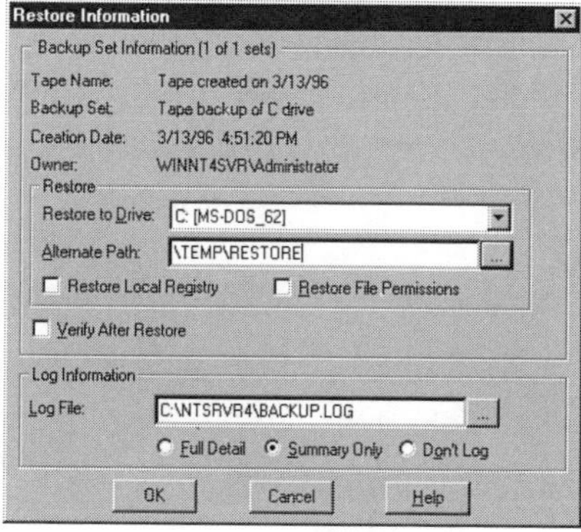

Fig. 17.6
Before files are restored to the hard disk, the Restore Information dialog box will be displayed.

The Restore Information dialog box displays the following information:

- *Tape Name.* Displays the tape name.
- *Backup Set.* The backup set name is shown here.
- *Creation Date.* Shows when the tape was created.
- *Owner.* The owner who created the backup set is displayed.
- *Restore to Drive.* Selects which drive to restore the data from the tape to.
- *Alternate Path.* Use of this text box is optional. You can specify an alternate path for the files on the tape instead of the original path recorded onto the tape.
- *Restore Local Registry.* Restores local Registry information to the drive. The computer must be restarted for the restored information to take effect.
- *Restore File Permissions.* Restores the original file permissions on the tape. Otherwise, the files inherit the permissions of the directory to which they are restored.
- *Verify After Restore.* Verifies the information written to the disk after the restore is performed.
- *Log Information.* Displays the filename of the log file to be used and determines the logging options. The Log Information box allows for three types of logging: Full Detail, Summary Only, and Don't Log. Full Detail logs using verbose messages for the logged events. The Summary Only option logs with just a brief summary of the event or error. The Don't Log option provides no logging of the restore process.

Monitoring the Restore Status

Once you choose the OK button in the Restore Information dialog box, the restore process starts with the settings you specified. Once the restore process starts, the Restore Status dialog box appears as shown in figure 17.7. The Restore Status dialog box contains essentially the same information as the Backup Status dialog box.

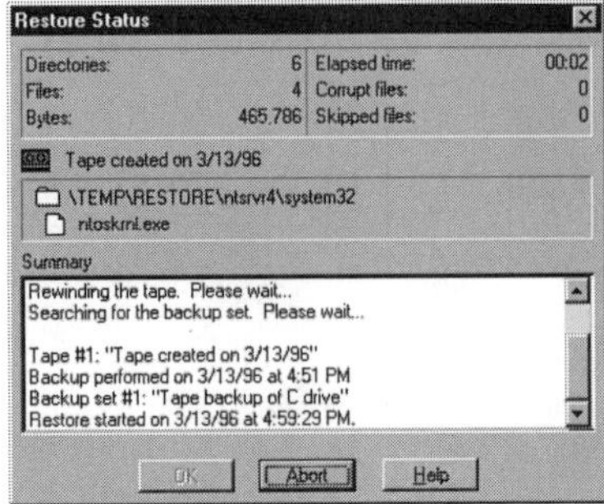

Fig. 17.7
Once the restore process is started, the Restore Status dialog box is displayed.

The Restore Status dialog box displays the following information:

- Directories processed
- Files processed
- Bytes processed
- Time elapsed in hours, minutes, and seconds
- Number of corrupt files encountered
- Number of skipped files due to read errors or open/locked files
- Selected disk, directory, and file currently being copied from the tape
- Summary information showing an event log of the current restore process

If you need to stop the restore process before it is completed, click the Abort button. This will display a message asking you if you want to abort the operation or continue the restore process.

Missing or Damaged Tapes in a Tape Set

If a tape is damaged or missing in a backup set that spans several tapes, the information on the tape probably won't be able to be restored. However, the last tape, which contains the catalog information of a multiple tape set, may sometimes be missing or damaged. When this occurs, the Backup utility can be forced to treat the remaining tapes as a single tape instead of a member of a tape set. To force the Backup program to do this, the /missingtape switch can be used with the Backup command on the command line.

This breaks the set into individual tapes. So, if you had four tapes in a set, and the fourth tape was missing or damaged, you could restore the data from the other tapes, one at a time, with the /missingtape switch from the command line.

Scheduling Backups

The Windows NT Backup utility does not allow for scheduled backups. However, the scheduler service and command line can be used to create and run a batch file to schedule backups. The Windows NT Backup Help file contains more information on how to create a batch file to handle backups.

To access Windows NT Backup in a batch file, use the NTBACKUP command. The NTBACKUP command has the following switches:

- */a*. This appends backup data to the tape; that is, it copies the new data after the old data on the tape. If this switch is not used, the old data will be overwritten.

- */v*. This switch causes the backup to perform verification. If this switch is not used, verification of the backed up data will not occur.
- */r*. This switch restricts backup access to the owner or the administrator.
- */d "text"*. This creates a text description of the backup.
- */b*. This switch causes the local registry to be backed up.
- */hc:(on/off)*. If /hc:on is used, then hardware compression is used. If /hc:off is used, then hardware compression is not used.
- */t (Normal, Copy, Incremental, Differential, or Daily)*. This switch specifies the type of backup type to perform.
- */l* "filename". This switch specifies the filename of the backup log.
- */tape:number*. Specifies which tape drive (0-9) to perform the backup if multiple tape drives are used.

So, the following line in a batch file

```
NTBACKUP Backup C:\WINDOWS /t Normal /v /d "Windows Backup" /l
➥"C:\backlog.txt"
```

would cause the backup program to perform a normal backup of files in the C:\WINDOWS directory, verify the backup, use "Windows Backup" in the description, and log to C:\BACKLOG.TXT. Keep in mind that using backup in a batch file should only be used by experienced batch programmers.

If more sophisticated backup scheduling is needed, there are many third-party backup programs on the market for both Windows NT Workstations and Windows NT Servers. Some titles include Arcada Backup Exec, Cheyenne ARCserve, Legato NetWorker, and Palindrome Backup Director. Many of these programs provide more advanced features as well as backup scheduling.

Tape Maintenance

The Windows NT Backup utility has three options on the Operations menu to help maintain tapes: Erase Tape, Retension Tape, and Format Tape. The Erase Tape command can either use a Quick Erase, where the header of the tape is deleted, or a Secure Erase, which erases the entire tape. The Secure Erase provides the best security, but can take a long time based on the tape type and length.

The Retension Tape command retensions QIC tapes to ensure proper winding of the tape. Retensioning a tape causes the tape to be rewound around the tape reel. This helps prevent tape errors and should be performed after about 20 uses of a QIC tape. This command is not available for 4mm or 8mm tapes since they do not require retensioning.

The Format Tape command formats a mini-cartridge tape.

Understanding Fault Tolerance

Although backups help to protect data by copying files to another medium, they require scheduled maintenance and are only as good as the most recent backup of the data. Disk fault tolerance supplements, but does not replace, backups of data. Disk fault tolerance helps protect data by spreading data across drives. That way, if a drive fails, all the data on the drive is not lost. There are different methods to restoring the data on the lost drive. One method simply copies the same data to two drives, while the other keeps information on how to rebuild the data from information kept on other drives.

RAID (Redundant Array of Inexpensive Disks) levels allow network servers to increase network disk performance and provide for fault tolerance of data. Windows NT supports RAID Levels 0, 1 (NT Server Only), and 5 (NT Server Only). Descriptions of the RAID levels follow:

- *RAID Level 0 (Disk Striping).* Distributes disk writes across two or more hard drives. This is used to increase the file performance because it allows simultaneous reading and writing of data from and to different drives. However, it provides no fault tolerance.
- *RAID Level 1 (Disk Mirroring).* Writes the same data to two separate drives, creating a mirror-image of the data. This allows one drive to fail without a loss of data since the other drive contains the exact same data. Read performance is increased over a single drive since data can be read off both drives to complete a disk read request. Write performance may diminish slightly, however. Raid Level 1 requires Windows NT Server 4.0 and requires two or more hard drives.

  Disk duplexing is a modification of disk mirroring. Disk duplexing still writes the same data on different drives, but each drive is connected to a different drive controller. By using this method, data is protected not only if a drive fails, but if a drive controller fails. Disk duplexing increases the fault tolerance of a computer, but also increases the computer's cost.
- *RAID Levels 2, 3, and 4.* All of these methods use disk striping, but they employ different error-correction strategies. These methods store checksum data on a single disk or multiple disks separate from data disks. These levels require disks to be dedicated to checksum information and can be very costly to implement. All of these methods contributed to the development of RAID Level 5. Windows NT 4.0 does not support RAID levels 2, 3, or 4.
- *RAID Level 5 (Disk Striping with Parity).* This method writes data across two or more hard disks similar to Level 0, but writes a parity bit or

checksum operation on the other disks. If a drive fails, the contents of that drive can be rebuilt using the parity information on the other drives. RAID Level 5 requires Windows NT Server 4.0 and requires three or more hard disk drives.

- *Combining RAID Level 1 and RAID Level 5.* Disks can also be mirrored and striped. This allows for improvements in read/write operations and provides for fault tolerance. However, this requires a larger investment of hard drives.

> **Note**
>
> Only Windows NT Server 4.0 provides fault-tolerance options like disk mirroring, disk duplexing, and disk striping with parity. Windows NT Workstation 4.0 only provides disk striping. If you need fault-tolerance options to protect data, you should use Windows NT Server instead of Windows NT Workstation.

Software versus Hardware RAID Solutions

Windows NT 4.0 uses software-based RAID solutions that support Level 0, 1, and 5. However, many hardware vendors may use hardware-based solutions when building fault-tolerant computers. These solutions usually bypass the Windows NT software drivers and may offer some performance advantages. Also, some users may want to use different levels of RAID than Windows NT supports.

One of the disadvantages of a hardware-based RAID solution is that it may lock you into a single-vendor solution. Also, hardware-based solutions are usually more expensive than using the software-based solution that Windows NT provides. Which type of RAID solution to use depends on the requirements and results desired by the users of the Windows NT computer.

Sector Sparing

Sector sparing, also known as "hot fixing," is another fault tolerance feature of Windows NT Server 4.0. With normal disk formatting, if a disk sector is found to be bad, it will be marked so data is not written to the bad sector. However, if a sector goes bad after the disk is formatted, it's possible that data will be written to that bad sector.

Sector sparing allows all read/write operations to check for a bad sector. If a bad sector is found during the read/write operation, the following steps occur:

1. The data that exists on the bad sector is removed by Windows NT.
2. The data is transferred to a valid sector that does not have any errors.

3. The bad sector is "mapped out" so data is not sent to the bad sector again.
4. The data is read from the transferred sector if needed again. The Administrator is notified through the Event Viewer program of the sector sparing operation.

> **Note**
>
> Sector Sparing is only available on Windows NT Server 4.0 with Small Computer System Interface (SCSI) devices. Windows NT Server 4.0 computers with Integrated Device Electronics (IDE) or Enhanced Integrated Device Electronics (EIDE) devices can't perform Sector Sparing. Windows NT Workstation 4.0 computers also can't perform sector sparing. If you need sector sparing to protect data, you should use Windows NT Server with SCSI drives.

Creating and Managing Fault-Tolerant Volumes

Windows NT 4.0 provides a tool called Disk Administrator which allows you to implement fault-tolerant volumes (see fig. 17.8). Disk Administrator also handles other aspects of disk management not related to fault tolerance such as disk partitioning, disk formatting, and extending volumes. To use the Disk Administrator utility, you must be logged on to Windows NT with the Administrator account or an account with administrative privileges.

The Disk Administrator displays all the disks and partitions currently located on the Windows NT computer. A legend, above the status bar, provides information about the colors used to signify different disk configurations currently used on the computer. If a disk configuration is not used, it will not appear on the legend. Disks on the system can have various configurations such as:

- *Standard Partitions*. Single partitions on a single disk. Standard partitions can be FAT, HPFS, or NTFS drive formats. Dual boot Windows NT configurations require at least one standard FAT partition and MS-DOS won't recognize any other drive configuration.
- *Volume Sets*. Take multiple free disk areas and combine them into a single volume where the data is written to the areas in sequential order. For example, the first free area is filled before data is written to the second free area.

- *Stripe Sets*. Similar to volume sets, except data is distributed across all drives simultaneously determined by Windows NT. This allows for better performance over volume sets or standard partitions.
- *Stripe Sets with Parity*. Fault-tolerant stripe sets. In addition to the data being written to the disk, checksum information is also written to allow the rebuilding of data if a disk fails. These can only be created under Windows NT Server.
- *Mirror Sets*. Create exact duplicates of all data on each disk. What is written to one disk, is written to the other disk. These can only be created under Windows NT Server.

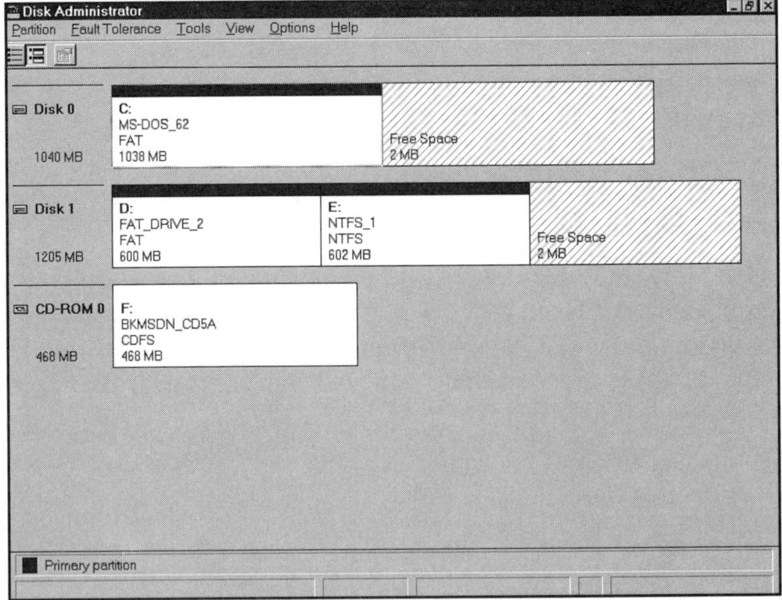

Fig. 17.8
The Disk Administrator utility shows all the available drives and partitions on a Windows NT Computer.

The fault-tolerance options in Disk Administrator are found in the Fault Tolerance menu on the menu bar. The Fault Tolerance item is only found in Windows NT Server 4.0, not Windows NT Workstation 4.0. However, standard partitions, volume sets, and stripe sets can be created and managed under Windows NT Workstation. Windows NT Workstation can also convert mirror sets and stripe sets with parity that were created by Windows NT server to drive types that Windows NT Workstation can use.

Implementing Mirrored Drives

Implementing a mirror set requires at least two drives on a Windows NT Server computer. When implementing mirrored drives, the second disk partition must be at least as large as the size of the first partition. However, the space should not be much larger than the first; otherwise, the space is wasted. Both the system and the boot partition can be mirrored with the Disk Administrator utility. The hard disks being mirrored can be of any type (SCSI, EIDE, or IDE) or any file type (FAT, HPFS, NTFS).

To create a mirror set, follow these steps:

1. Open the Start menu, and choose Administration Tools, Disk Administrator.
2. Select the first partition that you want to mirror.
3. Hold down the Ctrl (Control) key and click an area marked as free space that is at least the same size as the first partition.
4. Choose Fault Tolerance, Establish Mirror.
5. If you are mirroring a boot or system partition, a message appears informing you of the mirror. Choose OK to clear the message.
6. Choose Partition, Exit.
7. A message box asking you to confirm the current settings appears. Choose Yes to keep the mirror set you just created. If you do not want to keep the mirror set, choose No.
8. If you chose to keep the mirror set, a message box appears informing you that you must restart the computer for the changes to take effect. Choose Yes to restart the computer.
9. Another message box appears informing you that you should update the Emergency Repair Disk. Choose OK.
10. Finally, choose OK at the last message box to restart the computer. After the computer is restarted the mirror set is established, and you can check the Disk Administrator tool to verify the creation of the mirror set.

Implementing Duplexed Drives

To implement disk duplexing, simply connect each drive to a different drive controller and create a mirror set with the drives. No additional steps are required since creating the mirror set automatically uses the different disk controllers of each drive.

Implementing Disk Striping with Parity

Implementing disk striping with parity requires a minimum of three drives on a Windows NT Server computer. Each drive should have a minimum of 5M of unpartitioned free space available and each should be about the same size. If the partitions are not of equal size, the smallest partition of the set is used to determine the amount of space available for files in the set. System or boot partitions can't be part of a stripe set with parity when using the Disk Administrator tool. The hard disks can be of any type (SCSI, EIDE, or IDE) or any file type (FAT, HPFS, NTFS).

To implement disk striping with parity, follow these steps:

1. Open the Start menu, and choose Administration Tools, Disk Administrator.
2. Select the first area of free space that is at least 5M on a drive.
3. Hold down the Ctrl key and click an area marked as free space that is at least the same size as the first partition. Repeat this step with at least another area of free space.
4. Choose Fault Tolerance, Create Stripe Set With Parity.
5. A message window appears showing the size of the stripe set. The default size for the stripe set is three times the smallest area of free space selected. Choose the size of the stripe set space and click OK.
6. Choose Partition, Exit.
7. A message box asking you to confirm the current settings appears. Choose Yes to keep the stripe set with parity you just created. If you do not want to keep the stripe set with parity, choose No.
8. If you chose to keep the stripe set with parity, a message box appears informing you that you must restart the computer for the changes to take effect. Choose Yes to restart the computer.
9. Another message box appears informing you that you should update the Emergency Repair Disk. Click OK.
10. Finally, choose OK at the last message box to restart the computer. After the computer is restarted, the stripe set with parity must be formatted before it can be used. This can be done either in the Disk Administrator utility or from the command prompt.

Recovering Fault-Tolerant Volumes

It is important to know how to recover data after a fault-tolerant volume fails before a data failure occurs. This section covers how to handle the recovery process using fault-tolerant volumes.

Creating a Fault-Tolerant Boot Disk

A fault-tolerant boot disk is needed if a system or boot disk has been mirrored. Since DOS cannot recognize mirrored volumes, the disk must have Windows NT files that allow mirror sets to be recognized. This disk isn't required for disk striping with parity.

> **Caution**
>
> You can't create a system boot disk on a failed machine. Be sure to create a system boot disk *before* a systems failure occurs. If you have access to another Windows NT Server machine, you can also create a system boot disk. However, whenever you use a mirror set with a system or boot partition, make sure you create a system boot disk just to be safe.

To create a system boot disk, follow these steps:

1. From Windows NT Server, format a floppy disk. Be sure to use Windows NT Server to format the disk, not DOS. DOS will *not* correctly create a proper boot disk to load Windows NT.
2. Copy the following files from the primary partition of your Windows NT Server computer to the boot disk. For Intel x86 computers, copy: NTLDR, NTDETECT.COM, NTBOOTDD.SYS, and BOOT.INI. For RISC-based computers, copy: OSLOADER.EXE and HAL.DLL.

> **Note**
>
> The NTBOOTDD.SYS file for Intel x86 machines is only needed for SCSI computers when the SCSI BIOS is not used. If your computer does use the SCSI BIOS or you use an IDE drive, the NTBOOTDD.SYS file will not be located on your drive.

3. Remove the read-only and system file attributes of BOOT.INI to allow modification of that file. Modify the BOOT.INI file so that it points to the mirrored copy of the boot partition. This requires knowledge of ARC names to know how to point to the mirrored copy. After the file is modified, restore the read-only and system file attributes to BOOT.INI. For more information on modifying the BOOT.INI file, see Chapter 4, "Installing Windows NT."
4. Be sure to test the boot disk to ensure that it points to the right partition.

Recovering a System Mirror Set Using the System Boot Disk

To recover a mirror set that contains system or boot information, follow these steps:

1. Replace the bad system drive.
2. Boot the system with the System Boot Disk that you created. The boot disk loads Windows NT Server from the second mirrored drive.
3. Break the existing mirror. See "Recovering or Removing a Mirror Set" later in this chapter for information on breaking mirror sets.
4. Create a new mirror set to the free space on the replaced drive. See "Implementing Mirrored Drives" earlier in this chapter for more information on creating mirror sets.
5. Reboot the system without the System Boot Disk to ensure that the mirror set is working correctly. If it is not working correctly, the drive or cables are not connected properly. Verify that the drive connection is correct and repeat the procedure. If the drive connection is correct, then you will need to contact technical support from the drive manufacturer.

Understanding Advanced RISC Computing (ARC) Names

When creating a System Boot Disk, knowledge of Advanced RISC Computing (ARC) names is important when modifying the BOOT.INI file. ARC naming conventions are used for both Intel x86 and RISC-based computers to identify devices. An example of an ARC name is

```
scsi(0)disk(1)rdisk(0)partition(2)
```

The ARC name consists of several components: the type of disk controller, the ordinal number of the hardware adapter, the disk parameters, and the partition number.

The Disk Controller Type

The first part of the ARC name identifies the type of disk controller used. This setting can either be SCSI, for SCSI drives, or Multi for IDE or EIDE devices or SCSI drives accessed by the SCSI BIOS. For example, an IDE drive would have an ARC name similar to

```
multi(0)disk(0)rdisk(0)partition(1)
```

The Ordinal Number of the Hardware Adapter

The ordinal number of the hardware adapter refers to the physical controller in the computer. The number `0` is used to refer to the first disk, `1` for the second, and so on. So, if only one controller existed in the computer, the ordinal number would be `0`.

The Disk Parameters

The next two parameters are `disk()` and `rdisk()`. The `disk()` parameter refers to the hard drive of the controller you are using if you are using an SCSI drive. For an SCSI disk with the target ID of 0, the parameter would also be `0`. For IDE and EIDE drives, the `disk()` parameter is always `0`.

The `rdisk()` parameter refers to the ordinal number of the IDE or EIDE disk you are using. The number `0` represents the first IDE or EIDE disk on the controller. The `rdisk()` parameter is always `0` for SCSI drives.

The Partition Number

The `partition()` parameter refers to the partition number of a disk. Partition numbers start at 1. Primary partitions are assigned numbers first. Then, any drive letters in extended partitions are assigned numbers. So, `partition(1)` refers to the first primary partition on the specified disk.

So, an IDE drive with one controller and the Windows NT system files located on the second primary partition of the second drive would have an ARC name as follows:

```
multi(0)disk(0)rdisk(1)partition(2)
```

An SCSI drive with the same configuration would have the following ARC name:

```
scsi(0)disk(1)rdisk(0)partition(2)
```

Recovering or Removing a Mirror Set

When a member of a mirror set fails, you must first break the mirror set relationship. You may also just want to break the mirror set relationship if you decide that you no longer want the mirror set. To break the mirror set, follow these steps:

1. From the Disk Administrator utility, select the mirror set that you want to break.
2. Choose Fault Tolerance, Break Mirror.
3. A message appears notifying you of the changing of the mirror set into two separate disk partitions. You are asked to confirm the procedure. Choose Yes if you want to break up the mirror set. Choose No if you don't want to break the mirror set.
4. Choose Partition, Commit Changes Now.

5. A confirm message box appears; choose Yes to commit the changes you just made.
6. Another message appears to inform you that you should update the Emergency Repair Disk. Choose OK.
7. Choose Partition, Exit to close the Disk Administrator. The mirror set is now broken into two separate partitions. The second partition that was created with the breaking of the mirror set now has a new drive letter assigned to it.

After the mirror set is broken, you should assign, if it isn't assigned already, the working partition the drive letter that was previously assigned to the mirror set. The failed partition should be assigned another drive letter. Then, you can use free space on another drive or replace the failed drive and use the free space on the new drive to create a new mirror set.

Recovering a Stripe Set with Parity

A stripe set with parity contains parity information that can be used to rebuild a failed partition. If a member of the stripe set with parity fails, you can rebuild all the information that was contained on that member. To rebuild a failed member of a stripe set with parity, do the following:

1. From the Disk Administrator, select the stripe set with parity.
2. Select either a new area of free space on a different drive or a new drive. Make sure the new area of free space is at least as large as the other members of the stripe set with parity.
3. Choose Fault Tolerance, Regenerate.
4. Exit Disk Administrator and restart the Windows NT Server computer. When the computer restarts, the missing member is rebuilt.

Ensuring Server Redundancy

Many networks utilize Windows NT as the primary network operating system for user authentication, file and printer access, and database access. Since Windows NT servers are so vital to these networks, the ability for the network to stay operational even with a server failure or power outage is very important.

Uninterruptable Power Supply (UPS)

An uninterruptable power supply or UPS is a very important component for Windows NT computers. A UPS is an emergency power source that can deliver power to a computer if the main electrical power fails. UPS systems provide power during a temporary loss of power, known as a "black out" or a reduction in voltage to levels below normal operating range, known as a "brown out." Many UPS systems also act as surge suppressers to prevent damage to the computer system if the voltage levels temporarily exceed the normal levels, known as a "surge."

There are two types of UPS devices, online UPS systems and standby UPS systems. An *online UPS* supplies constant power through a battery. A *standby UPS*, also known as a standby power supply or SPS, supplies power only if the main power fails. For the purposes of this discussion, UPS represents both online and standby UPS systems.

Many UPS systems can also communicate their status, usually via a serial port, to a Windows NT 4.0 computer. UPS systems that can shut down a Windows NT computer properly when the power fails are known as smart UPS systems. Since data can be lost or corrupted if Windows NT is not shut down properly, a smart UPS helps to ensure that if power is lost, a Windows NT computer can be shut down properly. This feature is critical if Windows NT Servers are going to be powered constantly or used unattended.

UPS Service Configuration

The Windows NT UPS Service can be configured through the Control Panel folder. In the UPS item in Control Panel, you can configure which port the UPS uses, set the time delay for various settings, and specify a command file to execute when power fails. Configuring the UPS service is covered in Chapter 29, "Customizing Hardware and System Settings."

Power Failures and the UPS Service

If the power is lost while a Windows NT computer is connected to a UPS, the following occurs:

- Initial power failure. The Server service is paused. A Power Out event is logged in the Event Viewer and a Power Out alert is sent to the administrator.
- Power restored before Time Between Power Failure and Initial Message setting. The Server service is restarted. A Power Back event is logged into the Event Viewer and a Power Back alert is sent to the administrator.
- Time Between Power Failure and Initial Message setting expires without power restored. A Power Out message is sent to users based on the Delay Between Warning Messages setting.
- Power restored is restored before the automatic shutdown procedure. A Power Back message is sent to the users connected to the server and the Administrator. A Power Back event is also logged to the Event Viewer.

- Low battery signal or battery time equals zero. The Server service is stopped and a Power Shutdown message is sent to the users, administrator, and the error log. Windows NT saves data and shuts down.

> **Tip**
>
> UPS systems are *strongly* recommended for all Windows NT systems, from networked business systems to personal systems. UPS systems also provide power protection against electrical surges and eliminate the need for a separate surge protector.

Using Primary Domain Controllers and Backup Domain Controllers for Server Redundancy

When using Windows NT Server 4.0 domains on a network, it is recommended that the network have both a Primary Domain Controller (PDC) and at least one Backup Domain Controller. This way, if the Primary Domain Controller fails, the Backup Domain Controller can authenticate user logins and requests for resources. However, data and files may not be available if they exist only on the Primary Domain Controller. Copying data to a BDC will allow users to access the files, but users may have to re-map drive locations to the new BDC.

Mirroring Servers

Windows NT does not directly support mirroring of servers. However, third-party programs can be used to mirror Windows NT servers. Mirroring servers allows for data to be automatically copied to different servers, similar to the way mirrored drives work. This allows for a server to fail or be taken offline and still allow the data to be accessed by users.

One such third-party utility is Octopus by Octopus Technologies, Inc. This utility allows real-time mirroring of data from one server to another. Octopus also has an option to allow a mirrored server to automatically assume the role of a failed server on the network. The need for mirrored servers depends on the fault-tolerance requirements of an organization's network. ❖

CHAPTER 18

Optimizing Hardware: Processors, Video, and I/O Systems

by Richard Neff

Unlike other operating systems, Windows NT is designed to be a self-optimizing operating system. This means that Windows NT tries to adjust how it operates to accommodate a particular system for optimal performance. Other operating systems were designed with the idea that the user should handle the details of system configuration for optimal performance. However, many users did not have the time or the willingness needed to tweak operating systems and create the optimal system. Also, as hardware was added or removed from the system, the operating system configuration would have to be adjusted for the new configuration.

This does not mean that users can't improve the performance of Windows NT. Modifying certain hardware and software components may provide performance improvements under Windows NT. The most dramatic improvements come from upgrading hardware components that create bottlenecks for Windows NT. There are also certain steps to the Windows NT configuration that enhance system performance.

In this chapter, you learn to

- Recognize the different factors that affect processor performance and video performance
- Optimize processor performance
- Optimize video performance
- Recognize the different factors that affect input/output (I/O) performance
- Optimize I/O performance

Understanding Processor Performance

Windows NT runs on a variety of processor types such as: Intel, DEC Alpha, MIPS, and PowerPC processors. This prevents Windows NT users from being locked into a vendor-specific solution. Windows NT also allows the use of multiple processors, further increasing the performance of a Windows NT computer. To maximize the processor performance of Windows NT, you should understand the advantages and disadvantages of each processor type.

Intel Processors

Intel Processors (486, Pentium, and Pentium Pro) are currently the most popular processors to run Windows NT. Due to the ability to run DOS and earlier versions of Windows, the Intel series has become the most popular type of personal computer in most business and home environments. The price of Intel-based computers also makes them a more practical computer for most companies and individuals.

Currently, the Pentium Pro is Intel's fastest processor designed for Windows NT. The Pentium Pro is best for the server role or high-end workstation role in a network with Windows NT Server. However, the Pentium is the most cost-effective while providing extremely fast performance. The 486 processor is being phased out of production, but is a very practical processor for Windows NT Workstation computers.

Mhz Speed

The speed of processors is measured in megahertz (Mhz). The Mhz rating can be used to compare the speed of a processor in the same family. For example, a 100 Mhz Pentium processor is faster than a 75 Mhz processor. However, a 100 Mhz 486 processor is not comparable to a 100 Mhz Pentium processor because the processors are different types. Different types of processors may have features or enhancements that improve overall speed. A higher megahertz number indicates a faster processor of the same type.

Cache Memory

While regular RAM memory is practical for most memory operations, it is dynamic RAM (DRAM) that needs regular refreshing in order to hold the current data. A special type of RAM, known as static RAM (SRAM), is able to hold data without refreshing. Static RAM also provides much faster access times than dynamic RAM; however, the price of static RAM is much more expensive than dynamic RAM. While the price prevents static RAM from completely replacing RAM memory on personal computers, small amounts of static RAM are used as cache memory.

Cache memory holds information that has been passed from the regular DRAM memory to the CPU. Later, if the CPU needs the information again, it comes from the faster cache memory. Cache memory often increases the overall performance of a computer, and most personal computers currently made, including Intel-based computers, which have some sort of cache memory.

Internal Cache. An internal cache is the amount of cache memory physically built into the processor. One of the performance advantages of Intel 486, Pentium, and Pentium Pro processors, as well as many RISC (Reduced Instruction Set Computing) processors, is that the cache memory is internally built into the processor. This allows for very fast cache access and increases the overall processor performance in many instances.

External Cache. Because the internal cache memory of processors is usually very small, many motherboards have an external memory cache. An external memory cache also allows the user to increase the amount of cache memory for a computer. Increasing the amount of an external memory cache can improve overall system performance under Windows NT.

RISC Processors

RISC (Reduced Instruction Set Computing) processors usually provide faster performance than Intel processors that are CISC (Complex Instruction Set Computing) processors. However, RISC computers are usually more expensive than Intel processors and are usually used as servers or high-end workstations. Also, the availability of computers and peripherals may not be as common as the Intel-based computers and components.

> **Note**
>
> RISC-based computers are usually very fast when running 32-bit Windows NT code. However, RISC-based computers do not fare as well when running 16-bit legacy code designed for older Windows environments running on Intel machines. If you are running a lot of 16-bit applications, Intel machines usually perform much better than RISC-based machines.

DEC Alpha

Digital Equipment Corporation's (DEC) Alpha AXP processors are usually the fastest processors that can run Windows NT. These processors are well-suited for Windows NT Servers on a network. The disadvantage of the Alpha AXP processor is that it currently locks the user to a single-vendor solution with

Digital.

MIPS

The MIPS processor is made by MIPS Computer Systems, but can be found in many computers made by other manufacturers. The MIPS R4000 processors are equivalent in most regards to the DEC Alpha AXP processors. It offers very good processor performance and is designed for server or high-end workstation use. MIPS processors can be found in computers from different manufacturers, which prevents the user from being locked into a single-vendor solution.

PowerPC

The PowerPC processor is a joint effort by IBM, Apple, and Motorola to compete directly with Intel's family of processors. Windows NT 3.51 was the first version of Windows NT that could run on PowerPC computers. The PowerPC offers better performance than most Intel processors and can be a very good Windows NT Workstation or Server.

Effects of Memory on System Performance

Although it may first appear that the processor has the greatest impact on system performance, memory plays a very important role in this area. The processor performance also depends on how much physical memory is available and how virtual memory is handled. Virtual memory also affects disk performance on a computer. A lot of virtual memory activity reduces the amount of regular data that can be sent to or from the disk drives.

Improving Processor Performance

Processor performance is the starting point to overall system performance. The processing horsepower of a computer determines how well a processor-intensive operating system such as Windows NT will run. Here are some things you can directly do to the processor to improve the performance of Windows NT:

- If you are using 8-bit network, disk, or video cards, replace them with 16- or 32-bit cards. 8-bit cards use more processor time under Windows NT.
- Some processor types, such as 486 or Pentium processors, can be replaced with clock-doubler and clock-tripler replacement processors. This

method is usually cheaper and easier than complete motherboard replacement.

- Increase the size of your external memory cache. This is discussed in more detail in the following section "Adding External Cache Memory."
- Also discussed in the following section, increase the size of your physical memory. Windows NT likes a lot of memory to work with.
- Configure Windows NT's virtual memory to use multiple drives. This is discussed in the section "Using Virtual Memory on Multiple Drives."
- You may benefit if you are using multithreaded applications by adding additional processors. This topic is discussed in the section "Multiple Processors."

Adding External Cache Memory

As mentioned before, increasing the amount of external cache memory can often increase performance of a Windows NT computer. You should check with your computer manufacturer or documentation for the type of cache memory needed and the amount of cache memory that can be installed.

Tip

Keep in mind that, in some instances, you'll need to increase the external cache memory if you add regular DRAM memory to improve performance. This is due to degraded performance of external cache memory because of lower hit rates for the external cache. This is caused by more data being transferred to and from the memory and processor.

Adding Regular DRAM Memory

Adding more DRAM memory into a personal computer is a relatively simple and straightforward process. Most computer memory chips are arranged on a board with multiple chips known as a Single Inline Memory Module (SIMM). The purpose of the SIMM is to make it easier to install RAM memory by inserting a SIMM board into a slot, rather than individually trying to install the chips into the circuit board. SIMM modules simply slide into place and are held in place by clips.

However, before purchasing and installing SIMM boards into your computer, be sure to verify the type of SIMM modules that the computer accepts. SIMM modules can have a variety of storage capacities on a board as well as different numbers of pin connections. The computer's documentation or manufacturer should be able to provide the correct information regarding SIMM modules.

Caution

Computer chips, such as processor or memory chips, are very sensitive items. Common static electricity can do significant damage to these sensitive pieces. Be sure you are grounded and static-free before adding memory or processors into your computer.

Using Virtual Memory on Multiple Drives

If your system has multiple hard disks, creating a virtual memory pagefile for each disk may offer performance improvements. This will offer a performance gain if your disk controller allows simultaneous reading and writing to multiple disks.

Also, you may want to move the virtual memory pagefile completely off of the drive that contains the Windows NT systems files. This avoids disk attempts for both system file reads and writes and pagefile reads and writes. However, you may not want to do this to help facilitate recovery features of Windows NT.

To change the virtual memory pagefile settings, choose the Start button, Settings, Control Panel, and the System option. Then click the Performance tab and select the Change button in the Virtual Memory box. You need Administrator privileges for the Windows NT machine you want to modify. You can add multiple pagefiles, remove pagefiles, or modify the size of pagefiles. Virtual memory pagefiles must be 2M or larger. Figure 18.1 shows the Virtual Memory settings window.

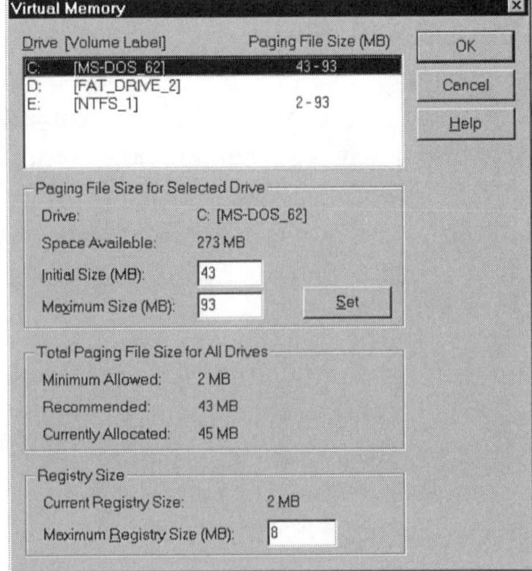

Fig. 18.1
Virtual memory pagefiles can be created for each disk.

Multiple Processors

One of the advantages of Windows NT over other operating systems is the support for multiple processors, known as multiprocessing. There are two types of multiprocessing: asymmetric and symmetric. Asymmetric multiprocessing assigns specific operations to a processor. Symmetric multiprocessing uses any available processor as needed, which helps balance the computer's workload. Windows NT uses symmetric multiprocessing when operating with multiple processors.

Multiple processors provide improved performance with applications that are designed with multiprocessing in mind. Most major applications designed for Windows NT will have performance improvements on a computer with multiple processors. However, a lot of older 16-bit applications or other applications that do not support multiprocessing may not have any noticeable performance improvements. If the Windows NT computer will run a lot of these applications, you may want to consider upgrading the processor or motherboard instead of adding another processor.

The procedure for adding an additional processor on a Windows NT system depends on the number of processors originally installed on the system. If the computer had two or more processors already installed, the new addition will automatically be detected and used by Windows NT the next time the system starts.

However, if the system only contained a single processor and a second one is added, then some adjustments have to be made. Windows NT has two versions of the Kernel, a uniprocessor version and a multiprocessor version. When a second processor is added, the uniprocessor version of the Windows NT Kernel has to be replaced with the muliprocessor version. Microsoft recommends using the Uni- to Multi-Processor program (UPTOMP.EXE), found in the Windows NT Resource Kit, to update the Windows NT Kernel. Otherwise, you will need to reinstall Windows NT before it will recognize and use the second processor.

Measuring Processor Performance with Performance Monitor

Of course, with so many different components affecting system performance, how do you know what area needs improvement? Windows NT provides a very useful utility, the Performance Monitor, to help diagnose performance bottlenecks. You can access the Performance Monitor by clicking the Start button, then selecting Programs, then Administration Tools, and finally the Performance Monitor item on the menu. The Performance Monitor program is displayed in figure 18.2.

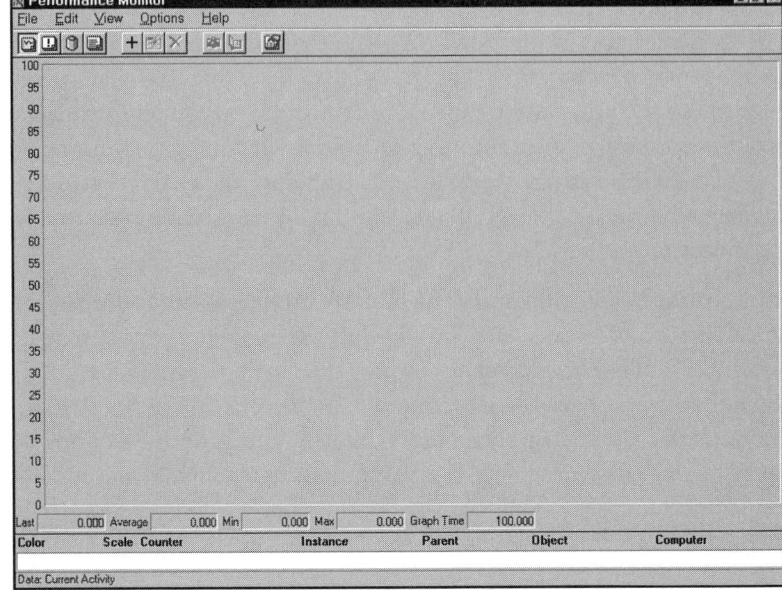

Fig. 18.2
The Performance Monitor program allows you to graphically display performance statistics for different Windows NT items.

The Performance Monitor can visually graph data or send it to a log file. The Performance Monitor program can track a variety of computer functions, such as: processor performance, disk performance, memory performance, process performance, and many more. To add an item to a Performance Monitor chart to track processor performance, do the following:

1. Choose Edit, Add To Chart. You can also choose the Add Counter toolbar button.
2. The Add To Chart window appears. From this window, you can choose the Object and the Counter to be added to the chart. For example, to chart % of processor time, Choose Processor in the Object list and % Processor Time in the Counter list.
3. You can also choose the color and line time representing the selected item to chart. If the Explain button is clicked, a Counter Definition box gives a brief overview of what that item represents.
4. After you have selected the item to chart and its display characteristics, choose the Add button on the left side of the window. The item will then be charted in the Performance Monitor.

There are some key objects you should check when monitoring processor performance: Processor:% Processor Time, Processor: Interrupts/sec, and System:Processor Queue Length. The Processor:% Processor Time is the most significant item to chart. This object shows how much of the time the processor is actually being used. The Processor: Interrupts/sec item shows how many interrupts from hardware devices are being serviced by the processor. The System:Processor Queue Length shows how many threads are currently in the processor queue waiting to be processed.

If the Processor:% Processor Time reached 80% or greater on a regular basis, it indicates the processor is constantly being utilized. If this is the case, either a second processor or a more powerful processor may be needed.

Also, if a dramatic increase occurs in the Processor Interrupts/sec counter when there is not a significant amount of system activity, this could signal I/O devices utilizing an excessive amount of processor time. If the System:Processor Queue Length consistently reaches values above 2, then this could also indicate a processor bottleneck.

Understanding Video Performance

Since Windows NT uses a graphical user interface, video performance is a very important component of system performance. If video performance is slow, the user may believe that the entire system is slow. Also, many high-end graphics programs require a lot of video horsepower for best results.

Bus Types

A *bus*, when discussing personal computer hardware, describes the path for communication between the CPU and any peripheral hardware. Personal computers have many different bus type standards. Video performance is dramatically affected by the different bus types. Choosing the right bus type can mean the difference between sluggish or fast video performance.

ISA

The ISA (Industry Standard Architecture) bus was used in the original IBM PC. It provides for 8- and 16-bit access to attached hardware. It's the most common bus used for most cards. However, it's the slowest bus available and isn't recommended for video cards. Video performance under Windows NT will be noticeably sluggish if used in any resolution other than 16-color VGA.

EISA

The EISA (Extended Industry Standard Architecture) bus was created to increase the performance of the ISA bus, but still retain backward-compatibility with existing ISA cards. It offers 32-bit access to EISA cards and allows 8- and 16-bit access with ISA cards. EISA is comparable to IBM's MicroChannel Architecture in performance. It offers better video performance than ISA, although EISA video cards are becoming hard to find because they are being replaced by VL bus and PCI cards.

MicroChannel Architecture

The MicroChannel Architecture bus was developed by IBM for the PS/2 series of computers. The MicroChannel Architecture bus provides for 32-bit access to hardware, but is not backward compatible with ISA cards. This means that new MicroChannel Architecture hardware has to be purchased to replace ISA hardware. MicroChannel Architecture provides reasonably fast video performance, but as with EISA video cards, MicroChannel Architecture video cards are hard to find as VL Bus and PCI bus become more popular.

VESA VL Bus

An association of video adapter manufacturers known as VESA (Video Electronics Standards Association) created a direct bus standard known as VL bus (VESA Local bus). The advantage of a direct or local bus is that it allows direct communication with the hardware rather than communication through the bus controller. The VL bus allows 64-bit communication to attached VL bus hardware. It's most commonly found on Intel 486 machines and provides very good video performance on 486 machines.

PCI

Another direct bus standard created by Intel is the PCI (Peripheral Component Interconnect) bus. The PCI bus allows 64-bit communications just like the VL bus. It also has many other speed-enhancing features to allow faster data communication between the processor and the PCI hardware. The PCI bus is most commonly found on Intel Pentium or better processors. The video performance on PCI hardware is very good and is well suited for Windows NT.

Video Memory

Many video cards sold today are actually graphic accelerator cards that have dedicated graphics processors and video memory built into the board. By dedicating a processor to handle graphics, overall performance is increased.

However, in order for the dedicated video processor to operate effectively, video memory, often known as VRAM, is needed.

Video memory requirements depend on the resolution displayed, the number of colors displayed simultaneously, and the number of objects displayed. Without enough video memory, higher resolutions with large color ranges can't be displayed or displayed at an acceptable speed. Minimum video memory requirements usually start at 512K, but many video cards supply 2M-4M built-in.

Improving Video Performance

The best way to ensure good video performance is to plan ahead when purchasing hardware. Since bus types can't be changed without replacing the entire motherboard, be sure to purchase a computer or motherboard that uses either the VESA VL bus if you want a 486 machine or a PCI bus if you are using a Pentium or other machine.

Of course, you may be installing Windows NT on a computer that you've already purchased. If that is the case, there are some things you can try to do to improve the video performance of the Windows NT machine.

Adding Video Memory

If video performance is sluggish, increasing the video memory can sometimes improve the situation. If you do a lot of graphics work or use higher resolutions and color depths, increasing the video memory can help achieve the best video performance. Be sure to check with the manufacturer to determine the type of memory needed and how much memory space is available on the video card. If you can't add any more video memory to your card, you may need to consider buying a faster or more expandable video card.

Using Current Video Drivers

The bus type and video memory are not the only factors to video performance. The Windows NT software driver written for a specific video card is also very important. Some drivers may have bugs that reduce the performance of the hardware under Windows NT. Make sure you use the newest driver from the manufacturer of the video card. The driver is usually available directly from the manufacturer, on a manufacturer's BBS or Internet site, or on an online service such as CompuServe, Prodigy, or America Online.

On the Web

You can get updates to video drivers at Microsoft's Web site at:

http://www.microsoft.com

You can also get updates to manufacturer-specific video drivers from the following Web sites:

http://www.atitech.ca ATI Technologies, Inc.

http://www.diamond.mm.com Diamond Multimedia Systems, Inc.

http://www.elsa.com ELSA, Inc.

http://www.hercules.com Hercules Computer Technology

http://matrox.com Matrox Graphics, Inc.

http://www.nine.com Number Nine Visual Technology

Overview of I/O Performance

Input/Output (I/O) performance deals with the performance of disk drives, disk controllers, parallel, and serial ports. In many instances the disk controller and port controller are located on the same expansion card or motherboard. The following sections deal with all of these devices even though they are independent of each other.

Bus Types and I/O Performance

As with video performance, the bus type used on a computer affects the I/O performance of a computer. I/O cards that use direct bus cards, either VL bus or PCI bus, are noticeably faster than regular ISA boards. Some computer manufacturers integrate the I/O board onto the main motherboard. These configurations may also yield faster performance than regular ISA I/O boards.

Disk System Performance

Disk systems consist of two parts: the disk drive itself and the disk controller. The disk drive I/O performance is composed of two parts: the access time and the transfer rate. The access time is measured in milliseconds (ms). A lower access time in milliseconds means faster accessing of data on the disk drive. So, a 10ms drive accesses data faster than a 15ms drive. The transfer rate is given in Megabytes (M) per second. Typically, modern hard drives have an external transfer rate between 10M/sec and 20M/sec.

Disk controllers are often integrated with other I/O devices on a single adapter card. The bus type of the adapter card is very important to disk performance, the same as video performance is linked to the bus type of the video adapter. Direct bus adapters provide better performance over other types of adapters. The original ISA adapter is the slowest bus type of all.

Memory may also affect disk performance under Windows NT. The virtual memory pagefile uses disk resources on a regular basis that may, at times, slow down regular disk access. Therefore, disk bottlenecks may not be due to a poor performing drive or controller.

Also, disk accesses are cached under Windows NT and the second time data is read from a disk, it may load faster than the original access of the data. The initial loading of programs usually takes the longest amount of disk time, hence the large initial use of disk resources when Windows NT starts.

Disk file systems can also become fragmented with heavy use. This slows disk performance because the disk heads must jump to multiple areas of the disk trying to read or write data belonging to a single file. This can be improved by third-party defragmenters, such as Diskeeper from Executive Software, that reorganize the file structure on the disk to improve file-access performance.

On the Web

To obtain more information about defragmenting drives under Windows NT, you can view Executive Software's Web site at:

http://www.execsoft.com

Bidirectional Parallel Ports

Bidirectional parallel ports not only provide a performance increase, but allow communication between the computer and printer. Not all computers have bidirectional parallel ports. Bidirectional ports are also known as extended capabilities ports (ECP) or enhanced parallel ports (EPP).

Windows NT supports bidirectional parallel ports. However, to modify bidirectional support, a printer and driver must be installed under Windows NT. To enable or disable bidirectional support for an installed printer, display the Properties window for the printer. Select the Ports table to display the Ports property sheet. Then, the port can be modified from the Ports tab and bidirectional support can be modified by the Enable Bidirectional Support checkbox.

High-Speed Serial Ports

The Universal Asynchronous Receiver/Transmitter (UART) controls the processing of serial communication ports on a personal computer. The original IBM PC used the 8250 UART chip. However, as the need for faster serial transmissions increased, the 8250 UART became too slow. In the IBM AT series of computers, a faster 16540 UART is used and the 16550A UART is found in most 486 and Pentium class computers today.

The 16550A UART provides much better reliability of high-speed transmissions than its predecessors. Windows 3.x did not take advantage of the buffering techniques of the 16550A UART. Windows NT, however, can take advantage of the 16550A UART performance increases.

Optimizing I/O Performance

As mentioned before, I/O performance depends on a variety of items. However, there are things you can do to improve I/O performance using Windows NT. Some things to consider are:

- If you've discovered a disk bottleneck, determine whether the disk system is really at fault or whether you really need more physical memory. If you have a disk bottleneck because the virtual memory pagefile is preventing other important disk data from being transferred quickly, more physical memory may be the answer.
- If a hard disk or partition is under 400M in size, you probably should not use NTFS as the file system on that drive. NTFS is designed to work on partitions greater than 400M. Conversely, if a disk or partition is over 200M in size, don't use the FAT file system. The FAT file system slows down on partitions greater than 200M.
- If disk performance is still a major problem, consider using a stripe set if you have multiple drives. Stripe sets increase I/O performance even though they provide no fault tolerance. When using any disk systems that are not fault-tolerant, make sure you make backups on a regular basis. Stripe Sets are discussed in the section, "Creating Stripe Sets," later in this chapter.

Performance Monitor and Disk Performance

In order to use Performance Monitor to measure disk performance, you need to run the following utility before using the Performance Monitor Utility: diskperf -y.

You also need to shutdown and restart the computer for the diskperf utility to take effect. You also need to have administrator access to use this utility.

There are two objects, LogicalDisk and PhysicalDisk, that contain items used to monitor disk performance. The LogicalDisk object contains performance measurements for logical drive letters or partitions on a disk. The PhysicalDisk object measures the performance of a physical disk on the system.

Some items to watch when determining disk bottlenecks are: PhysicalDisk:% Disk Time, PhysicalDisk:Disk Queue Length, PhysicalDisk:Avg. Disk sec/Transfer, and Avg. Disk Bytes/Transfer. If the PhysicalDisk:% Disk Time is high, check the PhysicalDisk:Queue Length item. If the PhysicalDisk:Queue Length item is two times the number of spindles on the physical disk, then the disk is being accessed more than it can handle.

If the PhysicalDisk:Avg. Disk sec/Transfer value is high, usually greater than .3 seconds, the system may be retrying the disk because of failures. If the Avg. Disk Bytes/Transfer drops below 20K on a regular basis, then applications may be accessing the disk inefficiently.

Creating Stripe Sets

Creating a stripe set allows data to be simultaneously read from or written to multiple disk drives. This process can improve disk I/O performance in most instances. Stripe sets are the most useful if the drive controller for the disks can handle simultaneous I/O processes. Usually, SCSI drives are better used for stripe sets than IDE or EIDE drives. Keep in mind that system and boot partitions cannot be part of a stripe set. Do *not* use stripe sets as a way to increase fault-tolerance! Stripe sets are used to increase disk performance and are not used as a security feature.

Note

For more information on creating stripe sets and the Disk Administrator utility, see Chapter 16, "Optimizing the File System."

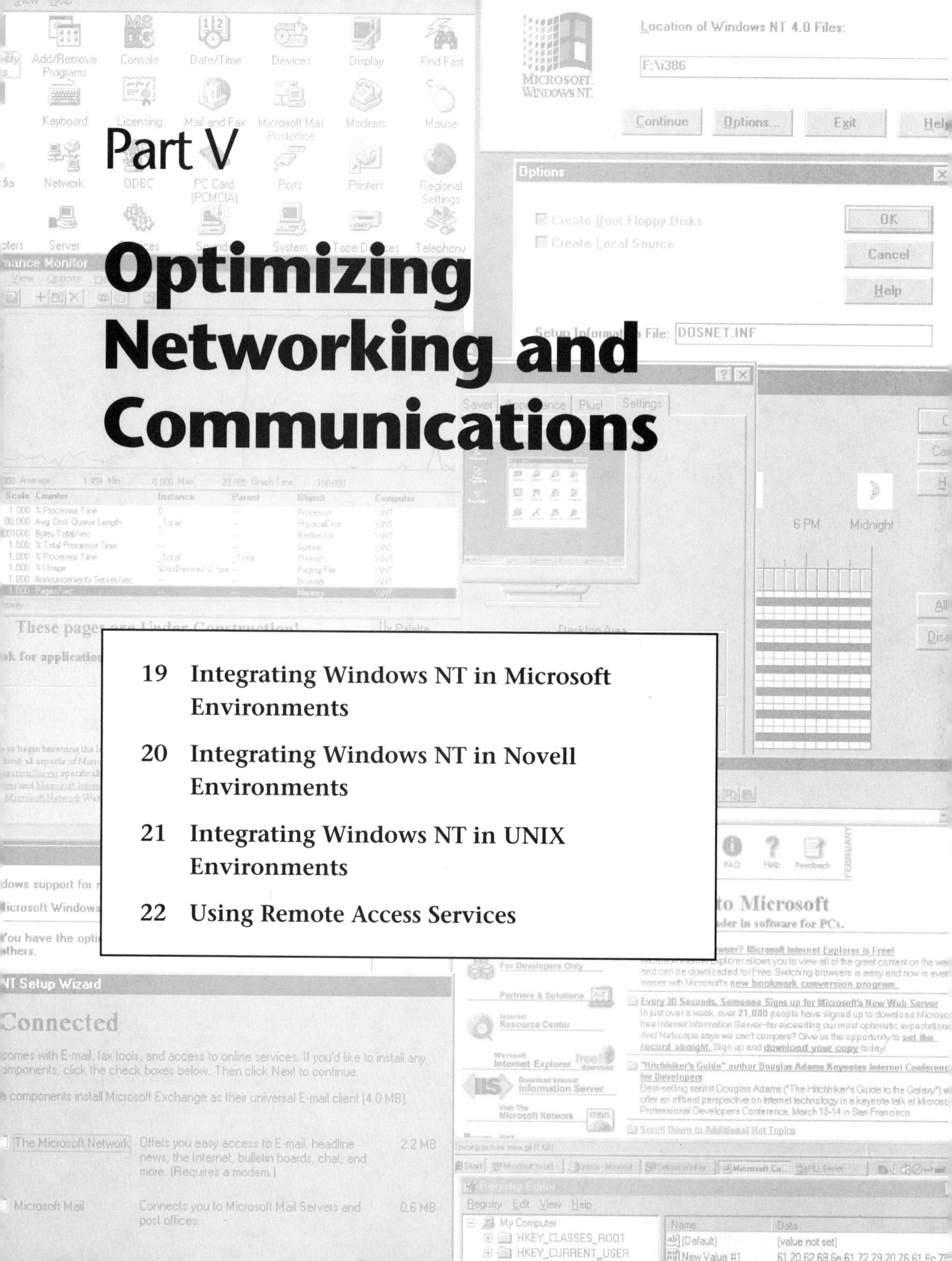

Part V

Optimizing Networking and Communications

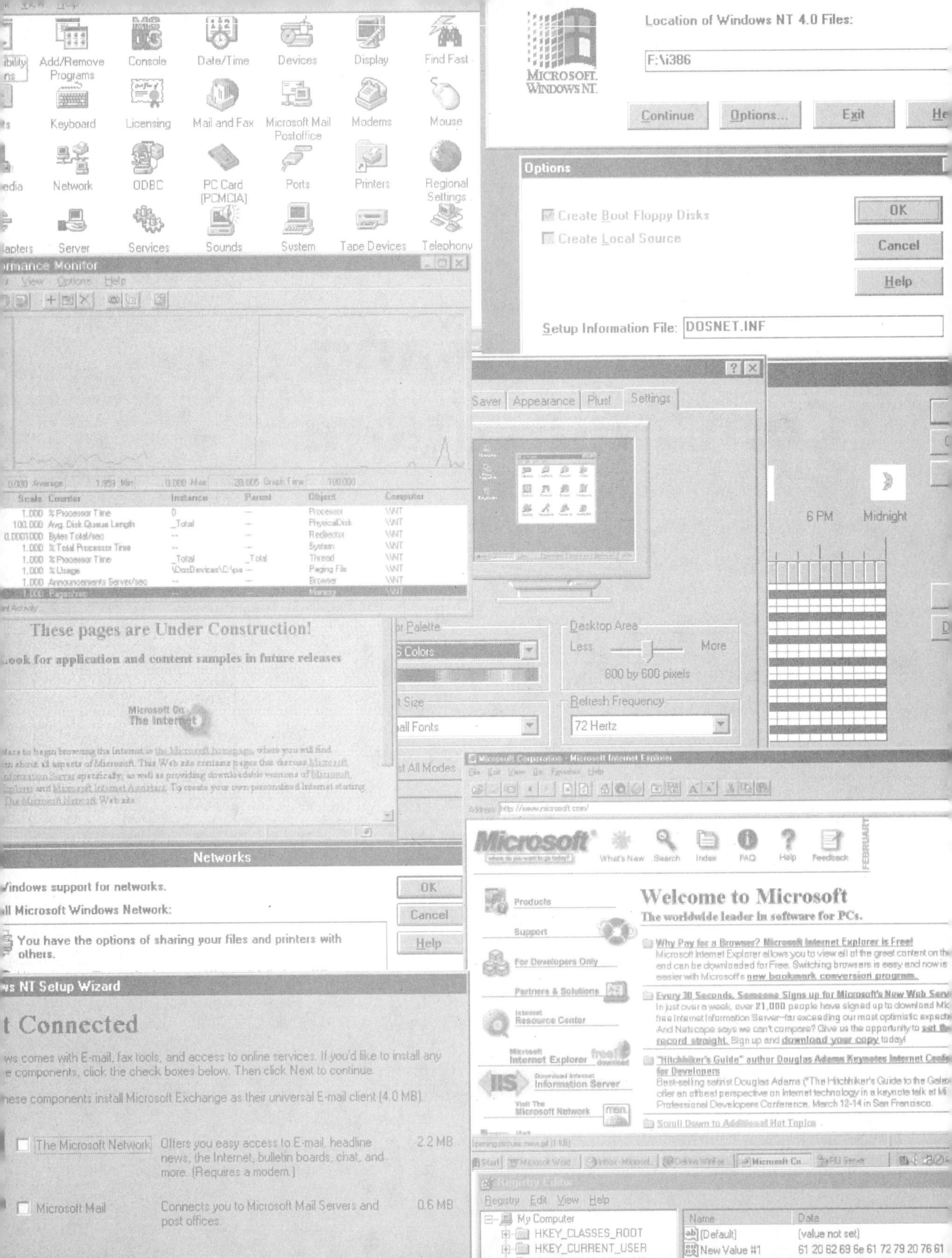
Add/Remove Programs
Console
Date/Time
Devices
Display
Find Fast
Keyboard
Licensing
Mail and Fax
Microsoft Mail Postoffice
Modems
Mouse
Network
ODBC
PC Card (PCMCIA)
Ports
Printers
Regional Settings
Server
Services
Sounds
System
Tape Devices
Telephony
Location of Windows NT 4.0 Files:
F:\i386
MICROSOFT. WINDOWS NT.
Continue
Options...
Exit
Options
Create Boot Floppy Disks
Create Local Source
OK
Cancel
Help
Setup Information File: DOSNET.INF
Saver
Appearance
Plus!
Settings
6 PM
Midnight
Desktop Area
Less
More
800 by 600 pixels
Refresh Frequency
72 Hertz
These pages are Under Construction!
Look for application and content samples in future releases
Microsoft On The Internet
Networks
Windows support for networks.
Microsoft Windows Network:
You have the options of sharing your files and printers with others.
OK
Cancel
Help
NT Setup Wizard
Connected
comes with E-mail, fax tools, and access to online services. If you'd like to install any components, click the check boxes below. Then click Next to continue.
These components install Microsoft Exchange as their universal E-mail client (4.0 MB).
The Microsoft Network
Offers you easy access to E-mail, headline news, the Internet, bulletin boards, chat, and more. (Requires a modem.)
2.2 MB
Microsoft Mail
Connects you to Microsoft Mail Servers and post offices.
0.6 MB
Microsoft
What's New
Search
Index
FAQ
Help
Feedback
Products
Support
For Developers Only
Partners & Solutions
Internet Resource Center
Microsoft Internet Explorer
Information Server
Visit The Microsoft Network
Welcome to Microsoft
The worldwide leader in software for PCs.
Why Pay for a Browser? Microsoft Internet Explorer is Free!
Registry Editor
Registry
Edit
View
Help
My Computer
HKEY_CLASSES_ROOT
HKEY_CURRENT_USER
Name
Data
(Default)
(value not set)
New Value #1
61 20 62 69 6e 61 72 79 20 76 61

CHAPTER 19

Integrating Windows NT in Microsoft Environments

by Dan Balter

The Windows NT network operating system (NOS), and Windows NT Server in particular, provide an extremely robust and fault-tolerant platform upon which you can base your crucial business operations. You might already be familiar with many of the benefits of Microsoft networking: peer-to-peer connectivity; strong integration between Windows for Workgroups, Windows 95, and Windows NT computers; multi-protocol networking support; relative ease of use and administration; and more.

Many smaller offices have implemented a peer-to-peer computer network using one or a combination of all three of the Windows products just mentioned. There are definite advantages for offices that connect all their computers together rather than leaving them as standalone machines. Instituting a proper electronic information sharing strategy can rocket a business to a new level of effectiveness and efficiency.

In this chapter, you learn to

- Employ a dedicated server
- Integrate DOS systems
- Integrate with Windows 3.x and Windows 95 systems

Employing a Dedicated Server

A *dedicated* server computer can act as a central repository where a company's important documents and other data can be stored and retrieved with ease. Without some sort of central organization, a peer-to-peer network that does not sport a dedicated server can become an endless maze of miscellaneous directories and files. If you've ever tried to locate a specific file on a network that does not have a dedicated server, you know how difficult it can be.

Security becomes a major problem without a dedicated server. Administration can be a nightmare because each user can keep different files on his/her own PC. As the number of workstations increase, the job of keeping track of all of the critical business data files (as well as application programs) becomes truly monumental. Furthermore, asking each user on a peer-to-peer network to perform regular and frequent backups is the cyberspace equivalent of trying to part the Red Sea; it's just not going to happen.

A dedicated server computer is a system administrator's security blanket. You control administration and backups. You're in charge of access permissions and directory and file organization. A dedicated server computer lets your users know that their important documents can be found, worked on, and saved in the same secure place.

"Dual Purpose" versus Dedicated Server

Don't get caught in the dual-purpose trap! File server computers are meant to focus on file and print services for their network users. Workstation computers should be focused on getting users' work done. These two important tasks ought not to be combined on one computer.

Applications used on the server can sometimes lock up a computer, even in Windows NT. The more access users have to any computer—a workstation or a server—the greater possibility for user error, accidents, or other mishaps. Even if nothing catastrophic occurs, allowing users to work on a server computer as just another client on the network means that memory resources on that machine will always be more taxed. As with any computer, the more open applications you have, the more memory is consumed by those programs. This leaves less RAM for the network operating system itself. It doesn't take long for a few RAM-hungry applications to bring a standalone computer to a crawl, let alone a network server that is trying to simultaneously service multiple file I/O and printing requests from its users.

All of these potential problems are compelling reasons to leave a server computer as just that: a computer that is dedicated to serving the needs of its users on a network.

Configuring NT Server Tasking Priorities

You can configure Windows NT Server for optimal multi-tasking performance based on its primary network function. By default, Microsoft assigns the most CPU cycles to *foreground* applications—programs that are being used by a local user on the system interactively. This means that *background* applications—all programs except the one a local user is immediately working on—do not receive as much priority from the microprocessors installed on the Windows NT Server computer.

In most cases, you should change this tasking setting to give equal CPU time priority to foreground and background applications. For a network server, such a balanced configuration is a must for good performance.

To change Windows NT Server's multi-tasking responsiveness, follow these steps:

1. Right-click the My Computer icon located on the Windows NT Desktop and choose Properties from the pop-up menu.

   or

   Click the Start menu, point to Settings, and click Control Panel. Double-click the System icon.

2. The Windows NT System Properties window appears. Click the Performance tab to configure the foreground application performance boost setting (see fig. 19.1).

3. In the Application Performance section, click and drag the Boost slider bar. The slider bar defaults to Maximum performance for foreground applications. For a dedicated server computer, slide the bar all the way to the left so that the performance boost for foreground applications is None.

4. Click OK to save your setting or click Cancel to abort any changes and keep the original setting.

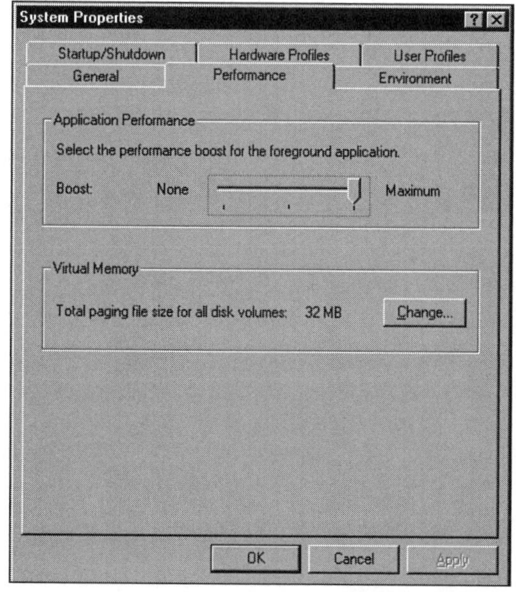

Fig. 19.1
The Windows NT System Properties window allows you to customize the performance boost for foreground applications.

Windows NT Server versus Windows NT Workstation

You might be wondering why there are two kinds of Windows NT: Workstation and Server. Although they are part of the same family, there are many key differences between these two network operating system cousins (see Table 19.1).

Table 19.1 Similar Products with Some Different Features

Functionality	Windows NT Server	Windows NT Workstation
SMP (Symmetric Multiprocessor) Support	Four processors supported in the shipping version	Two processors supported in the shipping version
Network Connections Support	No limit on connections	As a server, limit of 10 client connections
Apple Macintosh Services Support	Built-in	Not supported
Disk Fault Tolerance Features	RAID levels 1 and 5	Not supported
Domain Logon Authentication	Built-in	Not supported
Remote Access Services	Up to 256 simultaneous remote connections	Limit of one remote connection
Directory Replication Services	Can act as an importer and exporter	Can only act as an importer
Microsoft BackOffice Server Products Platform	Built-in	Not supported

Windows NT Domains versus Workgroups

All Microsoft networks conform to a Workgroup model or to a Domain model of network organization. The Workgroup model often works better for small organizations where computer resources and user accounts are maintained by individual users. No central point of administration is provided. If a user wants access to other computers in the workgroup, the user must be explicitly added as a user account on each of the computers that he wants to access. Redundant user accounts become necessary to share resources between several users and computers. In addition, each user is responsible for permitting or refusing access to his own computer resources. In a large organization, this scheme can become quite unwieldy.

The Domain model provides for a central point of administration for user accounts, resource sharing, access rights, and permissions. Domains allow users to log onto the network only once while gaining access to all network resources, even in a multiple-server environment. Users can even be permitted to access domains besides their own using trust relationships. *Trust Relationships* link together two or more domains.

> **Note**
>
> Windows NT Servers can *only* be members of a domain. Windows NT Workstation computers can become members of a workgroup or a domain, as is the case for both Windows for Workgroups 3.x and Windows 95 computers.

A Windows NT Server domain consists of at least one *primary* server, which is called the Primary Domain Controller (PDC). The PDC provides user authentication for users to log on to the network domain. Often, especially in large organizations, a domain will have at least one other server known as a Backup Domain Controller (BDC) that maintains a copy of the PDC's user accounts database. Should a PDC server go down, a BDC server can take over to allow users to continue to log on to the domain. A third type of server can also exist in a domain: it's simply called a Server. A Domain Server does not authenticate user logons. Its only purpose is to run application programs or to act as a dedicated application server for products like SQL Server, Exchange Server, or other back-end client/server applications.

Large-scale enterprise networks must choose from one of four major Windows NT Server Domain models:

- Single Domain
- Master Domain
- Multiple Master Domain
- Complete Trust

Domains and their associated design issues are covered in Chapter 3, "Planning the Installation." Trust relationships are covered in Chapter 9, "Administering Servers and Sharing Resources."

Microsoft Networking Transport Protocols

Windows NT Server supports the three major networking transport protocols that are most commonly used:

- IPX/SPX (NWLink, Novell NetWare-originated protocol)
- NetBEUI (often used within Microsoft networking environments)

- TCP/IP (a time-tested, proven protocol often implemented in UNIX environments and the Internet)

When you install Windows NT Server, two transport protocols are selected by default: NetBEUI and NWLink. You can change these default settings during or after installation.

NWLink: Native Novell NetWare Routable Protocol

NWLink is Microsoft's implementation of Novell NetWare's proprietary IPX/SPX protocol. NWLink is required if you are integrating Windows NT Server in an existing NetWare environment. NWLink is still a valuable protocol even outside of a NetWare environment. For larger networks, routing becomes an important factor for local area networks (LANs) and wide area networks (WANs). NWLink is a routable protocol, which has a reputation as a very robust network transport mechanism. NetBEUI, however, is not a routable protocol. If routing is important to your network and you don't want to bother with IP addressing, you might want to consider NWLink.

NetBEUI: Fine for Smaller Networks

Microsoft originally developed the NetBEUI protocol for its now-retired LAN Manager network operating system. As mentioned in the previous section, NetBEUI is not routable. As the native Windows NT Server protocol, it works well in smaller environments where the number of network users and nodes are limited and where routing is not required. NetBEUI requires the use of unique 10-character computer names for its network addressing. NetBEUI is simple to set up and its performance is more than adequate for most small network setups.

TCP/IP: Protocol of the Internet

TCP/IP stands for Transmission Control Protocol/Internet Protocol (that's "internet" with a lowercase "i," meaning between networks—not referring exclusively to *the* Internet so popular today). This protocol has withstood the test of time; it was invented by the U.S. government over 20 years ago for military use. TCP/IP uses unique numeric addressing for funneling data across network territory. This numeric style of network addressing, called *dotted quad* format, can be difficult to keep track of. Tools such as Domain Name Servers (DNS), Dynamic Host Configuration Protocol (DHCP), and Windows Internet Naming Service (WINS) were invented to assist with the tracking and mapping of TCP/IP addresses to computer names. TCP/IP is the network protocol standard used by UNIX computer systems and is the required telecommunications protocol of the Internet (with a capital "I"). If you are going to communicate with UNIX hosts, browse the World Wide Web, use telnet or ftp, peruse newsgroups, or set up an Internet server, you definitely need to utilize TCP/IP.

Note

Windows NT Server supports concurrent multiple protocols. You can have TCP/IP, NetBEUI, NWLink, and other NT-supported protocols loaded at the same time. Windows NT can connect to the Internet, NetWare servers, and many other types of networks simultaneously!

Integrating DOS Systems

Originally called the Microsoft Workgroup Add-On for MS-DOS, the Microsoft Network Client 3.0 for MS-DOS is widely available. You can download it from CompuServe, the Microsoft Download Service (MSDL), The Microsoft Network (MSN), Microsoft's ftp server site (**ftp.microsoft.com**), or from Microsoft's World Wide Web site (**www.microsoft.com**). Most conveniently, this DOS client connectivity software is packaged as a part of the Windows NT Server CD-ROM. You can find it in the \Clients\Msclient\Disks\Disk1 folder.

Connecting MS-DOS Workstations to Windows NT Environments

Insert a blank formatted floppy disk into a computer that has access to a CD-ROM drive. Insert the Windows NT Server CD-ROM into the drive. Copy all the files from the \Clients\Msclient\Disks\Disk1 folder on the CD to the root folder of the floppy disk. You now have a DOS client software installation disk.

Insert the floppy disk into the DOS machine you want to connect to a Windows NT Server network. At the DOS prompt, type **a:** (or **b:** depending on the computer's configuration) and press Enter. Type **setup** and press Enter. The installation process begins (see fig. 19.2).

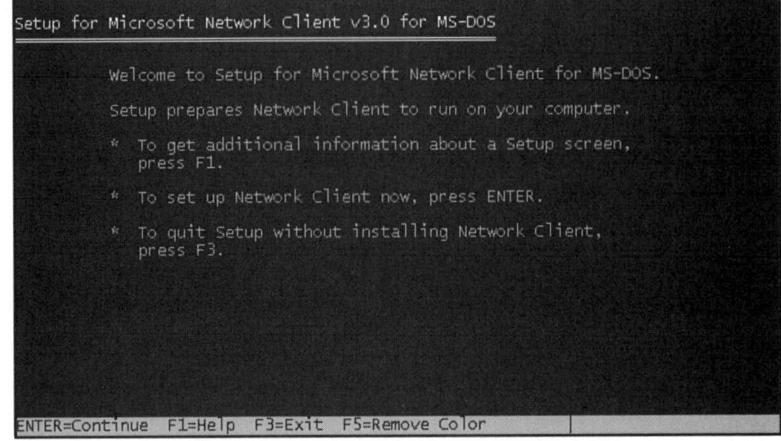

Fig. 19.2 The Microsoft Network Client for MS-DOS gives you three options when you first launch its setup program.

Installing the Microsoft MS-DOS Network Client Software

To set up your DOS workstation for network access, follow these steps:

1. Press Enter to proceed to the next setup screen.
2. The setup program asks you for a location to load the installation files. The default location is C:\net. Press Enter to accept this location or type a different location and press Enter to continue. The setup program tells you it's examining your system, then it displays a list of network adapter card drivers (see fig. 19.3).

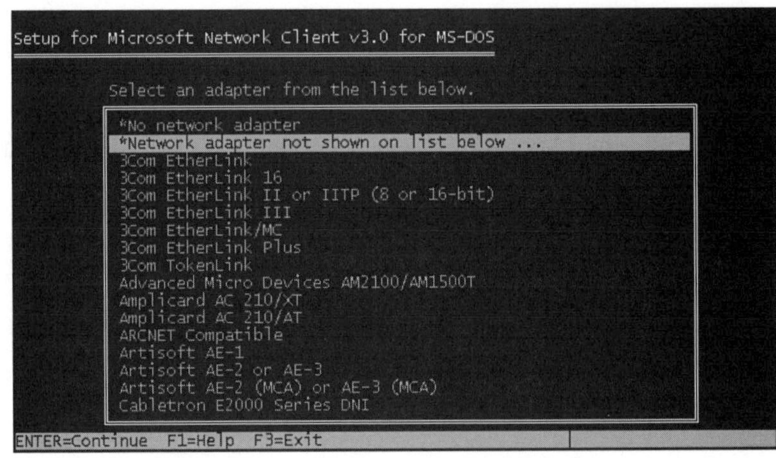

Fig. 19.3 MS-DOS client setup asks you to choose from a list of available network adapter card drivers.

3. From the list, select the specific network adapter card installed in the DOS computer you're working on. If the name of your specific network adapter is not shown, select the option `*Network Adapter Not Shown on List Below`. You need to have a manufacturer's disk of the network card so the setup program can install the appropriate driver.
4. After you select the appropriate network adapter card driver, press Enter. A pop-up message appears telling you about setting network buffers. Press Enter to optimize performance and continue.
5. You must assign a 20-character or less computer name to the DOS workstation computer. Only letters, numbers, and the following special characters are allowed in a computer name: ! # $ % & ( ) ^ _ ` { } ~. Press Enter to continue.

The setup program displays a configuration screen (see fig. 19.4). From here, you can make any necessary changes, additions, or deletions to the network client configuration. This is a very important step, especially if you want this DOS workstation to become a member of a Windows NT Server domain.

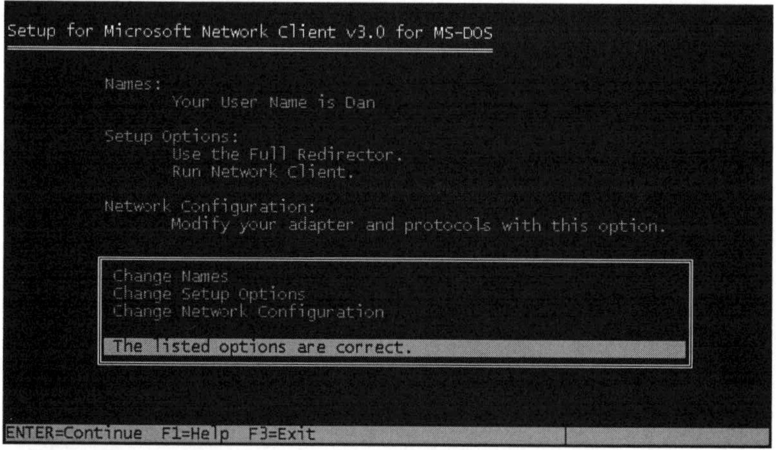

Fig. 19.4
MS-DOS client setup configuration settings screen where you can specify the user name, network client options, as well as network adapter and protocol.

V Communications

Configuring MS-DOS Network Client Software

By default, the setup program assigns your DOS workstation only as a part of a workgroup. The setup program does not permit domain logon by default. It assigns the computer to a workgroup with the name of Workgroup. You can't log on to a domain by filling in the workgroup name with the name of a domain!

Note

Remember, you can always press the F1 function key to view a Help screen related to the specific portion of the setup process you are working on.

Often you will find that the MS-DOS network client defaults are not sufficient. Since I am usually connecting to a Windows NT Server domain, I almost always have to modify the default options. Here's how you can change the default settings:

1. To change configuration options, use the arrow keys on the keyboard to highlight an option and press Enter. Use the Tab key to move between two sets of option boxes. Choose the Change Names option to change the user name, computer name, or more importantly, to correctly enter a workgroup or domain name. If you're logging on to a domain, enter the proper domain name and leave the workgroup name as it is.
2. When all the name choices have been selected and entered correctly, select The Listed Names are Correct and press Enter.
3. Next, select Change Setup Options and press Enter. Notice that under the Change Logon Validation option, the setup defaults to Do Not Logon to Domain. You must change this setting if you want to log on to a Windows NT Server domain. Select Change Logon Validation and press Enter (see fig. 19.5).

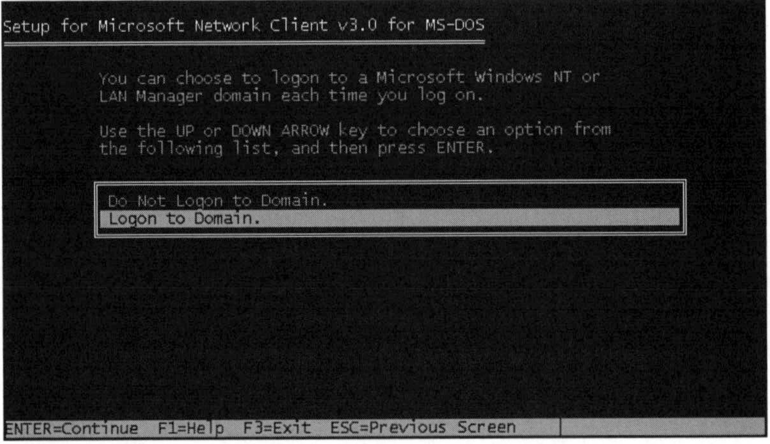

Fig. 19.5
You can adjust the MS-DOS client setup to allow for domain logon by highlighting the Logon to Domain option and pressing Enter.

4. After you select and correctly enter the setup options, select The Listed Options are Correct and press Enter.

5. Finally, to modify the network configuration, select Change Network Configuration and press Enter.
6. Make any necessary changes, such as adding or deleting a network transport protocol stack (the default is NWLink IPX-compatible transport), and select Network Configuration is Correct.
7. When you've made all the necessary adjustments to the network client settings, select The Listed Options are Correct and press Enter. The setup program copies all the requisite files to the computer's hard drive. When the program is completed, the final setup screen appears (see fig. 19.6).

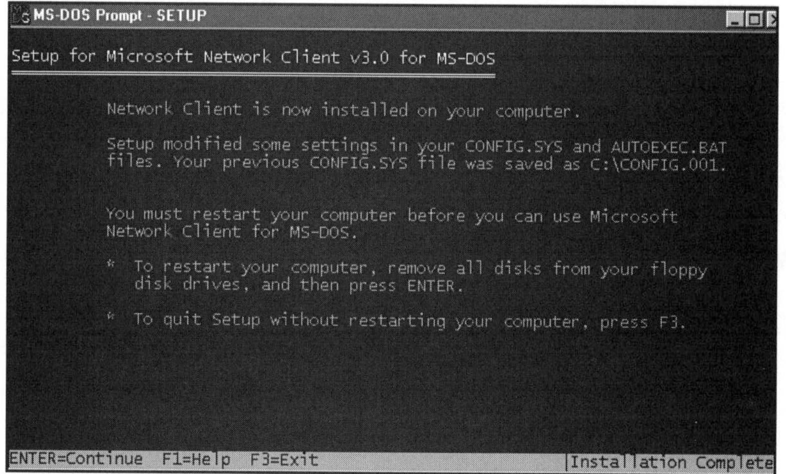

Fig. 19.6
Final MS-DOS client setup screen where you can press the Enter key to complete the installation process and have the computer rebooted so that your changes will take effect.

8. Now, you can press Enter to restart the computer or press the F3 key to return to the MS-DOS prompt without rebooting. You *must* reboot before the MS-DOS network client software will work.

Accessing Windows NT Server Network Resources

After the DOS client system reboots, the changes that the setup program made to the AUTOEXEC.BAT file and the CONFIG.SYS file should take effect. At a minimum, the setup program adds a network driver file named IFSHLP.SYS to the CONFIG.SYS and it adds the `Net Start` command to the AUTOEXEC.BAT in addition to adding the MS-Client directory to your path statement.

When the system now boots, it should ask you if your user name is the default name you entered into the setup program. Press Enter if this is the correct user name for the network; otherwise, type the correct user name. You are next asked for your network password. Type the proper user password for the workgroup or domain you want to log on to and press Enter.

The first time you log on to the network from that workstation, the MS-DOS client software asks you if you want to create a password-list file. If you do, you must retype your password to confirm it. Next, you are asked for your Windows NT Server domain password (if you are logging on to a domain). Type the password again and press Enter. If the user name and password are correctly entered, you should be granted access to the network domain. The MS-DOS Network Client software informs you of your privilege level in the domain and then states that the net Start command was completed successfully.

Working with the Net Command. If you type the command **`net /?`** at the DOS prompt, you can view a complete listing of the available net commands. Type **`net`** by itself and press Enter to display a pop-up utility that's designed to help you browse available network drives and printers and attach to them. Unfortunately, this pop-up utility doesn't always work properly. Use the net command often to connect to network resources.

Attaching to Shares and Assigning Drive Letters. Before you start wildly mapping drive letters to network share points, it's a good idea to set the `lastdrive=` line in the workstation's CONFIG.SYS file to Z or a letter higher than the default, which is E. This gives you a wider choice of drive letters to choose from when mapping to network directory shares.

Using the DOS command line to map drive letters is really quite easy. The command syntax is:

```
net use drive: \\servername\sharename
```

That's it! If you want to map the local computer's P: drive to the network share point named Programs located on a Windows NT Server named bigkahuna, here's all you have to do:

```
net use P: \\bigkahuna\programs [Enter]
```

The net command should then echo back the words `The command completed successfully` if all goes as planned. If the command does not complete successfully:

- A network connection has not been established with that server computer.

or

- The server computer that you are trying to connect to happens to be out of service at the moment.

or

- You mistyped the server name (maybe it's just *kahuna)* and/or the share name (perhaps the name is apps, *not* programs).

Attaching to Remote Printers. Connecting to network printers is very much the same as connecting to network directory shares. You use the net use command to map your local printer ports to network print queues. The proper syntax is

```
net use lpt?: \\computername\SharedPrinterName
```

If you want to redirect your lpt1 printer port to a network printer named HP4Sales located on a computer called Mrktg-3, the command line would look like this

```
net use lpt1: \\mrktg-3\hp4sales
```

Running Applications, Accessing Files, and Printing via Remote Resources. After you set up a local workstation's network drive mappings and network printer connections, the MS-DOS client software remembers those settings as defaults. When the user logs back onto the network, all the drive mappings and printer connections are automatically restored (assuming those network resources are up and running).

Basically, network drives and remote printers work the same as local resources—when they have been established. User rights and access permissions can and should be established on Windows NT Servers that limit a user's capability to read, write, delete, execute, change permissions, and take ownership of files. Without proper access rights and permissions, working with data files and programs remotely can prove to be an impossible task. For example, a user can't modify a document that resides in a network directory that allows read-only access. However, with proper access rights and permissions, working with files, applications, and printers in a networked environment differs little from working on local computer resources.

Integrating with Windows 3.x Systems

Most computer users seem to prefer Windows-style graphical computing to the character-based command line. However, Windows 3.0 and 3.1 were not really designed with networking in mind. You can connect to Windows NT computers in Windows 3.x by first loading the Microsoft Network Client for MS-DOS, but most of your computer's conventional memory will be used up by the MS-DOS client software. Your computer then can only run as a network node, not as a peer-to-peer server.

Windows for Workgroups: The Ideal Windows 3.x Network Client

Microsoft engineered Windows for Workgroups 3.1 primarily in response to the lack of network support in Windows 3.x. Windows for Workgroups could act as a workstation and a server with all of the necessary connectivity components already built in. Windows for Workgroups highlighted the idea of independent workgroups being connected in a point-and-click environment. Because of its built-in network functionality, Windows for Workgroups became the ideal Microsoft networking client.

Advantages of Using Windows for Workgroups 3.11 as a Windows NT Network Client

About a year after Windows for Workgroups 3.1 came on the scene, Microsoft brought out an upgraded version. Windows for Workgroups 3.11 offered several advantages over Windows 3.x and the earlier Windows for Workgroups version. Windows for Workgroups 3.11 offers the following:

- Fast, 32-bit networking drivers for better performance
- Support for Windows NT Server Domain logon authentication
- Support for Windows NT Server administration tools
- Improved resource sharing security
- 32-bit disk access and 32-bit file access features
- Microsoft Mail Workgroup Client software plus Microsoft Schedule+ calendaring program included with the system

Using Windows for Workgroups Optional 32-bit TCP/IP Client Software

If you're a system administrator in a TCP/IP-based network environment, you can install Microsoft's 32-bit TCP/IP protocol stack as an add-on to Windows for Workgroups 3.11. You can download this software from CompuServe, MSN, MSDL, or Microsoft's ftp and Web sites on the Internet. You can also install it directly from the Windows NT Server CD-ROM from the \clients\tcp32wfw folder. Read the READ.ME file that accompanies the software. This TCP/IP 32-bit client for Windows for Workgroups 3.11 boasts these advantages:

- Same code base as the Windows NT 3.5 TCP/IP protocol stack
- Support for Windows Sockets 1.1
- Supports Windows Internet Naming Service (WINS) for network browsing
- Built-in support for automatic TCP/IP addressing through the Windows NT Server Dynamic Host Configuration Protocol (DHCP)
- Does *not* utilize conventional MS-DOS memory through its design as a virtual device driver (VxD)

Installing or Upgrading to Windows for Workgroups 3.11

Installing the product or upgrading from Windows 3.x is fairly straightforward. You can purchase the packaged software from your favorite vendor or you can install it from the Windows NT Server CD-ROM. Remember, Windows for Workgroups is certainly *not* freeware. Client licenses must be purchased for every copy installed.

From DOS computers, simply type **setup** at the installation directory's command line (from floppy disk, CD-ROM, or a network drive) and follow the instructions the setup program provides.

To upgrade Windows 3.x computers, first be sure to close down all running applications. Next, go to Program Manager and choose File, Run (or press ALT+F+R on the keyboard). Select SETUP.EXE from the installation media and you're off and running.

When you get to the Network Setup part of the installation, you see the Network Setup dialog box (see fig. 19.7). You can access the Network Setup dialog box by double-clicking the Network Setup icon in the Network program group (one of the Windows for Workgroups default program groups). By default, no support for networks is installed. To add support for networking, click the Networks button. The Networks dialog box appears (see fig. 19.8).

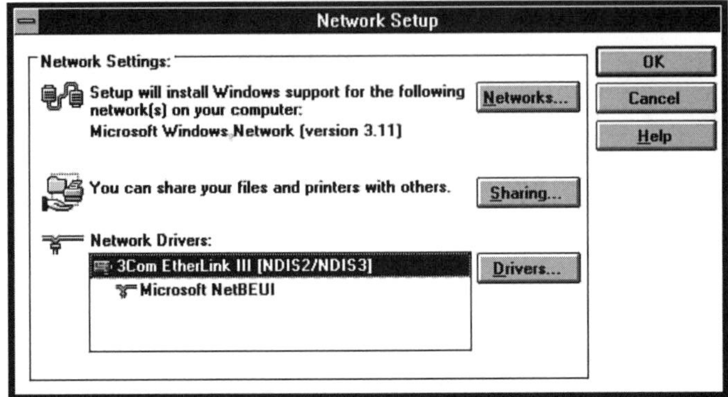

Fig. 19.7
The Network Setup dialog box where you specify the type of network, file sharing properties, and network drivers.

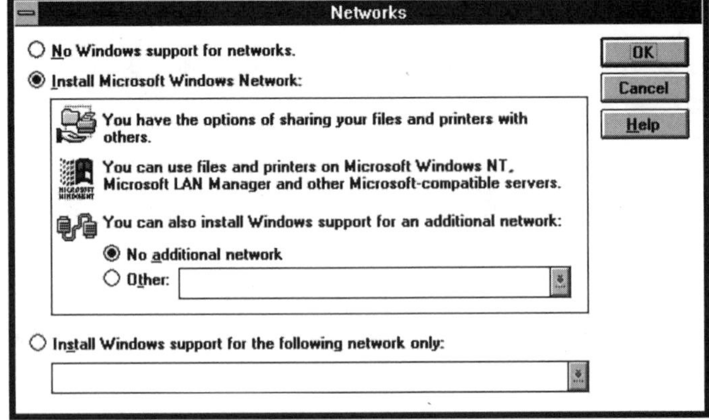

Fig. 19.8
The Networks dialog box for installing Microsoft Windows networking as well as other types of networks.

Select the Install Microsoft Windows Network option button to set up support for Microsoft networking. You can also specify support for one additional network service, such as Novell NetWare. Click OK to accept your networking choice and return to the Network Setup dialog box.

In the Network Setup dialog box, click the Sharing button if you want the Windows for Workgroups workstation to be capable of sharing its files and attached printers with other users on the network. From the Sharing dialog box, select the appropriate checkboxes to provide file sharing and printer sharing, then click OK.

Finally, click the Drivers button (or press ALT+D) to install the appropriate network adapter card driver. The Network Drivers dialog box will appear. Click Add Adapter (or press ALT+A) to select the appropriate driver for the network interface card installed in the computer workstation. The Add Network Adapter dialog box appears (see fig. 19.9). You can click the Detect button to have Windows for Workgroups detect the installed network adapter. If that is unsuccessful, select the proper adapter name from the list box. If the installed network card is not on the list, select Unlisted or Updated Network Adapter. Click OK, and you're prompted to insert a driver disk from the manufacturer of your network card. When the correct network adapter has been selected, click OK.

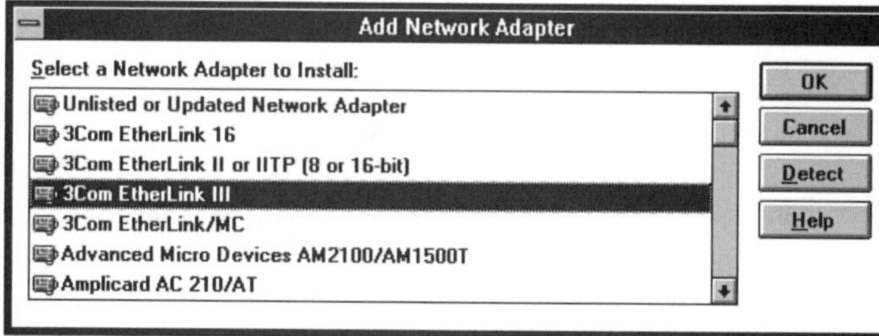

Fig. 19.9
The Windows for Workgroups Add Network Adapter dialog box allows you to select the proper network adapter card driver for the network adapter card that is installed in your computer.

The name of the network adapter you select is placed in the Network Drivers list box with two protocols: Microsoft NetBEUI and IPX/SPX Compatible Transport with NetBIOS (see fig. 19.10). As long as you do not need both protocols, remove the one you don't need by selecting the protocol and clicking Remove. Otherwise, select the protocol you want as the default and click the Set As Default Protocol button. You can also add more network card drivers and additional protocols by clicking the Add Adapter or Add Protocol buttons, respectively. You can further configure network drivers and protocols by selecting the one you want to configure and clicking Setup.

Click Close to exit the Network Drivers dialog box and return to the Network Setup dialog box. Click OK to have Windows for Workgroups save and implement the new network settings. Your system might need access to the Windows For Workgroups setup files. After copying the necessary network files, Windows for Workgroups tells you to restart the computer for the new network settings to take effect (see fig. 19.11). Close any open applications and click Restart Computer.

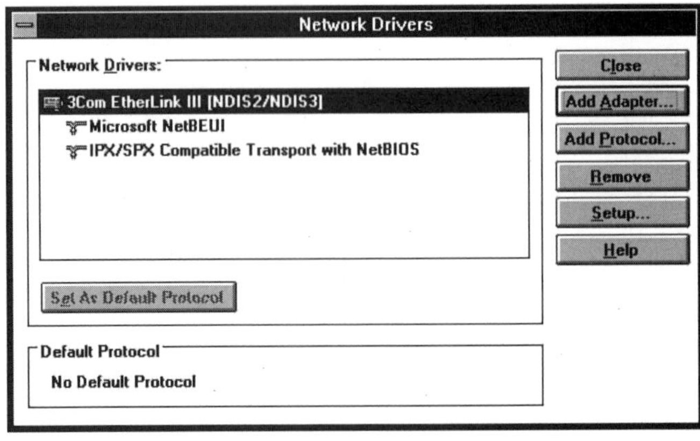

Fig. 19.10
The Windows for Workgroups Network Drivers dialog box where you can add or remove network adapter card drivers and their associated network protocols.

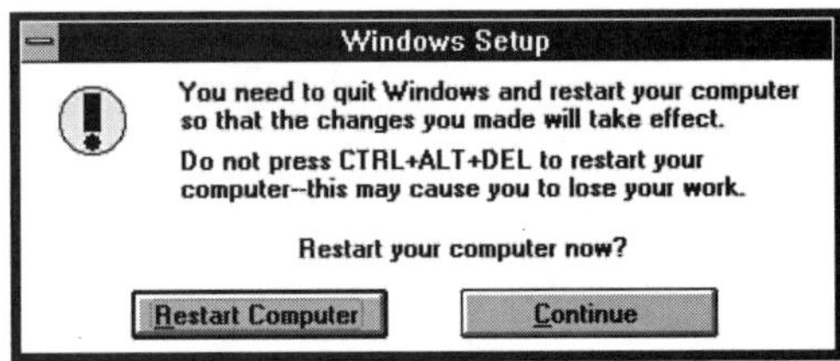

Fig. 19.11
The Windows for Workgroups Setup message box informs you that you must restart the computer for the new network settings to take effect.

Configuring Windows for Workgroups 3.11 to Connect to Windows NT Server Domains

The tricky part about configuring the networking portion of Windows for Workgroups is that it only prompts you for a workgroup name during installation of the product—not a domain name. Hooking up to a Windows NT Server domain requires an extra step that can only be performed *after* the installation process is complete.

You're prompted for a workgroup name during the setup process; Windows for Workgroups gives your workgroup a default name of Workgroup. You can change your workgroup name in the same location where you allow the workstation to become part of a Windows NT Server domain. Go to the Main program group, double-click the Control Panel icon, then double-click the Network icon. You can change the workgroup name in the Microsoft Windows Network dialog box (see fig. 19.12).

In the Options area, click the Startup button to open the Startup Settings dialog box (see fig. 19.13). Pay close attention to the Options for Enterprise Networking box. This is where you tell Windows for Workgroups that you want to log on to a Windows NT Server or a Microsoft LAN Manager domain.

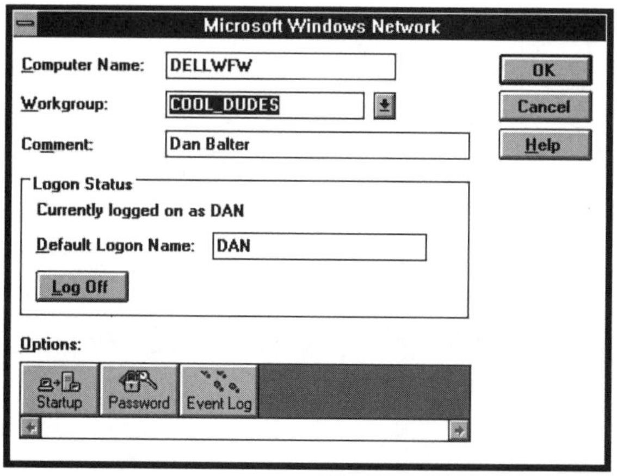

Fig. 19.12
The Microsoft Windows Network dialog box lets you type in the name of your network workgroup or configure your workstation to log on to a Windows NT Server domain.

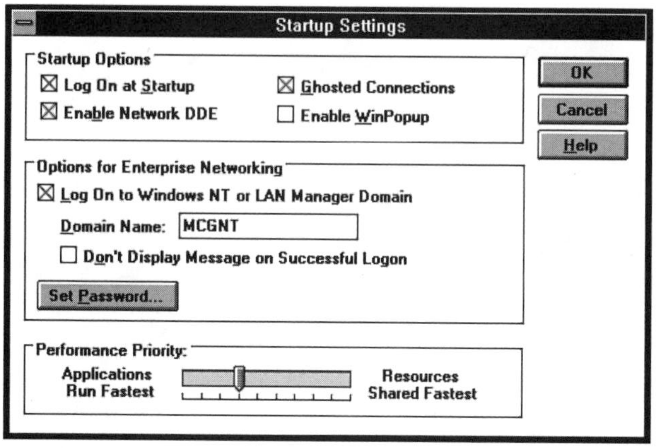

Fig. 19.13
The Startup Settings dialog box provides for entering in the name of the domain that you want to log on to.

Select the Log On to Windows NT or LAN Manager Domain checkbox if you want to use domain authentication. Type the name of the network domain in the Domain Name text box. Click OK to return to the previous dialog box and click OK again. Close the Control Panel. The next time the user logs on to this Windows for Workgroups computer, he will have to enter the Windows for Workgroups password. Then, the user will be asked to enter and confirm the domain password for his user account (see fig. 19.14). If the Windows for Workgroups password and the domain password are the same, each subsequent time the user logs on to the system, he only has to enter the password once for Windows for Workgroups and domain authentication (see fig. 19.15).

Fig. 19.14
The Welcome to Windows for Workgroups dialog box requests your Windows password and the Domain Logon dialog box asks for your NT Server domain password.

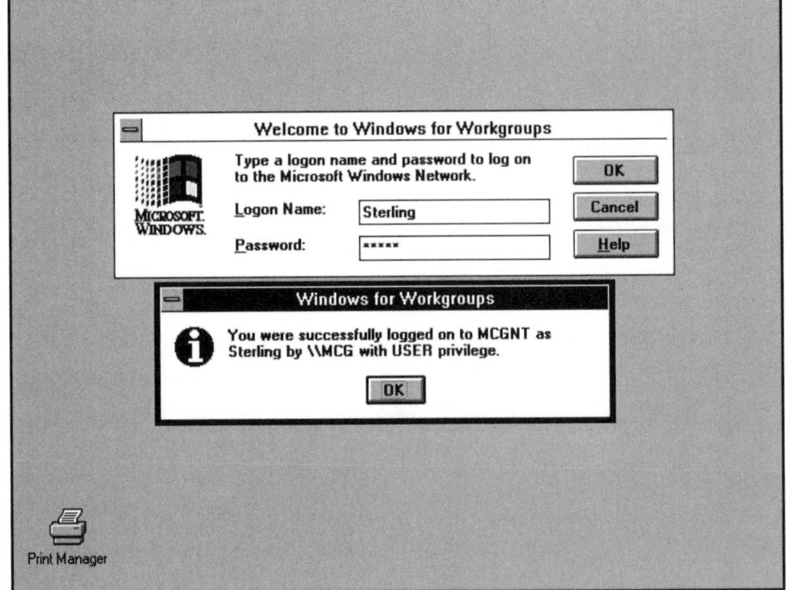

Fig. 19.15
After you have correctly entered your domain user name, password, and the name of the domain you want to log on to, your logon request will be authenticated.

Connecting to and Disconnecting from Network Resources

When a user successfully logs on to a Windows NT Server domain or is a member of a network workgroup, File Manager and Print Manager become the connectivity tools. The Windows for Workgroups edition of File Manager has some enhancements from its Windows 3.x counterpart.

When you launch File Manager, you'll notice that the Windows for Workgroups version has some buttons on the toolbar that don't exist in the Windows 3.x version. Some of the menu options are also different. The Windows for Workgroups edition of File Manager provides you with the ability to share directories on your computer with other users on the network. It also gives you the option of connecting to other computers on the network. To connect to a network directory share, follow these steps:

1. Click the Connect button on the toolbar or choose Disk, Connect Network Drive. The Connect Network Drive dialog box appears (see fig. 19.16).

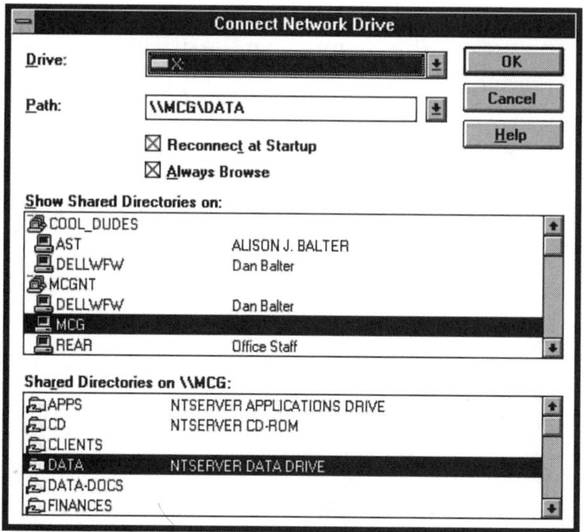

Fig. 19.16
The Connect Network Drive dialog box from File Manager allows you to connect to any of the available shared network directories.

2. Select a drive letter from the Drive drop-down list. The shared resource will map to this drive on the local computer.
3. Windows for Workgroups displays a list of the workgroups and domains currently part of the network in the Show Shared Directories On list box. A plus sign (+) to the left of the workgroup and domain names means you can expand these entries to display the computer names in each workgroup and domain. A minus sign (–) means the entry is already expanded. Click an available computer name to select it.
4. The Shared Directories On list box lists the available shared directories. Select the shared directory you want to access.

5. By default, the Reconnect at Startup checkbox is selected. Deselect this checkbox if you do not want the connection to be automatically restored when you log back on to Windows for Workgroups.
6. Click OK to accept the settings for this network connection. If you are accessing a shared directory from a computer that is part of a workgroup, and if a password is required for access to that shared directory, Windows for Workgroups requests the proper password.
7. A new window displays the name of the drive letter you assigned to the connection and it displays the actual network (UNC) path for the connection \\computername\SharedDirectoryName (refer to fig. 19.16).

Creating a shared directory on your local computer for other network users to access is easy. In File Manager, select the directory you want to make available as a network share. Click the Share Directory button on the toolbar, or choose Disk, Share As. The Share Directory dialog box appears (see fig. 19.17). You can assign a different share name than the default if you want. Deselect the Re-share at Startup checkbox if you want this to be a one-time only share. Choose the type of access permission you want to allow. Click OK. You just created a shared network directory.

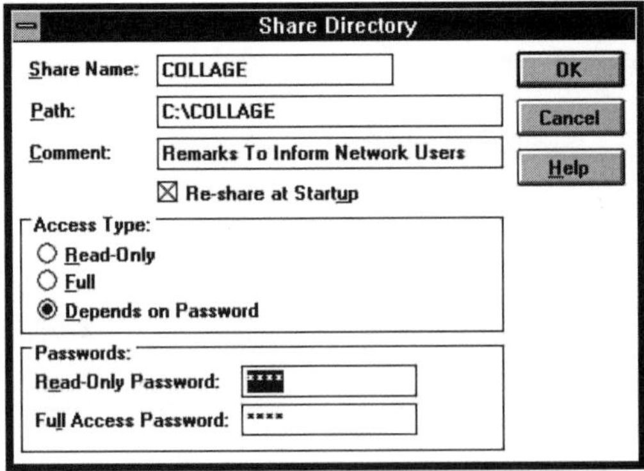

Fig. 19.17
The Share Directory dialog box gives you the ability to assign a unique name to the directory that you wish to share on the network and you can limit users' access to it by implementing read-only and/or full access passwords.

To disconnect from a network directory, follow these steps:

1. Click the Disconnect button on the toolbar, or choose Disk, Disconnect Network Drive.
2. Select the drive you want to disconnect and click OK.

To stop sharing one of your own directories on the network:

1. Click the Stop Sharing button on the toolbar, or choose Disk, Stop Sharing.
2. Select the shared directory you no longer want to share and click OK.

Integrating with Windows 95 Systems

Windows 95 really shines when it comes to integrating with Microsoft networking in general, and with Windows NT in particular. From the very beginning of its development, Windows 95 was designed to be the best PC network client.

Configuring Windows 95 to Connect with Windows NT

To set up a standalone Windows 95 computer for network access, click the Start button and choose Settings, Control Panel. From the Control Panel window, double-click the Network icon. The Network property sheet appears with only the Configuration tab showing. Click the Add button so you can start adding the necessary network components. The Select Network Component Type dialog box appears (see fig. 19.18).

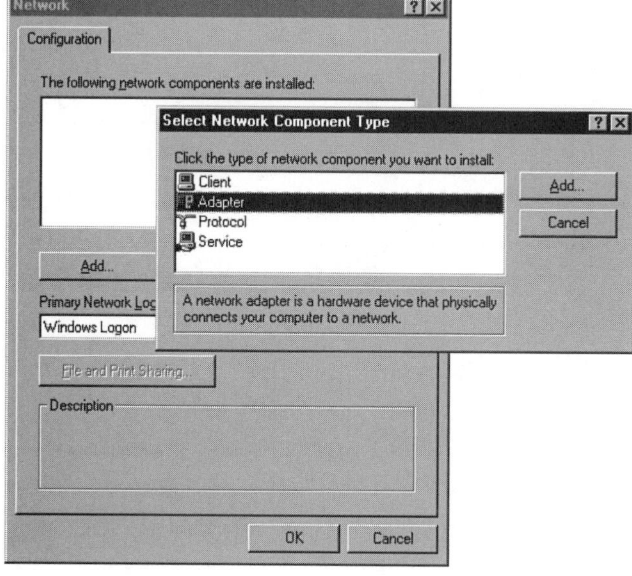

Fig. 19.18
The Network property sheet and the Select Network Component Type dialog box let you add network clients, adapter card drivers, protocols, and services.

First, select Adapter and click Add. Select the appropriate network adapter installed in the computer you're working on (see fig. 19.19). If your network adapter is not listed, click Have Disk and insert the driver disk from the network card manufacturer. After you select the proper network adapter, click OK.

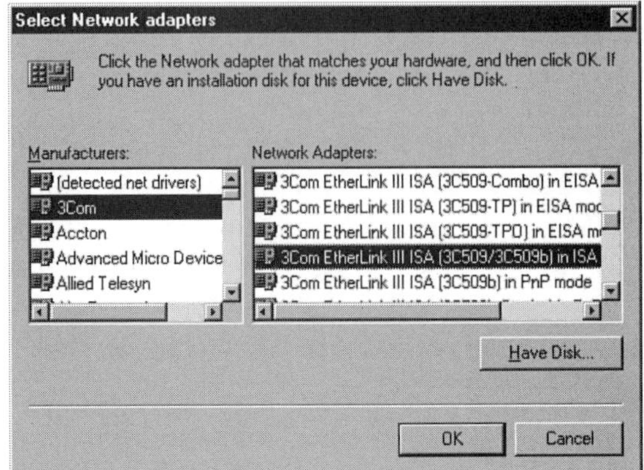

Fig. 19.19
The Select Network Adapters dialog box prompts you to choose the appropriate network adapter card driver for the network adapter card that is installed inside of your PC.

In the Select Network Component Type dialog box, add one or more networking protocols by selecting Protocol and clicking Add. Select the manufacturer and then select the individual protocol (see fig. 19.20). Click Have Disk if you have a protocol vendor's disk. Click OK after you select a manufacturer and its associated protocol. Repeat this process to add multiple protocols.

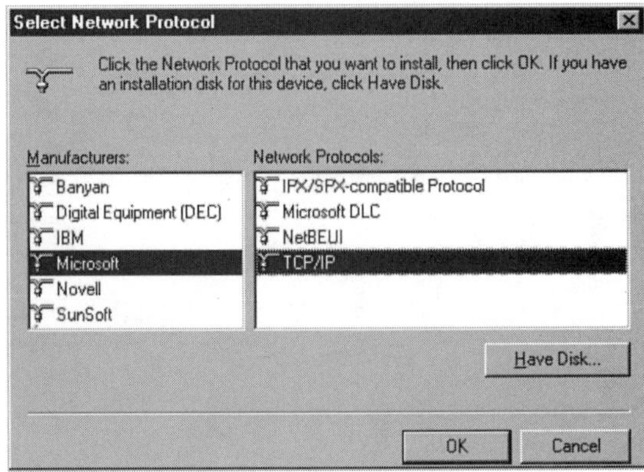

Fig. 19.20
The Select Network Protocol dialog box displays a list of available networking protocols that your PC workstation can use to communicate with other computers over the network.

Now choose the type of networking client you want to utilize. Select Client and click Add. Because this chapter is devoted to working with Microsoft networks, select Microsoft as the manufacturer and select the Client for Microsoft Networks as the network client. Click OK.

At this point in the configuration process, you should have at least three network components listed in the Network property sheet: the Client for Microsoft Networks, at least one network adapter card, and at least one protocol. The Primary Network Logon drop-down list should read `Client for Microsoft Networks`. Click the File and Print Sharing button. Select the I Want to be Able to Give Others Access to My Files checkbox if you want to share this computer's files over the network. Select the I Want to be Able to Allow Others to Print to My Printer(s) checkbox if you want to share this computer's attached printers with other PCs on the network. Another network component should be added if you select either of the two sharing checkboxes, File and Printer sharing for Microsoft Networks. The Network property sheet should now look similar to figure 19.21.

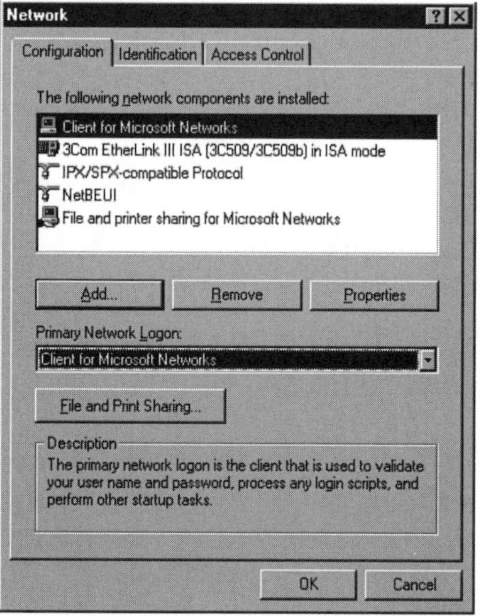

Fig. 19.21 The Network property sheet should look similar to this after networking components have been installed.

Select the network adapter component and click Properties to view detailed information on the network adapter card driver. This property sheet displays the network adapter card Driver Type, Bindings, Advanced settings, and Resources settings. Click the Resources tab to view the configuration type and I/O address range. Look for any hardware setting conflict in the I/O address range. An asterisk next to the I/O address indicates a conflict. Change that setting so the conflict no longer exists. Click Close.

Peer-to-Peer Workgroup Configuration

After you add the necessary network components, Windows 95 adds two tabs to the Network property sheet: Identification and Access Control. To set up workgroup networking, click the Identification tab. Be sure this workstation has a unique computer name; if it does not, enter one. Next, enter the name of the network workgroup. A computer description is optional.

Click the Access Control tab. Share-level Access Control is selected by default. User-level Access Control requires a server or domain type of network that maintains user- and group-level security, such as Windows NT Server or Novell NetWare.

Windows NT Server Domain Configuration

To enable Windows Server Domain logon authentication, click the Configuration tab. Select Client for Microsoft Networks and click the Properties button. Mark the Log On to Windows NT Domain checkbox and type the name of the Windows NT Domain you want to log on to. Next, select Quick Logon or Logon and Restore Network Connections. Click OK to return to the Network property sheet.

Working with TCP/IP Protocol Settings

To configure a Windows 95 client for TCP/IP, add the protocol first. Then, select the TCP/IP protocol in the Network property sheet and click Properties. A multi-tabbed TCP/IP property sheet appears. You can enter an IP address, a Gateway address, and primary and secondary WINS Server addresses. You can enable DHCP, specify a DNS configuration, and change other settings.

Finalizing the Network Settings

When you complete the necessary network configurations, click OK to close down the Network property sheet. Windows 95 might ask you for the location of the Windows 95 setup files so it can install the necessary driver files for the network. After this process, Windows 95 informs you that you must restart the computer for the new settings to take effect (see fig. 19.22). Close all running applications and click Yes to restart the computer.

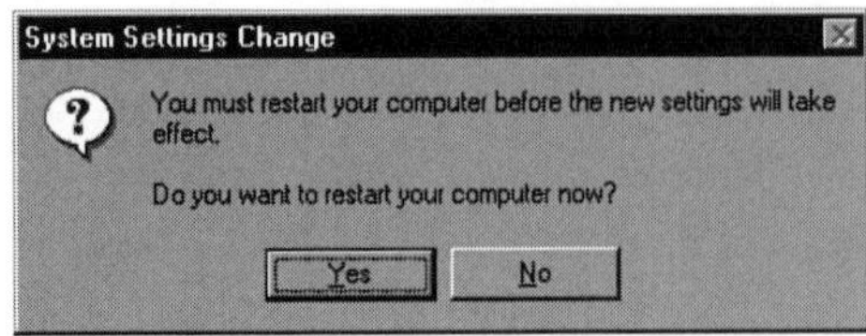

Fig. 19.22
For your changes to take effect, click Yes to restart the system.

Browsing Network Resources and Mapping and Unmapping Network Drives

When the Windows 95 system restarts, the user has to log on to the Windows NT Server domain (if the system was configured for domain logon) at the same time she logs on to Windows 95. The Enter Network Password dialog box appears (see fig. 19.23). For domain logon, the name of a domain must be specified the first time that a user logs on.

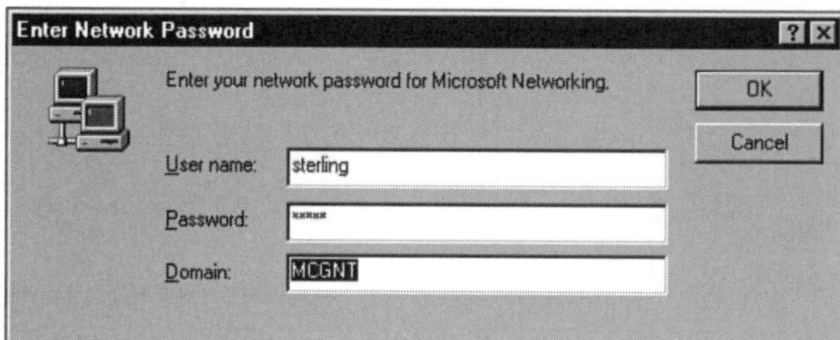

Fig. 19.23
The Enter Network Password dialog box for Microsoft networking will appear after you have successfully set up Windows 95 for networking. For domain log-ons, Windows 95 asks for the name of the domain that you want to log on to.

After the user logs on successfully, she can browse the network's resources with the help of a new desktop icon: the Network Neighborhood icon. Double-clicking the Network Neighborhood icon opens the Network Neighborhood window. The user can view all of the network computer's available in her current domain. Double-clicking the Entire Network icon in the Network Neighborhood window displays all of the domains and workgroups that reside on the user's network (see fig. 19.24). Double-clicking any of the other domains or workgroups inside the Entire Network window displays all associated computers. Double-clicking each computer shows each computer's shared folders.

To view the folder contents of any available networked computer, double-click its icon. To view any shared folder's contents (listing of files), double-click a folder icon. To assign a local drive letter to a shared folder, right-click the folder's icon and choose Map Network Drive, (see fig. 19.25). Choose a drive letter and click OK.

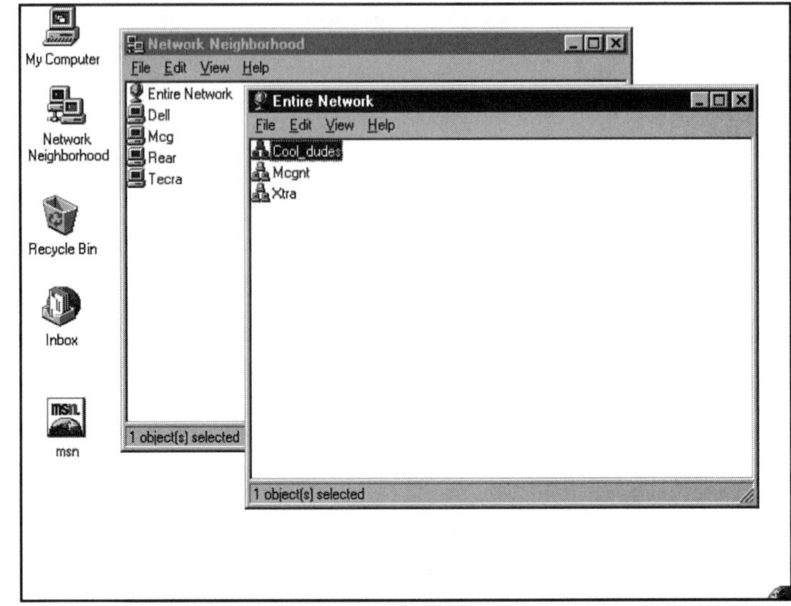

Fig. 19.24
You can access The Network Neighborhood window by double-clicking the Network Neighborhood desktop icon which is dislayed after Windows 95 networking parameters have been properly set up.

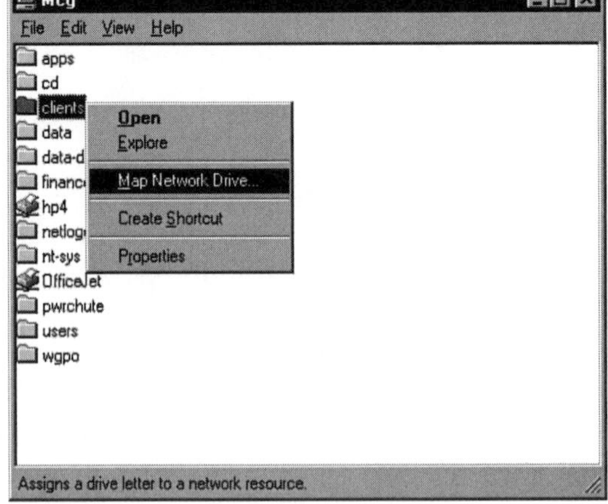

Fig. 19.25
You can use the shortcut menu to map a network drive.

Disconnecting from a shared network folder is just as easy. Right-click the network drive letter icon in the My Computer window, or use the Windows Explorer and choose Disconnect.

Sharing a Local Folder on the Network

To share a local folder on the network, open the Explorer or double-click My Computer to open its window. Right-click a local drive letter or folder and select Sharing from the shortcut menu. An alternate method for sharing is to click a local drive letter or folder, and choose File, Sharing.

The Properties sheet for the drive appears with the Sharing page open (see fig. 19.26). Select the Shared As option button and enter a Share Name and a Comment. Click the Add button to open the Add Users dialog box. Specify which network users can access this resource and assign those users network access permissions (see fig. 19.27). Click OK when you're done. Click OK again in the Properties sheet.

To stop sharing a folder, right-click the folder and choose Sharing. Select the Not Shared option button and click OK to apply the change.

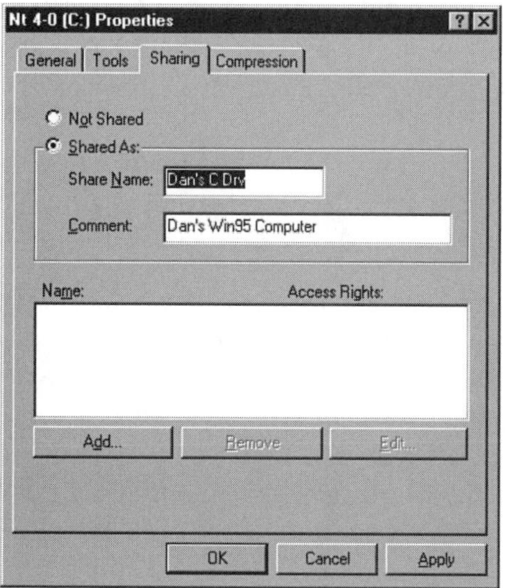

Fig. 19.26
The Sharing page of a local drive's Properties sheet gives you the option of sharing the local drive or folder with other users on the network.

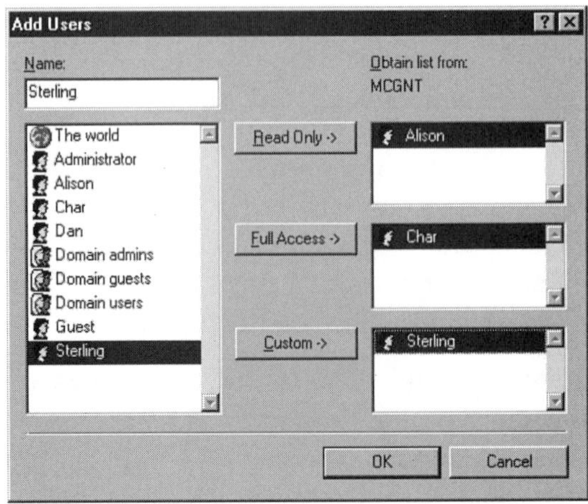

Fig. 19.27
The Add Users dialog box for adding network users and their associated permissions for accessing your PC's shared network resources.

Sharing and Connecting to Network Printers

To share a local printer that has already been set up, click the Start button and choose Settings, Printers, or, double-click the Printers folder located in the My Computer window. Right-click the local printer you want to share with the network and choose Sharing. You can also click the printer icon to select it and then choose File, Sharing. This procedure is very similar to the way in which a folder is shared. Click the Shared As option button and then click the Add button to add users and their permissions for accessing the printer. To stop sharing a printer, right-click the printer icon and choose Sharing or click the printer icon and choose File, Sharing. Select the Not Shared option and click OK to apply the change.

To connect to a network printer, click the Start button and choose Settings, Printers. Double-click the Add Printer icon to open the Add Printer Wizard. Click Next to proceed. Select Network Printer and click Next. Type the Network path for the printer you want to connect to, or click the Browse button. Select the network printer you want and click OK. Select Yes or No with regard to printer from MS-DOS-based programs and then click Next. Windows 95 might prompt you for the location of the installation files so it can install the appropriate printer drivers. Click Next to continue. Type a local name for the network printer and select whether you want to make this printer the system's default printer. Click Next. The Add Printer Wizard then asks if you want to print a test page. Leave this setting on Yes and click Finish. If the test page prints successfully, you are now connected to a network printer.

To disconnect from a network printer, click the Start button and choose Settings, Printers. Right-click the network printer you want to disconnect from and select Delete. Windows 95 asks you to confirm your choice. When you click Yes, the network printer icon disappears from your workstation's Printers folder. ❖

CHAPTER 20

Integrating Windows NT in Novell Environments

by Sue Plumley

Windows NT is perfectly suited for use with the Novell NetWare network. In most cases, you can install Windows NT over your existing software. If you're already connected to the NetWare network, NT detects this and automatically installs the Microsoft Client for NetWare. If you need to install the NetWare client and configure your workstation yourself, you'll find the task fairly straightforward.

Windows NT provides built-in drivers and protocols and 32-bit virtual device driver components for use with NetWare. Microsoft provides such excellent support for Novell NetWare because of NetWare's popularity and dominance in the network market. Being compatible with NetWare, Microsoft can more easily challenge Novell's hold over the marketplace.

This chapter shows you how to install the NetWare client and configure your Windows NT Workstation for use with the Novell network.

In this chapter, you learn to

- Use NetWare clients
- Employ NetWare file and print services
- Use NDS (NetWare Directory Services)
- Share resources in NetWare Environments
- Use the Gateway Service for Novell
- Migrate from Novell 3.12 to NT Server 4.0

Using Microsoft Client for NetWare

Using a NetWare client with your Windows NT Workstation provides you with access to file and print resources on NetWare servers as well as some NetWare utilities, such as drive mapping, volume information, and so on.

Additionally, using a NetWare client enables you to access a NetWare 4.x server that runs NDS (NetWare Directory Services). NDS is a Novell feature that displays shared objects on various NetWare servers in a hierarchical tree so you can easily locate the resources you want. You can also access a NetWare server that uses bindery-based and bindery emulation with the NetWare client. The bindery database contains definitions for entities such as users, groups, and workgroups.

You must configure the network to use a NetWare client before you can connect to the network. You also configure the adapter, protocol, service, bindings, and so on in the Network dialog box.

Tip

Novell will likely offer a client for Windows NT 4.0 that you can download from the Novell forum on CompuServe. Currently, that forum supplies a Windows NT 3.51 NetWare client.

On the Web

http://www.novell.com Novell's home page

http://support.novell.com/home/ Novell product support page

To open the Network dialog box, choose Start, Settings, Control Panel and double-click the Network icon. Figure 20.1 displays the Network dialog box.

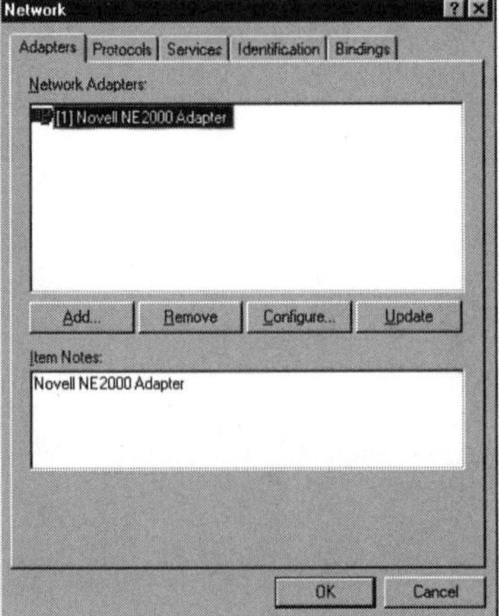

Fig. 20.1 Use the various tabs in the Network dialog box to configure for the NetWare network.

Installing Microsoft Client for NetWare

You must add the client service for NetWare before you can attach to a NetWare network. You can install either the Microsoft client for NetWare or a Novell client. The client you choose depends on your NetWare configuration.

◄ See "Installing the Network Hardware," p. 81

You should install the Novell client if any of the following are true about your NetWare site:

- Uses NCP (NetWare Core Protocol) Packet Signature
- Uses NetWare IP (Internet Protocol)
- Uses 3270 emulators that require a DOS TSR (Terminate and Stay Resident)
- Uses custom VLM (Virtual Loadable Module) components

If none of the preceding examples apply to your site, you can safely and successfully use Microsoft's client for NetWare. Microsoft's client for NetWare uses the NWLink IPX/SPX Compatible Transport protocol, which works well with NetWare.

> **Note**
>
> If you're using NetWare 4.x server configured for 802.3 protocol, you can use the NETX client; if you use the VLM client with the Novell NetWare 4.x server, you'll need to install the NetWare DOS Requester software to complete installation.

To install Microsoft's NetWare client, follow these steps:

1. In the Network dialog box, choose the Services tab (see fig. 20.2).

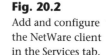

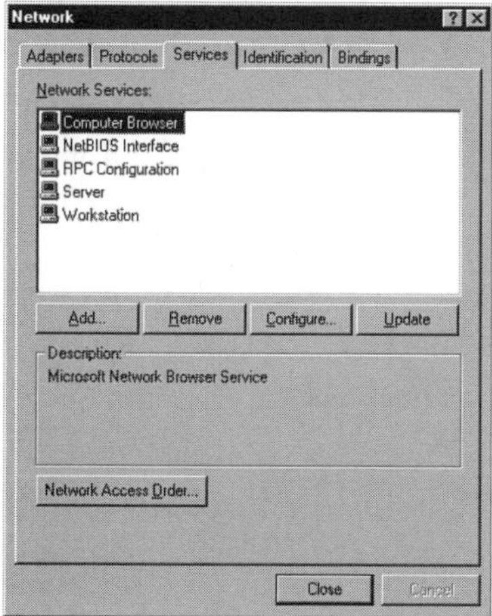

Fig. 20.2 Add and configure the NetWare client in the Services tab.

2. Choose the Add button. The Select Network Service dialog box appears (see fig. 20.3).

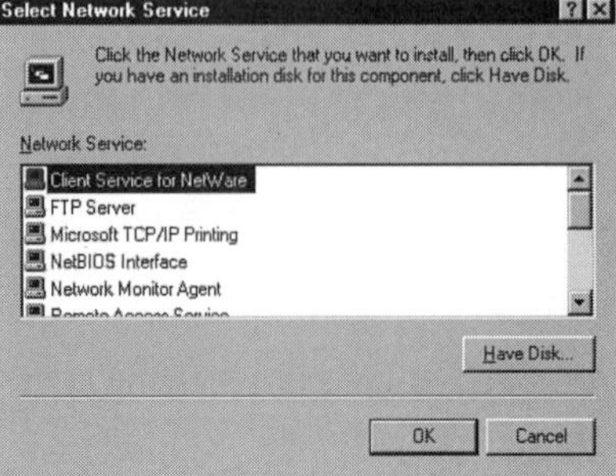

Fig. 20.3
Choose Microsoft's client for NetWare or install Novell's client.

3. To use Microsoft's client, choose Client Service for NetWare in the Network Service list.

   To use a Novell client, choose Have Disk. Insert the disk containing the client and enter the disk drive letter in the Insert Disk dialog box. Follow the instructions on screen to install Novell's client.

4. Choose OK to close the Select Network Service dialog box. Windows may prompt you for a drive and directory from which to copy files, usually the drive containing the Windows NT CD for the Microsoft client. When finished copying files, Windows returns to the Network dialog box and the client is added to the Network Services list.

5. Click the Close button to close the dialog box; alternatively, choose another tab in the Network dialog box to continue setting up the network.

> **Note**
>
> Check the Protocols tab of the Network dialog box to make sure you have the NWLink IPX/SPX Compatible Transport protocol, or a Novell protocol loaded for use with your client service. If not, choose the Add button and load the protocol.

Identifying the Computer

Your computer name is the name that identifies your computer to the network. You or your system administrator designate the computer's name but you can change it, if necessary. Make sure you discuss a computer name change with your system administrator before changing it, in case there are problems with the new name or in case you need permission to make the change.

To identify your computer to the network, follow these steps:

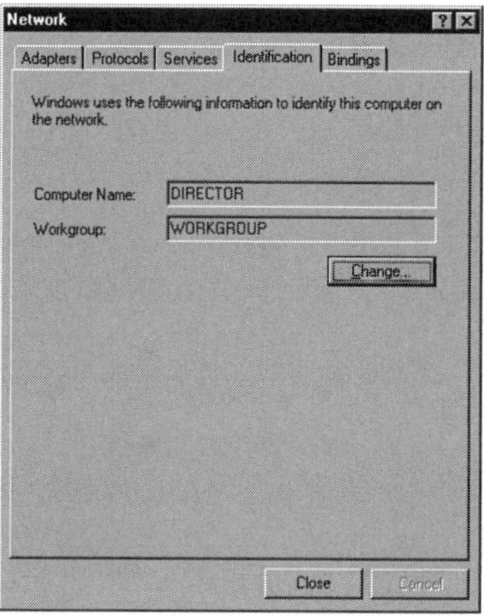

Fig. 20.4
You use a Computer Name with NetWare, but no Workgroup name.

1. In the Network dialog box, choose the Identification tab (see fig. 20.4).
2. Choose the Change button. The Identification Changes dialog box appears (see fig. 20.5).

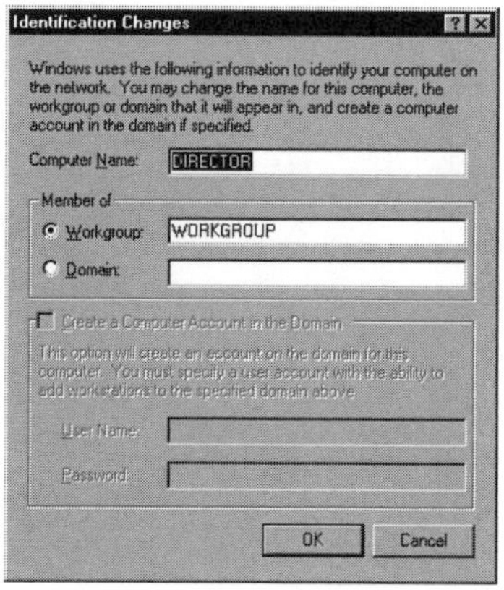

Fig. 20.5
You can designate a name to represent your computer, as long as you have your system administrator's permission.

3. In Computer Name, enter the new name for your computer.

> **Note**
>
> Workgroups and domains do not apply to Novell NetWare networks; they only apply to Windows-based networks, such as Windows NT Server or Windows 95 peer-to-peer networks.

4. Choose OK to close the dialog box and return to the Network dialog box. Choose Close or select another tab to configure.

Setting up Bindings

Binding is the process of assigning and removing protocols to and from the network adapter, protocol, and/or service. Each network adapter needs at least one protocol bound to the driver, else the driver cannot communicate across the network. You set bindings for the NetWare protocol in the Bindings tab of the Network dialog box.

To set the bindings for the NetWare client, follow these steps:

1. In the Network dialog box, choose the Bindings tab (see fig. 20.6).

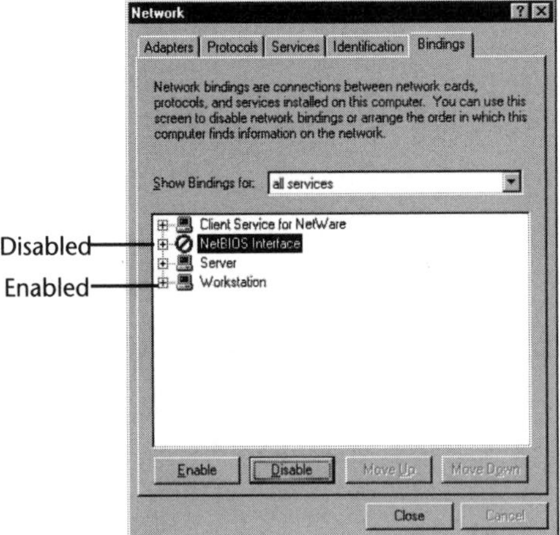

Fig. 20.6
Enable bindings so network communication can take place.

2. If the Client Service for NetWare is disabled, select the entry in the Show Bindings list and choose the Enable button.
3. Choose the Close button to complete the NetWare setup.

> **Note**
>
> Choose the Show Bindings For drop-down list box to set bindings for All Services, All Protocols, and/or All Adapters. A list of services, adapters, or protocols appears in the Show Bindings list box. Select the item and choose the Enable button.

Setting a Preferred Server

The preferred server is the default server you log on to when you log on to Windows NT. The preferred server checks your username and password to make sure you have permission to log on to the network; the preferred server also provides access to resources, such as files and printers.

> **Note**
>
> If your network is not an NDS environment, you should set a preferred server; if your network uses NDS, you'll use a default tree and context. Although NetWare enables you to use both a preferred server and default tree and context, Windows NT limits you to using one or the other; you cannot use both in the NT environment.

> **Caution**
>
> You can specify None as a preferred server and Windows NT will log you on to the nearest available NetWare server; however, you should specify a preferred server to avoid crowding a server that may be limited to a specific number of users or a server on which you are not a user.

To specify a preferred server, follow these steps:

1. In the Control Panel, double-click the CSNW icon. The Client Service for NetWare dialog box appears (see fig. 20.7).

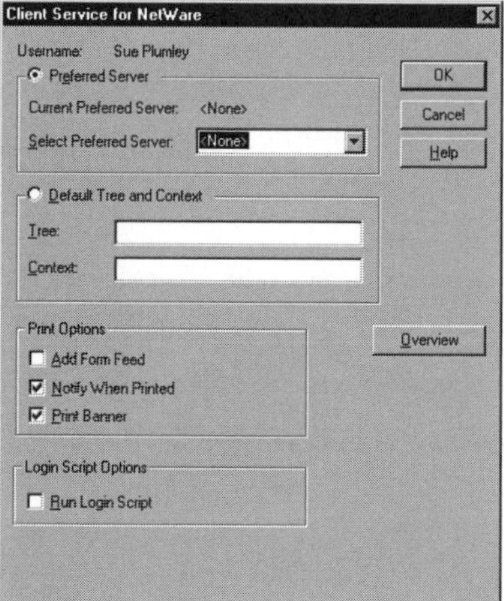

Fig. 20.7
You can choose to select a preferred server as a default.

2. In Preferred Server, select the server from the Select Preferred Server drop-down list box. If you do not see servers listed, see your system administrator for the exact name of the server you can enter into the text box.

3. Choose OK to close the dialog box. The changes will take effect the next time you log on to the network.

Note

You cannot use the NetWare login scripts with Windows NT; Windows NT does not support that scripting language. You can, however, assign a logon script in the User Manager using the User Environment Profile dialog box. NetWare uses the term "login" and Windows NT uses the term "logon;" both terms refer to the same process. You create the script file and store it in the logon script path: C:\SYSTEM32\REPL\IMPORT\SCRIPTS. If you use a login script, you must select the Run Login Script checkbox in the Client Service for NetWare dialog box (refer to fig. 20.7).

Tip

If your login scripts consist mainly of drive mappings, delete the script and map your drives through Windows NT, as described in the next section.

◄ See "Overview of System Administration," p. 164

◄ See "Managing User Profiles," p. 230

Troubleshooting

I can't get my Microsoft Client for NetWare to start.

The client services use NWLink, a protocol that enables your NT workstation to communicate with NetWare file and print servers. To make sure the NWLink is enabled, choose the Services icon in the Control Panel. In the list of services, find Client Service for NetWare. If it isn't started, select the service and choose the Start button.

If the client service is started, check the Event Viewer, System Log for any errors or problems that might be keeping the client from starting.

My client starts but I can't see the server.

You may not have the correct frame type selected for the NetWare. NetWare servers can use more than one frame type at a time. The default frame type for NetWare 3.11 and below is 802.3; default frame type for NetWare 3.12 and above is 802.2. Windows NT could have detected the wrong frame type. To check the frame type, click the Network icon in the Control Panel. In the Protocols tab, select the NWLink IPX/SPX Compatible Transport and choose the Configure button. In Frame Type, make sure the correct frame type is selected for your network. For more information about the network's frame type, see the network administrator.

I chose my preferred server but Windows displayed a message saying I cannot be authenticated on that server. Is there anything I can do?

Yes, if you have permission from the system administrator, you can choose Start, Programs, Administrative Tools, User Manager. In the User Manager, choose your name from the list of Usernames and choose the User menu, Rename command. Change your Windows NT username to your NetWare username. If you do not know your NetWare name or you cannot access the Rename dialog box in the User Manager, see your system administrator.

Using NetWare File and Print Services

Windows NT provides a way to map drives and capture printers without using Novell's NetWare utilities on your Windows NT workstation. Using the Windows NT features provides the same results without the memory problems or the headaches.

Mapping a drive through Windows NT is easier than using NetWare's MAP command. The MAP command enables you to quickly access any folder or directory on the server. Additionally, you can add any network printer to use from Windows NT quickly and easily.

Mapping Drives

You can avoid using NetWare's MAP command by mapping your drives through the Network Neighborhood in Windows NT. When you map a drive, you assign a drive letter to a network resource, such as a drive or folder. Mapping drives makes access to network resources faster and easier than opening several layers of windows to find the resource on the server or the network.

Tip

You can map your drives in Windows rather than adding search paths and mapped drives in a login script; it's easier and more efficient.

You might choose to connect a map as a root of the drive to help keep path statements from getting too long; for example, map to document directory F:\CARLOS\NOTEBOOK\WINWORD\DOCS so you use the mapped drive of J instead of the entire path. Not only is the path shorter and easier to type, but the path remains the same even if you access different folders in the NOTEBOOK directory.

To map a drive, follow these steps:

1. Open the Network Neighborhood and select the folder representing the shared directory you want to map to.
2. Choose File, Map Network Drive. The Map Network Drive dialog box appears (see fig. 20.8).

Fig. 20.8 Mapping drives makes getting to your work folders easier and more efficient.

3. In the Drive drop-down list, select an unassigned drive letter.
4. In Connect As, enter a username if you do not want to connect to the server using your logon name.
5. If you do not want to connect to the shared directory the next time you log on, disable the Reconnect at Logon checkbox.
6. Choose OK to close the dialog box and map the drive. Figure 20.9 shows the mapped drive connection in the My Computer window.

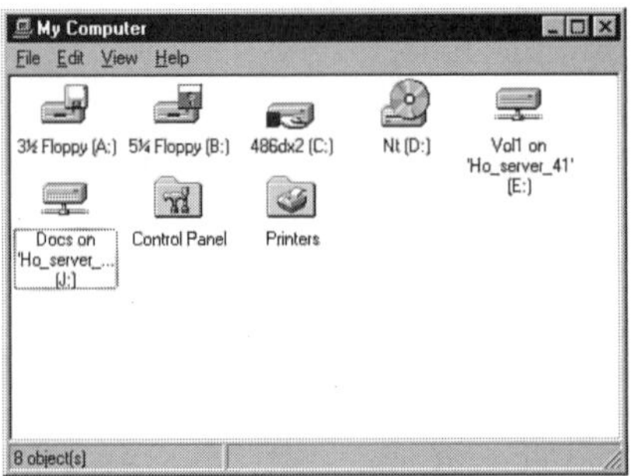

Fig. 20.9 Map a drive so you don't have to go through layer upon layer of windows and folders.

Capturing Printers

To use a printer on the network, you must connect to a NetWare print queue. You don't actually connect to a printer on the network; you connect to the print queue, and the server configuration determines which printer to send your job to. If one printer is busy, for example, the NetWare print queue may hold your print job or send it to another printer.

You capture a NetWare printer in Windows NT by using the Add Printer wizard. After adding the network printer, you can print to the NetWare print queue just as you would to a Windows NT printer.

To capture a printer, follow these steps:

1. Choose Start, Settings, Printers and double-click the Add Printer icon. The first Add Printer Wizard dialog box appears (see fig. 20.10).

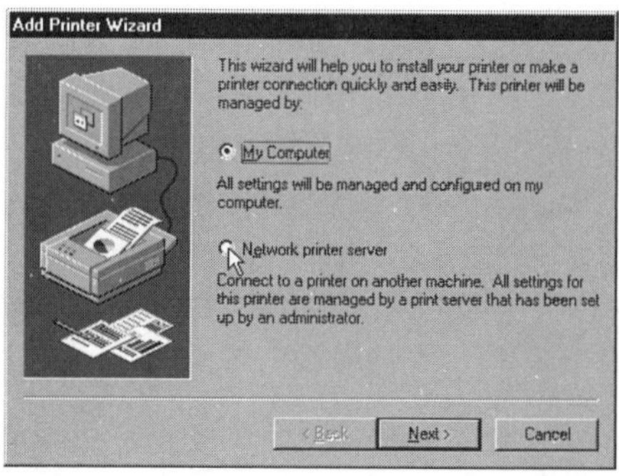

Fig. 20.10
A captured printer follows only those settings predetermined by the administrator.

2. Choose the Network Printer Server option and then choose Next. The Connect to Printer dialog box appears.
3. In the Shared Printers list, double-click the server to expand the list. Select the network printer you want to use. The printer's name appears in the Printer text box (see fig. 20.11).

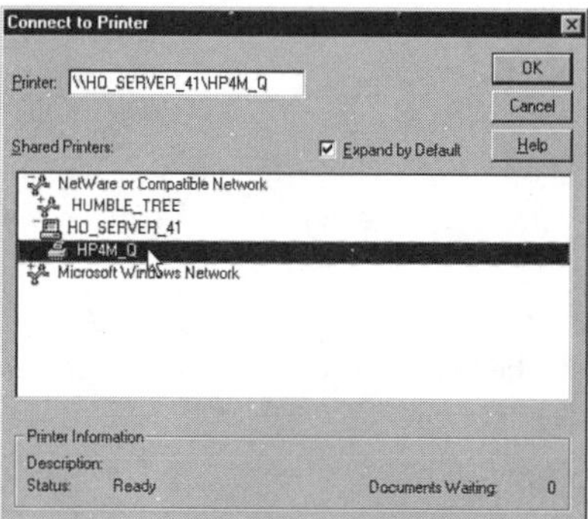

Fig. 20.11
Find the shared printer on the NetWare server or network.

Tip

You might need to double-click the tree in the Shared Printers list to see additional servers or computers on the network; then continue to expand those elements until you find the printer you want to use.

4. Choose OK to close the dialog box. The final Add Printer Wizard dialog box appears, telling you the printer was successfully installed.

5. Choose the Finish button. The printer appears in the Printers window (see fig. 20.12).

Fig. 20.12 The network printer is permanently installed to your system.

Note

You can set the print options: Add Form Feed, Notify When Printed, and Print Banner in the Client Service for NetWare dialog box (refer to fig. 20.7); double-click the CSNW icon in the Control Panel. These options are similar to those available directly on the NetWare server using the capture utility.

Troubleshooting

When I try to map using the NetWare MAP utility, I get a memory allocation error. Is it something I'm doing wrong?

The mapping table created by the NetWare MAP utility needs a default environment size in the Command Prompt window of at least 4,096 bytes. You can designate COMMAND.COM as the command interpreter for the Command Prompt window and reset the environment size by entering this command in the CONFIG.NT file:

```
shell=%systemroot%\system32\command.com /e:4096
```

Alternatively, you can use the Windows NT feature for mapping drives instead of using the NetWare MAP utility.

When I print to the captured network printer, no queues show up in the Print Manager. What's wrong?

If the print job is not showing up in your Print Manager, your Windows NT username and password don't match the username and password for the preferred server. The server validates your user credentials before it sends the jobs to the print queue. First you should check the Network Neighborhood to verify you can see the NetWare file server; if you cannot see the server, verify that your Client Service has started.

If the service has started and you have already logged in, you can use the SETPASS command at the MS-DOS Command Prompt to change your username and password on the NetWare servers. If you still have problems, see your network administrator.

Using NDS

NetWare Directory Services (NDS) is a NetWare feature that enables you to share resources on NetWare servers. NDS organizes the objects and displays them on a hierarchical tree that can span many servers. NDS provides you with global access to all network resources to which you have been given rights, no matter where the resources are located.

Understanding NDS

With NDS, users can log in to a multi-server network and view the entire network as a single information system, thus providing a more efficient view of the system.

NDS treats each network resource as an object. Some objects represent a physical entity, such as a user or a printer; some objects represent logical entities, such as a group or a print queue.

The NDS, also called the Directory, represents the network objects on a hierarchical tree structure, starting with a root object and then branching out.

When your system uses NDS, you become part of the tree as a physical object.

Specifying a Default Tree and Context

If your system uses NDS, you set a default tree and context to specify your position on the Directory. You cannot use a preferred server at the same time you're using NDS.

To set a default tree and context, follow these steps:

1. In the Control Panel, double-click the CSNW icon. The Client Service for NetWare dialog box appears (see fig. 20.13).

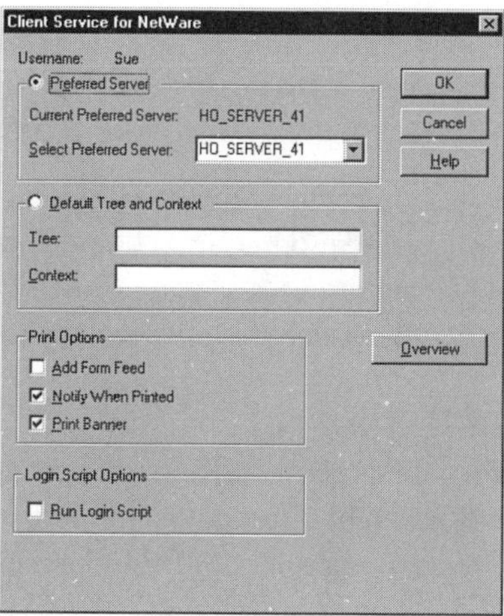

Fig. 20.13
You can choose either a preferred server or a default tree, but not both.

2. Choose the Default Tree and Context option.
3. In the Tree text box, enter the name of your default tree, such as humble_tree. Remember to use no spaces.

Tip

If you're unsure of your default tree, open the Network Neighborhood and double-click Entire Network. In the NetWare or Compatible Network window, your default tree should be listed beside a tree icon.

4. In the Context text box, enter the context of your user object.

Note

You can specify the context in either label-less or label format. You could enter MANAGER.WINNT.MICROSOFT or OU=MANAGER.OU=WINNT.O-MICROSOFT.

5. Choose OK to close the dialog box.

Sharing Resources in the NetWare Environment

You can share any resources—such as printers and folders—on the NetWare network as long as you have been granted the network rights by the system administrator. In Windows NT, you can view and connect to shared resources by using the Network Neighborhood window. To use the resources, you can capture the printer, open folders, and copy, read, or edit files as you would those on your own computer.

You cannot only view and connect to servers on the network, you can connect to other computers on the network and share their resources as well.

To share local resources—such as your printer or folders—with others on the network, you can right-click the resource and choose Sharing from the shortcut menu. Choose to share the resource as you normally would, by specifying a share name, user limit, and any permissions you want to add.

◀ See "Sharing File Resources," p. 164

◀ See "Sharing Printer Resources," p. 165

Browsing Shared Resources

You can view the network tree, the server, and other computers on the network through the Network Neighborhood. Expand any object, such as the tree or a server, by double-clicking the object. Available resources, such as files and printers, appear in the window. You can connect to any folder, for example, by expanding the folder and then opening, copying, or otherwise using that folder's contents. Naturally, you must have permission granted by the administrator to view and/or connect to network resources.

To browse shared resources, follow these steps:

1. Double-click the Network Neighborhood. If only the Microsoft network resources are shown, double-click Entire Network and then double-click NetWare or Compatible Network. The NetWare or Compatible Network window appears (see fig. 20.14).

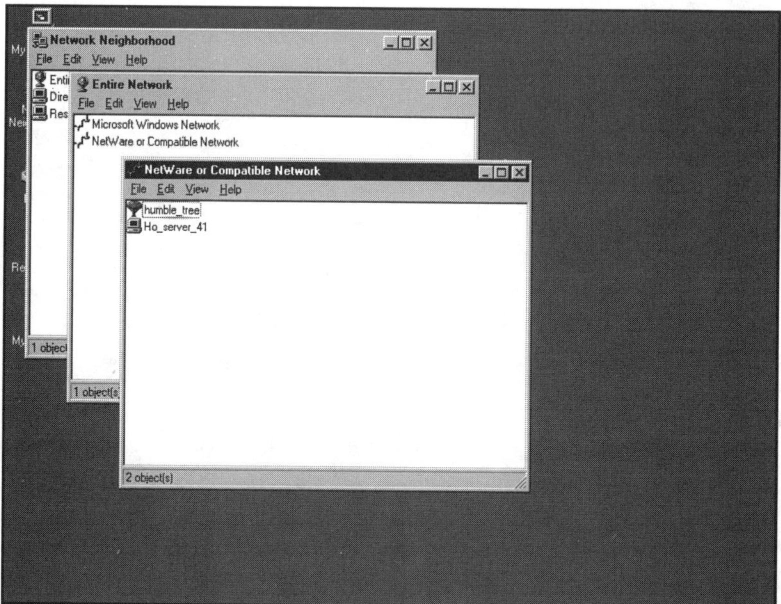

Fig. 20.14 The contents of the NetWare window depend on your system, the number of servers, NDS, and so on.

> **Tip**
>
> The Microsoft network resources include your computer and any other computer that uses Windows for Workgroups 3.11, Windows 95, or Windows NT.x, *and is* attached to the network.

2. To view the tree, double-click it. You can continue to double-click items in the window to expand them. Figure 20.15 shows the results of expanding the directory tree.

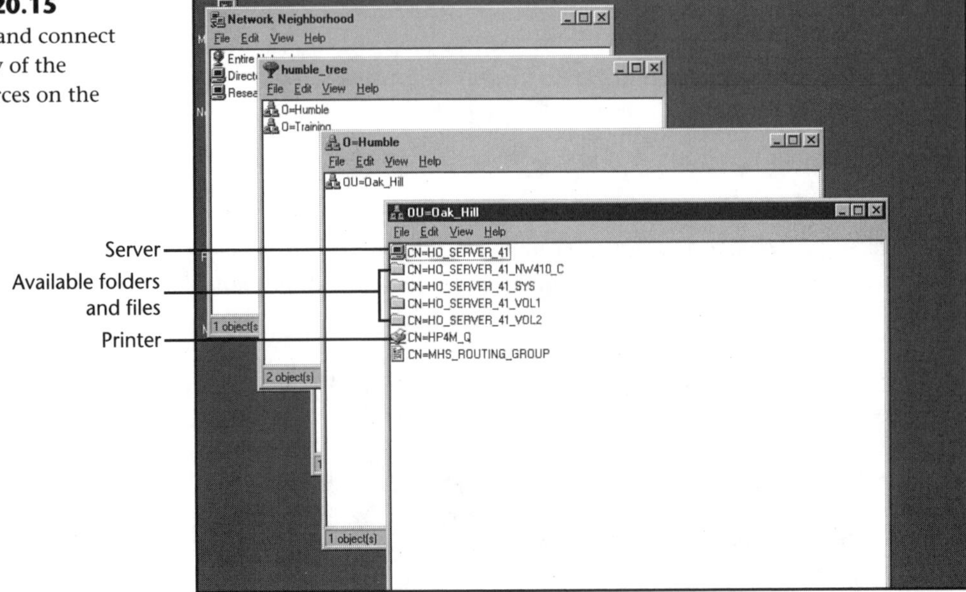

Fig. 20.15 View and connect to any of the resources on the tree.

3. To view the resources on any one server, double-click the server icon in the NetWare or Compatible Network window. Continue to expand by double-clicking the elements in the windows. Figure 20.16 shows the results of expanding the server.

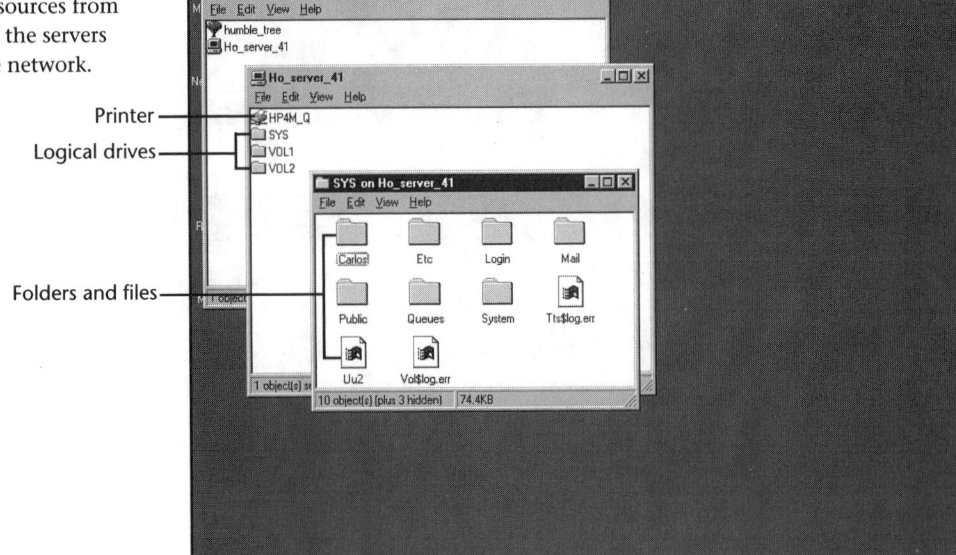

Fig. 20.16 Use resources from one of the servers on the network.

> **Note**
>
> You can use the NET VIEW command in a Command Prompt window to display servers and volumes on the network. To display volumes on a specific server, type: **net view \\<servername> /network:nw**.

Viewing Current Connections

You can view the current connections from the command prompt at any time using the NET VIEW command. The resulting screen tells you the local drive letter, the server name and volume and/or folders, and the network type.

To view the current connections from the Command Prompt window, follow these steps:

1. Choose Start, Programs, Command Prompt. The Command Prompt window appears.
2. At the command prompt, type **net use**. Figure 20.17 shows a resulting window.

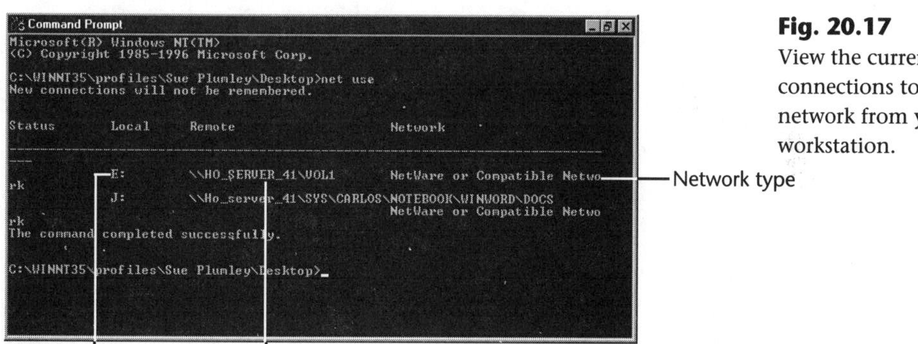

Fig. 20.17
View the current connections to the network from your workstation.

You also can view the current connections from the My Computer window, although you'll not see as much information as you would using the command prompt. Current connections in the My Computer window display the folder or volume name, instead of the path, the drive letter, and the server name (see fig. 20.18).

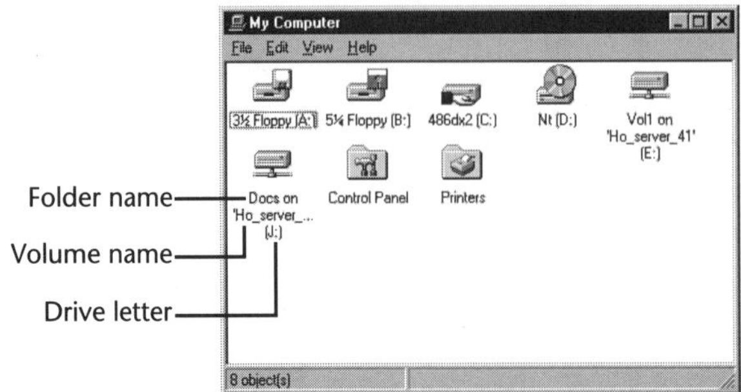

Fig. 20.18
Use resources from one of the servers on the network.

Tip

A red X appears through any connection that has been severed in the My Computer window, but the drive letter and server name remain.

Using NWLink

NWLink is a transport protocol that is IPX/SPX-compatible. Microsoft ships NWLink with Windows NT and enables you to use that protocol for communication with the NetWare network. NWLink supports the sockets application program interface (API) that some NetWare-based applications servers use to communicate with client computers. Thus, your Windows NT computers can act as clients in a NetWare client/server environment.

NWLink does not include a NetWare-compatible redirector, so you can't access NetWare file servers or shared printers solely with NWLink. That's why Microsoft ships with Windows NT NWBLink, a transport stack that runs alongside NWLink providing NetBIOS support similar to that provided by Novell.

When using NWBLink on an Ethernet, you may need to set your frame types; frame types refer to the format of IPX/SPX packets on your network. You can configure your network to run with either the IEEE 802.3 (CSMA/CD) or IEEE 802.3 (Logical Link Control) frame formats. You normally use 802.3 for NetWare 2.2 or 3.11 servers and frame type 802.2 with NetWare 4.x servers.

Note

In lieu of a gateway service, as supplied by Windows NT Server, using the NWLink is one connectivity solution.

By default, the NWLink IPX/SPX NetWare compatible protocol installs when you install the Microsoft Client for NetWare. Additionally, Windows generally detects the frame type used by the network and sets it for you. If, however, after installation you want to bind the NWLink to a different network card or for any other reason change the frame type, you can.

To configure NWLink, follow these steps:

1. In the Control Panel, choose the Network icon.
2. Choose the Protocols tab and select NWLink IPX/SPX Compatible Transport.
3. Choose the Configure button. The NWLink IPX/SPX Properties sheet appears (see fig. 20.19).

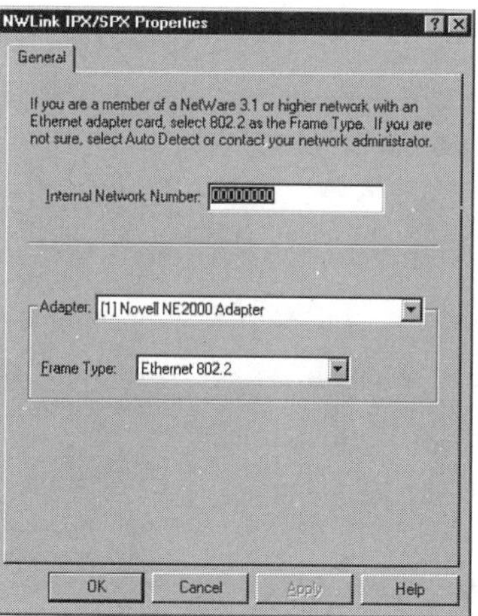

Fig. 20.19
Configure the frame type for your protocol using the NWLink IPX/SPX Properties sheet.

4. In Adapter, choose the correct adapter, if it's not already showing.
5. In Frame Type, click the down arrow and choose the frame type you need for your adapter card.
6. Choose OK to close the dialog box and apply the change. Choose Close to close the Network dialog box.

Using NetWare and Windows NT Clients

Windows NT is set up so you can view and connect to both a NetWare network and a Windows network, such as Windows for Workgroups, Windows NT Server, or Windows 95. You do not need to delete your NetWare client and configurations to attach to a Windows network.

The capability of attaching to two different servers adds multiple benefits for the user. With the two different types of servers comes two different types of users, computers, and resources available to each user on the network.

> **Note**
>
> Running two different server environments in parallel is a chore for the system administrator. User accounts, remote access services, and backup services aren't shared. Memory management as well as a lack of drivers may become problems.

To add the Windows network to your workstation, you'll need to install protocols you can use with Windows, such as NetBIOS/NetBEUI and/or TCP/IP. Your system administrator can clarify the protocol type you'll need. You don't want to remove the IPX/SPX protocol installed for NetWare; leave it set up as it is.

Other than that, all you need to do is open the Network Neighborhood to attach to the server and network of your choice. Figure 20.20 illustrates the path to the folders available on a Windows NT Server.

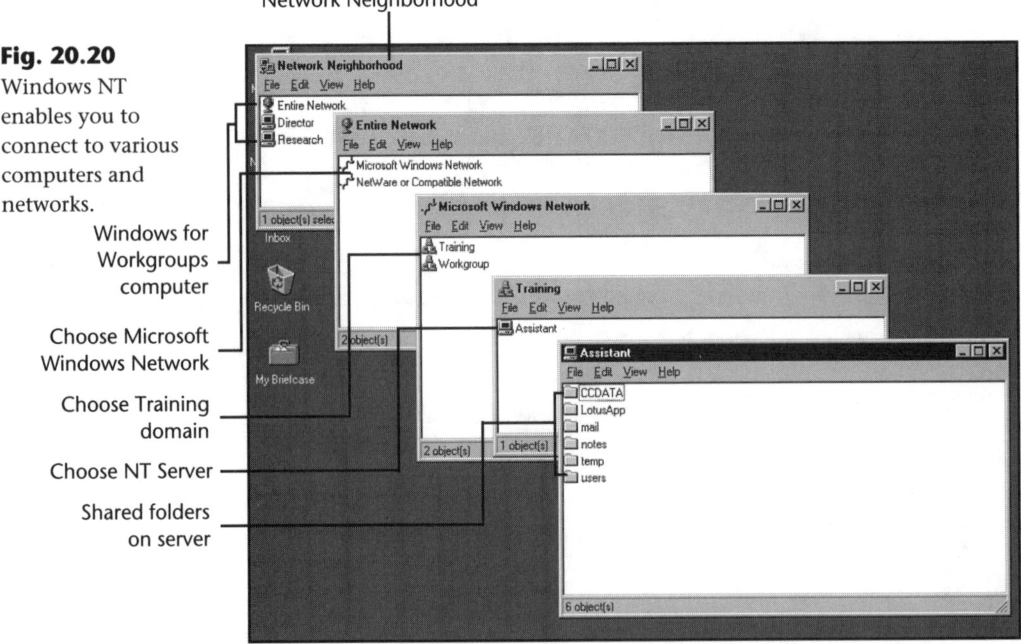

Fig. 20.20
Windows NT enables you to connect to various computers and networks.

Installing the Gateway Service for Novell

A gateway is a link between two networks that allows communication between dissimilar protocols, such as NetWare (IPX/SPX) and Windows NT Server (NetBEUI). Windows NTs Gateway Service enables all NetWare resources to become Windows NT resources as well. What this means is that you only need to run one set of network software on the client, backup and remote access services can be integrated, security can be integrated, and you can bypass NetWare user limitations.

> **Note**
>
> To use the Gateway Service, you must have the NetWare Client Service installed on the Windows NT computer, as described earlier in this chapter, and the Windows NT user must have a valid account on the NetWare server.

Installing the Gateway Service

You install the NetWare Gateway Service from the Windows NT Server. When you install the service, you also install NWLink.

To install the Gateway, follow these steps:

1. Open the Control Panel and double-click the Network icon. The Network Properties sheet appears; choose the Services tab (see fig. 20.21).

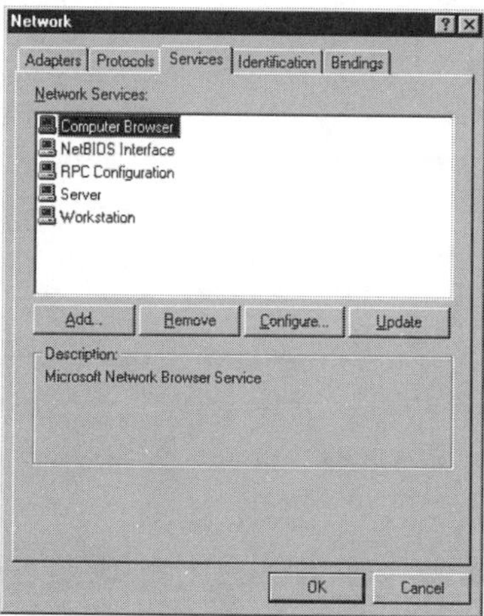

Fig. 20.21
Install the Gateway Services from the Services tab of the Network Properties sheet.

2. Choose the Add button to view the options for other add-ons to NT. The Select Network Service dialog box appears (see fig. 20.22).

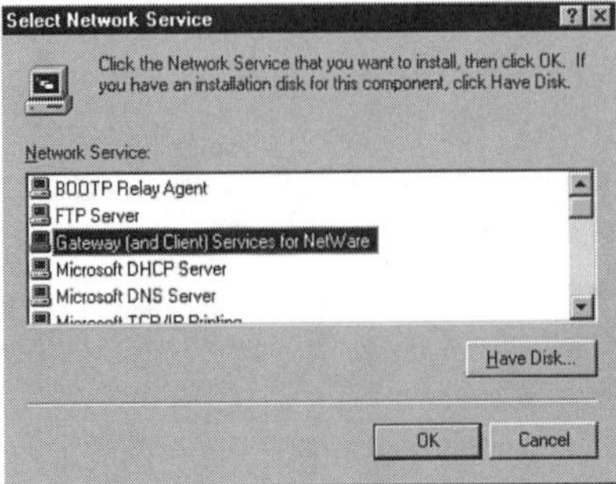

Fig. 20.22
Windows NT loads available services from which you can choose; locate the Gateway service.

3. Choose the Gateway (and Client) Service for NetWare in the Network Service list. Choose OK.
4. Enter the path to the setup files (generally to the CD). Windows NT copies files and then adds the Gateway Service for NetWare to the list of Network Services.
5. Choose OK to close the Select Network Service dialog box. When Windows NT returns to the Network Properties sheet, choose OK. Windows NT notifies you to shut the computer down for the new settings to take effect. Choose Yes. While the computer boots, you should prepare the NetWare server as described in the next section.

> **Note**
>
> If you're running Remote Access Services (RAS), setup displays a message asking if you want to configure RAS to support NWLink protocol. Choose OK if you want to configure RAS for IPX/SPX or Cancel if you do not.

Creating the User

While your Windows NT Server is rebooting, you need to create a user and Windows NT group on the NetWare server. You can prepare the NetWare servers for the Windows NT client from any NetWare-attached workstation.

To create the user, follow these steps:

1. Run SYSCON, NETADMIN, or NWADMIN from the NetWare-attached workstation.
2. Create a user on the NetWare server that matches the user that will log on from the Windows NT computer. Set the password for the user.

3. Create a NetWare group called NTGATEWAY and place the newly created user in that group.

   Now you can go back to the Windows NT Server to complete the process.

4. When the Windows NT Server has rebooted, the Select Preferred Server for NetWare dialog box appears. Choose Cancel.

5. The server displays a message dialog box asking if you want to continue; choose Yes.

6. Open the Control Panel and open the icon labeled GSNW; the Gateway Service for NetWare dialog box appears (see fig. 20.23).

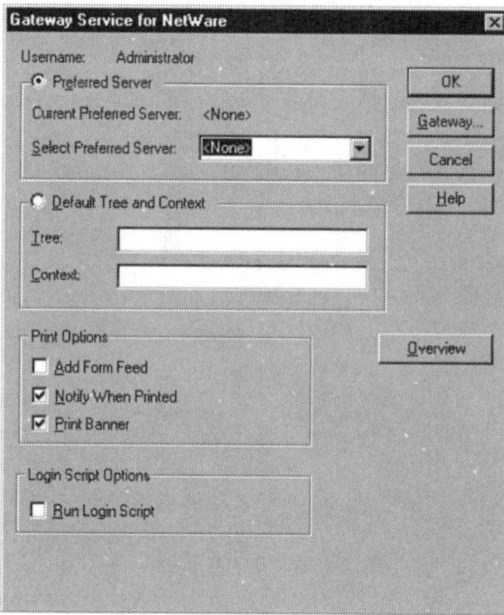

Fig. 20.23
Set preferred server and/or tree and context in the GSNW dialog box.

7. In the Select Preferred Server dialog box, choose your preferred server.

8. Choose OK to close the dialog box and then close the Control Panel.

Configuring the Gateway

After installing the Gateway service, you'll have to enable the service and create the user's account for the Windows NT clients to see the NetWare resources.

To configure the Gateway, follow these steps:

1. Open the GSNW icon in the Control Panel and click the Gateway button. The Configure Gateway dialog box appears (see fig. 20.24).

2. Choose the Enable Gateway checkbox and enter the user's name in the Gateway Account text box; fill in the user's Password, Confirm the Password, and choose OK.

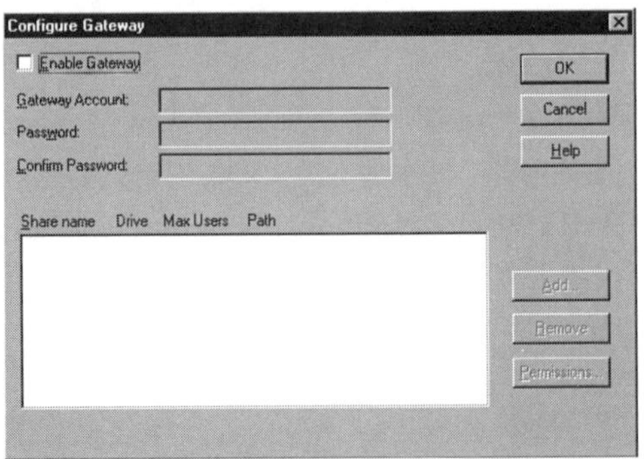

Fig. 20.24 Add clients and enable the Gateway by configuring the service.

Troubleshooting

My NetWare volumes are not available for sharing. How do I correct the problem?

Open the GSNW icon in the Control Panel and click the Gateway button. Choose the Add button. In the New Share dialog box (see fig. 20.25), enter the Share Name, Network Path, Comments, and the drive you want to use (Use Drive). Choose OK to return to the Configure Gateway dialog box and then choose OK again.

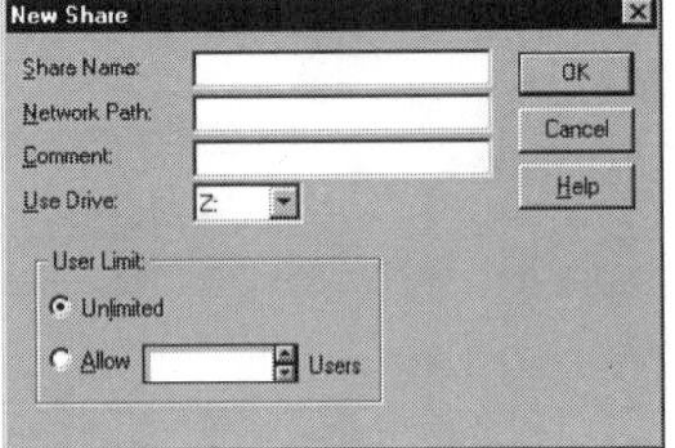

Fig. 20.25 Share NetWare volumes by specifying a share name and path to the volume.

Migrating from Novell to Windows NT

You might want to change from a Novell 3.12 or below network to a Windows NT-based network instead of upgrading to Novell 4.x because of Windows NT's graphical interface, administration tools, users' comfort with Windows, abundance of Windows applications, and so on. Normally, you use the Gateway Service as a preparation step to migrating completely to the Windows NT network. After installing and using the Gateway Service for a while, your users become more familiar and comfortable working with Windows NT.

Note

You cannot use Microsoft's Migration Tool to migrate from a Novell 4.x network to a Windows NT network. Since NDS is much too complicated to migrate, the Migration Tool does not enable you to access a 4.x server.

To change from a Novell-based network to a Windows NT-based one, you perform an over-the-wire migration, meaning you transfer all of your data to the Windows NT Server and rebuild all of your Novell users on the Windows NT server. You can, of course, migrate across more than one pair of servers at one time.

Windows NT's Migration tool helps you transfer data and rebuild your Novell users on the Windows NT server; however, this is no small chore. Luckily, the Migration Tool provides you with a trial migration so you can troubleshoot and solve problems before you perform the actual migration.

Caution

The Migration tool is not a tool for locking or joining Windows NT and NetWare accounts, it's a tool you use when you're completely abandoning NetWare for Windows NT.

To start the Migration Tool for NetWare, follow these steps:

1. Choose the Start menu, Programs, Administrative Tools, Migration Tool for NetWare. The Select Servers for Migration dialog box appears (see fig. 20.26).

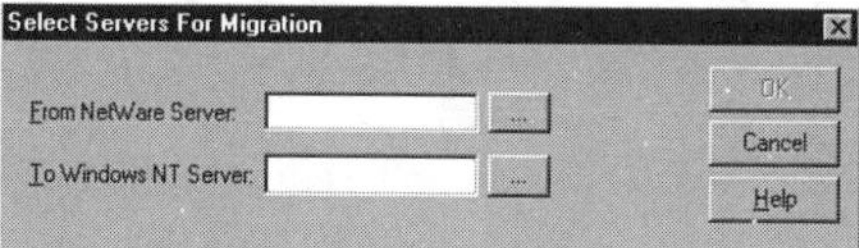

Fig. 20.26 Select one or multiple NetWare and Windows NT servers to migrate.

2. In the From NetWare Server text box, enter the NetWare server's name; in the To Windows NT Server text box, enter the Windows NT server's name.

Tip

Click the Browse buttons (the ones with an ellipsis on them) to view the servers and select them rather than typing in the servers' names.

Caution

To select a NetWare Server, you must be logged on as a Supervisor; to transfer data to a Windows NT Server, you must be logged on as a member of the Administrator's group. If your credentials are not verifiable, you cannot continue with the migration.

3. Choose OK to display the Migration Tool for NetWare dialog box.
4. Choose one of the following buttons to set options:

   Add. Add a NetWare or Windows NT server to the list; you can add multiple servers for migration.

   Delete. Select and then remove a pair of servers from the list for migration.

   User Options. Set options for transferring users, such as passwords, usernames, group names, and so on.

   File Options. Set options for transferring directories and files; use this option to choose which files you want to copy to Windows NT.

   Logging. Set up the log options to record the process in case you have problems and need to view the log files.

   Exit. Exit the Migration Tool without performing the migration.
5. When you're ready, choose one of the following:

   Trial Migration. Tests the migration process so you can see the results of the migration before you choose to actually start the migration.

   Start Migration. Starts the migration process.

Tip

It's a good idea to perform a Trial Migration in case there are unforeseen problems, such as user name or group name conflicts.

If you choose to go ahead with the migration, follow instructions on screen to complete the process. ❖

CHAPTER 21

Integrating Windows NT in UNIX Environments

by Chris Turkstra

The UNIX operating system has been around for over 20 years, and originally was a mainstay in the academic computing world. It has gained popularity more recently in the business world. UNIX systems were the first foray into client/server computing for many companies. Today, you can find UNIX running mission-critical applications in many corporations, as well as running many of the computers connected to the Internet.

Microsoft has put much effort into taking Windows NT beyond basic network connectivity to a level of UNIX interoperablility. More specifically, Windows NT users can use resources on UNIX systems and vice versa.

While Microsoft has provided much of the framework, it has relied on vendors to provide much of the software needed for full functionality. Specifically, very basic clients come bundled with Windows NT that allow you to use files, printers, and applications on UNIX systems—tools like ftp, lpr, and Telnet. In order to provide broader interoperability, you need to purchase third-party software like NFS and X Windows Servers.

This chapter is divided among three areas: file services, print services, and application services, which cover tools included with Windows NT and third-party products that add functionality.

In this chapter, you learn to

- Install and configure both Windows NT and third-party file transfer programs
- Get the most out of UNIX print services
- Use Telnet and X Windows to run most UNIX applications on Windows NT

- Use other UNIX services and commands such as SNMP, finger, nslookup, simple TCP/IP, and third-party tools

Since the native language of UNIX networks is TCP/IP, the central part of connecting your Windows NT systems with UNIX is the TCP/IP protocol. The TCP/IP Protocol must be installed before any of the programs in this chapter will run. See Chapter 24, "Installing and Configuring TCP/IP," for the details of installing TCP/IP.

File Services

The most basic network service is the ability to transfer data between systems. Windows NT comes with several text based client programs (ftp, tftp, rcp) to transfer data back and forth with UNIX systems, and a simple service (checkmark server) to allow UNIX systems the same capability. Third-party products enhance these capabilities.

ftp—File Transfer Protocol

ftp is probably the tool most often used for UNIX file transfer. The ftp client allows you to "get" and "put" files on remote systems, and is installed with the TCP/IP protocol.

> **Caution**
>
> Since the File Transfer Protocol was devised primarily for academic use, security was not a huge issue. As a result, ftp transfers usernames and passwords over the network as unencrypted text. A hacker attached to the network along the route your data flows could use a sniffer to capture your usernames and passwords.

The commands supported in the text mode ftp program are rudimentary, but have been enough to get the job done on UNIX systems for a long time. Chapter 25 has a detailed description of the command-line ftp utility, so I won't cover its usage in detail here. You've probably used ftp (maybe through a World Wide Web browser) to transfer files to and from systems on the Internet.

The text based ftp client (FTP.EXE) allows you to transfer files back and forth to UNIX systems, but the ftp server allows UNIX systems to transfer files back and forth to Windows NT computers.

Troubleshooting

My company has a firewall to the Internet. I can use my Web browser through it, but when I click an ftp site, I get errors. I can ftp to other computers on my company network, so why can't I get to a site past the firewall?

ftp uses TCP port 20 to send data and port 21 to send control information (the commands). If you are behind a firewall to the Internet, check with the firewall administrator to see if these ports are allowed passage. There may also be additional steps you need to take (like sending quoted commands) to get through.

On the Web

Many third-party versions of ftp are available that give you graphical interfaces, quick file viewing, and drag-and-drop functionality. After using one of these programs, you probably won't use the text program again. A popular one is called WS_FTP and is free to home users. It is available in the /pub/win32 directory at:

ftp1.ipswitch.com

In previous versions of Windows NT, you installed the ftp server by adding Simple TCP/IP Services to your network configuration. In Windows NT 4.0, ftp server is installed as a part of Microsoft Peer Web Services and is no longer installed with Simple TCP/IP Services. See Chapter 26, "Setting Up an Internet Server with IIS" for information on installing an ftp server.

rcp—Remote Copy Program

rcp is a file transfer program that allows you to exchange files with systems running the rshd (Remote Shell Daemon) program. rcp works somewhat like a DOS copy command, with the addition of source and destination computers and some security. If you need to, you can have one computer copy files to a second computer from a third with a single rcp command. You may find it useful to think of rcp as a single line ftp session.

Note

A daemon is a UNIX program that runs at all times, waiting for a request for service or connection, servicing that request, and shutting down the connection. Daemons are similar to the Windows NT services.

The parameters to use rcp are as follows:

- rcp [-a | -b] [-h] [-r] [host][.user:]source [host][.user:] path\destination

  -a. Specifies ASCII transfer mode for files. This mode is identical to the

ftp ASCII transfer mode and is only used for text files. This mode converts the EOL characters to a CR for UNIX systems. If you don't specify a binary transfer mode, ASCII will be used.

-b. Specifies binary image transfer mode. This mode puts and gets files without translation.

-h. Specifies that hidden files should be transferred.

-r. Recursive copy. This will copy all files in all directories below the directory specified in the command line. Both source and destination must be directories, not files.

Host. Specifies the host computer to copy to or from.

user:. If you want to use a username different from what your current login, or if you specify the host as an IP address, you must specify the user.

path\\. Specifies the path to copy from or to. This path is relative to the specified users' logon directory.

A sample rcp command to copy a binary file called /tmp/msg1.dat from a computer named "candygram" to a /tmp/newmsg.dat file on a computer named "landshark" with the username "joeb" is:

```
rcp -b candygram:\tmp\msg1.dat landshark.joeb:\tmp\newmsg.dat
```

> **Note**
>
> In order to use the rcp command, each computer must specify the other computer in a file called .rmhosts or .rhosts. You can find out the syntax of .rhosts by typing "man rhosts" at the UNIX shell. Be sure to read the man page—there are severe security implications surrounding the .rhosts file.

tftp—Trivial File Transfer Protocol

The trivial file transfer protocol is a less secure version of ftp primarily used for booting X Terminals or other devices that need to download an operating system or configuration at powerup. There is no user authentication with tftp and no file browsing capability.

While Windows NT does not come with a tftp server, the client (TFTP.EXE) is installed when you install TCP/IP. It has the following options:

- tftp [-i] host [GET | PUT] source [dest]

  -I. Specifies binary image transfer mode. This mode should be used for transfers of binary (non-ASCII text) files.

Host. The name or address of the tftp server.

GET | PUT. You can specify either GET to transfer a file from the tftp server to your computer or PUT to send a file to the tftp server.

Source. Specifies the name of the file to transfer.

Dest. Specifies where to transfer the file to.

nfs—Network File System

nfs is probably the most useful tool for sharing data with a UNIX system. nfs allows you to mount a UNIX file system as a logical drive. For instance, using nfs you can map your U: drive to /mount/shared on the UNIX system. The only bad thing about nfs is that it doesn't come with Windows NT—you have to acquire an nfs client from a third party in order to use nfs.

Tip

A free tool named SAMBA is available that allows for nfs-like file system access without buying an nfs client. While the software is not supported by a corporation, SAMBA provides bidirectional disk mounting without modification to Windows NT.

Before you can mount a UNIX file system on your Windows NT computer, you need to set up the UNIX system to export (share) the nfs directory you need. You need root equivalent access (root is the UNIX administrator) to export a directory.

Start by using Telnet to connect to the UNIX system from Windows NT either by entering "start telnet <hostname>" from a command prompt or from a run dialog box. Log into the system with a root (or equivalent) account.

The UNIX command "exportfs" is used to set up shared directories. Running exportfs by itself will produce a list of currently exported directories. To export a directory on a UNIX system, you can do one of two things.

1. Edit the /etc/exports file and run "exportfs -a" on the UNIX system. The -a parameter tells the nfs server to export all directories in the /etc/exports file.
2. Use the "exportfs -i <filesystem>" command. The -i parameter for exportfs translates roughly to "ignore the /etc/exports file and share this directory anyway."

For example, to export the /usr/bin directory on a UNIX system, the command

```
exportfs -i -o ro /usr/bin
```

grants any system on the network read only access to the /usr/bin directory.

Directories exported with the -i parameter will not be automatically re-exported after a UNIX system reboots. Only directories listed in the /etc/exports file will be re-exported at system startup.

For more information on the exportfs command, including security options, read the manual page by entering the command "man exportfs" at the UNIX prompt.

nfs Export

An "nfs export" on a UNIX system is conceptually identical to sharing a directory of filesystem on a Windows NT computer. The information about which directories are currently shared on the UNIX platform is kept in the /etc/xtab file, and the file /etc/exports contain the directories that are exported with the "exportfs -a" command, a command usually run at the UNIX system startup.

Caution

nfs is unfortunately both powerful and insecure. If misconfigured (something that can actually happen quite easily), nfs can allow any user on any system access to the entire UNIX filesystem. Many popular hacks on UNIX systems use nfs for breaking in. Please make sure you know exactly what the ramifications of each command you enter. Consult your local UNIX guru.

After you have set up the nfs directory on the UNIX system, follow the instructions for your nfs client to mount the filesystem as a network drive on Windows NT.

Print Service Interoperability

Windows NT is capable of interacting with most lpd (Line Printer Daemon) printers—a UNIX standard that has aged incredibly well. The generic UNIX printing mechanism is specified in RFC (Request for Comments) 1179, and includes communications specifications for lpd (the print server portion) and lpr (Line Printer Remote)—the client portion. This includes printers attached directly to a UNIX machine and lpd compatible print servers such as Hewlett Packard Jet Direct cards.

Printing from Windows NT to UNIX Printers

Before you can print to a UNIX printer, you have to install the Microsoft TCP/IP Printing service.

Installing the Microsoft TCP/IP Printing Service

Microsoft TCP/IP printing can be installed from the Windows NT Control Panel. You install this service the same way you install any Windows NT service—through the services tab in networking. To start the setup process, follow these steps:

1. Launch the Control Panel, and double-click the network icon.
2. Select the Services tab, then choose the Add button. Windows NT displays a Select Service dialog box.
3. Select the "Microsoft TCP/IP Printing" service from the list.

When you select OK, the service will be installed and you will have to restart your machine for the service to take effect.

Installing the UNIX Printer

In order to print to a UNIX printer, you will need to set up a printer port. To add the port, follow these steps:

1. Select Settings, then Printers from the Start Menu.
2. Double-click the Add Printer icon as if you were installing a regular printer.
3. Even though you are printing to a network printer, keep the My Computer button selected—you are actually adding a virtual printer port to your system that you can assign printer drivers to.
4. Select Add Port to bring up the available port types. Windows NT will display an Add LPR Compatible Printer dialog box like the one shown in figure 21.1.

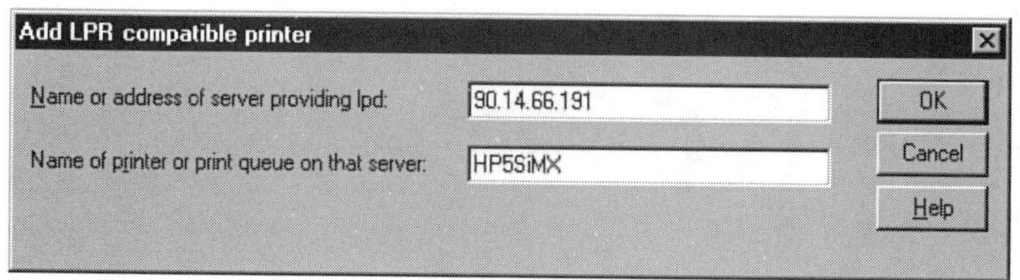

Fig. 21.1
The Add LPR Compatible Printer dialog box.

5. Fill out the first box with the DNS name or IP address of the print server, and the second box with the printer name.

Tip

If you are using a hardware print server, (such as a HP JetDirect Card) or you don't have the exact print queue name, it is usually possible to enter any text into the print queue name box—the default printer will be used.

At this point, Windows NT will attempt to send a test command to the UNIX Printer. A message box will pop up only if this command failed. If you are connected to the network and you get this message, you have probably entered something incorrectly. You'll need to check your settings and enter it again.

You should see your LPD printer listed in the printer port similar to the one in figure 21.2.

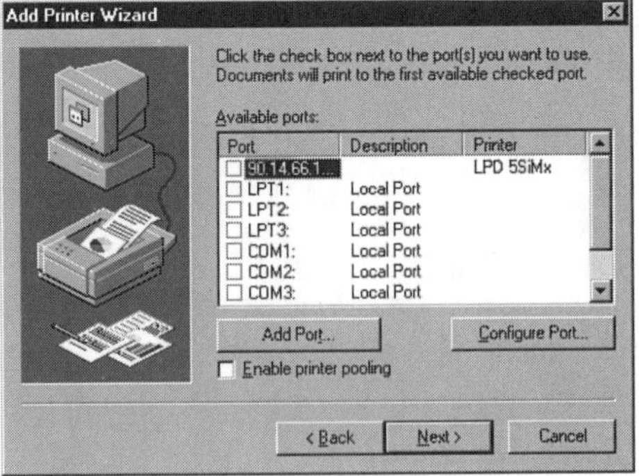

Fig. 21.2
Printer ports available with the LPD highlighted.

To assign a printer to your new port, do the following:

1. Make sure the box next to the UNIX printer port is selected and click Next.

2. From here, select the manufacturer and model of printer that you are printing to. Windows NT will probably need to copy some drivers from the NT CD-ROM at this point.
3. In the next window, type a name that you would like to see from your applications, such as "LPD Printer on HP box."
4. Now you have the opportunity to share this printer with other computers. If you choose to share the printer, you will need to enter a share name and select all the platforms that will be printing to it.
5. You should try to print a test page to test your setup. If you can successfully print the test page, you will be able to select this printer in your applications.

Sharing Your UNIX Printer with Other Workstations

You can share a UNIX printer and a Windows NT printer with other Microsoft network machines as long as you have a protocol (and security) in common with that machine. This means that you can set up one Windows NT workstation with both TCP/IP and IPX/SPX to act as a print UNIX printer server/gateway for a IPX/SPX only network. No other computers on that network require TCP/IP or Microsoft TCP/IP printing in order to print to a UNIX printer; they would simply print to the printer shared from your computer.

There are no special steps to sharing a UNIX printer. You can follow the steps outlined in Chapter 9, "Administering Servers and Sharing Resources" to create a printer share.

Printing from UNIX to Windows NT

Not only can you print to UNIX printers, you can let UNIX computers print to a printer connected to your Windows NT computer. The process of printing from UNIX to Windows NT involves starting the Windows NT lpdsvc and the UNIX command lpr. In the beginning of this section, we stated that Windows NT can print to any lpd compatible print server—starting the lpdsvc basically turns your Windows NT computer into an lpd compatible print server. Of course, you must have a printer you can print to (either networked or local) before you can share it with UNIX systems.

> **Note**
>
> Any printer you can print to from your Windows NT workstation, you can share with UNIX systems. This allows for many new configurations—including the possibility of printing to a Netware printer from a UNIX system through Windows NT.

To start the lpdsvc, either type

```
net start lpdsvc
```

at the command prompt; or open the Control Panel, double-click services, and select TCP/IP Print Services.

When you start the TCP/IP print service, printers that you have shared on your computer become separate print queues on a lpd print server. For example, if you have an HP LaserJet attached to your LPT1 port shared as "Local4Si" and your machine is named "Landshark," starting lpdsvc creates a printer named "Local4Si" on an lpd print server named "Landshark." You would print to this queue from UNIX with the command

```
lpr -S landshark -P local4si <filename>
```

You will need to substitute an IP address for "landshark" if you don't have a DNS or don't have an entry for "landshark" in the UNIX file /etc/hosts. See Chapter 24, "Understanding and Configuring TCP/IP," for more information on DNS and the hosts file.

Printing Utilities

The UNIX command lpq allows you to check the status of a print queue in a UNIX (lpd) print queue. The command syntax is

```
lpq -S <server> -P <printer> [-l]
```

The -S option is used to specify a lpd server name and is a required parameter. The server name can be an IP address, a UNIX host name, or a Windows NT computer with the TCP/IP print server (lpdsvc) started.

The -P option specifies a printer queue and is a required parameter. Because it is possible to have more than one computer at each lpd server, you must name the printer you need status for.

The -l option tells lpq to give verbose output about print jobs currently running. In practice, the -l option doesn't appear to actually add any information to the Windows NT report, but it may make you feel better when your jobs aren't printing.

The information returned by lpq from Windows NT's lpdsvc is: Owner, Status, Job Name (the filename), Job ID, Size, Pages, and Priority.

Application Interoperability

Microsoft has included the simplest UNIX application interface with Windows NT—Telnet. Telnet allows you to access the UNIX command prompt from a remote location. Because UNIX was designed to use a command-line interface (a shell), most UNIX applications and virtually all UNIX administration chores can be accessed from a simple Telnet session. Many UNIX gurus do 99 percent of their work from a Telnet session or a dumb terminal. Take a look in Chapter 25, "Using Internet Programs," for detailed information in Telnet.

X Windows

Like Windows NT, UNIX has a GUI called "X Windows." In X terminology, the server software runs on the computer that displays the program output, and the client software runs on the computer that does the processing. This means that when you talk about an X/server, you are referring to software running on the desktop computer. This GUI was only able to run on special X/Terminals until software companies came out with windows-based X/servers that turn your PC into an X/Terminal. Microsoft does not offer an X/server, but there is X/server software available from several vendors. Here are a few with information on how you can contact the vendors:

eXceed/NT
Hummingbird Communications Ltd.
(416)496-2200
www.hummingbird.com

eXcursion for NT
Digital Equipment Corp.
(800)344-4825
www.dec.com

PC Xware
Network Computing Devices, Inc.
(415)694-0650
www.ncd.com

Reflection
WRQ Corporation
(206)217-7500
www.wrq.com

Configuring eXceed for Windows NT

One of the popular X/server software for Windows NT is eXceed for Windows NT. Because this isn't an X Windows book, we won't cover how to install eXceed, but we will touch on how to use it.

Note

When installing eXceed, make sure you select Windows Sockets TCP/IP stack. Installing the stack supplied by Hummingbird (SuperTCP) may cause problems as Windows NT uses Winsock 2.0.

To start using eXceed, follow these steps:

- Start up the local X/server on your computer by running one of the Local X demos like Ico. This will allow you to see that the server is running.
- Use the Telnet application to connect and log in to the UNIX system.
- Run your application by entering its command and specifying your machine as the display parameter. The syntax for xclock (a simple graphical clock program) is

```
xclock -display <your IP Address>:0
```

If the path to xclock is present in your environment, an X window displaying your application should appear.

Tip

To run a UNIX command in the background (on most systems), add a "&" symbol to the end of the command. For example, entering

```
xclock -display <your IP Address>:0 &
```

will give you the UNIX prompt back in that Telnet session.

Other UNIX Tools

This section covers some of the other UNIX commands and services packaged with Windows NT.

Simple Network Management Protocol (SNMP)

SNMP is a protocol that provides basic administration information about devices attached to a network. SNMP is typically used by SNMP management software (Openview, Netview, SNMPc, and so on) that enables system administrators to get information on network connected devices from power conditioners to multiprocessor UNIX systems. In order to get information from a device, that device must be capable of broadcasting information or responding to SNMP queries. Windows NT 4.0 includes SNMP services that provide this functionality to SNMP management systems. This section will cover the installation and configuration of SNMP services on Windows NT.

Tip

Even if you don't use an SNMP manager, installing SNMP will give you some new capabilities. Performance Monitor will allow you to view and capture information about the TCP/IP protocol after your install the SNMP service.

You install the SNMP service the same way you install any Windows NT service—through the network windows services tab.

1. Launch the Control Panel, and double-click the network icon.
2. Select the Services tab, then choose the Add button. Windows NT displays a Select Service dialog box.
3. Select the "SNMP Service" service from the list.

When you select the OK button, the service will be installed and you will have to restart your machine for it to start.

Configuring SNMP

SNMP transfers information either as alerts (broadcasts) or in response to queries. With so many devices offering SNMP services, you can imagine how quickly a network can fill up with broadcast messages. Instead of flooding your network with messages indicating that all your devices are healthy, you should probably have important SNMP devices (servers, routers, and so on) send traps, but less important devices only respond to queries. If you choose not to send traps, your system could fail between the times your SNMP manager polls it, leaving you without any reason for its failure.

SNMP uses the concept of communities and destinations (hosts) as a method to help group your machines. A destination is a machine within a community. If you are familiar with TCP/IP, a community is like a network, and a destination is like a host—except there is no routing between communities. The Windows NT SNMP service automatically responds to queries from a community called "public" by default, but doesn't send traps to any community by default.

Agent tab. The Agent page (see fig. 21.3) tells the SNMP agent what information you wish to make available to SNMP management software.

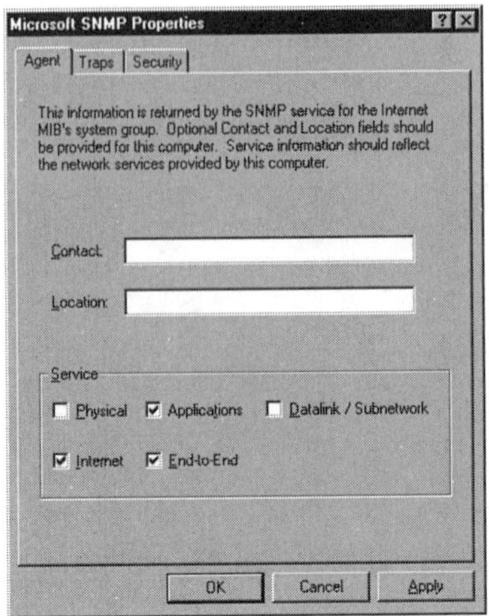

Fig. 21.3 The SNMP Agent page of the Microsoft SNMP Properties sheet.

You should type the name of the system administrator in the contact box and the machine's physical location or other identifying information in the location box. The Service group box allows you to specify what level of information you want to provide to SNMP queries or broadcasts. If you are broadcasting traps, minimize the number of boxes checked.

- *Physical.* Checking this box will enable physical medium network statistics.
- *Internet.* This box only applies if this workstation is an IP router. If so, this box will enable errors from higher level network software.
- *Applications.* Checking this box enables information and statistics from TCP/IP applications like WWW Services, ftp, and SMTP services.
- *End-to-End.* This box applies to computers that are end nodes on a network. If you are running TCP/IP, you should probably have this box checked.
- *Datalink/Subnetwork.* This check box only applies if your Windows NT workstation is acting as a part of a logical network—as a bridge, for example.

Traps tab. Traps are broadcast messages your SNMP service sends. This tab (see fig. 21.4) allows you to specify which community and destination to send traps to. If you leave the community box blank, the SNMP service will only respond to queries. After you have put in a community name or names, you can input a trap destination as a host name, IP address, or IPX address. If you specify a community or a host that doesn't exist, your SNMP traps will go unnoticed.

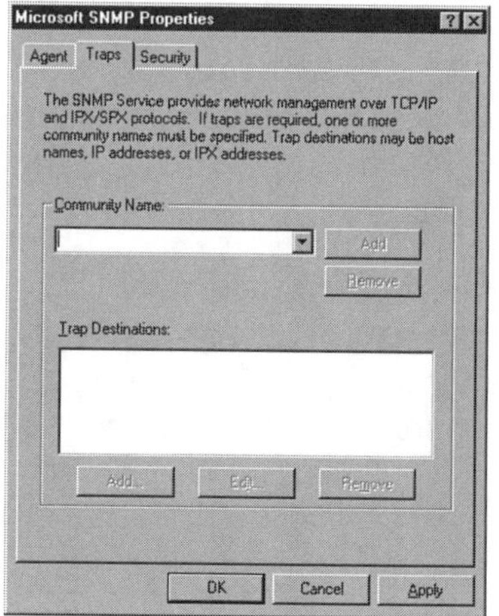

Fig. 21.4
The SNMP Traps page allows you to choose the community and destination to send traps to.

Security tab. The Security tab (see fig. 21.5) allows you to configure security options for the SNMP service. The check box at the top labeled Send Authentication Trap will direct the SNMP service to send an alert to the community and destination specified if unauthorized access is attempted. Unauthorized access is defined as a query coming from any community not listed in the Accepted Community Names list, or a host not listed in the Only Accept SNMP Packets from These Hosts list. To add communities or hosts, click the Add button and type in the desired name.

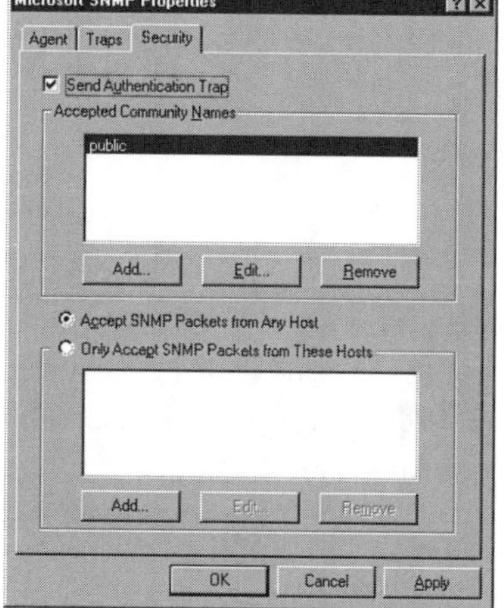

Fig. 21.5
The SNMP Security page lets you configure security options.

finger

While strangely named, finger is actually a useful tool. It allows you to find out information about a user or a domain from Windows NT. The basic finger syntax is

```
finger [-l] [user]@host
```

What information gets returned depends on the OS policies at the computer you are contacting. Some users have programs set up that will tell you some constantly updated information in their .project or .plan file. Others will tell you the last time the user logged in and their office and phone number. Finger can be a valuable tool for finding information from an e-mail address. If you finger with just an "@host" command, you may get information back about that computer system.

Nslookup

Nslookup is a diagnostic utility that gives you information culled from DNS (Domain Name Servers) servers. Nslookup basically allows you to convert IP addresses to host names and vice versa.

```
nslookup [-option ...] [computer-to-find ¦—[server]]
```

Although nslookup has an array of options, most people use it to test their DNS and convert IP addressed to DNS names. For the first argument, type the host name or IP address of the computer you want to look up. For the second argument, type the host name or IP address of a DNS name server. If you omit the second argument, the default DNS name server will be used.

The following code is output from NSLOOKUP:

```
C:\>nslookup 133.145.224.3 199.3.12.3
(null)    amerigo-fddi.cris.com
Address:  199.3.12.3
(null)    hitiij.hitachi.co.jp
Address:  133.145.224.3
```

Simple TCP/IP services

Windows NT supports Simple TCP/IP Services. In Windows NT 4.0 these services are truly simple. The TCP/IP services are installed from the networks services tab in Control Panel. They are

- Echo (RFC 862). Immediately returns characters.
- Discard (RFC 863). Discards sent characters.
- Character Generator (RFC 864). Returns a repeating pattern of characters.

- Daytime (RFC 867). Returns the system date and time.
- Quote of the Day (RFC 865). Returns a specified string.

These services each have a port assigned that you can look up in the "services" file. While these services may be of use in advanced TCP/IP testing, they should normally not be installed.

Other Tools

If you just can't get enough UNIX, it is possible to buy toolkits that are essentially Windows NT versions of popular UNIX programs. The MKS Toolkit from Mortice Kern Systems, Inc. includes almost 200 popular UNIX commands. Contact Information: Phone: (800)265-2797, Internet: **www.mks.com**. ❖

CHAPTER 22

Using Remote Access Services

by Richard Neff

One of the most powerful and useful items contained with Windows NT is the remote access service (RAS). RAS allows a Windows NT computer to allow remote users, such as telecommuters, to access the Windows NT network. The RAS client, known as Dial-Up Networking (DUN) in Windows NT 4.0, also allows a Windows NT computer to access outside networks, such as Internet Service Providers for access to the Internet. Windows NT provides this capability out of the box, so there is no extra software that needs to be purchased.

Security is also very important when transferring data across phone lines. Because network administrators have little physical control over who can dial into the network, stronger security measures have to be used to ensure network safety from unauthorized users. However, regular users should not be overly hampered by a complex security system. Windows NT RAS allows strong security options to be implemented without hindering remote access by authorized users.

Because Internet access is becoming very popular among Windows NT users, DUN provides a way of connecting to the Internet. After a DUN connection is established, most of the major Internet utilities can be run, such as Web browsers. Windows NT DUN provides a lot of flexibility with many types of remote access.

In this chapter, you learn to

- Install and configure a Windows NT RAS server
- Configure RAS Protocols on a RAS server
- Recognize supported RAS connection types

- Configure RAS security options
- Install and configure DUN clients
- Access remote resources using a Windows NT DUN client

Understanding RAS

Telecommuting is becoming very popular for many businesses. It allows a more flexible work arrangement for workers, and in some areas, laws have been created to force more companies to provide telecommuting options. RAS allows remote users access to a Windows NT network as if they were accessing the network from a computer in the office. Also, the Internet and other online services have become very popular areas for Windows NT users to connect, and DUN helps provide access to Internet providers.

Windows NT DUN provides both server and client software, so a Windows NT machine can receive incoming RAS calls as well as connect to a remote server. The server side of Windows NT's remote access is known as remote access services (RAS) and it is designed to handle remote users dialing into that computer to use network resources. The client side of Windows NT's remote access is Dial-Up Networking (DUN) and is designed to allow a Windows NT machine to connect to other servers via phone or other connections. This is a change from earlier versions of Windows NT, but the basic concept is still the same.

Dial-Up Networking (DUN)

A Windows NT computer using DUN can connect to the following Microsoft products:

- Windows NT 4.0 RAS Servers
- Windows NT 3.5 RAS Servers
- Windows NT 3.1 RAS Servers
- Windows 95 Dial-Up Networking Servers
- Windows for Workgroups RAS Servers
- LAN Manager RAS Servers

Additionally, Windows NT DUN can connect to other dial-in servers using the Serial Line Internet Protocol (SLIP) and Point-to-Point Protocol (PPP) standards.

Conversely, Windows NT RAS servers can be accessed by the following Microsoft client operating systems:

- Windows NT 4.0 DUN
- Windows NT 3.5 RAS
- Windows 95 DUN
- Windows for Workgroups
- MS-DOS
- LAN Manager

Also, any computers using non-Microsoft products can access Windows NT RAS with the Point-to-Point Protocol (PPP) standard.

Supported Network Interfaces for Applications

RAS also supports network applications that use the following:

- Windows Sockets
- NetBIOS
- Mailslots
- Named Pipes
- Remote Procedure Call (RPC)
- Windows NT (Win32) APIs
- LAN Manager APIs

Connection Limits

Both Windows NT Server and Windows NT Workstation can act as RAS servers. However, Windows NT Workstation can only allow one incoming or one outgoing remote user connection. Windows NT Server can have up to 256 simultaneous remote user connections to a RAS Server.

Tip

The inbound/oubound connections have an impact on how the Windows NT computer should be used. Using Windows NT Workstation as a RAS server is best for a user who wants to access their work computer at home. Windows NT Server is better for a dedicated RAS server.

However, when accessing NetBIOS resources over a RAS connection, the maximum number of simultaneous connections is 250 connections to a NetBIOS resource.

Software Compression

Software compression is supported in RAS. The compression type is based on the Microsoft DRVSPACE compression algorithm. This compression algorithm is used in MS-DOS 6.22 for disk compression and provides a 2 to 1 compression ratio, depending on the type of files being compressed. Compressing data under RAS provides faster connection speeds than uncompressed data.

WAN Support

Many connection types are supported between a RAS client and a RAS server. The different connection types provide different types of speed and cost benefits. The following connection types can be used:

- *Public Switched Telephone Networks (standard analog phone lines).* The most common type of remote connections are modem-to-modem connections over standard phone lines. This connection type is usually the least expensive type of connection. A modem and physical phone line are required for each client connecting to the RAS server.
- *X.25 Switched Networks.* X.25 switched networks send data called packets over a switched network. X.25 requires either direct access to a network via an X.25 card (required for the RAS server) or Dial-Up through an X.25 Packet Assembler/Disassembler (PAD). X.25 networks are usually provided through a commercial service and may not be available in all areas. Standard X.25 transmissions of up to 64 kilobits per second (Kbps) are supported. Revisions of the X.25 standard, developed in 1992, allow speeds of 2 megabits per second (Mbps) but are not widely used.
- *Integrated Services Digital Network (ISDN).* This standard is a purely digital communication link. It is designed to eventually replace the analog phone system used today. ISDN provides faster speeds than regular phone lines (about 64 or 128 Kbps versus 2.88 Kbps) and ISDN is quickly becoming popular for businesses that have a lot of remote telecommuters. However, ISDN requires either ISDN cards or adapters on both the RAS client and RAS server. Also, the phone company between the two points must set up an ISDN service to allow ISDN access. ISDN rates vary greatly between phone companies, so the cost benefit must be determined for the particular areas involved.

Protocols

The protocols that can be used to establish RAS connections are:

- *Serial Line Internet Protocol (SLIP).* SLIP was developed in 1984 to support TCP/IP connections over serial lines. SLIP is used to connect to UNIX and other hosts using TCP/IP. Windows NT RAS clients can use SLIP to connect to those hosts. However, Windows NT RAS servers can't be configured to be SLIP servers.
- *Point-to-Point Protocol (PPP).* PPP is an enhancement to the SLIP standard. PPP has become more common than SLIP for most remote access applications. It provides better management and security for remote connections. Windows NT RAS clients and RAS servers can use a PPP connection.
- *Point-to-Point Tunneling Protocol (PPTP).* This protocol is new to Windows NT 4.0. It allows RAS connections across the Internet. PPTP uses virtual private networks (VPNs) and uses encryption to help ensure security. Client computers using PPTP can access PPTP servers via a local Internet Service Provider (ISP).

When adding or modifying protocols, Multilink can be enabled. Multilink allows multiple physical links to be combined into one virtual link. Multilink is typically used for ISDN connections. Multilink allows full use of all available physical connections for a higher bandwidth connection.

Security

Security is a very important part of a network, especially when allowing remote users to access network resources. RAS provides many security measures to allow access to authorized users while preventing access by unauthorized users. RAS security is often stricter than local network security.

RAS can implement the following security measures:

- *Integrated Domain Security.* The RAS server uses the exact same account database for remote users as the Primary Domain Controller (PDC) of the Windows NT domain. This provides strong security by only allowing valid domain users to access the RAS server. Also, it allows easier administration of user accounts and does not require two different account databases.
- *Encrypted Authentication and Logon.* Authentication and logon information can be encrypted to ensure that even if the physical connection between the remote user and the RAS server is breached, the data is not readable to the unauthorized user.

- *Auditing of Remote Connections.* A key component to RAS security is not only keeping unauthorized users out, but being made aware of attempts to breach the security of a system. Auditing is the maintaining of accesses and attempts to the RAS system. Items such as authentication, logons, and connection failures can be audited.
- *Callback Security.* This type of security allows for the initial connection of a RAS client to a RAS server. The client is verified as a valid remote client, then the connection is broken. After the modem hangs up, the RAS server then dials the RAS client back at either a user-provided or preset phone number and is re-verified as a valid remote client.
- *Allowing Intermediary Security Hosts.* An intermediate device between the RAS server and remote clients provides a more secure remote network. A remote user is required to provide a code or password in order to gain access to the RAS server for authentication. This provides another layer of security for the remote network.

Remote Node versus Remote Control Access

Windows NT RAS is known as remote node access. Remote node access means that the remote client acts as if it were a local client on the network except it uses a phone or other remote connection rather than a direct network connection.

Another type of remote access is known as remote control access. This type of access uses a dedicated network computer at the Dial-Up site and the remote computer "takes control" of that computer. An example of a third-party utility that uses remote control is PC Anywhere.

The advantage of remote node access is that there is not a dedicated computer at the Dial-Up site for each remote user. Also, file and print access is easier to manage when using remote node access. RAS allows for one dedicated server with multiple incoming remote connections. However, when using RAS, executable files should reside on the RAS client machine for faster response.

Tip

For the best performance of a RAS client, be sure that only data is transferred over the remote connection. Trying to run large executable programs from the RAS Server may dramatically reduce the client response time. Also, database access should be limited to database systems that have been designed for remote access in mind.

Installing and Configuring RAS Server

RAS can be installed during the initial Windows NT setup if the Custom Setup option was used. Otherwise, RAS is later installed by using the Windows NT Control Panel, Network option. However, before installing RAS on a Windows NT computer, be sure the computer has the necessary equipment and you have the needed information. Also, you must be a member of the Administrators group on a Windows NT computer to install or configure RAS.

The Dial-Up Networking component can also be installed by double clicking the Dial-Up Networking icon in the My Computer folder. This will guide the user through the Dial-Up Networking installation, but will *not* install the RAS server component. You can install both the Dial-Up Networking client and the RAS server through Control Panel.

Installation Requirements

Before you install RAS services on a Windows NT computer, be sure to check that the following are available on your system:

- Approximately 2M of free had disk space for the client, server, and administration tools.
- One or more modems supported by Windows NT. Be sure to check the Windows NT compatibility list before installing a modem to verify that it will work properly under Windows NT.

The following are optional components that can be used with RAS server:

- Network adapter card with a NDIS 3.0 driver if other network resources are to be accessed from a RAS server
- X.25 adapter card to allow X.25 access
- ISDN adapter card to allow ISDN access
- Multiport adapter card, such as a Digiboard, to increase the number of available serial communication ports on a server. A modem can be connected to each of the additional ports.

Before installing RAS, be sure to check the Windows NT hardware compatibility list to ensure the hardware devices will be properly configured under Windows NT. If a hardware device is not on the compatibility list, check with the manufacturer to verify that the device will work properly under Windows NT. Windows 95-compatible devices are *not* guaranteed to work under Windows NT, so be sure to check the hardware for Windows NT compatibility.

Information Needed to Install RAS

In order to properly install and configure RAS, be sure to have the following information available before installing RAS:

- The serial communication port number (COM1, and so on) and the proper configuration settings for the port.
- The type of modem used with all the proper modem settings.
- The type of network to be accessed and protocols.
- The type of user access to network resources.

Installing RAS

Remote Access Services can be installed during the initial Windows NT installation if Custom Setup is used. Also, if the computer is not attached to a network, the Express Setup also offers to install RAS. If RAS is not installed with the initial Windows NT installation, RAS can be installed using Control Panel and the Network item.

To install Remote Access Services after Windows NT is installed, be sure the installation CD-ROM or disks are available, and do the following:

1. Click Start, Settings. Or, you can double-click the My Computer
2. Choose Control Panel.
3. When the Control Panel dialog box appears, choose the Network icon. Then, select the Services Property tab. The Services Property sheet is shown in figure 22.1.

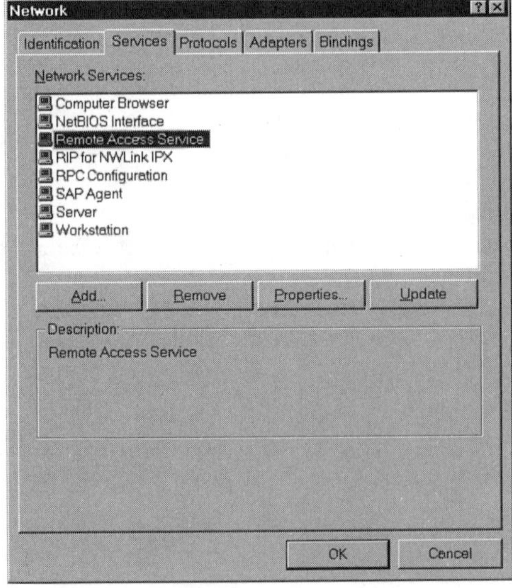

Fig. 22.1 The Network dialog box allows you to add Remote Access Services to the Windows NT computer.

4. Click the Add button. A drop-down list appears with the available software services that can be added to Windows NT.
5. In the drop-down list, select the Remote Access Service item. Then, click the Continue button.
6. You are prompted for the path of the distribution files. Insert the CD-ROM or disk into the drive and type the path into the text box. Then, click the OK button. The RAS files are copied to the hard drive.
7. After the files are installed, you need to specify a serial port. An Add Port dialog box appears listing all the ports, ISDN cards, or X.25 cards available. Choose the item you want to use with RAS and click the OK button.
8. The RAS setup offers to automatically detect any attached modems on the selected port. If you want to have the RAS setup detect the modem, choose the OK button. If you want to manually select the modem from a list, choose the Cancel button.
9. If you had RAS setup detect the modem, a dialog box appears showing the modem that RAS setup detected. Choose the OK button.
10. A Configure Port Usage dialog box appears and the modem is highlighted in the modem list. If you want to change the modem, select the modem you want from the list. The Configure Port Usage dialog box also has a Port Usage box. In the port usage box, you can select whether the port is to be used to dial out, receive calls, or both. When you are finished selecting items, choose OK. The Configure Port Usage dialog box is shown in figure 22.2.

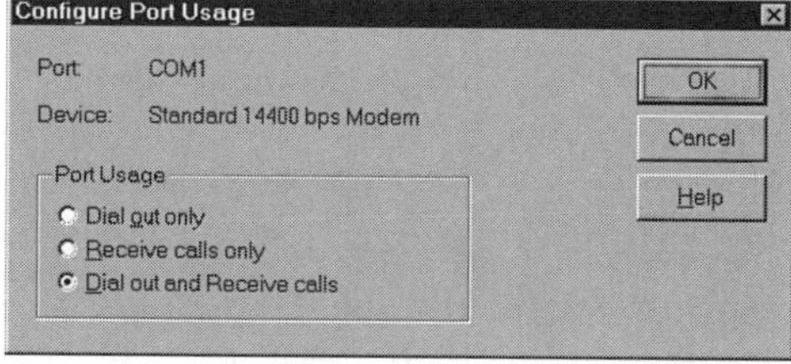

Fig. 22.2
The Configure Port Usage dialog box allows you to configure communication ports for use with Windows NT RAS.

11. RAS setup then displays Windows to set up protocol settings to be used with RAS. Details of these Windows are covered in the next section, "Configuring Protocols for RAS."
12. After protocol settings are configured, a Remote Access Service folder is created. A confirmation box appears. Choose OK to close the confirmation box.

13. The Network Settings dialog box is still open. Choose OK to close the Network Settings dialog box. Also, you may be prompted to confirm network protocol or other settings.
14. You are prompted to restart your computer for the changes to take effect. Before using RAS on your computer, be sure to restart Windows NT.

Configuring Protocols for RAS

A RAS server can allow many types of client protocols. A client can use: NetBEUI, TCP/IP, or IPX protocols. The most common procedure is to allow clients of all three protocols to access the RAS server. However, this might not be practical or desired in all instances.

Configuring NetBEUI

Configuring NetBEUI for RAS is probably the easiest of the three protocols to configure. In order to use the NetBEUI protocol, no extra addressing is needed. To configure NetBEUI, it must be selected in the Network Configuration dialog box and you must determine whether NetBEUI clients can access the entire network or just the RAS server.

Configuring TCP/IP

To allow remote computers that access the RAS server using TCP/IP, the TCP/IP protocol should be properly configured on the RAS server. Any clients using TCP/IP to access the RAS server require an IP address. This IP address has to be unique for each computer and provides a method of identifying the computer on the network. There are two methods to assign a remote computer an IP address. Either the computer may have a selected IP address or Dynamic Host Configuration Protocol (DHCP) may be used to dynamically assign IP addresses to remote computers as they connect.

Configuring IPX

Configuring the IPX protocol for remote users is similar to configuring the TCP/IP protocol. To configure IPX, you must determine whether the remote users will connect to the entire network or just the RAS server. Then, you must determine whether to have the unique IPX network numbers be assigned automatically or specify a range of network numbers to use.

Supporting Dial-In Users

As mentioned previously, the following systems can act as RAS clients to a Windows NT RAS server: Windows NT 4.0, Windows NT 3.5, Windows 95,

Windows for Workgroups, MS-DOS, LAN Manager, and any computers using the Point-to-Point Protocol (PPP) standard.

Installing and configuring Windows NT 4.0 clients is discussed later in this chapter. Other versions of Windows NT are configured in a similar manner as version 4.0. The installation procedures for Windows for Workgroups, MS-DOS, Windows 95, and other clients are discussed in the following section.

Configuring Windows for Workgroups RAS clients

Windows for Workgroups can be used as a RAS client if networking options are installed. If the networking options are installed, a Network program group will be available. In this program group are a variety of icons and programs such as: WinPopup, Chat, Netmeter, and so on.

To install RAS client software on a Windows for Workgroups machine, do the following:

1. From Program Manager, Open the Network program group. In the program group double-click the Remote Access icon.
2. If RAS has not been configured, a dialog box appears informing you that RAS needs to be installed. Choose the Install button.
3. Be sure to have the Windows for Workgroups system disks or CD-ROM available. A progress dialog box appears and you are prompted for the appropriate disk when files need to be copied.
4. After the needed files have been copied from disk, a Remote Access Configuration dialog box appears. This dialog box displays the available ports on your machine with the modem(s), if any, attached to those ports. At the bottom of the dialog box, there is an option to choose a modem type. Highlight the port you want to use to connect to a RAS server, and click the OK button.
5. Another dialog box appears informing you to restart the computer. Before using RAS on the Windows for Workgroups machine, be sure to restart the computer.

Configuring Windows 95 RAS Clients

Windows 95 uses the Dial-Up Networking feature to access Windows NT RAS servers. The Windows 95 Dial-Up Networking is very similar to the RAS client options in Windows NT. Dial-Up Networking creates a new icon for each type of connection installed on the system.

To install a Dial-Up Networking client on a Windows 95 machine, do the following:

1. Start Control Panel. In Control Panel, choose the Add/Remove Programs icon.
2. In the Add/Remove Programs dialog box, click the Windows Setup tab.
3. In the Components list, choose Communications, then the Details button.
4. In the Communications dialog box, select Dial-Up Networking. Then, choose the OK button.
5. The Dial-Up Networking software will be installed on your computer.
6. After the software is installed, you need to configure a Dial-Up Networking connection to a Windows NT RAS server. Open the My Computer icon, then double-click the Dial-Up Networking folder.
7. In the Dial-Up Networking folder, double-click the Make New Connection icon. This starts the Make New Connection wizard. Click the Next button.
8. You are prompted for the name of the connection, for example, Windows NT RAS Client. Also, you need to provide the modem type. Type the name of the connection and select the modem type. Then, click the Next button.
9. You are prompted for the area code, phone number, and country code of the Windows NT RAS server. After you have filled in the appropriate items, click the Next button.
10. A dialog box appears showing the connection name. To finish the new connection, click the Finish button. A new connection icon appears in the Dial-Up Networking folder.
11. By default, the new connection is a Windows NT 3.5 or 4.0 connection. To verify the correct connection type, choose Properties for the connection, then click the Server Type button. The type of Dial-Up Server is highlighted. To change the selection, select the correct server type from the drop-down list.

Configuring MS-DOS RAS Clients

Before installing RAS for DOS-based clients, the Networking Client for DOS should be installed and configured using the full redirector. If the Networking Client is not installed, the Windows NT Server CD-ROM has a directory containing the client software or the Network Client Administrator can be used to install the software.

RAS can be installed from the Windows NT CD-ROM, from separate RAS 1.1 for DOS disks, or by using the Network Client Administrator located in the

Administrative Tools folder. The exact installation procedures depend on how the RAS client is installed. Check your documentation for more information on installing the RAS client on a MS-DOS machine.

Other RAS Clients

Non-Microsoft clients using PPP can access a Windows NT 3.5x or 4.0 RAS server. The authentication with the PPP client will automatically be negotiated by the RAS server. Therefore, no special configuration for RAS server is needed to accept PPP clients. For information on how to install or configure PPP on a non-Microsoft client, refer to your software documentation.

The RAS Server Administrator Utility

The RAS Server Administrator utility provides many functions for the administrator to control the RAS server. An administrator can send messages or disconnect incoming remote users, view the current active connections, grant access permissions to remote users, and starting, stopping, or pausing RAS on a server. From the RAS Administrator utility, you can also control remote RAS server, not just the server where the utility is being used.

The RAS Server Administrator tool is shown in figure 22.3.

Fig. 22.3
The RAS Server Administrator utility allows the administrator to control the RAS server.

The initial screen of the utility shows the current RAS server being monitored or modified, the condition of the server (whether it is running, paused, or stopped), the total number of ports available and being used by the RAS server, and any comments about the RAS server. The current server name will also be displayed on the Windows' title bar. A menu at the top of the dialog box allows different servers to be viewed or changed as well as changing options for RAS servers.

Dial-In Permissions and Security

After Remote Access Services have been installed on a Windows NT computer, access permissions for remote users must be assigned. You must assign remote access permissions to users, otherwise they will not be able to successfully connect to a RAS server. Access permissions on a RAS server are granted through the RAS Administrator utility.

Note

Remote access permissions for users must be configured in the RAS Administrator utility. They cannot be configured using the User Manager or User Manager for Domains.

To grant access permissions to remote users:

1. Click Start, Programs.
2. Choose Administrative Tools, Remote Access Admin. This starts the Remote Access Administrator utility.
3. Choose the server or domain that you want to set remote access permissions for users for. You can select the server or domain by choosing Server, Select Domain or Server.
4. Choose Users, Permissions. The Remote Access Permissions dialog box appears as shown in figure 22.4.

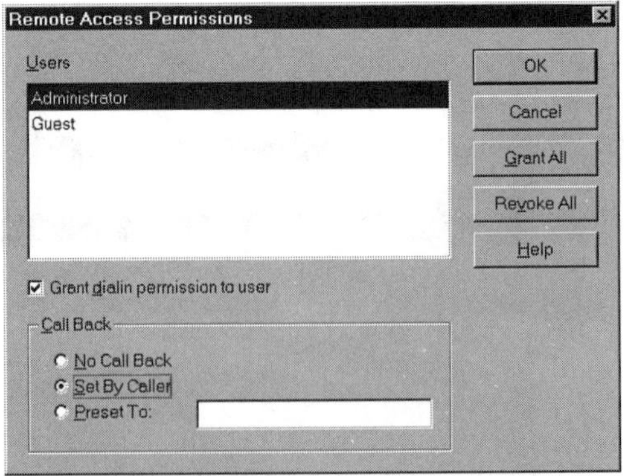

Fig. 22.4
The Remote Access Permissions dialog box allows you to set access permissions for remote users.

5. Highlight the user account that you want to set access permissions for in the Users list box.
6. Once the user account is highlighted, check the Grant Dialin Permission to User checkbox. This allows the account to dial in to the RAS server. To revoke access, clear the checkbox.
7. You can also click the Grant All or Revoke All buttons to either give all the users remote access rights or to remove remote access rights to all users.
8. After you have assigned all the remote access rights for the desired users, choose the OK button.

Caution

If you grant dial-in access to a guest account, be sure to assign a password to the account. Otherwise, unauthorized users will be able to access the network or RAS server through a remote connection. For the best security, it's usually a good idea not to assign dial-in permissions to guest accounts.

Authentication Methods

To understand the different methods of RAS security, you should be aware of what occurs when a RAS connection is made between a remote client and the server. The following steps occur when a RAS connection is made:

1. Once the connection is made, the RAS server sends a message challenging the RAS client.
2. The RAS client responds to the server's challenge, using one of the supported authentication methods.
3. The RAS server compares the client's response to the user account database to verify a valid remote user connection.
4. If the account is a valid account on the RAS server or Windows NT network, the RAS server then verifies the user's remote access permission.
5. If the user account is both valid and has remote access permissions, the user is connected as a RAS client. If the user account uses callback security, the RAS server disconnects, redials the user, and reverifies the user account and remote access permissions. At this point, the user has access to the network through a RAS session.

In step 2, the RAS client uses a supported authentication method to respond to the RAS server. Windows NT RAS supports the following authentication methods:

- *RSA Message Digest 5 (MD5) / Challenge Handshake Authentication Protocol (CHAP).* This method is only used by Windows NT RAS clients to dial out to third-party PPP servers. Windows NT RAS Server does not support this method for incoming clients. This method was developed by RSA, Inc. as a fast, simple, and compact method for 32-bit systems. However, since RSA MD5 requires the ability of clear-text (no encryption) passwords at the server level, it is not used by Windows NT RAS on the server level.
- *RSA Message Digest 4 (MD4) or MS-CHAP.* MS-CHAP is a Microsoft version of the MD4 method. This method is the default authentication method used between Windows NT RAS clients and Windows NT RAS

servers. It is also the most secure authentication method supported by Windows NT RAS.

- *Data Encryption Standard (DES).* The DES standard was designed by the National Bureau of Standards. It is used in Windows NT RAS for backward compatibility with LAN Manager systems and DOS-based clients.
- *Clear-Text Authentication Password Authentication Protocol (PAP).* Clear-text is text sent over the line without any encryption. This method is supported by Windows NT RAS for connection to SLIP servers or selected PPP servers, and should *not* be used for Windows NT RAS clients connecting to Windows NT RAS servers. This method is the least secure method supported by RAS.
- *Shiva Password Authentication Protocol (SPAP).* SPAP is a proprietary version of PAP for use with Shiva clients. Otherwise, it is the same as PAP and should be used to connect to SLIP and PPP servers.

The different types of authentication provide varying levels of security between the RAS server and a remote client. If there is an interception of communications between the two, the different authentication can prevent an unauthorized user from discovering a remote user's username and password. This is handled by a method known as encryption. For more information on RAS encryption, see the section titled "Using Data Encryption."

Server Security

Security is a very critical part of RAS because remote access to the network presents more network entry points. Also, these entry points can be from any geographical area and are much harder for an administrator to directly supervise. Therefore, RAS has more security options than a regular client on the network would normally have.

Even with the tighter security controls, authorized users should still be able to access the network remotely without too many security burdens. If remote user security measures become too complex or cumbersome, users will be less likely to use the features that RAS provides. With this in mind, RAS provides many security features that can be configured to provide the highest level of security to keep out unauthorized users, while allowing authorized users easy access to the network.

Using Callback Security. Callback security under RAS refers to a RAS server calling a remote user back after the user successfully dials in. Configuring a RAS server for callbacks can be used for security reasons, for reducing the cost of remote user phone access, or both. RAS servers can be configured to dial a specified number or to request the number to be dialed from the remote user.

Having RAS dial a specific number on callback provides the highest level of callback security. However, it is useful when the user will always be dialing from a fixed location, such as a home computer. Prompting the user for a number allows for users who are traveling with a portable computer.

Implementing callback options is very similar to granting remote access rights to users. To implement callback security for a user or group of users, do the following:

1. Click the Start, Administrative Tools, Remote Access Admin to start the Remote Access Administrator utility.
2. Choose the server or domain that you want to set callback permissions for users. You can select the server or domain by choosing the Server menu and then choosing the Select Domain or Server item on the menu.
3. Choose Users, Permissions. The Remote Access Permissions dialog box appears as shown in figure 22.5.

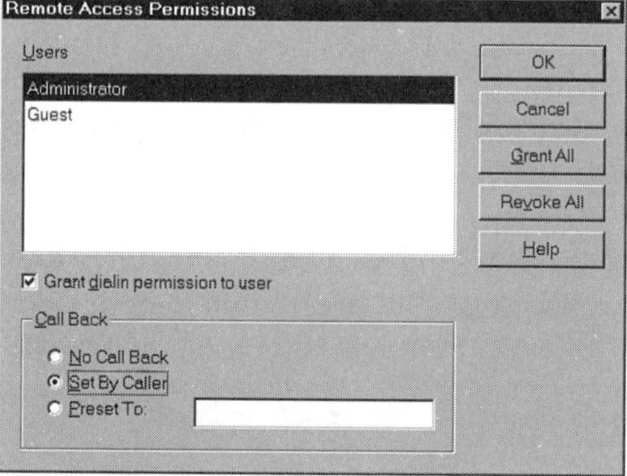

Fig. 22.5
The Remote Access Permissions dialog box also allows you to set callback options for remote users.

4. In the Remote Access Permissions dialog box, highlight the user account that you want to set callback permissions for in the Users list box.
5. Once the user account is highlighted, make sure the Grant Dialin Permission to User checkbox is checked. The bottom box contains callback options.
6. You can choose one of the following options: No callback, Set By Caller, and Preset To. Choose the option you want and if choosing the Preset To option, type the desired number into the box beside the Preset To option.
7. After you have assigned all the callback settings for the desired users, click OK.

> **Note**
>
> Callback security cannot be used on X.25 networks. Also, callback permissions should not be assigned to users who are connecting to a RAS server through a switchboard.

Although callback security can be properly used with a single modem using a single line, multiple modems and multiple lines can provide a higher degree of security. Using a single line, an unauthorized user can trick some modems and "hold" the line using callback security. With multiple modems and lines, the callback line can be a different line than the incoming line, providing better security.

To implement different incoming and outgoing lines, configure the COM ports in the Port Usage box to Dial Out Only or Receive Calls Only. For example, if you have a RAS server with four serial ports and modems, COM 1 and COM 2 can be set to receive RAS calls, then COM 3 and COM 4 can be set to dial out to remote users. Keep in mind this method requires multiple phone lines, serial ports, and modems.

Using Data Encryption. Data encryption is another important way to ensure data security when using RAS. Data encryption prevents unauthorized users from viewing intercepted transmissions sent between the RAS server and a remote user. Data encryption uses one of the supported RAS authentication methods. For more information on the supported RAS authentication methods, see the section titled "Authentication Methods" earlier in the chapter.

You can choose the following types of data encryption:

- *Allow Any Authentication Including Clear Text.* This is the lowest level of security. It allows remote connections with any of the authentication methods (MS-CHAP, SPAP, or PAP) to connect to the RAS server.
- *Require Encrypted Authentication.* This allows remote clients to connect that use an encrypted authentication method (MS-CHAP, MD5-CHAP, or SPAP).
- *Require Microsoft Encrypted Authentication.* This option requires the MS-CHAP authentication be used by remote connection into the RAS server. The is the highest level of encryption security used by RAS. If the Require data encryption is selected, all data sent to and from the RAS server is encrypted. If this option is selected, any clients dialing into the server must be able support data encryption.

Encryption types can be configured during the protocol support configuration when RAS is installed on the server or after RAS has been installed.

To configure Data Encryption on a RAS server after it has been installed, do the following:

1. You must be in Windows NT as a user with administrator rights. Click the Start, Settings, Control Panel, then Network.
2. Select the Services tab, then choose Remote Access Service. While Remote Access Service is highlighted, click the Properties button. This displays the Remote Access Setup dialog box.
3. In the Remote Access Setup dialog box, click the Network button to open the Network Configuration dialog box.
4. At the bottom of the Network Configuration dialog box, the Encryption settings appear.
5. Choose one of the following: Allow Any Authentication Including Clear Text, Require Encrypted Authentication, or Require Microsoft Encrypted Authentication. If you choose the Microsoft encrypted authentication option, you can also check the Require Data Encryption checkbox.
6. After you have selected the type of encryption, click OK.

Server Services

After a remote RAS user is connected, he can be allowed access to the entire network or just the RAS server. If he has access to the entire network, he may access any of the shared resources on the network as if he was connected as a local computer on the network. If the access is limited to the RAS server, any shares on that server may be accessed by the remote user.

You can configure whether a user can access the entire network or just the RAS server from the Network Configuration dialog box where protocols are configured. To change the type of access, do the following:

1. Click Start, Settings, Control Panel, and then Network.
2. Select the Services tab, then choose Remote Access Service. While Remote Access Service is highlighted, click the Properties button.
3. In the Remote Access Setup dialog box, click the Network button. This opens the Network Configuration dialog box.
4. Select a protocol in the Network Configuration dialog box and click the Configure button beside it.
5. At this point, you can choose whether to give users access to the entire network or access to just the RAS server. After you are finished, click the OK button.

Using DUN for Dial-Out

DUN can be used as a dial-out client to connect to a RAS server or a third party server, such as a PPP server connected to the Internet. To use DUN, you need to use the Dial-Up Networking client program. This program can be found in the My Computer icon on the desktop and by choosing Dial-Up Networking item in the folder.

The Dial-Up Networking Configuration dialog box is shown in figure 22.6.

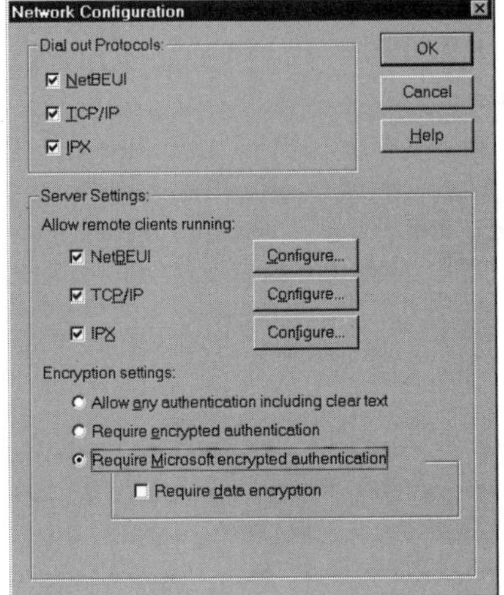

Fig. 22.6
The Dial-Up Networking program allows you to use RAS to dial out to other servers.

The Dial-Up Networking dialog box displays the following:

- *Phonebook Entry to Dial*. This listbox allows you to select the name of an existing phonebook entry that you want to dial. The New button allows you to create a new phonebook entry and the More button allows you to set different options. The More button is examined in greater detail in the next part of this section.
- *Phone Number Preview*. This textbox allows you to see the number to be dialed for this phonebook entry. You may also edit the number if you want to select a different phone number for this session. If you type a new phone number, it will only work for this session. To change the phone number permanently, you will need to edit the phonebook entry.
- *Dialing From*. This allows you to select an existing location that the session is dialing from. This is very useful if you travel and have to dial

from many different locations. There is also a Location button that allows you to create or edit a location or to add prefixes or suffixes.

The More button under the Phonebook Entry to Dial listbox has many different settings for Dial-Up Networking phonebooks or configuration options. The More button contains the following options:

- *Edit Entry and Modem Properties*. Allows you to modify an existing phone book entry. This item is discussed in greater detail in the next section, "Phonebook Entry and Modem Properties."
- *Clone Entry and Modem Properties*. This option allows you to copy the settings of an existing entry to a new entry. This item is also covered in the "Phonebook Entry and Modem Properties" section.
- *Delete Entry*. Removes an existing phonebook entry from the list.
- *Create Shortcut to Entry*. This creates a shortcut on the desktop for the selected entry. When you double-click the created shortcut, a login screen appears and the connection is dialed using the settings for the entry.
- *Monitor Status*. Sets Dial-Up Networking Monitor options such as Modem to Monitor, Display the Monitor Program in the Windows NT Tasklist, or Displaying the Monitor in a dialog box or on the taskbar.
- *Operator Assisted or Manual Dialing*. If selected, a checkmark appears beside this entry on the menu. When it is selected, it does not dial the phonebook number. This allows you to manually dial the number or use operator assisted dialing. Once a connection is made, Dial-Up Networking takes over.
- *User Preferences*. This sets the user preferences for Dial-Up Networking.
- *Logon Preferences*. Similar to User preferences, this option contains settings used if Dial-Up Networking is used to connect to a network with the Ctrl+Alt+Delete login box.
- *Help*. This displays the Windows NT help topic for the Dial-Up Networking program.

Phonebook Entry and Modem Properties

If you select the Edit entry and modem properties or Clone entry and modem properties, the Edit Phonebook Entry dialog box or the Clone Phonebook Entry dialog box will appear.

The Edit Phonebook Entry dialog box is shown in figure 22.7.

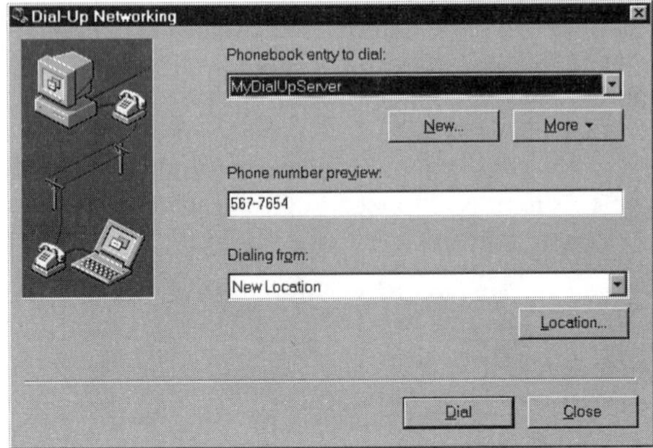

Fig. 22.7 The edit phonebook entry dialog box allows the remote user to configure Dial-Up Networking entries.

The dialog box has tabs allowing you to display different property sheets. The Edit and Clone Entry and Modem Properties sheets contain the following tabs:

- *Basic.* The Basic tab contains options such as: Entry Name, Comment, Phone number, Dial Using, and Use Telephony Dialing Properties. You can also add alternate phone numbers by clicking the Alternates button beside the Phone Number box.
- *Server.* This tab allows you to select the Dial-Up server type to connect to in the Dial-Up Server Type listbox. From this listbox, you can select PPP (default), SLIP, or Windows NT 3.1/Windows for Workgroups RAS. You also can select the network protocols from the Network protocols box to use for the RAS connection. At the bottom of the dialog box, you can select whether to use software compression or PPP LCP extensions used with newer PPP software.
- *Script.* The Script tab allows you to select a script to run after dialing. You can select scripts from a drop-down list or you can edit scripts. At the bottom of the sheet, there is a Before Dialing button that allows you to select any scripts to run before dialing.
- *Security.* The Security tab selects the type of encryption used for the Dial-Up Networking client. Similar to the settings in the RAS server encryption settings, this sheet determines how the client will send information to a server. You can Select Accept Any Authentication Including Clear Text, Accept Only Encrypted Authentication, or Accept Only Microsoft Encrypted Authentication. With the last option, you can also select to require data encryption or use the current username and password.

- *X.25*. If you are using Dial-Up Networking through an X.25 network, this tab allows you to set the Network and Address to use. There are two optional fields, User Data and Facilities.

User and Logon Preferences

The User Preferences and Logon Preferences dialog boxes allow you to set options such as: redial attempts, callback options, and phonebook selections. The User Preferences and Logon Preferences are almost identical in appearance, except for slightly different options on the property sheets.

The User Preferences dialog box is shown in figure 22.8.

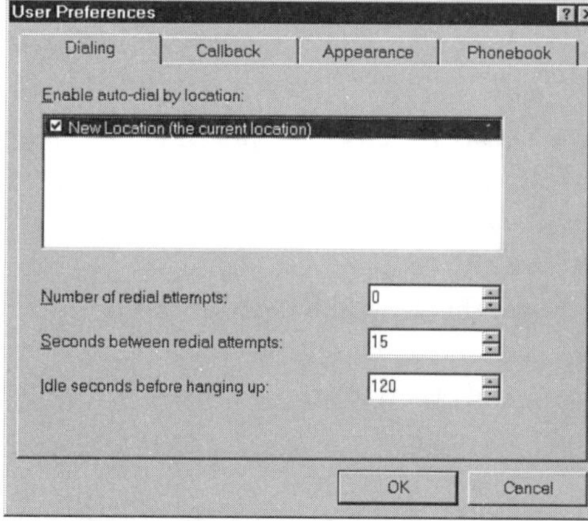

Fig. 22.8
The User Preferences dialog box allows the user to set dialing, callback, appearance, and phonebook properties.

The User and Logon preferences items contain the following tabs:

- *Dialing*. Both User and Logon Preferences Dialing property sheets allow setting for Number of redial attempts, Seconds between redial attempts, and Idle seconds before hanging up. These settings are used if the initial attempt fails or is interrupted. The User Preferences has an additional item at the top of the property sheet. The Enable auto-Dial By Location item displays a list of locations with a checkbox beside each location. This allows autodialing if a RAS connection is selected in an application.
- *Callback*. The Callback property sheet sets the callback options for a Dial-Up Networking client. You can choose No, Skip Call Back, Maybe, Ask Me During Dial When Server Offers, or Yes, Call Me Back at the Number Below. The last option also displays a list of modems and phone numbers available on the machine. Below the list are the Edit and Delete buttons to edit or delete items from the list.

- *Appearance*. The Appearance tab allows various appearance options to be modified. The User Preferences Appearance property sheet contains seven items that can be modified: Preview Phone Numbers Before Dialing, Show Location Settings Before Dialing, Start Dial-Up Networking Monitor Before Dialing, Show Connection Progress While Dialing, Close on Dial, Use Wizard To Create New Phonebook Entries, and Always Prompt Before Auto-Dialing. The Login Preferences contains two additional items: Allow Phonebook Edits During Login and Allow Location Edits During Login.
- *Phonebook*. The Phonebook property sheet allows you to set which phonebook is to be used with the Dial-Up Networking client. The Login Preferences Phonebook property sheet allows you to use the system phonebook or an alternate phonebook. The User Preferences Phonebook property sheet contains the same items in the Login Preferences Phonebook property sheet and also includes an option to use the user's personal phonebook.

Connecting to Servers

At the bottom of the Dial-Up Networking dialog box, there are two buttons: Dial and Close. The Close button closes the dialog box and exits the Dial-Up Networking program. If the Dial button is clicked, a Connect To dialog box appears as shown in figure 22.9.

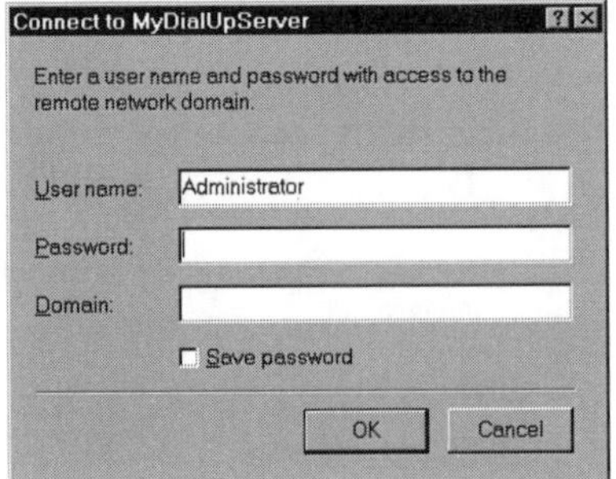

Fig. 22.9
The Connect to MyDialUpServer dialog box asks for the Username, Password, and Domain for the remote user.

This dialog box also appears if you've created a shortcut on the desktop of the phonebook entry. This dialog box allows you to type your username, password, and domain for the Dial-Up connection.

Dialing Prefixes and Suffixes

In some instances, remote users might have to dial a prefix in order to obtain access to an outside line or to disable call waiting on some phones. Also, there may be times when a suffix needs to be added to the end of the number. The RAS client can support prefixes and suffixes for phonebook entries. This option configures all phonebook entries to use the prefixes and suffixes for that location.

To add a prefix or suffix to a location, do the following:

1. Start the Dial-Up Networking program by double-clicking the My Computer icon on the desktop, then select the Dial-Up Networking item. The Dial-Up Networking dialog box appears.
2. Click the Location button to add a prefix or suffix for *all* phonebook entries for that location.
3. The Location Settings dialog box, shown in figure 22.10, appears. You should see a down arrow button beside the Prefix and Suffix objects allowing you to select items from a drop-down list. For example, you could choose 70# to disable call waiting as a prefix.

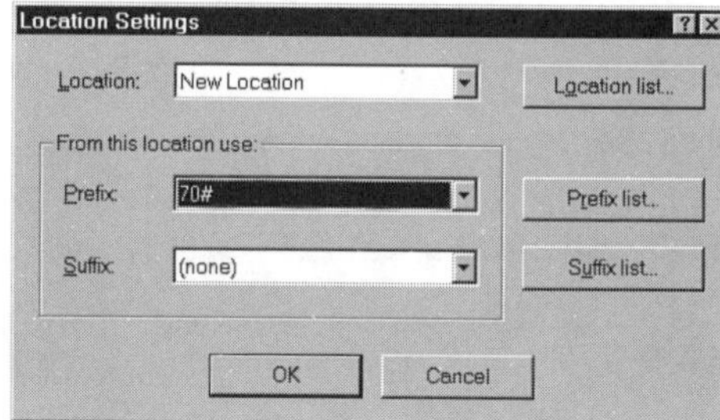

Fig. 22.10
The Location Settings dialog box allows you to select a prefix or suffix to use.

4. If you want to add or remove items from the drop down-lists, you can click the Prefix List or Suffix List buttons. These buttons allow you to modify items in the list to accommodate different dialing options. The Prefix List dialog box is shown in figure 22.11.

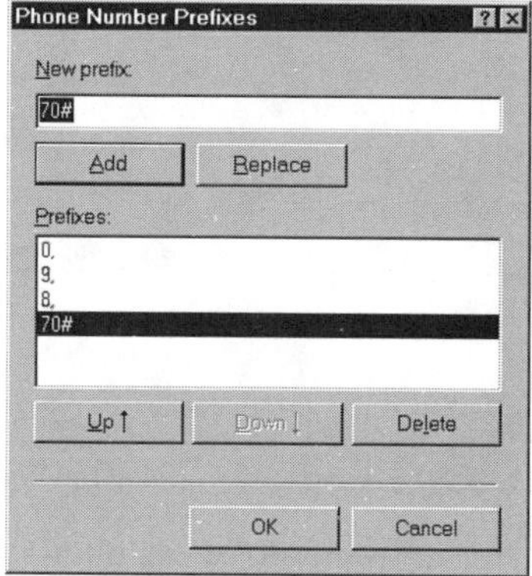

Fig. 22.11
The Prefix List dialog box allows you to add new prefixes to the list or to remove prefixes from the list.

5. When you are finished adding prefixes or suffixes, click the OK button to return to the RAS Client dialog box.

Multiple Phone Numbers

The Windows NT Dial-Up Networking program supports multiple phone numbers for a single phone book entry. To enter multiple phone numbers in a single phonebook entry, choose the Alternates button in the Basic page of the Edit Phonebook Entry property sheet. When the phonebook entry is dialed, the first number is dialed. If there is no answer, a busy signal, or another reason the first entry doesn't work, the second number will be dialed.

Setting and Using Telephony Options

Instead of using the Dial-Up Networking options for dialing, Telephony options, set in the Windows NT Control Panel, can be used. This option must be selected in the Basic page when editing or cloning a phonebook entry. Using the Telephony option is ideal if the computer is to remain in a fixed location with special dialing options.

The Telephony Dialing Properties sheet is shown in figure 22.12.

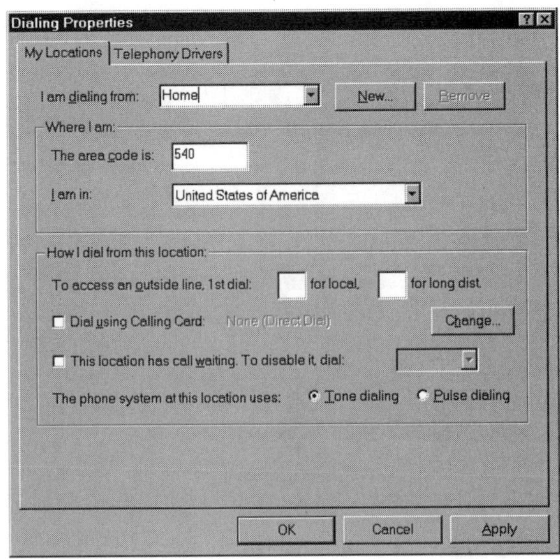

Fig. 22.12 The Dialing Properties sheet allows you to configure the Telephony options for Windows NT.

The Telephony item in Control Panel has the following options:

Under the My Locations tab:

- *I Am Dialing From*. This drop-down listbox allows you to select an existing location to dial from. Beside the listbox, there is a New button to add a new location to the list and a Remove button that allows you to remove a location.

- *Where I am.* This box contains an area code box and a listbox that allow you to select the country you are in.
- *How I Dial from this Location.* This box contains options on dialing from the selected location. You can add a prefix for both local and long-distance calls, set calling card options, turn off call waiting, and select tone or pulse dialing.

Under the Telephony Drivers tab:

- *The Driver List.* This box shows the drivers that are currently being used for Windows NT Telephony.
- *Add.* The Add button can be used to add drivers if they are missing.
- *Remove.* The Remove button can remove drivers that are no longer needed. Do not remove drivers unless you are sure that they are no longer needed. If a needed driver is removed, Telephony applications may not work properly.
- *Configure.* This allows you to set individual configuration options for the selected driver.

Using Remote Resources

Using remote resources, like drives and printers, is the same as using those resources on a local Windows NT machine on the network. However, certain things like browsing the network may be considerably slower.

Note

When using RAS, you may not see certain shared resources when browsing. Browsing is automatically disabled on a computer that is not networked, other than RAS. Therefore, the resources of the non-networked computer will not be displayed by the browser.

Using Remote Drives

Once you are connected to a server, you may access drives and files on that server or network, depending on your access privileges. You can also assign drive letters to remote disks and directories allowing them to be accessed as if they were local drive devices. Keep in mind that large file transfers may take a long period of time. You may want to compress files before sending into .ZIP format or other compression schemes to reduce transfer time.

Using Remote Printers

You may use remote printers in the same manner as remote drives. This allows you to print data to a printer located at the remote site. However, in most instances, you will probably want to send all of your print jobs to a printer connected to the local computer. Printing over remote connections may be very time consuming if the print job is large.

Using SLIP and PPP

Dial-Up Networking clients can connect to remote computers using either PPP or SLIP protocols. PPP connections have many advantages over SLIP connections. SLIP does not support encrypted authentication to a server, while PPP does. PPP connections can also be configured to have an automatic logon, while SLIP servers require an interactive logon. Also, PPP provides better handling of errors or noisy lines by using a frame checksum. SLIP does not provide this level of error handling.

By default, Dial-Up Networking uses PPP for its connections. However, some older UNIX machines and some Internet Service Providers (ISPs) still use SLIP to allow access to servers. You need to check with your ISP to see whether PPP or SLIP needs to be used.

Creating RAS Scripts

The RAS SWITCH.INF file can be used by the user as a script file to allow RAS to perform certain functions automatically. The SWITCH.INF file can be configured to have a different script for each device or service used by RAS. In order to modify the SWITCH.INF file, you will need to be aware of the six components used by the file. The six elements of the SWITCH.INF file are:

- *Section Headers*. The section headers are used for each device or service used by RAS. Similar to section headers to the old INI files, the section headers mark the beginning of a script. The section header must be enclosed in square brackets and should not be longer than 31 characters. The following is an example of a section header:

  [My Header]

- *Comment Lines*. Comment lines are used by the writer of the script to document or comment what the components of the scripts do. The comment lines are not processed and the only rule concerning comment lines is that they must begin with a semicolon (;). For example:

  ;This is a comment line

- *Commands*. Commands are used to send streams of text to the computer where the RAS client is connected. An example would be when the RAS client needs to send a username to the connected computer. Commands are preceded with COMMAND= and followed by the text that needs to be sent to the host or server computer. You need to be aware of the proper format and order of text that the connected computer expects. If the text is out of order or not typed properly, the command may not work. This may create an unusable script. An example of a command line is:

  COMMAND=WinNTUser<cr>

  This sends the text WinNTUser to the host computer followed by a carriage return. (The <cr> macro is discussed in the last item of this list.)

- *Responses*. A response is something that is sent from the remote computer to which the RAS client is connected. When writing RAS scripts, you need to know what responses will be sent from the connected server or computer. Responses use response keywords to handle the different types of responses.

- *Response Keywords*. The response keyword determines how to handle a response sent from the remote server or computer. The following response keywords are available:

  OK=*remote server text<macro>*. The OK keyword processes the text received from the remote server. If the text is the same as the text after the equals sign, the script continues to the next line of the script.

  LOOP=*remote server text<macro>*. If the text in the LOOP= response is encountered, the processing will jump to the previous line of the script.

  CONNECT=*remote server text<macro>*. The CONNECT response keyword is usually used at the end of a successful modem script.

  ERROR=*remote server text<macro>*. If the text in the ERROR= response is encountered, then RAS will display a generic error message. This is useful to highlight any errors that may occur when trying to make a remote connection.

  ERROR_DIAGNOSTICS=*remote server text*<diagnostics>. If the text is encountered, then the ERROR DIAGNOSTICS will return the specific device error. Be aware, however, that not all devices will report specific errors. If a devices does not report specific errors, try using the ERROR= response keyword.

  No Response. This is used when no response is expected from a remote server or computer.

- *Macros*. Macros are used in both commands and responses. One of the most common macros that can be used in both command strings and response strings is the <cr> macros, which sends a carriage return. Macros must be enclosed in angle brackets (< and >). Macros are designed to handle special functions or codes. The following macros are available:

  <cr>. This macro inserts a carriage return, which is the same as hitting the Enter key.

  <lf>. This macro inserts a line feed.

  <match>=*"string"*. This macro reports a match if the device response contains text identical to the text string enclosed in the quotation marks. The text string is case-sensitive when using the macro. This means that the text to be matched must have the same case as the text string in quotes.

  <?>. This macro is used as a wildcard character, similar to the wildcard characters used in a DOS session. For instance, the TE<?>T would match TEXT or TEST.

  <hXX>. (Where XX are digits in hexadecimal form). This allows any hexadecimal character to be included in the text string.

  <ignore>. This macro ignores the rest of the response string.

  <diagnostics>. This macro sends specific error information from a device that allows specific error messages to be sent. This macro is usually used with the ERROR_DIAGNOSTICS= keyword. If a device does not send specific error information, a standard RAS error message will be sent.

  <username>. This macro is not supported with SLIP connections. It allows the username typed in the RAS Authentication dialog box to be sent as a text string.

  <password>. This macro is also not supported with SLIP connections. It is the same as the <username> macro except it sends the password instead of the username.

Let's take a look at a sample script used to connect to a remote server. The remote server will ask for the assigned username and password in order to make a connection. The comment lines (lines that start with a semicolon) explain what the lines do. The script appears as follows:

```
[Remote Server Connection]
;The next command is used to initialize the connection to the
remote computer
```

```
COMMAND=
;The next lines are designed to loop until the username prompt is
➥reached
OK=<match>"Please enter your username:"
LOOP=<ignore>
;The next line sends the assigned username to the remote server,
➥followed by a carriage return
COMMAND=RichardN<cr>
;The next lines finds the password prompt
OK=<match>"Please enter your password:"
;The last line sends the password and a carriage return to the
➥remote computer
COMMAND=XM183E45
```

Note

You can modify the SWITCH.INF directly to create scripts, but it is a good idea to make a backup of SWITCH.INF before making any modifications. This allows for easy replacement of a script that does not work properly after editing.

Scripts can be activated before dialing, after dialing, or both. To activate a script in the SWITCH.INF file, do the following:

1. If you have not already started the Dial-Up Networking program, click the My Computer icon, then Dial-Up Networking.
2. Click the More button in the Dial-Up Networking dialog box.
3. Select Edit Entry and Modem Properties from the menu.
4. Click the Script tab to display the Script page.
5. If you want a script to run after dialing, click the Run this Script option. A listbox becomes active and allows you to select the script you want to run.
6. If you want a script to run before dialing, click the Before Dialing button. In the Before Dialing Script dialog box, click the Run this Script option. A listbox becomes active and allows you to select the script you want to run. Then click the OK button.
7. You may also edit RAS scripts by clicking the Edit scripts button. This starts Notepad with the SWITCH.INF file loaded. If you add a new script, be sure to refresh the list by clicking Refresh list so that it appears in the script list.
8. Click OK until you return to the main Dial-Up Networking dialog box. When you dial the modified entry the script will be executed. ❖

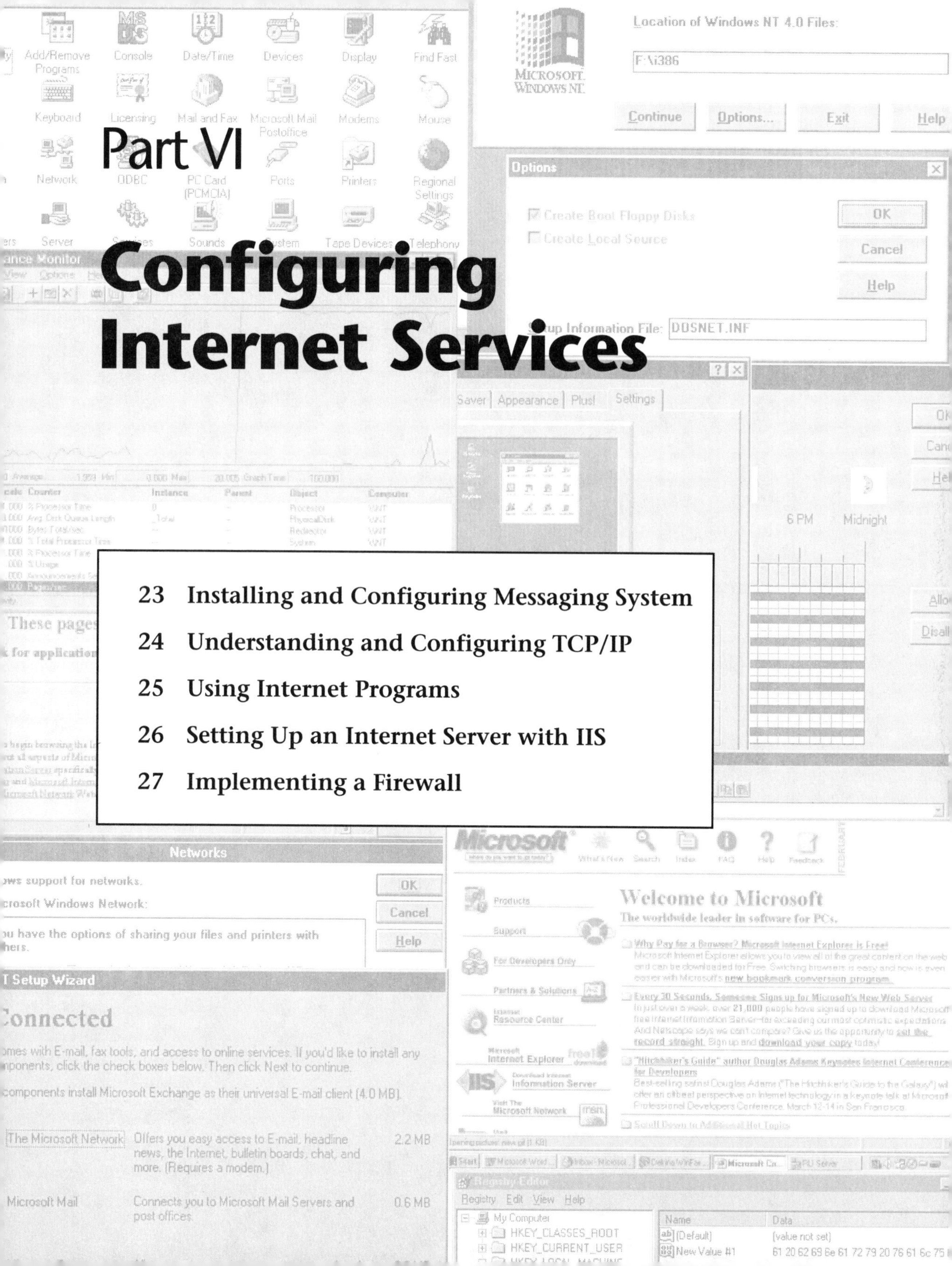

Part VI

Configuring Internet Services

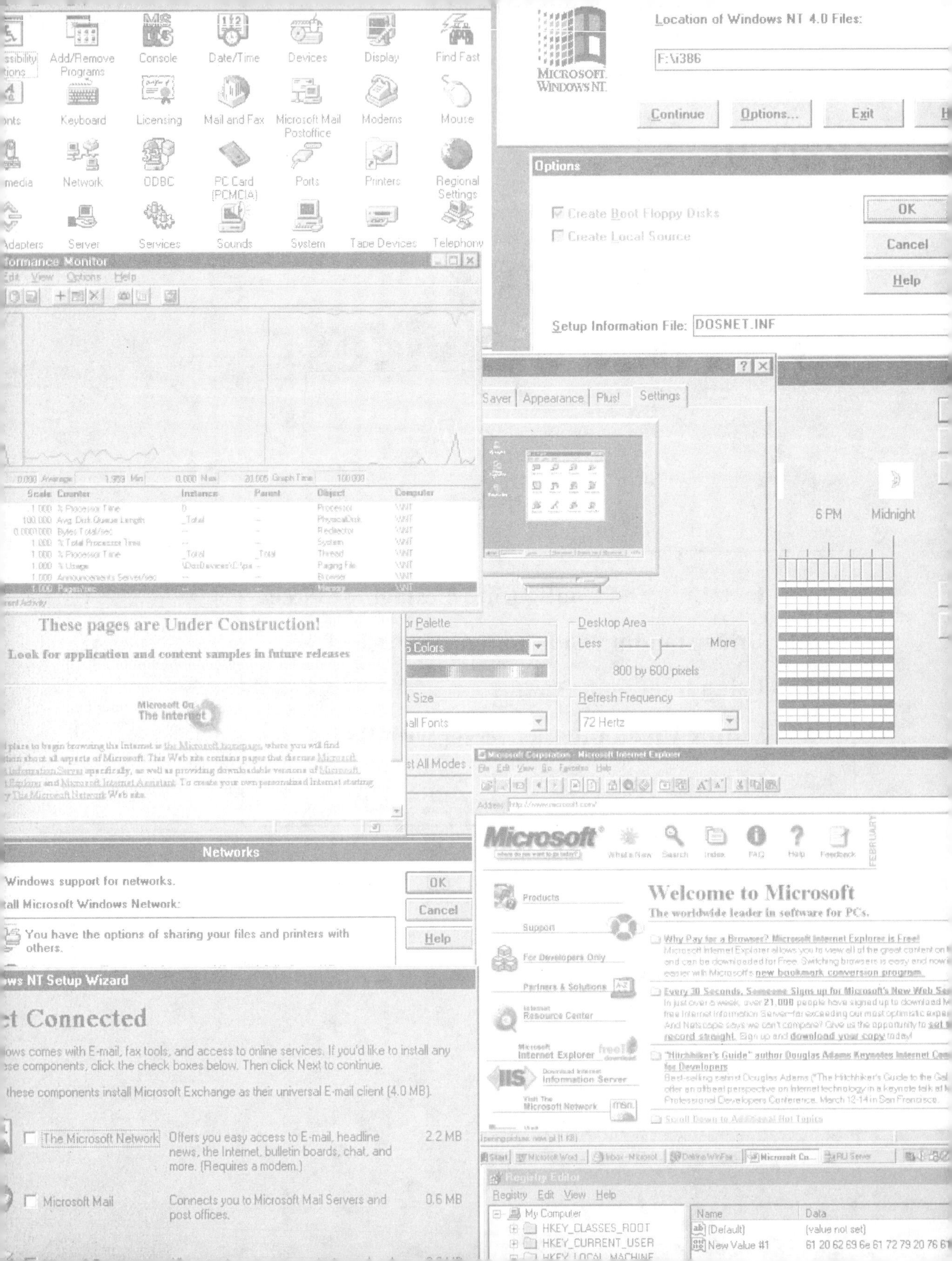

Add/Remove Programs
Console
Date/Time
Devices
Display
Find Fast
Keyboard
Licensing
Mail and Fax
Microsoft Mail Postoffice
Modems
Mouse
Network
ODBC
PC Card (PCMCIA)
Ports
Printers
Regional Settings
Server
Services
Sounds
System
Tape Devices
Telephony
Location of Windows NT 4.0 Files:
F:\i386
MICROSOFT WINDOWS NT
Continue
Options...
Exit
Options
Create Boot Floppy Disks
Create Local Source
OK
Cancel
Help
Setup Information File: DOSNET.INF
Saver
Appearance
Plus!
Settings
Desktop Area
Less
More
800 by 600 pixels
Refresh Frequency
72 Hertz
6 PM
Midnight
These pages are Under Construction!
Look for application and content samples in future releases
Microsoft On The Internet
Networks
Windows support for networks.
OK
Cancel
Help
You have the options of sharing your files and printers with others.
Welcome to Microsoft
The worldwide leader in software for PCs.
Products
Support
For Developers Only
Partners & Solutions
Internet Resource Center
Microsoft Internet Explorer
Microsoft Network
Registry Editor
Registry
Edit
View
Help
My Computer
HKEY_CLASSES_ROOT
HKEY_CURRENT_USER
Name
Data
(Default)
(value not set)
New Value #1
Connected
The Microsoft Network
Offers you easy access to E-mail, headline news, the Internet, bulletin boards, chat, and more. (Requires a modem.)
2.2 MB
Microsoft Mail
Connects you to Microsoft Mail Servers and post offices.
0.6 MB

CHAPTER 23

Installing and Configuring Windows Messaging

by Jim Boyce

Windows NT includes an e-mail feature named Windows NT Messaging (referred to in the remainder of the chapter as simply Messaging) that enables you to combine much, if not all, of your e-mail into a single inbox. With Messaging, you can send and receive e-mail to a Microsoft Mail post office, the Internet, and CompuServe. Messaging's support for Internet and CompuServe e-mail gives you a gateway to send and receive messages to almost anyone in the world who has an e-mail account on the Internet or on an online service such as CompuServe, America Online, Prodigy, or others.

Note

The Windows NT Messaging feature that is included with Windows NT is almost identical to the Microsoft Exchange client included with Windows 95. The Messaging client and the Microsoft Exchange client in Windows 95 are not the same as the Microsoft Exchange client designed by Microsoft for the Microsoft Exchange Server product. The Microsoft Exchange client for Microsoft Exchange Server provides additional features not supported by the versions included with Windows NT and Windows 95. In fact, Microsoft changed the name of the client to Windows NT Messaging (from Exchange) to differentiate between the "light" client and the full-featured client supported by the Microsoft Exchange Server product.

This chapter helps you install and configure Messaging to enable you to send and receive e-mail and faxes, both locally on your network and through your modem to remote sites and services.

In this chapter, you learn to

- Install Messaging
- Configure Messaging and service providers

- Create and edit a Messaging profile
- Set up your personal message store and address books
- Add other e-mail and fax services to Messaging
- Set up Messaging for remote mail access
- Customize Messaging

> **Note**
>
> Because the *Windows NT Installation and Configuration Handbook* focuses on installation issues, this chapter doesn't cover how to use Messaging. You can refer to Que's *Windows NT Communications Handbook* for more information on using Messaging.

Installing the Messaging Client

Microsoft Messaging is a typical Windows NT application (see fig. 23.1) that works in conjunction with various *service providers* to enable you to send and receive e-mail and faxes. You can think of a service provider as an add-on module that enables the Messaging client to work with specific types of mail and online services. For example, Windows NT includes service providers that enable it to work with Microsoft Mail and the Internet. (Messaging and Exchange are used interchangeably in this chapter.)

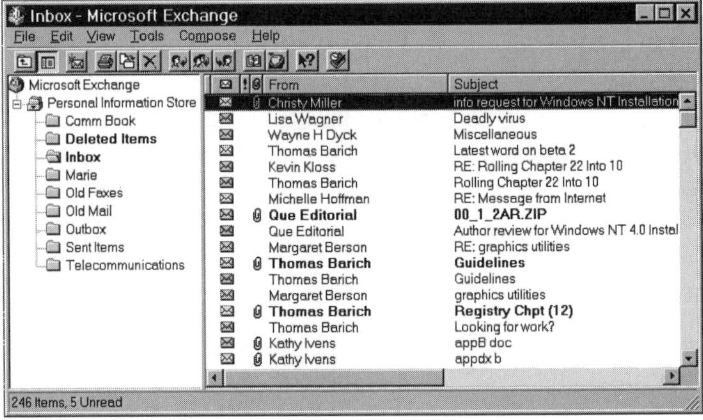

Fig. 23.1
Messaging provides a unified inbox for all of your e-mail.

Tip

You can expect other e-mail vendors to offer service providers for Microsoft Messaging that support their e-mail applications. Also look for online services, such as America Online and Prodigy, to provide Messaging service providers that work with their online services. CompuServe currently offers a Messaging service provider.

Installing and configuring Messaging consists of four phases, which are described in the following list:

▶ See "Installing and Configuring CompuServe Mail," p. 551

- *Install Messaging.* You can install Messaging when you install Windows NT, or you can easily add Messaging to your PC at any time after you install Windows NT.
- *Create at least one profile.* Your Messaging settings and service providers are stored in a Messaging *profile.* Each profile can contain one or more service providers to support different e-mail and fax systems. A profile is a collection of settings you can use to specify which service providers and settings you want to use with Messaging.
- *Add a personal information store and address book.* You need somewhere to store your messages, so the third phase in configuring Messaging is to add a personal information store to your profile, along with an address book to store e-mail and fax addresses. With Windows NT Messaging, the personal information store is referred to as your personal folders.
- *Add service providers.* The final phase of installing Messaging is to add the service providers you want to use to your profile. These could include Microsoft Mail, CompuServe Mail, and Internet Mail.

Note

The CompuServe Mail provider for Windows NT Messaging (called CompuServe Mail for Microsoft Exchange) was designed to work with the Windows 95 version of Messaging. It is included on the Windows 95 CD, but is not included with Windows NT. You can retrieve an updated version of the CompuServe Mail provider from CompuServe (**GO CSMAIL**). This updated version adds features not included with the original release (such as connection to CompuServe through the Internet) and works with Windows NT Messaging.

You can even get a cc:mail service for Messaging from Transend Corporation at: **http://www.transendcorp.com/**

On the Web

Setup doesn't automatically install Messaging when you install Windows NT. Instead, you must specifically select Messaging as an option to install when you run Setup. Or you can add Messaging after installing Windows NT. The following sections explain how to install the Microsoft Messaging client software. Later sections explain how to create and modify Messaging profiles, add service providers, and set other Messaging options.

Installing Messaging During Windows NT Installation

▶ See "Creating and Editing User Profiles," p. 523

If you have not yet installed Windows NT, you can install Messaging at the same time you install Windows NT. To install Messaging, use the following steps:

1. Start the Windows NT Setup program as explained in Chapter 4, "Installing Windows NT."
2. Proceed through the installation until the Setup Options dialog box appears (see fig. 23.2) and prompts you to select the type of installation you want. Choose Custom; then choose Next. (The Typical, Portable, and Compact selections will not install Messaging.)

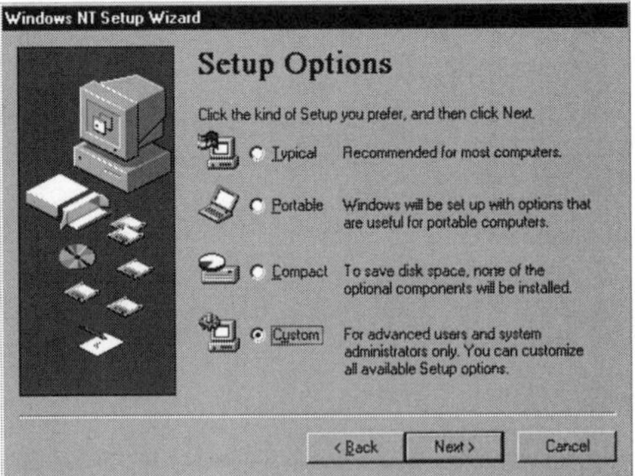

Fig. 23.2 Select the Custom option to install Messaging with the rest of the Windows NT components.

3. When the Select Components dialog box appears, mark the Microsoft Messaging checkbox, then click the Details button.
4. When the Microsoft Messaging property page appears, select the service provider you want to use with Messaging (see fig. 23.3). When you've made your selections, choose Next.
5. Follow Setup's remaining prompts to complete the installation process.

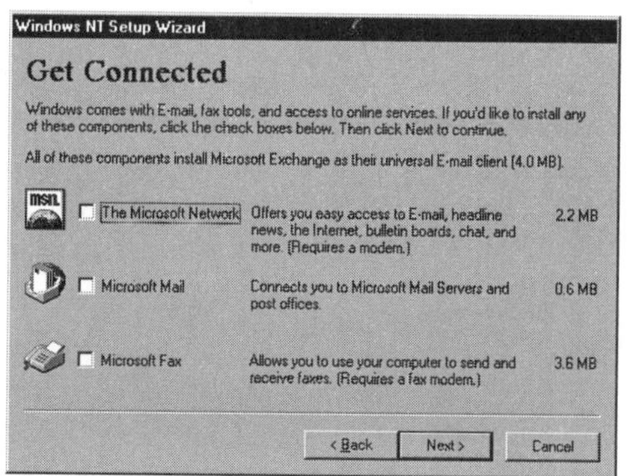

Fig. 23.3
Choose one or more service providers from the Get Connected dialog box.

> **Note**
>
> If you forget to add a service provider when you install Windows NT or add Messaging to your system, you can add the service provider later.

After Setup completes the installation process and you start Windows NT, you see an Inbox icon on the desktop. This is the object you will later use to start Messaging. Before using Messaging, however, you need to complete the configuration process. Skip to the section "Creating and Editing User Profiles" later in this chapter to learn how to complete the configuration process for Messaging.

▶ See "Creating and Editing User Profiles," p. 523

> **Troubleshooting**
>
> *When Messaging starts, I receive error messages that my Internet Mail server is not available. I don't have an Internet Mail server and don't use Internet Mail. What's wrong?*
>
> You probably have installed the Internet Mail service provider by mistake. Open Control Panel and choose the Mail and Fax icon. From the list of installed services, choose Internet Mail; then choose Remove. Windows NT prompts you to verify that you want to remove the Internet Mail service provider from your profile. Choose Yes to remove the service from your profile.

Adding Messaging After Installing Windows NT

If you didn't install Messaging when you installed Windows NT, don't worry—it's easy to add. Use the following steps to add Messaging after installing Windows NT:

1. Choose Start, Settings, Control Panel to open the Control Panel.
2. Double-click the Add/Remove Programs icon to open the Add/Remove Programs Properties sheet.
3. Click the Windows NT Setup tab, and the Windows NT Setup page shown in figure 23.4 appears.

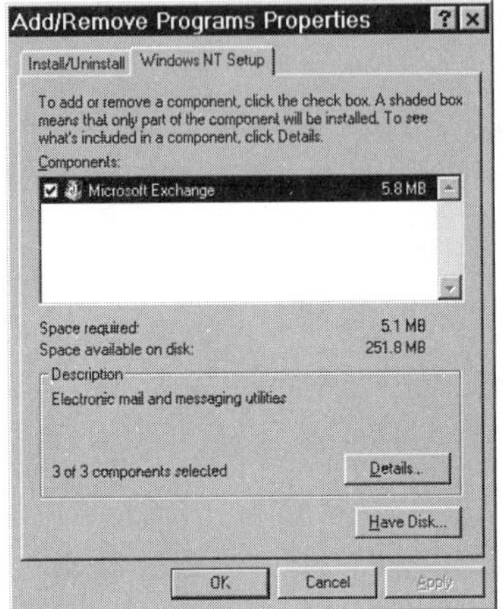

Fig. 23.4
Use the Windows NT Setup page any time you need to add a Windows NT component.

4. Scroll through the Components list to locate and select Microsoft Messaging (or Exchange); then choose Details.
5. In the Microsoft Messaging dialog box, place a checkmark beside Microsoft Messaging, then place a checkmark beside each of the service providers you want to use, and choose OK.
6. Choose OK again. Windows NT adds the necessary software to your system.

Note

If you will be using Messaging for local e-mail (on the LAN, for example) with the Microsoft Mail provider, you must first create a postoffice on a computer that will act as your mail server. For steps and tips on setting up a postoffice, see the section, "Setting Up a Workgroup Postoffice," later in this chapter. You should have the postoffice in place before you begin configuring your profile(s). If you are using only the Internet Mail or CompuServe Mail providers, you don't need a workgroup postoffice.

Creating and Editing User Profiles

Besides installing Messaging, you need to configure at least one user profile. The following section explains user profiles to help you understand how to create and edit them.

Understanding Profiles

A collection of information stores, address books, and service providers is called a *user profile*. For example, you might use a profile that contains your personal information store, one address book, a Microsoft Mail service provider, and a CompuServe service provider. In addition to giving you a means of grouping the service providers and information store you use most often into a named group, Messaging profiles also store the settings for each item in the profile. Figure 23.5 shows items in a typical Messaging profile.

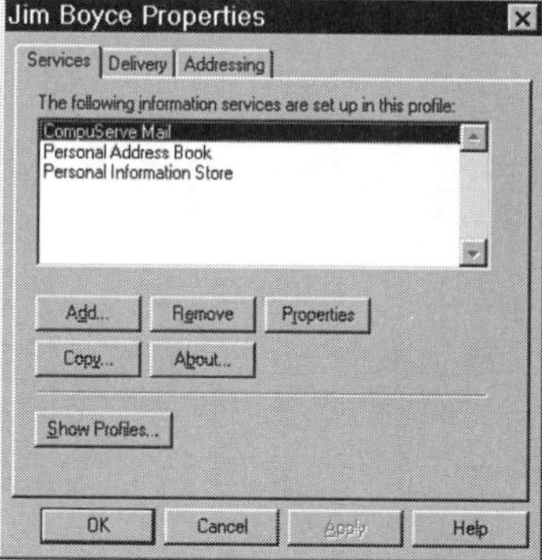

Fig. 23.5
A Messaging profile stores your Messaging settings by name.

If you're like most people, you will use a single profile. But you can use multiple profiles. For example, if you use CompuServe Mail very seldom but use Microsoft Mail all the time, you might want to place the CompuServe Mail provider in a separate profile. When you have to use CompuServe Mail, you can make the CompuServe Mail profile active (explained in the next section); then start Messaging to use it.

> **Tip**
>
> Information stores and address books are service providers, just like Microsoft Mail, CompuServe, and other service providers. All these service providers are often referred to as just *services*. A personal information store is really just a set of special Messaging folders in which you store your messages, and is something you must add to your default profile—Messaging doesn't create an information store for you automatically.

▶ See "Configuring Profiles," p. 524

Configuring Profiles

As with most configuration tasks in Windows NT, you create and edit user profiles from the Control Panel. When you install Messaging, Windows NT does not create a default profile for you. So, you must create your own profile after installing Messaging. To create a default profile, open the Control Panel; then double-click the Mail icon to display the Mail properties sheet similar to the one shown in figure 23.6.

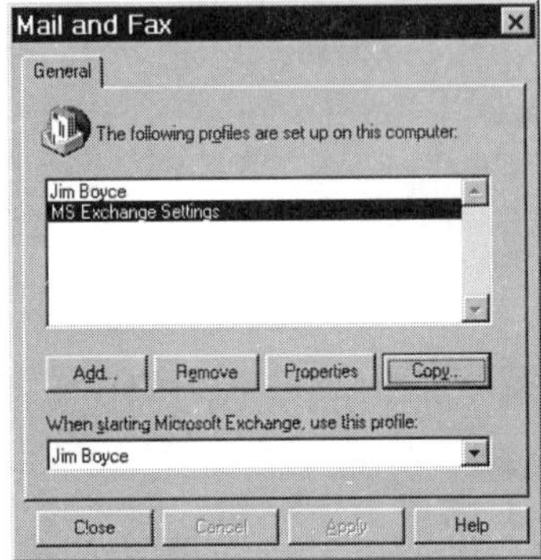

Fig. 23.6 Use the Mail property sheet to create and modify Messaging profiles.

From the Mail property sheet, you can add services to a profile, delete services, set properties for services, and create and view other profiles. You also can set the properties of services in a profile. If you are using the CompuServe Mail provider, for example, you can specify your CompuServe user ID, password, and other properties that control how and when the CompuServe provider logs on to CompuServe to send and receive your CompuServe mail.

Each service is different, so the properties that you can set for each service varies. Later sections, "Setting Up Personal Folders," "Setting Up Address Books," and "Adding Other Information Stores," explain how to add services and set their properties. The following section explains how to create and delete profiles.

Creating and Deleting Messaging Profiles

As explained earlier, you must create a default profile, or you might want to use more than one Messaging profile to store different sets of properties and services. You can create a profile in one of two ways—create a completely new profile or copy an existing profile. Regardless of which method you use, you can edit the profile to add, remove, or edit services after you create the profile.

You can easily create a Messaging profile from scratch or copy an existing profile. Windows NT provides a wizard to step you through the process of creating a profile. Use the following steps to create a new Messaging profile:

1. Open the Control Panel and double-click the Mail icon to display the Mail property sheet.
2. If one or more profiles already exist, click the Show Profiles button to display the Microsoft Messaging Profiles property sheet.
3. Click the Add button, and the Inbox Setup Wizard shown in figure 23.7 appears.

Fig. 23.7
Messaging provides a wizard to help you set up a profile.

4. Click the Use the Following Information Services option button.
5. Place a checkmark beside each of the services you want to include in your profile. Deselect any services you don't want included in the profile; then choose Next. If other profiles have already been created, the wizard displays a new dialog box prompting you for a name for your new profile (see fig. 23.8).

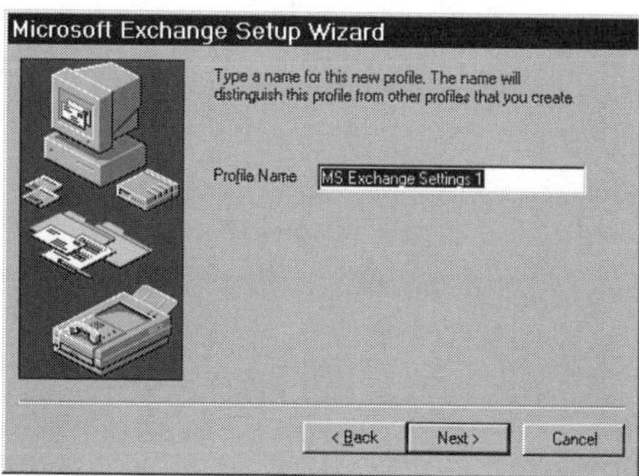

Fig. 23.8
Enter a unique name for your new profile.

6. Enter a unique name for your profile; then choose Next.
7. Depending on which services you selected, the wizard prompts you for information to configure the services. Refer to the sections later in this chapter that describe setup options for services to help you configure the services.
8. When you have finished configuring the services, the wizard displays a final dialog box showing the name for your new profile. If this is the first profile you've created, the wizard provides a name automatically. Choose Finish to complete the profile creation process.

Tip

If you use the preceding steps to create a profile and add services to the profile, Windows NT uses a wizard to step you through the process of configuring the services. If you add services manually as explained later in this chapter, Windows NT doesn't use a wizard, but instead displays a set of property sheets for the service. Use these sheets to set its properties. If you read through the following sections on configuring services manually, you'll have no trouble at all configuring the services using the wizard.

To copy an existing profile, follow these steps:

1. Open the Control Panel and double-click the Mail icon to display the default profile property sheet.
2. Click the Show Profiles button to display the Mail property sheet shown in figure 23.9.

Fig. 23.9
With the Mail property page, you can create a new profile or copy an existing profile.

3. Select the profile you want to copy; then click Copy A dialog box prompting you to enter a name for your new profile appears (see fig. 23.10).

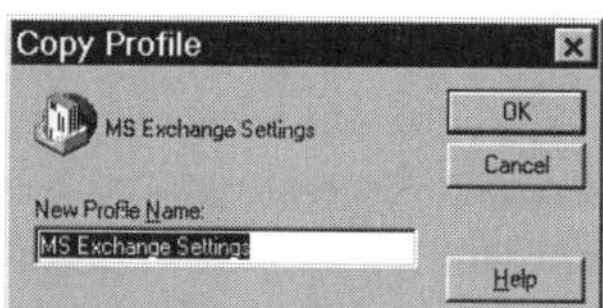

Fig. 23.10
Enter a unique name for your new profile.

4. In the New Profile Name text box, enter a unique name for your new Messaging profile; then choose OK. Windows NT then copies all the services and settings in the selected profile to your new profile.
5. Use the steps explained in the following sections of this chapter to configure the services in your new profile.

Tip

After you create a profile, you need to specify it as your default profile before you can use it with Messaging. See the section "Setting Your Default Profile," later in the chapter to learn how to begin using your new profile.

Setting Your Default Profile

Although you can create as many Messaging profiles as you want, you can only use one profile at a time. You have two options for specifying which profile Messaging uses. Each time you want to use a different profile, you must exit Messaging, use the Control Panel to specify which profile to use, and then restart Messaging. Or you can configure Messaging to prompt you to specify which profile to use each time Messaging starts.

To specify a default profile, follow these steps:

1. Open the Control Panel and double-click the Mail icon.
2. Click the Show Profiles button.
3. From the drop-down list labeled When Starting Microsoft Messaging, Use This Profile, choose the profile you want Messaging to use as a default.
4. Choose Close; then start Messaging to verify that it is using the correct profile.

To have Messaging prompt you to select a profile each time Messaging starts, follow these steps:

1. Start Messaging (double-click the Inbox icon on the desktop).
2. Choose Tools, Options to display the Options property sheet.

3. From the control group named When Starting Microsoft Messaging, choose the option labeled Prompt for a Profile to be Used. Then choose OK. The next time you start Messaging, you'll be prompted to select which profile you want to use.

To learn about other general Messaging options you can specify, see the section "Setting General Messaging Options," later in this chapter.

Setting Up Personal Folders

Without a place to store all your messages, Messaging wouldn't be much use to you. So each profile should include at least one *information store*. An information store is a special type of file that Messaging uses to store your messages, and Windows NT refers to a message store as Personal Folders. Whether the message is a fax, an e-mail message from your network mail post office, or another service, incoming messages are placed in the Inbox folder of your default information store. A typical information store contains the following folders:

- *Deleted Items.* This folder contains all the messages you have deleted from other folders. By default, Messaging does not delete items from your information store unless you select them in the Deleted Items folder and delete them. As explained later in the section "Setting General Messaging Options," you can configure Messaging to immediately delete a message instead of moving it to the Deleted Items folder.
- *Inbox.* Messaging places all your incoming messages—including error and status messages generated by the various service providers, e-mail, and faxes—in the Inbox.
- *Outbox.* Items that you compose are placed in the Outbox until the appropriate service delivers the message automatically or you manually direct Messaging to deliver the message(s).
- *Sent Items.* By default, Messaging places a copy of all messages you send in the Sent Items folder. You can configure Messaging not to keep a copy of sent messages (see the section "Setting General Messaging Options," later in this chapter).

In addition to the folders listed previously, you can add your own folders to an information store. And you're not limited to a single information store—you can add as many information stores to a profile as you like. The folders in each information store show up under a separate tree in the Messaging window. Figure 23.11 shows Messaging with two information stores being used, those stores are named Personal Folders and Personal Information Store.

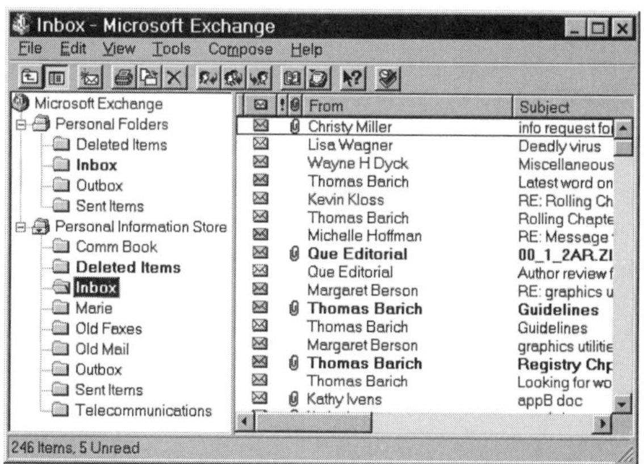

Fig. 23.11
You can use as many information stores in a profile as you like.

Adding multiple message stores to a profile is useful mainly for copying messages between message files. If you are using the latest version of the Microsoft Mail service provider that supports shared folders, however, you can add a shared folder message store to your profile. The shared folder enables you to share messages with other users.

There is one other reason to add a set of personal folders to your profile: you can't change the encryption method on an existing Personal Folders Store, but you specify the type of encryption to use on a secondary set of personal folders when you add the folders to a profile. The two stores are identical in function, so if you want to use a different level of encryption for your message file for extra security, add a Personal Folders item to your profile, copy your messages from the original Personal Folders to the new one, and then remove the original Personal Folders from your profile. Make sure that you configure Messaging to use the new personal folders to store incoming messages, as explained in the next section.

Configuring Your Personal Folders

You can change a handful of settings for Personal Folders. To change properties for a Personal Information Store, follow these steps:

1. Open the Control Panel and double-click the Mail icon.
2. If you want to set properties for Personal Folders in a profile other than the default profile, choose the Show Profiles button, select the profile you want to change; then choose Properties.
3. Select Personal Folders from the list of services in the profile; then choose Properties. The Personal Folders property sheet shown in figure 23.12 appears.

Fig. 23.12
Use the Personal Folders property sheet to set properties for the information store.

4. Set the properties for the Personal Folders according to the following descriptions and your needs:

   - *Name.* If you like, enter a new name for the Personal Information Store. This name will appear in the profile instead of "Personal Folders."
   - *Change Password.* Click this button to change the password for your Personal Information Store. The four properties you can set in the password dialog box are described in Table 23.1.

Table 23.1 Password Properties for an Information Store

Property	Purpose
Old Password	Enter in this text box the current password, if any, for the Personal Information Store.
New Password	Enter the new password you want to assign to the Personal Information Store in this text box.
Verify Password	Enter in this text box the new password you want to assign to the Personal Information Store to enable Windows NT to verify that you have entered the password correctly.
Save this Password in Your Password List	If you want the password stored in your password cache so you don't have to enter the password each time you open Messaging, place a checkmark in this checkbox.

   - *Compact Now.* Choose this button to compress (compact) your Personal Information Store. Windows NT compresses the file, reducing its size. Compressing a message store has no effect on your ability to use the file to store messages.
   - *Comment.* If you want to add a short comment about the Personal Folders, enter it in this text box.

After you have specified all the necessary properties, choose OK; then choose OK again to save the changes.

Adding Other Information Stores

As explained earlier, you can add as many information stores to a profile as you like. These additional stores are also called Personal Folders, and they have the same structure and function as your default Personal Folders. You can add a new Personal Folders file to a profile or add an existing file. Adding an existing file enables you to easily import messages from other information stores that you or others have created separately.

To add an information store to a profile, use the following steps:

1. Open the Control Panel and double-click the Mail icon.
2. If you want to add Personal Folders to a profile other than the default profile, choose the Show Profiles button, select the profile you want to change, and then choose Properties.
3. Choose Add; then from the Add Service to Profile dialog box, select Personal Folders and choose OK.
4. The Create/Open Personal Folders File dialog box appears. If you are adding an existing file, locate and select the file in the dialog box; then choose Open. If you want to create a new file, enter a name for the file in the File name text box, and then choose Open.
5. If you are adding an existing Personal Folders file, skip to step 6. If you are creating a new file, Windows NT displays a dialog box similar to the one shown in figure 23.13. The Name and Password properties are the same as those explained in the preceding section. From the Encryption Setting group, choose one of the following options:
   - *No Encryption.* Choose this option if you don't want the file to be encrypted. If the file is not encrypted, other users can open the file and read its contents with another program, such as a word processor.
   - *Compressible Encryption.* Choose this option if you want the file to be encrypted for security, but you also want to be able to compress (compact) the file to save disk space.
   - *Best Encryption.* Choose this option if you want the most secure encryption. You will not be able to compress the file if you choose this option.

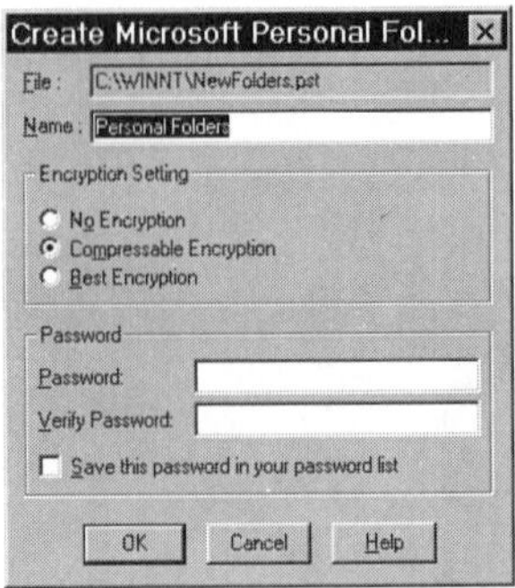

Fig. 23.13 The Create Microsoft Personal Folders dialog box enables you to set various properties for your information store.

6. If you are adding an existing Personal Folders file, adjust settings as explained previously.
7. Choose OK; then choose OK again to close the profile's property sheet.

Setting Delivery Options

Even though you can add multiple information stores to a profile, only one can be assigned to receive incoming messages. You can, however, assign an alternate information store to be used to store incoming messages if the primary store is unavailable for some reason.

To set these delivery options, follow these steps:

1. Open the Control Panel and double-click the Mail icon.
2. Click the Delivery tab to display the Delivery property page (see fig. 23.14).

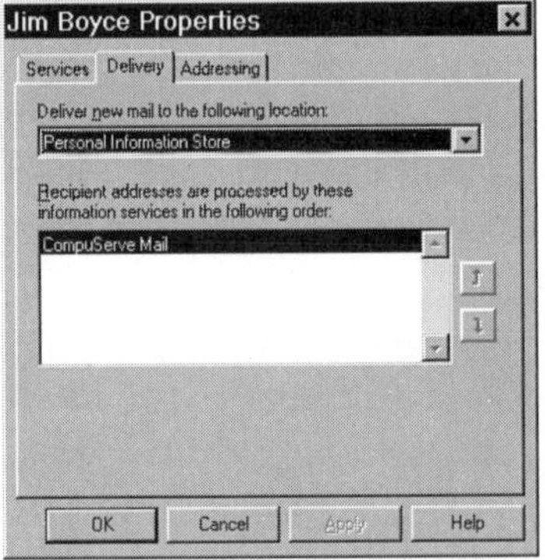

Fig. 23.14 Specify which store will receive incoming messages.

3. Specify settings in the Delivery property page based on the following descriptions:
    - *Deliver New Mail to the Following Location.* Select from the drop-down list the information store in which you want incoming mail to be placed.
    - *Recipient Addresses are Processed by these Information Services in the Following Order.* This control lists the order in which mail providers distribute mail when you direct Messaging to deliver mail using all services. To move an item in the list, select it; then click either the up or the down arrow.
4. After specifying the desired settings, choose OK to save the changes.

Setting Up Address Books

Although you can send and receive mail without an address book, adding an address book to your profile makes it possible for you to store addresses and quickly select an address for a message. You can add addresses to the address book yourself, or let Messaging add originating addresses of received mail.

A profile can contain only one Personal Address Book. When you install Messaging, Windows NT automatically adds a Personal Address Book to your default profile. You can add a new, blank address book, or add an existing address book that already contains address entries.

If you want to add a Personal Address Book to a new profile or you have accidentally deleted your Personal Address Book from your default profile, follow these steps to add the address book:

1. Open the Control Panel and double-click the Mail icon.
2. If you want to add a Personal Address Book to a profile other than the default profile, choose the Show Profiles button, select the profile you want to change, and then choose Properties.
3. Choose the Add button; then from the Add Service to Profile dialog box, choose Personal Address Book and click OK. The Personal Address Book property sheet shown in figure 23.15 appears.
4. In the Name text box, enter a name for the address book (or leave the name as is, if you prefer).
5. In the Path text box, enter the path and file name for the new address book file, or in the case of an existing address book, enter the path and filename of the existing file. If you prefer, you can choose the Browse button to browse for the file.

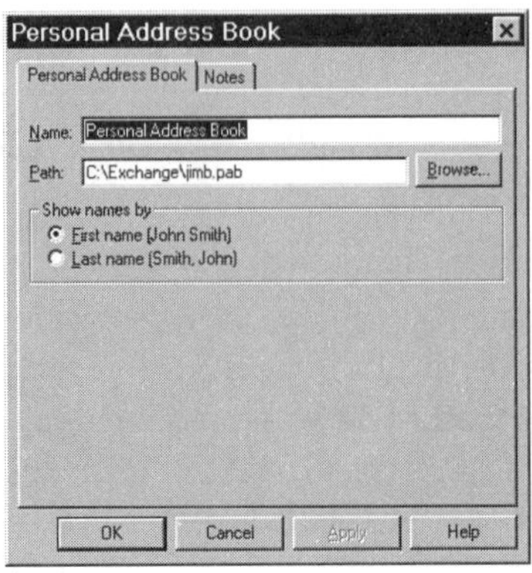

Fig. 23.15
Set properties for your Personal Address Book.

6. From the control group Show Names By, choose how you want names to appear in the address book (sorted by first name or last name).
7. Choose OK; then choose OK again to save the changes.

Setting Addressing Options

Although you can have only one Personal Address Book in a profile, you can add other types of address books. For example, a CompuServe Address Book is included in the CompuServe Mail provider. Other service providers that you add might also include their own address books. For this reason, you need a way to specify which address book Messaging displays by default and other addressing options.

To set addressing options, open the Control Panel and double-click the Mail icon. Then click the Addressing tab to display the Addressing property page shown in figure 23.16.

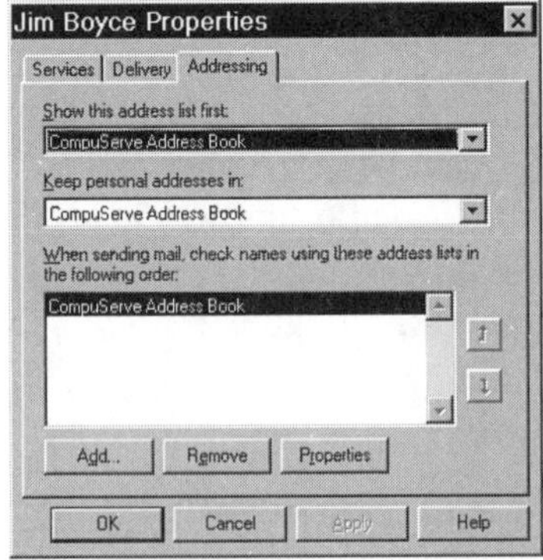

Fig. 23.16
Use the Addressing page to specify your default address book.

The properties you can specify on the Addressing page are described in the following list:

- *Show this Address List First.* Select from this drop-down list the address book you want Messaging to display when you click the To button in the compose window, or choose Tools, Address Book. You'll have the option in Messaging of selecting a different address book if more than one is installed.
- *Keep Personal Addresses In.* Select from this drop-down list the address book in which you want a new address to be added unless you specifically choose a different address book.
- *When Sending Mail, Check Names Using these Address Lists in the Following Order.* Use this list to set the order in which Messaging checks addresses for validity when you send a message or click the Check Names button in the compose window toolbar.

After you specify the Addressing properties you want to use, choose OK to save the changes.

Troubleshooting

I'm trying to add a second Personal Address List, but Messaging displays an error that the service can't be added twice to the profile.

Only one copy of the Personal Address List service can be present in a profile. If you want to add a secondary address list, you'll have to create a new profile to contain it, then switch between profiles when you want to switch address books.

Setting General Messaging Options

It might sometimes seem as if Messaging offers an overwhelming number of properties and options that you can set. This section helps you understand and set those properties and options. If you've read through the earlier parts of this chapter, you've already set some general Messaging options, including delivery and addressing options. The following sections explain the other options you can set. To reach the property pages referenced in the following sections, open Messaging; then choose Tools, Options.

Setting General Options

The General property page specifies a handful of properties that control how Messaging alerts you to new incoming messages and other common actions, such as deleting messages (see fig. 23.17).

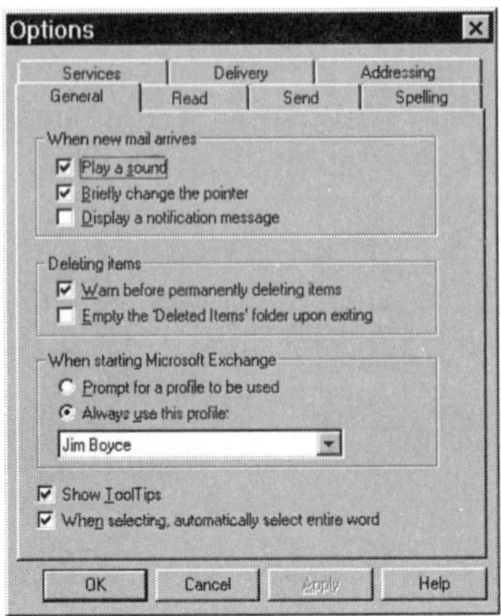

Fig. 23.17
Use the General property page to set general Messaging options.

The following list explains the properties you can set on the General property page:

- *When New Mail Arrives.* This group contains three options you can enable to control how Messaging notifies you of incoming messages.
- *Deleting Items.* Enable the option Warn Before Permanently Deleting Items if you want Messaging to warn you before you permanently delete a message (rather than deleting it to the Deleted Items folder). Enable the option named Empty the 'Deleted Items' Folder Upon Exiting, if you want Messaging to permanently delete messages from the Deleted Items folder when you exit Messaging.
- *When Starting Microsoft Messaging.* Use the options in this group to either specify a default Messaging profile or cause Messaging to prompt you to select a profile each time Messaging starts.
- *Show ToolTips on Toolbars.* Enable this option if you want Messaging to display a ToolTip for a toolbar button when you rest the pointer on the button for a second.
- *When Selecting, Automatically Select Entire Word.* Enable this option if you want Messaging to automatically select entire words when you drag over the words with the pointer.

Setting Read Options

The properties on the Read property page control the way Messaging handles messages when you read, reply to, or forward the messages (see fig. 23.18).

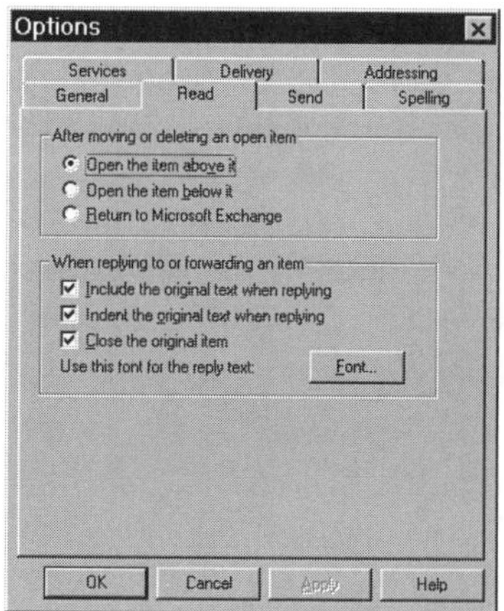

Fig. 23.18
Set options for reading messages using the Read property page.

The properties you can set with the Read property page are explained in the following list:

- *After Moving or Deleting an Open Item.* The three options in this group control Messaging's actions when you read, move, or delete a message. The options are self-explanatory—select whichever option suits your preferences.
- *When Replying to or Forwarding an Item.* These properties control how Messaging handles messages when you reply to or forward a message. Enable the option labeled Include the Original Text when Replying if you want Messaging to include the text of the original message in your reply. If you want the original message text to be indented in the message, with your new text at the left margin, enable the checkbox labeled Indent the original text when replying. Enable the option labeled Close the Original Item if you want Messaging to automatically close the original e-mail message window after you start your reply. Choose the Font button to specify the font used for your reply text.

Tip

If you indent original message text or use a special font in a reply or a forwarded message, the recipient sees those message characteristics only if he or she is using Messaging and a service provider capable of sending and receiving messages in RTF (Rich Text Format). An example of such providers is the Microsoft Mail service provider.

Setting Send Options

You also can specify a few properties that control the way Messaging handles items you are sending. Click the Send tab to display the Send property page shown in figure 23.19.

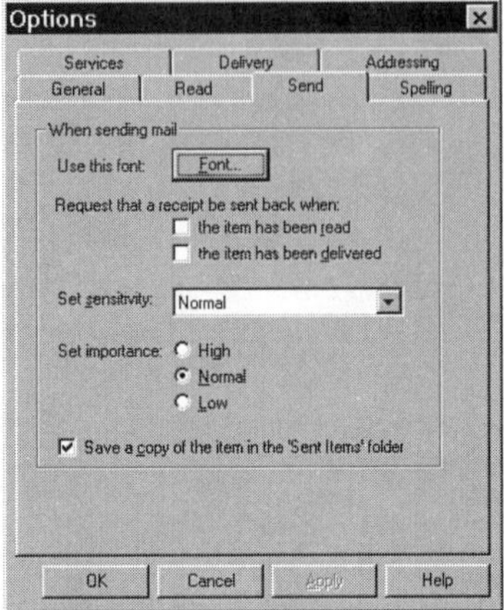

Fig. 23.19
Control outgoing message options with the Send property page.

You can click the Font button to choose the font Messaging will use by default for your outgoing messages. As with indented text, the recipient must also be using Messaging and a service provider that supports message transfer in RTF.

The two options in the group labeled Request That a Receipt Be Sent Back When control whether or not you will receive a return receipt from the recipient's mail system. The available options are as follows:

- *The Item Has Been Read.* If you choose this option, you receive a return receipt only after the recipient reads the message, which could happen well after he receives the message.
- *The Item Has Been Delivered.* Choose this option to receive a return receipt as soon as the message is delivered, regardless of whether the message has been read.

The Set Sensitivity and Set Importance options are self-explanatory. Choose the options you want to use by default. Note that you can override either of these settings when you create a message.

If you enable the option labeled Save a Copy of the Item in the Sent Items Folder, Messaging automatically places a copy of your outgoing message in the Sent Items folder. This is helpful if you need to review a message you previously sent. Just remember to periodically clean out the Sent Items folder to avoid having a huge message file filled with old messages.

Working with Microsoft Mail

If you are using Windows NT on a Microsoft-based network (Windows NT, Windows for Workgroups, or Windows 95), it's a good bet that you want to use the Microsoft Mail service provider—all of these Microsoft operating environments include a workgroup version of Microsoft Mail. Or, you might want to connect through Dial-Up Networking to a remote site, such as your district office, that uses Microsoft Mail. In either case, you need to create and configure a workgroup postoffice (WGPO) if your network does not yet include one. The following sections will help you do just that.

Tip

A *workgroup postoffice* is a special set of directories that Microsoft Mail clients and Microsoft Mail Messaging clients can use to send and receive e-mail. Before you can begin sending and receiving mail on your LAN using the Microsoft Mail provider, you must have a WGPO on your LAN. Fortunately, Windows NT makes it easy to create and manage a WGPO, as you will learn in the next section.

Setting Up a Workgroup Postoffice

The Control Panel contains an object specifically for creating and managing a workgroup postoffice. Open the Control Panel and double-click the Microsoft Mail Postoffice icon. Windows NT starts a wizard as shown in figure 23.20. This wizard lets you either create a new WGPO or administer an existing WGPO.

Note

When you create a WGPO, you also create an administrator's account. The administrator is responsible for creating and managing user mail accounts. Before you begin creating the WGPO, decide who will be administering the postoffice. In the following steps, you'll create an administrator account and should be ready to provide the name of the person who will be administering the postoffice.

To set up a new WGPO, follow these steps:

1. Start the Microsoft Workgroup Postoffice Admin wizard by opening the Control Panel and double-clicking the Microsoft Mail Postoffice icon.
2. Choose the Create a new Workgroup Postoffice option, then choose Next. Windows NT then prompts you for the name and location for your new postoffice (see fig. 23.21). Enter the name or choose Browse to browse for a folder for the WGPO.

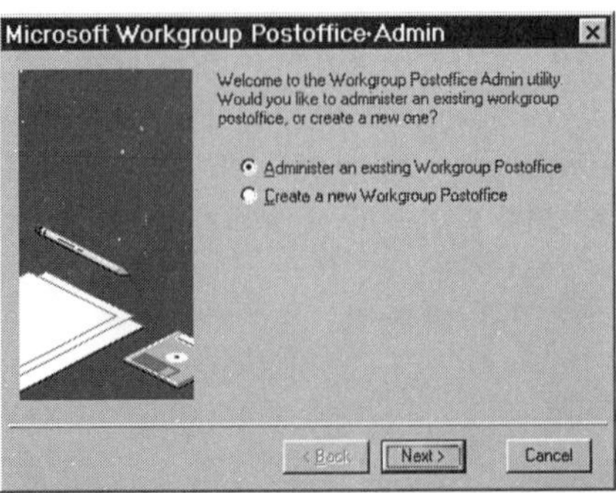

Fig. 23.20
You can create a new WGPO or administer an existing one.

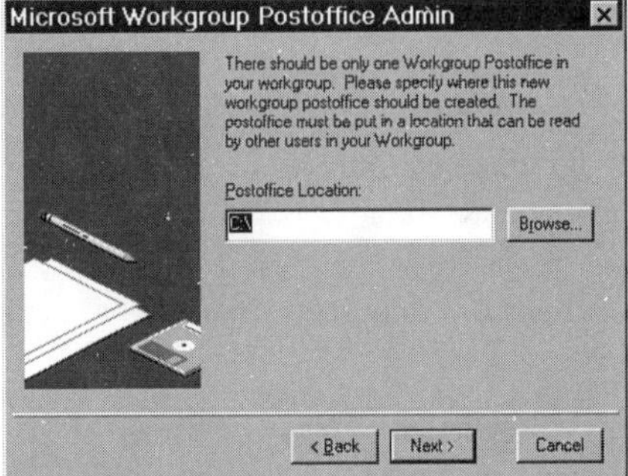

Fig. 23.21
Enter the path and file name for your new postoffice.

> **Note**
>
> You must choose an existing folder in which to create the WGPO. The wizard will not create a folder for you, but instead creates the WGPO folder structure in the existing folder that you choose.

3. After you click Next, the wizard prompts you to verify the path and filename you entered. Choose Next if the path and filename are correct, or choose Back to change the path or filename. After you click Next, the wizard displays the Enter Your Administrator Account Details dialog box shown in figure 23.22.
4. Fill out the fields in the account dialog box. You must provide entries for the following three items:
   - *Name.* In this field, enter the first and last name of the person who will be administering the postoffice.

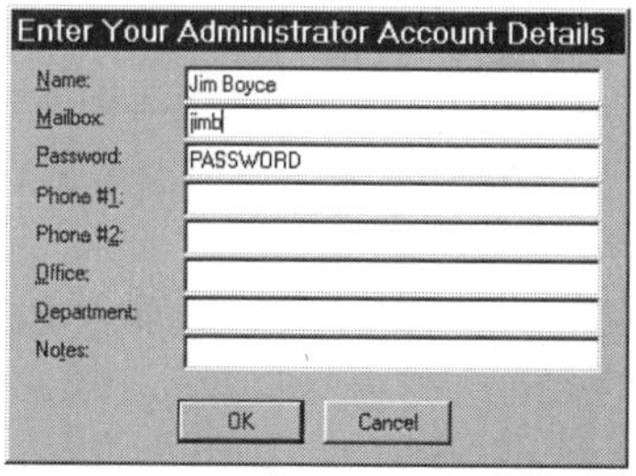

Fig. 23.22
You must specify details for an administrator account for your WGPO.

> **Tip**
>
> If you don't want to specify a particular user's name, use *Postmaster* as the Name and Mailbox entries for the account. When you or anyone else needs to log into the postoffice to administer it, simply log in using the Postmaster account.

- *Mailbox*. Enter in this field the name of the mailbox for the administrator's account. Windows NT suggests your Windows NT network name, but you should consider creating a general Postmaster account.
- *Password*. Although you can leave the password blank, it's a bad idea to leave your WGPO administrator's account unprotected. Windows NT uses PASSWORD as the default account password. You should enter a different password that others won't be able to guess.

> **Caution**
>
> Make sure you don't forget the account password. If you do, you won't be able to administer the WGPO without re-creating the entire WGPO (and losing all messages contained in it).

The remaining options in the account dialog box are optional, and are self-explanatory. They enable a system administrator to fine-tune individual user accounts and provide background information to others of your office information, such as phone number. Choose OK after you have specified the information you want included with the account. The general information (not the password) will appear to other users when they browse the postoffice list of accounts.

Administering a Postoffice

After you create the administrator account, you can begin adding, removing, and modifying mail accounts for users. To administer mail accounts, follow these steps:

1. Open the Control Panel and double-click the Microsoft Mail Postoffice icon.
2. Choose Administer an existing Workgroup Postoffice, then choose Next.
3. Enter the path to your WGPO (or choose Browse to browse for the WGPO), then choose next.
4. Windows NT prompts you for the account name and password of the administrator's account. Enter the mailbox name and password, then choose Next. A Postoffice Manager dialog box similar to the one shown in figure 23.23 appears.

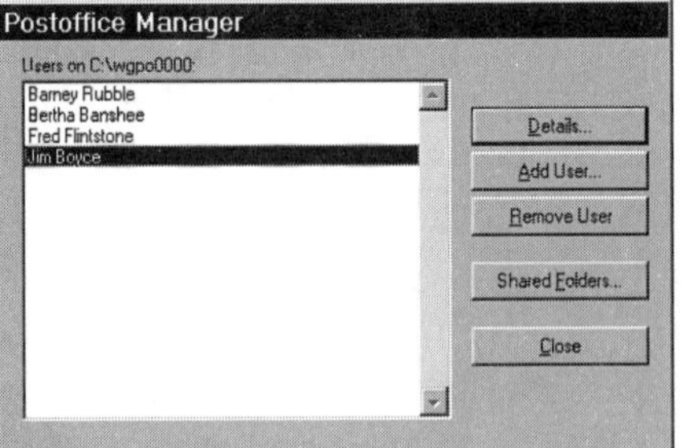

Fig. 23.23 The Postoffice Manager dialog box lets you manage user mail accounts.

5. To view the account details for a user's account, select the account and choose the Details button. A dialog box similar to the one shown in figure 23.24 appears. Modify any of the properties for the user, then choose OK.
6. To add a user, click the Add User button. Windows NT displays a dialog box nearly identical to the Details dialog box shown in figure 23.25. Enter the account details for the mail account, then choose OK.
7. To remove a user, select the user and choose Remove User. Windows NT will prompt you to verify that you want to remove the account. Choose Yes to delete the account, or choose No to cancel the deletion.
8. When you are finished administering the WGPO, choose Close.

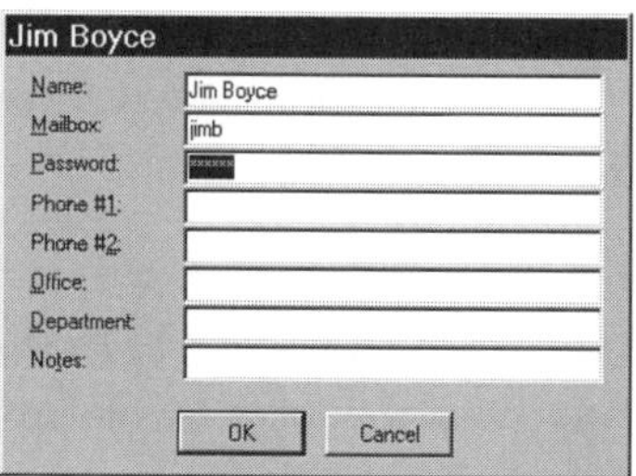

Fig. 23.24 You can modify any mail account property, including the password.

Changing Your Password

Your account in your Microsoft Mail WGPO is protected by a password to ensure that your messages are safe from snooping by others. To improve security, you should periodically change your mail account password. To do so, in Messaging choose Tools, Microsoft Mail Tools, and Change Mailbox Password. Messaging displays a simple dialog box in which you enter your current password, then enter your new password in two separate boxes to confirm the new password. When you're satisfied with your new password, choose OK.

Using the Postoffice Address List

You probably will most often use a Personal Address Book (PAB) to store addresses. When you're working with Microsoft Mail, however, you have an additional address source available—the postoffice address list, which stores the addresses of all accounts in the WGPO. As new accounts are added and as accounts change, those changes are reflected in the postoffice address list. To make sure you have available the most current copy of the postoffice address list, you should periodically download the postoffice address list to your PC. To do so, choose Tools, Microsoft Mail Tools, and Download Address Lists. Messaging will connect to your WGPO and download the postoffice address list.

To work with addresses in the postoffice address list, begin composing a message. Click the To button to display the Address dialog box. Choose Postoffice Address List from the Show Names drop-down list. Messaging will display the postoffice address list, and you can choose addresses from it just as you do with other address sources, such as the PAB.

Using a Session Log

For the most part, Messaging should have no problems connecting to your e-mail account in the WGPO and sending and receiving your messages. If you run into problems, however, the Microsoft Mail provider offers a means for you to troubleshoot the problem—you can direct the Microsoft Mail provider to maintain a log of its connection sessions. You can view the log to identify connection or other problems.

To turn on logging, follow these steps:

1. In Messaging, choose Tools, Services. Or, open the Control Panel and double-click the Mail icon. Either of these two actions displays the property sheet for your message service(s).
2. Choose Microsoft Mail from the list of installed services, then click Properties.
3. When the Microsoft Mail property sheet appears, click the Log tab to display the Log property page (fig. 23.25).

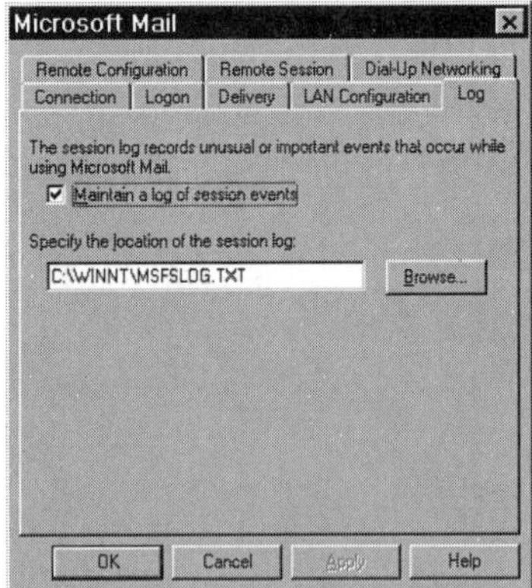

Fig. 23.25
Use the Log property page to turn on session logging.

4. Place a check in the checkbox labeled Maintain a log of session events.
5. If you want to specify a file other than the default (MSFSLOG.TXT) in which to store the file, enter the filename in the text box or click the Browse button to specify the file.
6. Choose OK to apply the change, then OK again to close the property sheet.

To view the log, simply locate it and double-click it. Windows NT will open Notepad (or WordPad if the file is too large for Notepad) and display the file.

Setting Microsoft Mail Options

Like each Messaging service provider, the Microsoft Mail provider offers many options that control how the provider sends and receives mail to and from your WGPO. To set these options, use one of the following two methods:

- From the Messaging window, choose Tools, Services.
- Open the Control Panel and double-click the Mail icon.

Either of these two methods displays the Services property page, although using the second method (through the Control Panel) displays the Delivery and Addressing pages.

After the Services page appears, select Microsoft Mail from the information services list, then click Properties to display the Microsoft Mail property sheet shown in figure 23.26.

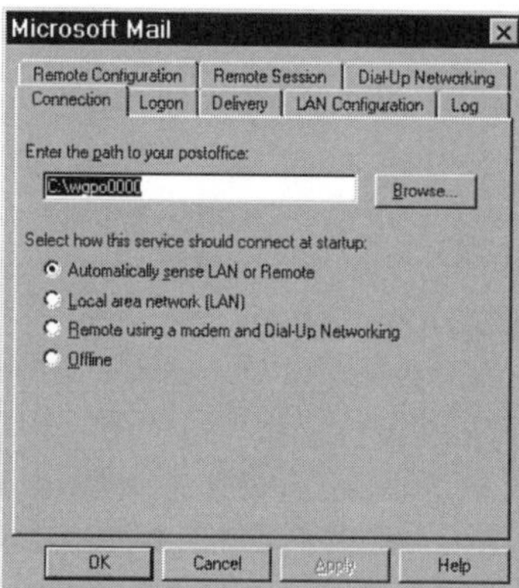

Fig. 23.26
The Microsoft Mail provider's property pages are similar to those of other service providers.

The following sections describe the settings found in each property page.

Connection

The following settings are found on the Connection page:

- *Enter the Path to Your Postoffice.* In this text box, enter the path to the shared directory containing your workgroup postoffice (WGPO). Or, click the Browse button to browse for the WGPO. If you are connecting to a WGPO on a remote system, you might map a local drive ID to the remote shared WGPO directory and specify the drive ID in this text box. Or, you can specify a UNC pathname to the postoffice.
- *Automatically Sense LAN or Remote.* Choose this option button if you want Messaging to automatically determine if you are connecting to the WGPO through a LAN or through a remote connection. If Microsoft Mail is unable to determine the type, it will prompt you to specify the connection.
- *Local Area Network (LAN).* Choose this option if you are connecting to the WGPO on your LAN.

▶ See "Configuring Messaging for Remote Access," p. 556

- *Remote Using a Modem and Dial-Up Networking.* Choose this option if you are connecting to the WGPO through a Dial-Up Networking connection.
- *Offline.* Choose this option if you are not connecting to your WGPO, but instead want to work offline to compose and reply to messages. Incoming and outgoing mail will not be delivered until you reconnect to the WGPO. Outgoing mail will be stored in your Outbox, and incoming mail will remain in your WGPO mail box.

Logon

The following settings are found on the Logon page:

- *Enter the Name of Your Mailbox.* Enter the name of your WGPO mail account (mailbox) in this text box.
- *Enter Your Mailbox Password.* Enter your mailbox password in this text box. The password will appear as asterisks for security. If you prefer to enter your password each time you log on and not store your password on your system, leave this text box blank.
- *When Logging On, Automatically Enter Password.* Enable this checkbox if you want Microsoft Mail to automatically enter your password for logon when you start Messaging. Clear this checkbox if you want Microsoft Mail to prompt you for the password before logging on.
- *Change Mailbox Password.* Click this button to display a simple dialog box you can use to change your password. You must supply your old password in order to specify a new one. You should change your password periodically to ensure security.

Delivery

The following setttings are found on the Delivery page:

- *Enable Incoming Mail Delivery.* Enable this checkbox to allow messages to be delivered from your WGPO mailbox to your Messaging Inbox.
- *Enable Outgoing Mail Delivery.* Enable this checkbox to allow messages in your Inbox to be delivered to the WGPO.
- *Enable deliver to...Address Types.* Click the Address Types button to specify address types to which you don't want messages delivered. A simple dialog box will appear that you can use to select the types of addresses to which you want messages to be delivered.
- *Check for New Mail Every nn Minutes.* Specify the frequency at which you want Microsoft Mail to check for new messages and send pending messages.

- *Immediate Notification.* Enable this checkbox if you want recipients of your messages to be notified when you send them messages. This option, when enabled, also causes you to receive notifications when others send you messages (if these other users have enabled this feature, also). This feature requires the use of a network protocol supporting NetBIOS.
- *Display Global Address List Only.* Enable this checkbox if you only want to work with the Global Address List (postoffice address list) and not your PAB.

LAN Configuration

The following settings are found on the LAN Configuration page:

- *Use Remote Mail.* Enable this checkbox if you want Microsoft Mail to retrieve message headers instead of messages, allowing you to preview your mail before retrieving it.
- *Use Local Copy.* Enable this checkbox to cause Microsoft Mail to use a local copy (stored on your computer) of the postoffice address list. To download the address list, choose Tools, Microsoft Mail Tools, and Download Address Lists.
- *Use External Delivery Agent.* Enable this checkbox if you want the EXTERNAL.EXE delivery agent to deliver your mail. EXTERNAL.EXE must be running on the server for you to make use of it.

Configuring the Internet Mail Provider

If you add the Internet Mail provider through the Control Panel, Windows NT automatically opens the property sheet shown in figure 23.27 as soon as you add the Internet Mail provider to a profile. You also can use this property sheet to configure the Internet Mail provider after you install it.

Note

Installing the latest version of Netscape installs the Netscape Internet Transport, a Windows Messaging service provider that performs essentially the same function as the Internet Mail provider included with Windows NT. If you already have Netscape installed, you shouldn't need the Microsoft Internet Mail service provider to send and retrieve Internet mail.

Setting Mail Properties

To set your Internet Mail properties, open the Control Panel and double-click the Mail icon. Select the Internet Mail provider, then choose Properties to display the General property page shown in figure 23.27.

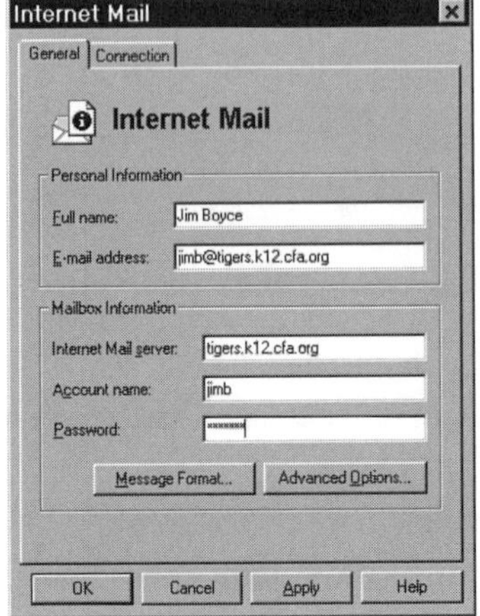

Fig. 23.27
Use the General property page to set general Internet Mail properties.

The following list explains the settings on the General property page:

- *Full Name.* Type your first and last name as you want it to appear in the message headers.
- *E-mail Address.* Type your e-mail address in the form *user@domain*, where *user* is your e-mail account name and *domain* is the domain name of your Internet Mail server. Example: **jimb@nowhere.com**.
- *Internet Mail Server.* Type the domain name of your Internet mail server. Example: **nowhere.com**.
- *Account Name.* Type your e-mail account name (generally, the account you use to log onto the Internet server). Example: **jimb**.
- *Password.* Type the password for your Internet e-mail account.
- *Message Format.* Click this button to specify whether or not the Internet Mail service uses MIME encoding to send your e-mail messages and attachments.
- *Advanced Options.* Click this button to specify the name of a server to which you want all of your outbound mail forwarded. This is necessary if your default Internet Mail server doesn't process outbound mail.

Configuring the Connection

In addition to specifying mail properties, you can also specify how Internet Mail connects to the Internet. To do so, click the Connection tab of the Internet Mail property sheet to display the Connection page shown in figure 23.28.

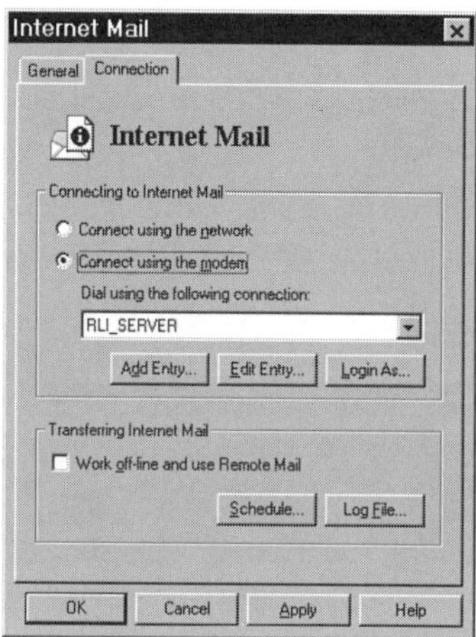

Fig. 23.28
The Connection page determines how Internet Mail connects to the Internet.

The following list describes the properties on the Connection page:

- *Connect Using the Network.* Choose this option button if you connect to the Internet through your local area network.
- *Connect Using the Modem.* Choose this option button if you connect to the Internet using Dial-Up Networking.
- *Dial Using the Following Connection.* If you selected the Connect using the Modem option, choose the correct Dial-Up Networking connection from this drop-down list. If you have not set up a Dial-Up Networking entry, click Add Entry (explained next).
- *Add Entry.* Click this button to create a Dial-Up Networking connection to your Internet service provider. Refer to the *Windows NT Communications Handbook* (Que) for help creating the connection.
- *Edit Entry.* Click this button to edit the selected Dial-Up Networking connection properties.
- *Login As.* Click this button to display the dialog box shown in figure 23.29. Specify the user name and password required to log onto the remote Internet server.

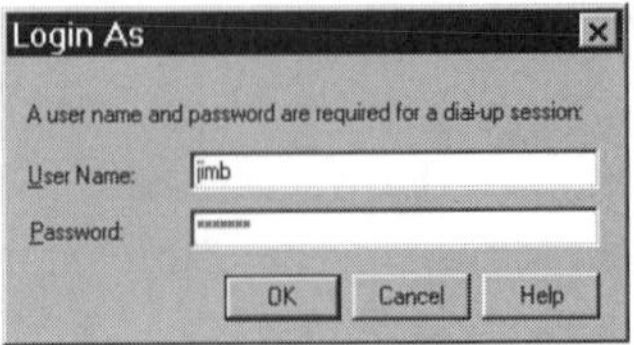

Fig. 23.29 Specify the login name and password required by your Internet server.

- *Work Off-line and Use Remote Mail.* Enable this checkbox if you want to use remote mail and not send and receive Internet mail automatically.
- *Schedule.* Click this button to display the dialog box shown in figure 23.30, which enables you to specify how often Messaging should check for new messages.

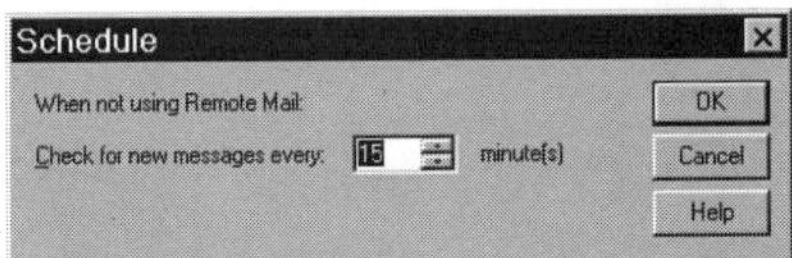

Fig. 23.30 Specify how often Messaging should check for new mail and send waiting mail.

- *Log File.* Click this button if you want the Internet Mail provider to maintain a log of your Internet connection sessions. The Log File dialog box appears, enabling you to select the logging method and location of the log file.

Troubleshooting

Occasionally, a message comes through that Internet Mail can't decode properly and I end up with a lot of gibberish in the message.

It's really not gibberish—that's what a coded file looks like. In these situations you often can save the message and use an external coding program to convert the message to a binary file. To acquire a MIME encoder/decoder, connect via ftp to **ftp.andrew.cmu.edu:pub/mpack/**. You'll find versions of a MIME coder to suit most operating environments, including DOS. If you need more advanced MIME capability, check the site ftp.thumper.bellcore.com:pub/nsb for a program called MetaMail that provides advanced MIME coding.

You also might need a program capable of uuencoding and uudecoding messages. One particularly good one is WinCode, which you can find in the WUGNET forum on CompuServe in Library 3.

On the Web

You also can find WinCode on the Internet at: **http://www.ccn.cs.dal.ca/Services/PDA/WindowsMisc.html**

Installing and Configuring CompuServe Mail

You probably use a front-end application such as WinCIM, CompuServe Navigator, or GoCIS to send and receive mail on CompuServe. These programs all work well, but you might prefer to use Messaging for your CompuServe mail, bringing all your messages into Messaging's common Inbox.

The CompuServe Mail provider for Messaging enables you to do just that. With the CompuServe Mail provider, you can connect to CompuServe to send and receive messages through CompuServe's mail system. Although you can't send and retrieve forum messages through Messaging, at least you can handle your CompuServe mail. You can enjoy the advantages of remote mail preview, a common Inbox, automatic scheduled send/receive, and the other features supported by Messaging.

The CompuServe Mail provider is not included with Windows NT. You can download the CompuServe Mail provider from the CSMAIL and CISSOFT forums on CompuServe.

Installing CompuServe Mail

The CompuServe Mail provider includes its own Setup program to automate the installation process. To install the CompuServe Mail provider, follow these steps:

> **Note**
>
> This installation procedure assumes you are installing the CompuServe Mail provider from the Windows NT CD. If you have downloaded the CompuServe Mail provider from CompuServe, first create a folder to contain the CompuServe Mail files. Open a DOS session and change to that directory. Extract the CompuServe Mail files to the directory by running the compressed file. If you downloaded the file to \Wincim\Download, for example, enter **\Wincim\Download\Csmail.exe**. If you renamed the file during the download, substitute the appropriate name in place of Csmail.exe. After extracting the files, proceed with step 3 (run the Setup program).

1. Create a folder to contain the CompuServe Mail for Microsoft Exchange source files.
2. Download the file CSMAIL.EXE from the CSMAIL or CISSOFT forums on CompuServe, placing the file in the folder created in step 1.

3. Run the CSMAIL.EXE file to extract its contents (it is a self-extracting archive).
4. Run the Setup program extracted from the CSMAIL.EXE archive. The Setup program will prompt you for a directory in which to store the CompuServe Mail files. The default is C:\Cserve.

The CompuServe Mail for Microsoft Exchange (version 1.1) was designed for Windows 95, but works with Windows NT. It does suffer, however, from one minor bug. You can't configure the location of your CompuServe files within the service provider's property sheet. Instead, you must manually edit the Registry to change the location. To do so, follow these steps:

1. Choose Start, Run, type **regedit** in the Open text box, then choose OK to start the Registry Editor.
2. In the Registry Editor, choose Edit, Find.
3. In the Find dialog box, type the string **001e661c** in the Find What text box, then click the Find Next button. Registry Editor should find the setting in HKEY_CURRENT_USER\Software\Microsoft\Windows NT\Windows Messaging Subsystem\Profiles*your profile*, where *your profile* is the name of the Messaging profile containing the CompuServe Mail provider.
4. Double-click the 001e661c setting after Registry Editor locates it in the registry. This will open an Edit String dialog box you can use to change the setting's value.
5. In the Value data text box, type the path to your CompuServe directory, such as C:\CSERVE, then click OK.
6. Close the Registry Editor.

Configuring the CompuServe Mail Service

After you add the CompuServe Mail service to your Messaging profile, you need to configure various settings that define how Messaging connects to CompuServe and sends and receives your CompuServe mail. To configure your user account information in the CompuServe Mail service, follow these steps:

1. Open the Control Panel and double-click the Mail icon.
2. Select CompuServe Mail from the list of installed services, and then choose Properties.
3. In the Name text box on the General property page (see fig. 23.31), enter the name you want to appear in mail message address headers (not your CompuServe account name).

Fig. 23.31
Use the General page to specify your CompuServe account information.

4. In the CompuServe Id text box, enter your CompuServe account ID.
5. In the Password text box, enter your CompuServe account password.

In addition to configuring your account information, you also need to specify how the service will connect to CompuServe. To do so, use the Connection property page and the following steps:

1. Click the Connection tab to display the Connection property page (see fig. 23.32).

Fig. 23.32
Use the Connection page to specify how the connection to CompuServe is made.

2. In the Phone Number text box, enter your CompuServe access number.
3. From the Preferred Tapi Line drop-down list, choose the modem you'll be using to connect to CompuServe.
4. From the Network drop-down list, choose the type of network connection provided by your CompuServe access number.
5. Choose the type of connection method you want to use from one of the following three options:

    - *Windows Modem Settings*. Choose this option to connect through one of CompuServe's access numbers using a modem (that you have already installed through the Modems object in the Control Panel).

- *Winsock Connection.* Choose this option if you want to connect to CompuServe through a Winsock Internet connection (such as through a Dial-Up Networking connection to your Internet service provider). Note that you must clear the Use CompuServe Dialer checkbox, as the CompuServe Dialer will not work properly under Windows NT.
- *Direct Connection.* Choose this option if you have a direct connection to the Internet through one of your computer's serial ports.

At this point, you can choose OK, then OK again to begin using your CompuServe Mail service in Messaging. (Choosing the Apply button saves your current settings without exiting the property sheet.) You might, however, want to set a few advanced options. The Default Send Options page contains a selection of properties that define how messages are sent (see fig. 23.33).

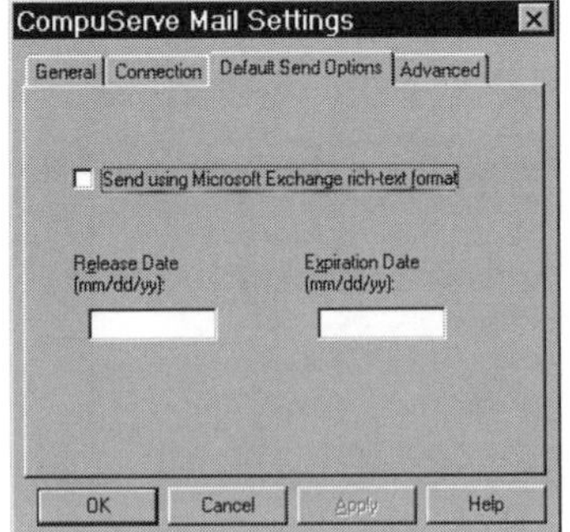

Fig. 23.33 The Default Send Options page controls how messages are sent.

The following list explains the properties on the Default Send Options page:

- *Send Using Microsoft Messaging Rich-Text Format.* Enable this checkbox if you want Messaging to include character (color, font, and so on) and paragraph formatting in your message. Only recipients who are using Microsoft Messaging will see the special formatting—other recipients will receive plain text.
- *Release Date.* If you enter a date in this field, messages will be held in your Inbox until the date specified, then forwarded on that date to the intended recipients. Leave this field blank if you want the messages to be sent as soon as the service connects to CompuServe.

- *Expiration Date.* If you enter a date in this field, the message will be deleted from the recipient's mailbox when the date is reached.
- *Payment Method.* Select one of the three option buttons in this group to specify who pays for surcharged messages.

You can use the Advanced property page to schedule automatic connection to CompuServe and other advanced connection options (see fig. 23.34).

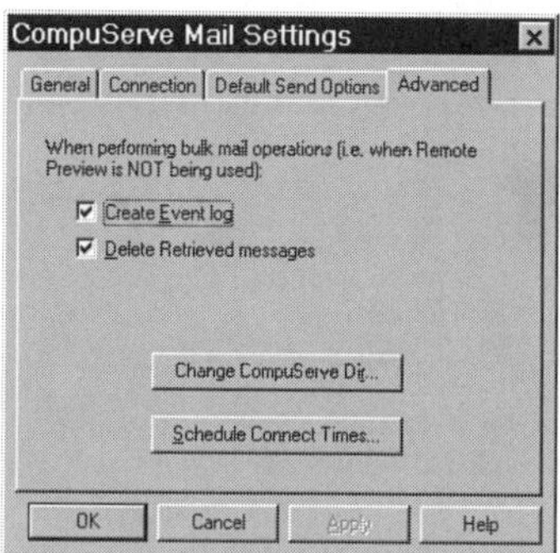

Fig. 23.34 Use the Advanced page to control advanced service options.

The following list describes the controls on the Advanced page:

- *Create Event Log.* Enable this checkbox if you want the CompuServe Mail provider to place log messages describing the results of each connection attempt in your Inbox. These log messages are helpful for troubleshooting connection problems.
- *Delete Retrieved Messages.* Enable this checkbox if you want the CompuServe Mail provider to delete mail from your CompuServe mailbox after the mail is retrieved and stored in your Messaging Inbox.
- *Accept Surcharges.* Enable this checkbox if you are willing to pay for messages that carry a surcharge. Messages such as those from the Internet generally carry a nominal postage-due fee.
- *Change CompuServe Dir.* Click this button to change the folder in which the CompuServe Mail provider stores configuration and address book settings. If you are using another CompuServe product such as WinCIM, the CompuServe Mail provider can use the same address book and connection settings as your other CompuServe product.
- *Schedule Connect Times.* Click this button to display the Connection Times dialog box (see fig. 23.35) and schedule automatic connections to CompuServe. If you want, you can use a selection of different scheduled connection times.

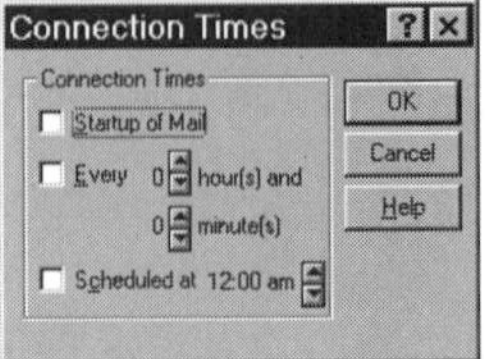

Fig. 23.35
You can schedule the CompuServe Mail provider to connect automatically to CompuServe.

After you have specified all the settings and properties you want to change for the CompuServe Mail provider, choose OK, then OK again to save the changes. Restart Messaging to begin using the new settings.

Connecting on Time

Assume that you configured the CompuServe Mail provider to check for messages at 8:00 AM and also every four hours, including times when you're away from your computer (like overnight). But, Messaging doesn't check at 8, 12, 4, and so on. It checks for mail at 8:00 AM, but the four-hour interval falls at odd times. You might be wondering why this happens.

The CompuServe Mail provider doesn't base its interval connection times on the explicit 8:00 AM setting you've specified. Instead, the provider checks at four-hour intervals based on the last time it automatically checked for mail. Open Control Panel and choose the Mail icon. Select the CompuServe Mail provider and choose Properties. Choose the Advanced tab, then choose the Schedule Connect Times option to display the Connection Times dialog box. Clear the Every checkbox and close the dialog box, then close the Profile property sheets. Shortly before the time when you want one of your interval connections to be made, open the Control Panel, choose the Mail icon, then enable the Every checkbox in the Connection Times dialog box and specify the interval you want to use. Close the property sheets. Messaging should then connect close to the time you want.

Configuring Messaging for Remote Mail

Messaging's Remote Mail feature enables you to dial into your mail server to Messaging e-mail when you are working from home or out of town. It also enables you to preview your messages, downloading only those messages you feel are important. You can use Remote Mail with the Microsoft Mail, Internet Mail, and CompuServe Mail service providers. All of these service providers support Remote Mail through a dial-up connection, and the Internet Mail and Microsoft Mail providers also support Remote Mail through a LAN connection.

The Microsoft Mail and Internet Mail service providers rely on Windows NT's Dial-Up Networking to provide a connection to a remote mail server. If you have not yet configured Dial-Up Networking on your computer, see Chapter 22, "Using Dial-Up Networking," to set up remote access on your system.

The following sections will help you configure each service for Remote Mail.

Setting Up Microsoft Mail for Remote Mail

After you install the Microsoft Mail service provider, you can configure it for either LAN access or remote access. Microsoft Mail supports Remote Mail for message preview for both types of connections. In most cases, however, it isn't necessary to preview messages when connecting to the postoffice over a LAN because the connection is much faster than a remote connection. Nevertheless, the option is still available to you.

To configure Microsoft Mail for a remote connection, follow these steps:

1. First create a Dial-Up Networking connection to your LAN's dial-in server using the Dial-Up Networking icon in My Computer.
2. Open the Control Panel and double-click the Mail icon.
3. Select the Microsoft Mail service, then choose Properties to display the Connection property page shown in figure 23.36.

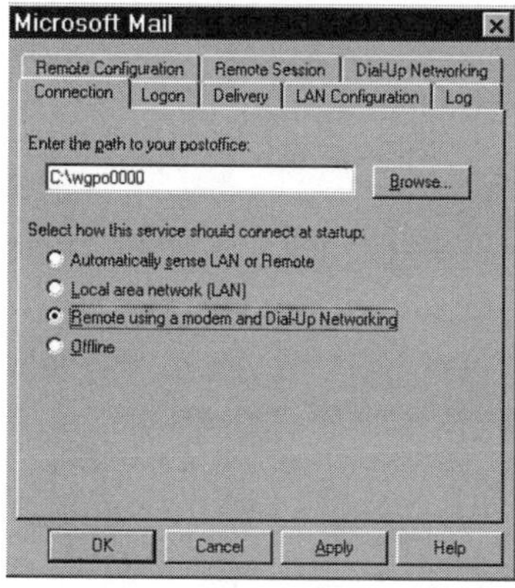

Fig. 23.36 Use the Connection page to configure Microsoft Mail for a remote connection.

4. Choose the option labeled Remote Using a Modem and Dial-Up Networking.
5. Click the Dial-Up Networking tab to display the Dial-Up Networking property page (see fig. 23.37).

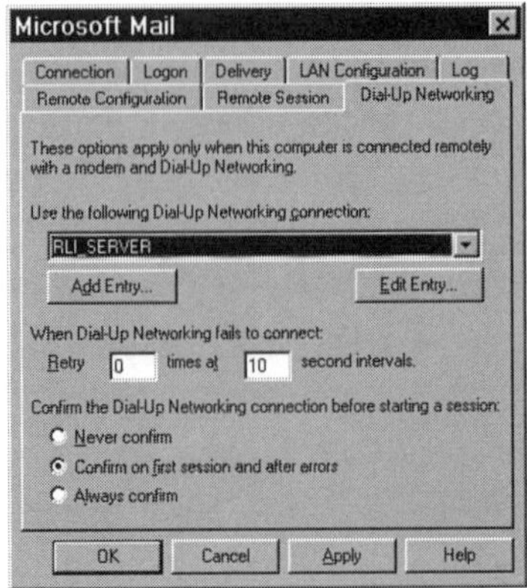

Fig. 23.37
Use the Dial-Up Networking page to specify which connection to use for remote mail.

6. From the drop-down list, choose the Dial-Up Networking connection you want to use for the remote mail connection (the one that points to your Microsoft Mail server). You'll only see connections you have previously created.
7. In the Retry text box, enter the number of times you want the connection to be attempted if the initial attempt fails, then use the times at text box to specify the frequency of connection attempts.
8. Choose one of the three confirmation option buttons to specify whether Windows NT will confirm that the Dial-Up Networking connection is working before starting the remote Microsoft Mail session. Configuring Remote Mail not to confirm the connection can save a little connection time. The Confirm on first session and after errors option is the default.
9. Click the Remote Session tab to display the Remote Session page (see fig. 23.38).

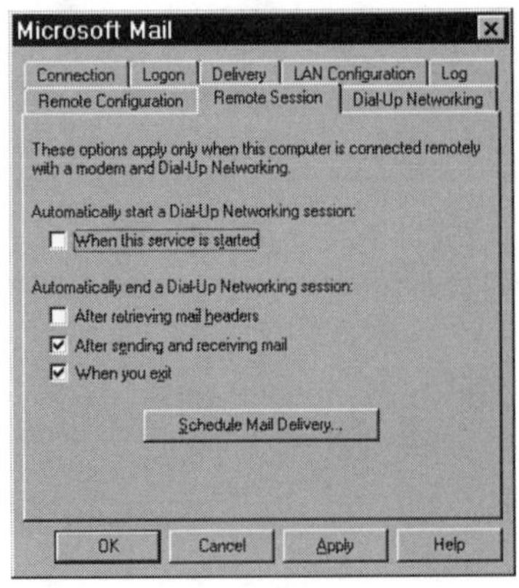

Fig. 23.38
Use the Remote Session page to control when the Dial-Up Networking session is started.

10. If you want the Dial-Up Networking session to start as soon as you start Messaging, enable the checkbox labeled When This Service is Started. If you don't want the Dial-Up Networking session to start until you direct Messaging to send and retrieve your mail, leave this checkbox cleared.

11. Specify when you want the Dial-Up Networking session to be terminated using any combination of the following checkboxes (if you leave all checkboxes blank, the Dial-Up Networking connection won't terminate automatically):

    - *After Retrieving Mail Headers.* Enable this checkbox if you want the Dial-Up Networking session to disconnect after Microsoft Mail retrieves your message headers.

    - *After Sending and Receiving Mail.* Enable this checkbox if you want the Dial-Up Networking session to disconnect after Microsoft Mail sends and receives pending mail.

    - *When You Exit.* Enable this checkbox if you want the Dial-Up Networking connection to disconnect when you exit Microsoft Messaging.

12. Choose OK, then OK again to save your configuration changes. Or, choose Apply to apply the changes without closing the property sheet.

If you want to use Remote Mail to preview messages when connecting to a WGPO (Workgroup Post Office) on your LAN, follow these steps:

1. Open the Control Panel and double-click the Mail icon.
2. Select the Microsoft Mail service, then choose Properties to display the Connection page of the Microsoft Mail property sheet.
3. Select the Local Area Network (LAN) option button or the Automatically Sense LAN or remote option button.
4. Click the LAN Configuration tab to display the LAN Configuration page shown in figure 23.39.
5. Place a check in the checkbox labeled Use Remote Mail to enable Remote Mail.

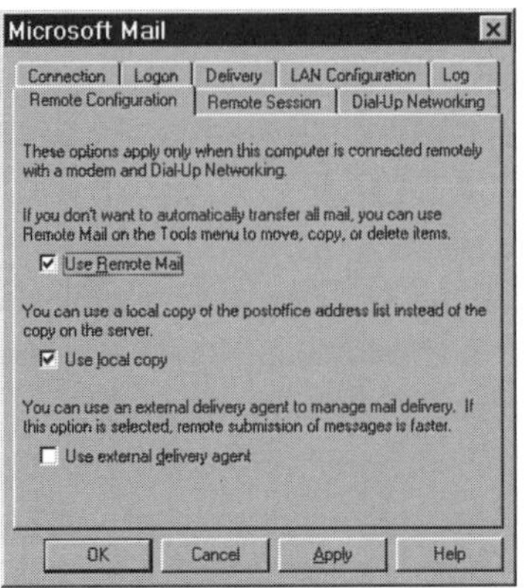

Fig. 23.39
Enable Remote Mail for a LAN connection through the LAN Configuration page.

> **Tip**
>
> Place a check in the Use local copy checkbox if you want to use a local copy of the post office address instead of checking addresses on the WGPO. When you're using Remote Mail through a Dial-Up Networking connection, you generally should check this box to enable Microsoft Mail to check addresses without connecting to the mail server. The Use external delivery agent checkbox controls whether or not Microsoft Mail uses the EXTERNAL.EXE program running on the server to expedite delivery. This checkbox does not apply specifically to Remote Mail.

6. Choose OK, then OK again to close the property sheets.

In the section "Working With Remote Mail," you learn how to preview messages, upload mail, and use other Remote Mail features. First, though, you need to decide how often Remote Mail will connect to your WGPO.

Setting Schedules

Although you can use Microsoft Mail interactively to check your mail, you also can configure the Microsoft Mail service to automatically connect at scheduled times to send and receive pending mail. This feature works with Remote Mail only if you're connecting to your WGPO over a Dial-Up Networking connection.

> **Tip**
>
> If your WGPO is located on the LAN, you can use Remote Mail to preview messages and control other message transfer options. But, you can't have Remote Mail automatically connect to the WGPO to update headers and perform other Remote Mail actions. Microsoft Mail's Remote Session property page, which enables you to specify

a connection schedule (using the Schedule Mail Delivery button), only applies if you are connecting to the WGPO through a Dial-Up Networking connection. The Check for New Mail Every xx Minutes control on the Delivery page controls how often Microsoft Mail checks your WGPO for mail, but is ignored by Remote Mail.

To configure scheduled connection times for a Dial-Up Networking connection to your WGPO, follow these steps:

1. Open the Control Panel and double-click the Mail icon.
2. Select the Microsoft Mail item, and then choose Properties.
3. Click the Remote Session tab, and then choose the Schedule Mail Delivery button to display the Remote Scheduled Sessions dialog box shown in figure 23.40.

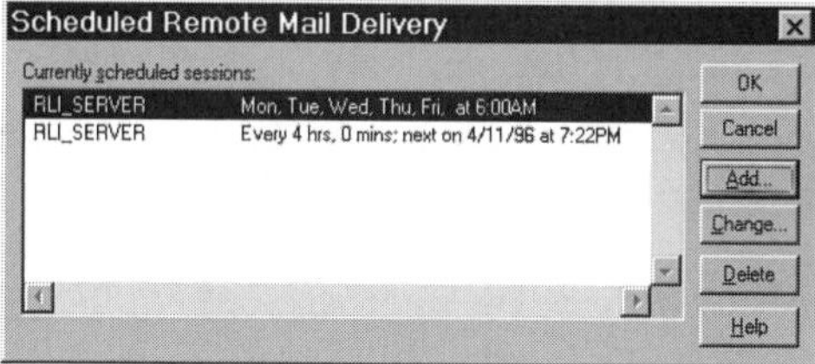

Fig. 23.40
You can schedule Microsoft Mail to connect automatically to check your mail.

4. Click Add, then use the Add Scheduled Session dialog box to specify the time at which you want Microsoft Mail to connect automatically. You can schedule connections at period intervals, weekly on the same day and time, or once only at a specific date and time. Choose OK after you specify the desired connect time.

Note

Fixed-interval connections (such as every four hours) are not executed based on a specific time such as 8:00 AM, 12:00 PM, 4:00 PM, etc. The connection times are based on the last connection's completion time plus the specified fixed time interval.

5. Repeat step 4 to add as many other connect times as you like. Then, continue to choose OK until you have closed the Messaging property sheet and saved your new settings.

Setting Up CompuServe Mail for Remote Mail

If you prefer to preview your CompuServe mail before downloading it, you can use Remote Mail. This is particularly useful if you routinely receive numerous messages or mail containing large binary attachments. When you install the CompuServe Mail provider, Remote Mail is enabled automatically. There are no additional configuration tasks to perform.

Setting Up Internet Mail for Remote Mail

Whether you connect to your Internet mail provider through a LAN or Dial-Up Networking connection, you can use Remote Mail to preview your messages and control message transfer. To configure Internet Mail for Remote Mail, follow these steps:

1. Install the Internet Mail provider.
2. Open the Control Panel and double-click the Mail icon.
3. Select Internet Mail from the list of installed services, and then click Properties to display the Internet Mail property sheet.
4. Click the Connection tab to display the Connection page (see fig. 23.41).

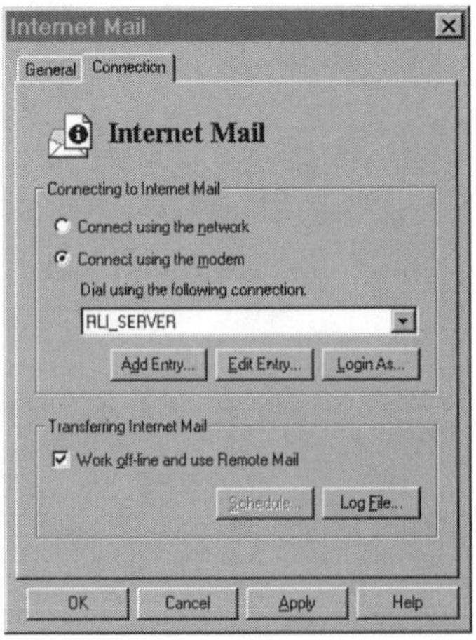

Fig. 23.41
Enable Remote Mail for Internet Mail through the Connection property page.

5. Place a check in the checkbox labeled Work Off-line and use Remote Mail.
6. Choose OK, then OK again to close the property sheets. ❖

CHAPTER 24

Understanding and Configuring TCP/IP

by Jim Boyce

The Internet's explosive growth in the last few years has stimulated a strong demand for support of TCP/IP (Transfer Control Protocol/Internet Protocol) and Internet-related utilities and programs. Windows NT offers a set of foundational components and general utilities that make it an excellent platform for TCP/IP internetworking.

This chapter helps you understand, configure, and use TCP/IP to provide connectivity between computers on your LAN as well as the Internet.

In this chapter, you'll learn to

- Install and configure TCP/IP in Windows NT
- Use Hosts and Lmhosts files for name resolution

> **Note**
>
> This chapter provides a general overview of Windows NT TCP/IP to help you understand how to configure and use TCP/IP. If you require a more technical description of how TCP/IP works, consult the *Windows NT Workstation Advanced Technical Reference* (Que), the *Microsoft Windows NT Resource Kit*, or one of the many resources and FAQs (Frequently Asked Question documents) available on the Internet. You might also want to consult Que's *Special Edition Using the Internet* and *Windows 95 Connectivity*.

An Overview of TCP/IP and the Internet

The two primary topics in this chapter—TCP/IP and the Internet—generally are closely related; you need the TCP/IP protocol to connect to and use the Internet. But even if you don't need to access the Internet, TCP/IP still offers an excellent means of interconnecting disparate operating systems on a single network. This section of the chapter provides a brief overview of TCP/IP and the Internet.

TCP/IP

TCP/IP stands for Transmission Control Protocol/Internet Protocol. TCP/IP is a network transport protocol widely supported by a majority of operating systems, including all versions of UNIX, Windows NT, Windows 95, Windows 3.x, Novell NetWare, Macintosh, Open VMS, and others. TCP/IP was originally developed through the Defense Advanced Research Projects Agency to support defense-related projects. TCP/IP offers a number of advantages that make it an excellent network transport protocol, particularly for connecting dissimilar computers and for enabling wide-area networking.

You can use TCP/IP as your only network protocol or in conjunction with another protocol. You might use NetBEUI within your LAN, for example, and use TCP/IP to connect to the Internet through a router or dial-up connection. Or, you might decide to use TCP/IP as your LAN protocol, as well. The following list describes some of Windows NT TCP/IP's features and advantages.

- *WinSock 2.0.* Windows NT TCP/IP supports the Windows Sockets (WinSock) 2.0 specification, which enables you to use WinSock-based TCP/IP programs without requiring an additional WinSock driver.
- *DHCP.* Windows NT TCP/IP supports Dynamic Host Configuration Protocol (DHCP), which enables a DHCP server, such as a Windows NT server, to automatically assign IP addresses to workstations on the network, including computers that connect to the network through a dial-up connection. DHCP enables you to more efficiently manage a pool of IP addresses for a given set of workstations.
- *WINS.* Windows NT TCP/IP supports Windows Internet Naming Service (WINS), which provides automatic resolution of IP addresses into logical computer names (such as resolving tigers.k12.cfa.org into 198.87.118.2).
- *Protocol support.* Windows NT TCP/IP supports Point-to-Point (PPP) and Serial Line IP (SLIP), enabling remote access to TCP/IP-based servers through dialup connections.
- *Core TCP/IP utilities.* Windows NT includes a number of TCP/IP applications for file transfer, terminal emulation, troubleshooting, and other general tasks.

Although setting up TCP/IP is not difficult per se, it can prove to be a complex task. Later in this chapter, you'll find more information about the technical aspects of TCP/IP. First, however, you should have some additional background about the Internet.

▶ See "Understanding TCP/IP," p. 565

The Internet

The Internet began as a small group of interconnected LANs and has grown into a worldwide network that spans many thousands of networks and millions of computers. Although the Internet began primarily as a defense- and education-related network, it has grown to encompass government and commercial networks and users, as well as individual users. The Internet really is nothing more than a huge wide area network. On that network, however, you can access an amazing variety of services and data. You can send and receive e-mail around the globe, transfer files, query enormous databases, participate in special-interest groups, and more.

Many ways exist to access the Internet. If you have a user account on one of the popular online services, such as CompuServe or America Online, or are a member of The Microsoft Network (MSN), you can gain access to the Internet through those services. Or, your network at work might be connected to the Internet through a dedicated or dialup connection. You might connect from your computer to an Internet service provider through a dialup connection. Regardless of the method you use to connect to the Internet, you can't do it without TCP/IP. Understanding TCP/IP is critical to configuring and initiating your Internet connection. The next section provides an examination of some key issues for TCP/IP networking.

Understanding TCP/IP

TCP/IP is versatile, but also complex. Before you can set up a TCP/IP network and correctly configure the computers and other devices on the network, you must understand many key issues. The following sections explain these issues, beginning with IP addressing.

Understanding IP Addressing

On a TCP/IP network, a *host* is any device on the network that uses TCP/IP to communicate, including computers, routers, and other devices. Each host must have a unique address, called an *IP address* (IP stands for Internet Protocol). An IP address identifies the host on the network so that IP data packets can be properly routed to the host. IP data packets are simply data encapsulated in IP format for transmission using TCP/IP. Every IP address on the network must be unique; conflicting (identical) IP addresses on two or more computers prevents those computers from correctly accessing and using the network.

An IP address is a 32-bit value usually represented in *dotted-decimal notation,* in which four octets (eight bits each) are separated by decimals, as in 198.87.118.1. The IP address actually contains two items of information: the address of the network and the address of the host on the network. How the network and address are defined within the address depends on the class of the IP address.

IP addresses are grouped into three classes: A, B, and C. These classes are designed to accommodate networks of varying sizes. Table 24.1 describes the IP address classes, where the variables w.x.y.z designate the octets in the address structure.

Table 24.1 IP Address Classes

Class	w	Network ID	Host ID	Available Networks	Available Hosts Per Network
A	1–126	w	x.y.z	126	16,777,214
B	128–191	w.x	y.z	16,384	65,534
C	192–223	w.x.y	z	2,097,151	254

Tip

The address 127 is reserved on the local computer for loopback testing and interprocess communication, and therefore is not a valid network address. Addresses of 224 and higher are reserved for special protocols, and can't be used as host addresses. Host addresses 0 and 255 are used as broadcast addresses and should not be assigned to computers.

As Table 24.1 shows, class A networks are potentially quite large, encompassing as many as 16,777,214 hosts. If you set up your own TCP/IP network, yours most likely falls into the class C network category, which is limited to 254 hosts.

You might wonder what's so important about an IP address. Routing data packets between computers is impossible without an IP address. By referencing the network portion of your IP address, a sending computer can route packets (with the help of intermediate routers and networks) to your network. The host portion of your IP address then routes the packet to your computer when the packet finally reaches the network.

Using Subnet Masks

A *subnet mask* is a 32-bit value expressed as a series of four octets separated by periods, just like an IP address. The subnet mask enables the recipient of an IP data packet to strip *(mask)* the IP address to which the IP packet is being sent into the network ID and host ID. Basically, the subnet mask enables the IP address to be broken into its two component parts. Table 24.2 shows the default subnet masks for standard class A, B, and C networks, with each subnet mask shown in binary and dotted-decimal forms.

Table 24.2 Default Subnet Masks

Class	Bit Value	Subnet Mask
A	11111111 00000000 00000000 00000000	255.0.0.0
B	11111111 11111111 00000000 00000000	255.255.0.0
C	11111111 11111111 11111111 00000000	255.255.255.0

In addition to enabling an IP address to be resolved into its network and host components, subnet masks also serve to segment a single network ID into multiple local networks. Assume that your large company has been assigned a class B IP network address of 191.100. The corporate network comprises 10 different local networks with 200 hosts on each. By applying a subnet mask of 255.255.0.0, the network is divided into 254 separate subnetworks, 191.100.1 through 191.100.254. Each of the 254 subnetworks can contain 254 hosts.

Tip

The subnet masks described in Table 24.2 are not the only masks you can use. Sometimes you have to mask only some of the bits in an octet. The network address and subnet mask must match, however, for every host on a local network.

Acquiring an IP Address

Although theoretically you could arbitrarily assign your own IP network address for your network, any address you might choose would probably already be assigned to someone else's network. If your network is self-contained and not connected to the Internet, duplicate addressing shouldn't cause any problems. If your network is connected to the Internet or you decide to connect it in the future, however, duplicate addressing causes serious routing problems for both networks.

> **Note**
>
> There is no charge to register an IP address. InterNIC does, however, charge for network domain name registration. Currently, the cost is $100 for the first two years, then $50 annually beginning in the third year.

To assure uniqueness of network addresses, a governing organization known as InterNIC (Internet Network Information Center) is responsible for assigning and maintaining IP addresses. If you set up a TCP/IP network, you should contact InterNIC to obtain a unique network IP address for your network. You also can register through the Internet by sending a registration request to **hostmaster@internic.net**. If you want more information about InterNIC and IP addressing, connect through the Internet to **is.internic.net**, log on as anonymous, and browse the directory /INFOSOURCE/FAQ for more information. To contact InterNIC through standard mail, phone, or fax, use the following information:

Network Solutions
InterNIC Registration Services
505 Huntmar Park Drive
Herndon, VA 22070
703-742-4777
Fax 703-742-4811

Understanding Gateways and Routing

To interconnect and provide routing of data packets, TCP/IP subnetworks interconnected with one another or connected to the Internet use gateways (routers). A default gateway generally is a computer or router that maintains IP address information of remote networks (networks outside its own network). Default gateways are required only on interconnected networks—standalone TCP/IP subnets do not require default gateways.

Before a host transmits an IP packet, IP inserts the originating and destination IP addresses into the packet. It then checks the destination address to determine whether the packet is destined for the same local network as the originating host. If the network addresses match (based on the subnet mask), the packet is routed directly to the destination host on the same subnet. If the network addresses don't match, the packet is sent to the subnet's default gateway, which then handles routing of the packet. The default gateway maintains a list of other gateways and network addresses, and routes the packet accordingly. Although the packet might pass through many gateways, it eventually reaches its destination.

If yours is a standalone subnet, you don't need a default gateway. Otherwise, you need at least one functioning default gateway to communicate outside of your subnet. If for some reason your default gateway becomes inoperative (a router fails, for example), you can't communicate outside your subnet, but you still can work within your subnet. If you need to ensure a connection, you might want to consider using multiple default gateways.

Tip

You can use the route utility from the command prompt to specify a static route and override the default gateway.

Using Dynamic Address Assignment

In TCP/IP networks that comprise relatively few nodes, or in which the network configuration is static (computers do not access the network remotely and the number of hosts don't fluctuate), IP address administration is relatively easy. The network administrator simply assigns specific IP addresses to each host.

On large or dynamic networks, however, administering IP addresses can be difficult and time-consuming. To help overcome this problem, Windows 95 supports Dynamic Host Configuration Protocol, or DHCP, which enables a host to automatically obtain an IP address from a DHCP server when the host logs on to the network. When you move a host from one subnet to another on your network, the host automatically receives a new IP address, and its original IP address is released, making it available for other connecting hosts.

By providing dynamic addressing, DHCP enables you to manage a pool of IP addresses for a group of hosts. Assume that your company has 100 employees who often dial into your subnet from remote locations, but not at the same time. At any one time, 25 to 30 remote users might be connected to the network, but your subnet has only 50 available subnet host addresses. If you assign IP addresses manually, you can accommodate only 50 of the remote users. You can't assign the same IP address to two users, because if they both connect to the network at the same time, routing problems prevent them from using the network.

Through DHCP, you can allocate a pool of 50 IP addresses to be assigned automatically to the dial in users. When a user dials in and connects, DHCP assigns the host a unique IP address from the pool. As long as no more than 50 users attempt to log on to the network remotely and acquire IP addresses, you can accommodate all 50 with unique addresses. If the number of users who need to connect exceeds the number of available addresses, the only solution is to expand your pool of available addresses or modify the subnet mask to accommodate more than 50 addresses.

▶ See "Installing and Configuring TCP/IP in Windows NT," p. 574

▶ See "Configuring IP Addressing," p. 576

DHCP in Windows NT relies on a Windows NT DHCP server that can assign IP addresses to hosts on the local subnet when the hosts start Windows NT, and can assign IP addresses to hosts that connect to the network remotely.

In addition to using DHCP, Windows NT can request an IP address from a PPP (Point-to-Point Protocol) dialup router. Whether you use DHCP or connect to a PPP dialup router, you use the same configuration option to configure dynamic address assignment.

Understanding Domains and Name Resolution

Computers have no problems using IP addresses to locate other networks and hosts. The average user, however, can have trouble remembering those dotted-decimal addresses. Domain names and computer names make specifying the addresses of other networks or hosts much easier.

A *domain name* is a unique name formatted much like an IP address, except that the domain name uses words rather than numbers. The domain name identifies your network and is associated with your network's IP address. If your company is Foo Fang Foods, Inc., for example, your departmental subnet might be known as **sales.foofang.com**. The first portion, sales, identifies your subnet. The second portion, foofang, identifies your corporate network. The last portion, com, specifies the type of organization, and in this example, indicates a commercial network. Table 24.3 lists common network type identifiers.

Table 24.3 Common Network Type Identifiers

Identifier	Meaning
com	Commercial entity
gov	Government entity
net	Networking organization
org	General organization
edu	Education
mil	Military

Tip

As with your IP address, your domain must be unique. If you connect your network to other networks or to the Internet, contact InterNIC to apply for a unique domain name.

A *computer name* specifies a host on the subnet. Your host computer name is combined with your domain to derive your Internet address. Your host name doesn't have to match your computer's name that identifies it in its workgroup, but it can. By default, Windows NT uses as your host name the NetBIOS computer name you specify during setup, but you can specify a different name when you configure TCP/IP. Whatever name you specify as the computer name in the TCP/IP configuration is registered with the network when Windows NT starts.

Note

The computer name you specify for your computer when you install Windows NT is its NetBIOS name. A computer's NetBIOS name bears no relationship to its host name under TCP/IP. The two names can be different or the same.

No direct translation or correlation exists between IP addresses and domain names and host names. Some method, therefore, is required to enable computers to look up the correct IP address when a user specifies a name rather than an IP address. Your Windows NT host can use one of two methods: DNS or WINS.

Note

For a technical discussion of DNS and WINS, you can consult the *Windows NT Advanced Technical Reference* (Que).

Understanding DNS

DNS stands for Domain Name System. *DNS* is a distributed database system that enables a computer to look up a computer name and resolve the name to an IP address. A DNS name server maintains the database of domain names and their corresponding IP addresses. The DNS name server stores records that describe all hosts in the name server's zone.

If you use DNS for your Windows NT workstation, you specify the IP address of one or more DNS servers in your TCP/IP configuration. When your workstation needs to resolve a name into an IP address, it queries the DNS servers. If the server doesn't have an entry for the specified name, the name server returns a list of other name servers that might contain the entry you need. The workstation then can query these additional name servers to resolve the name.

Tip

You can define multiple DNS servers in your Windows NT TCP/IP configuration.

▶ See "Using Hosts and Lmhosts Files," p. 581

Besides a DNS server, you can use the Hosts file to resolve host.domain-formatted names to IP addresses.

Understanding WINS

WINS stands for Windows Internet Name Service. WINS provides a dynamic database for managing name resolution. WINS relies on a Windows NT server to act as a WINS server. When you install TCP/IP on your workstation, the client software necessary to connect to a WINS server is installed automatically.

One advantage of using WINS is that it's dynamic, rather than static like DNS. If you use DHCP to assign network addresses, WINS automatically updates the name database to incorporate DHCP IP address assignments. As computers move from one place (and address) to another on the network, the WINS server automatically updates and maintains their addresses.

Another advantage of using WINS is that it includes NetBIOS name space, which enables it to resolve NetBIOS names into IP addresses. Assume that your computer's NetBIOS name is joeblow, your computer's TCP/IP host name is JoeB, and your domain name is bozos.are.us. A DNS server could only resolve JoeB.bozos.are.us, but a WINS server could resolve JoeB.bozos.are.us *and* joeblow.bozos.are.us into the correct IP address.

Tip

The *Windows NT Workstation Advanced Technical Reference* (Que) contains a good technical explanation of other advantages WINS offers.

When you configure TCP/IP in Windows NT, you can specify the IP addresses of up to two WINS servers to handle name resolution. If your network uses

DHCP, you can configure your workstation to resolve the addresses of WINS servers dynamically using DHCP.

If you don't have a WINS server available to provide name resolution of NetBIOS computer names to IP addresses (such as resolving your computer's name to its IP address), you can use the Lmhosts file to resolve NetBIOS names.

Preparing to Install TCP/IP

Now that you have a little background on how TCP/IP works, you're almost ready to install, configure, and begin using TCP/IP on your Windows NT workstation. Before you begin the installation procedure, however, you need to gather together the information you must provide when you configure TCP/IP. In particular, you need to know the following information:

- *Network address and domain.* If you set up a new TCP/IP network that you intend to eventually connect to the Internet, you must register with InterNIC for a unique domain name and network IP address. Even if you do not plan at this time to connect the network to the Internet, you should still acquire a unique domain name and network address from InterNIC for future compatibility.
- *IP address.* Determine whether your workstation will use static IP addressing or will obtain an IP address from a DHCP server. If you require a static address, contact your system administrator for an address, or if you are the administrator, assign an available address for the workstation. If you plan to use DHCP to acquire an IP address dynamically, or you dynamically acquire an IP address from a PPP dial-up router, you do not need to know the IP address of the DHCP server or router.
- *Subnet mask.* You must know the appropriate subnet mask for your subnet. If yours is a standard class C network with fewer than 254 hosts, your subnet mask should be 255.255.255.0. If you're not sure what your subnet mask should be, contact your system administrator.
- *WINS.* Determine whether your network provides one or more WINS servers for name resolution. If so, you need to know the IP address of the primary WINS server, as well as the IP address of a secondary WINS server if you choose to use a secondary server. If your workstation uses DHCP, however, you need not know the IP addresses of the WINS servers—DHCP automatically resolves them. If your network uses NetBIOS over TCP/IP, you might need a scope ID. If you're not sure, check with your system administrator.

- *Default gateway(s).* If your subnet is connected to other networks or to the Internet, you need to know the IP address of the gateway (router) through which IP routing is accomplished. If your network has access to multiple gateways, you can specify multiple gateways to provide fault tolerance and alternative routing.
- *Domain name resolution.* You must know the domain name of your network, as well as the host name you use. The host name defaults to the computer name assigned to the computer at startup, which you specify through the Identification property page for your Network settings. If you use DNS for name resolution, you must know the IP addresses of the DNS servers you use.
- *Bindings.* You must know which clients and services use the TCP/IP protocol. If you dial into a server for TCP/IP access (such as dialing into an Internet service provider or a Windows NT Server) to gain Internet access, you do not need to bind TCP/IP to any clients or services. If you use TCP/IP as your only protocol and want to dial into a server to access files and other shared resources, or you want to share your resources, you must bind TCP/IP to the appropriate client and service. If you use TCP/IP over a LAN, and no other protocol provides sharing services, you need to bind TCP/IP to your network client and sharing service.

Installing and Configuring TCP/IP in Windows NT

Before you can begin taking advantage of TCP/IP, you naturally have to install it. Of all network protocols, TCP/IP is the most complex to install and configure owing to its many settings and options. This section explains those settings and options, beginning with the installation process.

Note

If you have not read the previous section of this chapter, you should do so to learn what items of information you need before you install and configure TCP/IP.

Installing Windows NT TCP/IP

Windows NT TCP/IP installs like any other network transport protocol—through the Control Panel. To install TCP/IP, follow these steps:

1. Open the Control Panel and choose the Network object.
2. From the Protocols property page, choose the Add button. Windows NT displays a Select Network Protocol dialog box from which you can choose the protocol you want to install (see fig. 24.1).
3. From the Network Protocol list, select TCP/IP Protocol.

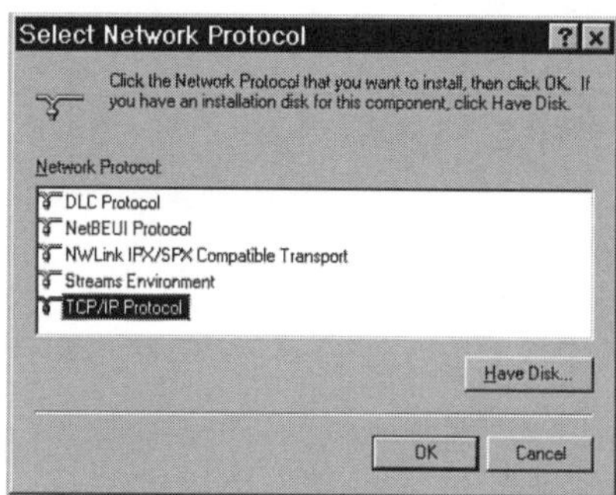

Fig. 24.1
The Select Network Protocol dialog box.

After you choose OK, Windows NT prompts you to specify whether you want to use DHCP to assign your IP address. Choose Yes to use DHCP, or No to assign an IP address manually.

Windows NT then prompts you for the location of the Windows NT source files (typically, the Windows NT CD). After you specify the location for the files, Windows NT adds the TCP/IP protocol to your PC, copying files as necessary.

If you have Dial-Up Networking installed on your system, Windows NT prompts you to specify if you want Dial-Up Networking to be configured to use TCP/IP. If you intend to use TCP/IP over a Dial-Up Networking connection, choose OK. Choose Cancel if you intend to use TCP/IP only on a hardwired connection on your LAN.

If you choose OK to enable TCP/IP for Dial-Up Networking, Windows NT displays the Remote Access Setup dialog box shown in figure 24.2. Use this dialog box to specify which port and device you want to use for the dial-up TCP/IP connection. When you've selected and configured the appropriate port, choose Continue. The TCP/IP protocol appears in the Network Protocols list on the Protocols property page.

Next, you need to specify a number of settings to properly configure TCP/IP, beginning with the IP address. To do so, choose Close on the Network property sheet. Windows NT will step you through the process of configuring settings for your TCP/IP protocol.

Tip

You can configure and use multiple sets of TCP/IP settings. You can use one configuration for your LAN TCP/IP connection, for example, and specify different settings for each dialup connection you use. For information on using TCP/IP over a Dial-Up Networking connection, refer to Chapter 22, "Using Remote Access Services."

Configuring IP Addressing

When Windows NT first displays the property sheet for the TCP/IP protocol, the IP Address page appears (see fig. 24.2). If you use a static IP address for your workstation, choose the Specify an IP address option button, then enter the IP address and subnet mask for your workstation in the IP address and Subnet mask text boxes. If you want to rely on a DHCP server or PPP server to assign an IP address automatically for your workstation, choose the Obtain an IP address from a DHCP server option button. You do not have to specify the IP address of the DHCP server.

If you specify an explicit IP address, take the time to verify that you have entered the correct address and subnet mask before you continue to the other configuration steps.

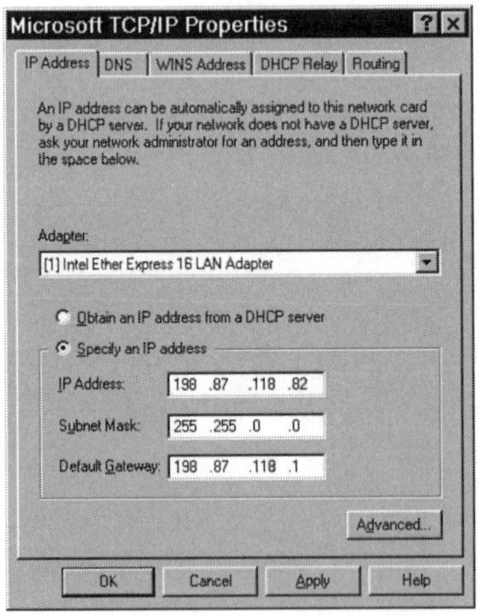

Fig. 24.2
Set basic IP values on the IP address property page.

Configuring a Gateway

If your subnet is connected to other subnets, to other networks, or to the Internet, you must specify at least one default gateway. To do so, click in the Default Gateway box and type the IP address of your default gateway.

Tip

Your network's router typically is the default gateway.

If your network is connected to multiple gateways, you can specify as many gateways as necessary to allow for fault tolerance if one gateway becomes unavailable. To add a gateway, click the Advanced button. In the Advanced IP Addressing dialog box (see fig. 24.3), click the Add button, located under the Gateways group. In the TCP/IP Gateway Address dialog box, type the IP address of the additional gateway, then choose Add. To change the search order for the gateways, use the Up and Down buttons on the Advanced IP Addressing dialog box to change the order of the gateways in the list. The gateways are listed in order of priority. Click OK when you're satisfied with the gateway entries.

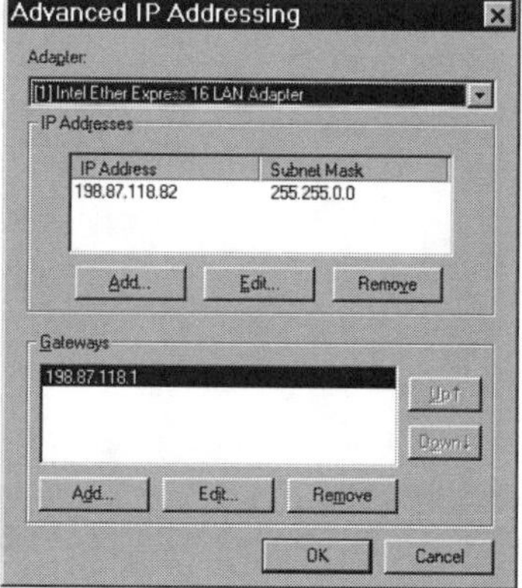

Fig. 24.3
Use the Advanced IP Addressing dialog box to specify additional gateways.

Troubleshooting

I can dial into my Internet service provider, but I can't seem to access any other sites on the Internet. How can I get past the service provider to other computers on the Internet?

(continues)

(continued)

Your default gateway setting is probably incorrect. Check with the service provider to determine the IP address you should use as the default gateway, as well as a secondary address, if applicable. Then, use the procedure explained in the previous section to configure the gateway. You'll have to restart your PC after changing the TCP/IP configuration. Then, connect again and try to connect to another computer on the Internet. If that fails, use the ping command to test the connection to the gateway. Refer to Chapter 25, "Using Internet Programs," for help using ping.

Using DNS

If your workstation requires Domain Name System (DNS) services, click the DNS tab to open the DNS property page shown in figure 24.4.

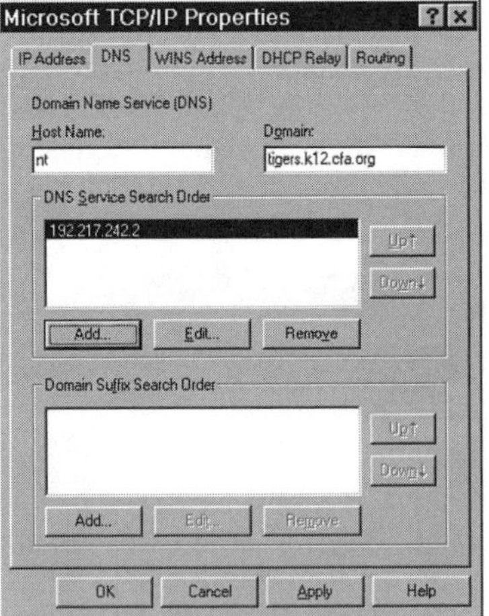

Fig. 24.4 The DNS property page.

Tip

If your computer needs to use Lmhosts to resolve network names, you must enable DNS.

Specifying Host and Domain Names

After you enable DNS, you need to specify some additional items of information. First, you need to specify the host name for your computer in the Host Name text box. By default, the host name is your computer's NetBIOS name. You can use any host name, however; you might use your own name as the host name, for example. You can use any combination of letters and numbers, a dash, or a period, but not a space or underscore character, in the host name.

Next, specify the domain name for your network in the Domain text box. TCP/IP combines the host name you specify with the domain name you specify to derive a Fully Qualified Domain Name (FQDN) for your computer. If your host name is JimB and your domain name is que.mcp.com, the FQDN for your computer is JimB.que.mcp.com.

Note

Some TCP/IP utilities use your host name, domain name, and FQDN to authenticate your computer name. Note that a computer's FQDN is not the same as a user's e-mail address. Although the FQDN might be JimB.que.mcp.com, the e-mail address might be jboyce@mail.que.mcp.com. Also, a DNS domain name and a Windows NT or LAN Manager domain name are in no way related.

Specifying DNS Server IP Addresses

If you do not use DHCP to define IP addresses, you must provide the IP addresses of the DNS servers you use. If you do use DHCP, the DHCP server can automatically provide the IP addresses of the DNS servers.

You can specify DNS server addresses in the DNS Service Search Order group of controls. First, determine the IP address of the DNS server you want to use by default. Then, click the Add button in the DNS Service Search Order control group. Windows NT displays a TCP/IP DNS Server dialog box in which you enter the IP address of the DNS server. Enter the IP address and choose Add. Windows NT returns to the DNS property page. Repeat the procedure to add other DNS servers, if desired.

Note

To change priority of DNS servers in the list, use the Up and Down buttons.

Adding Domain Suffix Entries

Normally, DNS appends the domain name specified in the Domain text box to your host name to resolve the FQDN of your computer. You can specify up to five additional domain suffixes that DNS can use if it can't resolve the FQDN using the default domain name. A DNS server attempts to resolve the FQDN using these additional suffixes in alphabetical order (which is how they appear in the list after you add them).

To add additional domain suffixes, enter a domain name in the Domain Suffix Search Order text box, then choose Add. Repeat the process to add additional domain names.

Troubleshooting

I can connect to other computers on the Internet using their IP addresses, but using domain names doesn't work. How can I get the domain names to work?

Something is wrong with your DNS configuration. Verify that you've specified a DNS server in your TCP/IP configuration as explained previously. If you have specified a DNS server, try to ping the server. If you can ping the server, it might not actually be a DNS server. If you're using a hosts file, verify that the domain name of the computer you're trying to reach matches the domain name specified in the hosts file, including case and spelling. See the section "Using Hosts and Lmhosts Files" later in this chapter for more help.

Using WINS

If your network includes one or more Windows NT servers configured as WINS servers, or access to WINS servers, you can configure your Windows NT TCP/IP stack to use WINS to resolve names. WINS offers numerous advantages over DNS, particularly in conjunction with DHCP. To configure WINS, click the WINS Address tab to display the WINS Address property page shown in figure 24.5.

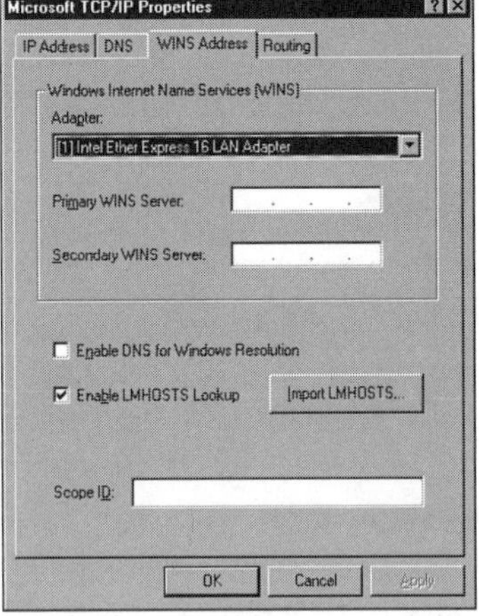

Fig. 24.5 Use the WINS Address property page to configure WINS settings.

You can specify a primary and a secondary WINS server by entering their IP addresses in the fields provided for that purpose on the property page. If your computer uses DHCP to resolve names, however, you can leave the IP address fields blank, and Windows NT queries the DHCP server for the WINS server addresses.

Tip

Mark the Enable DNS for Windows Resolution checkbox if you want Windows NT to use the IP address specified on the DNS page to locate the DNS server for Windows networking applications.

When you're satisfied with your TCP/IP settings, choose OK on the Microsoft TCP/IP Properties sheet, then choose OK on the Network property sheet. Windows NT will perform a binding analysis and bind the TCP/IP protocol as necessary.

Using Hosts and Lmhosts Files

DNS name servers resolve FQDN names provided in the host.domain format to IP addresses. A WINS server can resolve IP host.domain names to IP addresses, and it also can resolve a computer's NetBIOS name into its address name. Sometimes, however, being able to resolve names locally without relying on a DNS or WINS name server comes in handy. You might not have a DNS or WINS name server available to you, for example, or the server might be temporarily unavailable.

Windows NT provides two methods for resolving names to IP addresses locally, which you can use in conjunction with or in place of DNS and WINS name resolution. Both methods rely on simple ASCII files to store database entries for names and corresponding IP addresses. The first of these files, Hosts, resolves DNS-formatted names, and works with or in place of DNS. The second file, Lmhosts, resolves NetBIOS names into IP addresses, and works with or in place of WINS.

The following sections explain the Hosts file and the Lmhosts file, respectively.

Using the Hosts File for Name Resolution

If you can't access a DNS server, or you want to supplement a DNS server with your own entries, you can use the Hosts file to maintain a database of host names and their corresponding IP addresses. The Hosts file is called a *host table* because it contains a table of host names and their IP addresses. Windows NT can look up entries in the Hosts file to resolve names.

When you install Windows NT TCP/IP, Windows NT creates a sample Hosts file named HOSTS.SAM in the \WINNT\system32\drivers\etc folder. The HOSTS.SAM file is an ASCII file that you can edit using Notepad, WordPad, or any other ASCII editor. You should copy HOSTS.SAM to Hosts (omitting a file extension) and retain the sample file for future reference in case your Hosts file becomes corrupted or is accidentally deleted. In other words, edit the HOSTS file, not the HOSTS.SAM file. The following lists the contents of the default HOSTS file:

```
# Copyright (c) 1993-1995 Microsoft Corp.
#
# This is a sample HOSTS file used by Microsoft TCP/IP for Windows NT.
#
# This file contains the mappings of IP addresses to host names. Each
# entry should be kept on an individual line. The IP address should
# be placed in the first column followed by the corresponding host name.
# The IP address and the host name should be separated by at least one
# space.
#
# Additionally, comments (such as these) may be inserted on individual
# lines or following the machine name denoted by a '#' symbol.
#
# For example:
#
#      102.54.94.97     rhino.acme.com          # source server
#       38.25.63.10     x.acme.com              # x client host

127.0.0.1       localhost
```

The Hosts file uses the same format as the hosts file used on 4.3 BSD UNIX, stored in the /etc/hosts file. The HOSTS.SAM file contains comments identified by a leading # character and a single address entry for localhost. The localhost entry is always 127.0.0.1 and is used for loopback testing. You should not change the IP address for localhost or remove it from the Hosts file.

To add an entry to the Hosts file, enter the IP address, then tab to the second column and enter the host name. You can specify more than one host name for an IP address, but you must use multiple entries for the different domains, each with the same IP address, as in the following example:

```
102.54.94.97     tools.acme.com
102.54.94.97     TOOLS.ACME.COM
102.54.94.97     fooyang.gruel.com
```

Entries in the Hosts file are case-sensitive. The two entries for tools.acme.com and TOOLS.ACME.COM would enable the correct host name resolution if you specified the host name in lowercase or uppercase.

You can include a single host name for each entry or specify multiple host names for a single IP address. The following, for example, are valid entries:

```
198.87.118.72   me          theboss     tower.tigers.k12.cfa.org
198.87.118.50   TheServer   theserver   THESERVER
```

Each of the entries in this example specify three host names for each IP address.

Windows NT parses the entries in the Hosts file in sequential order until it finds a match. If you have a large Hosts file, you can speed up lookup time by placing the most often-used host name entries at the top of the file.

Using the Lmhosts File for Name Resolution

If you want Windows NT to be able to resolve NetBIOS computer names to IP addresses, you need to use a WINS or Lmhosts file. NetBIOS names are the computer names assigned to computers on Microsoft-based networks, such as the name you assigned to your computer during setup. As explained previously, your computer's NetBIOS name is not equivalent to your TCP/IP host name, although the two can use the same name.

Windows NT automatically resolves NetBIOS names for computers running TCP/IP on a local network. To resolve IP addresses of computers on other networks to which yours is connected by a gateway (when a WINS server is not available), you need to use Lmhosts.

> **Note**
>
> Like HOSTS, LMHOSTS is an ASCII file, and the format of an entry is similar to entries in a Hosts file. The LMHOSTS file, however, supports special keywords, which are explained later in this section. Windows NT includes a sample LMHOSTS file named LMHOSTS.SAM, located in the \WINNT\system32\drivers\etc folder. To use Lmhosts, copy LMHOSTS.SAM to LMHOSTS without a file extension, then modify LMHOSTS to add entries.

Windows NT TCP/IP reads the Lmhosts file when you start the computer. As it does the Hosts file, Windows NT parses each line sequentially, which means you should place often-accessed names at the top of the file for best performance. You also need to place entries that contain special keywords at specific locations in the file (these placement rules are explained later in the section). First, here are a few rules for structuring a Lmhosts file:

- Each entry must begin with the IP address in the first column, followed by its computer name in the second column. Any additional keywords appear in subsequent columns. Columns must be separated by at least one space or tab character. Some Lmhosts keywords follow entries, while others appear on their own lines (explained later).
- Place each entry on a separate line.
- Comments must begin with the pound (#) character, but special Lmhosts keywords also begin with the # character. Keeping comments to a minimum improves parsing performance. Place often-accessed entries near the top of the file for best performance.
- The Lmhosts file is static, so you must manually update the file to create new entries or modify existing entries.

Tip

Although Windows NT TCP/IP reads the Lmhosts file at system startup, only entries designated as preloaded by the #PRE keyword are read into the name cache at startup. Other entries are read only after broadcast name resolution queries fail.

You can use any or all of six special keywords (described in the following list) in a Lmhosts file:

- *#PRE.* This keyword causes the associated entry to be preloaded into the name cache, rather than loaded only after broadcast resolution queries fail. If you want names stored in a remote Lmhosts file to be added to the name cache at startup, use the #INCLUDE and #PRE statements in combination, such as the following:

  ```
  #INCLUDE     \\server\pub\lmhosts     #PRE
  ```

- *#DOM:*`<domain>`. This keyword designates a remote domain controller and enables you to identify Windows NT domain controllers located across one or more routers. Entries that use the #DOM keyword are added to a special Internet workgroup name cache that causes Windows NT TCP/IP to forward requests for domain controllers to remote domain controllers as well as local domain controllers. The following example identifies a domain controller named appserver in a domain named thedomain, and also causes the entry to be preloaded into the name cache at startup:

  ```
  184.121.214.2  appserver  #PRE  #DOM:thedomain
  ➥#This is a comment
  ```

- *#INCLUDE*`<filename>`. Use this keyword to include entries from a separate Lmhosts file. You can use #INCLUDE to include your own set of entries stored on your own computer, but you most commonly would use #INCLUDE to enable use of a centralized, shared Lmhosts file for multiple users. The following example includes an Lmhosts file from a local drive and directory:

```
#INCLUDE  c:\mystuff\Lmhosts      #Includes local file
```

> **Note**
>
> If you reference a remote Lmhosts file on a server outside of your network in an #INCLUDE statement, you must include an entry for the IP address of the remote server in the Lmhosts file. The server's entry must be inserted in the Lmhosts file before the #INCLUDE statement that references it. You also should not use #INCLUDE to reference an Lmhosts file on a redirected network drive, because your drive mappings might be different from one session to another. Use the UNC path for the file instead. Centralized Lmhosts files should never use drive-referenced entries, because the drive mappings in the file probably will not apply to all users who might use the file.

- *#BEGIN_ALTERNATE.* This statement signals the beginning of a block of multiple #INCLUDE statements (called a *block inclusion*). The statements within the block designate primary and alternate locations for the included file. The alternate locations are checked if the primary file is unavailable. The successful loading of any one entry in the block causes the block to succeed, and any subsequent entries in the block are not parsed. You can include multiple block inclusions within an Lmhosts file. The following is an example of a block inclusion:

```
#BEGIN_ALTERNATE
#INCLUDE       \\server\pub\lmhosts           #Primary source
#INCLUDE       \\othersrvr\pub\lmhosts        #Alternate
source
#INCLUDE       \\somewhere\pub\lmhosts        #Alternate
source
#END_ALTERNATE
```

- *#END_ALTERNATE.* This statement signals the end of a block of multiple #INCLUDE statements.
- *\0xnn.* This keyword enables you to specify nonprinting characters in NetBIOS names. You must enclose the NetBIOS name in quotation marks and use the *\0xnn* keyword to specify the hexadecimal value of

VI

Internet Services

the nonprinting character. The hexadecimal notation applies to only one character in the name. The name must be padded to a total of 16 characters, with the hexadecimal notation as the 16th character. Example:

```
109.88.120.45    "thename   \0x14"       #Uses special character
```

Adding an Entry to Lmhosts

NetBIOS computer names of computers on your LAN are resolved automatically. To resolve remote names when a WINS server is not available, add the NetBIOS names and their corresponding IP addresses to the Lmhosts file. To add an entry, use Notepad, WordPad, Edit, or any other text editor that enables you to edit and save ASCII files.

Each line consists of the IP address and NetBIOS name, and also can contain optional keywords and comments as explained previously. The following are examples of Lmhosts entries:

```
192.214.240.2     me                                  #Alias for my
➥computer
198.87.118.72     tower                               #Fred's computer
198.87.118.50     rli-server  #PRE                    #Application
➥server
120.89.101.70     server      #PRE   #DOM:tigers      #Some comment
➥here
182.212.242.2     sourcesrvr  #PRE                    #Source for
➥shared Lmhosts
182.212.242.3     source2     #PRE                    #Source for
➥shared Lmhosts
182.212.242.4     source3     #PRE                    #Source for
➥shared Lmhosts
187.52.122.188    images                              #Imaging server

#INCLUDE          c:\mystuff\lmhosts                  #My private
➥Lmhosts file

#BEGIN_ALTERNATE
#INCLUDE          \\sourcesrvr\pub\Lmhosts            #Primary central
➥Lmhosts
#INCLUDE          \\source2\pub\Lmhosts               #Alternate
source
#INCLUDE          \\source3\pub\Lmhosts               #Alternate
source
#END_ALTERNATE
```

In the preceding example, only the rli-server, server, sourcesrvr, source2, and source3 entries are preloaded into the name cache at system startup, because only they include the #PRE keyword. Other entries are parsed only after broadcast name resolution requests fail.

Tip

The addresses of servers you specify in a block inclusion must be preloaded through entries earlier in the file. Any entries not preloaded are ignored.

Troubleshooting

I'm using an Lmhosts file, and although it works, it takes a relatively long time to connect to some of the systems I use frequently. How can I speed it up?

If you have a large Lmhosts file, it's likely that the entries you're having trouble with are located near the end of the file. The names are processed sequentially during a resolution search, which means that the entire file has to be parsed before the needed address is reached. Either move to the top of the Lmhosts file the addresses of the systems you connect most often, or preload the entries as explained previously.

CHAPTER 25

Using Internet Programs

by Michael Marchuck

Windows NT provides a great deal of new tools that make Internet access easy. This chapter describes some of the tools available for Windows NT that allow you to take advantage of the Internet's vast information stores.

In this chapter, you learn to

- Configure Microsoft's Internet Explorer Web browser
- Install and configure Netscape Navigator
- Download files from the Internet
- Browse the USENET discussion groups

Configuring Internet Explorer

Microsoft's Internet Explorer is distributed on the Windows NT installation CD-ROM. This allows the Internet Explorer to be closely linked to the Windows NT operating system. Internet Explorer has been designed to take advantage of many low-level operating system functions to provide a seamless transition from local area network access to Internet access.

Installing Internet Explorer

Windows NT, by default configuration, installs the Microsoft Internet Explorer Web browser on to your system. If you have chosen to customize the installation, you will need to follow these steps to install Internet Explorer:

1. Open the Control Panel and choose Add/Remove Programs.
2. Select the Accessories option and click the Details button.
3. Select the Internet Jumpstart Kit option.
4. Click the OK button to install.

Managing Internet Explorer Options

In order to maximize your Internet exploration functionality, you need to understand the various options available for handling network connections and viewing documents. The following section covers some of the more common options and shows how you may want to adjust them to suit your needs.

View Options

In order to benefit from the information the Internet Explorer is providing to you, you need to adjust the default View settings. You can view any combination of the following three options:

- Toolbar
- Address Bar
- Status Bar

The toolbar allows you to select a number of commands by simply clicking the button associated with the command. The toolbar is shown by default.

The Address Bar is not shown by default, but you can enable this option by choosing View, Address Bar. This will allow you to type in addresses to explore without using the File, Open dialog box. Additionally, you will be able to see the current address of the document you are viewing within the Address Bar.

The Status Bar is also shown by default. However, you can adjust the level of detail that is displayed within the Status Bar. By default, the addresses shown in the Status Bar are simplified to show only the document name and the server from which it came. If you want to know the full Uniform Resource Locator address (URL) which details the directory in which the document is found, you can follow these steps to enable the full URL within the Status Bar:

1. Choose View, Options.
2. Select the Appearance property sheet (fig. 25.1)
3. Click the Full Addresses (URL's) option from the Addresses section of the property sheet.
4. Click OK to accept the changes.

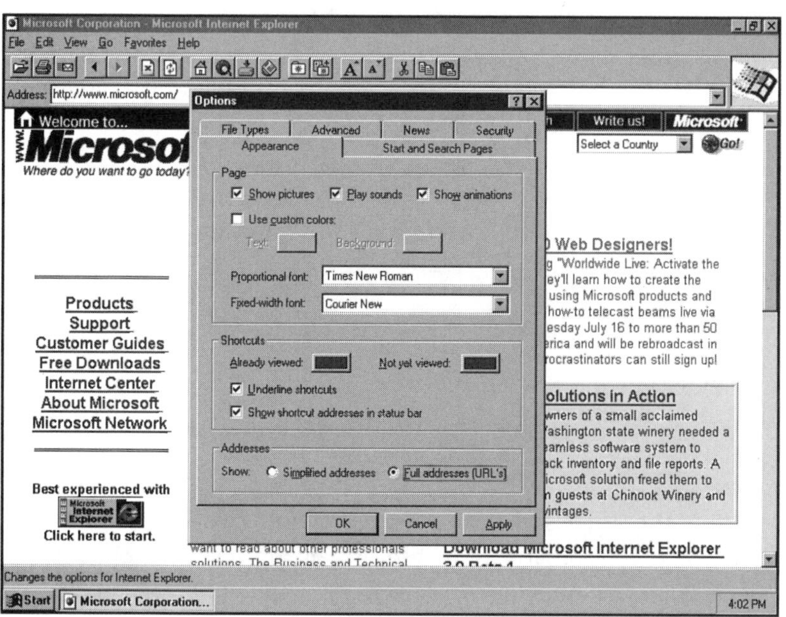

Fig. 25.1
The addresses shown in the Status Bar can be modified using the Appearance property sheet.

Internet Explorer Cache Management

While you are surfing the Internet, you'll probably pass through many of the same pages more than once. As you load World Wide Web pages and images, Internet Explorer stores them locally in a directory in order to speed up the retrieval of those pages should you return to them later. This document storage method is called caching. Whether you are simply going back to a previous page, or you are returning to a site you viewed an hour earlier, retrieving documents from your computer's cache is far quicker than reloading them from the Internet.

Internet Explorer holds the most recently viewed pages and graphics in a cache folder on your hard drive. This cache area can be defined to provide you with the best combination of retrieval speed and storage space. You can change the amount of cache space that Internet Explorer uses by following these steps:

1. Choose View, Options.
2. Click the Advanced tab (see fig. 25.2).

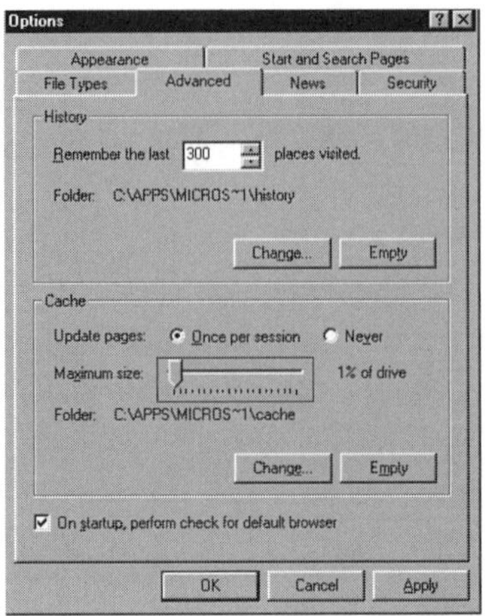

Fig. 25.2
The cache settings are modified on the Advanced property sheet.

3. Within the Cache section of the property sheet, you can adjust the amount of space that you want to allocate for the cache folder. The default space allotment is 10 percent of your hard drive.

> **Tip**
>
> When setting the cache folder allotment, try to set your hard drive space usage to match one day of your normal Internet exploration habits. For example, if you visit 20 sites in one day, chances are that you've only downloaded between 5 and 10M of data. If you leave your cache setting at 10 percent of your hard drive and you have a 500M drive, you will use 50M for caching Internet documents. That equates to between 10 and 20 days of data. Obviously, if you are a heavy user, this may only be one day's worth of exploring, but you'll want to adjust your cache setting to match your usage. A good way of measuring your cache needs is to empty the cache before you start exploring on an average day. At the end of the day, check the amount of data that is residing in your cache folder. Add about 10-20 percent more space to that amount when you set the cache folder allotment size.

4. Select the folder you want to use for storing the cached data. The default folder resides within the Microsoft Internet application folder.
5. Select the frequency in which the pages are checked for freshness. The Once Per Session option indicates that, after starting Internet Explorer,

the first time you access a page which has been stored in cache, the page will be checked to see if it has been updated. If you select the Never option, the page will only be retrieved from the cache folder. This will speed up your access to that page, but you may also be viewing information which is no longer current.

6. Adjust the number of sites you want to recall from the History section. Each time you visit a site, Internet Explorer remembers the address and name of the page you viewed. This way, you can go back to a previously viewed page if you have forgotten the address. The History setting does not affect the cache settings. Each address stored in the History folder only takes up between 50 and 100 bytes, so you do not need to set this number much lower than the default of 300 addresses.
7. Click OK to accept the changes made to the cache settings.

Start and Search Pages

When Internet Explorer starts, it begins loading the document at the address stored as the Start Page within the Internet Explorer options. In addition to the Start Page, most users will often access one of the many Internet indexing sites like Yahoo (**http://www.yahoo.com**), Excite (**http://www.excite.com**), or Alta Vista (**http://www.altavista.digital.com**) to help find the information they want. To facilitate the access to these sites, Internet Explorer includes the ability to connect to the Start Page (choose Go, Start Page) or the Search Page using the menu (choose Go, Search the Internet) or through the toolbar. Figure 25.3 shows the Internet Explorer's toolbar indicating the Start and Search buttons.

Fig. 25.3
The Start and Search pages can be accessed quickly using the Internet Explorer's toolbar.

You can modify which pages these toolbar or menu options point to. For example, if you wanted to change the Search Page to point to the Lycos search site (**http://www.lycos.com**) you would follow these steps:

1. Choose File, Open (or Ctrl+O).
2. Type **http://www.lycos.com** into the Address box and click OK.
3. After the page finishes loading, choose View, Options.
4. Select the Start and Search Pages property sheet. (see fig. 25.4)

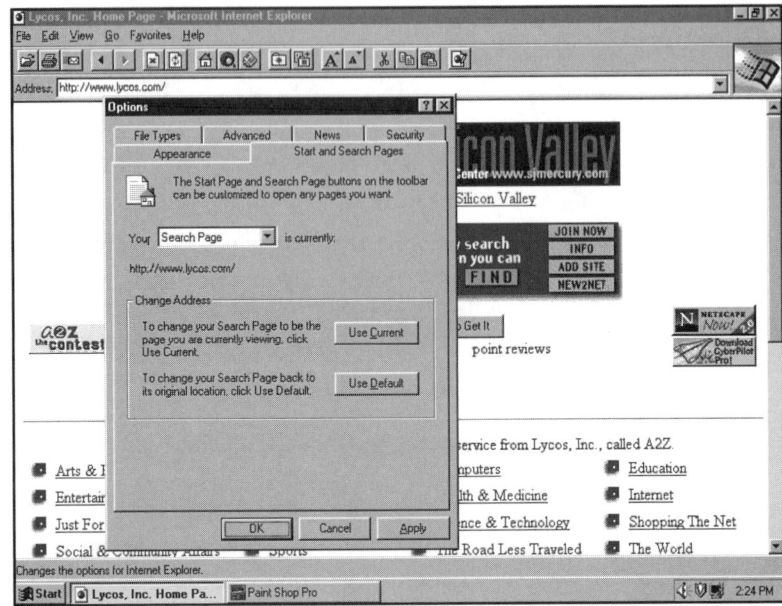

Fig. 25.4
The Search Page can be modified using the Start and Search Pages property sheet.

5. Choose the Search Page option from the drop-down list box.
6. Click the Use Current button to set the address of the Search Page.
7. Click OK to accept the changes.

You can follow the same steps for changing the Start Page by selecting the Start Page option in step 4.

Other Options

There are a great number of other options you can set to adjust how the Internet Explorer operates. Since this chapter is only designed to give you an overview of the applications, you may want to investigate the other property sheets available when you choose View, Options.

Using Internet Explorer

Once you have configured Internet Explorer to your liking, you need to understand the major usage techniques that will make your Internet exploration more enjoyable. The major techniques for managing your Internet Explorer sessions include:

- Using the Favorites folder to mark pages for future reference.
- Opening multiple Internet Explorer windows to view multiple documents simultaneously.

- Using the History folder to get back to places you've been before.

The following sections investigate these techniques to help you on your way.

Using Favorites

While you are busy exploring the Internet, you will undoubtedly run across sites that you'll want to return to in the future. Instead of having to write down multiple addresses, you can use the Favorites folder within Internet Explorer.

For example, you may run across a great Internet indexing site that you want to use to supplement the main Search Page site you've chosen. Perhaps your Search Page points to Lycos (**http://www.lycos.com**) but you also want to be able to easily get to Yahoo's categories (**http://www.yahoo.com**). You could create a Shortcut to Yahoo within Internet Explorer's Favorites folder. To do this:

1. Choose Favorites, Add To Favorites.
2. Verify or modify the name of the page to your liking (see fig. 25.5).

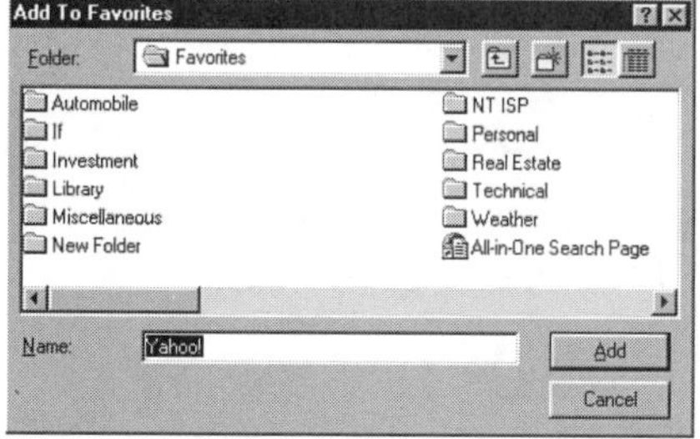

Fig. 25.5
You can change the name of the Internet Shortcut that you create within the Favorites folder.

You can even create subfolders within the Favorites folder to help organize your Internet sites. To create a new folder within the Favorites folder, click the Create New Folder button in the Add To Favorites dialog box (see fig. 25.6).

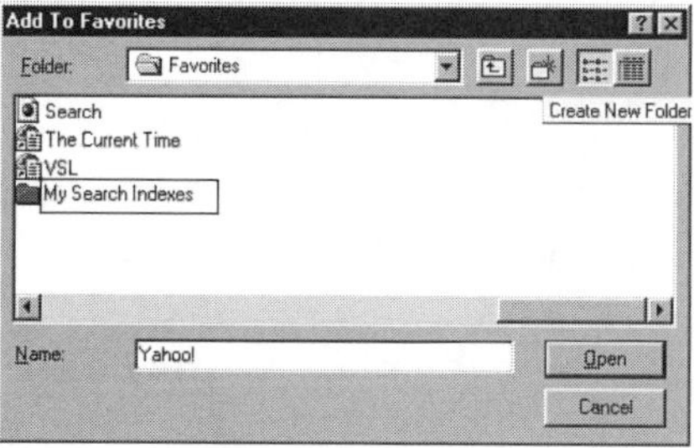

Fig. 25.6
By clicking the Create New Folder toolbar button, you can add folders within the Favorites folder to categorize your Internet sites.

Tip

You can also manage your Favorites folder from within Windows NT Explorer.

Using Multiple Windows

When you are exploring the Internet, you may want to see more than one page at a time. In these cases, you have two options. First, if you want to follow a link from within the current page you are viewing without losing the current page, you can right-click the link which brings up a menu like the one shown in figure 25.7.

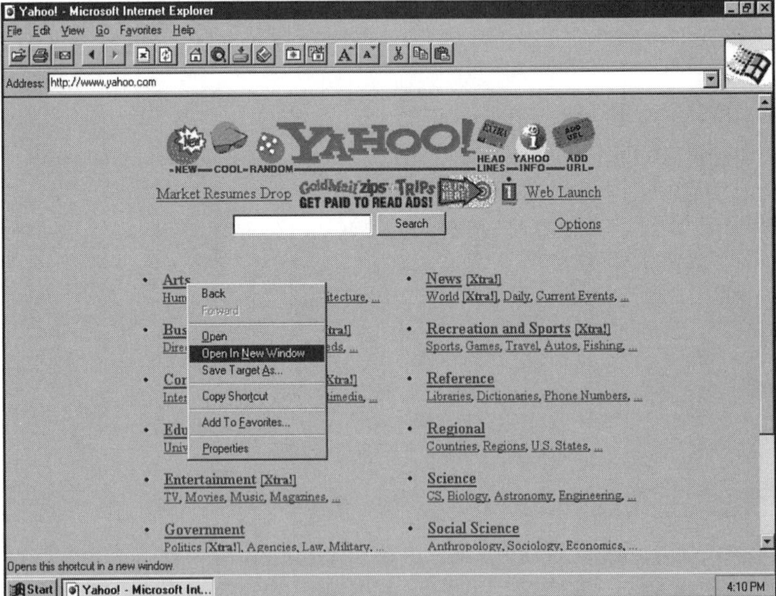

Fig. 25.7 A new window can be opened to follow a link from the current page.

By selecting Open in New Window from the pop-up menu, Internet Explorer preserves the current page you are viewing and starts a new window that will load the page from the link you selected.

The other option you can use to open a new window can be used when you want to open a page that is not linked from the current page, but might be in your Favorites folder or an address you know, like **http://www.microsoft.com**. To start a new window in this situation, choose File, Open, and then check Open in New Window. Then you can use the new window as a fresh copy of Internet Explorer.

Using the History Folder

Internet Explorer maintains a list of places you've been before even after the cached pages have been removed from your system. This is helpful for back-tracking to a site that contained information you know you saw "somewhere." To access the list of sites you've previously viewed, follow these steps:

1. Choose File.
2. Select one of the sites which appears within your File menu

   OR

   Select the More History option to display the History folder (see fig. 25.8).

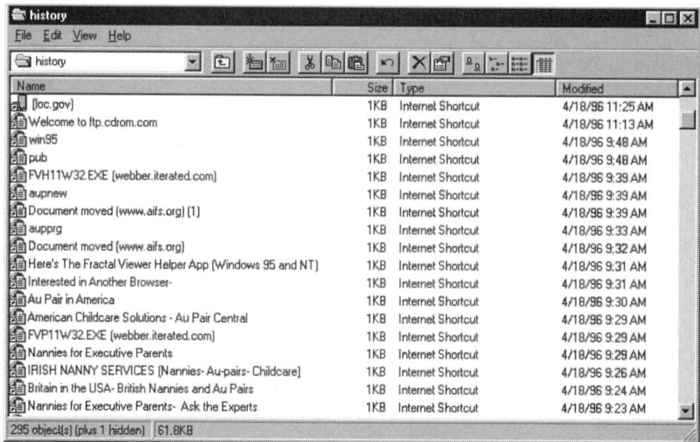

Fig. 25.8
The History folder shows the places you've visited over time.

You can sort the sites within the History folder simply by clicking the column headings, like Date Modified. This allows you to see the trail of sites in a chronological order. Double-click any one of the sites within the History folder to go back to that site.

Configuring Netscape Navigator

Like Microsoft's Internet Explorer, Netscape Navigator is a World Wide Web browsing tool. While the Internet Explorer is optimized for the Windows NT environment, the Navigator is a browser which shares its low-level programming code with several other environments like Macintosh and UNIX. Netscape Navigator has been considered the premier Web browser for a long time, and many of the features found on the WWW were pioneered by Netscape.

Since Navigator is a third-party application, you can obtain it by purchasing the shrink-wrapped program at your local software retailer, by mail-order, or even over the Internet. By attaching to Netscape's WWW site using Internet Explorer or an ftp client—which we'll explain how to do later in this chapter—you can download the application to your local hard drive.

On the Web

Netscape's World Wide Web site:

http://www.netscape.com

Installing Netscape Navigator

If you have purchased Netscape Navigator from a software retailer, you should follow the instructions contained in the package to install the Navigator application. This section covers the installation technique used to download and install Navigator from their Internet site using Internet Explorer.

To connect to the Netscape Web site, follow these steps:

1. Open an Internet Explorer window.
2. Choose File, Open.
3. Type **http://www.netscape.com** in the address box in the Open Internet Address dialog box.
4. Click OK.

Once you've connected to their Web site, you'll see a page similar to the one shown in figure 25.9.

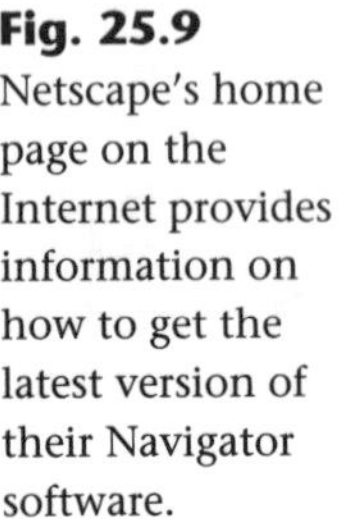

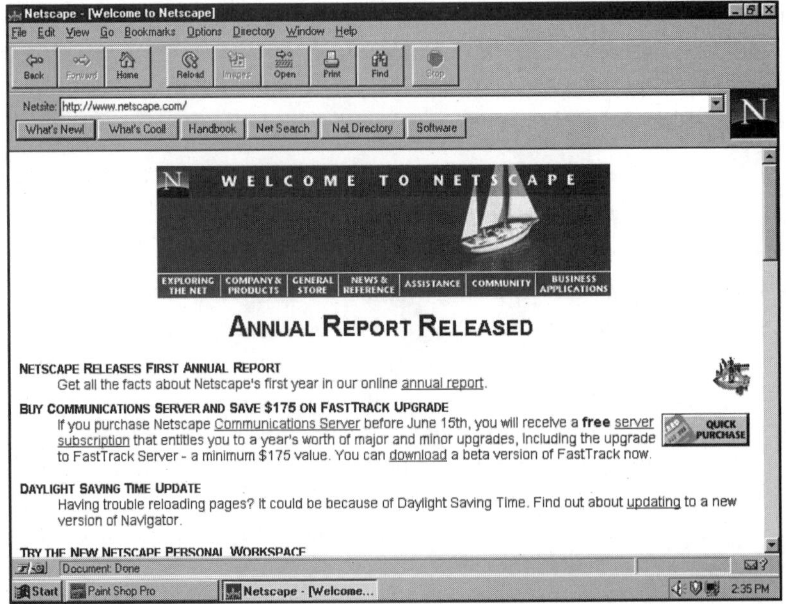

Fig. 25.9
Netscape's home page on the Internet provides information on how to get the latest version of their Navigator software.

Since the Internet changes so rapidly, the page you see when you connect may differ some from the one you see in figure 25.9. In any case, Netscape will provide you with links to download the latest version of their software for Windows NT. Follow these links and download the installation executable to your hard drive. The entire application, before installation, may be up to 7M. So your download at 14.4Kb/s may take a couple of hours or more to get the file.

> **Note**
>
> To minimize your download time, online charges, and your phone bill, you may want to consider purchasing the Navigator software at the store. Not only will it be far more convenient to install it from the disks or CD-ROM, but it will also contain additional documentation and registration information.

The Navigator installation is packaged as a self-installing program. You will have downloaded a file named something like AT3220E1.EXE (your exact file name may vary due to the version number of the software you download). Close your Internet Explorer window and open up Windows NT Explorer from the Start menu. Double-click the application file you downloaded to initiate the installation procedure. You will see a screen similar to the one shown in figure 25.10.

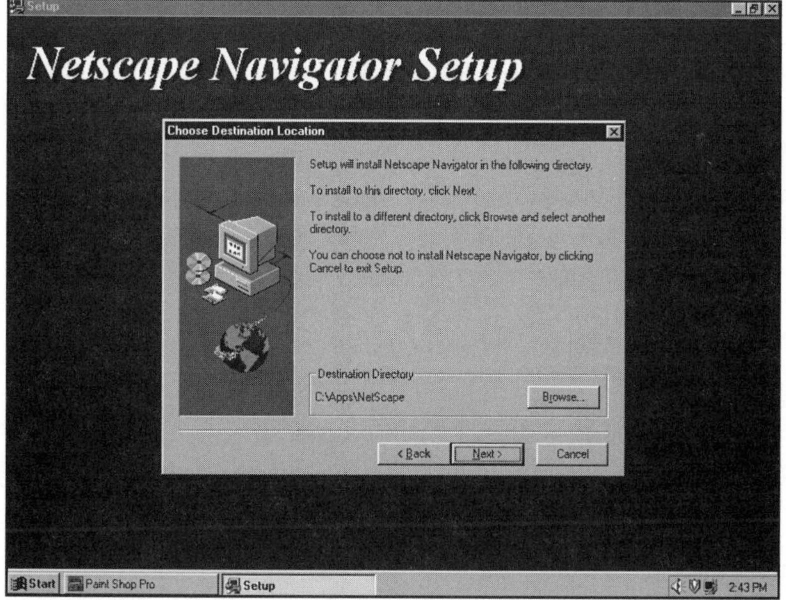

Fig. 25.10
The Netscape Navigator installation program guides you through the steps to install Navigator on your Windows NT system.

The installation program creates a folder within your Start menu from which you can run the Navigator application. Now that you've got the program installed, you can begin modifying the settings to suit your needs.

Managing Netscape Navigator Options

In order to maximize your Internet exploration functionality, you need to understand the various options available for handling network connections and viewing documents. The following sections cover some of the more common options and how you may want to adjust them to suit your needs.

Toolbar Options

The toolbar within Navigator contains buttons that can be configured to show just text, just icons, or icons and text. This will let you configure your toolbar to your liking. Figure 25.11 shows the Navigator toolbar without text.

To modify the toolbar icon options, follow these steps:

1. Choose Options, General Preferences from the main menu.
2. Locate the Toolbars section on the Appearance property sheet.
3. Select one of the options Pictures, Text, or Pictures and Text which suits your style (see fig. 25.12).
4. Click OK.

Navigator Cache Management

Like Internet Explorer, Navigator has a document cache to increase the speed at which you can reload documents you've previously viewed. For a more complete explanation of the cache function, see the section titled, "Internet Explorer Cache Management" earlier in this chapter.

Unlike Internet Explorer's cache management, Navigator uses a two-tier approach to managing previously viewed pages. The most recent pages are stored in memory up to a defined limit. After that, the pages are saved into the Navigator's cache folder in the same way that Internet Explorer does. This two-tier approach may provide somewhat better performance under other operating systems such as UNIX, Macintosh, or Windows 3.1. However, Windows NT uses an efficient disk cache which makes this two-tier approach unnecessary. You must reduce the memory cache to a very low amount to preserve operating system RAM and let Windows NT provide the hard disk caching instead. Figure 25.13 shows the cache configuration property sheet within Navigator.

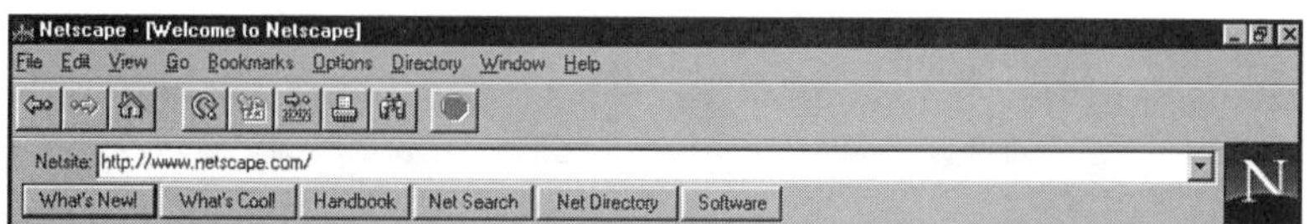

Fig. 25.11
The Navigator toolbar without text may be difficult to understand for new users but may be preferred by experienced users.

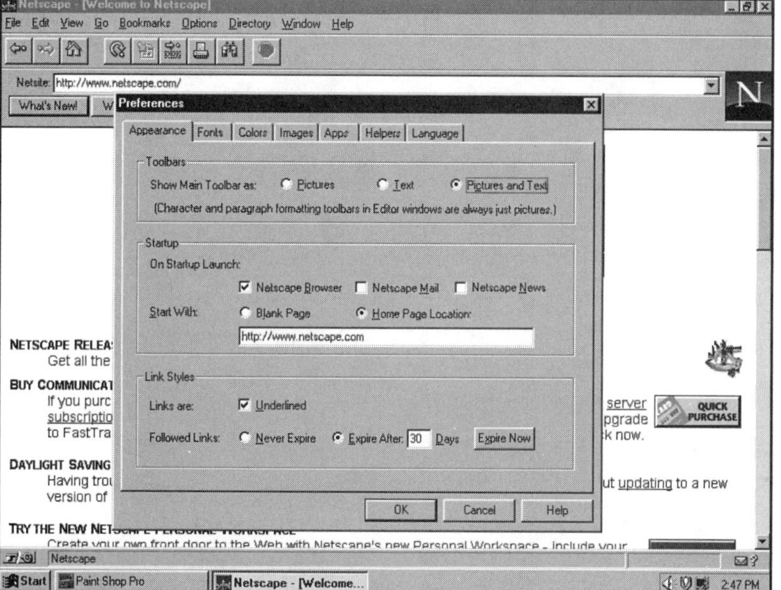

Fig. 25.12
The Navigator toolbar modifications are found on the Appearance property sheet.

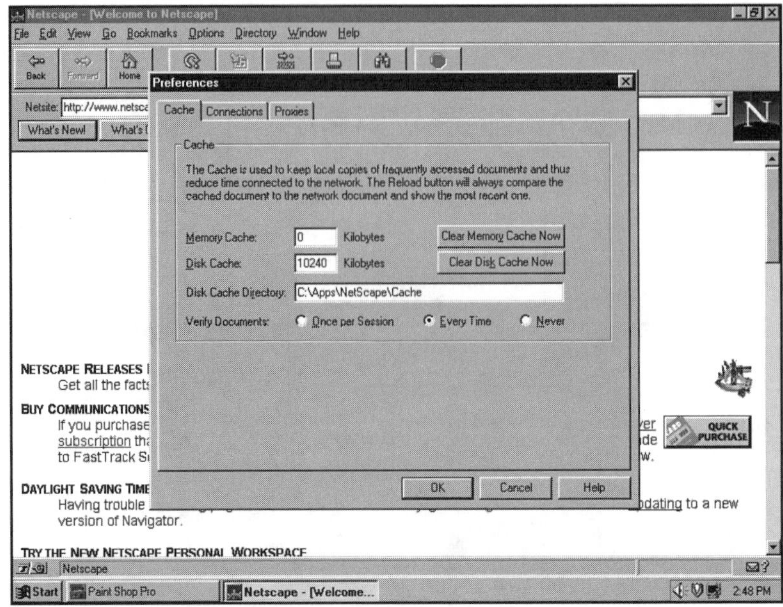

Fig. 25.13
Navigator's two-tier document cache should be configured to use less memory and more hard drive space.

To change the settings for Navigator's cache, follow these steps:

1. Choose Options, Network Preferences.
2. On the Cache property sheet change the Memory Cache from 1024K to 0K.
3. Increase the Disk Cache to equal about one day's worth of your normal browsing capacity. See the Tip in the Internet Explorer section which explains how to calculate this amount.
4. Click OK.

You should also check the length of time that Navigator will remember the links you have followed. Like the Internet Explorer's History feature, the Navigator will remember sites you've been to before. Instead of setting a particular number of sites to remember, you can set the amount of time you want to wait before the links begin expiring. If you explore the Internet frequently, your link history will consume a greater amount of disk space than if you browse infrequently. You may want to adjust the number of days before the links expire to a higher or lower number based on your Internet exploration habits. To do this:

1. Choose Options, General Preferences.
2. Locate the Link Styles section on the Appearance property sheet.

3. Adjust the Expire After setting to meet your needs. The default is 30 days.
4. Click OK to save these changes.

Configuring the Home Page

When Navigator starts, the Home Page is loaded by default. The choice of the Home Page can be set through the following steps:

1. Choose Options, General Preferences.
2. Locate the On Startup Launch section on the Appearance property sheet (see fig. 25.14).
3. Choose the Start With Blank Page option if you do not want Navigator to load anything from the Internet when it starts, or choose the Home Page Location option and fill in the address of the page you want to load when Navigator starts. This page can be a local page.
4. Click OK to save your changes.

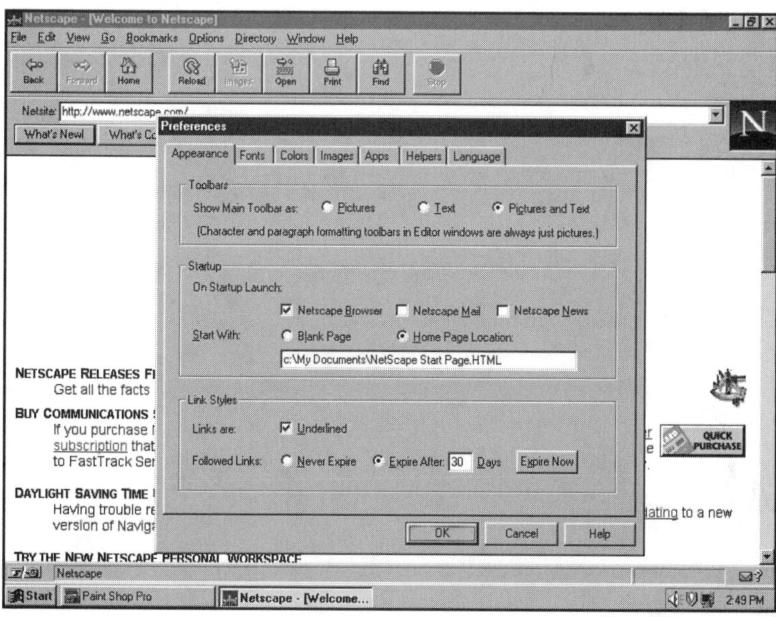

Fig. 25.14
Navigator's home page can be modified to show any site on startup, including a local page.

Using Netscape Navigator

Once you have configured Navigator to your liking, you need to understand the major usage techniques that will make your Internet exploration more enjoyable. The major techniques for managing your Netscape Navigator sessions include:

- Using the Bookmark option to mark pages for future reference.
- Opening multiple Navigator windows to view multiple documents simultaneously.

The following sections investigate these techniques to help you on your way.

Using Bookmarks

While you are busy exploring the Internet, you will run across sites that you will want to return to in the future. Instead of writing down the address of these sites, you can use the Bookmark option within Navigator.

For example, you may run across a great Internet indexing site that you want to use to supplement the main Search Page site you've chosen. Perhaps your Search Page points to Lycos (**http://www.lycos.com**) but you also want to be able to easily get to Yahoo's categories (**http://www.yahoo.com**). You could create a Bookmark to Yahoo within Navigator's Bookmark list. To do this:

1. Choose Bookmark, Add Bookmark.

   Your site will be added to the Bookmark list off of the main menu (see fig. 25.15).

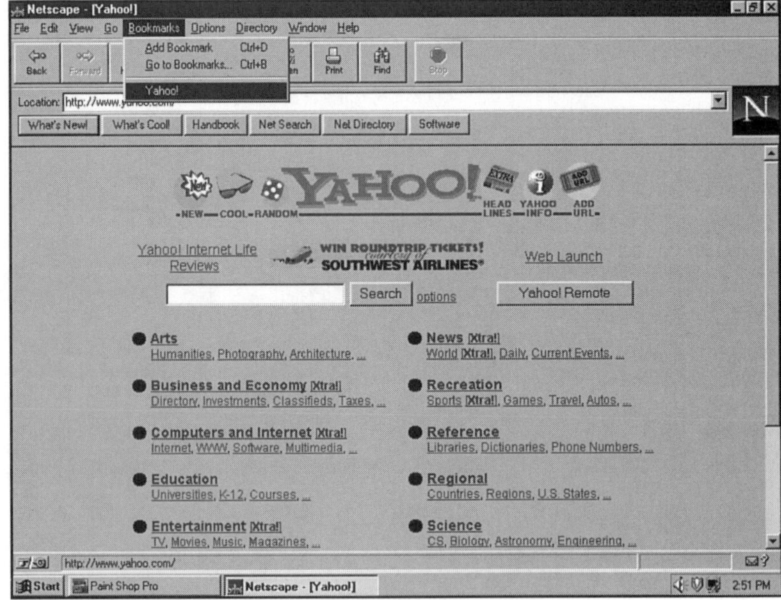

Fig. 25.15
Your Bookmarks can be accessed by selecting the Bookmark menu item from the main menu.

Using Multiple Windows

When you are exploring the Internet, you may want to see more than one page at a time. In these cases you have two options that you can use. First, if you want to follow a link from within the current page you are viewing without losing the current page, you can right-click the link within Navigator which brings up a menu like the one shown in figure 25.16.

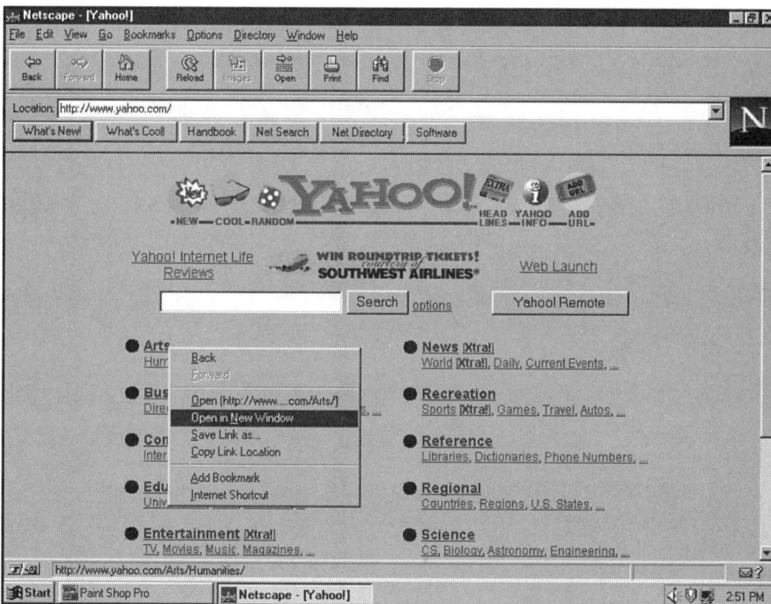

Fig. 25.16
A new window can be opened to follow a link from the current page.

By selecting the Open in New Window option from the pop-up menu, Internet Explorer preserves the current page you are viewing and starts a new window that loads the page from the link you selected.

The other option you can use to open a new window would be used when you want to open a page which is not linked from the current page, but might be in your Favorites folder or an address you know, like **http://www.microsoft.com**. To start a new window in this situation, choose File, New Web Browser. Then you can use the new window as a fresh copy of Navigator.

Integrating Multiple Programs

While Microsoft's Internet Explorer and Netscape's Navigator both can handle a wide array of Internet services, neither can handle them all. In order to provide additional functionality, other applications are used to open files or connect to services that are not included in the base Web browsing application. These other programs are called *helper applications*.

Understanding Helper Applications

Not every system needs the same capability as another system. Some people require the ability to hear real-time audio over the Internet while others want to watch short video clips or their favorite sports star. These audio, video, or external document files require a helper application to load and display or playback the data that is downloaded from the Internet.

These helper applications are usually configured by their document extensions and their Internet document types. Within the browser, the document types are configured to instruct the browser to execute a particular helper application when a certain document type is encountered. For example, figure 25.17 shows the helper application setup within Netscape Navigator which instructs Navigator to start WinZip when it encounters a file with the extension of ZIP or an Internet document type application/x-zip-compressed.

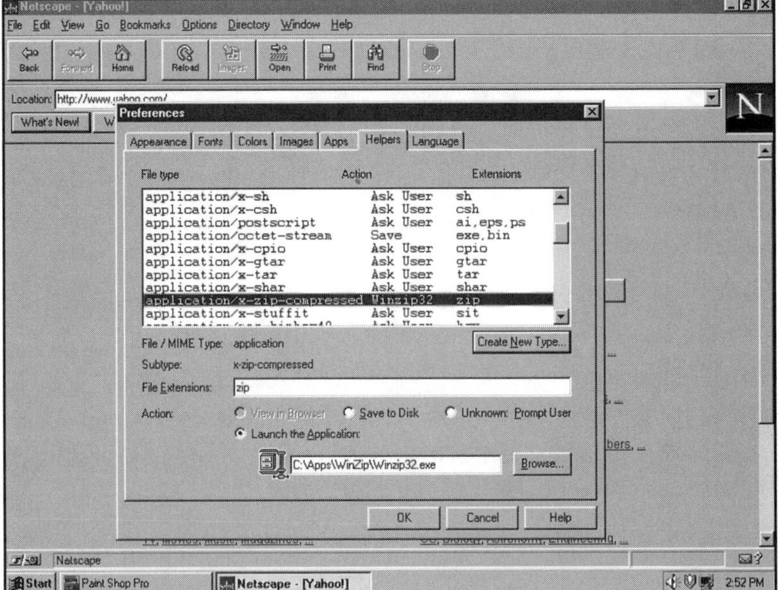

Fig. 25.17
Helper applications must be configured within the browser to be executed when a particular file type is encountered.

Understanding Plug-Ins

Browser plug-ins are similar to helper applications, however, the helper application actually runs within the browser window when it encounters a particular file type. One type of plug-in which allows external image types to be seen is the fractal image plug-in by Iterated Systems. *Fractal images* are encoded mathematically and the file sizes are usually very small. This type of image is ideal for transmission over the Internet where the size of the files dramatically impacts the speed of the display.

Iterated Systems fractal image plug-in:

On the Web

http://www.iterated.com

Installing plug-ins is unique to each application, but all plug-ins automatically register themselves with your Netscape Navigator. The next time you run Navigator, the plug-in will be available for you to use.

Now when you attach to a site which contains fractal images, you can view them inside your Navigator window rather than load them into an external helper application. Figure 25.18 shows a fractal image displayed using the fractal image plug-in.

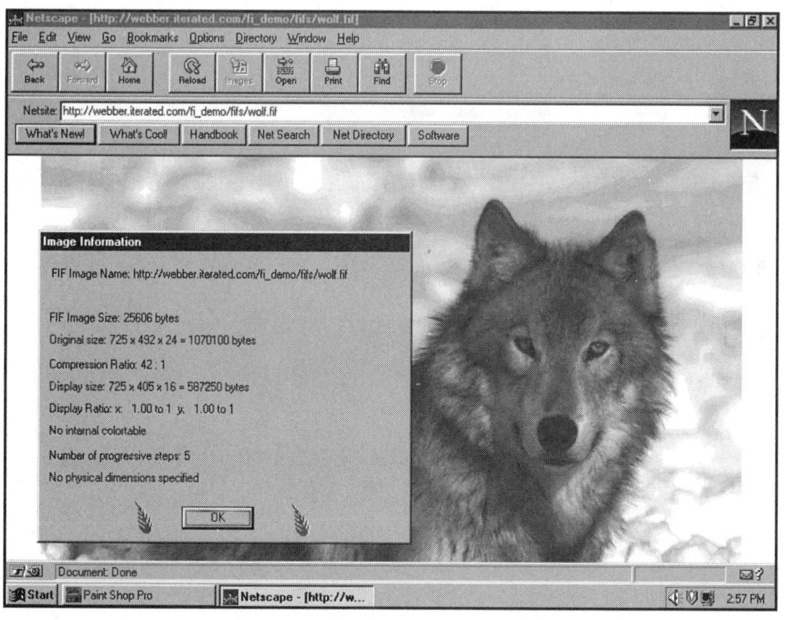

Fig. 25.18
Fractal images can be viewed within the Navigator window using the fractal image plug-in.

Using ftp and Telnet

Two of the classic Internet connection protocols are the File Transfer Protocol (ftp) and Telnet. ftp allows you to connect to another computer and download files to your local hard drive, while Telnet is a protocol which provides a test-based terminal-emulation for UNIX and mainframe applications. The following sections briefly cover these two Internet protocols and the client software you need to use them.

Using ftp

Both Internet Explorer and Netscape Navigator contain ftp clients that allow you to connect to remote ftp sites and download software. To illustrate how you can download files from the Internet using ftp, let's connect to a large ftp site at Walnut Creek that contains thousands of shareware files. The site is located at **ftp.cdrom.com**.

To connect to this site follow these steps:

1. Open an Internet Explorer window.
2. Choose File, Open.
3. Type **ftp://ftp.cdrom.com** in the Address box in the Open Internet Address dialog box. The *ftp://* tells Internet Explorer to use the ftp protocol to connect to the address *ftp.cdrom.com*.
4. Click OK.

When Internet Explorer connects with the site, you'll see a page similar to the one shown in figure 25.19.

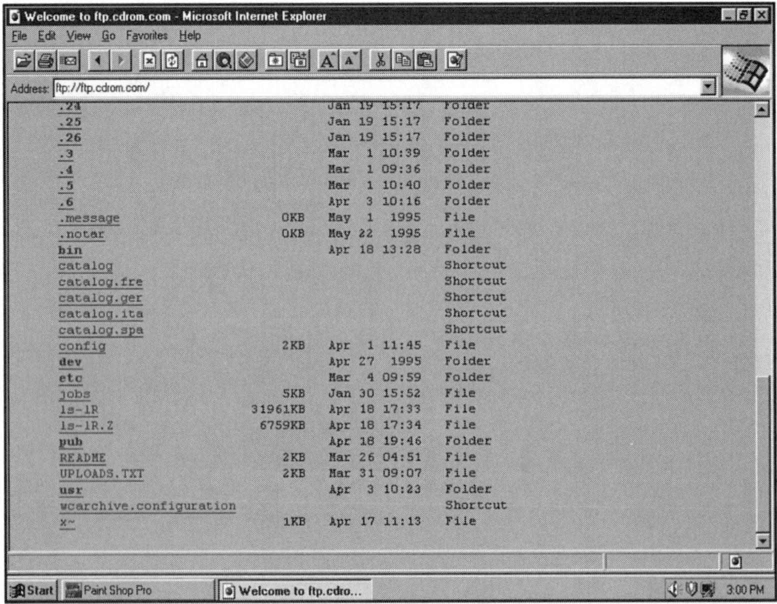

Fig. 25.19
The Internet Explorer displays any notes along with the folders you can access via ftp.

You may notice that the ftp interface is not as friendly as an average WWW page. The ftp site interface should be considered a type of long-distance file manager. You can see the folders and files but there isn't much else to help you determine what to click. Most ftp sites will have a README.TXT or an

INDEX.TXT file which explains what files are located in the current folder or in other folders on the ftp site.

To change into a folder, you simply click the folder name which links you to that directory. In most sites, the PUB folder will contain the files that you have permissions to access.

To download a file, just click the file name and Internet Explorer prompts you to choose a location in which to save the file (see fig. 25.20).

Tip

You may want to create a folder on your system to contain any new files you download from the Internet. As a suggestion, try creating a folder called "Internet Files" off of the root of your hard drive (such as, c:\Internet Files).

Caution

Files you download from the Internet may contain viruses or may not work as you might expect them to. You should *always* scan any files you download from the Internet for viruses.

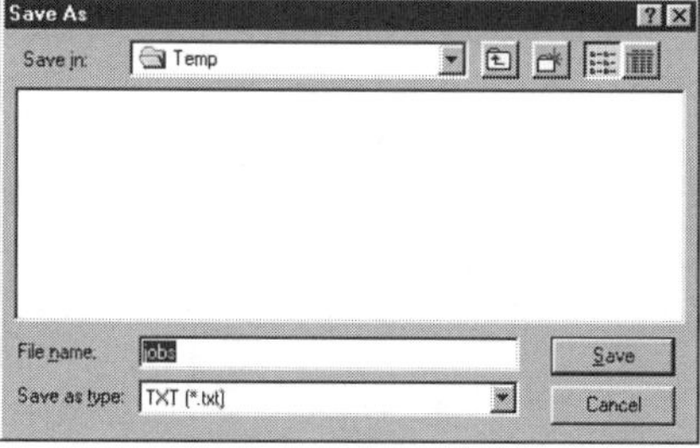

Fig. 25.20
Internet Explorer prompts you for a location to save the files you download from an ftp site.

Often, an Internet site will have a Web page that lists the files and their names. When you click the file name links to download the file, Internet Explorer automatically connects to the specified ftp site and prompts you for a location in which to store the file on your local system.

Using Telnet

Telnet usage is declining on the Internet with the introduction of more sophisticated Web forms and embedded programming languages like Java. But there are still many sites which use Telnet to access data on their system. For example, many library systems are only accessible via Telnet on the Internet.

Telnet is an auto-configured helper application within Internet Explorer. When you click a link that takes you to a Telnet session, Internet Explorer automatically starts the Telnet application and connects you to that site. Figure 25.21 shows an example of how a Web site can point you to a Telnet session.

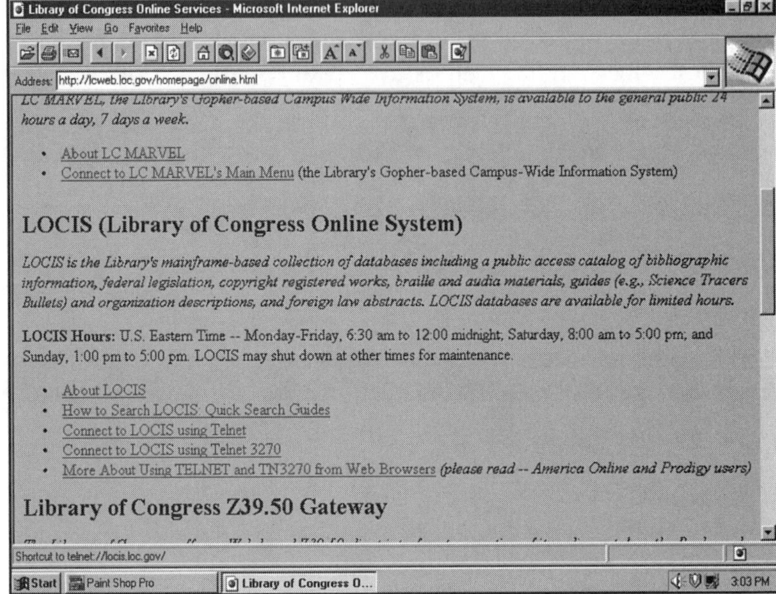

Fig. 25.21 The Library of Congress Telnet session can be accessed via their WWW page at **http://lcweb.loc.gov/homepage/online.html**.

Once you have started a Telnet site, the character-based application prompts you with instructions on how to sign-on to the site and use the application.

> **Note**
>
> Telnet sites vary in terms of their usage specifics and the keys you need to push to control your session. Make sure you read all instructions before you start a Telnet session.

Using Other Internet Tools

Several other Internet tools worth mentioning include Internet Relay Chat (IRC), E-mail, and Network News. These Internet services also require client software to connect and use. Internet Explorer only contains the Network News client within the browser, while Netscape Navigator includes Network News and E-mail clients. Neither Internet Explorer nor Netscape Navigator includes an IRC client.

Using an Internet Relay Chat Client

The IRC clients allow you to have real-time conversations with others from around the world. IRC is organized into chat channels that are accessed using an IRC client. A popular IRC client for Windows NT is the mIRC client. Figure 25.22 shows the mIRC client main screen after connecting to an IRC server.

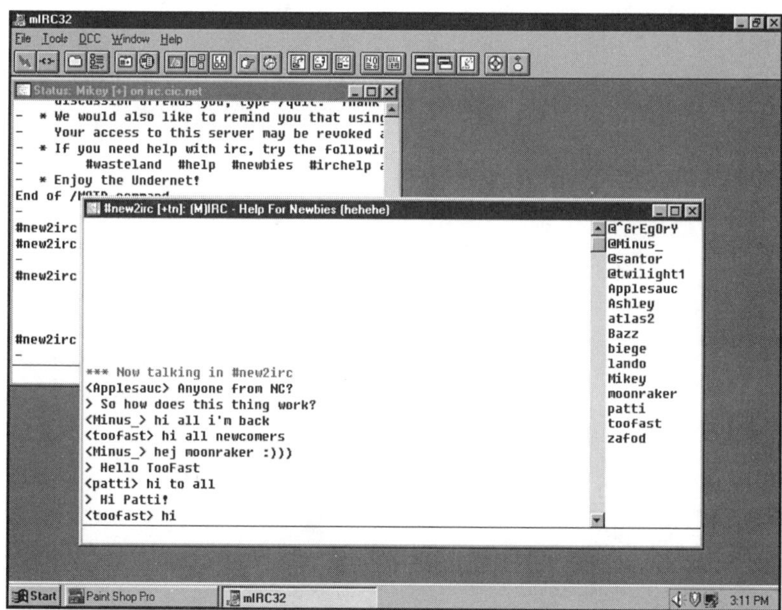

Fig. 25.22
The mIRC client allows you to connect into the IRC network.

The mIRC client provides an overview of how to chat in IRC as well as a few predefined chat channels like #ircNewbies, #ircHelp, and #new2irc. You may want to explore these channels for inexperienced users since the chatting in some other channels can get hostile when new users ask questions.

Using an E-mail Client

Windows NT provides a great way to get your Internet mail by using Exchange. You can also use the e-mail functions within Netscape Navigator, but the built in Exchange mail client can handle all the mail and file attachments you need for sending mail on the Internet.

Using a Network News Client

The Network News system is a type of electronic message board that allows users to converse about many different topics. You need to know the address of your Network News server which can be obtained from your Internet Service Provider (ISP). Most ISP's run their own Network News server so you can access news groups and articles quickly. The name Network News may imply a headline news articles, but actually each news group is a categorized message board which allows users to view and post new messages called articles.

When you connect to your news server for the first time, Internet Explorer asks you if you want to download the list of newsgroups on that server. You need to do this the first time you connect since you don't know which newsgroups are available to you. After you have connected and downloaded the list of newsgroups, you see a list something like the one shown in figure 25.23.

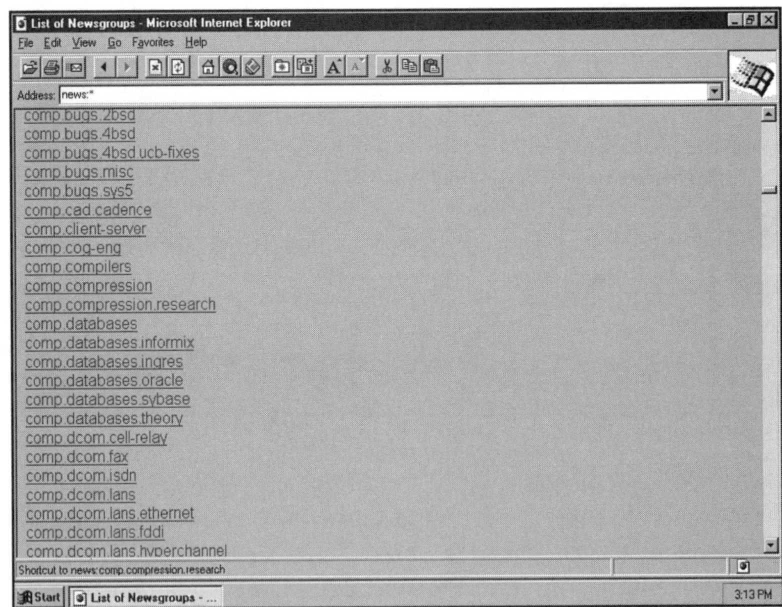

Fig. 25.23
Network News can be viewed from within Internet Explorer.

Notice that each newsgroup has an identifying name such as comp.compression.research which gives you a hint as to the discussion that is hosted there. In this case COMP defines this group as computer-related; COMPRESSION.RESEARCH suggests that the discussion focuses on researching data compression issues. Browse through the newsgroups which are hosts on your Network News server to find one that interests you. ❖

CHAPTER 26

Setting Up an Internet Server with IIS

by Craig Zacker

Internet services are now a major concern of nearly every software producer in the market today, and Microsoft is surely no exception. Both the Windows NT 4.0 Server and Workstation products are bundled with an Internet services package that could well make World Wide Web and ftp services as ubiquitous a feature of the modern desktop environment as a Web browser is now.

Designed primarily for internal use on corporate networks (so-called intranets), the Microsoft Peer Web Services allow any user of Windows NT 4.0 Workstation to publish personal Web pages and make ftp and Gopher services available to coworkers. The Windows NT 4.0 Server product includes the Microsoft Internet Information Server, which provides the same basic services, but is designed for the high volume usage that a corporate Internet site is likely to attract.

The Peer Web Services (PWS) and the Internet Information Server (IIS) are very much alike. Sites using both packages can even be administered from the same Internet Services Manager, which ships with both products.

In this chapter, you learn how to:

- Prepare your system to run the Microsoft Internet services
- Install the appropriate package for your Windows NT machine
- Configure the Microsoft Internet services

Introducing the Microsoft Internet Services

Both the Internet Information Server and the Peer Web Services offer the same suite of TCP/IP server modules. You can use your computer as a World Wide Web Server, an ftp or a Gopher server, or any combination of the three.

Depending on the package that you elect to use and the volume of traffic that you receive, you can even run the services while you use the computer for your typical daily activities.

The World Wide Web server allows your computer to serve HTML documents and graphics files to users through the HTTP protocol. You can also use tools provided by Microsoft and many other companies to build truly interactive Web pages that interface with other resources on your network, such as databases and order entry systems.

ftp is the File Transfer Protocol, an application-level protocol that allows users to transfer files to and from your system. The Windows NT ftp service allows remote users to connect anonymously, or it can use the native Windows NT security features to control access to specific files. The ftp service from Windows NT Server 3.51 and earlier, which was administered through the Control Panel, is now gone, having been replaced by this module in the Internet Information Server.

Gopher is another method of making files available for user download, which can be configured to present a friendlier interface to the client than ftp. You can include descriptions in your file listings, create customized menus, and link to files or services at other locations. It does not allow for anything like the graphical flexibility of the World Wide Web, however, which has eclipsed Gopher's popularity.

All three of the services are integrated into a unified Windows NT application that is installed and administered through a common interface. The Internet Services Manager is the same for both the Peer Web Services and the Internet Information Service. It allows you to administer the Internet service modules running on servers and workstations all over your network.

Both of the Internet service packages support a full range of high-end Web server features, including:

- Support for both NCSA (National Center for Supercomputing Applications) and CERN (Conseil Europeén pour la Recherce Nucléaire) image map files.
- The ability to host multiple independent Web sites, each with its own IP address and root directory.
- Support for CGI (Common Gateway Interface) scripts and applications, as well as the Microsoft Internet Server Application Programming Interface (ISAPI), providing a robust development environment for client/server applications.

- ODBC (Open Database Connectivity) drivers for database connectivity and the ability to log service activity directly to an SQL database.
- Centralized administration of all of the Internet services on the network with the Internet Service Manager application, or individual server administration through a Web browser with the HTML Administrator.
- Support for the Secure Sockets Layer (SSL) Internet security standard.

The Microsoft Peer Web Services

The Microsoft Peer Web Services ship with the Windows NT 4.0 Workstation product. Although the modules are functionally identical to the IIS, the operating system imposes a 10-user limitation on the TCP/IP stack. This means that the product would not be suitable for use as a dedicated high-volume Web server, but could serve very well as a means to share information between users on an internal network, or for light duty as an Internet server.

Note

The 10-user TCP/IP limitation is an extension of the same limitation imposed on drive-sharing connections through Windows NT network clients. Note that the limitation is on user, not individual protocol connections. Opening 10 ftp sessions from one workstation to the PWS ftp server would therefore occupy only one user connection, as would a Web browser that uses concurrent TCP connections to speed up the access rate.

The Internet Information Server

The Internet Information Server is Microsoft's high-volume Internet services package, which is now being included free with the Windows NT 4.0 Server product, along with the Microsoft Search Server and the Front Page Web publishing package. These tools can turn a Windows NT server into a self-contained, full-featured Internet site, offering users access to a virtually unlimited scope of information, files, products and services, all for the price of the operating system.

The difference between the IIS and the PWS is primarily one of degree. The products offer most of the same services, but the IIS running on Windows NT Server is designed to handle the large number of connections and the heavy TCP/IP traffic that public Internet sites can require.

Before Installing the Services

The Peer Web Services and the Internet Information Server both require additional resources and services beyond the base requirements for the Windows NT operating system itself. What you will need depends on how you intend to use the services, the amount of traffic you expect to receive, and what other expectations you have of the machine. Whether Internet or intranet, server or workstation, you must have the infrastructure to support the services properly.

Hardware Requirements

As for the hardware for your Windows NT machine, whether you will be running the IIS or the PWS, it will be necessary to have enough hard disk space for the files that will be served to your users (including space for any ftp file uploads that you may allow), and more importantly, enough RAM in the machine to support the services that you will run. Internet services may have to handle dozens or even hundreds of client connections at once, and the official memory requirements for Windows NT are quite modest. You will also have to consider the needs of any other services that you will be running on the computer, as well as whether or not you will be using the machine for your regular workstation activities.

Additional Protocols and Services

All of the Internet services require that the TCP/IP protocol be installed on the computer, as well as on all client computers. TCP/IP is the *lingua franca* of the Internet and the high level protocols used by the services (such as HTTP and ftp) require the transport mechanism provided by the combination of TCP and IP.

> **Note**
>
> See Chapter 24, "Understanding and Configuring TCP/IP," for more information on installing and configuring TCP/IP on your Windows NT machine.

If you intend to use either the IIS or the PWS to make your services available on the Internet, you must, of course, have a connection to an Internet Service Provider (ISP). This can be a network link through a router, or a direct connection from the Windows NT machine using a dialup or ISDN line.

If you want your users to be able to connect to your Web, ftp, or Gopher site using a host or machine name, rather than a numerical IP address, you will require a name resolution service. For Internet use, the standard is the domain name system (DNS), a distributed host name look-up mechanism that allows a client anywhere on the Internet to connect to any service by its host name (such as **www.microsoft.com**). Windows NT Server ships with a DNS service or your ISP should be able to provide you with access to a DNS server. In any case, you must register a domain name (such as microsoft.com) with the Internet Network Information Center (InterNIC) before you use it on the Internet.

If you will only be using the services on a private intranet, you can use NetBIOS names to identify your machines. The machine name that you assign to your Windows NT server or workstation during the operating system installation is its NetBIOS name. You can use an LMHOSTS file (which is a static table of IP addresses and NetBIOS names) on each computer to resolve names into addresses, or you can use the Windows Internet Naming Service (WINS) that ships with Windows NT Server. WINS is a dynamically updated and replicated database that can track the NetBIOS names for all of the machines on your network.

Finally, you must be sure to disable any other ftp, World Wide Web, or Gopher servers that are running on your machine, whether they are manufactured by Microsoft or not. Open the Windows NT Control Panel, launch the Services application, and check the listing shown for any other Internet services that may be running. You can use this dialog box to stop those services immediately, and also to modify their Startup status. The new services you are installing will be configured to start automatically when Windows NT boots. If any competing services also try to load automatically, unpredictable conflicts may result.

Types of Installations

Finally, you will need access to the Windows NT installation files. Although the installation processes for the IIS and the PWS are all but identical, each installation can be performed in several different ways. Both the Server and Workstation CDs have a directory called \Inetsrv that contains the files needed to install the IIS and the PWS, respectively. You can elect to install the Internet services during the Windows NT operating system installation process, or you can install them later.

You can perform a default installation of the IIS or the PWS directly from the CD-ROM, simply by running the INETSTP.EXE file (located in the \Inetsrv directory), using the Windows NT Explorer, the My Computer window, or the Run command on the Start Menu. You can also copy the files to a network drive and run the executable file from there.

A text file called UNATTEND.TXT is included in the \Inetsrv directory that allows you to supply answers to the installation prompts in advance. By modifying this file on a network copy of the \Inetsrv directory, you can create an unattended installation routine that will ease the task of setting up the services on a large number of machines. To execute a scripted installation, you run the INETSTP.EXE file with the -b switch and the name of the script file, as follows:

```
inetstp -b unattend.txt
```

Instead of executing the INETSTP.EXE file to perform the installation, you can also choose to install the services through the Windows NT Network Control Panel by selecting the Services tab, clicking the Add button, choosing the appropriate service, and specifying the location of the \Inetsrv directory.

Once you have Internet services running on your network, you can install just the Internet Services Manager application to any Windows NT machine by running the SETUP.EXE file found in the \Inetsrv\Admin directory. This allows you to administer the Internet services on your network from any Windows NT computer that you want.

Installing the Microsoft Internet Services

Whichever method you choose to execute the setup program for the Internet Information Server or the Peer Web Services, you will be presented with a screen like that shown in figure 26.1, allowing you to select which modules you want to install and the directory where the files are to be located.

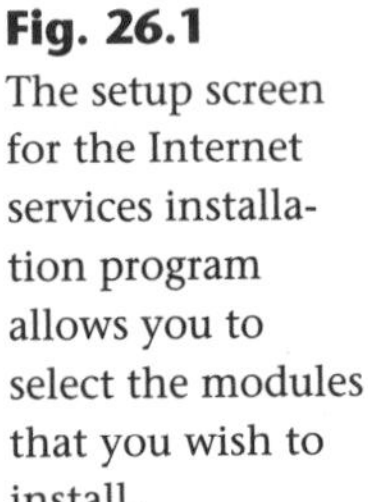

Fig. 26.1
The setup screen for the Internet services installation program allows you to select the modules that you wish to install.

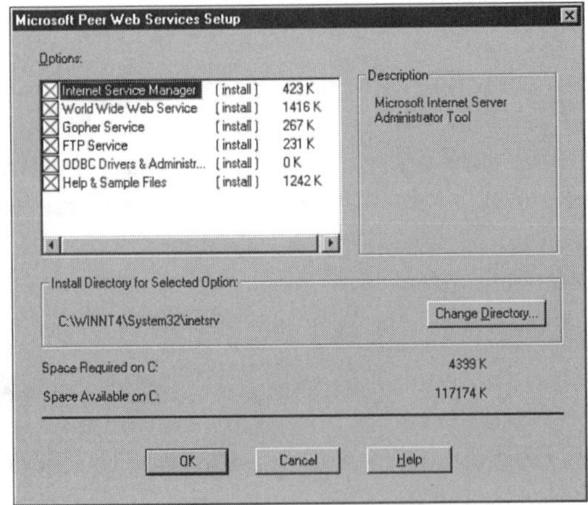

Caution

Keep in mind that although the disk space requirements for the services are relatively modest, the amount of system resources they require to run may not be (depending on your machine's hardware configuration). Since the installation process not only copies the files needed for the services, but automatically starts them as well, it is not a good idea to install a greater number of modules than you think your machine can handle safely. You can always run the setup program again at a later time to add or remove any modules that you wish.

Both the IIS and the PWS consist of the following modules, any or all of which you may choose to install or omit:

- *Internet Service Manager.* The administrative front end for all of the Internet services, this program allows you to configure all of the operating parameters for each instance of the Internet services, running anywhere on your network.
- *World Wide Web Service.* Allows you to publish programs and documents to remote clients using the HTTP protocol and a compatible Web browser.
- *Gopher Service.* Allows you to publish collections of files with greater flexibility than ftp. A Gopher site can contain links to other files or services, show file descriptions and other notations, and use custom menus for a more personalized display.
- *ftp Service.* Allows users with an ftp client program running on any computing platform to use the File Transfer Protocol to download and upload files to and from your computer.
- *ODBC Drivers and Administration Tools.* These provide your services with database connectivity that can be used to log server activity directly to an existing SQL database or to develop Web applications that allow clients to interact with your databases using a Web browser as a client.
- *Help and Sample Files.* These include the entire administration guide for the Internet services package in HTML format, as well as the initial sample content for your sites that is automatically activated when the services are installed. Installing these files is a good way to test your site without worrying whether your own documents may be at fault, in the case of a malfunction.

Once you have selected the modules that you wish to install, the Publishing Directories dialog box will appear, prompting you for the directories that will become the home, or *root*, directories of your new sites. Note that the directories specified here should reflect the location where you intend to store the documents that you will publish on the services. They do not indicate the location of the services' program files. The entries for services that you chose not to install are grayed out.

The root directory is that which is made available to a client program when it specifies your computer's IP address as its destination. If your IP address is 141.1.24.10 and your root directory is C:\WINNT\System32\inetsrv\wwwroot, then the contents of that directory will be displayed when a user points his or her browser to **http://141.1.24.10** or to an equivalent host name. Any subdirectories off of \wwwroot will appear to the client as subdirectories off of your host name or IP address.

Caution

If you decide to change the location of the root directories from their defaults, be sure to consider the security of your machine while doing so. Users will be able to access files located in any directory branching off of the root. Do not endanger important programs or data files for the sake of convenience by specifying a root that is too high up in your directory structure.

Once you have made these selections, the setup program will copy the appropriate files for each service in turn and attempt to start that service. Once the process is complete for all of the services you have selected, they should be fully operational (assuming you elected to install the sample content files). If you've installed the World Wide Web service, for example, launch the Internet Explorer (that is installed with the Windows NT operating system), enter your IP address, and you should see the screen shown in figure 26.2.

You may at this time begin to build your own Internet (or intranet) sites by placing other content files into the designated root directories, or you can proceed to the next section and customize the configuration of your services.

Note

If you run the IIS or PWS setup program again, you will be presented with the option to add or remove any of the modules listed earlier. Be aware that removing any installed service will cause only the program files to be deleted. Content files placed into the root directory or any of its subdirectories will be left intact.

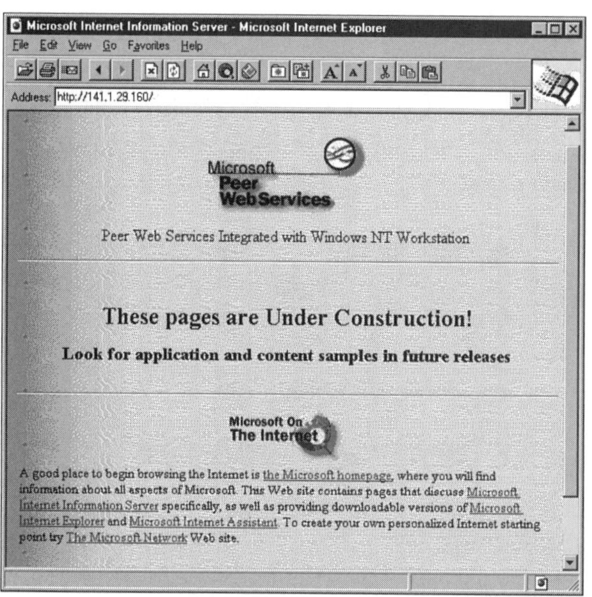

Fig. 26.2
The Microsoft Internet services are installed using basic default values that should leave them in an operational state upon completion of the setup process.

Configuring the Microsoft Internet Services

One of the primary advantages of the Internet Information Server and the Peer Web Services is the centralized administration provided by the Internet Service Manager. Through a single interface, all of the Microsoft Internet services on your network are displayed. Each service can then be configured through a single-tabbed dialog box that contains all of the settings that you will need to perform normal site administration tasks.

As mentioned earlier, the Internet Service Manager need not be installed on the same Windows NT machine that is hosting the services themselves. You can therefore place that machine running the services in a secure location, such as a server closet or data center, and still administer the services from your desktop. Alternatively, if you are supporting an intranet environment in which a large number of users are publishing documents using the Peer Web Services, you can perform technical support and administration chores on the services of any machine on the network without having to travel to that machine and interrupt the activities of the person using it.

Using the Internet Service Manager

When you launch the Internet Services Manager from the Windows NT Start Menu, you see the screen shown in figure 26.3, which is called the Report View. This view displays each of the Internet services on a separate line, grouped by server name.

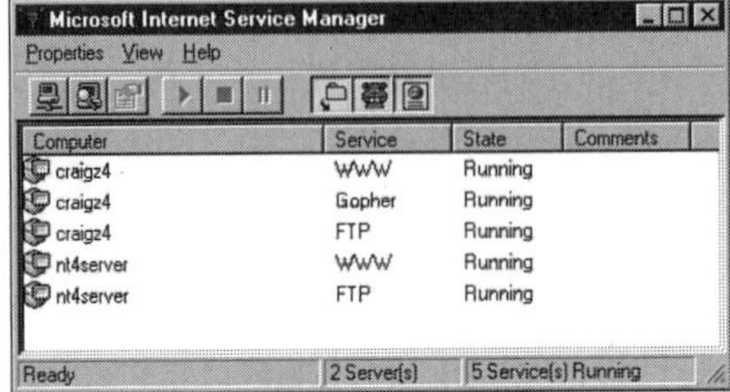

Fig. 26.3
The Report View of the Internet Services Manager individually lists each of the services running on the network.

Initially, the manager will display only the Internet services running on the local machine, if any. To add the services running on other Windows NT computers to the display, select Connect to Server from the Properties menu or click the Connect to Server button on the toolbar and specify another Windows NT machine on the network whose services you want to monitor. You can identify the other machine using either its IP address, its host name, or its computer (i.e.: NetBIOS) name.

You can also search the network for the Internet services by selecting Find Servers (also on the Properties menu) or by clicking the Find Servers button on the toolbar. Each of the services found will be added to the display.

> **Note**
>
> The Find Servers function will only locate Internet Information Server services. Servers running the Peer Web Services must be manually added using the Connect to Server option.

Once you are displaying several servers, you can sort the display by clicking one of the column headings, or by selecting the desired sort criterion on the View menu.

The manager also provides two other views of the Internet services on your network. Select Services View from the Views menu to invoke a collapsible display of server names with the services installed on each, as shown in figure 26.4. Figure 26.5 illustrates the Services View, which displays the three Internet services and the computers running each one.

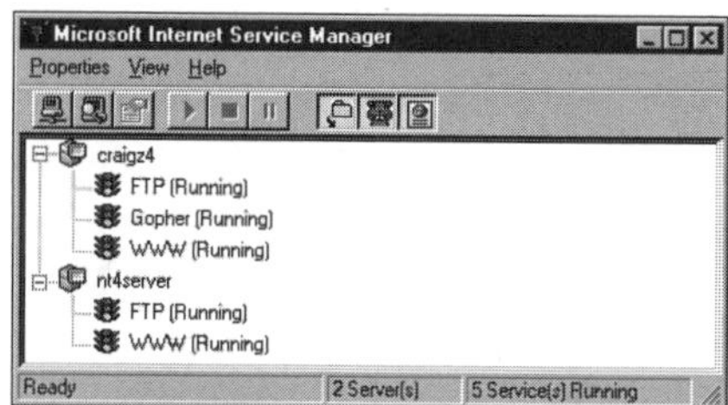

Fig. 26.4
You can choose to display your network's Internet services hierarchically by server.

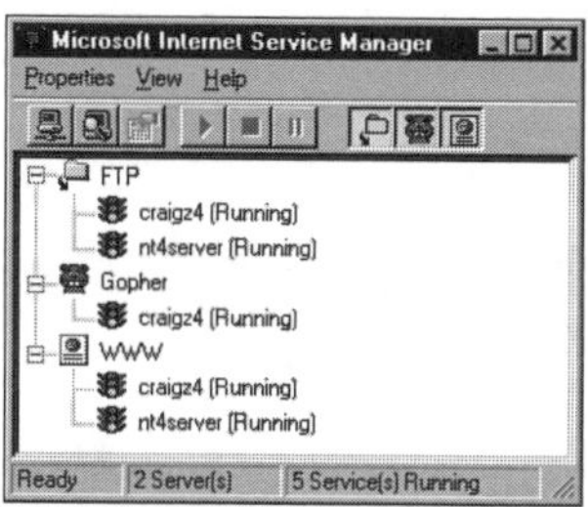

Fig. 26.5
You can also use the Services view.

By default, all of the services are displayed by the manager. You can use the View menu or the three rightmost buttons on the toolbar to select only the services that you wish to display.

Select a service by highlighting it and the toolbar buttons become active that allow you to start, stop, and pause the service. You can also perform these tasks from the Properties menu, or from the Services application in the Windows NT Control Panel (on the machine where the service is running). The latter also allows you to modify the Startup status of each service. By default, all of the Internet services are launched when Windows NT loads. You can switch any of the services to Manual, if you wish, in which case you must explicitly start that service whenever you boot the machine.

> **Note**
>
> It is recommended that you do not run Internet services that you are not actively using. This practice wastes system resources and can negatively affect the performance of the other services. By installing an occasionally-used service and configuring it for manual startup, you can activate the service whenever you need it and not overtax your system unnecessarily.

Configuring Service Properties

Once you have highlighted a service running on a particular server, clicking the Properties button on the toolbar or selecting Service Properties from the

Properties menu opens the Properties dialog box for that service. In most cases, individual settings are maintained for each of the services, although the screens of the dialog box for each service may be identical. The sections that follow cover each of the Properties screens; unless otherwise specified, it is to be assumed that particular settings apply to all three of the Internet services.

The Service Screen

The Service screen contains the basic login control parameters for each of the services. The differences in the services themselves dictate that this screen should vary slightly for the ftp, the World Wide Web, and the Gopher servers. The ftp Service screen is shown in figure 26.6.

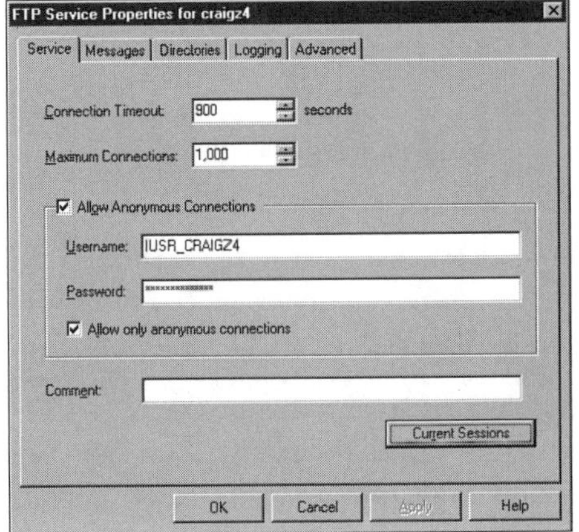

Fig. 26.6
The Service screen contains the account information for the default user of each Internet service.

Common to Service screens of all three services are the following:

- *Connection Timeout—(0 to 32,767; default=900 for PWS, 32,767 for IIS).* Specifies the maximum length of time (in seconds) that a client can remain connected to the service with no activity. Used to terminate TCP connections that are not properly closed by the client.
- *Maximum Connections—(0 to 32,767; default=1000 for PWS, 32,767 for IIS).* Specifies the total number of simultaneous service connections that are to be allowed by the server. Used to limit the amount of bandwidth and system resources allocated to a particular service or machine. (The number of connections is not necessarily equivalent to the number of users.)
- *Anonymous Logon—(username and password).* Most client logons to Internet services are anonymous, yet all users must be authenticated by

the Windows NT security system. The !USR_<*computername*> user appearing here by default is a Windows NT user account created during the installation of the IIS or PWS, through which all anonymous client users are authenticated. This account must have the appropriate rights to all of the files and programs that you intend to make available to anonymous clients. You can change the properties of this account in the Windows NT User Manager or specify a different account, as long as the correct account name and password appear on this screen.

- *Comment.* The text entered in this field appears in the Comments column of the Internet Service Manager. It can be used to identify the service in any way that you wish.

The ftp Service screen also contains the following options:

- *Anonymous client logons.* The ftp Service screen allows you to specify whether or not you wish to allow anonymous client logons as well as whether you wish to restrict your service only to anonymous logons. Clients not logging on anonymously must use a valid Windows NT user name and password with the appropriate rights to the files that they will be served.

Caution

Use of Windows NT accounts other than the designated Anonymous Connection user for Internet service file transfers can cause a breech in network security. Unlike Windows NT itself, the ftp and HTTP protocols do not encrypt the passwords that they transmit over the network. A user with a protocol analyzer (such as the Windows NT Network Monitor) can easily capture ftp packets and read the user passwords in clear text. The use of the anonymous account or other limited-access accounts especially created for Internet use is strongly recommended.

- *Current Sessions.* Clicking the Current Sessions button displays the users that are currently connected to the ftp site (see fig. 26.7), by password (if using an anonymous connection) or by username. The IP addresses of the users and the duration of the current connection are also displayed. You can immediately disconnect a single user or all users with the buttons provided.

The Gopher Service screen also contains the following option:

- *Service Administrator.* Enter the name and the e-mail address for the administrator of the Gopher server in the fields provided.

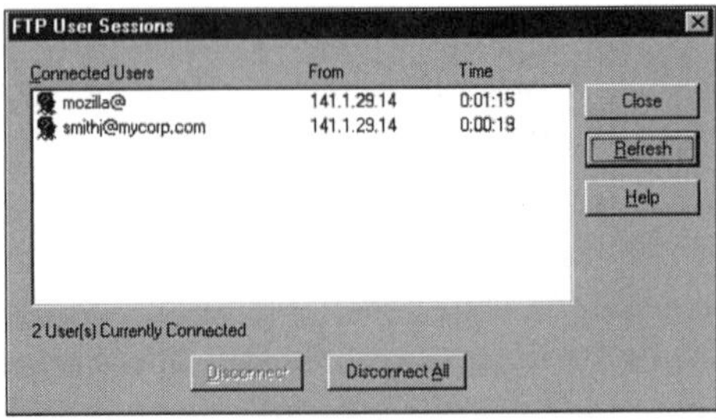

Fig. 26.7
The ftp User Sessions window allows you to monitor the current activity on your ftp site.

The WWW Service screen allows you to select the Password Authentication options that you would like to use to secure your site. They appear as follows:

- *Allow Anonymous.* When you elect to allow anonymous logons to your Web site, users will first attempt to connect using the anonymous account specified on the Service screen. It is not possible for a client to be authenticated using either of the options below when this box is selected, and anonymous access can be successfully granted.
- *Basic (Clear Text).* Users attempting to access a file to which the anonymous account does not have rights will automatically transmit their current Windows network username and password to the server for authentication. This user account must be valid on the computer running the WWW service (or on a common Windows NT domain), and have the appropriate rights to the desired files in order for transmission to take place. The Basic option causes usernames and passwords to be transmitted in clear text, resulting in a potential network security breech, but it allows the client to use any Web browser to establish an authenticated connection.
- *Windows NT Challenge/Response.* This option permits the same user authentication to occur as the Basic selection above, except that all passwords are transmitted using the Windows NT data encryption algorithm, preventing any lapse in security. To take advantage of this option, the client must be using a Web browser that supports the Windows NT Challenge/Response protocol. At this time, the only browser supporting this protocol is the Microsoft Internet Explorer, versions 2.0 and above.

The Messages Screen

The Messages screen (see fig. 26.8) is unique to the ftp Service Properties dialog box. It allows you to enter the text that you wish to display to your ftp users under various conditions.

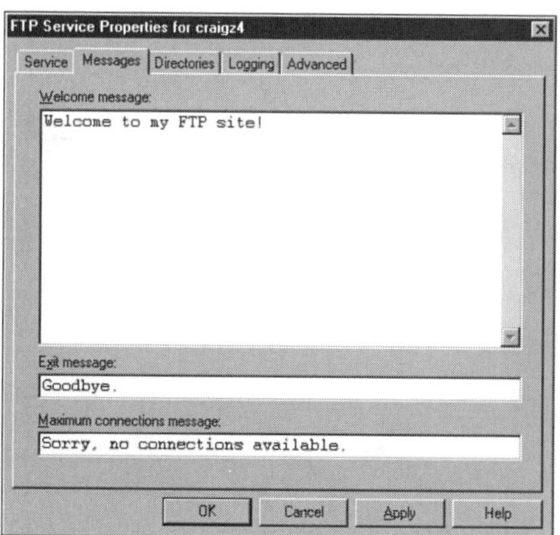

Fig. 26.8
The ftp Messages screen is used to configure the only personalized communication possible with an ftp client.

- *Welcome Message.* This text is displayed immediately after an ftp client is successfully authenticated and allowed access to the server. A large comment space is provided because this message is typically used to identify the site and inform the clients of any policies and restrictions that they are expected to observe.
- *Exit Message.* This text is displayed when a client terminates his or her TCP connection with the site in an orderly fashion.
- *Maximum Connections Message.* When a client attempts to connect to an ftp server that is currently servicing the maximum number of connections specified in the Service screen, the text in this field is displayed, allowing you to apologize to clients that have been refused.

The Directories Screen

The Directories screen is used to specify what files and directories are to be accessible to clients of each service. There are some differences in the options provided for the various clients, but each one allows you to specify the home or root directory for the service as well as additional virtual directories that may be located on any drive, but which will appear to the client as a subdirectory of the service being accessed. You set the root directory during the installation of the IIS or the PWS. Retaining the default settings was recommended during the installation because they provide sample content that allows you to test the functionality of the software. Once the sites are operating, however, you can use the Directory screen to modify the location of the root to a directory where your own content files are already located.

The main directory listing is common to all of the Internet services, but other options in this dialog box are used to configure properties of specific server modules.

The Directories screen for the WWW server (see fig. 26.9) contains the following settings:

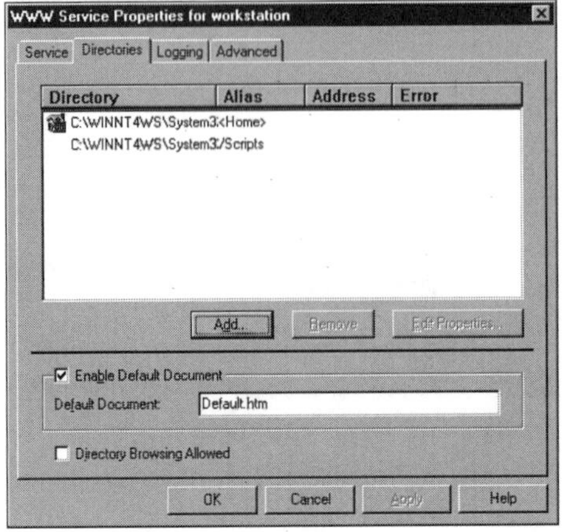

Fig. 26.9
The Directories screen is where you specify the location of the content files that you will publish on your services.

- *Enable Default Document—(default=default.htm).* Enabling this feature causes a file of the specified name to be automatically displayed when a client enters only a site address or a directory name in a Web browser. For example, if the HTML file that contains the home page of a Web site at **www.mycorp.com** is named DEFAULT.HTM, and a client specifies only the URL **http://www.mycorp.com** in his or her browser, then the default file will be displayed. If this feature is disabled, the client will instead see a listing of the files in the directory (if the Directory Browsing Allowed option is enabled), from which a selection can be made of the file to view. The same rule applies if the client specifies only a directory name, such as **http://www.mycorp.com/files**. The default.htm file located in the /files directory will then be displayed. You can change the default filename to anything you want in this screen. (By far, the most commonly used default filename is INDEX.HTML.)
- *Directory Browsing Allowed.* This option allows a client to see the contents of any directory on the Web site simply by specifying just the directory name in the Web browser. When this option is disabled, specifying just a directory name in the Web browser will generate an error message, unless there is a file of the default name in that directory and the Enable Default Document option is enabled.

The ftp server's Directories screen contains these Directory Listing Style options:

- *UNIX*. Issuing the LS -L or the DIR command from the ftp prompt (when connected to a PWS or IIS ftp server) causes filenames to be displayed in a UNIX-style format, as follows:

```
ftp> ls -l
200 PORT command successful.
150 Opening ASCII mode data connection for /bin/ls.
-r-xr-xr-x   1 owner    group           6672 Jun 30  1996 00index
-r-xr-xr-x   1 owner    group        1306112 Mar 30  1996 BOOTDSK.ZIP
-r-xr-xr-x   1 owner    group        1256896 Jan 11  1995 ADISK1.ZIP
-r-xr-xr-x   1 owner    group        1409876 Jan 11  1995 ADISK2.ZIP
-r-xr-xr-x   1 owner    group         984578 Jan 11  1995 ADISK3.ZIP
-r-xr-xr-x   1 owner    group        1398763 Aug 22  1995 BDISK1.ZIP
-r-xr-xr-x   1 owner    group         988358 Aug 22  1995 BDISK2.ZIP
dr-xr-xr-x   1 owner    group              0 Jun 30 16:18 Files
-r-xr-xr-x   1 owner    group        2048000 Jul 11  1995 QDISK.ZIP
226 Transfer complete.
1234 bytes received in 0.05 seconds (24.68 Kbytes/sec)
ftp>
```

- *MS-DOS*. Causes the LS -L or DIR command to display filenames in MS-DOS format, as follows:

```
ftp> ls -l
200 PORT command successful.
150 Opening ASCII mode data connection for /bin/ls.
06-30-96  08:45AM                      6672 00index
03-30-96  02:50PM                   1306112 BOOTDSK.ZIP
01-11-95  04:56AM                   1256896 ADISK1.ZIP
01-11-95  04:59PM                   1409876 ADISK2.ZIP
01-11-95  05:04PM                    984578 ADISK3.ZIP
08-22-95  12:25AM                   1398763 BDISK1.ZIP
08-22-95  12:31AM                    988358 BDISK2.ZIP
06-30-96  04:18PM       <DIR>                  Files
07-11-95  01:50PM                   2048000 QDISK.ZIP
226 Transfer complete.
894 bytes received in 0.05 seconds (17.53 Kbytes/sec)
ftp>
```

When you first display the Directories screen in the Internet Service Manager, you should see the home directory that you specified during the installation of the services in the main Directory window. If you wish to change the home directory setting, highlight it and click the Edit Properties button. To create additional directories, click the Add button. In either case, a Directory Properties dialog box like that shown in figure 26.10 appears.

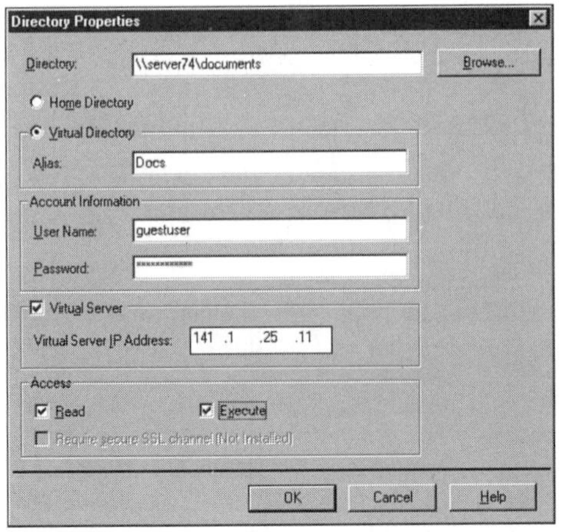

Fig. 26.10
You can create virtual directories for your site from actual directories located anywhere on your network.

Using the Directory Properties Dialog Box

When adding or modifying a service directory, you can type a path to the directory you wish to add in the field provided, or you can click the Browse button to open a standard Windows NT file management dialog box. Once you have specified a directory, select the appropriate radio button to signify whether this will be your home or a virtual directory. You can only have one home directory. If you try to create a second one, you will be asked if you want to replace the existing home directory specification with the new one.

If you choose to create a virtual directory, you must specify an alias name in the space provided. The contents of the virtual directory will appear to the users of your site within a subdirectory named for the alias you provide, located off of the root directory.

The location on your network of the actual files that appear in a virtual directory is completely irrelevant to your service clients. You can therefore point virtual directories to locations all over your network and have them appear to clients in a simple, unified directory structure. You can also create virtual directories for several different services that all point to the same network files, if desired. In this way, you can support large numbers of users and provide fault tolerance by spreading the client load over several different servers, and still only have to update your content files in one place.

Caution

When creating virtual directories, files on the server's local drives can be specified using drive letters, but you must provide UNC pathnames for directories on network drives (even for drives on servers running another network operating system, such as NetWare). You cannot use redirected drive letters in this dialog box, although the Browse option will mistakenly allow you to insert such drive letters into the field. Access to the directory will only be granted when a UNC name is specified.

Further, you must supply a valid username and password (with appropriate rights) in the Account Information box in order for access to a network directory to be granted to clients. (The Account Information box remains grayed out unless a UNC path name is specified in the Directory field.)

Finally, directories on NTFS drives that are packaged as virtual directories, whether they are located on the local or a remote server, must have the appropriate file and directory permissions set for the users that will be accessing them. These permissions are set using the Windows NT Explorer in the usual manner.

Additional options may be provided in the Directory Properties dialog box, depending on the service being modified. The World Wide Web variant (refer to fig 26.10) contains the following options:

- *Virtual Server.* This option allows you to assign a separate IP address to a particular virtual directory. With this feature, you can operate multiple independent Web sites using the same service. Users connecting to the IP address specified in this field (once the checkbox is activated) will be taken right to the virtual directory specified earlier.
- *Access.* You can specify whether clients are to be allowed the right to read files in the specified directory, execute applications or scripts there, or both. If you have installed the Secure Sockets Layer protocol on your site, you can also require that a client be using a secure channel before access to the directory is granted.

The Directory Properties dialog box for the ftp services allows you to specify whether clients should be allowed the rights to read (download) files in the specified directory, write (upload) files, or both.

Once you have specified or modified all of the desired options for the new directory, click the OK button and it will appear in the main Directory screen listing, along with the alias you have assigned it. An Error column is also provided on this screen to inform you when a client has had a problem accessing the directory in question. Errors are most often caused by incorrect or incomplete permissions having been set for the directory, its component files, or the user account accessing it.

The Logging Screen

The Logging screen is the same for all of the Internet services. It allows you to control whether and how client accesses of your services are to be recorded—in a text file or database. Logging accesses is the best way to track the usage of your sites, but the process can have some drawbacks, both in performance and in stability.

On busy Internet sites that are accessed hundreds or thousands of times a day, log files can grow to huge proportions very quickly. Windows NT requires large amounts of disk space for its paging functions as well, and will perform very erratically when hard drive space is short. If you do enable logging on busy sites, make sure that you have sufficient disk space for the log files, or that you move or purge them regularly.

Logging of Internet transactions can also slow down the performance of a service, particularly a Web site. Unlike ftp, which is used for explicitly downloading or uploading one file at a time, a single Web page may be composed of many different text, graphic, script or application files, each of which must be transmitted using a separate TCP connection. Multiply this by the number of users accessing the system and you have a much greater overall burden on system resources than either ftp or Gopher. Forcing the system to log every access as well adds to this burden and can cause access times to increase slightly for each transaction. This can add up to a perceptible decrease in the speed of a busy site.

Therefore, enable logging if you intend to use the information, but do not do so unnecessarily.

Note

You can configure each Internet service to log only successful activities, only errors, or both (which is the default). Logging only a service's errors can reduce the disk space, processing and I/O burden on your Windows NT machine.

To turn off the logging of successful activities, leaving error records only, use the Windows NT Registry Editor to locate the HKEY_LOCAL_MACHINE\SYSTEM\CurrentControlSet\Services\<*servicename*>\Parameters\LogSuccessfulRequests key, where <*servicename*> is replaced by one of the following:

MSftpSVC	(for the ftp service)
GOPHERSVC	(for the Gopher service)
W3SVC	(for the WWW service)

Then change the key's value from 1 to 0, save your changes, and restart the service.

The Internet Service Manager provides for two basic methods of storing the site activity logs, as shown in figure 26.11. Once you have enabled the logging function, you can choose to send the access records to a file or to a database.

> **Note**
>
> Since the Internet Service Manager is designed to administer sites using both the Internet Information Server and the Peer Web Services, it may appear as though both the file and database logging options are available to all services. However, only the Internet Information Server can log service activities using the ODBC Database Connector.

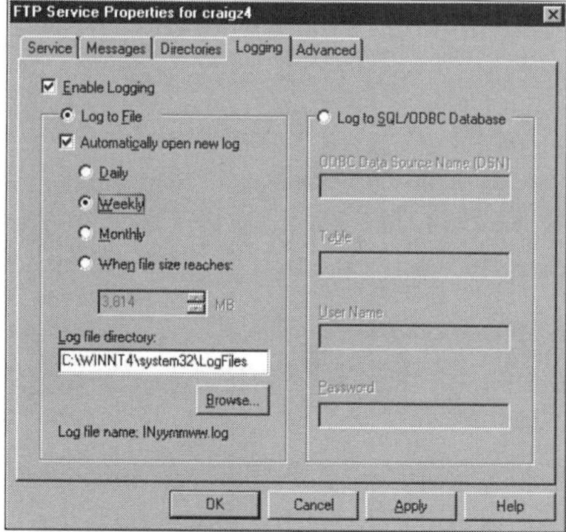

Fig. 26.11
The Logging screen provides the options by which service access records can be saved for later processing.

The Log to File option is much like that found in nearly all Web server products. If you disable the Automatically Open New Log feature, a single file is created, which will be allowed to grow indefinitely.

If you elect to open a new log file on a daily, weekly, or monthly basis, the name of each new log file reflects the time that it was created, using the following formulae:

Rotation Frequency	Log File Name	Key
Daily	IN*yymmdd*.LOG	*yy*=year; *mm*=month; *dd*=day
Weekly	IN*yymmww*.LOG	*yy*=year; *mm*=month; *ww*=week
Monthly	IN*yymm*.LOG	*yy*=year; *mm*=month

You can also configure the log file to be rotated when it reaches a size that you specify. In this case, the file is called INETSRV*n*.LOG, where *n* is replaced by a number that is incremented each time a new file is created.

You can also select the directory where the log files are kept by entering or browsing for a new pathname in the Log File Directory field. Note that, by default, the same log file directory is specified for all of the services on a particular Windows NT machine. This will cause the records from all of the services to be logged to the same file in that directory. To maintain separate log files for each of the services, you must specify a different log file directory for each one.

To send the service access records to a database, click the Log to SQL/ODBC Database radio button on the Logging screen of an IIC service. To log to a database, you must have ODBC version 2.5 installed on the Windows NT server, and you must install the appropriate driver for the database you wish to use during the IIS installation.

You also must create the database itself, using the tools provided with the database manager software. Create a Data Source Name (DSN) and protect the database in the usual manner. The database to which you write your service logs need not reside on the same machine as the Internet service itself.

Once the database is in place, enter the DSN, Table name, and a valid User Name and Password into the Service Properties Logging screen so that the service can access the database.

Table 26.1 lists the types of information that are captured to the service log, as well as the field names and lengths that you should use when creating your database.

> **Note**
>
> While the service log files maintain a historical record of site accesses, you can also monitor the performance of your Internet services in real time using the Windows NT Performance Monitor. The installation procedures for both the Internet Information Server and the Peer Web Services insert numerous additional counters for each of the services into the Performance Monitor configuration.

Table 26.1 Microsoft Internet Service Log Data Types and Field Names

Data Type	Field Name	Field Size
Client IP Address	ClientHost	char(50)
Client User Name	username	char(50)
Date	LogDate	char(12)
Time	LogTime	char(15)
Service	service	char(20)
Computer Name	machine	char(20)
Server IP Address	serverip	char(50)
Processing Time	processingtime	int
Bytes Received	bytesrecvd	int
Bytes Sent	bytessent	int
Service Status Code	servicestatus	int
Windows NT Status Code	win32status	int
Operation Name	operation	char(200)
Target of Operation	target	char(200)
Optional Parameters	parameters	char(200)

Logs captured to a plain text file place all of the fields for each record on a single line, delimited by commas. Both the IIS and the PWS ship with the Microsoft Internet Log Converter (CONVLOG.EXE), a command-line utility with which you can convert the log files to the European Microsoft Windows NT Academic Centre (EMWAC) or Common Log File format.

The Advanced Screen

The options on the Advanced screen (see fig. 26.12) allow you to specify the clients that are to be permitted access to the Internet service. You can also impose a limit on the bandwidth used by the Internet services on that computer.

Select the appropriate radio button to specify whether users should be Granted Access or Denied Access to a site, by default. Then you can click the Add button to specify the IP addresses of users or the subnet addresses of groups of users that will be the exceptions to the default. With these options, you can create a private site with a limited clientele, or bar certain users from accessing what is otherwise an open site.

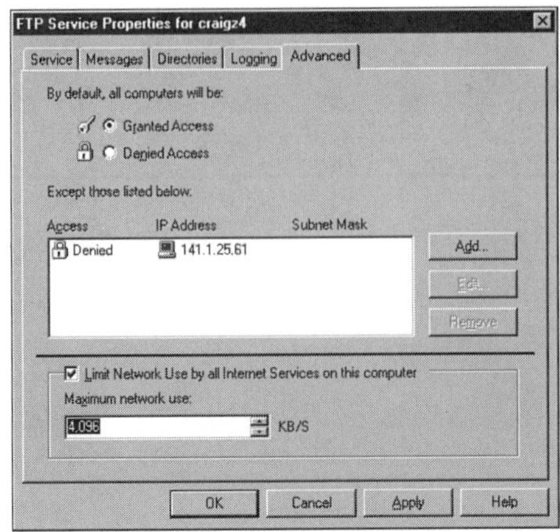

Fig. 26.12
The Advanced screen provides access control for the Internet services and a bandwidth throttle.

If you are running your services on the Internet, you may wish to limit the amount of bandwidth used, so as not to monopolize an Internet connection that is shared with other network services (such as e-mail, and so on). Check the Limit Network Use by all Internet Services on this Computer box to restrict the combined bandwidth of the installed IIS or PWS services to the number of kilobytes per second that you specify. Note that this option affects all of the Internet services running on this computer, while the access control options on this screen affect only the service whose properties you are editing.

Saving Configuration Changes

Once you have modified your service configuration changes, close the service Properties dialog box by clicking the OK button. In most cases, any changes that you have made will immediately take effect in the running service. This feature allows you to modify your site configuration at any time, without interrupting service even to users that are currently connected.

Using the HTML Administrator

The Internet Information Server and the Peer Web Services both provide other means for configuring the properties of the various services. Beneath the \Inetsrv directory in which the services are installed is a directory called \Htmla, where World Wide Web pages are installed containing an interface to scripts that allow you to modify virtually any of the parameters available in the Internet Service Manager through a Web browser.

By pointing your Web browser to HTTP://<*machinename*>/htmla/htmla.htm (where *machinename* is the NetBIOS name of the Windows NT machine running the services), you arrive at the HTML Administrator page, which is laid out in the same manner as the Service Properties dialog box in the Internet Service Manager, with tabs that provide links to HTML pages containing the various options (see fig. 26.13).

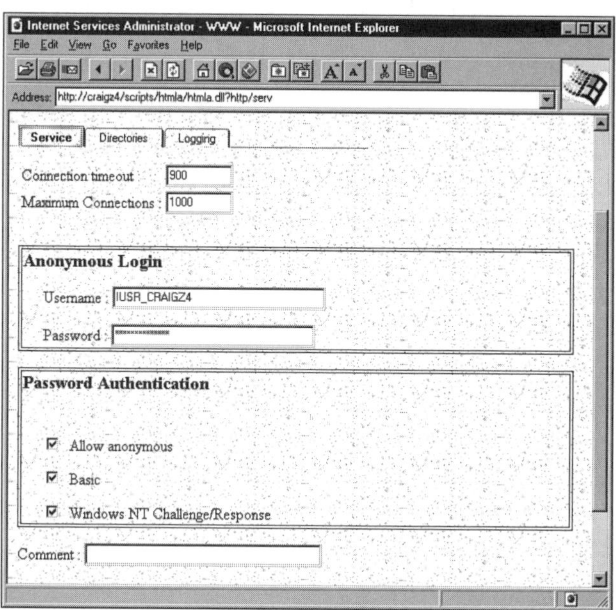

Fig. 26.13
The HTML Administrator allows a Web browser to access the maintenance interface of the Internet services.

With the HTML Administrator, you can configure your Internet services from any workstation with the proper Web browser installed. The computer need not be running Windows NT, and it need not be connected to the server by an internal network connection. You can even configure your site's settings over an Internet connection from any remote location, if you set up the security options to allow you to do so.

The HTML Administrator can only configure the services on the actual computer where the pages reside, however. It also cannot be used to start, stop, and pause services, as in the Internet Service Manager.

As configured by the installation program, the HTML Administrator page is a perfect example of the way in which the Windows NT security features are integrated into the Internet services. You cannot access this page using an anonymous connection (unless you have modified the service's anonymous account or the permissions of the Administrator files). The account that you used to log on to the computer where you are running the Web browser must have administrative rights on the Windows NT machine running the Web service.

What happens is that the browser attempts to access the HTML Administrator page using the anonymous account first (assuming that anonymous access is enabled). When this access is denied, a connection will be attempted again with the browser user's logon name and password instead of the anonymous account. The way in which this authentication takes place depends on the options you selected in the Password Authentication section of the WWW Properties Service screen.

If you selected only Windows NT Challenge/Response, then you must be running the Microsoft Internet Explorer version 2.0 or greater, or you will again be denied access. If you selected Basic, then you will be granted access if you are logged in to the workstation with the proper account. However, you will also be sending the username and password of an administrator-equivalent account over the network (or the Internet) in clear text. This information could easily be intercepted, allowing network users (or worse, Internet users) to gain administrative access to your Windows NT computer. ❖

CHAPTER 27

Implementing a Firewall

by Michael Marchuk

Internet security has become a hot topic over the past year. The number of security breaches continues to escalate as newer and more sophisticated tools become available to criminals and mischievous users. To adequately protect your organization's network from the threat of an Internet attack, the network should have a buffer between the Internet and the inside network. This buffer is called a *firewall.*

While firewalls can't protect your company from every threat, they can protect your network from the anonymous Internet users who want to break into your organization's systems.

In this chapter, you learn to

- Evaluate your organization's security profile
- Recognize the basic types of firewalls
- Choose the best hardware and software to fulfill the firewall's role
- Choose among the options that many firewalls offer

Understanding Security and Firewalls

This section covers the concepts behind implementing a firewall in your organization. These concepts will help you determine the best type of Internet security for your organization by revealing the types of threats that your network may encounter.

Security Concepts

While you may have heard about firewalls, you may not have a clear picture of how they work and what they actually do. To help you understand the role of a firewall, it's important that you understand the functions that can be served by the firewall system.

A firewall is a buffer between your internal network and the Internet. Figure 27.1 shows how a firewall connects your network to the Internet using two network connections, one for the internal local area network and one that connects to the Internet.

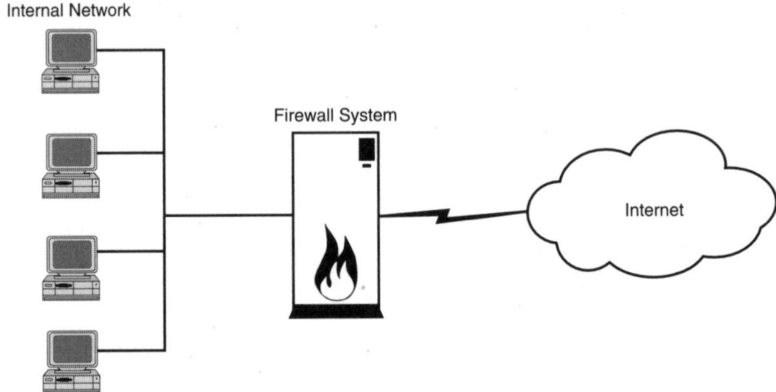

Fig. 27.1
A firewall connects to both your internal network and the Internet to provide a network security buffer.

There are a couple of basic designs that are used to actually make the connection between the internal network and the Internet. This first design is illustrated in figure 27.1. The firewall server contains two network interface cards that route the traffic through the firewall according to specific rules. We'll cover these rules and the traffic routing later in the chapter, so just concentrate on the concepts right now. The Internet connection is made directly into the firewall from the Internet routing hardware. This forces all traffic to be subjected to the screening process that the firewall provides.

While this method is very secure, it may also limit your organization's ability to provide services on the Internet. Since all traffic is screened rigorously, new services introduced on the Internet may not work through the firewall unless the firewall is upgraded. Also, some questionably secure services may use the same transport mechanism as a relatively secure service. In this case, the firewall may allow security breaches because it is allowing the secure transport mechanism to be used to access unauthorized internal network services.

To overcome the possibility of an intrusion to the internal network, the other alternative is to create a sort of demilitarized zone (DMZ) intermediate network between the Internet and the internal network. The DMZ network is shown in figure 27.2. Notice how the DMZ network allows unsecured servers to be part of the organization's Internet services along with secured servers that sit behind the firewall.

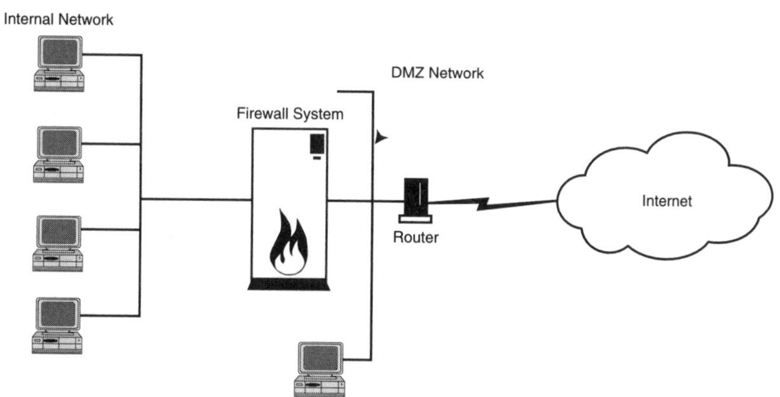

Fig. 27.2
The DMZ network provides connections for unsecured servers within the organization.

You may ask why anyone would want to place a server outside of a firewall. The answer lies in the shortcomings of the firewall's protection and the general limitations behind firewalls. For example, if your organization was beginning to offer short video clips of its new manufacturing process as part of the company's Web site, you may want to put the video clips on a server that sits outside of the firewall system for performance reasons. There's no need to screen each video packet through the firewall causing a performance hit on the firewall's routing ability.

Of course, in putting the video's or any data on an unsecured server, the company has to concede to the operating system's security flaws. If the unsecured server is compromised, the company may lose all the data on the server, or worse, have it replaced with data it would not want its customers to see. In 1995, a motion picture studio created a Web site to advertise its movie called "Hackers." Unfortunately, the studio's systems were broken into and the pictures of the movie posters were altered with graffiti. The studio replaced the pictures several times but finally conceded to the attacks on its systems and eventually took the site offline.

Unsecured servers in the DMZ network may also be used to provide services that your organization would not want to pass into the internal network. Such services as a file uploading area that could introduce viruses would be best left outside of the firewall and moved to the internal network only after being scanned for viruses.

Security Profiles

People generally fall into one of two general security profiles: those who spend too much time, effort, and money on network security, and those whose systems can be shut down by a 14-year-old hacker in an afternoon.

Seriously, security profiles can be described by two attitudes toward Internet access: permit or deny.

The individuals who choose the environment of permission often do so when a great number of services are required to be accessible through the organization's firewall, or when the services that need to be accessed cannot be limited by a conservative firewall strategy. In these cases, the organization's security profile may require that all services be permitted except for those that are expressly denied.

For example, all outbound access is unrestricted, but inbound access is restricted for services that could be used to access internal systems like Telnet or Network File System (NFS) services. This type of security is illustrated in figure 27.3.

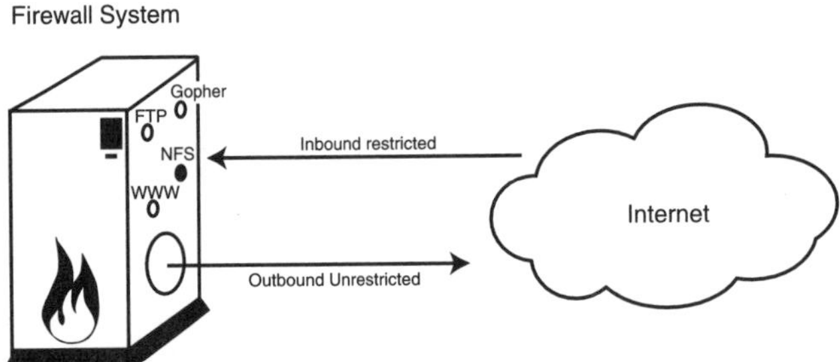

Fig. 27.3 Outbound access to the Internet is permitted without restriction, but inbound access is blocked for services that may be used to access internal systems.

While permitting all unrestricted access is a common security tactic, because it often leaves the users free to access any external service, it also poses the greatest threat to the company. Operating system flaws and hidden services may allow intruders easy access to your network if you are not monitoring traffic at all times. Your users may be happy with this type of security profile, but so are the hackers.

Many network managers opt for the other security profile. While some may call it the "paranoid" profile, it certainly lets network managers sleep a little easier at night. The organization that chooses to deny all traffic other than that which is expressly allowed will find that it can keep external Internet threats from breaching the firewall far easier because only a select few services are allowed to pass through to the internal network. These services can be closely watched by the firewall system which can detect and stop intruders before they do damage to the internal network. Figure 27.4 illustrates the basic principles behind the security profile that denies all but the expressly allowed services.

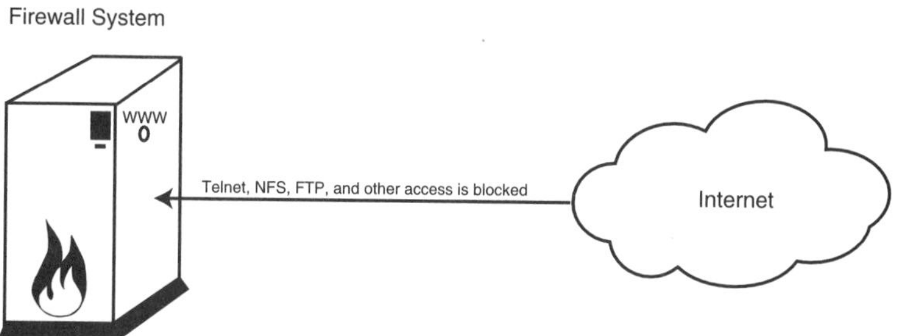

Fig. 27.4
Firewalls that deny all but a selected group of services are more likely to stop an attempt to break into the internal network.

A user behind a firewall with these access restrictions may also have a difficult time accessing systems that are outside the firewall. For example, a user who wants to access an e-mail server outside the firewall may be blocked because most e-mail systems send unencrypted passwords which can be easily intercepted. The firewall won't allow the user to send the password through because that same password may be used to get back in from outside the firewall. The user may be unhappy because a service has been restricted, but the constraints of the system have the best interests of the network in mind.

Note

Many firewall systems can be configured with either the permit or deny security profiles. Most allow some sort of blend that allows your users greater access to external services while minimizing the threats from outside the firewall. Only you can make the best judgment as to which services to block and what sort of risks are posed when accessing external services or providing internal services to users outside of the firewall.

Tip

When dealing with Internet security, it may be better to start off overly restrictive and ease the restrictions slowly as you become more aware of the risks that are present with your current network.

Firewall Types

There are two basic types of firewall systems that must be considered when implementing a firewall. The two firewall types can be described in terms of the OSI protocol stack model. The OSI protocol stack model consists of seven layers of a network protocol, like TCP/IP. Figure 27.5 shows the seven layers of the OSI protocol stack model.

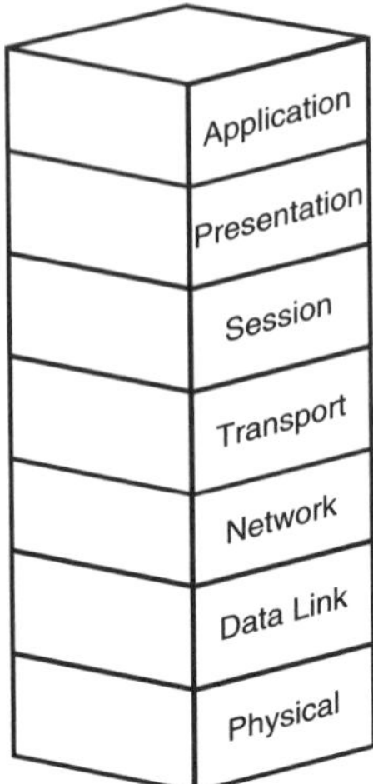

Fig. 27.5
The OSI protocol stack model illustrates the various functions that occur within a network protocol like TCP/IP.

The protocol stack builds from the physical layer, composed of the electrical signals that travel along the wires of the network, on up to the application layer, composed of the various protocols used on the network, such as HTTP, ftp, or Telnet.

The protocol stack model helps in understanding how each of the firewall types handle traffic and protect the internal network. The first type of firewall can be called the network-level firewall because it only looks at the layers up to the network and transport layers in the protocol stack model. The Transmission Control Protocol (TCP) part is located at the transport layer while the Internet Protocol (IP) is located at the network layer of the protocol model.

> **Note**
>
> Network-level firewalls can also be used with other protocols such as IPX/SPX, but this chapter concentrates solely on the TCP/IP protocol used on the Internet.

The network-level firewall filters out traffic based on rules that are focused at the network and transport layers. For example, the network-level firewall can filter network traffic from specific Internet addresses or only allow traffic from particular addresses. It can also filter traffic based on the TCP ports that are being requested. If the filter is set to only allow packets to pass through on TCP port 80 (the standard HTTP port), then any packets that request services on other ports such as port 23 (the standard Telnet port) are blocked as shown in figure 27.6.

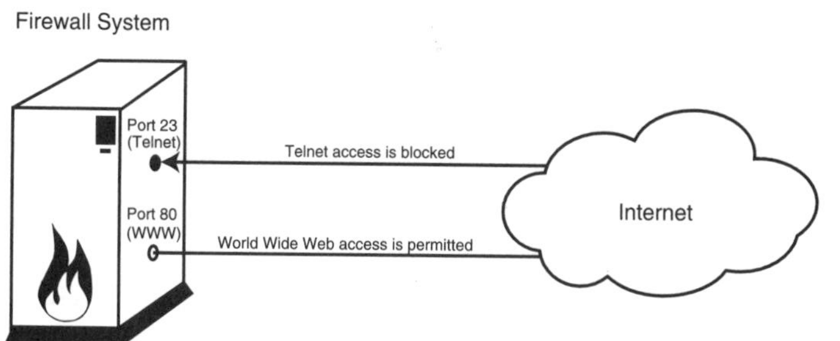

Fig. 27.6 Network-level firewalls filter traffic based on TCP/IP addressing information such as host addresses or port numbers.

Network-level firewalls allow direct access into the internal network for authorized services and hosts. The filtering mechanism works in the outbound direction also. The firewall can be set to filter specific ports or Internet addresses from the internal users or can be left wide open for outbound traffic.

The other type of firewall can be called the application-level firewall since it can evaluate the entire protocol stack before it passes on the network traffic. This type of firewall can also be called a proxy server since the outside traffic never really mingles with the internal traffic. The application-level firewall runs specific services that interact with both internal and external requests without actually allowing the other systems to communicate.

With an application-level firewall running an HTTP proxy service, systems from the internal network that send requests to Internet hosts are actually sending requests to the HTTP proxy service on the firewall which then makes the connection to the external Internet host as shown in figure 27.7. This is not unlike the situation where you and a friend are trying to fix a leaking faucet and have called a plumber for help. The plumber is describing the repair procedures to you while you relay them to your friend under the sink. In the same way, your World Wide Web browser is asking the local HTTP proxy server on the firewall to contact a particular site and download a Web page for you. The HTTP proxy server then contacts the site, downloads the page, and passes it on to you. Many application-level firewalls can also perform network-level traffic filtering functions in addition to servicing proxy requests.

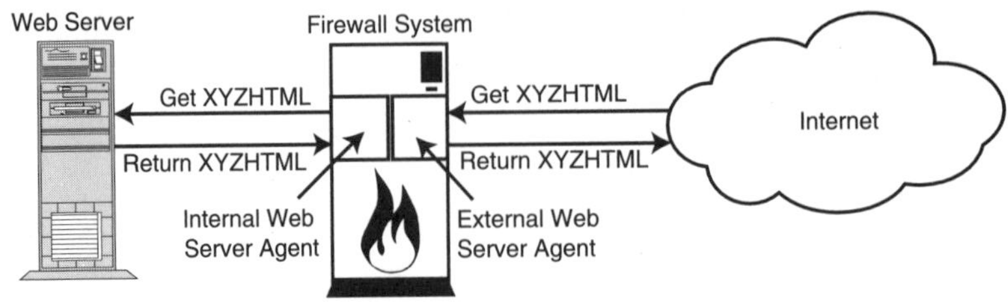

Fig. 27.7 Application-level firewalls connect to both internal and external systems without allowing the traffic to actually pass through the firewall.

Choosing the Right Firewall

Because their are so many types of organizations with varying needs and budgets, the right firewall for one network may be unmanageable for another. This section discusses the environments in which each of the two basic firewall types make the most sense. While this section will be a good starting point, you may want to consult with security experts regarding specific packages and maintenance agreements that are not covered here.

Network-Level Firewalls

As mentioned earlier in this chapter, network-level firewalls focus on the TCP/IP addressing and ports to prevent unwanted traffic from accessing the internal network. In terms of the relative complexity of installing and maintaining firewalls, the network-level firewall is easier than an application-level firewall. Focus on the word "relative," because firewall installation and configuration require a good knowledge of your current networking needs, Internet protocols, and known security holes.

This section covers some of the basic configuration options, but use this chapter as an introduction to this material. If you are not an expert in these things, you may want to seek the help of security consultants who can assess your current networking environment and recommend particular configuration options that will offer your organization the protection and flexibility you want.

Network-level firewalls have particular strengths that have made them quite popular. First, they are relatively inexpensive when compared to the application-level firewalls. Most network-level firewall functionality can be instituted in the router which connects your network to the Internet. Smaller organizations may not have the financial resources to purchase application-level firewall software and hardware in addition to their router, so configuring the packet filtering options in the router allows the organization to stretch its networking budget.

In addition to the financial benefits of network-level firewalls, the administration of the filtering rules is simple to maintain. Because the setup of the routers must be managed anyway, the additional time and effort to maintain the filtering rules is negligible. Since no UNIX firewall system is necessary, the administration and configuration complexity is greatly reduced.

The weaknesses of the network-level firewalls, however, may force larger or more sophisticated organizations into purchasing an application-level firewall. Using a router to filter your packets may effectively deter criminals from entering your internal network, but you may never know when your system has been attacked or be able to trace any attacks back to their sources because there are no logs or reporting modules to assist you. If the router blocks the attack, the packets are never allowed to enter; thus, you don't have a record of them. If a criminal does bypass your router's filters, you will never know how the system was breached nor by whom. Also, the entire internal network is available to be attacked from the Internet. Since all the internal network addresses are visible from the Internet, a criminal can browse the internal network for the weakest entry point.

Additionally, the network-level firewall may be only capable of providing basic statistics for your records. Application-level firewalls can have many reporting, statistical, and monitoring capabilities that you may want to keep your network running.

To summarize the situations in which you would want a network-level firewall instead of an application-level firewall:

- Your organization has limited financial resources for network security.
- Your organization lacks expertise in managing the more complex application-level firewalls and cannot afford to outsource this function.
- Your organization has low-risk systems that offer few Internet-accessible services (such as Telnet, WWW, and e-mail).

Application-Level Firewalls

An application-level firewall offers your organization a great deal of functionality and flexibility, but often at a much higher price than the network-level firewall. Since the application-level firewall acts on the application's protocol, many options are available for filtering, monitoring, and reporting. For example, you may set up an application-level firewall to deny access to all internal servers unless a secure channel between the external host and the firewall can be established. Additionally, an application-level firewall can monitor connection attempts by external hosts and, using heuristical analysis, determine whether a criminal is attempting to break into the network. These attacks can immediately alert an administrator so that law-enforcement officials can be notified. Detailed reports of suspicious activity can be maintained to allow administrators to investigate potentially hazardous Internet hosts and take precautionary measures.

The application-level firewall also allows the internal network to be completely isolated from the external network. Unlike the network-level firewall, which required that all the internal hosts have correctly assigned addresses that can be accessed by any system on the Internet, application-level firewalls allow the internal network to have any addressing scheme because the only system that is really communicating with the Internet is the application-level firewall. This allows administrators the flexibility of addressing their internal network without constraints, and it allows those networks that may have already assigned thousands of bogus TCP/IP addresses to servers and workstations prior to their Internet connection to be spared from an address-reassignment nightmare.

In addition to the external firewall protection, the application-level firewalls can also provide beneficial internal networking functions. For example, application-level firewalls may be set up to cache frequently accessed Internet pages, such as **www.microsoft.com**, so that the internal response times for accessing these pages is reduced. Network administrators may also set up the firewall to refuse internal connections out to sites with questionable business value.

While the application-level firewall can provide all of these functions, the administration of this type of firewall can be quite involved. Not only will the administrator need to know the basics behind the TCP/IP protocols, he or she will need to determine the best settings for caching, monitoring, and reporting.

To summarize why an organization would want an application-level firewall over a network-level firewall:

- Your organization has internal expertise to manage the more complex application-level firewall software and hardware.
- Your organization has a large budget for Internet security.
- Your organization's management needs detailed reporting and statistics for monitoring the network connection.
- Your organization wants to keep the internal network isolated from the Internet.

Defining Hardware Needs

Now that you understand the different firewall types, you may be formulating your future firewall system's requirements. This includes the hardware and software your organization will need for the firewall. This section covers the hardware aspects of the firewall while the next section, "Defining Software Needs," outlines some of the software needs you can evaluate.

Sizing Your Organization's Traffic

Obviously, more active sites require faster machines than sites without as much traffic. But if your organization is not on the Internet now, how can you accurately predict the traffic to and from your site? The simple, and perhaps obvious, answer is you can't.

So if you can't estimate your Internet site's traffic, how can you purchase the right hardware? There are several indicators that will clue you in to the answer. First, the connection that you have to the Internet ultimately decides how much traffic your network will experience.

If you have a 56 kilobit-per-second (kb/s) leased line connection to the Internet, your maximum throughput between your internal network and the Internet is only 7 kb/s (56 divided by 8-bits per byte is 7). The throughput on your internal Ethernet networks is around 1250 kb/s (10 megabits divided by 8-bits per byte) or more than 175 times faster. In this scenario, your router to the Internet won't impose much delay, even if it is a low-end model. Even application-level firewalls on low-end hardware are able to keep up with the connections at the 56 kb/s rate.

But often, the 56 kb/s line is outgrown quickly and a higher bandwidth line is installed. As your organization scales up the connection to the Internet, the firewall may begin to pose a potential bottleneck for your network traffic. If you have been in the networking arena for at least a few months, you understand that there is never enough bandwidth for your user's needs and the budget for the additional bandwidth won't be available until next year.

Tip

As difficult as it may seem initially, you may want to overestimate your Internet traffic to anticipate bandwidth additions within the next three years. If you are installing a 56 kb/s line now, estimate that you will have at least one T1 (1.54 megabits-per-second) connection within the next three years. This will help you determine the firewall solution that can grow with your network.

Buying for the Future

Network protocols change often, even as much as a few times each year. The Internet is growing and expanding so rapidly that no one can predict what type of challenges lie ahead for network security. For this reason alone, your hardware should be expandable and reusable. When you've outgrown the Pentium firewall server you purchased today, you can turn around and use it as a workstation tomorrow. Additionally, the server you purchase should be designed for heavy network traffic and application CPU utilization. The faster the server you purchase, the less delay introduced as a result of the firewall.

At the very least, your application-level firewall system should include the following hardware:

- Pentium 100 Mhz
- 32M of RAM
- 500M hard drive
- Two PCI Ethernet network interface cards

Your system may require more memory or hard drive space depending on the options you install. These options are discussed in greater detail in the next section, "Defining Software Needs."

If you are implementing a network-level only firewall system, you may choose to purchase a router that can filter packets. These routers have various router operating systems that require particular RAM and network configurations. Check with your router vendor to purchase the options you need.

Buying the Right Hardware

Assuming you are implementing an application-level firewall, you have the option of installing software onto a hardware platform that you purchase separately, purchasing hardware bundled with preinstalled software, or purchasing a dedicated firewall server "black box." These dedicated firewall servers offer a complete solution on proprietary hardware that allows the vendor to guarantee performance and compatibility. There are benefits and drawbacks to each of these systems, which are outlined in Table 27.1.

Table 27.1 Firewall Hardware Options

Hardware Option	Benefit	Drawback
Separately purchased hardware and software	May purchase a higher-quality system or one that matches the current installed base of the organization. Hardware can be reused later.	Must install and configure hardware and software from scratch. Expertise required to choose the best hardware platform.
Hardware and software bundled	Firewall and operating system software are preloaded saving time and effort. System may be easier to troubleshoot.	Hardware may be more expensive or of lower quality than current installed base. Hardware may not be able to be used later.
Proprietary hardware	Turnkey installation. No hardware configuration is necessary. Performance may be tuned for firewall tasks.	May be more expensive than software-only solutions. Cannot reuse hardware.

Before making any purchasing decision, make sure you have consulted the vendor regarding its maintenance, warranty, and upgrade policies that may influence your hardware purchasing decision.

Defining Software Needs

If you have purchased a system to function as your firewall, or have a current server that will begin fulfilling the role of a firewall server, you need to evaluate the various options available for firewall software. These options are broken down into the two firewall categories to allow you to evaluate your software needs.

Network-Level Firewalls

If your current router does not contain any protocol-specific packet filtering options or you want to protect a server that is on a network segment outside the firewall, you may choose to implement the protocol security options of Windows NT.

Built into the TCP/IP protocol options for Windows NT is the ability to filter certain addresses, ports, or services before they reach the server. This allows the server to act as a network-level firewall for itself, or if routing is enabled, for the internal network.

To manage the network-level firewall functionality of the Windows NT TCP/IP protocol, you must open the Network control panel found in the Control Panel folder. To access the Network control panel:

1. Choose Start, Settings, Control Panel.
2. Select the Network Control Panel application.

   OR

   Right-click the Network Neighborhood icon on the desktop and choose the Properties option.
3. Once you have started the Network control panel, select the Protocols property sheet.
4. Next, choose the TCP/IP protocol and click the Properties button.
5. Click the Advanced button to open a dialog box like the one shown in figure 27.8.

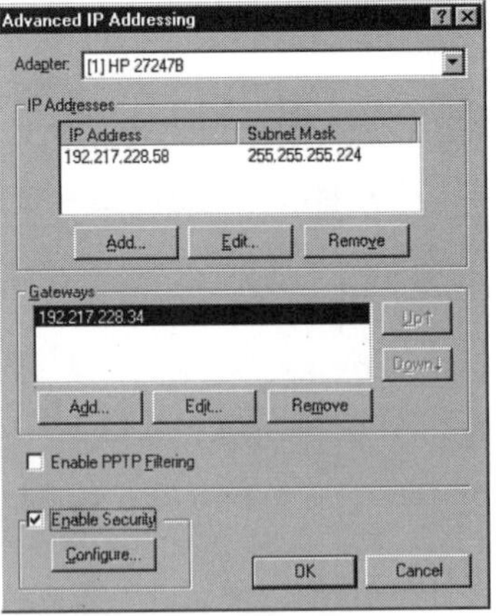

Fig. 27.8
The advanced TCP/IP protocol property sheet allows you to turn on the firewall functionality of Windows NT.

To turn on the firewall capabilities of Windows NT, select the Enable Security checkbox and click the Configure button below it. This brings up a dialog box like the one shown in figure 27.9. This figure shows the dialog box that contains the filtering options for Windows NT's TCP/IP networking.

Notice that TCP ports, UDP ports, and IP protocols may be filtered from the server. This allows the network-level firewall options to be set to the needs of your internal network. The default options permit all ports to be accessed from the outside. If you choose to enable the firewall security, you will be forced to accept the pessimistic security profile that denies all services that are not explicitly allowed. Again, you need detailed TCP/IP port knowledge to set up the filtering options that will keep your network safe.

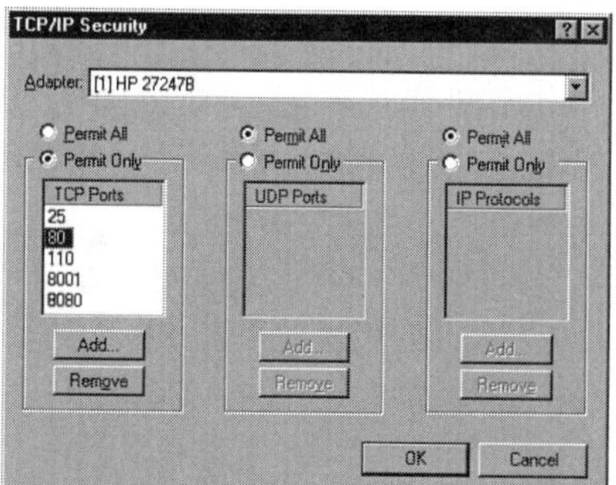

Fig. 27.9
Windows NT has built-in network-level firewall protection.

> **Caution**
>
> If you are unaware of the TCP/IP ports used for various services, you may unknowingly shut off access to your server by enabling this security. Check your setup with reference material to verify your choices for the ports you've enabled.

Application-Level Firewalls

Application-level firewalls have begun to appear for the Windows NT platform. Until recently, the only platform on which firewall software was available was UNIX. Windows NT-based firewalls offer advantages over UNIX firewalls for organizations that do not have UNIX expertise, or do not want to install a UNIX system as a firewall. Since the UNIX operating system is so open, many security flaws have been exploited by intruders. Some organizations are unwilling to install a UNIX firewall because they fear that the operating system may be compromised.

If you choose to install a Windows NT-based firewall system, you may be able to provide additional functionality for your users and your administrators. For example, the administrator who is familiar with Windows NT can quickly learn the new firewall software. Additionally, the administrator may be able to send notices or security alerts through the Windows NT network rather than e-mail. Windows NT firewall services may even offer remote management or performance monitoring through tools already in use by network administrators.

Application-level firewalls, like the one shown in figure 27.10, allow the organization to provide the monitoring, reporting, and filtering options that were explained earlier in this chapter. Systems like the Raptor Eagle-NT firewall are often priced on a per-user basis since the functionality of an application-level firewall is so much more intensive than a network-level firewall. These per-user costs may be expensive, but the costs are well worth it when the company's data is at stake.

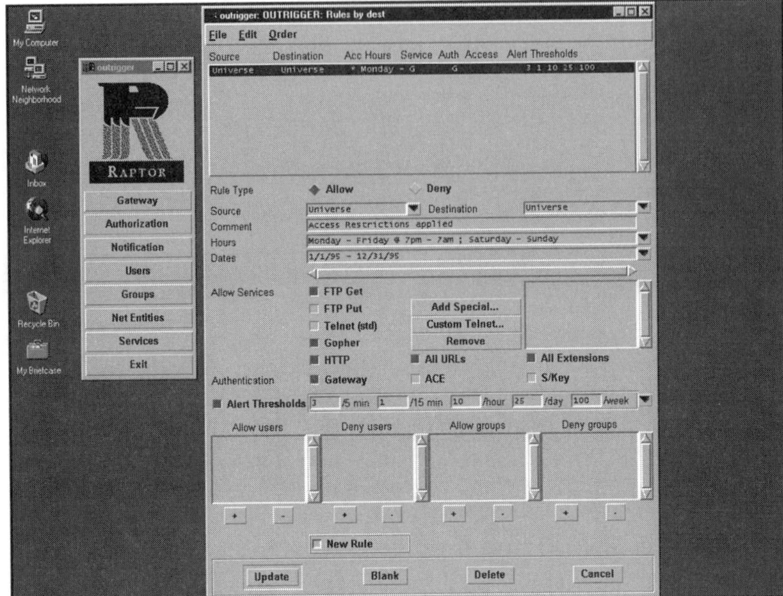

Fig. 27.10 Raptor's Eagle-NT is an application-level firewall system.

Figure 27.11 shows some of the notification features of the Eagle-NT firewall illustrating the flexibility of an application-based firewall system. Notice how the administrator has the ability to set notification times for particular types of alerts.

> **Note**
>
> Raptor's Eagle-NT software was carried over from their popular UNIX-based systems, so the displays shown in figures 27.10 and 27.11 have distinctive UNIX X-Windows characteristics.

When evaluating Windows NT firewall systems, you should verify that the firewall software runs as a service under Windows NT and will run on the workstation version of Windows NT. If your vendor requires the server version of Windows NT, your firewall will be more costly than one that will run on the workstation version.

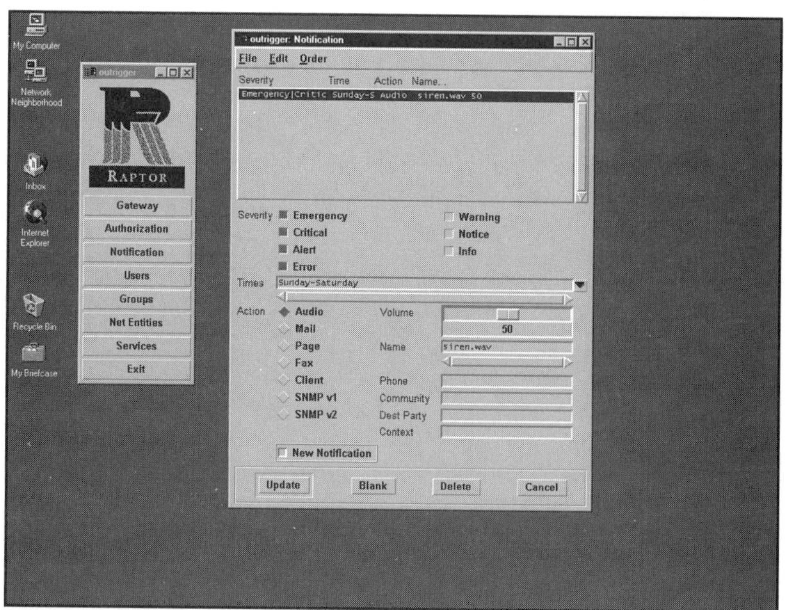

Fig. 27.11
Raptor's Eagle-NT software allows time-specific alerts for various conditions.

Additional Firewall Software Options

In addition to the firewall functions, many firewall software vendors also include secure versions of:

- E-mail servers
- Web servers
- ftp servers
- Gopher servers

You may want to look into these options since they eliminate the need to install different software on your firewall. These firewall options may not be as advanced as other popular Windows NT Internet servers such as Microsoft's Internet Information Server, but they may not need to be. You should evaluate your network's needs to determine if the firewall server will be sufficient. ❖

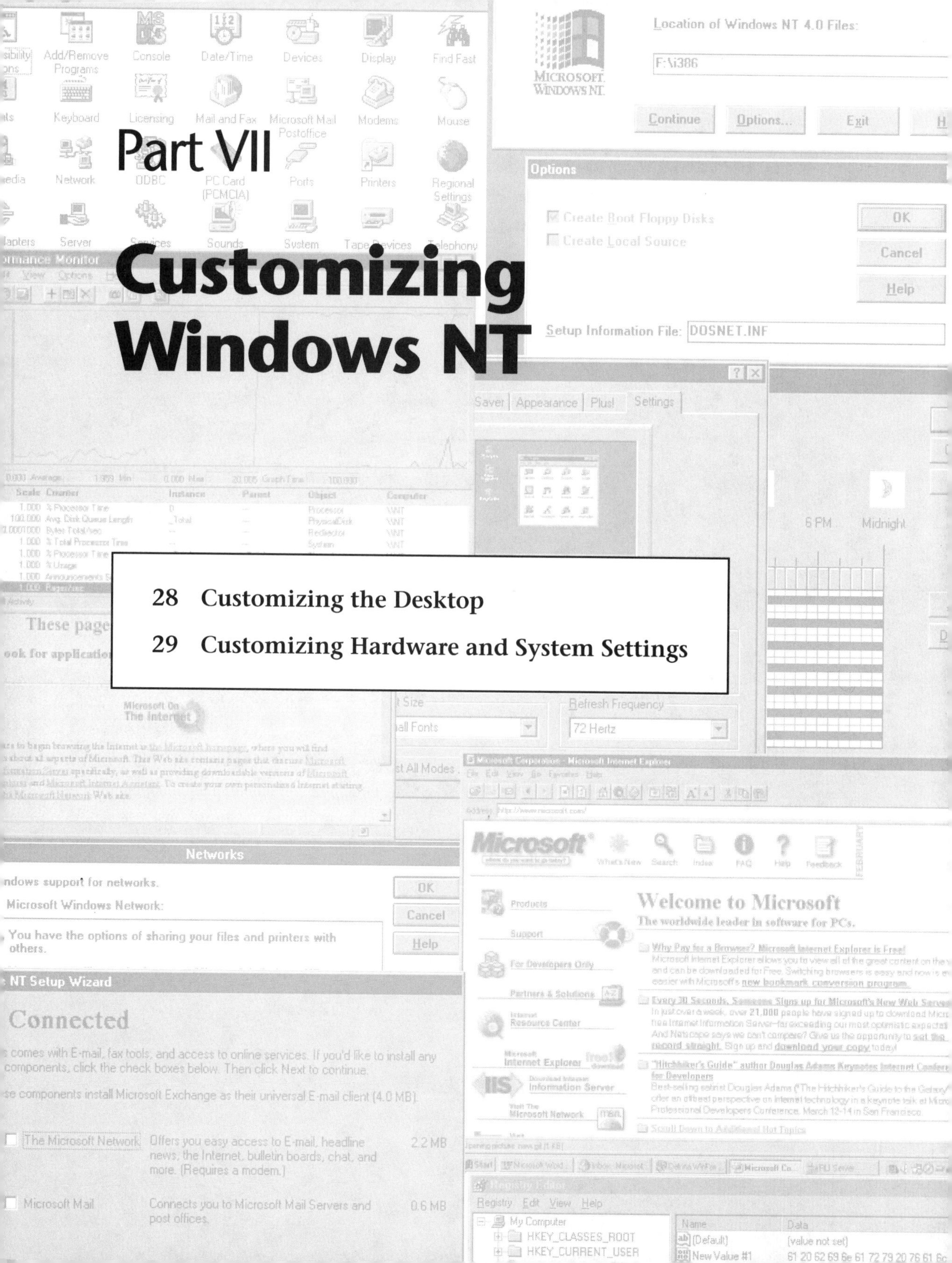

Part VII

Customizing Windows NT

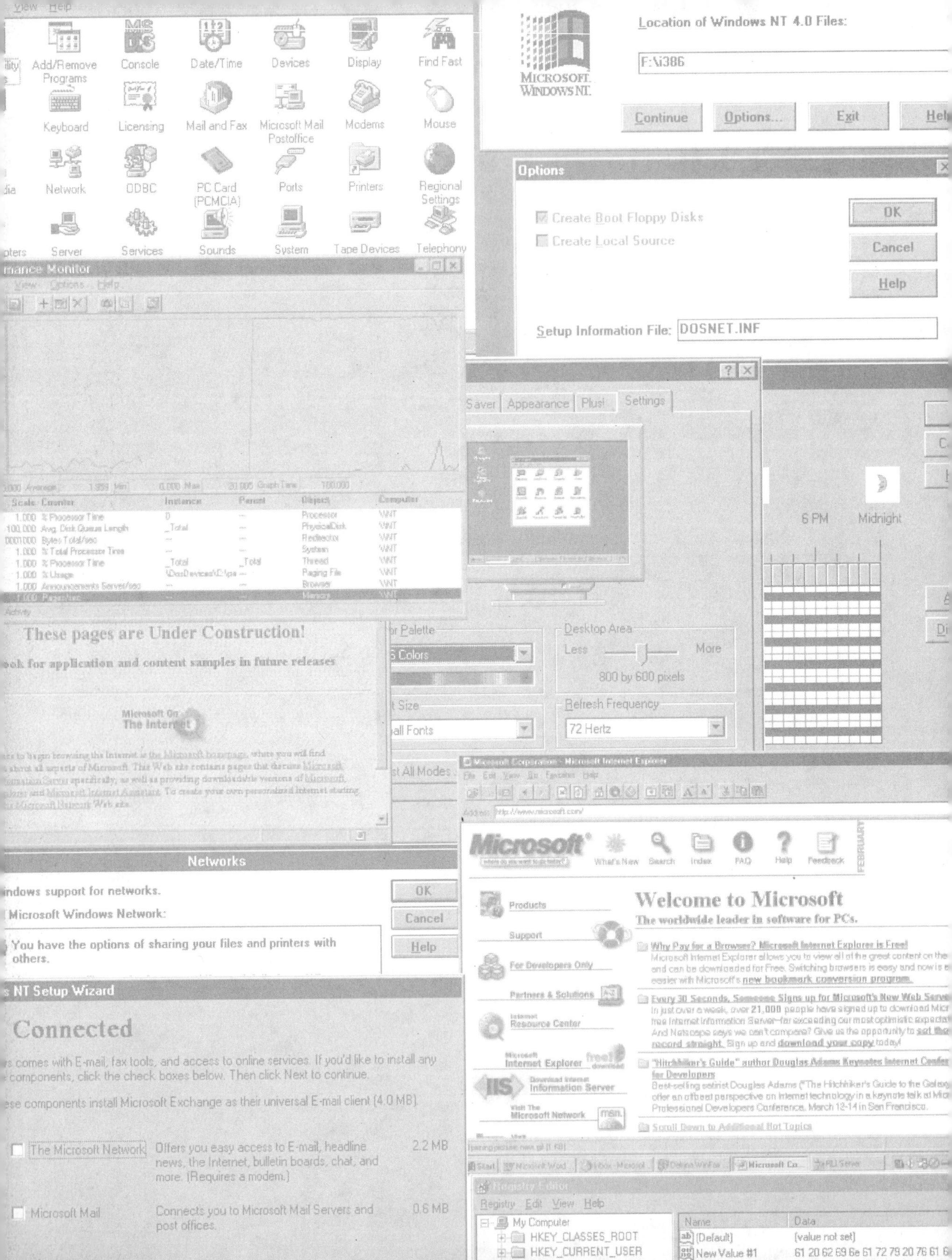
Add/Remove Programs
Console
Date/Time
Devices
Display
Find Fast
Keyboard
Licensing
Mail and Fax
Microsoft Mail Postoffice
Modems
Mouse
Network
ODBC
PC Card (PCMCIA)
Ports
Printers
Regional Settings
Server
Services
Sounds
System
Tape Devices
Telephony
Location of Windows NT 4.0 Files:
F:\i386
MICROSOFT WINDOWS NT.
Continue
Options...
Exit
Options
Create Boot Floppy Disks
Create Local Source
OK
Cancel
Help
Setup Information File: DOSNET.INF
Saver
Appearance
Plus!
Settings
6 PM
Midnight
Desktop Area
Less
More
800 by 600 pixels
Refresh Frequency
72 Hertz
These pages are Under Construction!
Networks
OK
Cancel
Help
You have the options of sharing your files and printers with others.
Connected
These components install Microsoft Exchange as their universal E-mail client (4.0 MB).
The Microsoft Network
Offers you easy access to E-mail, headline news, the Internet, bulletin boards, chat, and more. (Requires a modem.)
2.2 MB
Microsoft Mail
Connects you to Microsoft Mail Servers and post offices.
0.6 MB
Microsoft
What's New
Search
Index
FAQ
Help
Feedback
Products
Support
For Developers Only
Partners & Solutions
Internet Resource Center
Microsoft Internet Explorer
Download Internet Information Server
Visit The Microsoft Network
Welcome to Microsoft
The worldwide leader in software for PCs.
Why Pay for a Browser? Microsoft Internet Explorer is Free!
Every 30 Seconds, Someone Signs up for Microsoft's New Web Server
"Hitchhiker's Guide" author Douglas Adams Keynotes Internet Conference for Developers
Scroll Down to Additional Hot Topics
Registry Editor
Registry
Edit
View
Help
My Computer
HKEY_CLASSES_ROOT
HKEY_CURRENT_USER
Name
Data
(Default)
(value not set)
New Value #1

CHAPTER 28

Customizing the Desktop

by Robert Parker

Now that you've set up your NT system, decided on the file system, established security, configured the network, and wrestled with the dozens of technical details those entail—you deserve to sit back and make yourself comfortable. This chapter is all about configuring your desktop environment: how to add a personal touch to the desktop's "look and feel" and make working with NT comfortable (or even fun).

In this chapter, you learn to

- Configure the desktop wallpaper background
- Select colors and fonts for windows and other on-screen elements
- Choose and configure screen savers
- Add a "soundtrack" to system events
- Automatically start applications whenever you log in
- Use accessibility options

Customizing the Display

In Windows NT, all display options are controlled through a central control: the Display Properties sheet (see fig. 28.1). To display this property sheet, just right-click anywhere on the desktop. When the pop-up menu appears, select Properties.

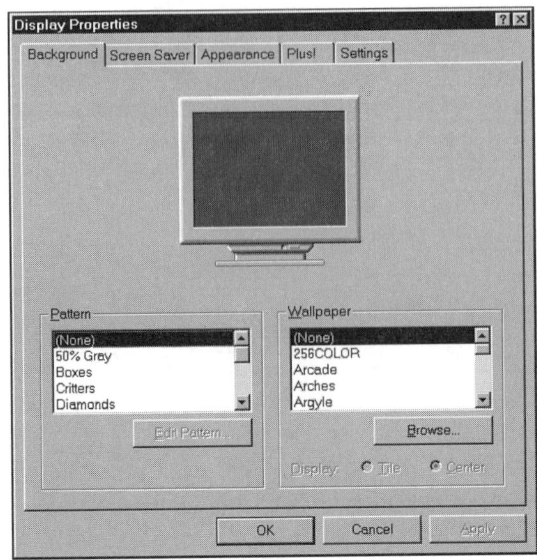

Fig. 28.1
Use the Display Properties sheet to change any display setting.

> **Tip**
>
> You can also display the Display Properties sheet by double-clicking the Display icon in the Control Panel.

Setting Wallpaper and Background Options

As you know, the desktop is the background over which windows, icons, and the taskbar are displayed. When you first install Windows NT, the desktop is a light apple green. Your desktop sets the tone for your Windows NT environment, the same way a frame complements the picture within. Desktops can be frugal or fanciful, ranging from a simple color or pattern to photographs or highly detailed digital artwork.

Selecting a Wallpaper

A wallpaper is simply a Windows bitmap graphic (a BMP file) displayed on the background. Generally, wallpaper bitmaps are either large files that cover most of the screen, or small files that are *tiled* (repeated and laid side by side) to cover the screen.

To select a wallpaper, open the Display Properties sheet. The Background tab should be selected (refer to fig. 28.1). If it isn't, click that tab. Select a wallpaper from the Wallpaper list. To display the wallpaper in the center of the screen (better for larger images), click the Center option button. To cover the screen with the image (better for smaller images), click the Tile option button. After you have selected a wallpaper, click Apply to add the wallpaper to your desktop.

You aren't limited to the wallpaper that comes with Windows NT; you can use any BMP file as a desktop wallpaper. You can create your own BMP files using Windows Paintbrush (or any graphics editor that can create BMP files). You can also use a graphics conversion utility to convert other graphics (such as GIF or JPG files downloaded from the Internet) to BMP format. To use a custom wallpaper, click the Browse button, and select the custom BMP file.

Tip

When should you Center a wallpaper and when should you Tile it? Centering works best for large images that cover the desktop. Tiling works best for smaller images, generally no larger than a quarter of the desktop. If you have a mid-sized image that's not quite large enough to center but too big to tile, you can stretch it to fit the desktop using a Plus! option (see "Using Plus! Options" later in this chapter).

Selecting a Background Pattern

Patterns are another way to customize your desktop. A *pattern* is literally a pattern of black dots, tiled to cover the screen and overlaid on the background color. Patterns are generally much simpler than wallpaper, and less colorful.

To select a pattern, open the Display Properties sheet. Make sure the Background tab is on top. Select a pattern from the Pattern list. You can preview each pattern in the "monitor" in the center of the property sheet. Click Apply to add the selected pattern to your desktop.

Tip

Patterns are displayed "behind" wallpaper on the desktop. You can combine a pattern with centered wallpaper (tiled wallpaper will cover the pattern) to create a nice "frame" for your wallpaper.

Use the 50% Gray pattern to create a muted background color.

You can change a pattern, or create a pattern of your own, by using the Pattern Editor (see fig. 28.2). Just select a pattern from the list and click Edit Pattern.

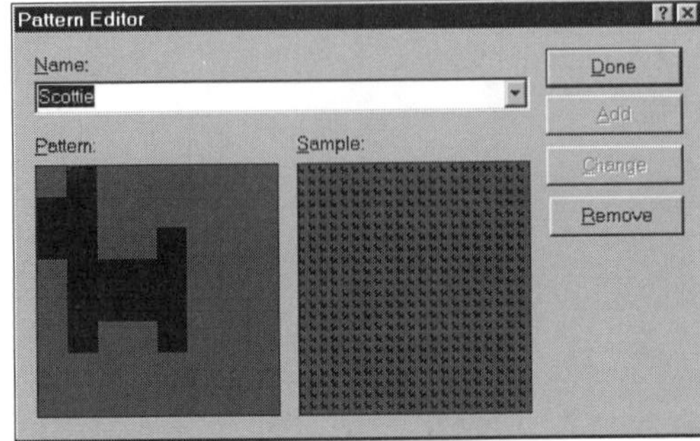

Fig. 28.2
Use the Pattern Editor to customize your desktop's background pattern.

To exit the Pattern Editor and save your changes, click Done. To delete a pattern from the pattern list, click Remove.

After you have selected the pattern or wallpaper you like, click OK to close the property sheet. Figure 28.3 shows just one combination of a pattern and a wallpaper.

Fig. 28.3
You can combine patterns and wallpaper to create a more complex desktop.

Changing Colors and Fonts

You can change the whole mood of your Windows NT environment by customizing the color scheme. You can select a scheme that's easier to read, one that complements your decor, or one to match your mood.

To change desktop colors, display the Display Properties sheet and select the Appearance tab (see fig. 28.4).

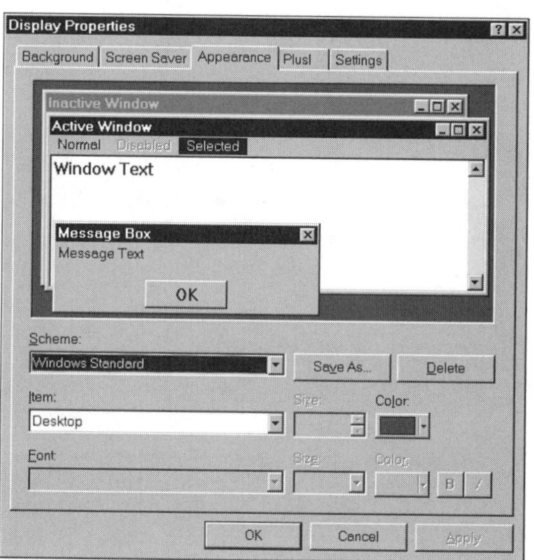

Fig. 28.4
Use the Appearance page to change desktop colors.

Selecting a Color Scheme

Windows comes with a wide variety of predefined color schemes, ranging from simple black-and-white to extremely colorful. To select a predefined color scheme, just scroll through the choices in the Scheme list. The choices marked VGA will display on any VGA monitor; the High Color choices require a video adapter capable of displaying 16-bit colors. This black-and-white book can't do justice to the desktop color choices Windows provides—take a look for yourself!

> **Tip**
>
> To change the number of colors your video adapter displays, use the Settings tab in the Display Properties sheet described in the section "Sizing the Desktop" later in this chapter.

Creating Your Own Color Scheme

If the predefined color schemes don't suit you, you can customize the color schemes, or create an entirely new scheme of your own.

Selecting Colors

Selecting colors for your desktop is extremely easy. Here's all you have to do:

1. In the "sample desktop" in the middle of the property sheet, click the desktop element for which you want to select a new color.
2. Click the Color drop-down menu to display a short menu of colors (see fig. 28.5).

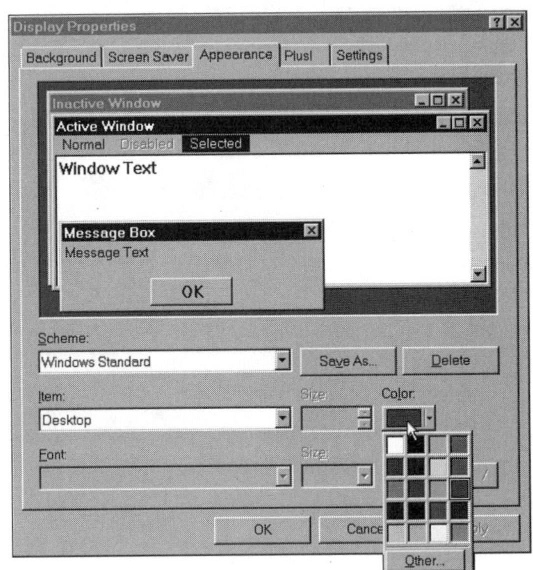

Fig. 28.5 Use the Color drop-down menu to select new desktop colors.

3. To use a color in the color menu, click it. If you don't see the color you want, click Other. The Color dialog box appears. You can select a color from the Basic Color list, or create your own custom color (see the next section to find out how).

Creating Custom Colors

If you still don't see the color you want in the basic color selections, you can use the Color dialog box (see fig. 28.6) to create your own custom color.

1. When the Color dialog box appears, click in any of the blank (white) Custom Color boxes.

2. Click in the "color matrix" (Windows NT's term for the large spectrum palette) to select a color.
3. Use the color slider at the right of the color matrix to select how light or dark to make your custom color.
4. The Color|Solid box shows the color you have selected. Repeat steps 2 and 3 until the color you want appears in the box.
5. When you have selected your custom color, click Add to Custom Colors.

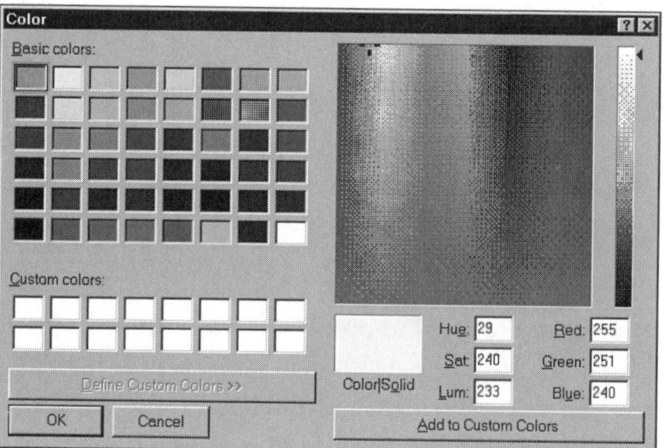

Fig. 28.6
The Color dialog box enables you to select more colors, or to mix your own.

To incorporate the custom color into your desktop color scheme, click the custom color's box and then click OK.

> **Note**
>
> The Color side of the Color|Solid box shows the currently selected custom color. Depending on the setting of your display adapter, custom colors may be *dithered* (a mix of distinct, different colors). The Solid box illustrates the closest solid (single) color that matches your selected custom color. You may want to experiment when selecting dithered colors; they don't work equally well on all desktop elements.

Selecting Fonts

In addition to selecting new colors, you can also select new fonts for drop-down menus and window title bars. To select a new font, click the object on the sample desktop for which you want to change the fonts. Then, use the Font and Size menus to select a new font.

> **Note**
>
> There are two Size selectors. The Size selector next to the Item list selects the size of the menu bar and its controls. The Size selector next to the Font list controls the font size.

Saving Your Customizations

Once you have created a new look for your desktop with new color and font selections, you should save it. If you modified an existing scheme, you can save it under that name; or, you can give the scheme a different name.

To save a color and font scheme, click Save As. You are prompted to enter a new name; type in the name and click OK. You can use spaces and punctuation in the name if you like.

Selecting a Screen Saver

Screen savers were first designed to prevent monitor burn-in on unattended systems (a problem many automated tellers suffer from—you can see traces of text literally burnt into their screens). Monitor burn-in is no longer the concern it once was because the Windows desktop is much more dynamic than the earlier DOS character-mode screens. But screen savers remain as popular as ever and now, screen savers have become almost an art form in themselves. Windows NT comes with a nice selection of screen savers that you'll enjoy exploring and using.

To select a screen saver, open the Display Properties sheet and select the Screen Saver tab (see fig. 28.7).

Use the Screen Saver list to select a screen saver. The list contains some Windows favorites (such as the starfield simulation) and some unique Windows NT additions, such as 3D Pipes. The monitor in the middle of the property sheet demonstrates the selected screen saver.

Customizing the Screen Saver

Each screen saver has different customization options (for example, to control how fast objects should move). To configure the selected screen saver, click Settings. Make any changes you like to the settings, and click OK. Then, to test the settings, click Preview. The screen saver displays until you move the mouse.

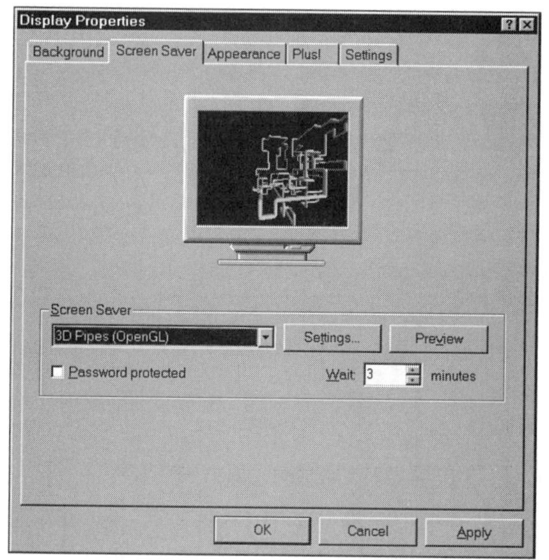

Fig. 28.7
Windows NT comes with a unique library of screen savers.

Locking the Screen with a Password

If you like, you can lock your screen saver with your login password (you cannot specify a separate screen saver password). Locking your screen is useful if you have sensitive material on your screen that you want to shield from prying eyes, if you are running applications that should not be disturbed, or if you just want to keep others from fiddling with your system. When your screen saver is locked, no one can exit the screen saver and return to the desktop without entering the proper password. To password protect your screen saver, just check the Password protected box.

After you have selected and customized your screen saver, click OK to implement your changes.

Changing Video Options

When Windows NT is installed, it uses a very basic video mode. Depending on your video adapter and the applications you will be using, you can run Windows NT in higher resolutions or with more colors.

To change your video options, open the Display Properties sheet and click the Settings tab (see fig. 28.8).

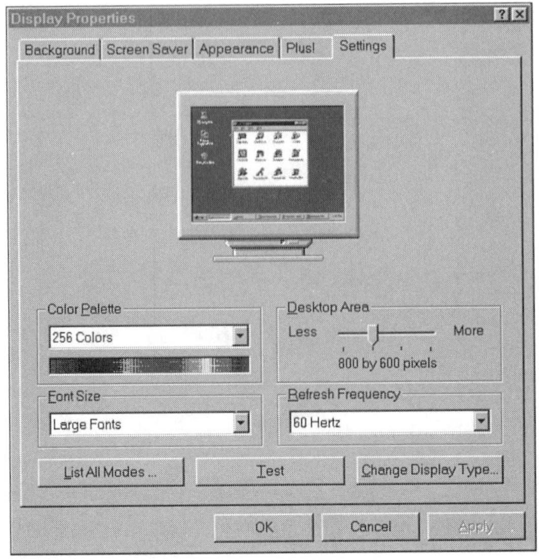

Fig. 28.8
The Settings page controls video options.

> **Note**
>
> As you work with the video options settings, you might notice that changing one option causes another option to change (for example, selecting a high number of colors decreases the size of your desktop, or changing the size of the desktop changes the refresh rate). Don't be concerned if this happens—it's normal. The video options available depend upon the capabilities of your particular video adapter; Windows NT tailors the options it presents to your video adapter's requirements and capabilities. You can click the List All Modes button to display a list of your adapter's supported settings.

Sizing the Desktop

The size of the desktop is an extremely important factor in the quality of your Windows NT display. The larger your desktop, the better your display. There is a trade-off, though—the larger your desktop, the slower your video response. With a high-quality video adapter, this speed difference is much less noticeable.

To change the size of your desktop, drag the Desktop Area slider to select a new resolution. The resolution is measured in pixels: 640 × 480 means that the desktop measures 640 pixels across and 480 pixels down. 640 × 480 is the lowest resolution (and will probably be the resolution Windows NT uses when it first installs). 800 × 600 is a very good compromise between resolution and speed, and is the upper limit for some video adapters. Most video adapters can display resolutions of 1024 × 768 or even as high as 1280 × 1024.

After you select a desktop size, you must test it. Click the Test button, then click OK. A test pattern displays for a few moments, then the Display Properties sheet appears again. If the test pattern displayed correctly, click Yes.

Determining the Number of Colors

When you configure your video display, you can also select the number of colors the video adapter can display at once. Simple Windows controls (such as dialog boxes and property sheets) don't require a wide palette of colors to look good; the system default of 16 colors will work fine for many applications. However, if you want to display finely colored digital art or photographs with appropriate fidelity, you should increase your display adapter's number of colors to at least 256. Many display adapters can easily display 65,000+ colors, and some higher-quality adapters can display more than 16 million colors. Better display adapters also have "high color" and "true color" modes, both of which afford an enormous range of color.

To change the number of colors in your palette, select the appropriate option in the Color Palette list.

Tip

Although Windows controls look fine in the basic 16 or 256 color modes, you can create a much more refined desktop using a wider palette of colors. Some color schemes are designed specifically for "high color" modes.

Selecting Font Size

The Display Properties sheet also controls the size of the system font used on the desktop and in Explorer windows. There are two sizes: small and large. How do you choose which size to use? It's easy—if you think the fonts under your icons are too big or too small to read comfortably, select the *other* option.

Use the Font Size list to select the font size. You must reboot your system if you change the font size.

Selecting the Refresh Rate

The Refresh Rate adjusts the way the video adapter works with the monitor. Some video adapters require certain refresh rates to display certain modes (for example, some video adapters require a different refresh rate for a 1024 × 768 desktop than for a 800 × 600 desktop). If you select a desktop size or color palette that doesn't display the test bitmap properly, try adjusting the Refresh Rate. The Refresh Frequency list selects the refresh rate.

After you have selected new video modes, click OK. Depending on the options you changed, you may be prompted to restart your system.

Using Sound Schemes

You can control more than the look of your desktop—you can control its sound as well. Windows NT can assign sounds to anything on its list of system events, including error messages, system startup and shutdown, and even pop-up menus.

Sounds are controlled on the Sounds Properties sheet (see fig. 28.9). To display this property sheet, double-click the Sounds icon in the Control Panel.

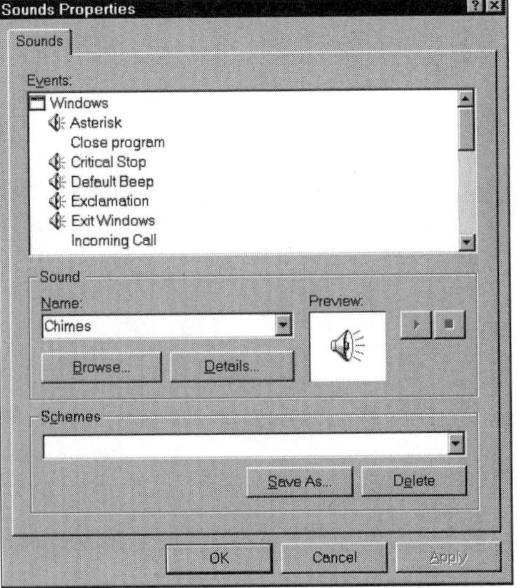

Fig. 28.9
Assign sounds to system events using the Sounds Properties sheet.

> **Note**
>
> You must have a sound card and an amplifier/speaker system installed to hear system sounds.

Selecting a Sound Scheme

Windows comes with a basic sound scheme that assigns a set of sounds to a set of events. At the time of this writing, only one sound scheme was installed with Windows NT. If more than one scheme is available (for example, additional Windows schemes or schemes you create yourself), you can select a new scheme from the Schemes list.

Creating a Custom Sound Scheme

You can customize your Windows NT "soundtrack" almost as easily as you can change the colors on your desktop. First, in the Events list, choose the system event to which you want to assign a new sound. Then, select the sound to assign to the event. The Name list contains the sounds currently installed in the default Windows sounds directory. You can select from one of those sounds, or use the Browse button to select another sound. System sounds must be WAV files.

> **Tip**
>
> Where can you get additional sounds? There's a wealth of WAV files available on the Internet. You can get all kinds of clips from news, TV, cartoons, and movies. Or, if you have a recording sound card, you can make your own WAV files using the Sound Recorder.

After you have configured the system sounds to your liking, click the Save As button to save your sound scheme. You are prompted for a name for the scheme; type in a name (you can use spaces if you like) and click OK.

To implement the sound scheme you have created, click OK.

Using Plus! Features

Plus! features are named after some of the desktop enhancements in Microsoft's Windows 95 Plus! Pack. They provide some extra features you can use to customize your desktop.

To use Plus! features, open the Display Properties sheet and select the Plus! tab (see fig. 28.10).

Selecting Desktop Icons

Windows NT's desktop by default contains icons for your computer, the Network Neighborhood, and the Recycle Bin. You can change the icons to any icon currently installed with Windows NT, or you can use your own ICO files.

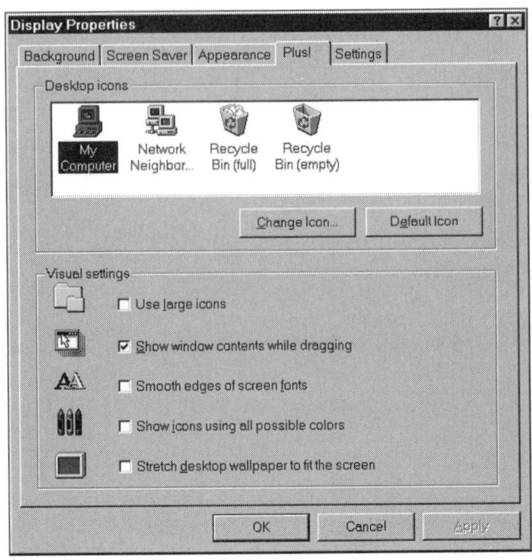

Fig. 28.10
You can enhance your desktop with Plus! features.

To change a desktop icon, select the icon you want to replace, then click Change Icon. A Change Icon dialog box appears; you can select an icon from the list or use the Browse button to select another. To restore the default icon for a desktop icon, select the icon and click Default Icon.

Changing Visual Settings

The Visual Settings provide some additional customizations for your desktop:

- Select Use Large Icons to use larger icons on the desktop. Large icons are most useful when you run your desktop at larger sizes (greater than 800 × 600). Small icons (the option unchecked) are preferable for lower desktop sizes.
- Select Show Window Contents When Dragging for a "live" picture of the window as you reposition or resize it. The default is to show only a window border as you reposition or resize a window. If you have a fast system with a good video card, this can be a very nice special effect.
- If you are running with a video adapter in high-color or true-color mode, you can select Smooth Edges of Screen Fonts to give your screen fonts a more polished look. Selecting this option in other video adapter modes has no effect.
- Select Show Icons Using All Possible Colors to create more colorful icons. Depending on the icon you select, you may or may not see much difference using this option.

- Select Stretch Desktop Wallpaper to Fit Screen to enlarge a centered wallpaper until it covers the entire screen. How well this will look depends on the original size and resolution of the wallpaper and the size of the desktop.

After you have changed the desired Plus! options, click OK to apply them to the desktop. Changing some options might require you to reboot your system.

Controlling Startup

There may be applications you want to start automatically whenever you start Windows NT. For example, you might want to start your schedule program to remind you of the day's events. The Startup program group enables you to start a program automatically whenever you log in.

1. Click Start, then select Settings, Taskbar. The Taskbar Properties sheet appears.

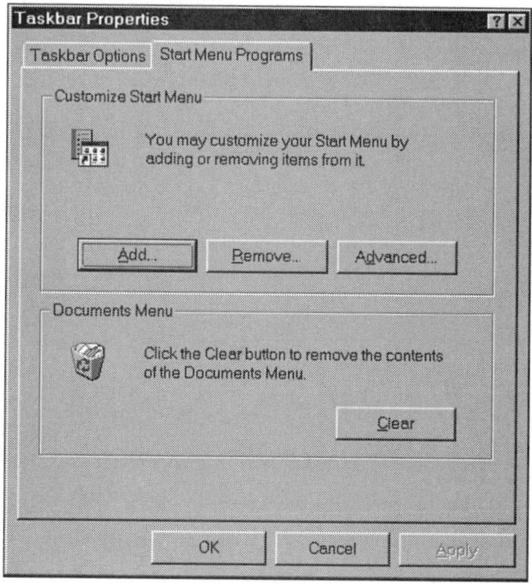

Fig. 28.11
You can configure the Start menu.

2. Click the Start Menu Programs tab (see fig. 28.11).
3. Click Add. The Create Shortcut dialog box appears. Enter the name of the program you want to start in the Command line box, or use the Browse button to help select the file.
4. Click Next. The Select Program Folder dialog box appears (see fig. 28.12).

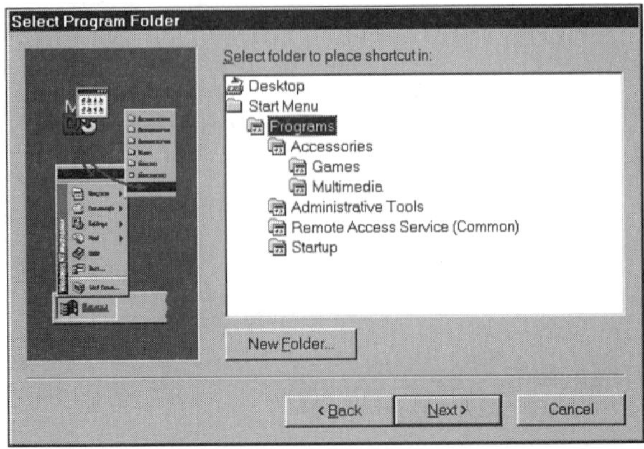

Fig. 28.12
Use Explorer to select the Startup group.

5. Click the Startup group, then click Next.
6. The Select A Title For The Program dialog box appears. Type the name of the program that you want to appear in the startup group (the same name appears on the taskbar when the program is started).
7. Click Finish. You return to the Taskbar Properties sheet; click OK.

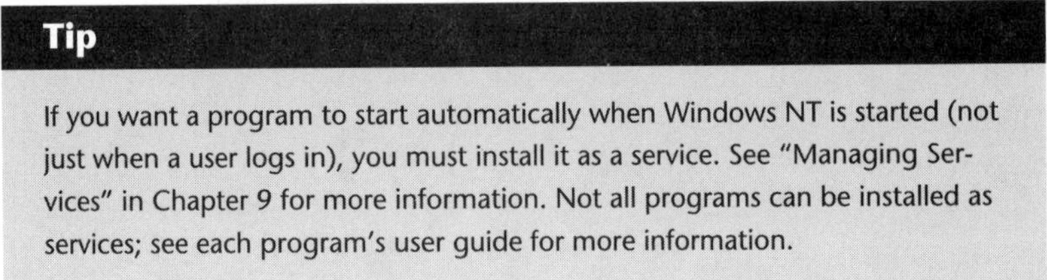
Tip

If you want a program to start automatically when Windows NT is started (not just when a user logs in), you must install it as a service. See "Managing Services" in Chapter 9 for more information. Not all programs can be installed as services; see each program's user guide for more information.

Using Accessibility Options

Microsoft has very thoughtfully provided Accessibility Options for users who otherwise might not be able to use Windows NT. To control the Accessibility Options, double-click the Accessibility Options icon in the Control Panel (see fig. 28.13).

Changing the Keyboard Options

There are three keyboard options on the Keyboard page. Sticky Keys is designed to help users who have trouble pressing multiple keys at once. When Sticky Keys is on, you produce Shift, Ctrl, or Alt keys by pressing the Shift, Ctrl, or Alt key, *then* the second key. Filter Keys ignores brief or repeated keystrokes, and slows the rate at which the key repeats when it is held down. Toggle Keys plays an audible tone when any of the Lock keys (Num Lock, Caps Lock, or Scroll Lock) are pressed.

To activate any of the keyboard options, check the appropriate box. Each option has a Settings button you can use to customize the option.

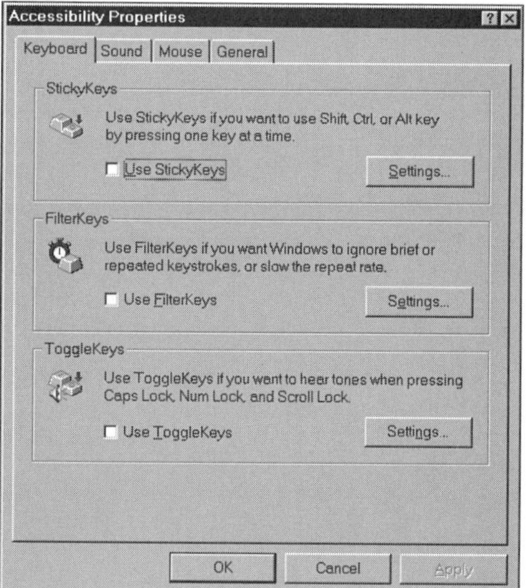

Fig. 28.13
Accessibility Options can assist users who have difficulty using standard hardware configurations.

Adding Visual Captions to System Sounds

The options on the Sound page enable hearing-impaired users to "see" system sounds. Sound Sentry converts sounds into visual events (for example, instead of a warning beep, it will flash the desktop). Show Sounds displays a caption appropriate to the sound the system makes.

To activate any of the sound options, check the appropriate box.

Using the Keyboard as a Mouse

The option on the Mouse page enables you to control the mouse using the number pad. Activate the option by clicking the checkbox; use the Settings button to select speed and acceleration.

Resetting Accessibility Options

You can automatically reset the Accessibility Options to return the computer to normal operations. This is useful if one of your users requires these options, but others do not. To enable the automatic reset feature, click the General tab, and click the Turn Off Accessibility Options After Idle For checkbox. The default idle time is five minutes (options range from five to 30 minutes). ❖

CHAPTER 29

Customizing Hardware and System Settings

by Michael Reilly

Windows NT does a good job of configuration during setup, automatically detecting hardware and software already installed. But sometimes we need to adjust the settings, or add new devices and applications. There are several tools that allow us to do so, including the Setup program, and the Control Panel.

In this chapter, you learn to

- Adjust the system time and date settings
- Customize your mouse and keyboard
- Configure Windows NT for international use by using Regional settings
- Connect a UPS
- Use and customize the Mandatory logon process
- Use the Hardware Profile to allow different configurations

Using the Control Panel

The Control Panel folder contains many of the icons for the system configuration utilities. Some configure the system hardware and software such as network cards, while others configure personal preferences, including screen colors and cursors. We will look at some of the options for customizing the hardware and system settings.

Setting Date and Time Options

Gone are the days when a personal computer asked for the time and date when you started it up. No more do we see directories full of files apparently created in 1980. But one minor problem is still with us. The clocks on personal computer motherboards are not all that accurate, and drift, normally losing a few minutes per month. This may not seem like much, but it gradually adds up. The problem will go away, along with the flashing 12:00 on VCRs, when computers and home appliances can access the signals from the atomic clocks which broadcast standard time signals. When that happens, remember, you read it here first.

There are some good reasons for taking a moment every now and then to keep your computer clock close to correct. When the computer is first set up, the clock may be correct—half way around the world. Some people never bother resetting their computer clock, except for the switch to daylight saving time—perhaps. But now, we don't even have to remember to do that. Windows NT 4.0 and Windows 95 change the time for us.

When a personal computer was a standalone device used by one person, the clock time did not matter very much. But now, most computers, at least in a business setting, are networked. Many employees dial in from home to access the corporate network. Multiple users may contribute to a file, or work on versions of the file. It has become more important to be able to tell which version of a document or file is the most recent. There are several software packages that synchronize files and directories on desktop and portable computers, and they use the data stamp on a file to decide which is the most recent version of a file. Windows NT 4.0 adds the Briefcase Replication feature, which can go beyond keeping the files synchronized: if the software has the capability, and Access 95 is a good example, the difference in the files can be reconciled. Having different times on the two computers is inviting trouble with this kind of software.

The Control Panel contains an icon for Date/Time, and clicking this icon brings up a clock display, as shown in figure 29.1. The display shows a calendar for the current month, with the current day highlighted, and the month and year shown in drop-down boxes so that they can easily be changed. The time is shown in both analog and digital format. The specific format can be changed using the Regional settings discussed later in the "Specifying Regional Settings" section.

The time can be adjusted by typing in the correct values in the box, or by highlighting the hour, minute, second or AM/PM indicator and using the spinner control or the up and down arrows to set the value. The month can also be selected by typing in the first letter. Typing in a second letter does not work the way you might expect, as each letter is taken to be the starting letter. So to reach July, press J twice. If you start to type JAN you will cycle through January, April, and November. You can once again use the up and down arrows to select a month, or drop down and select from the list. The year cannot be selected by typing a value; you must use the spinner control or the up and down arrows. While the methods of setting the various values are not consistent, they are easy to figure out.

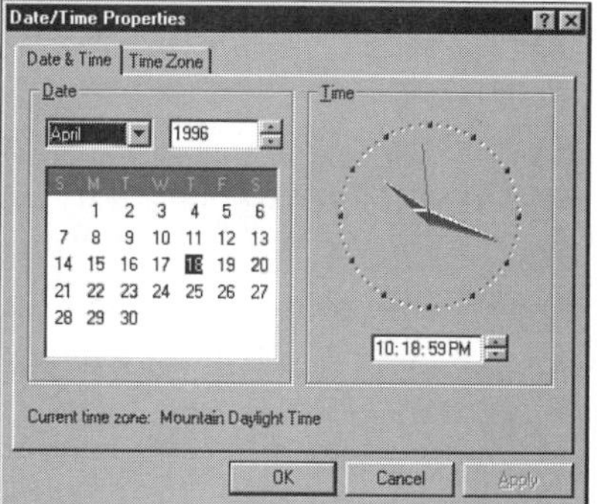

Fig. 29.1
The Control Panel Date/Time icon brings up this window, from which you can adjust the time and date, and the time zone.

Time Zones

The time settings in Windows NT have allowed for time zone settings since the first release of version 3.1. To set the time zone for your computer from the clock window, select the Time Zones tab. Then choose the correct time zone, and click the Apply button. While you are doing this, notice that there are even time zones for places like Arizona, and East Indiana which do not go on daylight saving time. On this screen, as shown in figure 29.2, you can instruct Windows NT to adjust for daylight saving.

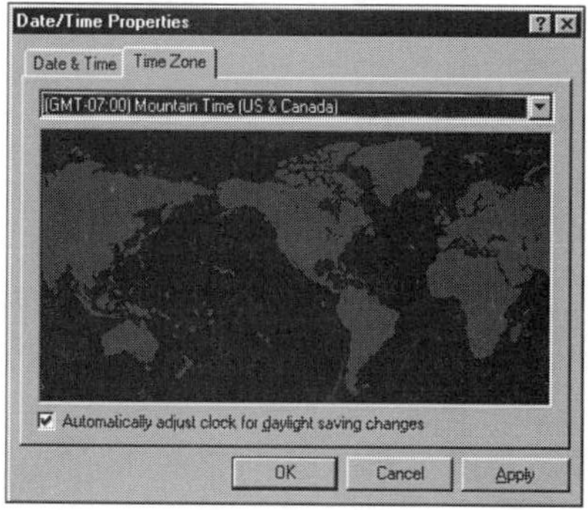

Fig. 29.2
You can select from a list of time zones, and choose whether to apply the daylight saving time change.

An interesting feature is that whatever time zone you select moves to the center of the map. Note the difference between figures 29.2, which is mountain time and 29.3, where Greenwich Mean Time (GMT) has been selected. Notice also in the list that eastern standard time and Bogota both show as GMT -5 hours. They are defined separately because Bogota would not have the same daylight saving setting as the east coast of the United States.

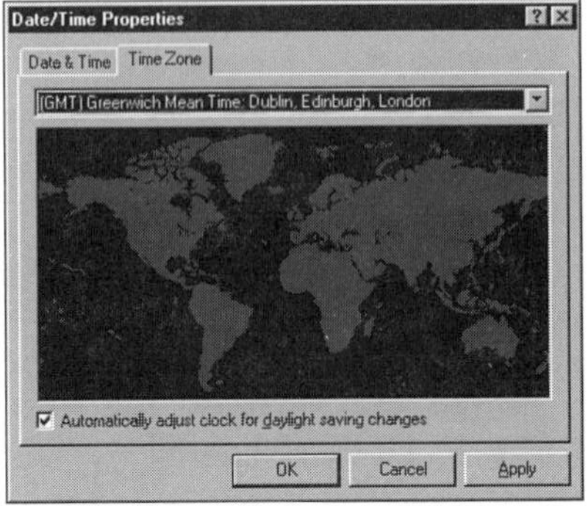

Fig. 29.3 When you select the time zone the map shifts so that it is centered on the chosen zone.

Implications for WAN Computing. The time zone setting feature is not just to keep you on track for daylight saving time. It's important when trying to synchronize files across a wide area network. The time zone feature does not just affect the setting of the clock, or daylight saving time. When a file is saved in Windows NT, the time stamp of the file is actually referenced to a standard. So if a user modifies a file at 4:30 PM in New York, and another user modifies the same file at 2 PM in Seattle, the Seattle file is the later version by 30 minutes.

You can try this for yourself. Check the time on a file on your computer. Now bring up the clock window and set the time zone to a zone other than your own. Now go back and check the file. You will see that the time on the file, and possibly the date, has been changed. But it is still the same absolute time. (Don't forget to reset your time zone after doing this.)

For a WAN administrator, it's important to be able to keep track of files across time zones. There are issues such as synchronization and replication of files that look at time stamps. When time zones are handled transparently, the latest version of a file is easily determined. If a backup is to be done of all files created since 6 AM this morning, what exactly does 6 AM mean? Do you want to back up all files created since 6 AM as defined at the location of the backup server, or since 6 AM the location where they were created? Because you are really working with absolute time references, it is the former. So yet another worry has been removed from the life of the network administrator.

So should the mobile computer user adjust the time setting on a portable computer to local time? If the issue is keeping file times correct, then the answer is either do not bother, or change the time and the zone, and your files will have the correct time. Don't change just the time without changing the time zone, because that causes confusion. The best bet is to leave the time alone rather than trying to keep track of where you are—unless, of course, you are using your computer to schedule appointments and sound alarms, in which case it makes more sense to synchronize it with local time.

Define Your Own Time Zone with the Resource Kit

The time zones are very comprehensive but may not cover all possibilities. For example, a minor problem is that England has to be set for GMT, but does go on to daylight saving time; a separate setting specifically for GMT would be handy. The Time Zone Editor in the Resource Kit allows you to edit or modify the time zones and the daylight saving settings, or even create a new zone. So as an example, let us create a new entry for GMT that doesn't use daylight saving time. (For anyone who assumes that daylight saving was invented in the U.S., the British have what is called British Summer Time, which they think they invented; but they switch on the last Sunday in March, not the first Sunday in April. This is why the Time Zone Editor utility is so useful.) The following steps are used to set up a new time zone:

1. Start the Time Zone Editor in the Resource Kit, which opens to the screen shown in figure 29.4.
2. Choose the GMT zone from the list, then click Edit. The Edit screen is shown in figure 29.5

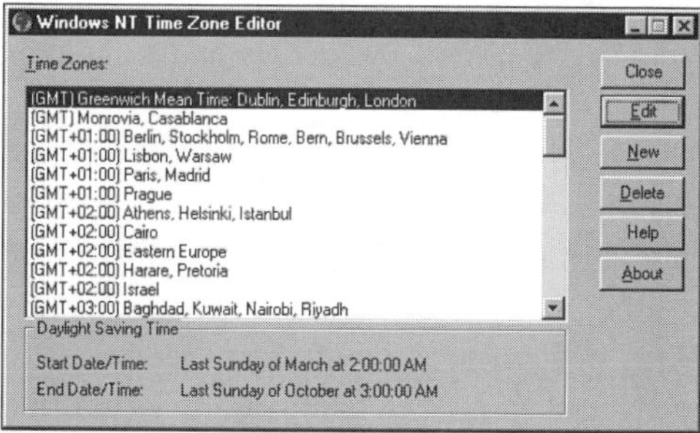

Fig. 29.4
This resource kit utility allows you to set up your own time zone.

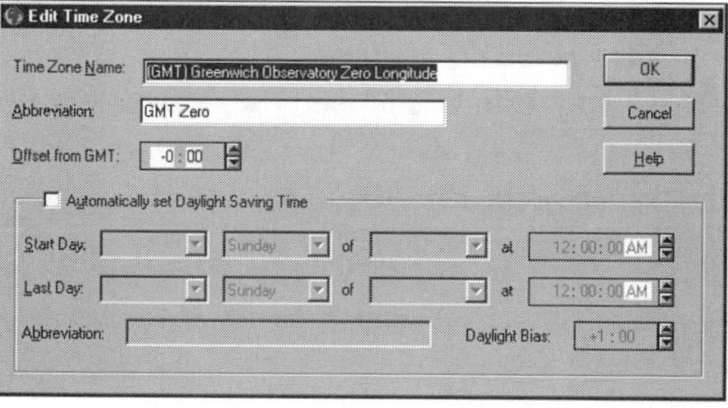

Fig. 29.5
Edit and Modify the time zones in this dialog box.

3. Type **(GMT) Greenwich Observatory Zero Longitude** in the Time Zone Name box.
4. Type **GMT Zero** in the Abbreviation box.
5. Leave the Offset from GMT as zero.
6. Leave the Automatically set Daylight Saving Time settings turned off, and click OK.
7. If you wish, edit the GMT setting that uses daylight savings so that it applies to the United Kingdom and Ireland, not to GMT. The results are shown in figure 29.6.

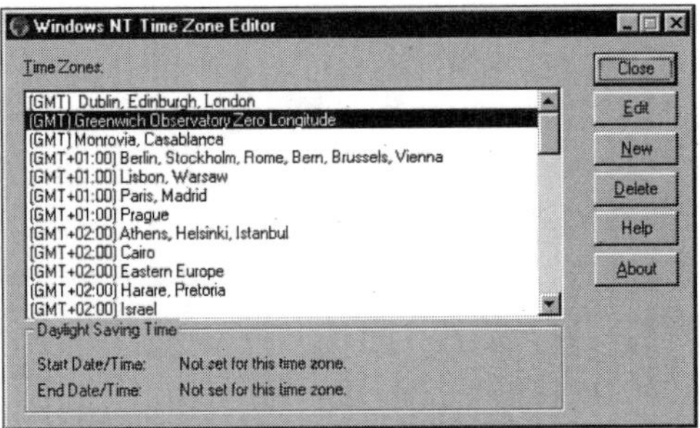

Fig. 29.6
Now you can keep synchronized with your company's office in the U.K.

As an alternative to using the Control Panel to get to the Date and Time Setting window, you can double-click the clock and bring up the Date and Time Window (if you have the clock turned on in the Task Bar properties); or you can right-click the clock and choose Adjust Data and Time from the pop-up menu.

Setting Keyboard Options

The user interface for Windows NT offers the capability of tuning the keyboard and mouse to the preference of the individual. Because the settings are stored in the user profile, each person who logs on to the system can have their own settings, without having to compromise with other users. And if you choose to use server-based profiles, your preferences can follow you to any computer on the network.

The keyboard only has a couple of parameters that can be tuned. However, there are some other options on this property sheet worth noting so that you know where they are if you need them. The keyboard settings icon is in the Control Panel. The keyboard properties sheet is shown in figure 29.7

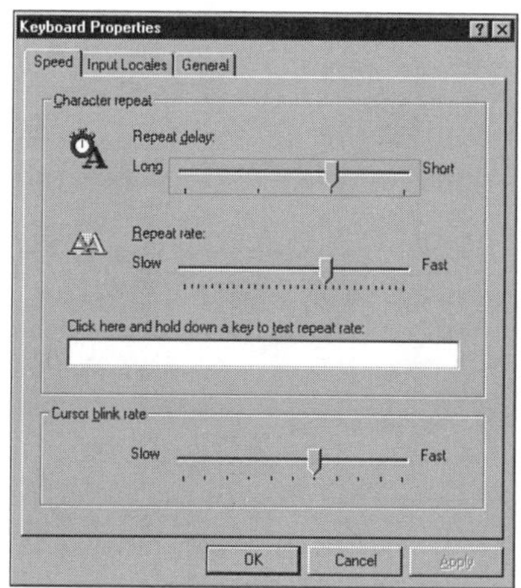

Fig. 29.7
The keyboard repeat rate and repeat delay can be set for each use of the system.

Repeat Delay

The Repeat Delay sets the amount of time that elapses before a character begins to repeat when the key is held down. Although this control looks like a slider which should be continuously variable, it actually only has the four settings and jumps from one to another. You can adjust the setting with the mouse, or select the control with the hot key and use the horizontal arrow keys to change the value.

Repeat Rate

The Repeat Rate controls the speed at which the character repeats when you hold down the key. This slider control has much finer adjustments than the repeat delay, and is adjusted with the mouse or the arrow keys.

There is a box on the properties sheet that is used to test the settings; you can test the new settings and adjust them to your liking before you exit from here. The Cursor Blink Rate is also adjusted from the Keyboard Properties sheet, again using the mouse or the arrow keys.

Input Locale

There is a second tab on the Keyboard Properties sheet that is used to set up the input locale, and thereby control which language and keyboard layout is loaded into memory when Windows NT starts. This property sheet is shown in figure 29.8, with the U.K. version of English added to the default U.S. English.

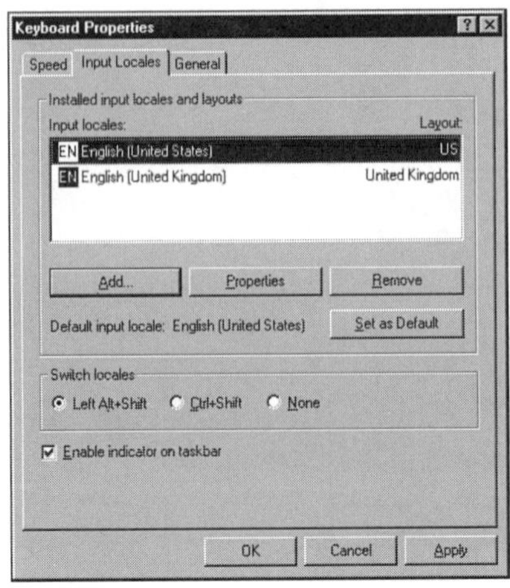

Fig. 29.8
The language and keyboard layout specified here are loaded into memory when Windows NT starts.

When the Enable Indicator on Taskbar option is chosen, you can switch between installed languages by clicking the indicator, as shown in figure 29.9.

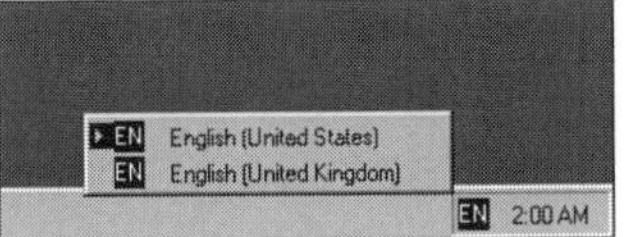

Fig. 29.9
The language used can be quickly changed by clicking the indicator and selecting the new language.

The General tab in the Keyboard properties sheet allows you to specify the type of keyboard you have installed. If it is a nonstandard keyboard, you need a disk from the manufacturer containing the Windows NT driver.

Configuring the Mouse

As with the keyboard, the mouse can be configured for individual preferences using the Mouse icon in Control Panel. The Mouse Properties sheet with the Buttons tab selected is shown in figure 29.10.

Swapping the Buttons

The Buttons tab on the Mouse properties sheet allows left-handed users to swap the functions of the two mouse buttons. You can try this for yourself: select the Left-handed option and click the Apply button. Just remember that to return to right-handed operation, you have to select the Right-handed option and click the Apply button using the right mouse button, not the left one. You can also use the Alt+R, Alt+A hot keys.

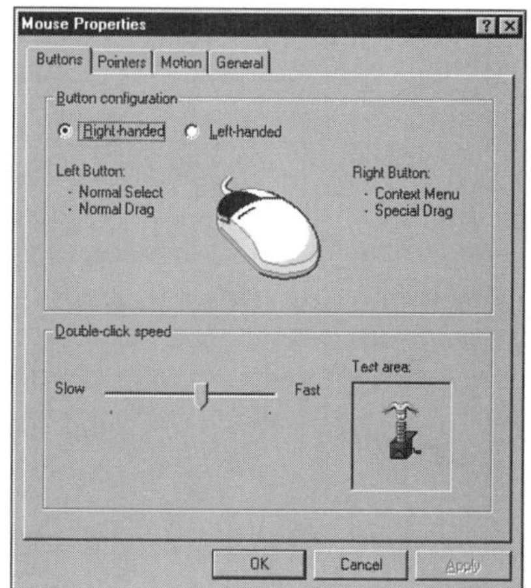

Fig. 29.10
The Buttons tab on the Mouse Properties sheet allows you to swap the buttons on the mouse.

Tracking and Click Speeds

The double-click speed is set from the Buttons tab in the Mouse property sheet. It is a slider control, and there is a test for the double-click speed. When you click the box with the right settings, a jack-in-the-box appears. High-tech stuff, don't you agree? It might have been better if when you clicked with the wrong setting, a tech support person appeared.

Pointers

Those animated cursors are still here, and they can be configured from the Pointers tab of the Mouse Properties sheet. As shown in figure 29.11, the default is to use plain old mouse pointers. But you can select different animated or non-animated pointers from a wide range of choices.

Fig. 29.11
You can use default mouse pointers or choose from a list of many others.

You can select a specific cursor theme, such as Dinosaurs, from a list. Figure 29.12 shows the list of available schemes. And you can configure your own combination, using the Browse button to search for the animated cursors (in the %WINNT_ROOT%\CURSORS directory) and save it—or save several different schemes if you wish, each with an identifying name. As you browse you will notice that the animated cursors have filenames that end with ANI and the non-animated end with a CUR filename extension.

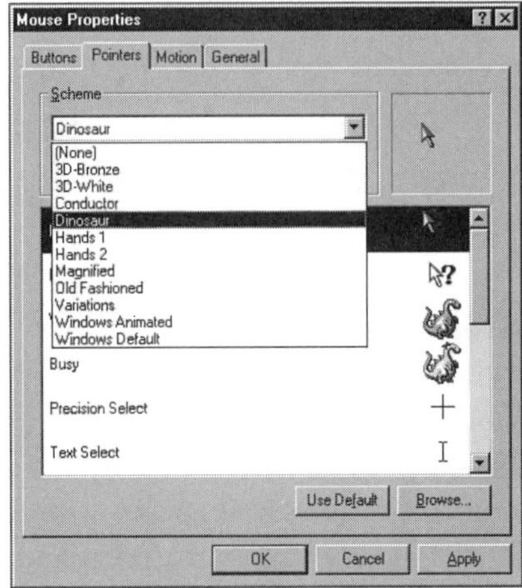

Fig. 29.12
Choose from the available schemes.

Pointer Speed

The speed at which the pointer moves in response to a mouse movement is very much a personal preference. It may also need to be adjusted if you change the pointing device, as the sensitivity of the new device may differ from that of the previous one. The Motion tab of the Mouse Properties sheet allows you to control the responsiveness of the mouse, as shown in figure 29.13.

Snap to Default

The Snap to Default option causes the cursor to jump to the default button whenever you open a dialog box, property sheet, or window. It reduces the mouse movement required, and speeds up many applications. This handy option is also on the Motion tab of the Mouse Properties sheet, and is shown in figure 29.13.

General

The General tab allows you to specify the type of mouse you are using. Several types are supported, and most mice emulate a Microsoft mouse anyway. But if you want to use a nonstandard pointing device, you will need a disk from the manufacturer from which you can load the Windows NT driver for the mouse.

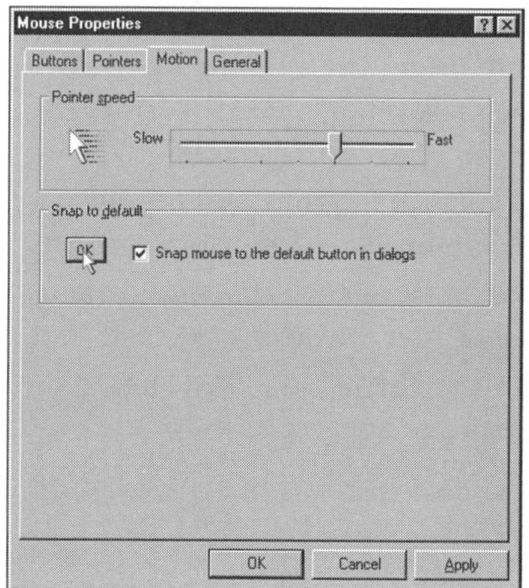

Fig. 29.13
The Motion tab on the Mouse Properties sheet allows you to control the responsiveness of the mouse.

Specifying Regional Settings

There is a wide variation in how data is formatted around the world, and Windows NT has included the flexibility to configure the user interface to reflect these regional differences. The variations include date formats, currency symbols, how decimal numbers are written, and so on. The Regional Settings Properties sheet is accessed from Control Panel. It contains six different tabs, each of which configures some aspect of the user interface. Actually these settings are chosen on a language-by-language basis, so perhaps Language settings would have been a better name for them. Figure 29.14 shows the first tab of the Regional Settings Properties sheet.

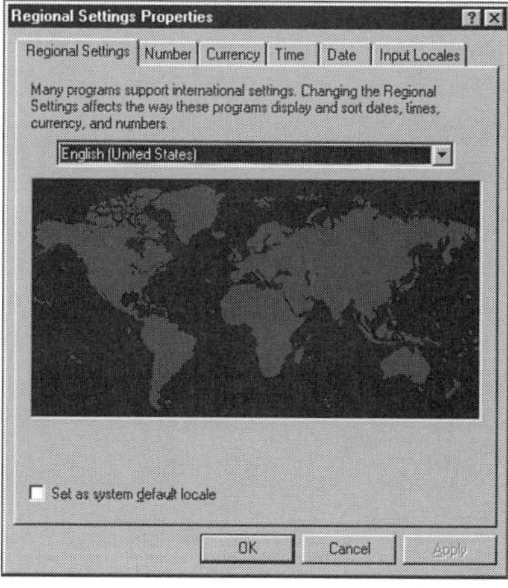

Fig. 29.14
The Regional Settings Properties sheet controls how information is formatted and displayed in Windows NT to allow for differences in regional standards.

Regional Settings: Language Preference

The country settings can be chosen from the Regional Settings tab. When you drop down the list, you see a list of languages rather than countries or regions. This makes sense in places such as Switzerland where French, German, and Italian are spoken, or even in Canada or Belgium, with more than one official language. There are multiple versions of English, French, and Spanish, for example. Once you choose a language setting and apply it, the default values for that language appear in the other tab sheets, but can be changed. You have to restart Windows NT if you have chosen a regional setting that requires loading a different character set.

Number Formats

The Number page on the Regional Settings property sheet, shown in figure 29.15, allows you to change the way numbers are displayed. The decimal indicator and thousands separator vary between countries, and you can't even take for granted that the separator will be every three digits as it is in the U.S. Some countries use counting systems where there is a name for ten thousand, and then they count in multiples of that unit. So what we might call the thousands separator is now called the digits grouping symbol. From this sheet, you can also specify a system on units for measurements: the United States is now almost alone in the world in not using the metric system. Note that changing the format of the numbers does not change their value, as they are stored in binary form anyway. But changing the units of measurement does nothing to convert values. These settings are just for the presentation of the stored values.

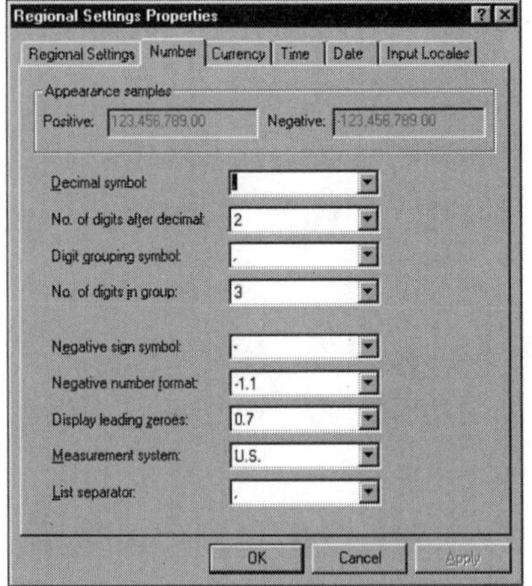

Fig. 29.15
The Number page allows you to change the way numbers will be formatted for display.

Currency Formats

The options on the various currency formats are shown in figure 29.16. The previous comments about decimal separators and grouping digits still hold true, and these parameters can be set up differently for currency than for the regular numbering system.

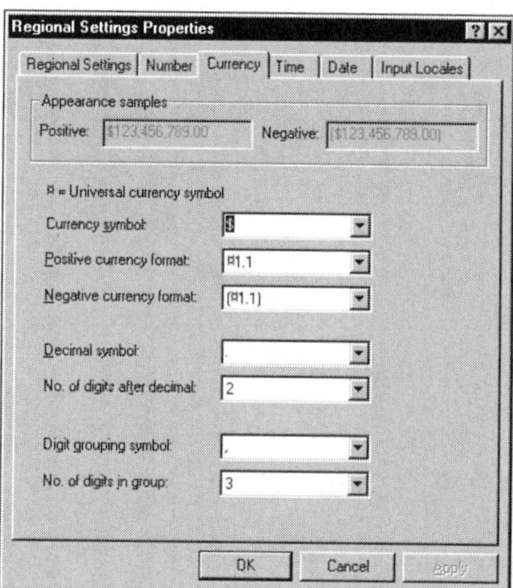

Fig. 29.16
The Currency page allows you to change the way currency will be treated for display.

Some countries put the currency symbol before the amount, as in the United States and Britain. Others put the currency symbol after the amount, so watch out for that variation. Perhaps the most common difference from the standard numbering format is the use of parentheses instead of the minus sign for negative numbers when dealing with currency.

Time Formats

Figure 29.17 shows how the time can be formatted differently in various countries. It's common in Europe, for example, to express all timetables and schedules in 24 hour format. (The English still have tea at 4 o'clock in the afternoon, not 1600 hours. Some things never change.) To change to this format, select one of the options that shows HH for the hours instead of hh in lowercase. Using the 24-hour format means that the AM and PM equivalents are not needed.

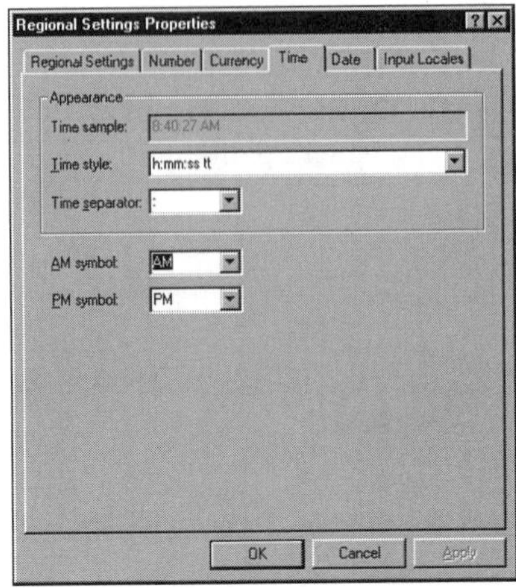

Fig. 29.17
The Time page can switch from 12-hour to 2-hour format.

Date Formats

The date format is the cause of a lot of confusion between Europe and the United States. The European date format, with the day, then the month, then the year, is shown in figure 29.18. The best idea, especially if you have to work with overseas offices, is to standardize on a format that shows the month in letters, as in JAN, FEB, and so on. This way there will be no confusion. You may wish to make this the default format in your applications also. Applications such as Word and Access can handle these variable date formats.

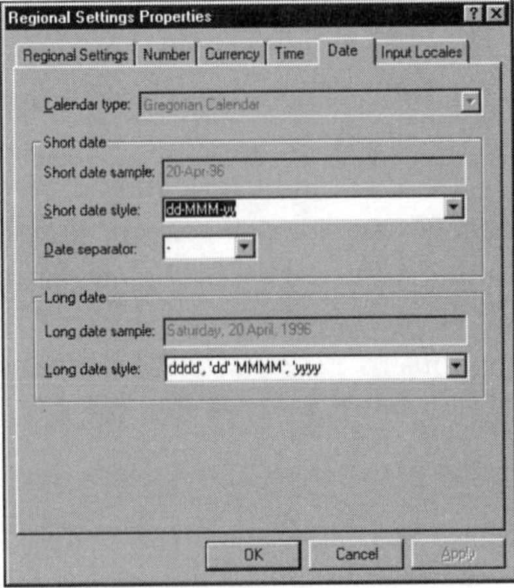

Fig. 29.18
The Date page is shown with the month clearly indicated using letters, not numbers.

Input Locale

This option actually shows the same information as shown in figure 29.8 when we discussed Keyboard settings, and is just a different way to get to the same property sheet.

Setting Security Options

The Windows NT security model is based on the concept of a single user logon to access resources anywhere in a workgroup, domain, or trusted domain. There are some changes you can make to reduce the level of security, although you should consider that users do not like having to log on.

Mandatory Logon

The Windows NT mandatory logon is the dialog box you normally see when you start the computer, or log in again. The username normally defaults to the name of the last person who logged in, although this is a breach of C-2 level security and can be turned off. If someone is trying to break in, why give them half of the information they need? If they walk up to a computer and can get the name of the previous user, they may even be able to guess the password just by knowing some facts about that user. So for a secure environment, this option should be turned off. To do so, you will have to edit an entry in the Registry. The Registry Editor is covered in Appendix A, "Working with the Registry Settings." Find the Registry key

\HKEY_LOCAL_MACHINE\SOFTWARE\Microsoft\Windows NT\
CurrentVersion\WinLogon

and add the value "DontDisplayLastUserName" with a data type of REG_SZ and value of 1.

This change offers a double level of security because Windows NT will not tell you if the username is not a valid account: it waits for the password, then states that it can't log you on. So a hacker gets no feedback about whether the username is valid or not. To be even more secure, remember to change the name of the administrator account if you have not already done so.

Logging on with Default Username and Password

During the mandatory logon, the computer name or name of the domain for logon authentication is shown in the Domain box, and the password is required. Placing all these values in the Registry will bypass the logon dialog box. Again, this is a serious breach of C-2 level security, but it can be set up for users who want to be able to start their computer and bypass the logon dialog box. Obviously, only one user can log on like this; there is no way for another user to override the default logon. One possible option is to configure a computer that has a default Guest logon and make it accessible to anyone who needs limited access.

To configure this option, you must change the following Registry entries.

In the key:

\HKEY_LOCAL_MACHINE\SOFTWARE\Microsoft\Windows NT\
CurrentVersion\WinLogon

set the DefaultDomainName and the DefaultUserName to the correct values. Then add a value called "Default Password" to this key. Give it a data type of REG_SZ and type in the default password for this default account.

Then add a value called "autoAdminLogon" to your computer. Make it a datatype REG_SZ and a value of 1.

Log out, and when you log back in, the system logs you back in with this account. Keep in mind that if the default user has insufficient privileges to edit the Registry, you can't log on to this computer as a system administrator to remove the default logon. As long as you can connect over the network, you can change the Registry remotely, of course, but be careful with standalone computers.

Setting UPS Options

Any system that is running as a server must have a UPS (Uninterruptible Power Supply), and many other systems, such as CAD workstations, can also benefit from having backup power so that no work is lost when the main power fails. Windows NT can receive signals from many types of UPS power supplies that tell the operating system that it is now running on backup power. The user can then shut the system down in an orderly manner. For the UPS to notify the operating system, it must be connected to the computer by a cable. This cable plugs into the UPS and into a serial port on the computer, but *it is not a standard serial cable*. It is specifically designed for the UPS and should be obtained from the UPS manufacturer. *Do not* use a normal serial cable for this purpose.

There are some configurable settings that refer to the characteristics of the UPS and how the messages will be sent to the computer. The configuration screen, again accessed via the Control Panel, is shown in figure 29.19.

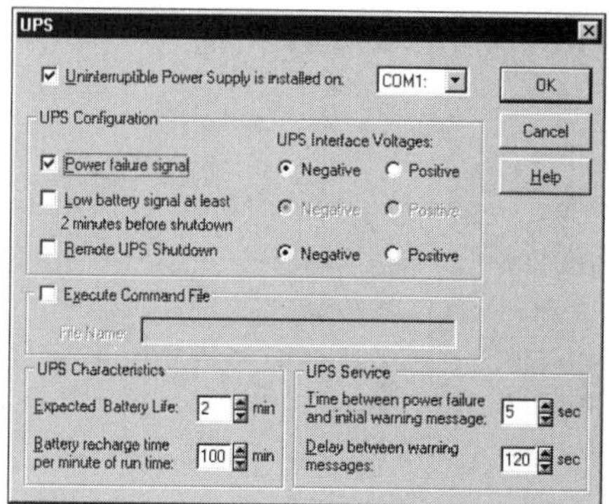

Fig. 29. 19
The characteristics of the UPS and how Windows NT handles a power outage are configured from this menu.

First, you must specify which COM port is to be used for the connection to the UPS to make other settings accessible. The Power Failure signal will have either a positive or negative voltage, which must be specified. Some UPSs can send a signal two minutes before they run out of power, and again, this signal must be specified as positive or negative. If the UPS can't send this signal, you can supply some parameters that let the operating system make an estimate of when the reserve power will run out. The Expected Battery Life and Battery Recharge per Minute of Run Time set the battery characteristics upon which the estimate is based.

The UPS Service can be configured with the time between the power failure and the first alert message, so that you do not keep seeing alerts whenever the power drops for a few seconds. And the delay between successive messages can be configured, so that you can shut down without being constantly reminded that the main power is out.

In order for this all to work, the Messenger Service and the UPS service must be running on the computer to which the UPS is attached. They should therefore be configured to start automatically when the computer is started. Check under Services in Control Panel to make sure that this is the case. And from time to time, when convenient, check that the UPS is still working, and that its batteries are still good. Better to find out that you need to replace the battery under controlled conditions than in a real emergency. And, like all rechargeable batteries, they have a finite lifetime.

If you really want to control what happens in the event of a power outage, the UPS service can be configured to run an executable file, such as a batch file, that will take the actions that you program into it. These actions can include sending messages, and shutting down the system. The batch file is especially important for an unattended server.

Using Hardware Profiles

Hardware profiles were introduced with Windows 95, and are very useful for portable computer owners in particular. The idea is that the computer won't always be configured the same every time it starts. For example, a laptop computer may be in a docking station, or it may be connected to the network through a PC card (these used to be called PCMCIA cards) or it may be out of the office entirely. Perhaps the owner connects into a token ring network in one office, and an Ethernet network in another. By setting up various hardware profiles, we can control which hardware is expected to be present for any given situation. To change from one state to another, we just reboot and select a new profile, instead of having to activate and deactivate hardware item by item. Modern portable computers are adding *hot-docking* capabilities, where they can be docked and undocked while running, and the required hardware drivers are loaded and unloaded as necessary.

The hardware profile is perhaps not as important to the desktop user, but there are still some situations in which it can be useful. For example, suppose we have SCSI cards in several computers, and a portable tape backup unit that is moved from computer to computer. We want to avoid problems when the tape unit is added or removed, so we can build two profiles, one with and the other without the tape drive. Then we just select the appropriate configuration when starting the system. The default profile will be the one without the tape unit attached.

The profiles in Windows NT 4.0 are in some ways more sophisticated than the profiles introduced in Windows 95, because when the profile changes, certain services may or may not be required. Therefore, the various services must be configured, along with the hardware, to start up automatically with some profiles and not with others.

The easiest way to set up a hardware profile list is to modify an existing profile. A good starting point is the profile that Windows NT set up when you first installed the software. To copy an existing profile:

1. Open the System folder in the Control Panel folder.
2. Click the Hardware Profiles tab to switch to the Hardware Profiles sheet, as shown in figure 29.20.
3. On the Hardware Profiles sheet, select the Original Configuration, then Copy, as shown in figure 29.21.
4. Supply a new name for the profile, and click OK.
5. Select the Original Configuration, and then click the Properties button as shown in figure 29.22.

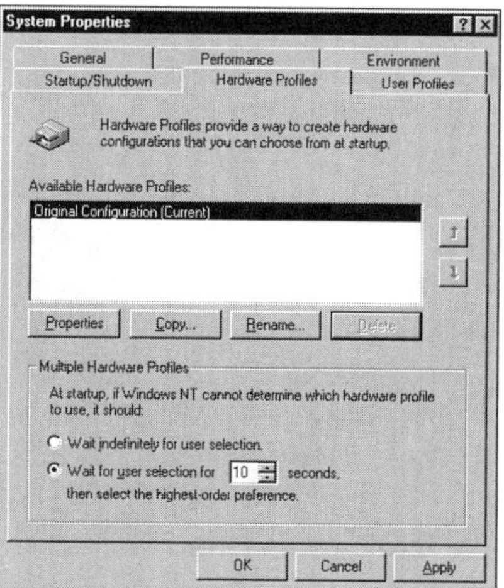

Fig. 29.20
This menu is accessed from the Control Panel, System folder.

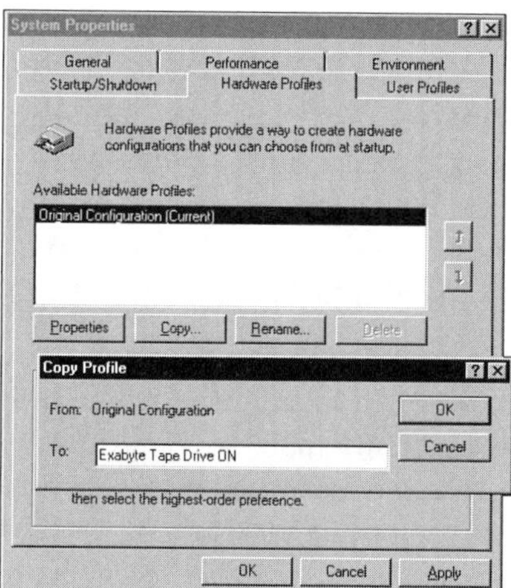

Fig. 29.21
Copy a known good hardware profile and then make the changes for the new configuration.

The Hardware Profile Properties sheet, as shown in figure 29.22, will be of interest to portable computer owners. It asks if this is a portable computer, and if so, is the configuration for the computer when it is docked or undocked. The idea is to support hot docking and undocking, where the computer will automatically load and unload device drivers to reconfigure itself as it is inserted into or removed from the docking station. The Network tab allows you to completely disable all network components, without having to configure each individually, for a particular profile. Again, for a portable computer on the road, this is a useful option.

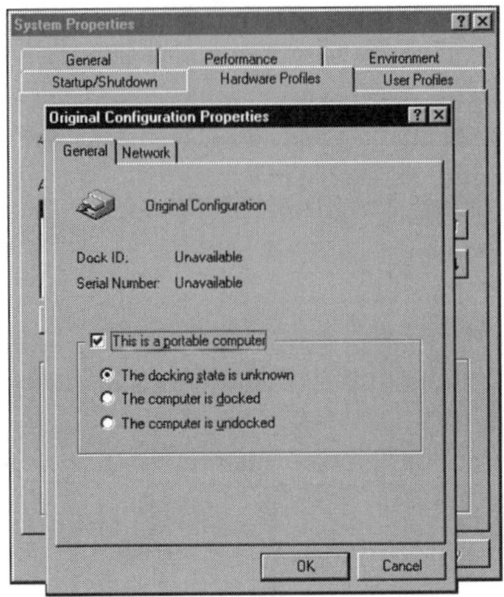

Fig. 29.22
You can configure the profile for a portable computer in or out of its docking station.

Now return to the Hardware Profiles tab as shown earlier in figure 29.20. Notice the startup options. Windows NT can be configured to pause for a specified number of seconds before taking the highest order profile (that is, the one at the top of the page), or it can be set to hold indefinitely until the user selects a profile. The order of the profiles can be changed to ensure that the default profile is the one you want. Select the profile and then use the arrows to the right of the list to move it to the top of the list.

Each new profile must be configured with the correct hardware combination, and the corresponding services configured in the Control Panel using the Services and Devices icons, as shown in figures 29.23 and 29.24. As with the hardware, services can be set to start with one profile, but not with another. For example, there is not much point in enabling the Netlogon service if the computer does not have a network card installed, or starting RAS if no modem is present.

The ability to configure profiles should eliminate messages about "Service Failed on Startup" from your system whenever the configuration changes.

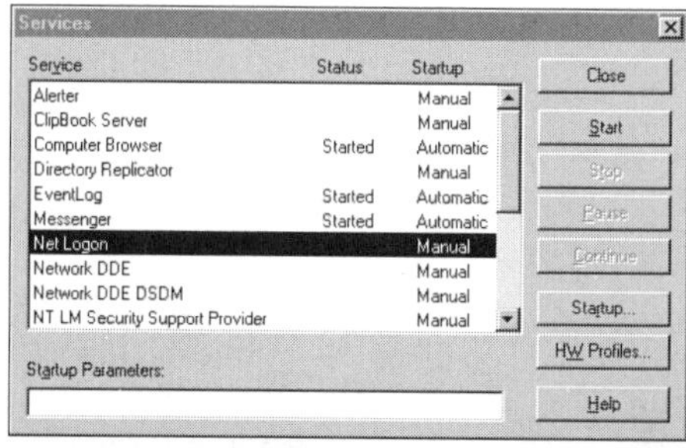

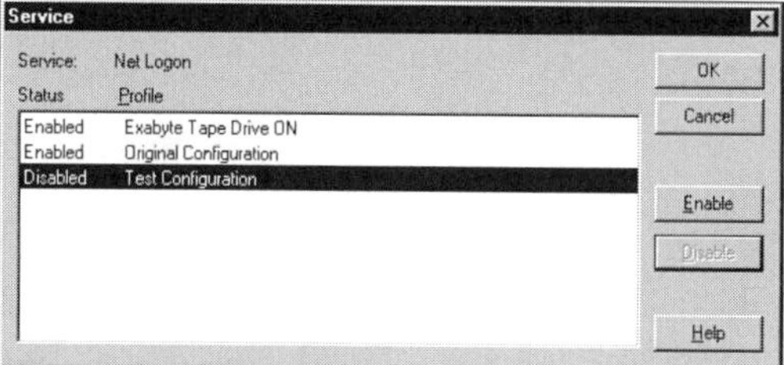

Fig. 29.23
In this example, the *Netlogon* service is disabled in a test configuration.

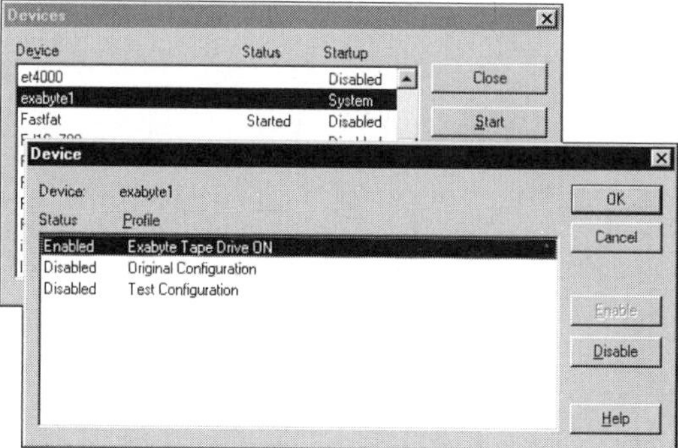

Fig. 29.24
The device *exabyte1* is configured to start only when the hardware profile that includes the tape drive is selected.

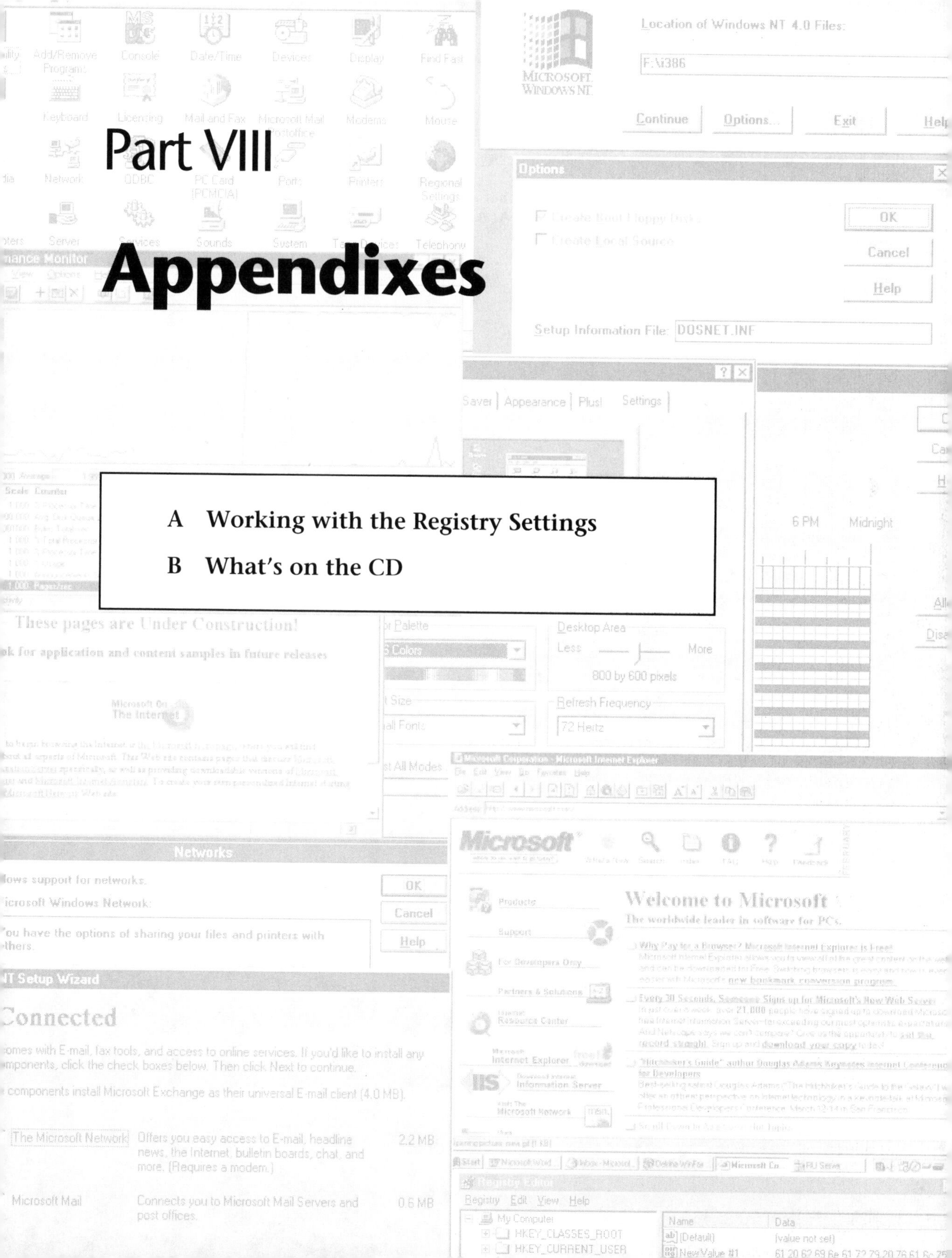

Part VIII

Appendixes

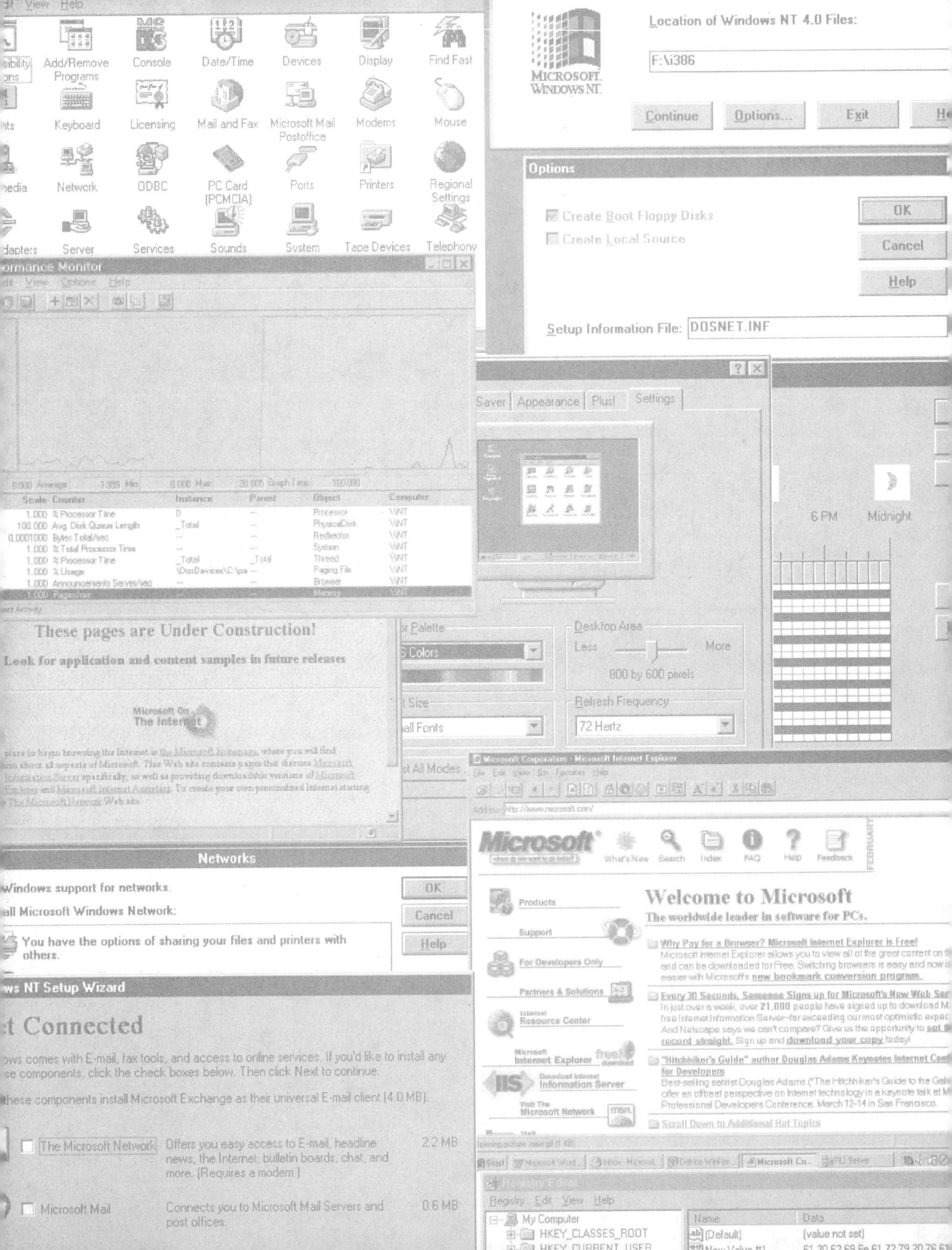
View
Help
Add/Remove Programs
Console
Date/Time
Devices
Display
Find Fast
Keyboard
Licensing
Mail and Fax
Microsoft Mail Postoffice
Modems
Mouse
Network
ODBC
PC Card (PCMCIA)
Ports
Printers
Regional Settings
Server
Services
Sounds
System
Tape Devices
Telephony
Location of Windows NT 4.0 Files:
F:\i386
MICROSOFT. WINDOWS NT.
Continue
Options...
Exit
Options
Create Boot Floppy Disks
Create Local Source
OK
Cancel
Help
Setup Information File: DOSNET.INF
Appearance
Plus!
Settings
6 PM
Midnight
Desktop Area
Less
More
800 by 600 pixels
Refresh Frequency
72 Hertz
These pages are Under Construction!
Look for application and content samples in future releases
Networks
OK
Cancel
Help
You have the options of sharing your files and printers with others.
Welcome to Microsoft
The worldwide leader in software for PCs.
Products
Support
For Developers Only
Partners & Solutions
Resource Center
Internet Explorer
Information Server
Microsoft Network
Why Pay for a Browser? Microsoft Internet Explorer is Free!
"Hitchhiker's Guide" author Douglas Adams Keynotes Internet Conf
Registry Edit View Help
My Computer
HKEY_CLASSES_ROOT
HKEY_CURRENT_USER
Name
Data
(Default)
(value not set)
New Value #1
The Microsoft Network
Offers you easy access to E-mail, headline news, the Internet, bulletin boards, chat, and more. (Requires a modem.)
2.2 MB
Microsoft Mail
Connects you to Microsoft Mail Servers and post offices.
0.6 MB

APPENDIX A

Working with the Registry Settings

by Kevin Jones

When Windows NT starts up, it needs to know all the information about your system. It needs to know the configuration settings of your hardware; the rights, privileges, and preferences of all users; and information about your installed software. All this information is stored in a database called the *Registry*. This database is critical to getting and keeping your system up and running.

Although you may never need to directly modify the Registry, it is still important to understand what the Registry is and how it works. Not only does this knowledge help you maintain your system, but if you ever need to directly modify the Registry, you'll have the understanding and tools needed to make any necessary changes.

Understanding the Registry

The primary function of the Registry is similar to the function of the INI files found in Windows 3.x (WIN.INI and SYSTEM.INI), as well as CONFIG.SYS and AUTOEXEC.BAT. When Windows NT starts, it gets information from the Registry about the device drivers that it needs to load, hardware installed in your system, and user information. However, the Registry also serves many other functions.

For instance, the Registry also serves as the central clearing house for applications supporting Object Linking and Embedding (OLE). This is where all the OLE-enabled applications store information about themselves—information that other OLE applications may need to know. This kind of information allows you, for example, to edit a Microsoft Excel spreadsheet from within Microsoft Word.

The Registry also is the preferred place for applications to store their own data (for example, the last window position or default font). Before Windows NT, applications used to store this kind of information in their own INI files. This resulted in many INI files scattered about on your hard disk. Now, each application can create a section within the Registry where it can neatly and efficiently store its information.

> **Note**
>
> In a perfect world, INI files would have disappeared in Windows NT. But it is very likely that you are still running one or more old, 16-bit Windows applications. These programs don't use the Registry and still read and write to their own private INI files. But they also expect that WIN.INI, SYSTEM.INI, and other standard INI files are available to them. Windows NT goes to a lot of trouble to make these worlds coexist, but the bottom line is you'll still find INI files on your system.

A Brief History of the Registry

The Registry had its beginnings as the humble Registration Database in Windows 3.1. This database was required so that Windows could make Object Linking and Embedding (OLE) work between applications. Windows needed a central repository where all OLE-enabled applications could store information on the programs and interfaces used to support OLE (for example, displaying, editing, and printing object data).

When Microsoft began engineering Windows NT, they decided to extend the functionality of the Registration Database. Besides just storing information for OLE-enabled applications, Microsoft decided to create a single database to store all the configuration information about the computer—its hardware, software, networking, security, and user profiles. This information collectively is known as the Registry.

> **Note**
>
> Windows 95 also has a Registry. While this Registry contains the same type of information as the Registry in Windows NT, the files that make up the Registry are different. While there are some other differences—some good and some bad—it's clear that INI files eventually will be completely replaced with the Registry.

Structure of the Registry

The Registry is a hierarchical database—in other words, it is organized in a tree structure. This tree is divided into five main subtrees. These are listed in Table A.1. Each branch or subtree is called a *key*.

Table A.1 Registry Keys

Key Name	Description
HKEY_CLASSES_ROOT	Contains information on file type associations and Object Linking and Embedding
HKEY_LOCAL_MACHINE	Contains information about the local computer, including information about hardware, startup options, and system parameters
HKEY_CURRENT_USER	Contains information about the user currently logged on, including the User Profile, preferences, and network settings
HKEY_USERS	Contains information about all User Profiles defined on this machine
HKEY_CURRENT_CONFIG	Contains information about hardware configuration settings

Each key serves a main function and is further divided into additional keys. These keys also may be further subdivided, and those keys divided again, and so on. Each key has a name unique within its key and may have one or more associated values. Each value has three parts—a name, a data type, and an actual data value. (Each key can have one default value that has no name. All other values must have a name.) For example, the key HKEY_CLASSES_ROOT\.DOC has a default (no name) value of type REG_SZ and an actual value of Word.Document.6.

Table A.2 lists the five possible data types for Registry values.

Table A.2 Registry Data Types

Data Type	Description
REG_BINARY	Contains raw binary data
REG_DWORD	Contains a four-byte value
REG_EXPAND_SZ	Contains a string (text) that contains a replaceable parameter; for example, in the string notepad.exe %1, the %1 will be replaced with a valid filename
REG_MULTI_SZ	Contains several strings, separated with a NULL character
REG_SZ	Contains a text string; this is often used for description values, program names, and so on

HKEY_LOCAL_MACHINE

The HKEY_LOCAL_MACHINE key contains all the data required to specify the configuration of the local machine. It does not contain data about software programs installed on this computer or information about users defined for this computer. It is divided into five keys—HARDWARE, SAM, SECURITY, SOFTWARE, and SYSTEM.

The HARDWARE key is a dynamic branch of the Registry that is computed each time the computer is booted. It contains information broken down into three more keys—DESCRIPTION, DEVICEMAP, and RESOURCEMAP. Together, these keys contain data that Windows NT requires to boot up your computer to the logon screen. They describe all the hardware in your computer, where additional information about each device is stored within the Registry, and the resources (for example, interrupts, I/O addresses) that each device requires.

Tip

Because the HARDWARE key (and all its subkeys) is dynamically created each time the computer is started, it doesn't make sense to try to modify this key. Any changes you make would be overwritten the next time the computer is started.

The SAM key contains data about users and group accounts. Collectively, this data is known as the Security Account Manager database—hence, the key name SAM. The majority of the data in this key is changed by using the User Manager program. This key is also mapped to the key HKEY_LOCAL_MACHINE\SECURITY\SAM.

The SECURITY key contains security related information, such as user rights, password policy, and local group membership. To change most of the information in this key, use the User Manager program.

The SOFTWARE key contains information about the software installed on this computer. The information is general configuration information and is not user specific. User specific information is stored under HKEY_USERS\SOFTWARE. The SOFTWARE key is further subdivided into Classes, Program Groups, Secure, and description key. Classes is the same key as HKEY_CLASSES_ROOT (see the section "HKEY_CLASSES_ROOT" later in this chapter). The Program Groups key contains information about common programs shared by all users of this local computer. (Information about programs used by specific users is stored under HKEY_CURRENT_USER.) The Secure key provides a secure location where applications can store information that should only be changed by a system administrator. Finally, the description key contains the names and version numbers about the software installed on this computer.

The SYSTEM key contains information needed during the startup of the computer. Similar to the HARDWARE key, the SYSTEM key contains information stored about the computer. (The HARDWARE key contains data computed at startup.) Because this data is critical to getting your computer up and running, multiple copies of the settings are maintained in control sets. These appear as ControlSet00x keys, where "x" is replaced with a number (for example, HKEY_LOCAL_MACHINE\SYSTEM\ControlSet001). These are kept so that if you (or someone like a system administrator) makes a change to the Registry that prevents you from starting your computer, you can revert back to an earlier, good configuration.

HKEY_CLASSES_ROOT

This key contains the same information that the Registration Database contained under Windows 3.1. This information defines all the file associations and Object Linking and Embedding data. The data is divided into two types of keys: *filename extensions* and *class definitions*. The filename extensions map file types to class definitions. For example, the file type key ".DOC" has the value "Word.Document.6." Under the class definitions are all the data needed to perform basic shell and OLE functions. For example, this data is used to enable you to double-click a Word document in File Manager and have the system launch Word and automatically load the selected document.

This key is actually only required to provide compatibility with Windows 3.1 apps that read and write to the Registration Database. This entire key is actually mapped to HKEY_LOCAL_MACHINE\SOFTWARE\CLASSES.

HKEY_CURRENT_USER

This key contains all the information required for Windows NT to set up the computer for the user logging on to the computer. This includes information like user rights, application preferences, and environment settings. There are seven default keys with HKEY_CURRENT_USER. They are as follows:

- Console
- Control Panel
- Environment
- Keyboard Layout
- Printers
- Program Groups
- Software

Tip

You may have noticed that similar types of data appear in different parts of the Registry. You also may have noticed that parts of HKEY_LOCAL_MACHINE and HKEY_CURRENT_USER are the same. In this case, the values in HKEY_CURRENT_USER supersede the values in HKEY_LOCAL_MACHINE. Think of it in this way: HKEY_LOCAL_MACHINE contains the default values that every new user gets; however, as each user changes his preferences, these new values are saved under HKEY_CURRENT_USER.

HKEY_USERS

HKEY_USERS is the key where the data for each user (the user profile) is saved. When a user logs on to the computer, his data is copied from HKEY_USERS*Security ID String* to HKEY_CURRENT_USER. Also, the key HKEY_USERS\.DEFAULT contains the default data for any new users added to the computer.

HKEY_CURRENT_CONFIG

HKEY_CURRENT_CONFIG is a new key that was added with Windows NT 4.0. It contains configuration for the current hardware setup. It is subdivided into two keys, SOFTWARE and SYSTEM.

INI Files and the Registry

As previously described, the Registry fulfills a function similar to the Windows 3.x INI files. If you look in the Windows NT directory of your system, you notice that you still have INI files. These include the standard WIN.INI and SYSTEM.INI files. You may be wondering why you have both the Registry and WIN.INI files. The answer is compatibility. Even though you are running Windows NT, there is still a good chance that you are running at least one old 16-bit, Windows 3.x program. And this program doesn't know anything about the Registry. It is trying to read and write data to WIN.INI and SYSTEM.INI.

What happens when one program writes data to an INI file and another program tries to read the same data from the Registry? To keep all the programs working together, Windows NT can map data contained in an INI file to particular keys in the Registry. This mapping is defined by the data contained under HKEY_LOCAL_MACHINE\SOFTWARE\MICROSOFT\WINDOWS NT\CURRENTVERSION\INIFILEMAPPING. This key has subkeys that define particular INI files and particular entries within those INI files. To understand how to interpret the values for these keys, you need to know five symbols used within those keys. These values are listed in Table A.3.

Table A.3 INI Mapping Symbols

Symbol	Description
!	Write any data to both the Registry and the INI file.
#	When a user logs in, set the Registry value to the value contained in the INI file.
@	Don't read data from the INI file if the data isn't in the Registry.
USR	The INI file data for the entry should be mapped HKEY_CURRENT_USER plus the text value for the key.
SYS	The INI file data for the entry should be mapped HKEY_LOCAL_MACHINE\Software plus the text value for the key.

For example, the value for HKEY_LOCAL_MACHINE\SOFTWARE\MICROSOFT\WINDOWS NT\CURRENTVERSION\INIFILEMAPPING\WIN.INI\WINDOWS\BORDERWIDTH is "#USR:Control Panel\Desktop." The # means that the value for the BorderWidth should be reset from the WIN.INI file each time a new user logs in. The USR means that the value for the border width should be stored at HKEY_CURRENT_USER\CONTROL PANEL\DESKTOP\BORDERWIDTH.

Modifying the Registry

Editing the Registry is not recommended by Microsoft. Changing Registry data can result in programs failing to function properly, your losing data, or your computer failing to startup. Even given all these dire warnings, there may be times when you do want—or need—to edit the Registry. Windows NT comes with two tools to help you edit the Registry—both called Registry Editors. You won't see options on the Start Menu for either of these tools. Microsoft doesn't want the uninformed user blindly playing with these tools—that would create a technical support nightmare. However, for the informed user, these tools are available.

Note

In Windows NT 3.51, there was a Registry Editor call the Registration Info Editor. This program was used primarily to add file association information—information about how to open and print each particular type of file (that is, *.doc, *.xls, *.txt). This program has been removed from Windows NT 4.0 and has been replaced with the Registry Editor from Windows 95. If you still want to work with this type of information, see the section in Chapter 4, "Understanding File Types."

The Registry Editor REGEDIT.EXE is located in the Windows NT root subdirectory (that is, C:\WINDOWS). This is the same Registry Editor found in Windows 95. It provides an Explorer-like view of the Registry, using a single window split into two panes to view the Registry data. This editor is best suited for individual users to make adjustments to their own particular Registry settings.

A more "high powered" Registry Editor, REGEDT32.EXE, is located in the Windows NT system subdirectory (that is, C:\WINDOWS\SYSTEM). This Registry Editor uses multiple child windows to view the Registry data, with each major key displayed in its own window. This editor provides some functionality not found in REGEDIT.EXE. For example, REGEDT32 allows loading individual hives, setting user security permissions, and auditing settings. Because of these types of features, this editor is ideal for administrators to use.

Caution

When you are using either Registry Editor, you may make a mistake that could stop one of your programs from running correctly, or from even running at all. If you aren't so lucky, that mistake could disable your computer, prevent you from connecting to the network, or accessing devices attached to your computer. You read it again and again in this chapter—be careful when using the Registry Editor. It is a very good idea to make a backup copy before making any changes.

Using Regedit

Regedit externally appears to be same Registry Editor that comes with Windows 95 (see fig. A.1). However, because the way the Registry is stored on the disk is different for Windows NT and Windows 95, and because Windows NT has more security features than Windows 95, the internals of the programs are different. Although the programs appear the same, actually only about 40 percent of the keys are the same between the Windows 95 and the Windows NT Registries.

Note

The Registry for Windows NT is stored as a collection of different files. The Registry for Windows 95 is stored as only two files, System.dat and User.dat (with two backups—system.da0 and user.da0—of course).

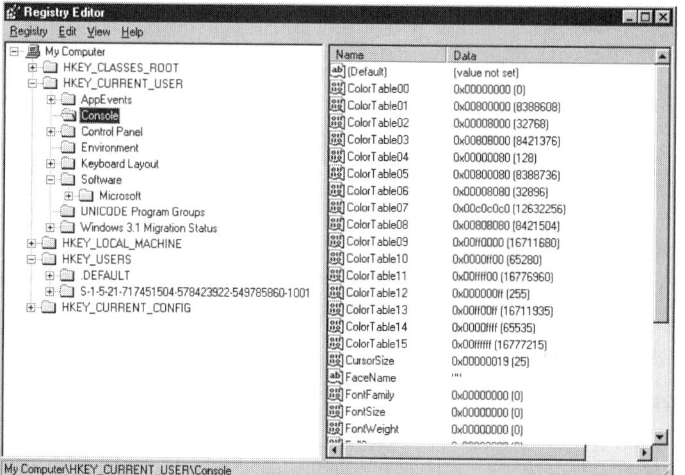

Fig. A.1
Use Regedit to view settings for the Console Application.

Working with Registration Files

Many applications provide a registration file (*.REG) that contains all the Registry keys that the application requires to function properly. Following is a portion of a registration file that comes with Microsoft's Word for Windows. This particular portion contains all the information Word needs to make its wizards function properly:

```
HKEY_CLASSES_ROOT\Word.Wizard = Microsoft Word Wizard
HKEY_CLASSES_ROOT\Word.Wizard\DefaultIcon = winword.exe,4
HKEY_CLASSES_ROOT\Word.Wizard\CLSID = {00020900-0000-0000-C000-
➥000000000046}
HKEY_CLASSES_ROOT\Word.Wizard\shell = New
HKEY_CLASSES_ROOT\Word.Wizard\shell\New\ddeexec = [FileNew("%1")]
HKEY_CLASSES_ROOT\Word.Wizard\shell\New\ddeexec\Application =
WinWord
HKEY_CLASSES_ROOT\Word.Wizard\shell\New\ddeexec\Topic = System
HKEY_CLASSES_ROOT\Word.Wizard\shell\New\command = winword.exe /n
```

With the Regedit, you can merge these settings into the Registry. You can also export a portion of the Registry to a registration file. You might do this to make a backup of some Registry settings or to copy some settings from one Registry to another.

Importing a Registration File

There are instances when you will need to import, or merge, a registration file. Three common instances are:

- When you've installed an application for one user, and then need to update the Registry for another user. If the application has provided a registration file, you can log in as the new user and import the file.
- When you need to copy Registry settings from one Registry to another. You would do this by exporting the necessary settings and then importing that registration file (see the next section).
- When you want to make a backup copy of the settings before you begin making changes to the Registry (a smart thing to do).

To import a registration file, follow these steps:

1. Choose Registry, Import Registry File. The Import Registry File dialog box appears (see fig. A.2).
2. Browse to the folder that contains the Registry file you want to import.
3. Choose Open or press Enter.
4. A message box appears telling you whether or not the file was successfully imported. Choose OK.

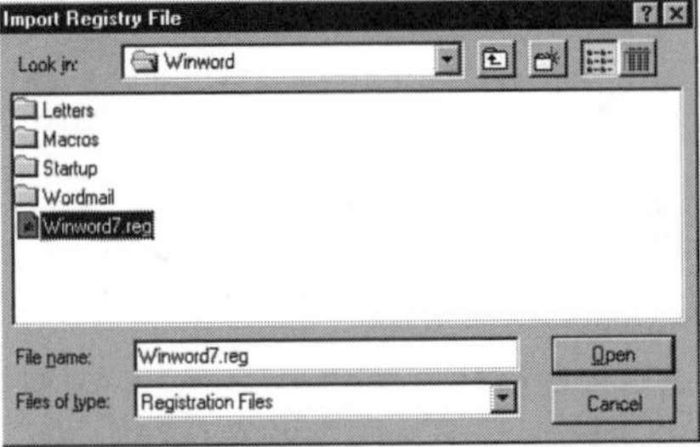

Fig. A.2 Importing the Registration File for Word for Windows 7.0.

Exporting a Registration File

Exporting registration settings is necessary when you need to copy settings from one Registry to another, or when you want to back up a portion of a Registry for safety or later use.

To export a portion of the Registry, follow these steps.

1. Browse to the key that you want to export and select it. For example, if you want to export the entire HKEY_CLASSES_ROOT key, select that

key in the left-hand pane. If you only wanted to export the "txtfile" key (found within the HKEY_CLASSES_ROOT), you would expand the HKEY_CLASSES_ROOT key and select only the "txtfile" key.

2. Choose Registry, Export Registry File. The Export Registry File dialog box appears (see fig. A.3).

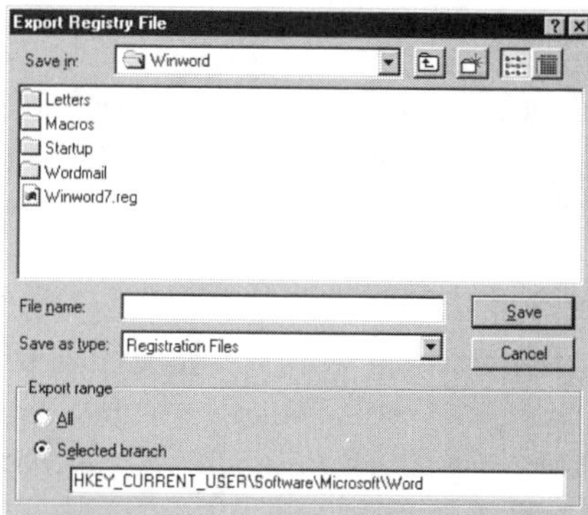

Fig. A.3
Exporting the Registry settings for Word for Windows.

3. Browse to the folder where you would like to store the Registry file.
4. Type in the name you want to use for the Registry file in the File name edit field.
5. You can select to have the entire Registry export by selecting the All option in the Export Range group box.
6. Choose Save or press Enter.

Connecting to a Remote User's Registry

You can connect to a remote user's Registry using REGEDIT. This allows you to view their Registry to try and diagnose problems, check settings, and make adjustments if necessary. To be able to connect to another user's Registry, you need to have proper access permissions.

To connect to a remote user's Registry, follow these steps:

1. Choose Registry, Connect Network Registry. The Connect Network Registry dialog box appears.
2. If you know the computer name that you want to connect to, type in the name in the Computer Name edit field.

3. If you don't know the computer name that you want to connect to, choose Browse. The Browse for Computer dialog box appears. Use this dialog to select the computer you want to connect to, and choose OK.
4. Choose OK.

> **Tip**
>
> When you use REGEDIT.EXE to connect to a remote user's Registry, you are connecting to the Registry for the user currently logged on. With REGEDT32.EXE, you can load specific hives. In other words, you could load the Registry settings for a user that isn't logged on.

Disconnecting a Remote User's Registry

After you are finished looking at or working with another user's Registry, you can disconnect from their Registry. To disconnect, follow these steps:

1. Choose Registry, Disconnect Network Registry.
2. Choose OK.

Printing the Registry

If you want to make a hard copy of a Registry, REGEDIT allows you to print out either the entire Registry or specific branches.

If you want to print out the entire Registry, follow these steps:

1. Choose Registry, Print. The Print Registry dialog box appears (see fig. A.4).
2. Select the printer you want to print to in the Printer Name drop-down list.
3. Choose All in the Print Range box.
4. Choose OK.

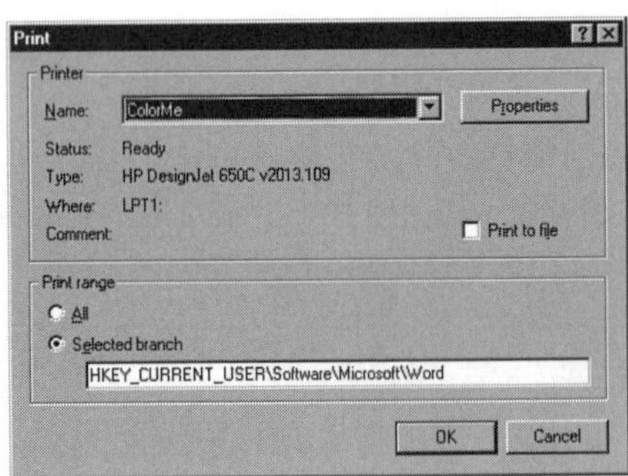

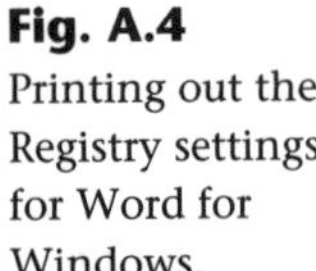
Fig. A.4
Printing out the Registry settings for Word for Windows.

If you want to print out a specific portion of the Registry, follow these steps:

1. Select the key in the Registry Editor that you want to print. For example, if you wanted to print the "txtfile" key under HKEY_CLASSES_ROOT, expand the HKEY_CLASSES_ROOT key and select the "txtfile" key.
2. Choose Registry, Print. The Print Registry dialog box appears.
3. Select the printer you want to print to in the Printer Name drop-down list.
4. Choose Selected Branch in the Print Range box. The edit field contains the name of the key you selected. If the name is wrong, type in the correct name.
5. Choose OK.

Editing the Registry

There are times when you need to change only a specific value or add a single key to the Registry. While this is easy to do with the Registry Editor, please be careful. Making the changes may be easy, but the results can be disastrous.

> **Tip**
>
> The steps listed in the following sections use the menus for REGEDIT to perform the tasks. In Windows NT 4.0, much of the functionality is directly accessible using context menus. So, try directly selecting the key or value and then clicking with the right mouse button. This will bring up a context menu that may have the command you want.

Adding a New Key

To add a new key, follow these steps:

1. Select the Registry key in the left-hand pane under which you want to add your new key. For example, if you wanted to add a new file extension, you would select HKEY_CLASSES_ROOT. However, if you wanted to add a Default Icon key for a particular file type, you would select that file type (HKEY_CLASSES_ROOT\wrifile) in the left-hand pane.
2. Choose Edit, New. A cascading submenu appears (see fig. A.5).
3. Choose Key.
4. The new key appears in the left-hand pane. The name will be New Key # and will already be selected and ready for renaming. Type in the key name you want.
5. Press Enter.

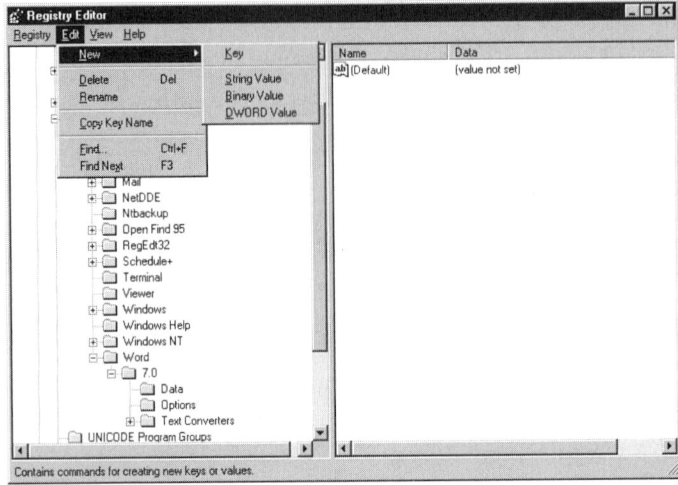

Fig. A.5 Use the cascading submenu to add new keys and values.

Deleting a Key

To delete a key, follow these steps:

1. Select the Registry key in the left-hand pane that you want to delete.
2. Choose Edit, Delete, or press the Del key.
3. A message box appears, asking you to confirm that you really want to delete the key. Choose OK.

Renaming a Key

To rename a key, follow these steps:

1. Select the Registry key in the left-hand pane that you want to rename.
2. The name in the left-hand pane will become selected and ready for renaming. Type in the key name you want.
3. Press Enter.

Adding a New Value

To add a new value, follow these steps:

1. Select the Registry key in the left-hand pane under which you want to add the new value.
2. Choose Edit, New. A cascading submenu appears.

3. Choose the type of value you want to add—String Value, Binary Value, DWORD Value.
4. The new value appears in the right-hand pane with the name New Value #. The value name will be selected and ready for renaming. Type in the new name you want and press Enter.

> **Tip**
>
> The REGEDIT.EXE Registry Editor only allows you to add three types of values—string, binary, and DWORD. If you want to add either of the additional string types—expandable strings or multistrings—you'll need to use REGEDT32.EXE.

Deleting a Value

To delete a value, follow these steps:

1. Choose Edit, Delete.
2. A confirmation message box appears, asking you if you really want to delete the value. Choose Yes.

Renaming a Value

To rename a value, follow these steps:

1. The value name will become selected. Type in the new value name.
2. Press Enter.

Changing a Value's Data

To change a value's data, follow these steps:

1. Select the Registry key in the left-hand pane that contains the value you want to modify. The right-hand pane will display all of the values contained in the selected key.
2. Select the value you want to modify in the right-hand pane.
3. Choose Edit, Modify. An Edit dialog box will appear. This will be one of three edit dialogs: one for strings, one for binary data, and one for DWORD data.
4. Type in the new data in the Value Data edit field.
5. Choose OK.

Using REGEDT32

REGEDT32 is the most powerful Registry Editor available with Windows NT. If you make a mistake using REGEDIT, an application may not work properly. It might not even run. OLE functionality like In Place editing may stop working, if you are lucky. If you aren't lucky and you make a mistake using REGEDT32, you may cripple Windows itself or even prevent another user from logging on. Normally, you should use the various administrative tools and Control Panel programs to modify the Registry. However, some applications may not provide tools to modify all its keys, or if you are a developer, you may need to create or modify the keys for your application by hand. When you need to directly modify the Registry, REGEDT32 allows you full and complete access to all the Registry keys.

To run this Registry Editor, follow these steps:

1. From Program Manager, choose File, Run. The Run dialog box appears.
2. Type **regedt32** in the Command Line edit field.
3. Choose OK. The Registry Editor starts.

Understanding the Display

Unlike the simple display of REGEDIT, REGEDT32 has a multiple document interface (MDI). It displays several windows (normally five), where each window displays the contents of one of the five major keys (see fig. A.6). In much the same way that File Manager displays the contents of a drive (subdirectories and files), this Registry Editor displays the contents of a root key (subkeys and values). You can expand and collapse keys by double-clicking the little folder icons. Icons with a "+" in the folder icon indicate that the key has subkeys. You can also expand and collapse the tree by using the keyboard in the following ways:

- Expand the selected level by choosing Tree, Expand One Level or clicking the + (plus sign) key.
- Expand the entire branch (all the keys underneath the selected key) by choosing Tree, Expand Branch or clicking the * (asterisk) key.
- Expand the entire tree by choosing Tree, Expand All or clicking Ctrl+*.
- Collapse the selected branch by choosing Tree, Collapse Branch or clicking the - (minus) key.

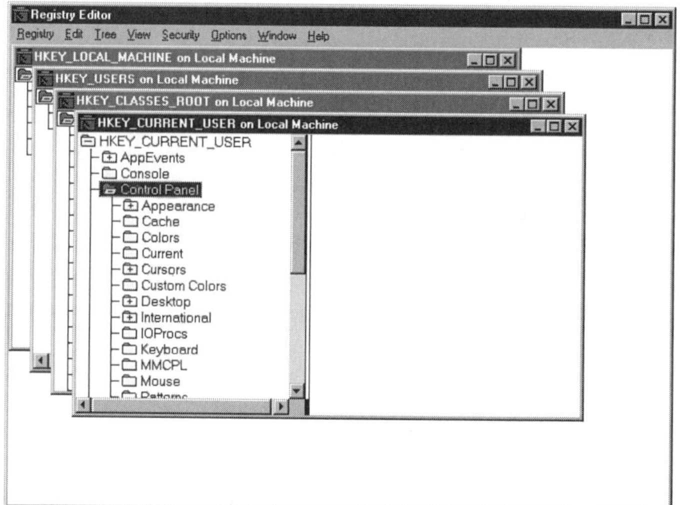

Fig. A.6
You can view Registry data by using the Registry Editor.

Understanding Hives

The way the Registry is actually stored on your hard disk is as a collection of distinct files. Each of these collections is called a *hive*. The standard hive files are listed in Table A.4. Each hive consists of two files, the actual data and a backup copy (with a LOG extension). In addition, because the system hive is so critical, it has an additional backup copy (with the ALT extension). By default, these files are stored in the SYSTEM32\CONFIG subdirectory of the root Windows subdirectory (that is, C:\WINNT35\SYSTEM32\CONFIG).

Table A.4 Standard Hives

Hive	Filenames
HKEY_CURRENT_USER	USER####(.LOG) and ADMIN###(.LOG)
HKEY_LOCAL_MACHINE\SAM	SAM(.LOG)
HKEY_LOCAL_MACHINE\SECURITY	SECURITY(.LOG)
HKEY_LOCAL_MACHINE\SOFTWARE	SOFTWARE(.LOG)
HKEY_LOCAL_MACHINE\SYSTEM	SYSTEM(.LOG) and SYSTEM.ALT
HKEY_USERS\.DEFAULT	DEFAULT(.LOG)

> **Note**
>
> LOG files are used to make sure that Registry hives don't get corrupted when hives get updated. To do this, Windows NT writes all changes to the LOG file. Then it marks a part of the Registry to indicate that the Registry is about to get updated. It then performs the update by processing the changes listed in the LOG file. Finally, it unmarks the Registry, indicating that it is done processing the LOG file. If anything happens during the update and your computer crashes, Windows NT can use the LOG file, with its list of changes, to recover the hive when Windows NT restarts.

It is possible to use REGEDT32 to actually load and work with hives of another user and with hives from another computer. You might want to load such a hive if you are making changes to another user's hive because of a change in software or because the other user is having problems running Windows NT.

To load another hive, follow these steps:

1. Choose File, Load Hive.
2. Browse to the drive and subdirectory where the hive you want to load is located.
3. Select the file and choose OK.

After you have worked with the hive, you need to unload it so that it can be loaded by the other user or machine. To unload the hive, choose File, Unload Hive.

Editing the Registry with REGEDT32

REGEDT32 provides a much richer set of controls when you need to edit the Registry. Not only does it allow you to add keys and values, but it allows you to work with all types of values—binary, string, expandable string, DWORD, and multistring. See Table A.5 for descriptions of each data type.

Table A.5 Registry Data Types

Data Type	Description
Binary (REG_BINARY)	Simple binary data. It is often used to store configuration information for hardware components.
String (REG_SZ)	Text data. It is often used for filenames, component descriptions, and so on.
Expandable string (REG_EXPAND_SZ)	Text that contains a variable that will be replaced. For example, many system components add Registry entries that

Data Type	Description
	contain %SystemRoot%. When this value is requested by an application, %SystemRoot% is replaced by the actual path of the Windows system files.
DWORD (REG_DWORD)	A number 4 bytes long.
Multistring (REG_MULTI_SZ)	Multiple text strings. Each string is separated by a NULL byte (a byte of all zeros). It is often used for device driver information.

Adding a Key

To add a key, follow these steps:

1. Select the primary key you want to add your new key under by clicking the child window's title bar, or choose Window, *primary key name* (for example, HKEY_CLASSES_ROOT).
2. Navigate down the subkey tree until you are at the subkey you want to add your new key under (for example, \AVIFILE\SHELL). Navigate by double-clicking the key names in the left-hand pane.
3. Choose Edit, Add Key. The Add Key dialog box appears.
4. Enter the key name in the Key Name edit field (for example, **PRINT**). Although there is a field for entering the class of the Registry key, you can ignore this field. This may be used in the future, but for now it is not used.
5. Choose OK.

Adding a Value

To add a value, follow these steps:

1. Select the primary key you want to add your new value key under by clicking the child window's title bar, or choose Window, *primary key name* (for example, HKEY_CLASSES_ROOT).
2. Navigate down the subkey tree until you are at the subkey you want to add your new value under (for example, \AVIFILE\SHELL\PRINT\COMMAND). Navigate by double-clicking the key names in the left-hand pane.
3. Choose Edit, Add Value. The Add Value dialog box appears (see fig. A.7).

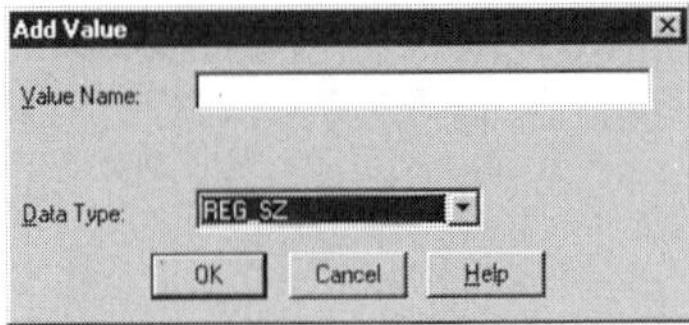

Fig. A.7
Add a string value to the DDEXEC Registry key.

4. Enter the name of the new value in the Value Name edit field (for example, **PRINT**). Each key may contain one value that does not have a name. This is represented in the display by `<No Name>`. For example, the `<No Name>` value for the key `HKEY_CLASSES_ROOT\TXTFILE\SHELL\OPEN\COMMAND` is `notepad.exe %1`. This is often used when the key only has one data value.
5. Select the class of the key in the Data Type drop-down list box.
6. Choose OK.
7. An Editor dialog box (there is one for each data type) appears. Type in the actual data value.
8. Choose OK.

Deleting a Key or Value

To delete a key or value, follow these steps:

1. Select the primary key that contains the key or value you want to delete by clicking the child window's title bar, or choose Window, *primary key name* (for example, HKEY_CLASSES_ROOT).
2. Navigate down the subkey tree until you are at the subkey or value you want to delete (for example, `\AVIFILE\SHELL\PRINT`). Navigate by double-clicking the key names in the left-hand pane.
3. Select the key or value you want to delete.
4. Choose Edit, Delete, or press the Delete key.
5. A prompt appears asking you to confirm that you want to delete the key or value. Choose Yes.

Editing a Value

To edit a value, follow these steps:

1. Select the primary key that contains the value you want to edit by clicking the child window's title bar, or choose Window, *primary key name* (for example, HKEY_CLASSES_ROOT).

2. Navigate down the subkey tree until you are at the subkey that contains the value you want to edit (for example, \AVIFILE\SHELL\PRINT\COMMAND). Navigate by double-clicking the key names in the left-hand pane.
3. Choose Edit, *data type*. The *data type* can be one of four values—Binary, String, DWORD, Multistring. Although you can edit any value by choosing any data type, it is most useful if you choose the same *data type* command as the value's data type.
4. The *data type* Editor dialog box appears (for example, DWORD Editor). Type in the new data for the value.
5. Choose OK.

Changing the View

The normal default view of REGEDT32 should work fairly well for you. However, if you are working with very low resolution, such as on a laptop (640 × 480), you may find that you want to view only the key pane or the value pane. To change your view between these different views, do one of the following:

- Choose View, Tree and Data to view both the keys and data values.
- Choose View, Tree Only to view only the keys (the left-hand pane).
- Choose View, Data Only to view only the values (the right-hand pane).

When you are working in the Tree and Data mode, you can increase the width of either the Tree or Data pane. When you do this, you naturally decrease the width of the other pane.

To adjust the widths of the panes, follow these steps:

1. Choose View, Split, or click the separator between the Tree and Data window panes.
2. Move your mouse right to increase the width of the Tree pane, or left to increase the width of the Data pane.
3. When the widths are adjusted the way you want, single-click the left mouse button.

Refreshing REGEDT32 Display

The final control you have over the display is when to refresh the contents of the display. In other words, the data that is displayed in the Registry Editor is a copy of the Registry's data at the time you started the Registry Editor. It is possible, likely even, that some of the data will have changed since you started. This is especially true if you are working with a Registry on another computer. To update the display so that it displays the most current data, you need to force the Registry Editor to refresh its display. To do this, do one of the following:

- Turn on the automatic refresh by choosing Options, Auto Refresh. If the command already has a checkmark beside it, Auto Refresh is already turned on.
- To refresh the entire Registry, choose View, Refresh All or press Shift+F6.
- To refresh just the contents of the active child window, choose View, Refresh Active or press F6.

Caution

If you are working with the Registry of a remote computer and have turned on Auto Refresh, it still doesn't show any changes. Auto Refresh only works when you are editing your own local Registry. To make matters worse, Refresh All and Refresh Active are disabled. So if you are working with a remote computer's Registry, turn off Auto Refresh and periodically refresh the data yourself.

Using the Security Features of REGEDT32

Although it is very important that you don't carelessly use the Registry Editor—you don't want to cripple your computer or your programs—it is also important that you protect the Registry from changes from other users. There are three basic ways you can help protect the Registry on your computer:

- Protect the actual files themselves using the file security features of Windows NT.
- Use the security features available within the Registry Editor to only allow users to have access to certain keys.
- Set up auditing of Registry changes.

The rest of this section discusses the last two preceding options.

Tip

You can take a couple of other easy precautions to protect your Registry. First, remove or restrict access to REGEDIT.EXE and especially, REGEDT32.EXE. Second, restrict access to administrators only. No user should need access to your Registry.

Restricting Users from Registry Keys

Much like you can use File Manager to restrict access to files on a user/group basis (if the files are on an NTFS volume), you can use REGEDT32 to restrict access to Registry keys on a user/group basis. However, unlike File Manager, even if you are not running on an NTFS volume, the user-based restriction for the Registry will still work.

To set user permission for Registry keys, follow these steps:

1. Select the primary key that contains the key you want to restrict access to, by clicking the child window's title bar, or choose Window, *primary key name* (for example, HKEY_CLASSES_ROOT).
2. Navigate down the subkey tree until you are at the subkey you want to restrict access to (for example, `\AVIFILE\SHELL\PRINT`). Navigate by double-clicking the key names in the left-hand (tree) pane.
3. Select the key you want to restrict access to.
4. Choose Security, Permissions. The Registry Key Permissions dialog box appears (see fig. A.8).
5. Select the user or group that you want to set the access privileges for. If the user or group isn't shown, choose Add to add that user or group to the list.
6. Set the type of access by choosing one of the options in the Type of Access drop-down list box.
7. If the key you are restricting has subkeys and you want your new settings to override whatever settings those subkeys may have had, click the Replace Permission on Existing Subkeys checkbox.
8. Choose OK.

Tip

If you make any restrictions to Registry keys, always make sure that administrators and the system have full access to all keys. Then, if something goes wrong, an administrator can go back in and reset the changes.

After you make any changes, it is a good idea to turn on auditing changes to those keys you've restricted and then test your system, logging on as different users and administrators. This is simply to make sure that the restrictions you've set haven't caused any problems in the normal running of your computer and programs.

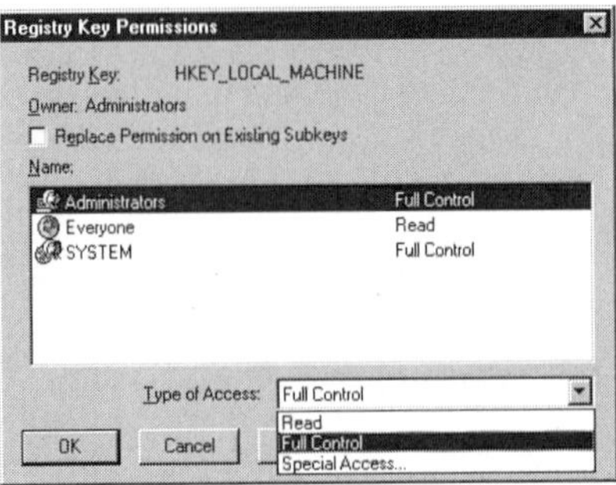

Fig. A.8 Set Access Permissions on the HKEY_LOCAL_MACHINE Registry Key.

> **Note**
>
> Although REGEDT32 allows permissions to be set on any key, the system automatically assigns permissions to all the hives except for user profile hives. You really shouldn't need to override this behavior.

Auditing Registry Editor Changes

When you need or want to monitor what is changing in your Registry—and who is making those changes—you can use the auditing features of the Registry Editor. There are three separate steps that you must do to use auditing:

1. Use the User Manager administrative tool to turn on auditing.
2. Use the Registry Editor to set up the auditing parameters for Registry changes.
3. Use the Event Manager to view the audit logs.

To set the auditing parameters using the Registry Editor, follow these steps:

1. Select the primary key that contains the key you want to audit, by clicking the child window's title bar, or choose Window, *primary key name* (for example, HKEY_CLASSES_ROOT).
2. Navigate down the subkey tree until you are at the subkey you want to audit (for example, `\AVIFILE\SHELL\PRINT`). Navigate by double-clicking the key names in the left-hand (tree) pane.
3. Select the key you want to audit.
4. Choose Security, Auditing. The Registry Key Auditing dialog box appears (see fig. A.9).
5. Select the user or group that you want to audit. If the user or group isn't shown, choose Add to add that user or group to the list.

6. Set the type of auditing by choosing one or more of the options in the Events to Audit box. See Table A.6 for more details. You can choose to audit either the success or failure, or both. For example, you can choose to audit every time a key is successfully set, every time a failure occurs when trying to set a key, or both events.

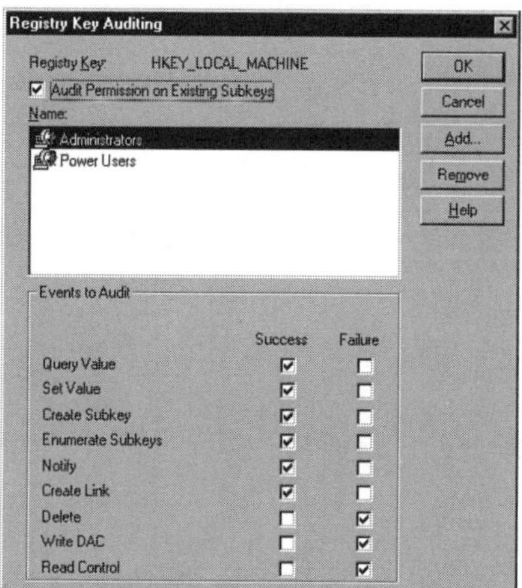

Fig. A.9
Set auditing parameters on the HKEY_LOCAL_MACHINE Registry key.

7. If the key you are auditing has subkeys and you want to audit those keys also, click the Audit Permission on Existing Subkeys checkbox.
8. Choose OK.

Table A.6 Auditing Options

Audit Event Type	Description
Query Value	Audit any event that tries to open a key for purposes of reading its value.
Set Value	Audit any event that tries to open a key for purposes of settings its value.
Create Subkey	Audit any event that tries to open a key for purposes of adding a new subkey.
Enumerate Subkeys	Audit any event that tries to open a key for purposes of reading its subkeys.
Notify	Audit any event that tries to open a key for purposes of monitoring when the key will be changed.
Create Link	Audit any event that tries to open a key for purposes of creating a symbolic link.

(continues)

Table A.6 Continued

Audit Event Type	Description
Delete	Audit any event that tries to open a key for purposes of deleting the key.
Write DAC	Audit any event that tries to open a key for purposes of finding out who has access to the key.
Read Control	Audit any event that tries to open a key for purposes of determining the owner of the key.

When Should You Modify the Registry?

So far in this chapter, you learned about the Registry and how to use the provided tools to modify it. But you really haven't learned when to modify it. It most cases, you'll probably use tools other than the Registry Editor(s) to make changes—maybe without even realizing that you are changing the Registry. Control Panel applications, the User Manager, and the Windows Setup program all make changes to the Registry. But there are a few times when you need to roll up your sleeves and work directly on the Registry.

Increasing the Size of the Registry

The size of the Registry is limited. The system puts some limits on it so that the Registry can't grow too large and prevent your system from working. The default value for the size of the Registry is set to be 25 percent of the size of the paged pool, which by default is 32M. That makes the default maximum size of the Registry 8M. This means, that by default, the Registry cannot grow beyond 8M. Why would it grow? The primary reason for the Registry to grow is when you add new users. But at 8M, the Registry can support about 5,000 users. Unless you are maintaining a very large network, this probably will never be a problem. You also can restrict the Registry from growing very large at all. If you are the only user on your computer, you may want to restrict the size of the Registry to only a few megabytes.

To approximate the current size of your Registry, look in the SYSTEM32/CONFIG subdirectory of the directory where you installed Windows NT (for example, C:\WINNT35\SYSTME32\CONFIG). Total the size of the following files:

- SAM and SAM.LOG
- SECURITY and SECURITY.LOG
- SOFTWARE and SOFTWARE.LOG
- SYSTEM and SYSTEM.LOG
- USER#### and USER####.LOG (for the current user, for example KEVIN000 and KEVIN000.LOG)
- ADMIN### and ADMIN###.LOG (if present)
- DEFAULT and DEFAULT.LOG

While this is not exactly the amount of memory the Registry will take, it serves as a quick approximation.

To set the maximum size of the Registry, follow these steps:

1. Run the Registry Editor, REGEDT32.EXE.
2. Select the HKEY_LOCAL_MACHINE\SYSTEM\CURRENTCONTROLSET\CONTROL key.
3. Add (or modify if it is already there) the value RegistrySizeLimit. This value should be a REG_DWORD type.
4. Set the value to the maximum size (in megabytes) that you want the Registry to be able to grow to.
5. Exit the Registry Editor by choosing File, Exit.

What to Do When a System Won't Start

When a system just won't start, you can do a number of things. Hopefully, you've been proactive and have done things like creating an Emergency Repair disk and making regular backups of critical system files. If you have, you have a great leg up. If you haven't, you probably have a lot of work in front of you.

If your system has just failed to start properly, you can force Windows NT to start using the last known good configuration. To do this, follow these steps:

1. Reboot your computer.
2. At the startup prompt, select Windows NT. Press Enter.
3. Immediately press the spacebar.

4. At the Configuration Recovery menu, choose Use Last Known Good Configuration. Press Enter.

> **Note**
>
> To be considered a good configuration, Windows NT must do two things. First, it must successfully load all startup drivers. Second, a user must have successfully logged on to the computer. After these two events have happened, Windows NT copies the current configuration to the Last Known Good Configuration key in the Registry.

If your computer still fails to load, you may have physical damage to one or more of the Registry hives (the actual files). To solve this type of problem, see the next section.

Restoring Damaged System Files

If you think the Registry is actually damaged—that it isn't a configuration problem—then you will need to restore the damaged files. For this to work, you must have already created backup copies of your Registry.

▶ See "Changing the Registry on a Remote System," p. 729

> **Note**
>
> Windows NT itself maintains a separate backup copy of the system hive, called SYSTEM.ALT. If during startup, Windows NT can't properly load the system hive, it automatically switches and tries to load its backup copy.

The following procedure backs up your Registry files:

1. Boot your computer into another instance of Windows NT, or if Windows NT is installed on a FAT volume, you can boot into MS-DOS.
2. Copy the files in the Windows SYSTEM32/CONFIG subdirectory to another directory. These are your backup copies.

To restore these files, reverse the process by following these steps:

1. Boot your computer into another instance of Windows NT, or if Windows NT is installed on a FAT volume, you can boot into MS-DOS.
2. Copy the backup files to the Windows SYSTEM32/CONFIG subdirectory.
3. Restart your computer, booting into Windows NT.

After you restore these backup files remember that any changes you made to the Registry between the time that you backed up and restored the files are lost. For example, if you installed a new program, any Registry keys created by the new program are lost. You will either have to merge the program's registration file (if it has one) into the Registry or reinstall the program. The same goes for any newly installed hardware.

Changing the Registry on a Remote System

If booting into the last known good configuration didn't get your system up and running again, if you don't have backup Registry files, or if restoring the backups didn't fix your problems, you may still be able to fix your problem by using the Registry Editor from another Windows NT system.

For example, if your system won't start into Windows NT because you had to replace some failed hardware (maybe a hard disk controller card), but you can boot into MS-DOS and connect to the network, you can make configuration changes using the Registry Editor on another system.

To load the Registry of a remote computer, follow these steps:

1. Run the Registry Editor.
2. Choose File, Select Computer.
3. Select the computer in the Select Computer list.
4. You can now edit HKEY_USERS and HKEY_LOCAL_MACHINE if you are not a member of the Administrators group. If you are a member, you can edit all keys. This is subject to any access controls that may be in place for the remote Registry.

Using REGEDT32 to Find Configuration Problems

Probably one of most useful ways of using the Registry Editor isn't to perform any editing. Rather, you will find that you can quickly look at a lot of configuration data using the Registry Editor. Then you can use another program—a Control Panel program or the User Manager program—to actually make the changes.

When this is coupled with the capability to view the Registry on a remote computer, one user (usually an administrator) can help another user diagnose problems.

For example, if a user had problems running software and environment variable problems were suspected, an administrator could attempt to solve the problem by following these steps:

1. Run the Registry Editor.
2. View the Registry on the remote computer. See "Changing the Registry on a Remote System," earlier in this chapter.
3. View the values of the HKEY_LOCAL_MACHINE\SYSTEM\CURRENTCONTROLSET\CONTROL\SESSIONMANAGER\ENVIROMENT.
4. If an incorrect value is found, the administrator can immediately fix the problem—remotely.

Tip

Although you can use the Registry Editor to view data when you're looking for conflicts, sometimes the data in the Registry just isn't very helpful. This is especially true when viewing the data for the HKEY_LOCAL_MACHINE\HARDWARE key. Looking at a bunch of bytes just doesn't help. To see this data in a friendlier form, run the Windows NT Diagnostics program. This organizes and displays all the data in an easily understood format.

Customizing Your Windows NT Logon

You can customize the Windows NT logon in two different ways. First, you may want your computer to automatically log on when it boots up. You might want to do this because the machine is running some service—such as an ftp Internet service—and you want the machine to automatically restart if the power should go out and come back on. To do this, follow these steps:

1. Run the Registry Editor.
2. Select the HKEY_LOCAL_MACHINE\SOFTWARE\MICROSOFT\WINDOWS NT\CURRENTVERSION\WINLOGON key.
3. Add a value called AutoAdminLogon. This should have a data type of REG_SZ and a data value of 1.
4. Add a value called DefaultPassword. This should have a data type of REG_SZ, and the data value should be set to the password of the user listed in the DefaultUserName value.

Second, you can have Windows NT display a custom logon prompt. You would do this to force the user to click OK to your prompt prior to logging on, maybe for a licensing agreement or disclaimer. To add the custom logon prompt, follow these steps:

1. Run the Registry Editor.
2. Select the HKEY_LOCAL_MACHINE\SOFTWARE\MICROSOFT\WINDOWS NT\CURRENTVERSION\WINLOGON key.
3. Add a value called LegalNoticeCaption. This should have a data type of REG_SZ, and the data value should be the text that appears as the caption for the logon prompt.
4. Add a value called LegalNoticeText. This should have a data type of REG_SZ, and the data value should be set to the text of the message for the logon prompt. ❖

APPENDIX B

What's on the CD

by Brian Underdahl

The CD-ROM that accompanies this book contains a wide variety of useful tools, shareware products, and evaluation versions of software. The items on this CD-ROM are high powered technical tools intended to make installing and configuring Windows NT 4.0 a lot easier. Whether you're a system administrator or perhaps just an everyday Windows NT user, you'll find software to help you automate tasks, tweak system settings, and make your mail system work your way.

Because many of the programs on the CD-ROM are very powerful tools, it's important that you exercise caution when using them. This is especially true with tools that modify the Registry. Always make certain you make backups of important files so you'll be able to recover from any errors you might make.

You'll also find the Macmillan Electronic Catalog.

Using the CD-ROM

When you insert the CD-ROM into your system, a program called Autorun automatically displays a graphical interface to the files on the CD. The first time you run the CD, you may need to run the Setup program to install several interface support files. Later, you'll only need to click the Start button to view the file listings. Simply select a category and you'll see all the files in the category. To see each file's description, select the file in the file listing. Once you've selected a program you'd like to try, you can use the buttons to view the files, install the program, or in some cases, run the program from the CD.

If you wish, you can also use the directory and filename information in this appendix to browse the CD. Each program listing in the appendix includes the name of the directory, the filename, a short description, and contact information for the software author.

Because of the fast moving nature of the computer world, many of the programs we've included may have newer versions available than what you'll find on the CD-ROM. Some software authors release new versions almost every week, so it's just not possible for us to have the latest versions on the CD-ROM in every case. If you like a program enough to keep using it, you may want to see if a newer version is available. We've included contact information along with each software description to make this much easier for you.

Important Information About Shareware

Shareware distribution gives users a chance to try software before buying it. If you try a shareware program and continue using it, you are expected to register. Individual programs differ on details. Some request registration while others require it. Some specify a maximum trial period, either a set number of days or uses. With registration, you get anything from the simple right to continue using the software to an updated program with a printed manual.

Copyright laws apply to both shareware and commercial software. The software authors have not given you the right to continue using their software without registration simply because they have chosen to use shareware distribution.

Software authors use shareware distribution methods for several reasons. One of the most important is that this method enables the authors to keep the cost to you as low as possible. But this system only works if you keep up your end of the bargain. Remember, if you don't register shareware you use, there's no incentive for the software authors to produce new shareware products, or even updated versions of existing ones.

So once you've tried out the shareware on the CD, make one of these choices; register the software you find yourself using, and uninstall any you don't find useful.

A Special Note to Shareware Authors

We're constantly looking for top quality software to include with our books. As the largest publisher of computer books, we reach a broad market of computer users. If you are the author of high quality shareware, freeware, or evaluation version software and you would like us to consider including your software on a future CD, please let us know. Send your program name, a brief description of the software and its intended audience, and your complete contact information to:

kkloss@que.mcp.com

On the CD

AUTOSTART 1.0

Filename: AUTOSTRT.ZIP

Directory: Auto

AUTOSTART is a Windows NT service that will automatically run a batch file when a Windows NT server or Windows NT workstation is booted. AUTOSTART is freeware from Camellia Software Corporation.

For more information:

Camellia Software Corporation
Bill Goforth
7807 126th St. SE
Tenino, WA 98589

Phone: (360)264-5307

Fax: (360)264-5307

Auto Task for Windows NT, 1.3d

Filename: ATNT13D.ZIP

Directory: Auto

Auto Task is an automated task processor/manager for Windows NT. Auto Task that lets you schedule any MS-DOS or Microsoft Windows application to run at specific times without user intervention. Individual tasks can be scheduled to run by Interval, Day, Week, Month, or Date. Task processing can be monitored using the automated task manager which provides information on current tasks running, or those still waiting to run. Task processing can be enabled or disabled globally, or on a per-task basis. Tasks that are currently running can be terminated both manually or automatically. In addition, task logging can be activated to write the status of each processed task to a file.

For more information:

Brian K. Freese
2393 N. Rosewood Lane
Round Lake Beach, IL 60073

Phone: (847)265-8252

bfreese1@aol.com

102377,422 on CompuServe

Batch Job Server, Evaluation 1.26

Filename: BJSA126.EXE

Directory: Auto

Batch Job Server is a batch job management environment for Windows NT. It manages the queuing and execution of Windows NT batch files (batch jobs) submitted by users, programs or other host systems (Mainframes, UNIX servers, and so on). Batch Job server is a 32-bit Windows NT service. It can be installed on either a Windows NT server or a Windows NT workstation.

Two 32-bit client applications, BJS Client and BJS Administrator, are included with Batch Job Server. BJS Client is used by Batch Job Server users to access Batch Job Server. It allows users to submit batch jobs and to monitor and control their batch jobs. BJS Administrator is used by system administrators and server operators. In addition to the functions provided by BJS Client, it provides functions to manage the Batch Job Server environment. BJS Client and BJS Administrator can be installed on a Windows NT workstation (or server), a Windows 95 workstation, or a Windows for Workgroups workstation.

For more information:

Camellia Software Corporation
Bill Goforth
7807 126th St. SE
Tenino, WA 98589

Phone: (360)264-5307

Fax: (360)264-5307

Catalog 1.2

Filename: CATAL121.ZIP

Directory: Dskfile

Catalog 1.21 Shareware (for Windows 95 and Windows NT 3.51) allows you to catalog a drive unit (floppy, hard disk, optical disk, or CD-ROM) into a file. It also allows you to search for files in your archive. You can run Catalog in French or in English.

For more information:

Benjamin Bourderon
9 rue magenta
69100 Villeurbanne France
100735,2646 on CompuServe

Benjab@msn.com

CleverWatch 4.0.2

Filename: CW40NT.ZIP

Directory: Tools

CleverWatch is an intelligent agent for monitoring and managing Lotus Notes Servers. It is designed to detect Notes server problems, notify Notes administrators, and to even automatically take user-specified corrective actions. CleverWatch is based on two simple concepts: commands and triggers. Triggers specify what should be monitored, and commands specify what actions will be taken once a trigger occurs. CleverWatch can detect all types of server crashes—even the hardest Notes crashes like transport protocol communication problems and operating system crashes.

For more information:

CleverSoft, Inc.
Bill Cronin
27 Gorham Rd, Suite #1
Scarborough, ME 04074

Phone: (207)883-3550

Fax: (207)883-3369

http://www.cleversoft.com

bcronin@cleversoft.com

Cuneiform OCR 2.0 (CD-Book Bundle/Internet Version)

Filename: CUNE120C.EXE

Directory: Auto

Cuneiform OCR is an extremely accurate, fast, and easy-to-use optical character recognition package. Cuneiform OCR works with all popular Twain-compatible scanners. It also reads faxes from the Messaging Inbox, Fax Group 3, PCX, and TIFF sources. This 15-day evaluation version is the complete, working version of the software, and will make your scanner much more useful than it is with the OCR software packaged with the scanner.

For more information:

Cognitive Technology Corporation
Yefim Schukin
9 El Camino Drive
Corte Madera, CA 94925

Phone: (415)925-2323

Fax: (415)461-4010

http://www.ocr.com/

ctc@ocr.com

76600,1623 on CompuServe

Datum Directory

Filename: DD32.ZIP

Directory: Dskfile

DATUM Directory is a UNIX "LS" clone with an added feature of coloring the extensions to make recognizing or finding files much quicker and easier! It has all the main commands that LS supports as well as many more and supports long filenames. The program was written in MS Visual C++ for the WIN32 subsystem and is best run under Windows NT (Optimized for NT but does run under Windows 95).

For more information:

Nader Eloshaiker
10 Mulkarra Dve
Chelsa Vic, Australia 3196

u3917231@scrooge.ee.swin.oz.au

Drag and View for Windows 95/Windows NT

Filename: DV95.ZIP

Directory: Dskfile

Drag And View For Windows 95/Windows NT 1.0 enables you to view files with the right mouse button. It views most popular database, word processor, spreadsheet, graphic and multimedia formats, plus ASCII and HEX formats. It allows you to rotate graphics and save them in other bitmap formats. It plays AVI, MRI, MID and WAV files. It allows you to edit text files, copy to the clipboard, print, search, and go to text.

For more information:

Canyon Software
Daniel
1537 Fourth Street, Suite 131
San Rafael, CA 94901

74774,554 on CompuServe

Drag and Zip for Windows 95/Windows NT

Filename: DZ95.ZIP

Directory: Dskfile

With Drag and Zip you can zip and unzip files with just a right-click of the mouse. It includes built in zipping, unzipping, extraction of TAR and GZ files, and virus scanning. The program also supports long filenames and pathnames. Drag and Zip link to Mosaic and Netscape, and make Windows hosted SFXs. It includes password encryption and multiple disk zip files.

For more information:

Canyon Software
1537 Fourth Street, Suite 131
San Rafael, CA 94901

74774,554 on CompuServe

EasyHelp/Web 2.81a

Filename: EZY281A.EXE

Directory: Tools

EasyHelp/Web is a set of Microsoft Word macros contained in a template called EASYHELP.DOT. These easy-to-use macros can be executed either from the Word toolbar or by using shortcut keys, and they enable you to mark up a document with topics and hypertext links and graphics. You can process the marked-up document, then build and view the resultant help file directly from within Word. EasyHelp/Web also allows you to maintain one document that can be printed out as a hard copy manual or can be viewed as a help/HTML file. No complicated footnotes or extra page breaks clutter the document. In fact, the only formatting changes made to the document are colored text, to let you see where the topics and hypertext links are.

For more information:

Eon Solutions Ltd.
Jeff Hall
Eon House, 8 Bottrells Lane
Chalfont St. Giles, Buckinghamshire, HP8 4EX, England

eonsol@cix.compulink,co.uk

100130,2471 on CompuServe

http://www.eon-solutions.com/

ftp://ftp.u-net.com/com/eon/ezy281.exe

Fastkey 1.2 for Windows 95 and Windows NT

Filename: FKEY.EXE

Directory: Tools

FastKey is a utility program for Microsoft Windows NT that allows you to control and extend the function of any key on your keyboard. It provides the ability to assign a command, text string, key script, and sound to any key.

For more information:

Reed Consulting
2312 Belvedere Dr.
Toledo, OH 43614

76237,516 on CompuServe

FaxMail Network for Windows

Filename: FAX_N103.ZIP

Directory: Mail

FaxMail Network for Windows adds a faxbar to your Windows programs, giving you access to all the Fax/Modems and Fax/Machines in the world, and making them your printers. FaxMail Network for Windows attaches itself to the actual Microsoft Windows environment, thereby adding its features to all Windows applications. FaxMail Network for Windows has many features such as dynamic viewing, editing cover pages, FaxBook import/export, Windows dynamic all class FaxModem driver, and technical support. You can import up to 1000 names and phone numbers into each FaxBook (Phone Book) at a time from any xBase database program, and you can have as many FaxBooks as you want. FaxMail Network for Windows gives you laser quality fax output, making it a great tool to send an occasional fax or large numbers of high-quality faxes from the background while you work on other tasks. It bundles the most useful fax features, and it is fast! FaxMail Network for Windows supports most FaxModems, Group 3 CLASS 1, CLASS 2, and CLASS 2.0.

For more information:

ElectraSoft
Jon Krahmer

3207 Carmel Valley Dr.
Missouri City, TX 77459-3068

Phone: (713)261-0307

Fax: (713)499-8423

BBS: (713)499-5939

jonk@blkbox.com

http://www.blkbox.com/~jonk/

ftp://garbo.uwasa.fi/windows/comm/

File Reader Win95 1.1

Filename: FR95.ZIP

Directory: Dskfile

The File Reader program allows you to look at the contents of any type of file. It displays the contents in both hexadecimal and ASCII format if the byte is an ASCII character, otherwise as a period. Using the Find option, you can search for a string fragment and change that string information. For example, if an application expects to find a file on the C: drive and you moved it to the D: drive, the application will fail to find the file it expects if the information is hard coded in the executable. Using this program, you can find the string fragment in the executable and change it from C to D. This program will not allow you to increase or decrease the size of any file. You must match any changes character for character. This unregistered version will not allow you to save your modifications until you have registered the application.

For more information:

Floersch Enterprises
Richard H. Floersch
7307 W. 89th Terrace
Overland Park, KS 66212

http://www.sunflower.org/~dflo/

Grep++ for Windows NT and Windows 95

Filename: WINGREP.ZIP

Directory: Tools

Grep++ is a convenient utility designed to search for text strings in a set of files. Although it was designed to be used from the Tools menu in Visual C++, it can be used from within any Software Development Environment or as a standalone utility.

For more information:

Foundation Software System
Scott P. Leslie

sleslie@e55.webcom.com

http://www.webcom.com/~sleslie/shareware.html

Internet Idioms

Filename: INETXIDM-ALPHA.ZIP—for Alpha Processors

Filename: INETXIDM.ZIP—for Intel Processors

Directory: Mail

Internet Idioms is part of Ben Goetter's Widgets for Microsoft Exchange collection. This extension patches Messaging System to behave more like a traditional Internet mail client. Are you sick of staring at Arial 10 text? Do you miss automated signatures and prefixed replies? Then you'll want to give Internet Idioms a try. Both Intel and Alpha versions are included.

For more information:

Ben Goetter

http://www.angrygraycat.com/goetter/widgets.htm

goetter@halcyon.com

Janitor in a DLL

Filename: MTWB.ZIP—for Alpha Processors

Filename: MTWB A1.ZIP—for Intel Processors

Directory: Mail

Janitor in a DLL is part of Ben Goetter's Widgets for Microsoft Exchange collection. This extension patches Messaging System to add a purge command to empty the Deleted Items folder. If, instead of setting Messaging System option Empty upon exiting, you use your Deleted Items folder as a long-term repository, you might find a one-step Purge command more convenient than opening that folder, selecting all the messages, pressing delete, and confirming that you want to delete them permanently.

For more information:

Ben Goetter

http://www.angrygraycat.com/goetter/widgets.htm

goetter@halcyon.com

Link&Run 1.2

Filename: LINK RUN.ZIP

Directory: Auto

Link&Run links up to five network drives and/or runs up to five programs simultaneously or one after another. Link&Run can be forced to link the first available drive letter from a specified set, or can link the first available of all drive letters. When all programs have ended, the network drives are disconnected. If no programs are specified, the network links will not be disconnected. Virtual paths can be used when specifying Programs (such as, \\Server1\Programs\MYPROG.EXE). A network is not required if Link&Run is used only for running programs. There is a Setup Wizard included that prompts you for required network link and program information and then adds an icon to a new or existing group. Link&Run is fully compatible with Windows 3.1, Windows 3.11, Windows NT, and Windows 95.

For more information:

James Dean
48 Steeles Ave East
Thornhill, Ontario, Canada, L3T 1A2
Phone: (905)889-6479

74754,2630 on CompuServe

MAPI Download

Filename: MFETCH.ZIP—for Alpha Processors

Filename: MFETCH1.ZIP—for Intel Processors

Directory: Mail

MAPI Download is part of Ben Goetter's Widgets for Microsoft Exchange collection. MAPI Download connects and downloads messages without ever starting the Exchange mail client, making it suitable for running from scheduler programs. Like MAPI Logon, it allows you to specify the profile to use on the command line. If you would like to dial your mail provider every 12 hours and download your messages to your personal folders, you need MAPI Download.

For more information:

Ben Goetter

http://www.angrygraycat.com/goetter/widgets.htm

goetter@halcyon.com

MAPI Logon

Filename: MLOGON.ZIP—for Alpha Processors

Filename: MLOGON1.ZIP—for Intel Processors

Directory: Mail

MAPI Logon is part of Ben Goetter's Widgets for Microsoft Exchange collection. This extension patches Exchange to enable you to specify Exchange's profile on its command line. That way you can open a shortcut from the desktop and never interact with the Choose Profile dialog box, going instead directly to mail. MAPI Logon does just that.

For more information:

Ben Goetter

http://www.angrygraycat.com/goetter/widgets.htm

goetter@halcyon.com

NT Backup Scheduler

Filename: BACKSCHD.ZIP

Directory: Auto

NT Backup Scheduler is a full featured tape backup scheduling package used with the backup software that ships with Windows NT. Windows NT Backup Scheduler allows you to create a backup schedule with easy access to all the features of Windows NT Backup. The scheduled backup can be run in the background, and in unattended mode. You can also save backup schedules for future use.

For more information:

Software by JAKE
Ed Crabb
8814 S.E. Alder
Portland, OR 97216
Phone: (503)254-1574

72570,1130 on CompuServe

jake@hevanet.com

NetScanTools 32 Bit 2.20

Filename: NST32220.ZIP

Directory: Tools

NetScanTools contains a number of ports of UNIX functions:

- *nslookup*. Name server lookup of host names or IPs.
- *Finger*. Gets info on users on remote systems.

- *ping*. Determines ability to connect to a remote host.
- *Traceroute*. Determines route taken to reach a remote host.
- *Whois*. A lookup utility for determining registered Internet names and so on.
- *Daytime*. The time of day on a remote host.
- *Quote*. Returns quote of the day from a remote host.
- *What's new at NWPS' Web site*. A bare bones URL grabber.
- *NetScanner*. An easy way to sequentially ping an IP address range to find the active computers. Will also resolve the IPs to host names. Hosts file management.

Also included are functions to determine the services your version of sockets can connect to; the protocols understood by your version of sockets; and general info about your version of Windows sockets.

For more information:

Northwest Performance Software
Kirk Thomas
P.O. Box 148
Maple Valley, WA 98038-0148
Phone: (206)630-7206

http://www.eskimo.com/~nwps/index.html

Network Message Sender 2.1

Filename: NMS21U.ZIP

Directory: Mail

NMS runs on Windows NT workstations or servers and is used to send messages to a user/machine or to multiple users/machines at one time. A group feature allows you to place multiple recipients in a group. To send a message to everyone in that group, you simply specify a group, enter your message, and click the Send button. NMS will search your LAN/WAN for the specified users/machines, send the message, and report the results.

For more information:

Pierson Software
Mike W. Pierson
P.O. Box 993218
Redding, CA 96099-3218

71726,316 on CompuServe

NotifyMail 32-bit 1.0.2

Filename: NMAIL32.EXE

Directory: Mail

NotifyMail is an application that listens for a finger connection. When it receives the connection (for the appropriate user) it will notify you of new e-mail. This can be done by having QUALCOMM's Eudora, Pegasus, or any MAPI compliant e-mail client check your mail, displaying a dialog box or playing a sound.

For more information:

NotifyMail Software
5383 Chelsea Ave, #101
La Jolla, CA 92037-7959

http://www.notifymail.com/

OpalisRobot for Windows NT, 2

Filename: OPR_V2.ZIP & ODBC321.ZIP

Directory: Auto

OpalisRobot automates administration, production, maintenance, and communication tasks on Windows NT systems. You can use OpalisRobot to do things like daily planning of backup or administrative tasks, automatic night control of client sites, automation of client/provider communications, and database maintenance. You can use OpalisRobot to easily customize the Windows NT environment.

For more information:

Opalis
Laurent Domenech
27, BLD PEREIRE
75017 Paris, France

71524,27 on CompuServe

PageMaster 1.71 for WinNT

Filename: PM32.ZIP

Directory: Auto

PageMaster allows you to compile lists of numeric and alphanumeric pagers. Pages may be sent to groups of pagers, or just a single pager. PageMaster monitors a phone line for rings, and can automatically send Microsoft Mail (or any MAPI or VIM mail system) e-mail to a pager.

For more information:

Omnitrend Software, Inc.
Thomas R. Carbone
15 Winchester Court
Farmington, CT 06032-3423

Phone: (860)678-7679

Fax: (860)678-7679

72662,455 on CompuServe

Pping 0.3

Filename: PPING.ZIP

Directory: Tools

Pping is a multithreaded console utility for Win32 (Windows NT and Windows 95). It is similar to the ping program that comes with operating systems that have TCP/IP. Ping sends an ICMP message to the remote machine and waits for a response. The output of the standard ping program is verbose and needs some explanation to the inexperienced. Pping, on the other hand, gives a simple go/no-go type of response that is more suitable for checking if the remote machine is responding. Further, Pping accepts multiple remote machine names as well as wildcards for IP addresses.

For more information:

Intellisoft, Inc.
Raju Varghese
Stockmatt 3
CH 5316, Leuggern, Switzerland

100116,1001 on CompuServe

raju@intellisoft.ch

Random Password Generator 5.0 (Shareware Version)

Filename: PASSGEN.ZIP

Directory: Tools

Random Password Generator 5.0 is a secure method for creating passwords. Random Password Generator randomly selects from a group of numbers, lowercase letters, uppercase letters, and special characters or any combination and select passwords. You have the ability to identify up to 1,000,000 (yes, that's 1,000,000) different passwords, using as many as 25 characters per password. This application randomly selects passwords that have not been previously selected (if desired) and sorts them in order. You can copy selected passwords or save them all as text files. The generator uses numbers, upper- and lowercase letters, and special keyboard characters. You can select any combination of these choices to generate passwords. A total of 94 characters are available for the randomizer to select from.

For more information:

Tim Hirtle

102705,2261 on CompuServe

RegFind 0.7

Filename: REGFIND.ZIP

Directory: Registry

Regfind is a utility for searching through a win32 Registry. This utility does not write to the Registry and should, therefore, not cause any damage to it. Microsoft has stated that modifications to the Registry can render the system unusable. Regfind does not modify the Registry in any way. Regfind is a console application: You can run it from a DOS box just like other command-line programs. With this program you will be able to unearth vestiges of obsolete data, such as old host names that are no longer valid. Applications waiting for old hosts to respond only continue after a time-out error is reported. Thus removing those names from the Registry may allow the application to start faster.

For more information:

Intellisoft, Inc.
Raju Varghese
Stockmatt 3
CH 5316, Leuggern, Switzerland

100116,1001 on CompuServe

raju@intellisoft.ch

Remote Process & Shutdown Service 1.2.0c

Filename: RPSSRV.ZIP

Directory: Auto

Remote Process & Shutdown Service 1.2.0c allows processes to be started remotely by another system attached to the same network. It can even be run from a dialup remote access link. It will also allow a system to be remotely logged off or shut down. This is a 32-bit application designed to operate on Windows 95 or Windows NT. This release contains improved interactive control panel and client programs.

For more information:

Digital Control Systems
Royce W. Shofner
P.O. Box 505
Hermitage, TN 37076
Phone: (615)889-6357

Fax: (615)889-9595

BBS: (615)889-9595

73347,145 on CompuServe

Rich Text Sentry

Filename: RTFGUA1.ZIP—for Alpha Processors

Filename: RTFGUARD.ZIP—for Intel Processors

Directory: Mail

Rich Text Sentry is part of Ben Goetter's Widgets for Microsoft Exchange collection. This extension patches Windows Messaging to prevent you from accidentally sending out rich text messages to recipients running a client other than Windows Exchange. Windows Exchange makes it very easy to send a rich text message to such a recipient, and all they will see is a huge, unreadable chunk of encoded binary data. If that recipient happens to be an Internet mailing list, 5000 users will receive that chunk. Rich Text Sentry helps guard against such embarrassing accidents.

For more information:

Ben Goetter

http://www.angrygraycat.com/goetter/widgets.htm

goetter@halcyon.com

SeNTry ELM—Windows NT Event Log Management

Filename: SENTRY.ZIP

Directory: Tools

SeNTry ELM is the industry standard tool for Windows NT Event Log management. SeNTry is extremely easy to install and configure. The SETUP program installs a complete working SeNTry system—it only needs the services to be started for events to be collected in an Access database and displayed using the SeNTry monitor. SeNTry ELM also includes support for Microsoft SQL Server Databases. The included online user manual shows you how to configure SeNTry ELM to handle complex matters, such as SQL Server and MAPI Configuration.

For more information:

Serverware Group plc of Denton House
Peter Seldon
40-44 Wicklow Street
London WC1X 9HL, England

sales@serverware.com

support@serverware.com

http://www.serverworld.com

70630,640 on CompuServe

Search Replace Win95 2.3.1

Filename: FDREPL95.ZIP

Directory: Tools

Search Replace allows you to change a keyword or phrase in many lines of many text files quickly and efficiently. Application developers can, for example, wire it into the Microsoft C++ visual work bench through its Options/Tools menu to enrich the editing capability. It can also be used standalone by developers or administrators who need to change a piece of information in one or more lines of many files located in multiple directories.

In today's networking environment, many files can be manipulated on foreign machines. A UNIX file type option is available for those who need to remotely alter text files that conform to the UNIX file standard. UNIX saves files with just a newline (\n) while DOS saves files with a carriage return (\r) -newline (\n) combination. This program enables you to correctly handle UNIX files on your PC.

For more information:

Floersch Enterprises
Richard H. Floersch
7307 W. 89th Terrace
Overland Park, KS 66212

http://www.sunflower.org/~dflo/

ShutDown 1.56

Filename: SDOWN156.ZIP

Directory: Auto

ShutDown 1.56 makes it easier to shut down your computer in Windows 95 and Windows NT. Rather than click Start or File, Shutdown, and then shutdown, ShutDown provides the same shutdown service Windows NT's Program Manager and Windows 95's Start button does. Make it a shortcut on the desktop or put it on the Microsoft Office Toolbar. You can also run ShutDown from the command line. This is also great for shutting down the computer from a batch file or a scheduling program. The standard shutdown procedure is used, so don't worry about losing data during the shutdown. Windows NT or Windows 95 will ask every running application if they want to quit or not. ShutDown also supports timed shutdowns and running of a batch file or program before shutting down.

For more information:

Chris Bluethman
2302 N. Star Drive
Stillwater, OK 74075

72347,3306 on CompuServe

http://www.excalibur.net/~cdb

cdb@excalibur.net

Somarsoft ACTSNT 1.7

Filename: ACTSNT.ZIP

Directory: Tools

Somarsoft ACTS sets the PC time via your modem. This is a Windows NT/Windows 95 program that dials the NIST or USNO time source using a modem, obtains the current time, and uses this time to set the time on your PC. Similar programs designed for DOS will not work under Windows NT because of security issues. Version 1.8 accommodates USNO phone number changes. The unregistered version is fully functional.

For more information:

Somar Software
Frank F. Ramos
P.O. Box 642278
San Francisco, CA 94164

Phone: (415)674-8771

Fax: (415)674-8771

72202.2574@compuserve.com

http://www.somar.com

Somarsoft DumpAcl 2.6

Filename: DMPACL.ZIP

Directory: Tools

Somarsoft DumpAcl is a Windows NT program that dumps the permissions and audit settings for the file system, Registry, and printers in a concise, readable listbox format, so that "holes" in system security are readily apparent. Somarsoft DumpAcl also dumps user/group info. The shareware version is fully functional, except for printing.

Windows NT contains the mechanisms for providing strong system security, using permissions to control access to objects, and auditing to log access. However, it can be very difficult to determine if all permissions and audit settings have been set correctly, because there are so many files and Registry keys on the typical system. The situation is analogous to having a building with unbreakable locks on each of 10,000 doors. The problem is not with the locks themselves, but rather with one person walking around and checking that none of the 10,000 doors is unlocked.

Somarsoft DumpAcl provides a solution to the problem of too many files and Registry keys to check on a regular basis, by producing a consise and readable report of permissions and/or audit settings. By reviewing this report, you can determine if users have more access than you want to allow. You can then use File Manager, Registry Editor, or Print Manager to set permissions and audit settings differently.

For more information:

Somar Software
Frank F. Ramos
P.O. Box 642278
San Francisco, CA 94164

Phone: (415)674-8771

Fax: (415)674-8771

72202.2574@compuserve.com

http://www.somar.com

Somarsoft DumpEvt 1.5

Filename: DUMPEVT.ZIP

Directory: Tools

Somarsoft DumpEvt is a Windows NT program to dump the eventlog in a format suitable for importing into a database. It is similar to DUMPEL utility in the Windows NT resource kit, but fixes various defects of that program that make the output unsuitable for importing into databases such as Access or SQL server. This program is used as the basis for an eventlog management system for long-term tracking of security violations and other problems. The unregistered version is fully functional.

For more information:

Somar Software
Frank F. Ramos
P.O. Box 642278
San Francisco, CA 94164

Phone: (415)674-8771

Fax: (415)674-8771

72202.2574@compuserve.com

http://www.somar.com

Somarsoft DumpReg 1.0

Filename: DUMPREG.ZIP

Directory: Registry

Somarsoft DumpReg is a program for Windows NT and Windows 95 that dumps the Registry, making it easy to find keys and values containing a string. For Windows NT, the Registry entries can be sorted by reverse order of last modified time, making it easy to see changes made by recently installed software, for example. This is a must-have product for Windows NT systems administrators.

For more information:

Somar Software
Frank F. Ramos
P.O. Box 642278
San Francisco, CA 94164

Phone: (415)674-8771

Fax: (415)674-8771

72202.2574@compuserve.com

http://www.somar.com

Somarsoft RegEdit 1.4

Filename: RGEDIT.ZIP

Directory: Registry

Somarsoft RegEdit is a DLL (RGEDIT.DLL) that can be called from 32-bit Visual Basic programs. It allows a network administrator to write a short Visual Basic program to dump or modify the Windows NT user profiles for a large number of users at once. For example, a 10-line VBA for Excel program can change the mail server path in the Registry profiles of all users at once. This fully functional shareware version is a must have utility for Windows NT network administrators.

For more information:

Somar Software
Frank F. Ramos
P.O. Box 642278
San Francisco, CA 94164

Phone: (415)674-8771

Fax: (415)674-8771

72202.2574@compuserve.com

http://www.somar.com

SuperMonitor

Filename: SUPERMON.ZIP

Directory: Tools

SuperMonitor displays your system's resources (such as memory) in windows you can start and stop, thus providing an accurate picture of the resources used. With SuperMonitor, you can easily see how much memory individual programs use, not just the overall picture. The program can display continuous, average, or maximum values in different windows, as well as logging the figures to disk. This shareware version is limited to three minutes of monitoring per window, after which you can start a new monitor window.

For more information:

Tessler's Nifty Tools
Mary Tessler
P.O. Box 1791
San Ramon, CA 94583

71044,542 on CompuServe

TaskView 4.2 for Windows 95 and Windows NT

Filename: TVIEW.EXE

Directory: Auto

TaskView is a utility program for Microsoft Windows 95, and Windows NT that provides the ability to view and manage the active tasks currently operating on the computer. Virtual View capability expands the desktop working area for application programs. It is also particularly useful for terminating programs that are no longer cooperative and to set the priorities of operating tasks.

For more information:

Reed Consulting
2312 Belvedere Dr.
Toledo, OH 43614

76237,516 on CompuServe

TimeSync 0.6

Filename: TIMESYNC.ZIP

Directory: Tools

TimeSync is a Windows NT service that keeps the local clock of the machine in sync with a reference source. Currently, time reference sources may be one of the following: the PDC of a domain, a specific Windows NT machine, a UNIX (or any) machine that understands TCP and has a time server (RFC868) or an NTP server (RFC 1305). As a service, it does not require that a user be logged in: it starts off as soon as the machine boots up and runs unobtrusively in the background.

For more information:

Intellisoft, Inc.
Raju Varghese
Stockmatt 3
CH 5316, Leuggern, Switzerland

100116,1001 on CompuServe

raju@intellisoft.ch

WFI 32-Bit Registry Control, 1.06

Filename: WREG.ZIP

Directory: Registry

The Wright Registry Control lets your Access95 and VB4 applications easily interact with the Windows 95\Windows NT Registries using properties, methods, and collections. In the old days, we had INI files and life was good. It was no huge chore to read and write INI files, and it was common for Visual Basic applications to use them. Life changed with the release of Windows 95 and Windows NT. INI files were no more, we were told, as all settings should be stored in the system Registry. Unfortunately, writing to the Registry is not as simple as writing to an INI file. An application that uses the Registry must successfully deal with keys, subkeys, values and value types, using APIs that are geared more toward C and C++ development than Basic development.

For more information:

Wright Futures

Fax: (206)889-2465

74001,2244 on CompuServe

WinImage 2.50

Filename: WIMANT25.ZIP

Directory: Dskfile

WINIMAGE 2.50 enables you to create copies of DMF format disks. You can also open a CD-ROM ISO image file in read-only mode, make a disk image from a floppy disk, extract a file from the image, make an empty image, inject file into the image file, and put the image on a blank disk. This program can read, write, and format DMF format disks.

For more information:

Gilles Vollant
13, rue Francois Mansart
F-91540 Mennecy, France

100144.2636@compuserve.com

WinZip 6.0a for Windows 95

Filename: WINZIP95.ZIP

Directory: Dskfile

WinZip brings the convenience of Windows to the use of ZIP files. Windows 95, Windows NT, and Windows 3.1 versions are available. It includes PKZIP-compatible built-in zip and unzip, so PKZIP is not needed for basic archive operations, and built-in support for popular Internet file formats: TAR, gzip, and UNIX compress.

WinZip includes a powerful yet intuitive point-and-click, drag-and-drop interface for viewing, running, extracting, adding, deleting, and testing files in ZIP, LZH, and ARC files, including self extracting archives. Optional virus scanning support is included.

For more information:

Nico Mak Computing
Nico Mak
115 James P. Casey Rd.
Bristol, CT 06010
Phone: (203)585-5376
Fax: (203)585-7352
70056.241@compuserve.com
support@winzip.com
http://www.winzip.com

Index

Symbols

A

C

D

G

H

J

K

L

M

N

O

P

Q

R

S

U

V

X–Z